Civilian in Peace, Soldier in War

Civilian in Peace, Soldier in War

THE ARMY NATIONAL GUARD, 1636–2000

Michael D. Doubler

University Press of Kansas

Preface to the Paperback Edition
© 2003 by the University Press of Kansas

First published as
I Am the Guard: A History of the Army National Guard, 1636–2000

Published by the University Press of Kansas (Lawrence, Kansas 66049), which was
organized by the Kansas Board of Regents and is operated and funded by Emporia
State University, Fort Hays State University, Kansas State University, Pittsburg
State University, the University of Kansas, and Wichita State University

Library of Congress Cataloging-in-Publication Data

Doubler, Michael D. (Michael Dale), 1955–
Civilian in peace, soldier in war : the Army National Guard, 1636–2000 /
Michael D. Doubler.
p. cm. — (Modern war studies)
Previously published: I am the Guard. Wash, DC : U.S. GPO, 2001. With new preface.
ISBN 0-7006-1249-1 (pbk.)
1. United States—Militia. 2. United States. National Guard Bureau. I. Title. II. Series.

UA42 .D68 2003
355.3'7'0973—dc21

2002035851

British Library Cataloguing in Publication Data is available.

Printed in the United States of America

10 9 8 7 6 5 4 3 2 1

The paper used in this publication meets the minimum requirements of
the American National Standard for Permanence of Paper for
Printed Library Materials Z39.48-1984.

Freedom is not free!

To all Army National Guard soldiers
who have given their lives
in order to keep America free.

I Am the Guard

Civilian in Peace, Soldier in War . . . of security and honor, for three centuries I have been the custodian, I AM THE GUARD.

I was with Washington in the dim forests, fought the wily warrior, and watched the dark night bow to the morning. At Concord's bridge, I fired the fateful shot heard 'round the world. I bled on Bunker Hill. My footprints marked the snows at Valley Forge. I pulled a muffled oar on the barge that bridged the icy Delaware. I stood with Washington on the sun-drenched heights of Yorktown. I saw the sword surrendered . . . I AM THE GUARD. I pulled the trigger that loosed the rifle's havoc at New Orleans. These things I know—I was there! I saw both sides of the War Between the States—I was there! The hill at San Juan felt the fury of my charge. The far plains and mountains of the Philippines echoed to my shout . . . On the Mexican border I stood . . . I AM THE GUARD. The dark forest of the Argonne blazed with my barrage. Chateau Thierry crumbled to my cannonade. Under the arches of victory I marched in legion—I was there! I AM THE GUARD. I bowed briefly on the grim Corregidor, then saw the light of liberation shine on the faces of my comrades. Through the jungle and on the beaches, I fought the enemy, beat, battered and broke him. I raised our banner to the serene air on Okinawa—I scrambled over Normandy's beaches—I was there! . . . I AM THE GUARD. Across the 38th Parallel I made my stand. I flew MIG Alley—I was there! . . . I AM THE GUARD.

Soldier in War, Civilian in Peace . . . I AM THE GUARD.

I was at Johnstown, where the raging waters boomed down the valley. I cradled the crying child in my arms and saw the terror leave her eyes. I moved through the smoke and flame at Texas City. The stricken knew the comfort of my skill. I dropped the food that fed the starving beasts on the frozen fields of the west and through the towering drifts I ploughed to rescue the marooned. I have faced forward to the tornado, the typhoon, and the horror of the hurricane and flood—these things I know—I was there! . . . I AM THE GUARD. I have brought a more abundant, a fuller, a finer life to our youth. Wherever a strong arm and valiant spirit must defend the Nation, in peace or war, wherever a child cries, or a woman weeps in time of disaster, there I stand . . . I AM THE GUARD. For three centuries a soldier in war, a civilian in peace—of security and honor, I am the custodian, now and forever . . . I AM THE GUARD.

Courtesy of National Guard Association
of the United States

Contents

Tables

Foreword

FOR THE 225 YEARS OF OUR HISTORY as an independent nation, the general defense policies of the United States have reflected George Washington's *Sentiments on a Peace Establishment.* Washington's *Sentiments* was written in response to a request from the Continental Congress immediately after the cessation of hostilities in the Revolutionary War. Washington sought the advice of those stalwarts of the Revolution: Knox, Pickering, Huntington, Heath, Hand, Von Steuben, and Rufus Putnam. The *Sentiments* reflects not only the experience of that group in the Revolutionary War but certainly also the experience of the colonists in the previous hundred years of intermittent involvement in the North American extensions of Europe's wars as well as the colonists' own security problems with Native Americans. The *Sentiments* also reflected Washington's great respect for the principles of the Declaration of Independence, his adherence to the principle of subordinating the military to civil authority, and the desire to stay at peace with the rest of the world while remaining secure in our homeland at the least possible cost to our citizens.

Washington's *Sentiments* articulated five fundamental pillars of the national defense. The first was a "regular and standing force" large enough to take on the immediate tasks of the day. Washington listed "to awe the Indians, protect our trade, prevent foreign encroachments, guard us from surprises..." as the purposes of Regular forces. The defense establishment would include a Navy "as rapidly as the national budget would allow." It is quite clear that Washington envisioned Regular forces as being as small as possible but adequate to take on all those tasks for which the nation's citizen-soldiers would not be equipped.

The second element of the national defense was, in Washington's words: "A well organized Militia; upon a Plan that will pervade all the States, and introduce similarity in their Establishment, Maneuvres, Exercise and Arms." This particular point reflects Washington's continuing frustration with the lack of standardization and poor quality among many of the militia units provided him by the colonies during the war. It also reflects his understanding that we were a nation of separate colonies, soon to be States, and that our militia tradition was a bulwark of our democracy and necessary for both the States and the national government. National defense problems requiring major forces were to be resolved, not in the European fashion of the day with professional armies, but rather with the employment of the citizens in their own defense.

Washington's third and fifth points covered the need for arsenals with war reserve supplies and the need for what we would today call a "defense industry." His fourth point called for "Academies, one or more for the Instruction of the Art Military." Washington, like every senior military commander who followed him, understood that better trained officers and soldiers from both the Regulars and the militia would have made victory in the Revolutionary War much easier.

The five major points of Washington's *Sentiments* were indeed general, as the Congress had requested. They were also simple, understandable, and, like other of the Founding Fathers' thoughts, adaptable to the unforeseen problems the nation would face in the years ahead. The halls of Congress have echoed with many long and lively debates on each of the five points in the *Sentiments*. For the most part, senators and representatives, many of whom have probably never read Washington's *Sentiments,* have voted to maintain national security policies that reflected the *Sentiments*.

In this volume, Michael Doubler has given us a remarkably comprehensive examination of the history and development of the second point in Washington's *Sentiments,* the "Militia." He has also given us a balanced look at the interactions, often contentious, sometimes smooth and harmonious, but always necessary, between Washington's first point, the "regular and standing force," and point two, the "Militia." The book is a good read, one that should give pleasure and pride to every Guardsman. Far more important, it brings invaluable lessons from history to policy makers of today. It should be required reading for defense policy makers in both the executive and legislative branches of our government and for military officers dealing with force structure and mobilization planning.

Washington didn't mention it when he wrote the *Sentiments,* but I'm sure he said to himself at the time that tension would always exist between the Regulars and the militia. With one part of the total force consisting of professional soldiers convinced that soldiering is full-time work requiring undivided attention and the other part of the force consisting of citizen-soldiers who train intermittently and whose livelihoods in other fields require a lot of attention, conflicting views were bound to rise. Washington himself wrote some scathing comments about some of the militia of the Revolutionary War. Two hundred years later, I heard the echoes of those criticisms from Regular officers in the Pentagon. On the other side of the coin, many a militia (later National Guard) officer has been heard disparaging the Regulars and suggesting that whenever they were in trouble citizen-soldiers would "bail them out." While both views may be understandable, neither strengthens the total force. Doubler tells of the frictions, but he also tells of the wonderful accomplishments for the nation when Regulars and Guardsmen have reinforced each other effectively.

During the course of a 46-year military career, I have had the opportunity to look at America's defense establishment from different perspectives to get a good understanding of the wisdom and foresight in Washington's *Sentiments.* I was able to view the "regular and standing force," the "Militia," and their interactions from positions ranging from that of a private soldier in the National Guard to that of Chairman of the Joint Chiefs of Staff of the United States. My own experience was much influenced by two of the greatest Chiefs of Staff the Army ever had, George Marshall and Creighton Abrams; both had tremendous respect for—and from—the National Guard. Both understood the necessity of meshing the strengths of the Regular Army and the National Guard to produce the best defenses for the United States. I spent my first five years as a soldier in a National Guard infantry division; nearly three of those five years were in combat. My World War II division, the 34th, was the first to be sent overseas after Pearl Harbor, and as a consequence, it retained a richer mixture of Guardsmen than many of the other Guard divisions that were required to provide cadres for other new divisions being formed. My two wartime division commanders were both superb Regular Army officers, Charles W. "Doc" Ryder and Charles L. Bolte. Both understood and carried out Marshall's policy of giving National Guard officers full opportunity to prove their capacity to lead. Both retained and promoted competent Guard officers, and both were quick to dispose of incompetents whether they were Regulars or Guardsmen. We who served as enlisted soldiers and junior officers in the 34th Division were fortunate to serve under fine leaders from each of George Washington's first two pillars.

Many years later, after the Vietnam War, I had the good fortune of serving as Director of Operations on the Army Staff at the time General Abrams was reshaping the Army. His belief in the importance of closer integration of the Regular Army and the National Guard led us to the "Roundout" concept of the late 1970s. Being one of the authors of the idea, General Abrams detailed me to present the idea to the Army Reserve Force Policy Board. My briefing to the board was given on a warm day in Washington, DC; I was in shirt sleeves without my uniform coat with its 34th Division combat patch on the right shoulder. When I finished, the very first person to speak was the chairman emeritus of the board, who was also the longest serving Guard major general in the force at the time. He said, "General, I don't know who you are, or what your experience has been, but I can tell you one thing, and that is that you don't know a damn thing about the National Guard! This idea will never work!" I repressed my reaction to tell him that I had far more time in combat with Guardsmen than he had and simply continued to explain the benefits of the concept to the nation, the Army, and the National Guard. Fortunately, most of the board came to a different conclusion than the first speaker, and the concept was implemented. In my next job, I had the even greater good fortune of commanding a mechanized division that was "rounded out" by a fine National Guard brigade.

As this book is going to print, a new president and a new and experienced secretary of defense are conducting a much needed review of national security and defense policies. Those involved in the review would be wise to lean on the wisdom of our first Commander in Chief's *Sentiments on a Peace Establishment,* recognizing that Washington's two main pillars of the nation's defense forces—Regulars and the National Guard—are both necessary and that the nation's defenses can be strengthened greatly by the judicious reinforcement of both. This book provides wonderful examples from the past for building cooperation for the future. On the other hand, the future will be different from the past. When examining the defense structure of the future, the reviewers must consider both State and national needs. If I were the reviewer, I would look to a much richer integration of active duty forces and the reserve components. It may not be possible, but I would seriously examine combining the Guard and the Army Reserve to eliminate the overhead required for two reserve components. I would recommend major changes in the pay and retirement systems, emphasizing "pay for performance" and providing both Regular and Guard soldiers early vesting in a "portable" retirement system to help keep the force young and vigorous. With the size of the total force becoming an ever diminishing percentage of the overall population, the National Guard's longstanding ties to local communities become ever more important in keeping the support of "we the people" for a sensible national defense. The revolutions in communications and computing power hold hope for a training revolution that can support better readiness for Guard units and closer integration with the Regular Army. At the same time, the revolution in the speed of communications and modern transport also guarantees that potential enemies of the United States can pose the sort of immediate threats that can only be answered by active forces prepared for an almost instantaneous response. The Regular Army and the National Guard need each other perhaps more than at any other time in history. The nation needs both in a strong, mutually reinforcing posture.

John W. Vessey
General, USA (Ret.)

Preface to the Paperback Edition

T HE FIRST PRODUCTION MEETING for the publication of the original, official edition of *I Am the Guard: A History of the Army National
Guard, 1636–2000,* occurred on September 12, 2001. Though the
meeting occurred within twenty-four hours of the most horrific terrorist
attack to date in American history, the participants realized that an important, new chapter in the Army National Guard's history was already
unfolding. After some preliminary discussion of possibly postponing the
book's publication, the decision was made to proceed with the scheduled
release of the Army Guard's first official history. The Guard's story was too
compelling to be delayed any longer, especially in the light of unfolding
events. This new, paperback edition of *I Am the Guard,* retitled *Civilian in
Peace, Soldier in War: The Army National Guard, 1636–2000,* provides the
first opportunity to consider the role of the Army National Guard in
America's first war of the twenty-first century.

The Army Guard's introduction to the war on terrorism came suddenly and spectacularly on the morning of September 11. At 9:37 A.M.,
American Airlines Flight 77 unexpectedly roared over the rooftops of the
Army National Guard Readiness Center in Arlington, Virginia, the Army
Guard's national headquarters just outside Washington, DC. Startled
groundskeepers stared up at the hijacked airliner as it rushed overhead at
treetop level, its jet engines screaming at full throttle. In one brief instant,
workers saw the faces of several stricken passengers pressed hard against
the aircraft's windows in forlorn stares as the doomed airliner streaked
toward its final target. Seconds later, Flight 77 slammed into the western
side of the Pentagon, killing 189 people instantly in a tremendous blast
that rocked America's greatest symbol of military power. Two Army
National Guard officers working in the Pentagon perished instantly in the
attack, as did five other individuals with close family or professional ties to
the Guard. A number of Army National Guard medical personnel who
were attending a meeting in the Pentagon at the time became heavily
involved in the rescue, treatment, and evacuation of casualties. The next
day, military policemen from the Maryland and Virginia Army National
Guard helped to clamp a tight security perimeter around the Pentagon.

The nation's first, organized military responders in the war on terrorism were not elite ranger, airborne, or special forces units, but the men and women of the New York Army National Guard. On that bright, clear morning of September 11, citizen-soldiers in New York City responded to the attack on the World Trade Center in a manner reminiscent of the colonial minutemen of old, who at the sound of an alarm instantly abandoned their plows to take up arms. New York Guardsmen who witnessed the first airliner slamming into the north tower of the World Trade Center instinctively understood that their city was under attack. Not waiting for specific orders, they rushed to the scene of the crisis. A number of Guard soldiers were already at the World Trade Center when a second hijacked airliner struck the south tower, and they witnessed the horrible collapse of both towers. Over the next several hours, larger numbers of citizen-soldiers—some in uniform, others still in their civilian work clothes—rallied at the scene to assist policemen, firefighters, and emergency medical personnel. The first military unit to arrive at the disaster was a New York Guard civil support team whose members were trained in the detection of chemical, biological, and radiological contaminants. Authorities feared that the hijacked airliners might have carried harmful agents, but Guard survey teams were able to assure rescue workers that the smoldering, jagged debris field was free of deadly toxins. Meanwhile, Guard leaders quickly formed their available citizen-soldiers into a cordon sanitaire around the debris field to limit public access to the destruction and carnage. Governor George E. Pataki mobilized the entire New York National Guard, and the Empire State's Adjutant General, Maj. Gen. Thomas P. Maguire Jr., moved to assist in fashioning a comprehensive response to the ghastly disaster.

The New York Army National Guard performed a myriad of tasks in the wake of the cataclysm. Most were deployed to man a formal security perimeter surrounding the World Trade Center site. Roving patrols detained looters, souvenir hunters, curiosity seekers, and members of the media attempting to gain unauthorized access to the debris field. Other citizen-soldiers volunteered to work alongside firefighters and policemen in bucket lines used to remove the rubble. Guard soldiers searched the rooftops of adjacent buildings in an attempt to locate scattered airplane parts and human remains. Medical personnel assisted at first aid stations and makeshift morgues while maintenance crews deployed mobile generators and light sets that facilitated around-the-clock recovery operations. While lower Manhattan attempted to regain a degree of normalcy the following week, Guard soldiers manned security checkpoints and assisted returning workers in getting safely to their places of business and residents to their homes.

National Guard armories often become the focus of attention in local communities during traumatic national events, and in the days following the attack, that tendency manifested itself in New York City. A national drama unfolded in lower Manhattan at the armory of New York's 69th Infantry—The Fighting 69th—on Lexington Avenue. On the evening of September 11, agencies of the city government moved into the armory, converting it into a disaster relief center manned by city employees, aid workers, and grief counselors. Thousands of anxious New Yorkers soon descended on the armory hoping to gain the slightest scrap of information on those still missing. Friends and family members plastered the inner and outer walls of the old historic building with homemade flyers bearing images of loved ones in a final, desperate attempt to locate them. For millions watching on television across the nation, images from the armory captured the acute anguish of those most directly affected by the heinous attack.

Since September 11, the Army National Guard has been a key participant in Operation Noble Eagle, the homeland defense portion of the war on terrorism. On any given day, as many as 25,000 Guard soldiers have been on duty across the nation. In the weeks following the attack, over 9,000 citizen-soldiers helped to improve security at commercial airports across the country. In the face of a series of anthrax attacks delivered through the postal system, civil support teams conducted over one hundred inspections of suspicious letters and packages thought to have contained chemical substances or explosives. Army Guard troops augmented customs agents at the busiest crossing sites on the Canadian and Mexican borders and increased security at a number of ports of entry. In the nation's capital, members of the District of Columbia National Guard helped the Capitol Police to provide security at the Capitol Hill complex, the first time citizen-soldiers had been called upon to defend the Capitol since 1968. Guard men and women have served on extensive security details at the World Series, the New York City Marathon, the Super Bowl, and the 2002 Winter Olympic Games. In each instance, they helped to provide a safe and secure venue for these popular public events. For the first time since the Vietnam era, large numbers of Americans have seen National Guard members on duty and have appreciated their presence more than ever.

Based on its history of wartime service in the twentieth century, the Army Guard will most likely undertake four distinct missions during a protracted war on terrorism. First, citizen-soldier units of all types will deploy to overseas combat theaters to join Regular Army and Army Reserve units in direct action against the enemy. Already, two Army National Guard Special Forces soldiers have given their lives in Afghanistan, and a Guard engineer battalion is currently preparing to deploy to the region to help the Afghan people recover from more than two decades of war. Additionally, Guard units will deploy overseas to replace Regulars displacing to active theaters of war. Guard soldiers could help to sustain America's forward presence in Europe and Asia and assume even more responsibility for peacekeeping, deterrence, and security missions. Citizen-soldiers have already been posted to Guantanamo Bay, Cuba, to assist active duty troops in garrisoning the terrorist detention facility established there. Third, Guard units remaining in the United States will constitute an important strategic reserve against the outbreak of new hostilities around the globe. Whether they remain under State control or are ordered to active, federal service, Guard units constitute an important source of military power. Lastly, Guard soldiers will play a large role in homeland defense by conducting various missions designed to preserve the lives and protect the property of the American people from future terrorist attacks or the threat of attacks.

The militia and National Guard have always concerned themselves with homeland defense. Any time a foreign threat has had the capability to inflict harm within the United States, citizen-soldiers have been an integral part of the nation's defenses. In many ways, the militia in the American Revolution and in the War of 1812 performed homeland defense by helping to eject British forces. The modern concept of citizen-soldiers contributing to homeland defense began after the Spanish-American War when enemy battle fleets posed a threat to American shores. Starting in 1907 and lasting until World War II, a significant portion of the National Guard manned heavy defensive positions along the nation's extensive coastline. At the beginning of both world wars, the War Department deployed National Guard fighting units to protect dams, water reservoirs, industrial centers, and utilities from acts of sabotage. Citizen-soldiers standing guard on the platforms of railway stations in 1917 and 1941 helped to assuage the fears of the American people that came with the country's entry into the world wars. During the early Cold War, Army National Guard missilemen occupied Nike Missile launcher sites that protected centers of population and industry against attacks from Soviet heavy bombers laden with nuclear weapons. In the late 1990s, the Guard formed civil support teams capable of an early response to nuclear, chemical, and biological attacks by nontraditional threats employing weapons of mass destruction.

Throughout the past, America's citizen-soldiers have confronted and defeated evil. Over the last century, they have played a vital role in vanquishing imperialism, fascism, and communism. In much the same manner as those who have gone before them, the men and women of today's Army National Guard will help to defeat terrorism. When the war on terrorism finally comes to a close, the Guard's full role in the conflict will be detailed and examined. Until that day dawns, this new paperback edition of *Civilian in Peace, Soldier in War* will help to inform and educate the American people about the significant accomplishments of their nation's oldest military institution.

The militia and National Guard have had an enduring and powerful influence on America's development and eventual rise as a world power. When the first English settlers established their colonies in the New World, they brought to America the desires for freedom of speech, freedom of religious expression, the gaining of economic prosperity, and the defense of their lives and property. At the beginning of the twenty-first century, American society's major concerns have changed little. Over the past four hundred years, the militia tradition ranks with the free press, churches, and private enterprise as institutions that have had a lasting and profound effect on our society.

This book provides a broad, comprehensive view of the accomplishments of citizen-soldiers as the militia, the National Guard, and, since 1947, the modern Army National Guard. While much has changed since the creation of America's first citizen-soldier regiments in 1636, a number of the National Guard's important characteristics have remained constant. The National Guard has maintained its unique status as both a federal and State force. As a federal reserve in the first line of defense, the Army National Guard provides ready units for mobilization in time of war and national emergency. As a State force, it provides for the protection of life and property and preserves peace, order, and public safety. Another constant has been the dedication and service of its members. From the earliest engagements in the New World, Guard soldiers have performed exemplary, selfless service for both community and country. The National Guard has always been a community-based force, with citizen-soldier camps and armories appearing wherever the American people have ventured. At the same time, the National Guard has been a dynamic institution capable of responding to the nation's changing needs. From the musket to the microprocessor, Guard soldiers have quickly adapted to the new weapons and tactics of warfare.

Rooted in the English tradition of militia service and firmly established by the U.S. Constitution, the composition and service of the Army National Guard has evolved in three distinct phases during the past four hundred years. From its early beginnings in North America, the militia provided local protection and law enforcement and served as the basis for more ambitious military ventures. During the American Revolution, the militia fought the war's first battles, provided the foundation for the creation of the Continental Army, and contributed troop units of varying quality for a wide range of missions. Throughout the nineteenth century, militiamen enforced federal, State, and local laws, helped to create the vast volunteer armies of the American Civil War, and protected settlers during westward expansion. In the aftermath of the Spanish-American War, the long era of militia service surrendered to the rise of the National Guard. With the Militia Act of 1903, the National Guard became the organized, trained, and equipped federal reserve of the United States Army. In two world wars, the National Guard proved its worth during battles in Western Europe and the Mediterranean basin and throughout the far-flung archipelagoes of the Pacific Ocean. After World War II, the modern Army National Guard emerged as a bulwark against communist expansion. During the Cold War, Army Guardsmen fought in the Far East, and deployments to Europe and Central America helped to contain communism. Since the fall of the Berlin Wall in 1989, Army National Guard soldiers have ventured to Southwest Asia and the Balkans to implement a new national security strategy. In nearly four centuries, American militiamen have transformed themselves from a loose collection of local defense forces to a modern and ready Army National Guard that is perhaps the best reserve force in the world.

In 2002, the Army National Guard consists of nearly 350,000 men and women serving voluntarily in fifty-four States and Territories stretching from the U.S. Virgin Islands to Guam. The Guard's presence is felt in approximately 2,800 local communities across the nation. Perhaps the most unique aspect of the Army Guard is that it exists as both a federal and a State force. No other reserve military force in the world has such an arrangement, and the National Guard's dual allegiance to State and nation has often been the subject of much controversy and misunderstanding. The National Guard stands separate and distinct from the other federal reserve forces of the Army, Navy, Air Force, and Marines. National Guard troops serve at the direction of the State governors until the U.S. president orders them to active federal service for either domestic emergencies or overseas service. Still, Army National Guard men and women work in conjunction with Regular troops and other federal reserves. In its totality, the U.S. Army consists of three separate components: the Regular Army, the Army National Guard, and the U.S. Army Reserve. The Army Guard represents nearly 40 percent of the Army's total assets, and in certain critical combat functions, it contains more than half of the Army's entire capabilities.

Four predominant themes provide a useful analytical framework for an examination of the National Guard's history. First and foremost, the National Guard has provided valuable service to the nation, usually within the context of the constitutionally defined missions of executing the laws, suppressing insurrections, and repelling invasions. Second, the National Guard is a dynamic institution that constantly adapts to the political, social, and economic conditions that shape American society. Internally, the National Guard is an organization in transition and forever changing in terms of its personnel, force structure, weapons, and training. A third major theme in the Guard's history has been its relations with the Regular Army. Since the creation of the Continental Army in 1775, the history of America's military forces has been a tale of two armies. Regulars and Guardsmen have often quarreled over important policy issues while forging an uneasy alliance that has seen intermittent periods of mutual support and bitter rivalry. Once policy decisions are rendered, Regulars and citizen-soldiers usually work together to achieve the nation's goals. A summary of the successes and failures of the integrated efforts of Regulars and State soldiers during national crises constitutes a fourth major theme in the Guard's history.

In addition, two fundamental questions loom large in the National Guard's history. First, will the Guard show up in a crisis? While Guardsmen have time and time again displayed their dependability during national and local emergencies, the question of reliability goes far beyond the willingness of individual soldiers to serve. Various laws, court rulings, executive orders, and actions of the governors have either restricted or prompted the Guard's employment. And second, assuming the National Guard shows up, will it be ready? The ability of the National Guard to perform in wartime has always been a central concern of American military policy. Since colonial times, Guardsmen have responded to domestic emergencies and journeyed overseas to repel aggression and to carry out America's war aims. From the creation of its first regiments in the Massachusetts Bay Colony in 1636 to the current war on terrorism, the readiness of the National Guard has been measured by the effectiveness of its combat units.

The National Guard does not stand in isolation in American history, and the Guard's past yields significant lessons that go far beyond its own experience as an important national resource. The Guard is a reflection of the United States and its people during national emergencies and periods of peace and prosperity. America's social values, domestic laws, and foreign policy have all had a strong influence on the National Guard's development. The Guard's story is also a case study in American government. Important constitutional questions regarding the militia's status and the efficacy of the system of shared powers among the president, Congress, and the States are evident throughout National Guard history. Even more important, the long-term trends and lessons learned from the past four hundred years can illuminate strategic thinking regarding the proper roles, missions, plans, and policies for the U.S. armed forces and the Army National Guard in the twenty-first century.

Because the National Guard's history is so closely tied to the American people, *Civilian in Peace, Soldier in War* includes the story of many other organizations and personalities. Deeply imbedded in its history are the ongoing debates between Federalists and Republicans, competition between Nationalists and States' Righters, and the strained relations between Regulars and citizen-soldiers. Several organizations have had a profound influence on the National Guard's development, so the policies and actions of Congress, the War Department, the governors, the National Guard Bureau, and the National Guard Association of the United States figure prominently in the narrative. Important leaders in and out of the National Guard have exerted influence over citizen-soldiers. From George Washington through Senator Charles Dick and Secretary of War Elihu Root to Congressman G. V. "Sonny" Montgomery and Generals George C. Marshall and Colin L. Powell, legislative and military luminaries have shaped the National Guard.

No one work can cover all aspects of nearly four hundred years of National Guard history, and even an official account has its limits. By necessity, the narrative is not a history of the National Guard in the several States, but a centralized view of the Guard's overall development and contributions at the national level. While the National Guard's federal role is the primary focus, key actions by Guard soldiers in State service that have defined the Guard's standing in American society are closely examined. Part I, The Militia, and Part II, The National Guard, consider the origins and broad trends in the American militia tradition. Part III, The Army National Guard, takes a more in-depth look at the creation, contributions, and transformation of the Army National Guard during the Cold War and toward the end of the twentieth century. The origins and early history of the militia and National Guard have been previously well documented and recounted; therefore the early narrative draws extensively from the best secondary sources available. The use of primary source materials and official documents is most evident during the treatment and analysis of the National Guard in the twentieth century, especially after 1945. The story of the Air National Guard lies beyond the volume's intent; but the development of early National Guard flying units is included because of their important service and because their legacy is the foundation for today's Army National Guard aviation force.

One of the unfortunate effects of the Vietnam War and the implementation of the all-volunteer military in the 1970s has been a pronounced lack of knowledge among the American people regarding the armed forces. This is especially true regarding the heritage and contributions of citizen-soldiers serving in the National Guard and the other reserve components. The Persian Gulf War and the military's heavy involvement in peacekeeping operations throughout the 1990s has helped to raise awareness of the military's importance to American society. Now, the war on terrorism has propelled security and defense matters to the forefront of the national agenda. If *Civilian in Peace, Soldier in War* heightens awareness among the American people of the Army National Guard's long and proud service and its crucial role in the common defense, then this book will have achieved its highest purpose.

Acknowledgments

L IKE MOST SUCCESSFUL ENDEAVORS by the Army National Guard, the research, writing, publication, and distribution of its first official history was truly a team effort. General John W. Vessey, Jr. (Ret.), the former Chairman of the Joint Chiefs of Staff under President Ronald Reagan, graciously took the time from his busy schedule to write a particularly insightful and thought-provoking Foreword. I would like to recognize the Chief of the National Guard Bureau, Lt. Gen. Russell C. Davis, and the Bureau's Vice Chief, Maj. Gen. Raymond F. Rees, for their continued interest in the completion of the Army Guard's first official history. The Army National Guard History Project Editorial Board provided the content review and the significant resources required to complete this book, and each member deserves a special thanks. Maj. Gen. William A. Navas, Jr. (Ret.), the Director of the Army National Guard at the time, understood that an official history of the Army Guard was sorely needed and had the vision to begin the project. His successor, Lt. Gen. Roger C. Schultz, had the wisdom to continue the work and to give it his unwavering support. Brig. Gen. Michael J. Squier always provided welcome encouragement and valuable feedback. Brig. Gen. D. Allen Youngman, the Adjutant General of Kentucky, lent his considerable knowledge and analytical skills as well as his friendship to the completion of the task. Two Army National Guard chiefs of staff, Cols. Mark L. Juneau and Charles P. Baldwin, guaranteed the project's success by providing crucial administrative and logistical support.

A number of other institutions and individuals deserve special mention as well. The National Guard Association of the United States gave me complete access to the archival holdings of the National Guard Educational Foundation Library, which contains the best primary source materials on the National Guard in the entire nation. Lt. Col. Sherman Fleek, Ms. Renee Hylton, and Maj. Les Melnyk of the National Guard Bureau Historical Services Division provided yeoman's work in meticulously reviewing the manuscript. Capt. Mark Nelson of the Army National Guard Director's Staff Group performed valuable service in providing technical assistance with selected images. The staff of the U.S. Army's Military History Institute at Carlisle Barracks, Pennsylvania, did their usual outstanding work in assisting me with background research. Insightful comments from three preeminent scholars on the National Guard, Maj. Gen. Bruce Jacobs (Ret.), Col. Leonid E. Kondratiuk (Ret.), and Dr. Jerry Cooper of the University of Missouri–St. Louis, greatly improved the manuscript's analytical and interpretive worth. Chief Warrant Officer John W. Listman Jr. deserves full credit for gathering the photographs and performing essential research. The Army National Guard deputy chief of staff, Orville W. "Buck" Troesch Jr., provided key support at crucial moments of need throughout the three years required to complete the project. Karen Holly of the Army National Guard Installation Support Office worked tirelessly to make sure that publication and initial distribution of the original edition of the official history were completed in a timely manner.

I would like to extend a special word of thanks to the University Press of Kansas for making this new paperback edition of the Army Guard's first official history available to a broader reading audience. The press fully appreciated the significance and importance of the Army Guard's history, especially in light of the horrendous events of September 11, 2001. Mike Briggs and the entire staff did their usual professional job in moving the project quickly through to final publication.

In addition to the individuals named above, I would like to express a sincere word of thanks to all those who provided their interest, support, and encouragement as I toiled to finish the manuscript. The unfailing support of family, friends, and colleagues made an extremely challenging project all the more easier, and for that I am forever grateful.

Michael D. Doubler
Alexandria, Virginia
July 4, 2002

Part I
The Militia, 1636–1897

CHAPTER 1

The Colonial Militia, 1636–1775

E very Man therefore that wishes to secure his own Freedom, and thinks it his Duty to defend that of his Country, should, as he prides himself in being a Free Citizen, think it his truest Honour to be a Soldier Citizen.

> *Exercise for the Militia of the*
> *Province of the Massachusetts Bay,*
> Boston, 1758

Introduction

On the crest of a low, round hill, portions of two regiments of Massachusetts militia nearly five hundred strong stood in a line of battle, their weapons at the ready. None of the yeoman farmers wore uniforms, and their heavy work clothes and hats revealed no distinctions between officers and enlisted men. The regiment on the right was composed of new minute-man companies while the troops on the left were units of the standard, enrolled militia. They all stood quietly, awaiting orders as the morning sun climbed slowly into the eastern sky. Though it was already nine o'clock in the morning, most of the citizen-soldiers had been up well before sunrise. Pealing church bells, mounted couriers, rolling drums and the discharge of muskets in the hours before dawn had alerted the countryside of the approach of a heavy column of British infantry. Minutemen had dressed quickly, grabbed their muskets and rushed to the prearranged rally point of their town's company while enrolled militia companies assembled at a slow-er pace. Further to the west, the alarm had sounded just after sunrise when many farmers were already hard at work in the fields. Near the small farm-ing hamlet of Pepperel, Abel Parker was plowing when the alarm sounded. Parker left his plow in its furrow, and without stopping to unyoke his oxen, dashed to his house, seized his coat in one arm and his flintlock musket in the other and ran to his minuteman company's assembly point.

Colonel James Barrett was on horseback nearby. As the senior officer present, he commanded the minuteman and militia companies of the two regiments that had already rallied atop the hill. Barrett had full confidence in his men, and on the morning of April 19, 1775, he was ready to show the British Regulars that his militiamen were not afraid to fight. The citizen-soldiers all knew of the talk in Boston's barracks and rum houses where British Regulars voiced their utter contempt for the Yankee militia. But Colonel Barrett knew otherwise. Though most of his younger soldiers were inexperienced, many of the officers and sergeants were veterans of the French and Indian War and other campaigns. All of them had benefited during the past year from a thorough regime of drill and marksmanship training.

Beyond the hill at a distance of little more than two hundred yards, Barrett closely watched the British infantry positioned around North Bridge, a sturdy, arched wooden structure more than forty yards long that spanned the sluggish Concord River. The expected British raid sixteen miles deep into the Massachusetts countryside had finally come. A column of nearly 1,000 Redcoats had left Boston after midnight heading westward along the main road to Concord, intent on searching the town for weapons and war supplies. Just after sunrise, the British had engaged a militia company on the village common in Lexington, four miles east of Concord. There had been an exchange of musketry, with several of the Lexington men killed and wounded. As the British continued westward, the militia companies of Middlesex County had rallied at Concord. Before the British arrived, Barrett had withdrawn his men to the militia training field north of town to await the arrival of reinforcements. Even as he eyed the Redcoats, Barrett knew that other British soldiers were ransacking his own farm in their search for hidden war materials. Suddenly, a little more than a mile away, a thick, black plume of smoke arose from the center of Concord, a sure sign that the British had set a building afire.

"Will you let them burn the town down?" an officer suddenly asked. The unexpected challenge to Colonel Barrett's authority came from Lieutenant Joseph Hosmer, the acting regimental adjutant and a local firebrand who advocated open rebellion against the British Crown. Despite his abrupt manner, Hosmer was right; with the British setting fire to Concord, it was no longer possible for the militiamen to sit patiently atop the hill. Barrett turned and ordered his men to load their flintlocks. As the citizen-soldiers gripped powder horns and wooden ramrods to load their weapons, Barrett rode along the line reminding them not to open fire until fired upon, and that if shooting did erupt, they were to return fire as rapidly as possible. The soldiers had another standing order—they were to shoot the British

officers first in the hopes of making the other Redcoats break and run. At the far right of the battle line, Barrett gave orders to Major John Buttrick, the acting commander of Middlesex County's minuteman regiment. Buttrick was to march his minutemen down to the bridge and attempt a crossing of the Concord River without bringing on an engagement. Meanwhile, Barrett and the Middlesex militiamen would await the outcome of events from their position on top of the hill.

Down at North Bridge, Captain Walter Laurie of the 43rd Foot closely watched the Yankee militia. His orders that morning had been to occupy North Bridge and to prevent armed colonists from disrupting the search of Concord. With three companies of British infantry—nearly 120 soldiers in all—Captain Laurie held his position just beyond North Bridge. He had confidence in his soldiers and probably shared the Regulars' low opinion of the militia. A British officer leading the Concord expedition had bragged that if the lowly militia dared to appear they would surely scatter if he drew his sword only half way out of its scabbard. Yet, as the morning wore on and the two sides sat watching one another, the British became more aware that the Yankee militia greatly outnumbered them. The unexpected sight of the yeoman farmers loading their weapons only increased the Redcoats' concerns.

Suddenly, Captain Laurie noticed the line of minutemen leaving the distant hilltop. They descended from the height marching to the beat of a drum and began moving toward the bridge in a double file with loaded muskets at their sides. The British were astounded that the militia would dare to challenge them. Even more importantly, the citizen-soldiers' order and discipline surprised the onlookers. Slowly, as the British Regulars watched the steady, sure advance, they realized a trained and disciplined unit was approaching rather than an armed mob of disorganized farmers. Growing anxious, Captain Laurie ordered his three companies to fall back over the bridge quickly and to take up a close order firing formation on the far side. As the Redcoats withdrew across North Bridge, some of them pulled wooden planks from the roadbed. At the sight, a wave of anger swept through the approaching minutemen, and they shouted for the British to leave their bridge alone.

At the east end of the bridge, order broke down as the three British companies became intermingled. Redcoat officers attempted to sort out the confusion even as the minutemen neared the opposite end of the bridge. With Major Buttrick in the vanguard, the troops followed behind in a long column, marching two abreast, moving along an elevated causeway that led to the bridge. Suddenly, a shot rang out as one British soldier opened fire without orders. A second later, two other Redcoats shot at the minutemen, and finally the massed infantry let loose with a ragged volley. The Redcoats fired high, with most of their musket balls buzzing harmlessly over the heads of the minutemen. Several shots did find their mark, killing two citizen-soldiers instantly and wounding four others.

"Fire, fellow soldiers, for God's sake fire!" Major Buttrick shouted as soldiers fell around him. Immediately, the men behind took up the command, and shouts of "Fire! Fire!" rose along the entire length of the column. Minutemen scrambled out of formation, hastily forming a battle line at the west end of the bridge and along the narrow causeway and opened fire with a vengeance. Their muskets rang out with deadly accuracy as the minutemen carried out their standing orders; four of the eight British officers at the far end of the bridge fell in the opening shots. The minutemen loaded and fired with great accuracy as the roar of their discharging muskets echoed up and down the Concord River valley and a dense cloud of smoke boiled up over North Bridge. Before long, the weight of the militia musketry overwhelmed the Regulars. The British formation gave way, and the Redcoats turned and ran for their lives. As the minutemen peered through the dense smoke, the British infantry fled back toward Concord, abandoning their killed and wounded and ignoring the shouts of the surviving officers.

As the minutemen stood watching the British retreat, they perhaps did not fully realize that their actions had given birth to the world's greatest democracy. Years later, the triumph of the American minutemen at Concord's North Bridge would inspire Ralph Waldo Emerson to write:

> *By the rude bridge that arched the flood,*
> *Their flag to April's breeze unfurled,*
> *Here once the embattled farmers stood,*
> *And fired the shot heard round the world.*

The performance of American citizen-soldiers on April 19, 1775 was not a chance occurrence but rather the result of deliberate planning. The militia system that developed in Massachusetts in the late 18th Century embodied the natural evolution of nearly two hundred years of colonial military experience in North America. English settlers brought from their homeland two social attitudes that had a profound influence on America's continued development. Steeped in ancient tradition and codified into English law, the militia tradition called for the compulsory service of all free males between the ages of sixteen and sixty. In early North American settlements, colonial leaders readily adopted the philosophy and the specifics of militia service first learned in England. Additionally, the colonists brought to the New World a deep and abiding fear of standing armies as a repressive agent of ambitious monarchs. The eventual posting of British Regulars to America further deepened the feelings of distrust and bitterness that colonial militiamen had against full-time soldiers.

During the colonial period, the American militia performed a number of vital military functions. First and foremost, citizen-soldiers organized and armed themselves during prolonged struggles with Native Americans. In the absence of military assistance from Great Britain, the militia system alone guaranteed the success of early English colonization. As the Indian threat receded, militiamen found themselves more and more engaged against other colonial powers. Battles against the Spanish and French and service alongside British Regulars often revealed the militia's best and worst aspects. By the late 1700s, the militia was a bulwark against unwelcome British intrusion into colonial affairs.

The early militia expanded and developed in a number of different ways. All colonies (except Quaker-dominated Pennsylvania) initially adopted compulsory service and required militiamen to arm and equip themselves. Colonial legislatures, rather than Governors, regulated the militia and allowed the popular election of officers. Throughout the period, the quality of the militia varied greatly depending upon the proximity of an immediate threat. When danger neared, colonial leaders energized the militia, but as threats evaporated, militia units often fell apart from neglect. In New England, a society based on separate towns resulted in a militia system concentrated in closely knit, rural communities. In the South, economics and agriculture produced a plantation system that created militia units that were more widely dispersed, based on counties rather than towns, and concerned more often than not with the control of slave populations.

The English Militia Tradition

In Western civilization, the concept of an armed citizenry finds its beginnings in ancient Greece. The Greek city-states required military service of all able-bodied, free male citizens. Such service was usually of a short duration, and Greek citizen-soldiers fought locally to defend their own lands and city-state. The word "militia" comes from the Latin term *miles*, meaning "soldier".[1]

After the fall of the Roman Empire, the militia concept endured as the Saxon fyrd. The Saxon invasions of the 5th Century transplanted the fyrd to England. The Anglo-Saxon fyrd embodied two key concepts. Each male was obligated to military service and citizen-soldiers had to provide their own arms and equipment. Lacking any formal system of training, the real value of the fyrd was its ability to mass a great number of armed citizens at critical points on short notice.

The first legal roots of the American militia can be traced to the reign of King Henry II of England. Facing a civil war, Henry II turned to the militia for additional military support. In his "Assize of Arms" promulgated in 1181, the king formally levied the military obligation of every adult male in defense of the realm. Citizen-soldiers were required to arm and equip themselves based on their social status and economic standing. Henry II's Assize of Arms formally codified into English law the role of the militia and represented a turning point in the history of governments levying military obligations upon citizen-soldiers.

Subsequent laws provided better definition of the militia's characteristics. In 1285, the Statute of Winchester defined the militia as "every man between fifteen years of age and sixty years" and required every militiaman to maintain arms. In addition, the law required the inspection of arms twice annually. During the 14th Century, competition between the monarchy and Parliament resulted in constraints on the militia's employment. Under pressure from Parliament, the Crown promised that militia groups would not be used beyond the borders of their local shire unless there was the "sudden coming of strange enemies into the realm." Concerned over the Crown's power to impress all Englishmen into military service, Parliament passed other laws specifying that no citizen could be compelled to perform military service without the legislature's assent and that militiamen could serve outside their native shires only in the instance of "great necessity." With legal restrictions on the militia's employment overseas, the English monarchs turned increasingly to mercenaries for foreign ventures and the militia deteriorated significantly.

During Queen Mary's reign, domestic turmoil, religious fanaticism, and an increasing military threat from Spain resulted in a militia revival. Her Majesty's "An Acte for the Having of Horse, Armour and Weapon" added important new provisions to previous militia laws. Wealthy individuals were required to provide the resources for those too poor to arm and equip themselves. Each shire was to appoint a "Lord Lieutenant" responsible for mustering the local militia, inspecting arms and equipment, and conducting periodic training.

Queen Elizabeth's long reign from 1558 to 1603 witnessed an even bolder restructuring of the militia. The queen rejected the idea of increasing the effectiveness of the entire militia and instead decided to focus resources on a smaller portion of the militia population. Queen Elizabeth created "trained-bands," or trainbands, that represented a select group of militiamen chosen from each shire to receive proper arms and training. By 1573, London's trainbands included 3,000 militiamen who trained three times a week. Ten years later, 12,000 men out of the 180,000 carried on English muster roles were members of trainbands. The monarch called out the trainbands in the summer of 1588 as the Spanish Armada approached the British Isles. England would depend upon trainbands and the common militia for domestic defense until the establishment of the British Regular Army in 1661.

Increasingly, England's attention turned toward economic opportunities in the New World. In December 1606, three small English merchant vessels sponsored by the Virginia Company of London departed for the New World. The ships' crews and settlers on board hoped to establish a permanent English colony in North America. The colonists were fully aware of the dangers ahead and knew that their very survival depended to a large extent upon the ability to defend themselves. No organized group of professional soldiers accompanied the expedition, although a few experienced military adventurers were aboard. Citizen-soldiers were expected to fight and protect themselves, and the holds of the three ships contained arms and equipment. Perhaps more important to their survival, the English adventurers carried with them the centuries old tradition of militia service.

Military Forces in the New World

Well before the English set out to colonize North America, Native American, Spanish, and French military institutions existed in the New World. At the time of America's discovery, the powerful Aztec and Inca empires ruled Mexico and South America. Though the Spanish *conquistadores* brought new arms and tactics to bear against the Native Americans, the Indian empires fell victim to disease rather than weapons. Epidemics of typhoid, smallpox, measles, and other communicable diseases from Europe left only one million Native American survivors by the beginning of the 17th Century. At that time there were perhaps fewer than 300,000 Indians east of the Mississippi River. The Indian population was divided into numerous disparate tribes led by local chieftains. The most powerful group was the Iroquois Confederation centered between Niagara Falls and Lake Champlain. Indian warfare usually consisted of a war party of braves acting under the leadership of a local chieftain to exact revenge against a neighboring foe.[2]

The Spanish were the first to introduce European military institutions to the New World. On the heels of Columbus and other explorers, Spanish adventurers rushed to the New World in search of unimaginable riches. Only twenty years after Columbus discovered America, Hernando Cortez, one of the greatest Spanish *conquistadores*, ruthlessly destroyed the Aztec Empire and looted its treasures. The mining of vast deposits of gold and silver soon dominated Spanish interests. Military activity centered on protecting the mines, controlling the Indian populations and protecting the vital sea routes in the Caribbean that allowed convoys to carry precious metals back to Spain. Spanish military bases developed in Panama and at Veracruz, Havana, and Santiago. In 1509, Spanish settlers founded San Juan on the island of Puerto Rico, and King Ferdinand appointed Ponce De Leon as the Governor and "Captain of Land and Sea." With no Spanish Regulars available, Ponce de Leon organized the settlers and led them in two campaigns that subdued the island's Caribbean Indians. Afterwards, Ponce de Leon organized his *milicia* into the "Borinquen Regiment." ("Borinquen" was the original Indian name for Puerto Rico and has been a title of renown throughout Puerto Rico's history.) Spain commenced the fortification of Puerto Rico in 1527 and sent Regulars to garrison the island.[3]

In September 1565, the Spanish established St. Augustine, the oldest permanent European settlement on the North American continent. Florida became a Spanish military province with St. Augustine as its *presidio* or headquarters. Soon after its founding, the Spanish commander designated St. Augustine's civilian settlers as *milicia* and made them responsible for defending the outpost while Spanish Regulars defeated nearby French ventures. An early militia roster from St. Augustine in 1578 carries the names of forty-three citizen-soldiers. Through the years, Spain primarily relied upon Regulars to defend Florida while the Spanish militia performed auxiliary functions. Despite Indian uprisings and devastating raids from English privateers, St. Augustine survived as Spain's permanent outpost on the North American continent.[4]

Established Spanish bases in the south and abundant fishing grounds off Newfoundland drew French colonists to the upper regions of North America. The French soon occupied the St. Lawrence River valley, established a strong outpost at Quebec, and created a lucrative fur trade. The Iroquois represented a serious threat to the French. Alliances with Indian tribes hostile to the Iroquois allowed the French to establish outposts in the eastern Great Lakes and upper Ohio River valley. Eventually, France committed Regular troops to the St. Lawrence valley and organized the local population for defense. Militia companies soon formed in New France under the leadership of militia officers responsible for administration and training. By the mid-1600s, French ministers at Versailles viewed a militarized Canada as the best means of containing the expansion of English settlements beyond the Appalachian Mountains.[5]

The Virginia Militia, 1607–1646

On April 26, 1607, the vessels *Susan Constant, Goodspeed,* and *Discovery* rounded the head of Cape Henry on America's mid-Atlantic coast and entered the mouth of Chesapeake Bay searching for a suitable site for a permanent settlement. The small flotilla represented the investment hopes of the Virginia Company of London who intended to establish a profitable settlement based on trade with the Indians and the export of timber, tobacco, and precious metals. Concerns over security were second only to the profit motive. The Spanish to the south were a direct threat to English ambitions, and the settlers were acutely aware of the possibility of attacks from Native Americans. The only means of defense for the one hundred settlers on board was to serve as citizen-soldiers based on the English militia system. The vessels carried a substantial number of arms that included their own mounted cannon in addition to matchlocks, pikes, and swords.[6]

The settlers did not have to wait long to receive a clear demonstration of the need for security. On the evening of April 26th, a landing party splashed ashore near Cape Henry—the present-day site of Fort Story, Virginia—and before long a band of Indians shot arrows at the intruders. The English quickly withdrew without suffering casualties, and the engagement confirmed their perception of the Indians as inherently hostile. In subsequent days, the flotilla explored the environs of the lower James River searching for a suitable landing site that afforded concealment and early warning against Spanish maritime raids while offering suitable land defenses against Indian attacks. The settlers finally selected a marshy peninsula connected to the mainland by a narrow neck. On May 14th, the English unloaded their vessels and established the Jamestown colony. To protect the site from Indian intrusions, they erected a weak barrier of logs and brush.

Not long afterwards, curious Native Americans appeared to study the newcomers. In tidewater Virginia, a strong confederation of Indian tribes lived under the leadership of the chieftain Powhatan. All together, Powhatan's tribes could muster 2,500 braves against Jamestown's one hundred inhabitants. Before long, the Native Americans decided to eliminate the intruders. On May 26, 1607, 200 braves assaulted the settlement. A sharp engagement followed in which two colonists died. Their names unknown to history, the two settlers were the first English citizen-soldiers to die in America. Only gunfire and cannons from the three nearby ships saved the settlement from annihilation.[7]

In response, Jamestown took on the look of a fortified camp instead of a trading settlement. Within a week, standing orders were issued for organizing a defensive system. The constant carrying of weapons became customary, day and night watches were established, and organized training on Saturday became an established routine. A sturdy palisade fort replaced the ineffective barrier of brush and logs. They did not survive in written form, but the Jamestown orders might well be considered the first militia ordinances in American history.[8]

Though secure behind their defensive barrier, the settlers barely survived starvation and disease during the ensuing winter. In September 1608, Captain John Smith became Jamestown's undisputed leader. A mercenary by trade and a veteran of many campaigns on the European continent, Smith imposed military discipline and training in order to guarantee the settlement's survival and to provide the means for offensive action against the Indians. After further improving Jamestown's defenses and organizing the settlers for work details and guard duty, Smith began a training regime designed to prepare the citizen-soldiers to compete in open battle against Powhatan's braves.

By modern standards, early militia weapons were extremely crude. Troops frequently wore metal helmets and various pieces of body armor, including breast and back plates. Nearly one-third of citizen-soldiers carried pikes while others were armed with matchlocks, a dangerous and inaccurate gunpowder weapon. On muster days, militiamen practiced the complicated tactics and techniques more appropriate for European battlefields. One commonly used drill book described fifty-six steps for loading and firing a matchlock. In addition, the troops armed themselves with an array of knives and hatchets while leaders carried swords.

A musketeer armed with a matchlock from a European training manual published in 1608, the year after the founding of Jamestown, Virginia. The weaponry and equipment is typical of the earliest, American militia units. (Anne Brown Collection)

Once he was confident the militiamen could stand up in combat, Smith launched a series of devastating raids against Powhatan's people. The campaign first exposed the English to the unique style of Indian warfare that endured throughout the colonial period. An individual brave, his face carefully patterned with colorful pigments and armed with a bow and arrow and any variety of knives, clubs, and tomahawks, was a terrifying figure. Highly skilled in the techniques of wilderness fighting, an Indian warrior could cover great distances quickly while subsisting off the land or on a small supply of parched corn. A war party fought together on favorable ground either to make a stand or to launch an attack. No formal system of tactics prevailed except for the ambush, a form of attack in which the Native Americans were truly skilled. Over time, the Indians acquired gunpowder weapons and integrated them into their evasive fighting techniques.[9]

Smith's offensive terrorized the Powhatan tribes up and down the James River and introduced the English to the challenges of Indian warfare. Heavy helmets and body armor proved too cumbersome in forests and swamps, and militiamen only wore them when defending their fort. The colonists, deeply imbued with the linear tactics and feudal concepts of European warfare, developed utter contempt for the Indians' evasive tactics. Believing the Native Americans were little more than savages, the English were slow to adopt their unique fighting style. The English eventually discontinued the use of battle lines but persisted in moving along trails and paths in tight columns. Over time, the colonists developed a healthy respect for the fighting skills and mobility of their opponents. By the summer of 1609, Smith's offensive had resulted in an uneasy peace between Jamestown and Powhatan. Weeks later, an exploding powder charge badly burned Smith, and he returned to England for treatment.

After Captain John Smith's departure, the Virginia Colony continued strict military discipline and training to ensure Jamestown's continued existence and eventual profitability. More experienced soldiers arrived, assumed formal rank, divided the colony into standing units and imposed training regimes. The colonists waged a protracted war of raids and ambushes against Powhatan's warriors as even more English settlements grew up along the James River. A marriage in 1614 between Powhatan's daughter, Pocahontas, and one of the colonists resulted in a truce. Relieved that the struggle was over, the English abandoned their strict militia habits in order to focus all of their attention on growing tobacco.

Unfortunately, expanding English settlements and efforts to convert the Indians to Christianity caused a widening gulf between the two peoples. On March 22, 1622, the Indians launched a massive and coordinated surprise attack against all English settlements along the James River. In one awful day of bloody attacks, the Native Americans killed three hundred settlers, nearly one-quarter of the white population. After recovering from the shock, the colonists launched a series of bloody reprisals. Additional arms came from England, and for the first time, widely dispersed plantations and farms included an armed citizenry.[10]

In 1624, the Virginia Company went bankrupt and the English Crown assumed control of the colony. The Virginia Assembly moved to create a standing militia system to deter further Indian aggression. All males ages 16–60, except for "olde planters" and "newe commers," were liable for militia duty, and the legislators levied a series of taxes to buy arms and equipment. The assembly divided the colony into four military districts and created a responsive command structure based on county militia units. By the 1630s, Virginia mustered over 2,000 militiamen. When a second Indian uprising occurred in 1644, the militia struck back with powerful counterattacks. Over a two-year period the colonists gained the upper hand, and in 1646, the exhausted Powhatan confederation surrendered to English controls. Virginia's hard-won victory was the result of a militia system transplanted from England and successfully applied to the unique environment of the New World.[11]

The New England Militia, 1620–1676

On November 11, 1620, one hundred Pilgrims landed at Cape Cod and established the Plymouth Colony. Though they believed a hostile Indian population awaited them, the Pilgrims had taken only modest measures to arm and equip themselves. In an important step, the Plymouth Company had secured the services of Captain Miles Standish to act as a military advisor. The warning of an Indian raid on February 16, 1621 prompted action. The following day the Pilgrims met, formally elected Captain Standish as "their captain and military commander," and authorized him complete authority in militia matters.[12]

Standish moved quickly to impose order and discipline. He organized the Plymouth militia into four squadrons and instituted a thorough plan for watches, guards, and alarms. The colonists realized that their survival was at stake and gave Standish broad powers to instill discipline and levy punishments. When one recalcitrant Pilgrim refused to stand watch and called his commander a "beggarly rascal," Standish clapped the man into irons. Frequent musters and training sessions became common. Over time, militia activities became an integral part of the colony's social structure. In late 1621, the Pilgrims conducted a muster and an exercise of arms as part of the first Thanksgiving celebration, and two years later a militia muster and the "shooting off of many muskets" accompanied the festivities of one of Plymouth's first wedding celebrations.

In subsequent years, Plymouth's militia expanded and increased. As the original Plymouth Colony spread inland, the General Court ordered the creation of a militia company in every town under a local

"The March of Miles Standish" from a 1873 lithograph that portrays the early militia in the Plymouth Colony. (Anne Brown Collection)

commander who reported to Miles Standish. A Dutch visitor in 1627 witnessed a disciplined militia organization:

> They assemble by beat of a drum, each with
> his musket or firelock, in front of the captain's door;
> they have their cloaks on, and place themselves in order,
> three abreast, and they are led by a sergeant without
> beat of a drum…on the left hand [comes] the captain
> with his side-arms, and cloak on, and with a small
> cane in his hand; and so they march in good order,
> and each sets his arms down near him. Thus, they are
> constantly on their guard night and day.[13]

By 1639, the expanding Plymouth Colony included eight militia companies in as many towns. The ultimate responsibility for raising and maintaining the Plymouth militia remained in the hands of legislators rather than the Governor.[14]

Compared to their neighbors to the south, the Puritans of the Massachusetts Bay Colony took military matters much more seriously. A royal charter granted the colony extensive powers of self-government and permitted the shipment of arms and military supplies to America free of taxation. Aboard the first ships to arrive in Massachusetts Bay were the arms and equipment for a proposed company of one hundred soldiers. Captain John Endecott served as the colony's first militia leader and established a trading post at Salem in 1628. The following year Endecott completed the organization of Salem's first militia company.[15]

In June 1630, a Puritan fleet of eleven ships reached Massachusetts Bay, and settlements quickly sprang up along the coast. Almost immediately, the Puritans formed militia companies in Boston and Dorchester. As the population increased and spread inland, the Massachusetts General Court authorized the raising of additional companies, and by 1636, the colony included ten companies that ranged in size from sixty-four to two hundred men. A captain commanded each company and had the responsibility for musters, training, and discipline. Starting in 1636, the General Court permitted militiamen to elect their officers, and captains appointed noncommissioned officers. Musters occurred weekly on Saturdays. Money from fines levied against those absent or guilty of improper conduct during training went toward the purchase of arms and equipment.[16]

On December 13, 1636, the Massachusetts General Court directed the establishment of the first militia regiments in North America. A total of fifteen separate towns contributed as many companies with a combined strength of approximately 1,500 men to form three new regiments. The North, South, and East Regiments encompassed the entire colony in separate, geographic districts. A colonel commanded each regiment with assistance from a full-time, paid "muster master" who maintained unit rolls. All three regiments held elections for the choosing of company officers. Regiments eventually became the basis for all modern armies, and because Massachusetts was the first government in North America to raise militia regiments, December 13, 1636 has become recognized as the birth date of the modern U.S. National Guard. (Today, the 181st and 182nd Infantry and 101st Field Artillery as well as the 101st Engineer Battalion of the Massachusetts Army National Guard are the U.S. Army's oldest units because they directly trace their lineage to the North, South, and East Regiments established in 1636.)[17]

Increased tensions between colonists and Indians had done much to stimulate the formation of the regiments. New England's first serious war with the Indians occurred in 1637 when Massachusetts and Connecticut fought the Pequots. Hated and feared by other tribes, the bellicose Pequots resisted English migration into the Connecticut River valley and lived up to the meaning of their tribal name – "destroyer." After a series of incidents and reprisals in 1636, the colonists declared war on the Pequots. The decisive engagement of the war came on May 26, 1637 when a force of ninety Massachusetts and Connecticut militiamen aided by friendly Indians conducted a vicious surprise attack against a main Pequot stronghold on the upper reaches of the Mystic River. Attacking at dawn, militiamen broke through feeble fortifications and set fire to the village. Other militiamen and friendly Indians formed a solid ring around the flaming village and prevented the escape of survivors. In an orgy of violence, the attackers killed as many as 500 Pequots, including women and children, while suffering only two killed and twenty wounded. Within weeks, other militia units completed the near destruction of the entire Pequot tribe.[18]

The bloodshed of the Pequot War and the certainty of extended conflicts with other tribes resulted in the creation of the American minuteman, the most significant militia adaptation of the colonial period. To guarantee rapid responses against Indian raids along the colony's frontier, the Massachusetts General Court directed that a portion of the militia remain in a near constant state of heightened readiness. On August 12, 1645, legislators passed the first law to articulate the minuteman concept. Each militia company was to select a third of its members who "shall be ready at half an hour's warning" to respond to alarms. Minutemen were to have their arms, ammunition and equipment ready for immediate use day or night. For the next 130 years, Massachusetts retained the minuteman concept in various degrees of effectiveness depending upon the seriousness of perceived threats.[19]

In the aftermath of the military emergency of the Pequot War, Connecticut, Rhode Island, and New Hampshire created formal militia organizations. The Connecticut General Court retained for service three small militia companies raised during the war, and in 1650 passed broader legislation that enacted a more extensive militia system based on the Massachusetts model. By 1680, the Connecticut militia numbered 2,507 men. In May 1668, Portsmouth was the first town in Rhode Island to organize a trainband. All males ages 16–50 were liable for service—herdsmen and fishermen were exempted—and eight musters per year were required. Within three years, Rhode Island mustered two regiments. The New Hampshire militia came into existence with the chartering of the colony in 1679. The first militia units included four infantry companies, "one company of artillery...and one troop of horse."[20]

King Philip's War erupted in New England in 1675 becoming the first great war in American history and a traumatic conflict that threatened the very existence of the colonies. King Philip was the English name the colonists had bestowed upon the chieftain of the Wampanoag Indians who had considerable influence with the other New England tribes. Various acts of vandalism in the summer of 1675 soon led to a state of war between the colonists and Indian tribes inhabiting the lands from Cape

Cod to the upper Connecticut River. The war's most famous battle was the Great Swamp Fight on December 19, 1675. A combined force of 1,100 militiamen from Massachusetts, Plymouth, and Connecticut, aided by a number of Indian allies, raided the main settlement of the Narragansett Indians hidden away in Rhode Island's Great Swamp. Attacking in bitter cold and deep snows, the militia destroyed and burned the settlement. The Indians resisted valiantly with hundreds killed while the colonists lost approximately 200 men.[21]

After the Great Swamp Fight, the colonists became more effective fighters by adopting Indian tactics and employing additional Indian allies. The most effective Indian fighter of the period was Benjamin Church of Plymouth. Church organized a special company that combined militiamen and Indians into a single unit and blended European discipline with Native American stealth to create new tactics for forest warfare. Over the course of several months, Church's unit became the spearhead of the New England militia's efforts as he launched a series of punishing raids aimed at the destruction of Indian food supplies. The war effectively ended on August 12, 1676 when Church's men killed King Philip in an ambush. They beheaded Philip, cut off his hands, quartered his body and then hung each quarter from a different tree. King Philip's War rocked New England with its widespread devastation and loss of life. As many as 1,000 New Englanders were killed, and Indian losses were perhaps much higher. The most significant outcome was that the militia had provided an adequate defense of the colonies, broken the power of the New England Indian tribes, and gained the long-term security of the region's white settlements. The early Indian wars also proved that when the militia was not prepared and caught unawares at the opening stages of hostilities, it possessed the ability to rebound and organize itself into an effective fighting force.[22]

The Militia Expands and Evolves

In the decades following the first English settlements, all but one of the original thirteen colonies stretching from New Hampshire to Georgia established militia organizations. In all colonies, the militia included the obligated men actually or nominally enrolled for training and service at the local level. The legislatures normally granted service deferments to high government officials, ministers, university students, craftsmen, and fishermen and prohibited most African-Americans and Indians from serving. Citizen-soldiers carried on muster rolls and formed into geographically-based units available for immediate service became known collectively as the enrolled militia.

Adjacent to New England, the Dutch established the colony of New Netherlands in 1614 that initially relied upon the promise of Regulars rather than militiamen to provide defense. Fifty years later, a strong British military and naval expedition dropped anchor off the small city of New Amsterdam at the base of Manhattan Island and coerced the Dutch into surrendering. Shortly after capturing the colony and renaming it New York, the Duke of York established a militia. Before long, militia units protected the colony throughout the length of the Hudson River valley, from Albany in the north to New York in the south. In 1664, the General Assembly of New Jersey voted "to constitute trained bands" for the colony's defense. The legislators directed the militia "to suppress all mutinies and rebellions" and to wage war when necessary against "all Indians, strangers, and foreigners." William Penn established Pennsylvania in 1681, but the heavy pacifist influence of the Quakers and peaceful relations with the Indians precluded the establishment of a militia until the middle of the following century.[23]

In the mid-Atlantic region, the militia came to Maryland in 1634 with the founding of a settlement at St. Mary's on the western shore of Chesapeake Bay. Maryland very quickly established trainbands. Unlike Virginia and the New England colonies, Maryland refused to use the mili-

Infantry and cavalry units of the New York militia pass in review before the Governor in 1700. (Anne Brown Collection)

tia to intimidate or exterminate entire Indian villages for the wrong doings of a few renegade braves. However, the English Civil War did spark a prolonged, internal conflict in Maryland that often saw militia units fighting one another. The militia of the Swedish colony of Delaware was first called out on August 31, 1655 when a Dutch force threatened Fort Christina on the site of present day Wilmington. The fort's commander rode up and down the colony calling men into military service. The Dutch attack succeeded, and under their influence, the Delaware militia was given a formal peacetime structure that endured until the colony passed to English control. The continued existence of the militia drew Delaware away from the control of the Quakers in neighboring Pennsylvania and helped to maintain Delaware's status as a separate, political entity.[24]

In the South, the militia in the Carolinas developed along lines similar to those in Virginia where agriculture dominated the economy. Militia units in the North usually formed around towns, but in the South the larger tracts of land needed to support plantations and a more widely dispersed population resulted in militia units organized at the county level. The first English settlers came to the Carolina colony in April 1670, landing at Albemarle Point near present-day Charleston. The following year Carolina's Grand Council passed the colony's first militia law. In its early decades, the Carolina militia expended much effort fighting Indians, Spanish raiders, and pirates. In 1729, the colony split into North and South Carolina with separate militia organizations.[25]

Georgia became the last of the original thirteen colonies in 1733 when General James Oglethorpe established the city of Savannah on the high bluffs overlooking the Savannah River. One purpose for the founding of Georgia was to create a military buffer between the Carolinas and Spanish incursions from Florida. Because of constant attacks from the Spanish and Indians, Georgia created a three-tiered defense establishment of British Regulars, full-time colonial rangers, and enrolled militia. While Regulars and rangers saw service on an intermittent basis, the Georgia militia was the continuous bulwark that guaranteed the colony's survival.[26]

The use of full-time rangers in Georgia reflected the increasing use of different types of military forces throughout the colonies. As settlements moved further inland, the Indian threat to seaboard communities waned, and the enrolled militia deteriorated. In coastal cities and towns, enforcement of militia laws was lax. On the frontier, settlers based their defenses on widely dispersed blockhouses and stockades to provide protection against Indian uprisings. In 1645, Virginia built four forts along its frontier and raised suitable garrisons from the militia. The colony also created ranger units that patrolled the frontier hoping to detect or foil Indian attacks before they hit settlements. All along the forward face of the Appalachians, the colonies developed their own systems of forts and defense forces. Starting around 1675, the militia laid aside its matchlocks and pikes in favor of the sturdy, reliable flintlock musket that remained in service for nearly 150 years.[27]

Between 1689 and 1763, conflicting English, French, and Spanish interests involved the colonies in a series of near continuous wars. The typical colonial war pitted the American colonies against the French Canadians with Indian allies on both sides. When ambitious expeditions required more than the militia's local, defensive capabilities, the colonies relied more and more upon ad hoc organizations known as "provincial" troops for extended military operations beyond their borders. Colonial legislatures commissioned officers to raise and lead provincial units. Provincial units were formed from volunteers, draftees, substitutes and hirelings that came from the enrolled militia. The legislatures usually levied manpower quotas on each town, county or single militia unit. Volunteerism was the preferred recruiting method, but militiamen selected to serve who did not want to leave their families, farms, or shops for an extended period could avoid service by providing a substitute or paying a fine that allowed the colony to hire a replacement. As more members of the enrolled militia possessed the financial ability to find a substitute or pay a hefty fine in lieu of actual service, the members of provincial units came more and more from the lower rungs of society. Provincial troops serving for pay believed they had a binding contract with the government, and when their term of service was over or a perceived breach of contract occurred, they did not hesitate to stage a mutiny or desert in mass.[28]

The greatest accomplishment of provincial forces was the capture of the French fortress of Louisbourg in 1745 during King George's War. Located on Cape Breton Island off the coast of Nova Scotia, the huge fortress guarded the sea lanes in and out of the mouth of the St. Lawrence River and was perhaps France's most important strategic point in all of Canada. In a complex joint operation, the New England militia united with the Royal Navy to reduce the fortress. The New England colonies raised a provincial army of nearly 4,000 troops under the leadership of William Pepperell of Maine. When early recruiting efforts lagged, the colonial assemblies offered pay and the promise of plunder as compensation. On April 30, 1745, Pepperell's army successfully completed a hazardous landing on Cape Breton Island while British warships established a firm blockade. The provincials soon laid siege to the fortress, and the garrison surrendered thirty-nine days later. Louisbourg's capture by a militia army prompted enthusiastic celebrations in the colonies and in Britain. In following years, the successful siege took on near mythical proportions in the colonies as a clear demonstration of the native fighting abilities of American citizen-soldiers. However, New Englanders felt betrayed in 1748 when England returned Louisbourg to the French with the Peace of Aix-la-Chapelle. The diplomatic concession convinced Americans that Britain had scorned their sacrifices in favor of her own self interests and increased the widening social and political gap between England and the colonies.[29]

Minority participation in the militia usually centered on the utilization of African-Americans. Early militia laws defined and restricted the status of blacks. For example, a 1634 Virginia ordinance forbade free blacks and slaves from carrying firearms and ammunition or serving in the militia. In general, colonists believed that armed blacks would incite insurrections, force an end to slavery, and form alliances with Indian tribes. However, serious military threats eventually softened views on black militia service. New York used slaves to build fortifications and granted freedom to slaves who served with distinction in wartime. Eventually, the colonies passed laws that permitted slaves to accompany militia and provincial forces on campaign as musicians, teamsters, and laborers. A shortage of white manpower in the Carolinas resulted in the widespread use of blacks as armed militiamen. In 1705, nearly one-third of the men on Carolina muster rolls were African-Americans. During the Yamasse War of 1715, the South Carolina militia included units of armed blacks led by white officers. After the defeat of the Yamasse Indians, the Carolina militia restricted the use of blacks and turned its attention to controlling the growing slave population. Over time, the primary mission of the militia became the conduct of slave patrols that worked to ensure that slaves remained on their plantations.[30]

The French and Indian War, 1754–1763

The greatest of the colonial wars began out of a dispute over the control of the upper reaches of the Ohio River valley. England and France eventually engaged in the first true world war for the control of overseas possessions and the balance of power on the European continent. The outcome of the French and Indian War determined that England would become the dominant power in North America and added to the growing divide between the mother country and American colonists.[31]

During the early 1750s the French increased their presence in the upper Ohio Valley in order to block further English expansion. The arrival of Pennsylvania traders and Virginia land speculators in a region inhabited by Indian tribes and controlled by the French was a recipe for confrontation. In 1753, the French began construction of three forts between Lake Erie and the forks of the Ohio River where the Allegheny and Monongahela Rivers joined. Before the end of the year, Virginia sent Major George Washington to the contested region to demand a French withdrawal. The French politely refused Washington's demands and immediately began to reinforce and fortify their settlements in the region.

In an attempt to gain the upper hand, Virginia sent Washington back to the forks of the Ohio River in early 1754 with orders to build a fort. Washington supervised the construction work of forty Virginia militiamen until a large French force arrived. On April 17th, the Virginia militia conceded to French superiority. After Washington withdrew, the French went to work in earnest on the same site to complete a more formidable bastion they named Fort Duquesne. Determined to gain control of the region, Virginia sent Washington reinforcements. On May 28th, Washington ambushed and defeated a Canadian reconnaissance party, and knowing that French reprisals were certain, he built a circular palisade that became known as Fort Necessity. Additional reinforcements of Virginia and South Carolina militia brought Washington's strength to 400 soldiers, but they were not enough to stave off defeat. On July 3rd, a force of 700 French troops and Indians from Fort Duquesne attacked Washington's position. Short on food and ammunition, Washington surrendered after a nine-hour battle. The colonial militiamen were allowed to withdraw the next day under honorable conditions, and in return, Virginia was to keep its troops west of the Appalachians for a full year.

The crisis at the forks of the Ohio prompted the creation of the Pennsylvania militia, the last of the militias formed in the thirteen original colonies. Heavily influenced by the political dominance and pacifist religious beliefs of the Quakers, Pennsylvania had resisted the establishment of a formal militia system even though informal militia organizations known as "associators" had sprung up throughout the colony in the late 1740s. In the months following Washington's surrender at Fort Necessity, emboldened Indian raiding parties burned and looted a number of locations on the Pennsylvania frontier. On November 25, 1755, the Pennsylvania Assembly passed the colony's first militia law. Unlike the other colonies, militia service was voluntary rather than compulsory. No militiaman had to spend more than three days away from his home, and extended service was limited to three weeks. Additional legislation authorized the construction of a series of forts to guard the frontier along with a provisional regiment of full-time militiamen to serve as a garrison.

George Washington: Colonial Militiaman, 1753–1775

George Washington received his first experience as a military leader while serving as an officer in the Virginia militia. In his youth, Washington seemed destined for a life as a farmer and land surveyor. But with the death of his older brother in 1752, Washington moved to Mount Vernon, a large plantation on the Potomac River and received an officer's commission in the Virginia militia. In February 1753, the twenty-one year old Washington received the rank of major and a share of the responsibility for training Virginia troops. Ten months later, he volunteered for active service against French incursions in the upper Ohio Valley.

Anne Brown Collection

Washington's service in the French and Indian War gained him widespread recognition and valuable experience. His first command, which resulted in the surrender at Fort Necessity, only strengthened Washington's resolve. In 1755, he served as a volunteer aide to Maj. Gen. Edward Braddock during the disastrous expedition against Fort Duquesne. Washington's display of raw courage and tactical skills during Braddock's Defeat caused his personal reputation to soar. Afterwards, the Governor of Virginia placed him in overall command of the colony's frontier defenses. During the war, Washington learned the skills needed to lead soldiers in battle and observed the role discipline and training played in creating effective fighting units. He also learned that successful commanders paid attention to administrative matters, looked after the welfare of their troops and made do with limited resources. By 1758, Washington served as a brigade commander, the only American militia officer to achieve such rank in the war.

After the end of hostilities, Washington returned to Mount Vernon to resume his life as a planter and a local political leader. With the approach of the American Revolution, Washington remained loyal to Virginia. He accepted the command of the Virginia militia with the rank of colonel and represented the colony in the Continental Congress. After Lexington and Concord, the Congress appointed him to various committees dealing with military matters. On June 15, 1775, the Continental Congress unanimously elected Washington "General and Commander in Chief" of all Continental forces. For the next eight years, Washington led the Continental Army in battle and served as the Revolution's senior military officer while employing skills he first learned as a colonial militiaman.

In 1757, Pennsylvania passed a stronger law that created a militia system comparable to those in the other colonies.[32]

The news of French encroachment in the upper Ohio River valley prompted a swift British response. For the first time, London decided to commit British Regulars to North America. The British drew up an ambitious plan for four separate offensives against as many fortresses along the Canadian frontier. In early 1755, Maj. Gen. Edward Braddock arrived in Virginia with two regiments of British Regulars and the authority to recruit two additional regiments from among the colonists. Braddock also integrated colonial provincial regiments into his plans.

The most spectacular British failure of 1755 occurred directly under Braddock as he attempted to capture Fort Duquesne. Hacking its way through a vast, mountainous wilderness, Braddock's column of Regulars and provincials got to within a day's march of their objective. Along the banks of the Monongahela River on July 9th, a combined force of French and Indian troops collided with the British. The French force took up dispersed, hidden positions along both flanks of Braddock's column. Chaos and panic ensued as the Redcoats fought an invisible enemy hidden in the dense woods. Trained in the tactics of linear warfare, Braddock's soldiers were unprepared for the ambush. Braddock courageously attempted to rally his troops but fell mortally wounded, and the remnant of his shattered army fled in panic. "Braddock's Defeat" became familiar in the colonies as the symbol of the British Army's unwillingness and inability to adjust to the military environment of the New World.

The shock of Braddock's Defeat and a change in the government in London resulted in a more concerted war effort. The Royal Navy established a tight blockade of Canada while more British Regulars came to America for direct attacks against French strongholds. In 1758, British and colonial troops recaptured Louisbourg and took control of the site of Fort Duquesne; the latter the British renamed Fort Pitt, which became the genesis for Pittsburgh, Pennsylvania. Brig. Gen. James Wolfe conducted a spectacular campaign in 1759 that resulted in Quebec's capture on September 16th. The following year, the remaining French forces in Canada surrendered at Montreal. Victory in the French and Indian War gave England control of North America from St. Augustine to Hudson Bay and all lands between the Atlantic Ocean and the Mississippi River.

In spite of its successful outcome, the French and Indian War created a widening gulf between Great Britain and its American colonies. British Regulars developed a loathing for colonial provincial troops. British officers considered the Americans as ill-disciplined, prone to desertion, and lacking in basic military skills. Convinced of the limited aptitude of American troops, the British relegated most of them to support and auxiliary functions. Provincial troops built roads, drove wagons, constructed and repaired fortifications, and performed other menial tasks rather than fighting. All together, the British Army formed a low opinion of Americans as fighters, and it labeled the entire colonial militia as an ineffective institution. In many cases, the British Army's opinions were justified, but the aspersions cast upon the militia were based on an ignorance of colonial military practices. Most British officers confused ad hoc provincial forces with the enrolled militia and consequently misjudged the militia's ability to respond to crises closer to home. However, a minority of British officers did understand the difference between hired provincial troops and militiamen who chose to stay at home. "The Militia," one senior officer wrote, "are the real Inhabitants; Stout able Men, and for a brush, much better than the Provincial Troops, whom they hire whenever they can get them, and at any price."

Not all colonial units performed poorly, and provincial regiments from Pennsylvania, New York, and New Jersey established sound reputations. One of the best of these was the "New Jersey Blues" commanded by Col. Peter Schuyler. An experienced soldier, Schuyler organized his men as light infantry and trained, armed, and equipped them for forest combat. Unlike most provincial regiments, the New Jersey Blues were a standing unit with qualified leadership, well-trained and with good arms. Throughout the war, the regiment participated in almost all of the campaigns in upstate New York. With justifiable pride, the Governor of New Jersey reported to London that the New Jersey Blues were "universally allowed to be the best Provincial Regiment in America."[33]

If British Regulars formed a low opinion of colonial troops, the converse was true as well. British recruiting policies incensed Americans, especially when the English actively sought indentured servants for military service. Strict disciplinary measures that included the flogging of Redcoat soldiers for minor offenses appalled the colonists and further marked the British Army as a threatening and repressive institution. The quartering of British troops in colonial homes outraged Americans who insisted the practice was illegal. Still, British authorities pointed to the exigencies of the war and routinely placed troops into American homes. Braddock's Defeat emphasized the limits of the British Army in the minds of most Americans while the capture of Louisbourg endured as an example of the courage and innate abilities of militiamen. By the end of the French and Indian War, American citizen-soldiers held a high opinion of their own military prowess and a jaundiced view of the Regulars.

The Drift Toward Revolution

Great Britain established policies after the French and Indian War that eventually led to the American Revolution. The British Army remained in America after 1763 to protect the frontiers of the newly acquired territories, to maintain peace between settlers and Indians, and to regulate the fur trade. Many Americans were suspicious of a standing army posted on their land and argued that for nearly 150 years the militia alone had provided adequate security. Lastly, the British government for the first time instituted a series of colonial taxes designed to reduce its war debts and to pay the costs of maintaining Regular regiments in the colonies.

A continuing struggle over economic and political power during 1765–1775 created a gap between Great Britain and the colonies as wide and stormy as the Atlantic Ocean itself. In 1765, Parliament passed the Stamp and Quartering Acts that raised taxes in the colonies and required the colonists to provide the British Army with living accommodations and supplies. Colonial outrage caused the repeal of the Stamp Act, but the practice of Regulars quartered in American homes and public buildings endured. When the assemblies of New York and Massachusetts refused to provide supplies to the Redcoats and thumbed their noses at additional taxes, the British government disbanded the New York assembly and threatened the same action against Boston. The British government's reprisals against colonial political institutions sparked a growing resistance movement.

Increased agitation prompted most of the British Army to redeploy from the frontier to Boston, New York, Philadelphia, and Charleston. The close proximity of British Redcoats to political activists in Massachusetts sparked the infamous "Boston Massacre." On the night of March 5, 1770, a mob of dock workers and revolutionaries confronted British troops outside of a Boston customs house. After considerable provocation by the mob, panicked Redcoats opened fire on the angry crowd, killing five Bostonians. Afterwards, the British government withdrew its troops from the city. The Boston Massacre became a symbol of British political, economic, and military oppression and marked the British Army as a threat to liberty.

A political and economic impasse transpired until the night of December 16, 1773 when a group of militant Bostonians dumped three shiploads of tea into Boston harbor. The "Boston Tea Party" was a violent reaction to an effort by Parliament to coerce the colonies into purchasing the heavily taxed tea supply of a company granted a monopoly on tea sales in America. Parliament swiftly punished Massachusetts; the port of

Boston was closed until the city paid for the destroyed tea, the colony's charter was all but repealed, and the right to convene in town meetings was limited. In addition, Maj. Gen. Thomas Gage was appointed the new Governor and returned to Boston with 3,500 Regulars who were quartered in American homes and public buildings. In response to Parliament's actions, American political leaders convened a Continental Congress in Philadelphia on September 5, 1774 to fashion a collective response to the increasing political and economic tensions. The Continental Congress supported the civil disobedience in New England and called upon all colonies to strengthen their militias.[34]

Parliament's sanctions following the Boston Tea Party prompted an extraordinary response in Massachusetts. With their normal governing bodies all but eliminated, political activists assembled a new Provincial Congress in Worcester. Convinced that armed conflict with Britain was all but inevitable, the Provincial Congress viewed military preparedness as a top priority. The new government took control of all arms in the colony and organized Massachusetts for self-defense. The legislators created an intricate system of alarms and mounted messengers to facilitate quick, emergency communications across the countryside and to warn of unexpected British actions. Ringing church bells, discharging weapons, and shouting messengers on horseback formed the core of the alarm system.[35]

The Provincial Congress turned much of its attention to transforming the enrolled militia into a reliable field army. First, it insured the militia's loyalty and reliability by requiring all officers to resign. The extreme measure purged from the ranks all Loyalist officers, men with strong allegiance to the British monarchy who eschewed revolution and independence. All militia companies elected new officers, and in turn, the officers convened to elect battalion and regimental commanders and staffs from among themselves. Across Massachusetts, towns and counties expended considerable energy in preparing citizen-soldiers for action. All men were directed to carry firearms and to participate in more earnest and frequent musters. In the fall of 1774 militia units trained with a sense of urgency and determination not seen in years. New England ministers exhorted militiamen from the pulpit and compared them to a righteous David about to face off against an overbearing Goliath in the form of the British Regulars.[36]

The Provincial Congress' most important military measure was to resurrect the minuteman concept first created during the early wars against the Indians. The officers in each town enlisted as much as one-third of their soldiers who were prepared to react to an alarm at any time of day or night in a minute's notice and to meet at prearranged assembly points within thirty minutes. Each minuteman carried a clean musket and a bayonet, a knapsack, thirty rounds of ammunition and attended musters at least three times a week. Towns provided minutemen with enough supplies, provisions, and ammunition for two weeks of service. Across the colony, militia units met to select their minutemen, and no town had trouble in finding willing volunteers. Over time, minuteman regiments were organized along the same lines as militia regiments. In the minuteman regiments, Massachusetts drew from the manpower of its enrolled militia to create a well-armed and trained force of light infantry capable of rapid assembly and quick movement to any point in the colony.[37]

A strict regime of training and members with extensive military experience made the Massachusetts militia much more effective than outward appearances indicated. Frequent drill periods held on village commons instilled discipline and reinforced the chain of command. Many musters were dedicated entirely to marksmanship training. Captain Timothy Pickering of Salem wrote, published, and distributed simple instructions for the loading and firing of a musket as much as four times per minute while emphasizing aimed fire. "Lean the cheek against the butt of the firelock, shut the left eye, and look with the right along the barrel at the object you would hit," Pickering advised his fellow militiamen, "or, in other words, take good sight." All across the countryside, townspeople heard on nearly every day of the week the distant growl of company volleys from various militia units engaged in target practice. A large number of the militia officers and senior noncommissioned officers brought with them extensive military experience from the French and Indian War. In most cases, combat veterans replaced officers whose only prior qualification for service was loyalty to Britain or high social standing. Veterans were familiar with the challenges of leading soldiers in combat and tried to prepare younger men for the first shock of battle.[38]

The Provincial Congress well understood that arms and soldiers alone do not make an army and turned its attention to acquiring supplies. If armed conflict developed between the militia and the Regulars, the force that could sustain itself would eventually prevail. The Congress moved quickly to gain control of all of the arms, equipment, and ammunition available and established safe supply points and weapons caches in towns scattered throughout the colony. Concord held one of the greatest concentrations of war materials, making it a point of particular interest for the British.[39]

Lexington and Concord

A popular military maxim declares that when discussing war, amateurs speak of tactics while professional soldiers ponder logistics. It should come as no surprise then that the American Revolution began over a scramble to control the most precious commodity of 18th Century warfare: gunpowder. In Boston, General Gage received reliable intelligence reports of militia units forming, training, and gathering supplies in anticipation of hostilities. Hoping to prevent open conflict with the colonists, Gage decided to disarm the militia with a series of small, surgical raids secretly planned and carefully executed against known caches of war materials. His most important goal was to gain more secure control over cannons and gunpowder held in powder houses and forts ostensibly under British control. Few firearms were produced in America, and all gunpowder was imported from abroad. Without gunpowder, Gage knew the militia could not put up prolonged resistance.[40]

On September 1, 1774, British infantrymen descended on the main Massachusetts Powder House six miles west of Boston. The Redcoats discovered that the colonists had already removed a considerable amount of powder and quickly took possession of the remaining 250 half-barrels of gunpowder. General Gage's first "powder alarm" enraged the colonists, prompted militia units to muster on village commons, and further motivated efforts to raise militia units. A second powder alarm in mid-December against Fort William and Mary in New Hampshire was a British debacle. Learning of the raid beforehand, Boston activist and silversmith Paul Revere rode to New Hampshire with a warning. Four hundred New Hampshire militiamen soon captured the British fort, seizing 100 barrels of powder and 16 cannons before Redcoats from Boston arrived. In Rhode Island and Connecticut, militia units moved against British defenses at Newport, Providence, and New London to capture additional cannons and gunpowder.[41]

On February 22, 1775, Gage's troops moved against a cache of supplies in Salem. They conducted the raid on a Sunday in hopes that most colonists would be engaged in church activities. However, an early alarm caused the residents of Salem to stream from their meeting houses and delay the column while others removed arms and supplies to safer locations. The raiders finally reached their objective late in the day, only to find the war stocks gone. The withdrawal from Salem took on a new, ominous tone. As the Regulars returned to the coast to board ships for Boston, militia units took up positions in open fields along the escape route. Near the coast, the Marblehead Regiment, made up of rugged fishermen who respected the sea more than they did the British, stood in formation as the Redcoats passed. Both sides hurled shouts but neither opened fire. The militia's actions at Salem reflected the desire of political leaders who allowed the militia to demonstrate against the British but hoped the Redcoats would fire the first shot in a confrontation.[42]

The situation changed dramatically on April 14th when General Gage received direct orders from London to put down the insurrection by force. The ministers in London assumed that the "rebels" were nothing more than "a rude Rabble without plan, without concert and without conduct." Gage was directed to move quickly and decisively with all of the strength at his disposal to arrest the leaders of the rebellion, to disarm the militia and to restore order in the colony. He quickly approved a plan to strike a rapid, strong blow at the very heart of the uprising. A single column of British troops much larger than those used during previous powder alarms would strike far inland to arrest rebel leaders at Lexington and then destroy Massachusetts' largest cache of war supplies at Concord.[43]

If excellent British intelligence provided detailed information on colonial activities, poor security gave the colonists ample warning of Gage's massive raid. In a prodigious effort, they displaced nearly all of the supplies in Concord to safer locations. Community leaders reviewed plans for spreading a general alarm across the countryside. A lantern signal from the steeple of the Old North Church in Boston would indicate to adjacent towns that the British raid had begun while alarm riders spread the word further inland. Militia commanders received word that a threatening British raid was imminent and prepared both minuteman and enrolled militia units for action. Whenever the British raid came, the militia intended to react quickly and to muster their full strength against the Redcoats.[44]

Starting at ten o'clock on the night of April 18th, General Gage quietly mustered the troops required for the march on Lexington and Concord. Command of the expedition went to Lieutenant Colonel Francis Smith, an officer of good judgement and prudence but lacking in energy and decisiveness. Gage selected his best troops for the mission: twenty-one companies of grenadiers and light infantry with a total strength of nearly 900 soldiers. As the infantrymen boarded longboats and paddled their way across Boston harbor to a landing site near Cambridge, two lanterns glowing in the steeple of the Old North Church signaled to the surrounding countryside that the raid was underway. Meanwhile, Paul Revere rowed across Boston harbor to Charlestown where he acquired a horse and galloped further inland with the vital news. (It is an American myth that during his midnight ride Paul Revere shouted "The British are coming!" Instead he cried, "The Regulars are coming out!" a warning that had particular meaning for the militia.)[45]

Darkness, confusion, and marshy ground delayed the beginning of the march, and not until two o'clock on the morning of April 19th did the British begin moving toward Lexington. With clear skies and warm temperatures, the Redcoats made good time westward along the main highway. As the column moved deeper into the dark and hostile countryside, the troops grew concerned over the sights and sounds all around them of a general uprising. Across the entire countryside they heard the echoes of signal guns and church bells sounding the alarm. At a safe distance, dark figures on foot and on horseback lurked in the shadows keeping track of their progress. Nearly three miles short of Lexington, Lt. Col. Smith halted the column for a rest. It was clear that the Redcoats had lost the element of surprise, and Smith sent a messenger galloping back to Boston to inform General Gage that reinforcements might be necessary.

In Lexington, Captain John Parker had gathered his militia company on the village common around two o'clock in the morning. The forty-six year old Parker possessed more military experience than most of the British Regulars headed his way. In the French and Indian War he had fought with the British throughout Canada, including the capture of Quebec. Like a small number of towns, Lexington had declined to create a minuteman company under the control of the Provincial Congress, but did maintain a robust enrolled militia company. The composition of Parker's company reflected the militia's close family and social ties. Among the nearly seventy men in the company were eight pairs of fathers and sons, and nearly one quarter of the men were Parker's own blood

British infantry fire upon Captain John Parker's militia company on Lexington common just after sunrise on April 19, 1775. (Anne Brown Collection)

relatives or in-laws. Their ages ranged from sixty-five to nineteen. Among the citizen-soldiers was Prince Estabrook, an African-American slave who eventually gained his freedom because of his military service.

Lexington's decision not to raise a company of minutemen and the British route of advance determined that enrolled militiamen rather than minutemen would fire the opening rounds of the American Revolution. When it became apparent shortly after their muster that the British were still far away, the Lexington company retreated to the shelter of a large tavern just off the town common. At dawn a messenger brought word that the British column was approaching, and Captain Parker ordered his men to form up on the common. As the militiamen deployed into a line of battle, Parker shouted his orders: "Stand your ground! Don't fire unless fired upon! But if they want to have a war, let it begin here!" Moments later, the head of the British column reached the Lexington common. Seeing the militia, British officers directed the lead companies toward Parker's men. The Redcoats quickly deployed from a marching column to a line of battle as an officer barked, "Lay down your arms, you damn rebels!" Hoping to avoid a direct confrontation, Parker ordered his men to disperse. But before the militiamen could react, either a British officer on horseback or an American just off the village common fired one or more shots. The British infantry heard the shots and fired a few rounds without orders. Seconds later, at a range of no more than fifty yards, the British let loose with a volley followed by rapid, individual fire. A few Americans returned fire but most scattered under the unexpected shock of the British volley. In a matter of seconds, seven Lexington militiamen were killed and nine wounded.

After a lengthy pause to recover from the engagement, the British column continued westward toward Concord some five miles distant, arriving around eight o'clock. As the Redcoats approached, militia units assembling in Concord withdrew to a safer location north of town to await the arrival of reinforcements. By mid-morning, one regiment of minutemen and a second of enrolled militia had gathered north of Concord. Colonel Smith sent out detachments to occupy two bridges on the Concord River north and west of town in order to prevent militia units from interfering with the search. The British infantry conducted a thorough inspection of Concord but found few war materials. One prize was the discovery of a number of wooden gun carriages that the British made into a pyre and set ablaze. The smoke from the fire caused the militia regiments north of Concord to believe that the British were about to raze their town and prompted an attack on the Redcoat companies guarding the North Bridge. It was during this engagement that the "embattled farmers" fired the "shot heard round the world."

A detailed view from an early lithograph of the engagement at Concord's North Bridge on April 19, 1775. Heavy musketry from the minutemen (left) is prompting a British retreat (right). (Anne Brown Collection)

After fighting two engagements with the militia that morning and knowing that a general alarm was still spreading throughout the countryside, Colonel Smith's main concern became a swift return to the safety of Boston. With the unfruitful search of Concord completed, the column began the sixteen-mile return trip around noon. The British commander's concerns were well-founded. Militia companies from as far as twenty miles away were converging on the highway connecting Concord and Lexington. While popular history portrays the minutemen as firing upon the retreating British from hidden positions behind trees, rocks, and stone fences, the real battle was much more sophisticated. Militia commanders were intimately familiar with the terrain along the Boston highway and positioned their troops at critical points that afforded the best opportunities for inflicting casualties while minimizing their own losses. In reality, the retreating Redcoats faced a successive series of militia defensive positions that hampered their withdrawal all the way back to Boston.

One mile east of Concord, at a road junction named Meriam's Corner, the militia struck back at the British. For the first time that day, nearly 1,000 militiamen outnumbered their adversary. As the retreat toward Lexington continued, the combat was nearly continuous, and British losses soared. During the battle, Captain John Parker gathered his company of Lexington men, and in a remarkable feat of leadership, led them in an ambush that wounded the British commander, Colonel Smith. The timely arrival at Lexington of a British relief column 1,000-soldiers strong saved the original raiding party from all but certain annihilation. As the retreat continued eastward, the fighting intensified. Militia units fired and maneuvered skillfully to present a constant hail of musketry against the flanks and rear of the British column. The most vicious fighting of the day occurred in villages and farmhouses closer to Boston where the opposing sides gave no quarter in brutal hand-to-hand combat. At the Jason Russell house in Menotomy (present-day Arlington) the British trapped and killed some twelve Americans, the greatest single loss of the day. At Cambridge, a militia unit occupying a key bridge blocked the line of retreat to Boston. Desperately in seek of safety, the British column veered eastward toward the Charlestown Peninsula on the north side of Boston harbor, where good defensive terrain, darkness, and the protection of the British Navy finally put an end to the fighting. Before the day was over, as many as 14,000 Massachusetts militiamen from more than forty regiments had responded to the general alarm, but perhaps fewer than 4,000 had actually fired upon the Redcoats.

In the following days, both sides counted their losses. The militia suffered a total of ninety-four casualties: 50 killed, 39 wounded, and 5 missing. All together, twenty-three villages sustained casualties: Lexington alone suffered twenty men killed and wounded. Compared to the militia, the British suffered three times as much. Out of nearly 1,800 troops engaged, the Redcoats' casualties included 65 killed, 180 wounded, and 27 missing. Reluctantly, General Gage communicated to London his losses, the expedition's failed results, and a newfound respect for his adversaries. After the battle, one British commander wrote of the Yankee militia: "Whoever looks upon them as an irregular mob, will find himself very much mistaken. They have men amongst them who know very well what they are about..."[46]

Conclusions

The militia system that arose in the American colonies found its roots in the laws and traditions of England while adapting to the unique environment of the New World. Over time, the contributions of militia units in America far surpassed the limited roles that English militiamen had performed in the British Isles. The creation of the minuteman was a novel innovation that gave the American militia far greater capabilities.

By 1775, the colonial militia represented a revolution in military affairs. The old European system of limited warfare with small, professional armies led by aristocratic officers found a new and unusual challenge in an armed and trained citizenry fighting for principles rather than monarchical ambitions or personal gain. In this sense, the American militia foreshadowed the "nation in arms" that came with the French Revolution of 1789.

The American militia system developed its own unique traits and characteristics. The militia was a geographically-based, local defense force designed for limited service during short-term emergencies. The militia system served as both a training base and a reservoir of manpower. During local emergencies, entire militia units responded to alarms. For more ambitious and extended operations, the militia acted as a reservoir of trained manpower from which colonial leaders raised provincial units. Militiamen elected their own company leaders, and officers believed it was their responsibility to lead their men into battle, an obligation they were unwilling to cede to others. In general, citizen-soldiers believed they could not be sent beyond the borders of their own colony without their consent except under the most extreme circumstances. Legislators controlled the militia's organization and training while the Governors usually retained the right to commission senior ranking officers. In the New England and mid-Atlantic colonies, militia units formed around towns while the southern militias enjoyed county affiliations. Usually thought to reflect a universal military obligation of all males ages 16–60, the militia laws granted deferments to ministers, students, and certain key artisans while denying service to black slaves and Indians.

The militia made many important contributions during the colonial period. More than anything else, it insured the success of English colonization in America by protecting nascent settlements and colonies from attacks by Native Americans and other colonial powers. In a new and hostile land, the militia gave structure and security to settlements and became a critical, stabilizing element in colonial social life. As the Indian threat receded, the militia allowed the creation of provincial units for more ambitious and long-lasting operations during disputes with France and Spain. As America drifted toward conflict with England in the late 18th Century, a revised militia provided the means for combating British Regulars. In the end, the militia provided the foundation for military success in America, first against hostile Indians, then against France and Spain, and finally against England herself.

The Massachusetts militia in the battle of Lexington and Concord represented the zenith of the militia's accomplishments in the colonial period. In almost all respects, the militiamen on April 19, 1775 enjoyed conditions that ideally favored their system. The fight was a defensive battle of relatively short duration with militiamen serving under their own leaders on terrain they all knew intimately. The creation of minuteman units allowed an even faster, initial response and reflected the militia's tendency to allocate resources to meet the most serious and immediate threats. In addition, the militia benefited from an effective intelligence network, a complex system of alarms, experienced combat leaders, and a thorough regime of musters and marksmanship training. The failure of British Regulars to identify and understand the militia's inherent strengths and advantages largely explains their bloody failure at Lexington and Concord. But as an army of citizen-soldiers encircled Boston in late April 1775, the question of whether or not the militia could meet the demands of a protracted, far-flung war for American independence remained unanswered.

Chapter 2

Revolution and Early Nationhood, 1775–1794

B y keeping up in Peace "a well regulated, and disciplined Militia," we shall take the fairest and best method to preserve, for a long time to come, the happiness, dignity and Independence of our country.

George Washington,
Sentiments on a Peace Establishment, 1783

Introduction

Colonel William Prescott stood on the parapet of a stout, earthen redoubt studying the dazzling panorama of war that stretched out before him. The vantage point from atop Breed's Hill gave Prescott a commanding view of the entire Charlestown Peninsula, the city of Boston with its expansive harbor, and most of the surrounding countryside all of the way westward to Cambridge. On the afternoon of June 17, 1775 a battle was imminent, and curious spectators crowded the rooftops of Boston hoping to watch the first deliberate confrontation between the British Army and the American militia. In Boston harbor, a number of British warships lay at anchor, sporadically bombarding the increasing numbers of American militiamen flowing onto the Charlestown Peninsula.

However, the focus of Prescott's attention was nearly 2,000 British infantrymen drawn up in an attack formation some 400 yards east of Breed's Hill. The brilliant afternoon sun made the Redcoats shine bright with scarlet and steel. The long, upright bayonets gleaming in the afternoon sun caused Prescott serious concerns. His own Massachusetts militiamen had a limited amount of ammunition and lacked bayonets; if the fighting *became hand-to-hand, the British would have a distinct advantage. Still, Prescott felt better knowing that Colonel John Stark's New Hampshire militiamen had arrived to protect his left flank between the Breed's Hill redoubt and the Mystic River. It was now past three o'clock in the afternoon, and Prescott expected the British assault to begin at any moment.*

Colonel Prescott's Massachusetts regiment had been atop Breed's Hill for the past fifteen hours. Starting at midnight, his soldiers had worked diligently to construct a crude, square redoubt that by dawn was a credible defensive position. At sunrise, British lookouts observed that the Americans had occupied Breed's Hill, and a moment later British warships had opened fire on Prescott's position. One of the first shots struck and killed a militiaman at work in the redoubt. The first casualty came as a shock; work stopped as fellow citizen-soldiers gathered about to stare nervously at their dead comrade. Prescott intervened, gave instructions to bury the soldier in a shallow grave, and ordered his men back to work. Before long, another shell smashed the barrels containing the regiment's drinking water. Though hunger, thirst, fatigue, and fear took its toll on several soldiers, Prescott's men continued work on the redoubt as the Redcoats marshaled their forces for an all-out assault on the American positions across the waist of the Charlestown Peninsula.

The first British attack began at half past three o'clock. With flags flying, the British infantry marched up the front slope of Breed's Hill moving through waist high grass while negotiating stone and wooden fences that slowed the advance. British naval gunfire had set fire to the nearby town of Charlestown and smoke hung heavy over the battlefield as the entire settlement went up in flames. Prescott ordered his men to aim low, not to open fire until the Redcoats were very close and to concentrate on hitting the British officers. At a range of less than fifty yards, the Americans opened fire with a series of volleys that tore large gaps in the British ranks. The Redcoats hastily retreated, reformed, and attacked again. Now Prescott ordered his men not to open fire until the British were within thirty yards. The British infantry staggered before the militia's fire, and for the second time, fell back from Breed's Hill. All along the American lines, citizen-soldiers shouted wildly at their success in turning back the Regulars.

The militiamen's enthusiasm quieted when they observed the Redcoats forming for a third assault. In the redoubt, Prescott's men were desperately low on ammunition. Soldiers rummaged among the dead and wounded searching for powder horns and cartridge boxes. Enough ammunition remained for one last volley. The British soon charged again with an effort more determined than before. Prescott's men held their fire until the Redcoats were only twenty yards away and then let loose with a final, devastating volley that emptied their muskets. The British ranks staggered under the fire, recoiled and rushed headlong over the forward rampart of the redoubt. A desperate hand-to-hand fight ensued in which Prescott's militiaman used their empty muskets as clubs and wielded rocks, knives, and hatchets. Swinging his sword wildly, Prescott shouted orders for his soldiers to abandon the redoubt and to fall back to the safety of Bunker Hill at the western end of the Charlestown Peninsula. Before long, the British had complete control of the redoubt and counted the dead bodies of thirty militiamen they had run through with the bayonet.

Hours later, with his coat and trousers ripped by British bayonets but otherwise unhurt, Colonel Prescott told his superiors he was willing to retake the Breed's Hill redoubt if given command of three fresh regiments with sufficient ammunition and bayonets. Orders never came for the counterattack, but William Prescott and all of the militiamen on the Charlestown Peninsula forever remembered June 17, 1775 as the day they defied the British Regulars in open battle while inflicting twice as many casualties as they received.

In 1782, a year before the end of the American Revolution, the French scholar Abbe de Mably wrote to the Patriot leader John Adams seeking his thoughts on the writing of a comprehensive history of the war. The future President of the United States replied that any study of the Revolution required an understanding of the key institutions that had created American greatness in the colonial period and served as the basis of success during the recent war. To Adams, there were four critical institutions in American society: towns, religious congregations, schools, and the militia. Adams told the French scholar that the militia "comprehends the whole people…so that the whole country is ready to march for its own defense upon the first signal of alarm."[1]

Adams's belief in the importance of the militia to America's well-being was based upon a firsthand observation of citizen-soldiers during the American Revolution. The militia performed a myriad of functions during the eight years that marked America's second longest war. The militia fought the war's opening battles, formed the basis of the new Continental Army, reinforced the Continentals during crucial battles and campaigns, and performed other important auxiliary functions. Throughout all thirteen colonies, Patriot militiamen denied the British control of the countryside, stood their ground against Loyalist militia, and insured political support for their cause. However, the militia proved incapable of prevailing in battle alone against British Regulars and usually failed to provide sustained combat power during independent, extended operations.

The militia's predominant role in colonial society and its contributions during the American Revolution guaranteed the militia a permanent place as an enduring institution of the new United States. The creation of the Continental Army in 1775 resulted in a dual military system of American Regulars and militiamen that from the start was both complimentary and competitive. After the American Revolution, the proper place of Regulars and citizen-soldiers in a new national military establishment became a point of crucial debate between opposing political factions. The U.S. Constitution perpetuated a dual system of Regulars and citizen-soldiers for national defense and forever defined and affirmed the importance of the militia as an integral component of American society and government.

The Battle of Bunker Hill

In the days following the dramatic events of the battle of Lexington and Concord, a large, disparate collection of militiamen quickly gathered outside of Boston. The militiamen's wild-eyed enthusiasm was matched in intensity only by complete confusion. When it became apparent that a rematch with the British was not imminent, Massachusetts turned to the business of raising a more permanent army to conduct the siege of Boston. The Provincial Congress sent appeals to the neighboring colonies for reinforcements and then set about the task of organizing a New England army with a proposed strength of 13,600 soldiers. General Artemus Ward, the senior ranking officer in the Massachusetts militia, became the commander of the new army. Ward's first priority was to organize new regiments by recruiting men from existing minuteman and militia units who volunteered for service for the remainder of the year. On May 16th, Ward declared the first two regiments ready for service. By the second week in June, twenty-four regiments were organized, and the army mustered a total of 11,636 men. A dearth of quality leaders and chronic shortages of weapons, uniforms, and supplies greatly impeded training. The massive expenditure of ammunition on April 19th had reduced gunpowder supplies to dangerously low levels. General Ward prohibited marksmanship training and remained content to keep the British bottled up in Boston until more ammunition was available.[2]

The other New England colonies responded swiftly to the call for reinforcements. With a total strength of 1,400 officers and men, three regiments arrived from New Hampshire under the overall command of Col. John Stark. Tall and lean, Stark was a leader of daring and skill who had served as a captain in Rogers' Rangers during the French and Indian War. Perhaps more important than manpower, the New Hampshire militiamen brought with them the gunpowder they had captured at Fort William and Mary in advance of General Gage's failed powder

A gunner from the Rhode Island artillery in 1776. Rhode Island artillerymen acted as the first siege artillery during the investiture of Boston, 1775–1776. (Anne Brown Collection)

alarm the previous December. Connecticut sent two regiments that included the only militia company in the entire New England army to wear recognizable uniforms. Brig. Gen. Israel Putnam, a gregarious, stocky man of boundless energy, commanded one of the Connecticut regiments and developed a reputation as a man not afraid to fight. At the head of three Rhode Island regiments arriving in Boston rode Brig. Gen. Nathaniel Greene, a self-educated soldier who walked with a noticeable limp. In addition to 1,500 infantrymen, Rhode Island contributed twelve heavy guns that became the army's siege artillery.[3]

While the New England militia reorganized around Boston, other militiamen carried out the first American attack of the war. On May 10th, a militia force composed of Ethan Allen's Green Mountain Boys from Vermont and other militiamen under Col. Benedict Arnold captured Fort Ticonderoga on the southern shores of Lake Champlain. In a stealthy night attack, the militiamen entered the fort through an unsecured door and were on the fort's parade ground before a sentry challenged them. Ethan Allen received the fort's surrender from a surprised garrison commander still dressed in his nightshirt. The Americans eventually transported Fort Ticonderoga's heavy guns to Boston months later for use as siege artillery.[4]

Inside Boston, British infantrymen recovered from the trauma of Lexington and Concord while General Gage considered his next move. Appeals to London for additional troops fell on deaf ears. However, an unexpected form of aid appeared on May 26th when a warship arrived carrying Maj. Gens. William Howe, Henry Clinton, and John Burgoyne, a military triumvirate with considerable experience gained in Europe and America. In reality, the British government sent the commanders to goad Gage into action. On June 12th, acting under direct orders from London,

Gage imposed martial law, declared the New Englanders traitors, and offered a full pardon to all those willing to lay down their arms. At the same time, Gage agreed to conduct a limited offensive to capture the dominating heights on the Charlestown Peninsula on the north side of Boston harbor and the prominent terrain at Dorchester below the city. By occupying the surrounding high ground, the British intended to stop the militia from emplacing artillery that could dominate Boston and its harbor.[5]

Poor security in Boston allowed the Massachusetts Provincial Congress to learn of Gage's plan in short order. Hoping to prevent the British from gaining the upper hand, legislators ordered General Ward to occupy and fortify Bunker Hill, the highest of three hills on the Charlestown Peninsula. The assignment went to a Massachusetts regiment commanded by Col. William Prescott and reinforced by a large detachment of Connecticut troops. The 1,000-man expedition assembled on Cambridge Common on the late afternoon of June 16th with a wagon loaded with entrenching tools and a full equipage of weapons, ammunition, and food. After the president of Harvard College offered a divine blessing, the column headed for its objective under the cover of darkness. At Bunker Hill the reinforced regiment halted, and a council of war ensued. For reasons that remain unknown, Colonel Prescott decided to advance further down the peninsula and to entrench atop Breed's Hill, a steep, sixty-foot height on the outskirts of Charlestown. A supporting position was to be dug on Bunker Hill afterwards. Just before midnight the column reached Breed's Hill, and a militia engineer staked out the trace of a square redoubt measuring 132 feet on each side. New England farmers who had experience in clearing farmlands of rocks, trees, and stumps worked feverishly with picks, axes, and spades to dig their redoubt. By sunrise, the fort had taken on enough shape to give the soldiers cover against British naval gunfire.[6]

When General Gage learned of the surprise American encroachment, he abandoned his original plan for capturing the high ground above and below the city in favor of a single, strong riposte against the Charlestown Peninsula. Conferring with his other generals, they agreed that the Yankee militia's forward position on Breed's Hill presented an opportunity. The redoubt's location exposed a portion of the American army to destruction, and a stinging defeat of the militiamen defending Breed's Hill might spark the complete dissolution of the New England army and extinguish the entire rebellion. Gage committed five infantry regiments, a marine battalion and an artillery company—about 2,200 troops in all—to the assault and put General William Howe in overall command. Starting around one o'clock in the afternoon, British long

New England militiamen fight British grenadiers at close quarters during the battle of Bunker Hill, June 17, 1775. (Anne Brown Collection)

boats began ferrying the assault force from Boston's docks to a landing site on the eastern tip of the Charlestown Peninsula.[7]

The sight of British troops moving into attack positions prompted General Ward to rush reinforcements to Colonel Prescott. By three o'clock as many as 4,000 militiamen in various regiments and detachments from Massachusetts, Connecticut and New Hampshire defended a line that stretched continuously for 600 yards across the waist of the peninsula. The American defense in the south was anchored on Prescott's redoubt on Breed's Hill, and to the north two regiments of New Hampshire troops under Colonel John Stark defended a series of stone and rail fences. Further back on Bunker Hill, General Israel Putnam organized a collection of troops to construct defenses to support the forward positions.[8]

At half past three o'clock, General Howe launched his Redcoats in a main attack against John Stark's regiments while a second, supporting attack went straight toward Breed's Hill. High grass and broken terrain slowed the advance, and as the lines closed to within fifty yards, a sudden onslaught of American firepower from Stark's men posted behind a stone wall killed nearly 100 British soldiers in short order. On Breed's Hill, Prescott's men successfully defended their redoubt. Howe pulled his soldiers back, regrouped and launched the depleted regiments in a single, powerful blow aimed at the center of the American lines. From their prepared defenses on high ground, the militia again prevailed. Howe withdrew a second time, and around four-thirty in the afternoon concentrated his depleted forces in a single blow against the redoubt on Breed's Hill. Prescott's militiamen waited until the British closed within twenty yards before unleashing their last ammunition in a final volley. (While the last gunfire was surely at close range, there are no reliable accounts of anyone commanding "Don't fire until you see the whites of their eyes!") The Redcoats stormed into the redoubt and ejected the defenders at the point of the bayonet. Prescott's withdrawal sparked a general retreat back to Bunker Hill all along the American line. Howe's victorious and exhausted troops approached Bunker Hill but did not attack. By five o'clock the savage battle was over, and American units began withdrawing from Bunker Hill and the Charlestown Peninsula to the greater safety of the mainland.[9]

The Redcoats had successfully pushed the stubborn militiamen off the Charlestown Peninsula but at a staggering price. British casualties for the two and a half hour struggle totaled 1,034 men, or nearly half of the attacking force. Yankee marksmanship took a particularly heavy toll of British officers. Eighty-nine officers were killed or wounded, including all twelve members of General Howe's staff. A chastened General Gage reported the bloody victory to London, noting that "the loss we have sustained is greater than we can bear." The battle reinforced a healthy respect of the Yankee militia first gained at Lexington and Concord. "These people shew a Spirit and Conduct against us they never shewed against the French," Gage wrote to his superiors. "They are now spirited up by a Rage and Enthousiasm, as great as ever People were possessed of, and you must proceed in earnest or give the business up..."[10]

At Cambridge, General Ward reported American casualties as 450 killed, wounded, and captured, but total losses may have been higher. The militiamen had fought well by taking advantage of the terrain and demonstrating a surprising skill in fighting from hasty fortifications. Though forced to give up their defenses, the Americans took pride in the fact they had competed well in open battle against one of the best professional armies in the world while inflicting heavy losses. When the American Revolution ended eight years later, what became known as the battle of Bunker Hill remained the British Army's bloodiest single engagement of the war and took the lives of more British officers than any other battle.[11]

Congress Creates an Army

Despite the valor of American citizen-soldiers at Bunker Hill, the action revealed near fatal shortcomings in the New England army's discipline, staff work, and logistics. Obviously, a more professional fighting force was needed to compete on a level playing field with the British Army. The need was especially obvious to the Massachusetts Provincial Congress who nearly a month before Bunker Hill petitioned the Continental Congress to assume responsibility for "the regulation and general direction" of the army so that it might "more effectually answer the purpose designed."[12]

After lengthy debate, the Second Continental Congress acted on June 14, 1775—three days before Bunker Hill—to create the Continental Army, America's first standing force of Regulars. On that historic day in 1775, Congress voted to raise ten companies of riflemen from Pennsylvania, Maryland, and Virginia that became the first American troops to enlist directly into the Continental Army. (The designated birthday of the United States Army is June 14, 1775, nearly 150 years after the creation of the first militia regiments in 1636.) The following day, Congress appointed one of its own to serve as the commander in chief of the Continental Army. George Washington, a forty-three year old colonel in the Virginia militia and one of the Old Dominion's delegates in Congress, had made a profound impression on his fellow legislators with his imposing appearance, confident manner, and competent work in congressional military committees. Congress soon moved to appoint twelve general officers to serve under Washington. The promotions went to recognized leaders and were allocated among the thirteen colonies in proportion to the number of troops each contributed to the war effort. In raising the rifle companies from colonies beyond New England, appointing an army commander from Virginia, and designating general officers from throughout the colonies, Congress succeeded in creating broader support for the war and established the Continental Army as a national asset.[13]

Though it authorized a new, standing army, Congress in no way proposed any dissolution of the militia. Citizen-soldiers in organized units represented a vast reservoir of manpower for the Continental Army and at crucial times were to muster and fight alongside the new, American Regulars. Furthermore, Washington's army could not be in all places at any one time, and the militia would always be available to handle local emergencies wherever they might arise. Congress recommended to the colonies a number of plans for strengthening their militia that included the creation of minuteman units, the organization of standard regiments, and the creation of special committees in each of the colonial legislatures to oversee military matters.[14]

The actions of the Second Continental Congress created a series of important, historic precedents in the relationship between the country's highest legislative body and the military. Congress established itself as the country's principle policy making body in military affairs by involving itself in the organization, manning, and supply of the Continental Army. In its handling of military policy, Congress reinforced the concept of civilian control over the military first established by Parliament in Great Britain and then embraced by the colonial legislatures in their control of militia affairs. The clearest example of the exercise of civilian control was

Congress' selection of Washington as commander in chief followed by the appointment of subordinate general officers. In creating a Regular Army and maintaining a reliance on the militia, Congress produced a dual military system that would come to have a profound and enduring influence on nearly all matters of military policy.

Washington left Philadelphia on June 23rd, headed for his new command outside of Boston and escorted by a mounted militia unit, the Philadelphia Light Horse that later became known as the First Troop, Philadelphia City Cavalry. (The First Troop, Philadelphia City Cavalry remains today as the U.S. Army's oldest cavalry unit and serves in the Pennsylvania Army National Guard as Troop A, 104th Cavalry.) Washington arrived in Cambridge nine days later and quickly saw that building "a respectable army" would be a formidable task. All together, Washington's army numbered little more than 14,000 troops, and the shortage of gunpowder allowed each infantryman to carry no more than nine rounds. Short on ammunition and with only a handful of heavy artillery pieces, a classic siege of Boston was impossible. The situation forced Washington to maintain a solid infantry ring about Boston where a weakened British Army, now under the command of General Howe, suffered from a lack of food and the ravages of disease. Throughout the siege, Washington labored to create an American Army that was a close approximation of the British forces he had admired during the French and Indian War. For weeks on end, the new commander in chief worked tirelessly to establish better organization, training, and discipline while overcoming nearly insurmountable problems in administration and supply.[15]

Of all the obstacles Washington encountered, the most vexing was acquiring the manpower needed to maintain the Continental Army's ranks. The enlistments of most of the regiments in the New England army were set to expire at the end of December 1775. Efforts to recruit the militia into the Continental Army produced only 9,000 volunteers. The reluctance of militiamen to volunteer angered Washington. However, militiamen countered that they had born the burden of the struggle for nearly a year, starting with Gage's powder alarms and extending through Lexington and Concord, Bunker Hill, and the protracted siege of Boston, and that other fresh troops should volunteer to continue the struggle.[16]

On January 1, 1776, Washington published a general order establishing a Continental Army in the field consisting of twenty-seven regiments. Still short of personnel, the New England colonies provided replacement militia units at Boston so that by March 1776, 5,000 of the 14,000 troops available to Washington were citizen-soldiers. Congress eventually required the colonies to raise, organize, and equip regiments for the Continental Army that became known collectively as the "Continental line." For their efforts, the colonies were allowed to appoint regimental officers through the rank of colonel. Each colony maintained an interest in sustaining their Continental regiments as well as their local militia. The arrangement ensured that combinations of Continentals and militiamen would fight together in nearly all of the American Revolution's major engagements.[17]

The American Revolution in the North, 1775–1777

Great Britain clearly comprehended the need to quash the rebellious American colonies but never clearly formulated a coherent, long term strategy for winning the war. British planning and subsequent military operations focused alternately on capturing key, strategic points in America and in fomenting a general uprising among the Loyalist population. In general, British commanders believed that the occupation of major cities such as New York, Philadelphia, and Charleston would suffice to spark a Loyalist counterrevolution. British commanders counted on the Royal Navy to provide strategic mobility up and down the eastern seaboard and to control major river lines that provided easy access to the American interior.

At first glance, the war between Great Britain and the rebellious colonies appeared as an unequal contest. A powerful nation of more than ten million people with vast wealth and a professional army and navy confronted a loose confederation of colonies numbering two and a half million people that possessed no navy, a host of militia, and only a handful of Regulars. However, the British government failed to grasp the difficulties of asserting its authority over a widely dispersed population that lived throughout a vast tract of wilderness largely devoid of decisive, strategic points. British supply lines extended 3,000 miles across the hazardous North Atlantic, and supplies that Redcoats required often did not survive the passage. Rugged terrain and long distances made communications difficult, and jealous, egotistical British commanders on different fronts often failed to coordinate their efforts. Time and time again, British commanders overestimated the numbers and intensity of Loyalist support while underestimating the staying power and fighting abilities of American Continentals and militiamen. Recruiting adequate manpower for the British Army proved difficult, forcing London to resort to the widespread hiring of German mercenaries.[18]

During the American Revolution, the militia played a vital role in the winning of battles and campaigns and in controlling the allegiance of the populations scattered throughout the colonies. The northern campaigns during the war's early years demonstrate the important role the militia played in supporting conventional operations. While Washington formed the new Continental Army outside Boston, Congress authorized an ambitious venture against Canada designed to eliminate its use as a British base and perhaps lead to its assimilation as America's fourteenth colony.

Two American columns composed almost entirely of militiamen converged on the St. Lawrence River valley from different directions. Benedict Arnold, hero of Fort Ticonderoga and former commander of the Governor's Foot Guard of Connecticut, led a column of New York and New England militia in a direct, overland advance against Quebec. The only Continental unit with Arnold was a battalion of riflemen under the command of Colonel Daniel Morgan of Virginia, a veteran of Braddock's Defeat. With Washington's blessing, Arnold's troops left Massachusetts in mid-September and proceeded by boat to Maine. In one of the most grueling marches in American history, Arnold's soldiers struggled northward over a rugged, barren wilderness while suffering through bitter, winter weather. On November 9th, after a march of 400 miles in forty days, Arnold's haggard group of nearly 600 Continentals and militiamen reached the south bank of the St. Lawrence River across from Quebec. Despite the frigid weather, the energetic Arnold assembled a flotilla of small boats and began crossing the St. Lawrence on November 14th. As much as he wanted to capture Quebec, Arnold lacked the artillery and special equipment required to take the city. An impasse developed until reinforcements arrived from an unexpected quarter.[19]

While Arnold marched on Quebec from the south, a second column of American militiamen commanded by General Richard Montgomery approached from the west. Using Fort Ticonderoga as a base of operations, Montgomery had assembled an army of militiamen by late August and then advanced northward to threaten Montreal. On November 11th, Montgomery's troops captured Montreal and began preparations for a move on Quebec. Three weeks later, Montgomery and 300 men arrived at Quebec by ship carrying badly needed supplies, winter clothing, and weapons for Benedict Arnold's tattered force. On December 5th, Montgomery and Arnold deployed their combined force of approximately 1,000 men to besiege Quebec, but the British garrison showed no signs of surrendering.[20]

Aware that the militia's enlistments would expire at the end of the year, Montgomery and Arnold conducted a desperate night attack on December 30th during a blinding snowstorm. The struggle continued throughout the night, but the British, fighting from prepared defenses, retained the upper hand. By daybreak, Montgomery was dead, Arnold wounded and Morgan captured; nearly half of their troops were casualties. Arnold withdrew the survivors, established defensive positions a few miles from Quebec and begged for reinforcements. During the following spring both sides sent fresh troops to the St. Lawrence valley. Disease, starvation, and a series of setbacks at the hands of the British finally forced a withdrawal that ended with American troops returning to upstate New York in June 1776. For all its failures, the Canadian expedition showed that militiamen under proper leadership could fight during prolonged offensive operations. More importantly, the invasion bought precious time for the organization and training of the Continental Army and postponed British plans for an invasion of the colonies from Canada.[21]

George Washington's 1776 campaign illustrates the ways in which the Continental Army and the militia complemented each other. On March 17, 1776 the British finally evacuated Boston, and General William Howe sailed north to Halifax, Nova Scotia to organize British military and naval forces for a huge attack on New York City. Anticipating the British offensive, Washington moved his army from Boston to New York. The Declaration of Independence on July 4, 1776 buoyed recruiting, and Washington was able to put nearly 20,000 Continentals and militiamen into the field. During the ensuing battles around New York City, the performance of inexperienced Continentals and militia units ranged from the courageous to the ignominious. Maryland Continentals and the Delaware Regiment at the battle of Long Island first established their reputations as the hardest hitting troops of the Continental Line. In the last stages of the battle, the Marylanders counterattacked the British six times despite overwhelming odds. Watching the ardent effort from a short distance, an emotional George Washington exclaimed, "Good God! What brave fellows I must this day lose!" (Today the Maryland Continentals serve in the Maryland Army National Guard as the 175th Infantry, and the Delaware Regiment serves in the Delaware Army National Guard as the 198th Signal Battalion.) During the evacuation of Long Island, Washington relied upon the sturdy fishermen of Colonel John Glover's Marblehead Regiment from Marblehead, Massachusetts to man the longboats used to ferry the army to safety. At the opposite end of the spectrum, raw Connecticut militia broke and ran during a British landing at Kip's Bay on Manhattan despite the personal efforts of an enraged Washington to halt the rout. All throughout the New York campaign, the Americans suffered at the hands of superior British mobility and discipline while Washington took excessive risks that too often exposed his troops to unnecessary dangers.[22]

By early November Washington admitted defeat in New York and began a difficult retreat southward across New Jersey with the British in hot pursuit. The enlistments of Continentals and militiamen were due to expire at the end of December, and as Washington moved south his army slowly melted away. It was at this low point in the war that a frustrated Washington vented his spleen on citizen-soldiers. The commander-in-chief wrote to Congress that the militia "come in you cannot tell how, go, you cannot tell when; and act, you cannot tell where." Additionally, he said that they "consume your Provisions, exhaust your Stores, and leave you at least in a critical moment."[23]

In spite of Washington's condemnations, the militia made important contributions during one of the bleakest periods of the Revolution. As the British ranged further from New York City, New Jersey militia harassed Redcoat and Hessian outposts and attacked foraging parties. One British officer complained that the militia kept the army in a "perpetual harassment" and "lost us more men than the last campaign." After Washington's dwindling forces reached the safety of the Delaware River, an infusion of Pennsylvania militia and the arrival of detached Continentals raised the number of troops to 5,000. With the knowledge that his army might disappear at the end of the year, Washington planned a bold, surprise stroke against an isolated Hessian garrison at Trenton. Once again, Washington relied on the skills of John Glover's Massachusetts fishermen to ferry his troops across the ice-choked Delaware River on Christmas night of 1776. After the successful raid on Trenton, Washington defeated two isolated British regiments at Princeton on January 3, 1777. The twin victories offset the effects of earlier disasters around New York City and restored confidence in Washington's abilities. The Continental Army went into winter quarters in Morristown, New Jersey to prepare for coming campaigns while the militia returned to their homes.[24]

In 1777, the British Army moved by sea from New York City to the Chesapeake Bay, and Washington and Howe maneuvered against one another for several months in New Jersey, Delaware and outside Philadelphia, crossing swords at Brandywine and Germantown. Though Howe captured Philadelphia, Washington's mixed force of Continentals and militia fought well for the most part. Washington relied heavily on the Continentals but gained a greater respect for his militiamen. Many militia units had experienced several battles, and under improved leadership, they achieved better confidence and discipline.[25]

The militia's greatest contribution in the Revolution's northern theater occurred during the Saratoga campaign of 1777. Operating from Canada, a British army under General John Burgoyne aimed to attack southward along the line of Lake Champlain and the Hudson River valley to effect a juncture with British forces from New York City. By occupying the Hudson River valley, the British sought to split the colonies in two and to isolate New England, considered the hotbed of Patriot sentiment, from outside support. Burgoyne began his southward movement in June 1777 with a force of 7,200 British and Hessian Regulars and nearly 1,000 Loyalist militia and Indian allies. Fort Ticonderoga surrendered on June 27th, and Burgoyne decided in favor of a direct, overland advance on Saratoga, nearly one hundred miles away on the upper Hudson River. The British commander underestimated the transportation and logistical difficulties of moving and feeding a large force in the middle of a dense wilderness.[26]

A gathering multitude of Continentals and militiamen at first slowed Burgoyne's advance and finally forced the capitulation of the entire British force. As Burgoyne moved further southward, New York and the New England colonies realized the seriousness of the threat and sent militia units to upstate New York. The bad behavior of Burgoyne's Indian allies in scalping civilians motivated many militiamen to oppose the invasion. New Hampshire called upon favorite son John Stark, the hero of Bunker Hill, who had quit the Continental Army piqued over his inability to gain a promotion to brigadier general. New Hampshire commissioned Stark as a brigadier general of militia, and he quickly recruited 2,000 men and set out for the Hudson River valley. Meanwhile, Washington dispatched nearly 1,200 Continentals to the scene of the crisis, and General Horatio Gates assumed command of all American forces.[27]

Meanwhile, Burgoyne encountered increasing difficulties in feeding his troops and animals. More and more, the army spent its time foraging. On August 11th, Burgoyne dispatched a column of 650 Hessians to gather cattle and supplies reported at Bennington in southern Vermont. Unbeknownst to the Hessians, John Stark's army sat waiting for them at Bennington. On August 16th, the two forces collided in a sharp fight. Under Stark's leadership the militia performed magnificently and carried out all planned maneuvers as intended. Every Hessian mercenary was killed, wounded or fled. Later in the day, the militiamen attacked and defeated a second column of Hessians that Burgoyne had dispatched to reinforce the first expedition. The battle of Bennington gained the initiative for the Americans, denied vital supplies to Burgoyne's troops and eliminated about one-tenth of the enemy force.[28]

Despite the Bennington debacle, Burgoyne stubbornly pressed southward toward Saratoga. A coordinated British advance from New York City never materialized, and militia units put increasing pressure on the Redcoat column. In early September, Burgoyne informed London that whenever he attempted to advance that "militia in the amount of

"There, my lads, are the Hessians!" General John Stark shouted at the beginning of the battle of Bennington. "Tonight our flag floats over yonder hill, or Molly Stark is a widow!" The fight on August 16, 1777 was one of the few times militiamen in the American Revolution defeated European professional troops in open battle. (Anne Brown Collection)

three or four thousand assemble in twenty-four hours." Burgoyne managed to reach Saratoga, but south of the town Continentals and militiaman dug in their heels and allowed no further advance. The battles of Freeman's Farm and Bemis Heights convinced Burgoyne that further progress southward was hopeless. By October 8th, food supplies were low, forage was scarce, troops were deserting and the American militia had completely surrounded the Redcoats. Burgoyne finally surrendered his entire force of 6,000 troops at Saratoga on October 17th. As a result of the great victory, France negotiated an alliance with America in February 1778 that was tantamount to a declaration of war against England and provided the colonies with badly needed supplies, money, and French troops.[29]

The American Revolution in the South, 1778–1783

With the defeat at Saratoga and the return of the British Army to New York City in 1778, Great Britain abandoned its strategy of winning the war by capturing key, strategic points. A new strategy emerged that focused on subjugating the southern colonies where the British believed

British General John Burgoyne surrenders his sword and his army to General Horatio Gates and Colonel Daniel Morgan at Saratoga on October 17, 1777. (Anne Brown Collection)

most of the population held Loyalist tendencies. The British hoped to exploit the social and political divides between coastal planters and upcountry farmers while fomenting potential slave and Indian uprisings. After the British Army eliminated Continental and militia forces, Loyalist militia were to gain control of the countryside. The final phase of British strategy called for the reinstatement of Royal Governors. Starting in Georgia, the British hoped to spark a military and political groundswell that would allow them to reclaim the South and eventually all of the colonies.

With a paucity of Continental troops available for service in the South, much of the fighting fell to the militia. From the beginning of the Revolution, the militia had played a large role in promoting the Patriot cause below the Mason-Dixon Line. Virginia's Royalist Governor rallied sympathetic militiamen in an effort to retain the Old Dominion's allegiance to the Crown, but Patriot militia smashed the counterrevolution in December 1775 at the battle of Great Bridge. Two months later, a force of 1,000 North Carolina militiamen killed or captured a similar sized force of Loyalist militia at the battle of Moores Creek Bridge and prevented North Carolina from falling back into British hands. The South Carolina militia bore the lion's share of the burden of defeating a large

British expedition against Charleston in June 1776. The linchpin of the American defenses was a sturdy fort on Sullivan's Island that guarded access to the city's inner harbor. Col. William Moultrie defended the fort with his 2nd Regiment of South Carolina infantry. During the battle of Sullivan's Island on June 28, 1776, a combined force of militia and Continentals turned back a joint attack by British infantry and warships and prevented South Carolina from falling into enemy hands.[30]

The British return to the South began with the capture of Savannah in December 1778. By the end of the following summer a Royal Governor once again controlled Georgia, and the British began preparations for carrying the war into South Carolina. In the spring of 1780, a powerful British land and sea force clamped a tight hold around American troops defending Charleston. On May 12th, nearly 5,500 Continentals and militiamen surrendered in the greatest disaster to befall American arms during the entire war. Maj. Gen. Charles Cornwallis deployed his 8,000 British Regulars at outposts across South Carolina in an effort to reassert the Crown's control throughout the colony.[31]

The British occupation spawned a bloody guerilla war that pitted British Regulars and Loyalist militia against a dedicated contingent of

FORT MOULTRIE ON SULLIVANS ISLAND NEAR CHARLESTON, JUNE 28, 1776.

The successful defense of Fort Moultrie on Sullivan's Island on June 28, 1776 during Great Britain's first attempt to capture Charleston, South Carolina. (Anne Brown Collection)

South Carolina militiamen. Operating from secure bases in thick wood-lands and gloomy swamps, gifted leaders such as Thomas Sumter, Andrew Pickens and Francis Marion led their militiamen in raids against British and Loyalist outposts and foraging parties. Bloody, destructive reprisals by Loyalist militia against Patriot officials and property turned much of the neutral population against the British and the Loyalists. An increasing escalation of violence occurred between the opposing parties with the British using terror as a weapon against the Patriot militia. The mounted forces of Lt. Col. Banastre Tarleton gained an infamous reputation for brutality that included the execution of prisoners. In the Appalachian Mountains, the fear of spreading British control prompted small bands of militiamen to join forces with the South Carolina militia. On October 7, 1780 a small army of nearly 1,200 frontier militiamen armed mostly with long rifles encircled a small Loyalist militia force at King's Mountain in the northwest corner of South Carolina. The superior firepower and marksmanship of the frontier militia resulted in the eventual surrender of the entire Loyalist force. The Patriot militia proceeded to kill and scalp many of the prisoners mercilessly in retribution for Tarleton's previous excesses in slaughtering innocents and prisoners. King's Mountain was the turning point of the bitter guerilla war: it buoyed Patriot morale and deterred Loyalists from continuing their support of the British Army.[32]

While the guerilla war raged, General Cornwallis concentrated on defeating the Continentals. At the battle of Camden on August 16th, Cornwallis soundly defeated a mixed force of Continentals and militia attempting to advance into South Carolina. At the height of the battle, militiamen bolted in the face of vigorous attacks by British Regulars. After Camden, George Washington sent his trusted subordinate, Nathaniel Greene, southward with orders to redeem the situation. In a bold deci-sion, Greene split his army in two to prevent its complete annihilation at the hand of Cornwallis' Regulars and to buy time for the strengthening of his own forces. Greene put one wing of the army that headed into the interior under Daniel Morgan. In response, Cornwallis divided his own army and dispatched a fast-moving column of 1,100 infantry and cavalry under the ruthless Banastre Tarleton to destroy Morgan.[33]

Tarleton caught up with Morgan on January 17, 1781 west of King's Mountain at an open, sparsely wooded location known as the Cowpens. The unsuspecting Tarleton charged recklessly at the Americans, not knowing that Morgan had laid a trap for him through the clever deploy-ment of his mixed force of Continentals and militiamen. In the tactical masterpiece of the American Revolution, Morgan utilized the terrain and effectively maneuvered his soldiers—who were two-thirds militia—to crush the British with a double envelopment. The Redcoats surrendered

Anne Brown Collection

Maj. Gen. Nathaniel Greene
"Rise and Fight Again"

Nathaniel Greene was a self-made soldier whose stellar military career began as a private in the Rhode Island militia. By the end of the American Revolution, he served as a major general with a reputation for leadership second only to George Washington.

Nathaniel Greene was born in 1742 into a family of Rhode Island ironworkers. As a young man in charge of the family foundry, he gained valuable managerial and leadership skills. Raised a Quaker in the pacifist tradition, Greene nevertheless developed an avid interest in military affairs. In September 1773, Greene's congregation expelled him for attending a militia parade. In October 1774, he helped to form a militia company called the Kentish Guards, but fellow militiamen thought him unfit for command because of a noticeable limp caused by a stiff knee. Determined to remain in the militia, Greene served as a private. He became deeply involved in revising Rhode Island's militia laws and advising the General Assembly on defense matters. When Rhode Island raised three regiments in anticipation of war with Great Britain, the legislature considered the hobbling private as the best qualified military leader in the colony. After Lexington and Concord, Greene became a brigadier general of militia and led Rhode Island's troops to the aid of Massachusetts.

During the siege of Boston, Greene displayed exceptional leadership and managerial skills. The Continental Congress recognized his talents by appointing Greene as a brigadier general in the Continental Army. Greene served beside Washington during most of the army's early battles. In March 1778, he became the army's quartermaster general with the mission of improving a failed supply system. Greene's business background helped him immensely in improving the army's transportation system and in establishing an effective network of field supply depots.

After the battle of Camden, Greene became the senior American commander in the South. He skillfully combined the talents of militiamen and Regulars during a brilliant campaign that ultimately led to the exhaustion and withdrawal of the British Army. "We fight, get beat, rise and fight again," he once wrote in describing the fighting in the South. But Greene's characterization perhaps applied to all militiamen and Continentals who stoically endured through the many highs and lows of the Revolution.

Impoverished by the war, Greene accepted the ownership of a confiscated British estate near Savannah, Georgia in 1785. The following year, he died there unexpectedly of sunstroke at the age of only forty-four.

after suffering heavy losses, and Tarleton managed to escape with only a small band of cavalry. Together, the militia victories at King's Mountain and Cowpens stripped the British Army in the South of its most mobile troops, thus severely diminishing its ability to defeat the Americans.[34]

After Cowpens, Morgan marched north at a blistering pace to rejoin Greene's troops in central North Carolina. Cornwallis pursued the Americans as Greene withdrew his army northward into Virginia. Cornwallis pursued to the Virginia border but then retreated because of a lack of supplies. Greene followed the Redcoats back into North Carolina, and on March 5, 1781, the two armies collided at Guilford Court House. After a hard-fought battle, the British held the field but lost twice as many casualties as the Americans. With his ranks depleted and lacking supplies, Cornwallis withdrew to Wilmington on the coast and then decided to move his army northward by ship to Virginia. With the British Regulars out of action, Greene's army moved into South Carolina. One by one, the scattered British outposts throughout the colony fell to Greene's Continentals or to the militia. By October 1781, the British had withdrawn to the security of Charleston and Savannah as the Patriot militia reasserted its control over the countryside. Though Cornwallis had managed to defeat American forces in a number of standup battles, he never divined a way to overcome the militia. "I will not say much in praise of the militia of the Southern Colonies," Cornwallis once admitted, "but the list of British officers and soldiers killed and wounded by them...proves but too fatally that they are not wholly contemptible."[35]

The victory of Continentals and militiamen in the Carolinas created conditions for the final British defeat at Yorktown. The successful coordination of French troops and warships, along with Washington's march to the York-James Peninsula, resulted in the concentration of superior combat power against the British. With support from the Virginia militia, the Franco-American force hemmed the Redcoats in at Yorktown. After a short siege, Cornwallis surrendered his 8,000-man army on October 20, 1781. The largest British debacle of the war shook the British government and led to the suspension of military operations in America. Peace negotiations began in Paris in April 1782, but the participants did not reach a viable agreement until January 1783. The Continental Congress ratified the treaty in April, and the Peace of Paris ended the American Revolution on September 3, 1783.

At the end of eight years of war, the Continental Army and the militia shared credit for the profound victory. George Washington's cautious strategy of preserving the Continental Army as the most visible symbol and central rallying point of the American cause proved correct. Still, because of their persistently small numbers, Continentals did not win the war alone. The militia provided a vast reservoir of manpower for a multiplicity of military needs while fighting in a majority of the war's 1,331 recognized engagements and forming the basis for each colony's contribution to the Continental line. George Washington often condemned militiamen for their tendency to break in battle or to drift away at the end of a campaign. But during operations under his direct supervision, the militia provided valuable reinforcements at critical times and gave the commander in chief the numbers of troops required to mount successful, limited strikes against the British. Washington tended to ignore the militia's successes that occurred beyond the scope of his immediate supervision. In fact, the Patriot cause in the South, where Washington never served until the end at Yorktown, could not have succeeded without the militia. In most battles militiamen fought alongside Continentals, but the militia usually could not stand alone successfully in heads-on battle against British Regulars. The militia had a mixed record in open combat: for each militia rout, such as Kip's Bay or Camden, there were corresponding victories at Bennington and Cowpens. The Continental Army and the militia represented the two sides of a double-edged sword, and the victory would not have been possible without the achievements of both.

Away from the rattling musketry and booming cannon of deliberate battles, the militia performed essential work in sustaining the Patriot cause. More than anything else, the militia prevented native Loyalists from gaining the upper hand. Key Patriot militia victories at Moores Creek Bridge, Great Bridge, and King's Mountain stopped the Loyalists from regaining control of several colonies. The Patriots used militia enrollment as a litmus test to guarantee the allegiance and cooperation of the population. Militia patrols harassed British outposts, attacked Redcoat foraging parties, quashed pro-British activities and monitored enemy movements. One of the militia's greatest achievements in monitoring enemy activity came in September 1780 when a roving New York militia patrol captured Major John Andre and exposed Benedict Arnold's plot to turn the American defenses at West Point over to the British. Other militia activities included suppressing occasional Indian uprisings, repelling British maritime raids, enforcing local laws, garrisoning forts, guarding prisoners of war, transporting supplies, and patrolling against slave insurrections. Much more than the Continental Army, the British considered the militia as the greatest obstacle to winning back the sympathies and allegiances of American colonists. William Lenoir, an officer in the North Carolina militia, was almost constantly in the field or on alert for eight years. After the war, Lenoir probably reflected the experience of many militiamen when he recalled that during the war years he "slept with my wife on one side and my rifle on the other."[36]

The Militia and the Constitution

The Continental Congress remained the single ruling body over national affairs throughout the Revolution, but important changes in American government began well before the end of the war. In the Revolution's early years several colonies drafted new constitutions that created State governments. In the same vein, Congress created the Articles of Confederation in 1777 as a blueprint for a new national government. The States did not approve the Articles until 1781, and with the end of the war two years later, political leaders turned their attention to the creation of a more permanent, national government.

Two differing philosophies dominated the debate regarding the purpose and structure of a new government. The Federalists, led by Washington's former aide-de-camp Alexander Hamilton, believed that America needed a strong national government. To be successful, America had to become a vibrant nation-state, respected among foreign powers. The key ingredients in national success were a strong central government and a powerful, national bank to promote mercantilism and foreign trade. Thomas Jefferson, author of the Declaration of Independence and Governor of Virginia, became the principle advocate of an opposing view. Republicans—first known as Anti-Federalists— favored a central government stronger than that allowed by the Articles of Confederation but much weaker than the monarchies of Europe. To Republicans, the majority of the power in America belonged to the States because strong, central authority invited despotism and warmongering. The Federalists favored a vision of a country highly commercial and concentrated in urban centers; Republicans wanted America to remain rural and agrarian.

Differences between the two groups generated an acrimonious debate over the creation of a standing army that became a fundamental issue in the division of power between the States and the central government. The Federalists favored a strong defense establishment firmly under national control. They emphasized the militia's shortcomings during the Revolution and believed that reliance on the militia would weaken the new nation politically as well as militarily. An adequate, standing army was needed to support westward expansion and to serve as a model for the militia. A Regular Army needed support from a military academy, a system of arsenals, and munitions production facilities. To create a larger army in wartime, the central government would order into federal service militia units made more effective by the imposition of strict national standards for discipline and training. In cases of civil insurrection, the army and the militia together would restore order. For the Federalists, a strong reliance on the militia was anathema. A prominent

Federalist wrote that to rely primarily on the militia for national defense "was to lean on a broken reed."[37]

Republicans believed that for largely political reasons the nation had to trust its defense to citizen-soldiers rather than Regulars. The recent experience of the Revolution dominated Republican thinking. "Was it a standing army that gained the battles of Lexington and Bunker's Hill, and took the ill-fated Burgoyne?" one asked. "Is not a well regulated militia sufficient for every purpose of internal defense?" Secure in North America and protected by the barrier of the Atlantic Ocean, America need not waste its precious resources or endanger its liberties with an expensive, standing army. If a major conflict erupted, the ocean barrier would buy enough time to raise a sufficient army. The entire people were armed and organized through the militia, and even though a small Regular Army might be needed to garrison western outposts, embattled citizens organized by the States could act in their own defense. Republicans argued that a large, standing army might lead to the neglect and even outright elimination of the militia, leaving the people with no armed bulwark to protect their liberties. The experience of the British Army in America reinforced and expanded fears of the evils of a standing army. In terms of internal security, Republicans believed that any government that relied on Regulars to enforce laws smacked of tyranny. The States were to institute laws and insure their compliance through a judicious use of the militia. "The militia...is our ultimate safety," declared Patrick Henry of Virginia. "We can have no security without it."[38]

Events at the end of the Revolution fueled the debate over the power of the central government, civil-military relations and the need for a standing army. From the last cantonment of the Continental Army at Newburgh, New York, officers sparked a civil-military crisis by threatening to march on Congress because of a long simmering dispute over pensions. Personal intervention by George Washington in March 1783 placated the officers and ended the Newburgh Conspiracy, but the episode provided Congress with a frightening example of a standing army's potentially subversive nature. Two months later, the officer veterans of the Continental Army created a public furor when they announced the creation of the Society of the Cincinnati, a supposedly fraternal and charitable organization. Membership was hereditary, and Republicans wondered if the society was the first step toward a new American nobility. With a war chest garnered from charitable contributions and State auxiliaries established to exchange regular correspondence on public issues, suspicious onlookers wondered whether or not the veterans' organization had sinister, political motives. In June 1783, another example of the possible dangers of a standing army occurred when Continental troops of the Pennsylvania line, bitter over pay problems, marched on the State House in Philadelphia where both Congress and the State government were in session.[39]

In an effort to seek guidance on a proper military policy for the new nation, Congress appointed a special committee chaired by Alexander Hamilton who quickly sought the advice of the most prestigious military authority of the day. In May 1783, George Washington replied to Congress with his "Sentiments on a Peace Establishment," America's first "white paper" on national defense. Washington opined that an effective military included at least four elements. The first, essential component was a small Regular Army to garrison posts on the frontier, to protect trade routes, to defend against raids from British Canada and Spanish Florida and to provide security against surprise attacks. An equally important component of defense was "a well organized Militia" that was to benefit from a series of recommended reforms. Washington proposed that the central government and the States establish a system of arsenals for stockpiling arms and equipment. Lastly, he urged the founding of one or more military academies to teach the more difficult aspects of military science, especially engineering and artillery.[40]

Washington's recommendations regarding citizen-soldiers called for a major overhaul of the colonial militia system with an aim toward creating a "National Militia" better prepared to respond to the fledgling nation's needs. The former commander in chief called for the enrollment of all males ages 18–50. Perhaps inspired by the minuteman concept, every State was to form a special militia "Corps" by enrolling a small percentage of the most motivated and physically fit young men into elite units trained and prepared to "resist any sudden invasion." Washington believed that during a national crisis a standing army could act in concert with the most prepared militiamen to buy time for the central government to raise additional Regular troops and for the States to ready the balance of the enrolled militia for active campaigning. Congress was to create national "Military Rules" that prescribed uniform standards for the organization, training and equipping of all State units in order to make them compatible with active forces. In a major departure from the colonial militia system, Washington argued that the government should pay militiamen for muster days and active service and provide weapons, equipment, and uniforms. He called for the appointment of an "adjutant general" in each State to assist the Governor in administering the militia.[41]

Washington's "Sentiments" regarding the militia were clearly aimed at eliminating many of the shortcomings he had observed firsthand during the Revolution. Washington desired to refashion the militia into a more responsive and reliable institution by extending the central government's controls at the expense of State authority. Standardizing the militia would allow citizen-soldiers of the several States to join together quicker and more effectively into a unified, national effort. At the same time, the former Virginia militiaman clearly understood the vital role the citizenry should play in national defense and recognized America's strong militia tradition. Washington viewed a Regular Army and the militia as complimentary rather than competitive. It would fall to others in future years to recommend reductions in the militia as the means of supporting a larger, standing army.

Washington's great prestige and respected views proved inadequate to settle the differences between Federalists and Republicans on military matters. The final catalyst to reach some type of agreement over the shape and authority of a new, national government and its military institutions came from an unexpected quarter. Burdened by debts, taxes, and the threat of land seizures, yeoman farmers in western Massachusetts led by Daniel Shays rebelled against the State government in September 1786. Shays, a veteran of Bunker Hill and a former Continental Army officer who had served at Saratoga, convinced many militiamen to join in his cause against the government. Word of Shays's Rebellion spread rapidly across the country, and political leaders feared the uprising was the harbinger of widespread anarchy. The inability of the Continental Congress to organize an effective defense of the national arsenal at Springfield and the willingness of local militiamen to side with the insurgents emphasized the central government's impotence. In January 1787 an expedition of volunteer militia from eastern Massachusetts overwhelmed Shays's men in an engagement at Springfield and finally ended the uprising. The specter of Shays's Rebellion persuaded Congress and the States that an organized central government with the power and authority to deal effectively with political, economic, and military problems was a dire necessity.[42]

The greatest showdown between Federalists and Republicans on defense matters occurred in the spring of 1787 when the Constitutional Convention met in Philadelphia to draft a constitution for the fledgling United States. The U.S. Constitution gave the republic a federal form of government with shared responsibilities between the central government and the States. Broadly speaking, the Founding Fathers agreed that the military authority of the new country needed strengthening, but they used a system of checks and balances to distribute and control power even in military matters. At the federal level, military authority was split between the president and Congress. The Constitution appointed the president as commander in chief of the armed forces to guarantee civilian control over the military and granted implied powers for the president to employ the military as needed during wartime. Congress reserved the right to declare war, to "raise and support Armies" and to control all military appropriations.

The Constitution's militia clauses articulated a complex, balanced system of shared responsibilities within the federal government. The Republican Founding Fathers viewed the enrolled militia as a potential counterbalance against a repressive, standing army in the hands of a despotic leader. If the president served simultaneously as the commander in chief of the Regular Army and the militia, what would prevent a corrupt president from disbanding the militia and threatening the States with his professional army? To achieve a balance of power in the control of military forces, the Constitution gave primary responsibility for controlling the militia to Congress rather than the president. Congress retained for itself the powers for "organizing, arming and disciplining, the militia, and for governing such Part of them as may be employed in the service of the United States." The Constitution granted Congress the power to call out the militia for three specific purposes. Article I, Section 8 reads:

> To provide for calling forth the Militia to execute
> the Laws of the Union, suppress Insurrections and
> repel Invasions.

Article II, Section 2 describes the only direct relationship between the president and the militia. Once Congress ordered the militia "called into the actual service of the United States," the president was to act as commander in chief "of the Militia of the several States."

The Constitution established a balance of power in militia affairs between the federal government and the States. Article II, Section 8 reserved to the States the right to appoint officers and the authority to train the militia "according to the discipline prescribed by Congress." To insure the militia's primacy and to prevent the States from creating extra-legal forces, Article II, Section 9 specified that no State could "keep troops" without "the consent of Congress." Republican extremists resented the intrusion of the federal government into the previously unfettered authority of the States to administer the militia. In limiting State powers, some Republicans grumbled that the Constitution had relegated the States to a role little more than that of a "drill-sergeant."[43]

Starting with Delaware in December 1787, the States ratified the Constitution. In May 1790, Rhode Island was the last of the original thirteen colonies to grant approval. However, the States urged Congress to adopt a specific enumeration of individual freedoms, and in 1791, the Bill of Rights became the Constitution's first amendments. Two of the ten amendments dealt specifically with military matters. Reflecting the recent experience of the British Army in America and acknowledging the potential abuses that might come with a standing army, the Third Amendment prohibited the quartering of troops in private homes without the "consent of the Owner" and only "in a manner to be prescribed by law."

The Republicans feared that the federal government might one day usurp excessive powers and dissolve the militia. In the minds of States' rights advocates, the defining characteristic of the militia was an armed citizenry. A generation of leaders who had just fought the Revolution clearly understood that in the most dire circumstances political authority ultimately came out of the barrel of a gun. A specific proviso guaranteeing the existence of an armed citizenry was designed to insure the militia's continued survival even in the face of extreme abuses from the federal government. The Second Amendment states:

> A well regulated Militia, being necessary to
> the security of a free State, the right of the people
> to keep and bear Arms shall not be infringed.

In the late 20th Century the Second Amendment became the center of a social and legal controversy between those wanting to restrict gun ownership and others who insist that Americans have the inalienable right to bear arms. In 1791, the Second Amendment's reference to "a free State" pertained to the individual States rather than to the entire country or the population at large, and it seems very likely that the States intended the amendment to apply exclusively to the weapons in the hands of the enrolled militia.[44]

The Militia Act of 1792

In the years immediately following ratification of the Constitution, defense matters competed with other demands for the time and attention of the first president and the Congress. After his inauguration in April 1789, George Washington grappled with a number of crises beyond the Appalachians between early settlers and various Indian tribes. Washington pressed Congress to pass legislation that better defined the president's military powers outlined in only general terms in the Constitution. In August 1789, Congress created the Department of War and appointed Henry Knox, a former Massachusetts militiaman who had served as the Continental Army's chief of artillery, as the first secretary of war. The Federalists continued to argue that if the American people were unwilling to support an adequate, standing army, more disciplined and reliable State forces were needed. As much as national legislators may have wanted to address military issues, questions over the nation's finances, foreign affairs, and wrangling over the location of a new capital city dominated the congressional agenda.

In January 1790, the Washington Administration attempted to goad Congress into action by putting forth its own plan for militia reform. The brainchild of Secretary of War Knox, the plan's principle objectives were to provide the militia with better training and organization and to bring State forces under increased federal control. A main feature of the plan was to organize the militia by age groupings so as to concentrate time and money on those segments of the militia best suited for field duty. Militiamen ages 18–20 would undergo thirty days of instruction each year at "camps of discipline" intended to teach basic soldier skills and to impart the best values of citizenship. Only attendance at militia camps would qualify American youth to vote, hold office and exercise other legal rights. The bulk of the militia was to form a "main corps" consisting of all citizen-soldiers ages 21–45. This corps constituted a national manpower pool for the creation of armies for prolonged conflicts. Militiamen ages 46–60 were to belong to a "reserve corps," a kind of home defense force that mustered only twice each year and was to be called out only in the event of an actual invasion. Echoing Washington's "Sentiments," the Knox plan called for the federal government to provide the militia with all arms, equipment, and uniforms. State units were to become compatible with federal forces by conforming with standard, approved designs for unit organization. A final provision required senior militia officers to render periodic status reports to federal authorities.[45]

Congress and much of the public greeted the Knox plan with skepticism and disbelief. The projected expense alone—a minimum of $400,000 annually—shocked most congressmen. Businessmen and craftsmen objected to sending young workers and artisans off to training camps for four weeks each year. The public feared that military camps would corrupt young men's morals and militarize the entire nation. Many congressmen and State officials questioned the value of implementing national standards for service and unit organizations. For example, the southern States needed more militia cavalry units for slave patrols while no such need existed in the North. Republicans saw the plan as a huge intrusion into State affairs that ran contrary to the intent of the Constitution's carefully crafted clauses regarding federal and State control over the militia.[46]

In May 1792, Congress countered by enacting into law a militia plan of its own. The Militia Act of 1792 required all free, able-bodied men ages

18–45 to serve in the enrolled militia and to provide their own weapons and equipment. Federal and State elected officials were exempt from duty, as were postmen, mariners, and a variety of other skilled workers. No federal monies were authorized for pay, equipment, training or any other purpose. Congress attempted to impose standard unit designs upon State units but stipulated that standard formations were to be created only "if convenient." The law authorized an Adjutant General (AG) in each State to enact the orders of the Governor. The AG was to supervise unit training, discipline, and administration and to provide formal, periodic reports to the Governor on the militia's "arms, accoutrements and ammunition" and on all matters relating to "the general advancement of good order and discipline." The law's greatest weakness was that it contained no sanctions for noncompliance. The act represented the triumph of the Republicans over the Federalists in militia affairs by reserving to the States near complete control over their soldiers.[47]

In the same month, Congress passed another statute vital to the militia's future. The "Calling Forth Act" clarified many of the Constitution's powers and delegated to the president some of Congress' authority to call the militia into federal service. Whenever the United States was invaded or a threat of invasion was imminent, the president received blanket authority to call out as many militiamen from as many States as necessary to meet the crisis. In the same manner, Congress gave the president power to call out the militia to suppress "insurrections in any State" but only after the legislature or the Governor of the affected State had requested federal assistance. However, the president had limited powers in using the militia to enforce federal laws. Before the president could dispatch militiamen for law enforcement, an associate justice or district judge had to inform the president that lawbreakers were too strong and pervasive for local law enforcement to control. While in federal service, militiamen were to receive the same pay and allowances as Regulars but could not be compelled to serve more than three months per year. Unlike the Militia Act of 1792, the Calling Forth Act included sanctions to force compliance. Militiamen failing to follow the president's orders "in any of the cases before cited" were subject to heavy fines and even courts martial.[48]

All fifteen States—Vermont and Kentucky joined the Union in 1791 and 1792, respectively—enacted their own militia laws in response to congressional action. State laws confirmed the right of the people to bear arms, installed the Governor as the commander in chief of the militia and appointed a State AG. As a general rule, State constitutions and laws specified that militia units could not serve beyond State borders without specific authorization. Most States retained the colonial practice of electing junior officers, but the appointment of more senior officers was usually reserved to the Governor or the legislature. However, State laws varied in a number of ways. In States where threats from Indians and foreign troops were real, muster days remained frequent. Militia units in more secure areas trained as little as once a year. In New England, the States began supplying muskets to poor militiamen who lacked the means to purchase their own firearms. Some States allowed blacks, Indians, and other minorities to serve but not to bear arms. The southern States required militiamen to participate in slave patrols whose main purpose was to discourage runaways and prevent slave uprisings by insuring that slaves remained on their plantations.[49]

The Militia in Federal Service, 1794

At the end of the Revolution, Congress had quickly disbanded the Continental Army. In October 1783, only six months after the Peace of Paris, all national troops who had enlisted in the Continental Army for the duration of the war were discharged. Over the following months, Congress released troops serving under other conditions of enlistment. On June 2, 1784, national military forces reached an historic nadir: only eighty broken-down veterans remained to guard the military stores at West Point and Fort Pitt. By its actions, Congress established an important precedent. The immediate dismantling of the very forces that had achieved victory was to occur after every major conflict in American history.[50]

Traditional fears over the evils of a standing army and the expense of maintaining Regular troops could not negate the growing need for some type of field force. The flow of settlers into the Ohio River valley and the threat from British forts in the Great Lakes region resulted in a national army of Regulars and militiamen. The focus of attention was the Northwest Territory, organized by Congress in 1787 and encompassing the region north of the Ohio River and east of the upper Mississippi River. A loose confederation of Indian tribes with British backing contested the white settlement of the territory. Treaties with the Indians attempted to restrict the white migration, but the great host of Americans floating down the Ohio River on flatboats to find new settlements resulted in deadly confrontations. Mounted Kentucky militiamen conducted frequent raids northward across the Ohio River in grim retribution for Indian attacks.

In June 1784 Congress asked the States to raise an army of 700 soldiers to intervene in the Northwest Territory. Connecticut, New York, New Jersey, and Pennsylvania supplied the soldiers, but only the Keystone

State provided its full quota. Commanded by Lt. Col. Josiah Harmar of Pennsylvania, the "First American Regiment" deployed to the Ohio River valley and established a series of isolated forts extending down all the way to Fort Washington on the future site of Cincinnati, Ohio. A rising tide of white settlements resulted in open warfare with the Indians. In October 1790, Harmar launched a punitive raid into northern Ohio that met with disaster. The mixed force of 320 Regulars and over 1,000 militiamen from Kentucky and Pennsylvania fell prey to a series of Indian ambushes. In most of the engagements, the ill-disciplined and untrained militia panicked and fled. The remnant of Harmar's column retreated to Fort Washington to lick their wounds. The expedition suffered over 200 killed and wounded with most of its equipment and weapons lost or destroyed. A War Department inquiry put the blame for Harmar's defeat squarely on the militia's poor performance. Harmar's own reputation survived the disaster, and after resigning from the Army in 1792, he returned home to Pennsylvania to become the commonwealth's first AG.[51]

Congress responded to Harmar's defeat by raising an additional infantry regiment and authorizing the president to call out 2,000 militia cavalry with the intent of launching a reprisal raid. Overall command went to Arthur St. Clair, the Governor of the Northwest Territory. St. Clair assembled a 1,000-man, ragtag army of Regulars, militia, and short-term levies. The force advanced cautiously northward from Fort Washington in August 1791, but the mix of troops never formed a cohesive team. On November 4th, 1,000 Indian braves descended on St. Clair's unsuspecting force and inflicted one of the greatest defeats in American history. Untrained militiamen fled the battlefield, and Regulars were too few in number to survive the onslaught. The Indians killed 623 soldiers and wounded another 258. St. Clair's defeat shocked the nation and resulted in the first congressional inquiry into a military operation. The militia once again came in for heavy criticism, but Congress concluded that a combination of administrative and logistical blunders had caused the calamity.[52]

The defeats in the Northwest Territory convinced even the Republicans of the need for a stronger standing army. The militia had built its reputation largely as a local, defense force, and the defeats in Ohio raised serious questions over the militia's ability to participate effectively in extended, offensive strikes against the Indians. In March 1792, Congress authorized an expansion of the army and gave the president permission to call out as much militia cavalry as needed to protect the frontier. Maj. Gen. "Mad" Anthony Wayne took command of the "Legion of the United States" and took advantage of two years of peace negotiations to drill his Regular regiments into a trained fighting force. After peace talks with the Indians collapsed, Wayne advanced into northwestern Ohio with a combined force of 3,500 Regulars and mounted volunteers. At the battle of Fallen Timbers on August 20, 1794, Wayne's "Legion" won a striking victory, opening Ohio and portions of Indiana to settlement and convincing congressional skeptics of the value of a small Regular Army.[53]

With all federal resources focused in the Northwest Territory, settlers south of the Ohio River relied on the militia for self-defense and to settle disputes with the Creek and Cherokee Indians. In 1790, North Carolina's western lands were designated the Southwest Territory, a region that eventually became Tennessee. Faced with increasing numbers of settlers into the territory, Governor William Blount organized a territorial militia that by the fall of 1792 included fourteen infantry companies and a cavalry troop. Increasing violence between settlers and Indians, fueled by hard feelings on both sides over the defeats of Harmar and St. Clair, resulted in open warfare. Late in 1793, General John Sevier led a force of mounted militia deep into Creek lands, defeating the braves and destroying villages. In September 1794, Tennessee militiamen vanquished the Creeks and Cherokees at the battle of Nickojack, a success in the Southwest Territory that mirrored the results of Fallen Timbers in the Northwest Territory. In the summer of 1794, the War Department finally authorized the construction of forts in the Southwest Territory manned by Regulars. With its lands secured by militia victories, Tennessee became the sixteenth State in June 1796 and the last State admitted to the Union in the 18th Century.[54]

In addition to Indian threats, the federal government faced a direct challenge to its obligation to enforce domestic laws. In 1791, Congress had passed an excise tax on distilled spirits to raise revenues to finance the national debt and to support the new government's rising costs. Opposition to the tax was widespread but centered in western Pennsylvania where angry distillers and consumers increasingly subjected tax collectors to threats and harassment. In the summer of 1794, mounting tensions exploded. A mob of 500 men looted and burned the home of a tax collector in mid-July and prompted 6,000 enemies of the tax to assemble at Pittsburgh two weeks later. In an echo of Shays's Rebellion, the enrolled militia of western Pennsylvania sided with the insurgents, making the restoration of order and the enforcement of laws in the region all but impossible.[55]

George Washington realized that the Whiskey Rebellion was a direct challenge to the federal government's power and credibility, and he refused to tolerate the escalating defiance of federal authority. With "Mad" Anthony Wayne's Regulars engaged in the Northwest Territory,

President George Washington reviews militiamen at Fort Cumberland, Maryland during the mobilization for the Whiskey Rebellion, 1794. (Anne Brown Collection)

the president called upon the militia to enforce federal law. The Calling Forth Act of 1792 had required the president to receive the opinion of the judiciary before mobilizing the militia, and on August 4, 1794, Supreme Court Justice James Wilson informed Washington that the situation in western Pennsylvania was beyond the "ordinary course of judicial proceedings." Three days later, the Washington Administration issued a proclamation ordering the rebels to disperse and stating its intention to call out the militia. The War Department issued orders to the Governors of Virginia, Maryland, Pennsylvania, and New Jersey to prepare a combined force of 12,950 militiamen to march on western Pennsylvania. Meanwhile, Washington sent official emissaries to Pittsburgh to offer amnesty to the lawbreakers in return for oaths of allegiance to the United States. However, the insurgents finally spurned the government's offer, leaving the administration with no choice but to use force.[56]

Widespread dissatisfaction with the whiskey tax existed throughout the country, and many militia units had problems filling their ranks. Pennsylvania had to resort to a militia draft, while New Jersey was the first State to provide its full complement of troops. Still, the States were successful in fielding the numbers of troops required. On September 9th,

Washington ordered militiamen from four mid-Atlantic States to march to forward assembly points. Citizen-soldiers from Virginia and Maryland rallied at Cumberland, Maryland while Pennsylvania and New Jersey troops converged on Carlisle, Pennsylvania. The Governors of Virginia, Pennsylvania, and New Jersey took their roles as militia commanders seriously and rode at the head of their contingents. On September 25th, Washington ordered the troops westward. The commander in chief himself took to the field to review the militiamen and to see them off. Bad weather and rugged mountains slowed the advance, but resistance melted away in the face of the overwhelming show of force. The militia army restored order and apprehended several men but held only a few lawbreakers for trial. The courts convicted two insurgents of treason, but both eventually received presidential pardons. By late November the militia's role in putting down the Whiskey Rebellion was essentially complete. Citizen-soldiers returned home with the satisfaction of knowing that they alone had greatly legitimized the new federal government by enforcing compliance with the laws of the land.[57]

Conclusions

The militia's greatest achievement of the 18th Century was its role in winning the American Revolution. Starting with the battle of Bunker Hill, militiamen fought in nearly every major battle and minor engagement of the war. Citizen-soldiers particularly distinguished themselves at Bennington, Saratoga, King's Mountain, and Cowpens. State commanders like John Stark, Francis Marion, and Charles Sumter provided militia leadership and influenced the outcome of the war. Of all the Revolution's battles, Bunker Hill became the most prominent in the public mind because militia advocates believed the bitter fight on the Charlestown Peninsula best demonstrated the native fighting ability of patriotic citizen-soldiers. Beyond set piece battles, the militia confounded British efforts to win back the hearts and minds of American colonists. By controlling a vast majority of the population and the countryside, the militia insured that pro-British sentiments and activities were short-lived.

The creation of the Continental Army in 1775 introduced a dual system of national defense that included both Regulars and citizen-soldiers. From the beginning, the relationship between Continentals and militiamen was both supportive and contemptuous. Washington welcomed militia augmentations to his army while complaining of the militia's shortcomings and the strain they placed on his weak supply system. On the other hand, militiamen were willing to serve with the Continental Army but preferred to fight in their own State under the leadership of their own officers. State units of the Continental line established the practice of the States raising manpower in wartime for service with a national army. After the war, Washington's "Sentiments" became the first of many documents throughout American history to call for a reformed national militia with diminished ties to the States and stronger, direct links to the federal government.

The U.S. Constitution codified a dual national defense system of Regulars and citizen-soldiers and firmly established civilian control over the military. Federalist desires for strong, national military forces were unable to overcome America's traditional fear of a standing army and the reluctance to shoulder the expense of maintaining large numbers of Regulars in peacetime. Within the federal government, Congress and the president shared powers and responsibilities in raising and commanding the Regular Army while Congress and the States had specified powers in administering and employing the militia. The Constitution chartered the militia as an institution to "execute the Laws of the Union, suppress Insurrections and repel Invasions" and all but explicitly identified the militia as an organization based on States' rights. National leaders friendly to the militia were willing to accept a certain degree of inefficiency in State soldiers as the price they paid for insuring the active participation of an armed citizenry in the country's defense. At the same time, the militia was to act as a check on federal powers and to curb the potentially dangerous machinations of a standing army.

The Militia Act of 1792 and the Calling Forth Act enabled the enduring role of the citizen-soldier and guaranteed the States a continuing responsibility as the provider of manpower in times of national crisis. In the broadest sense, the Militia Act placed into federal law the militia tradition transplanted from Europe and reflected the main features of the militia laws the various colonial legislatures had already enacted. The law clearly identified the militia as a State-run institution and governed the administration, organization, and training of State soldiers for more than a century. If Indian fights in the Northwest Territory called into question the militia's worth as an offensive force, the Whiskey Rebellion identified the militia as a reliable instrument for domestic law enforcement. Ironically, the Federalists had to employ a force they largely derided in order to defend the credibility and power of the very government they sought to establish. The Whiskey Rebellion established an important precedent for the exercise of presidential power in calling upon the militia to enforce the laws of the land.

In 1794, victorious Regulars at Fallen Timbers and militiamen rallying against the Whiskey Rebellion represented the twin foundations of America's military establishment. As the population migrated westward into the Ohio and Mississippi River valleys, it was far from certain if America's dual military system could meet the diverse threats sure to challenge the inevitable expansion across the North American continent.

The Volunteer Militia, 1795–1897

way off in the wilds of America a soldier had been found totally different from any that had ever walked a battlefield. Upon one day
he was a citizen, quietly following the plow; upon the next he
became a soldier, knowing no fear and carrying a whole destroying battery in his trusted rifle. He was a soldier from conviction to principle,
from loyalty to his country, from duty to his family.

> Maj. Gen. John A. Logan in
> *The Volunteer Soldier of America*

Introduction

*The soldiers of the 1st Minnesota Volunteer Infantry lay prone along
the low crest of Cemetery Ridge watching intently as a military rout unfolded before them. Panicked Union soldiers of the Army of the Potomac's
III Corps came reeling back from their forward positions near the Peach
Orchard and the Emmitsburg Turnpike. On the late afternoon of July 2,
1863, the second day of the battle of Gettysburg, James E. Longstreet's
I Corps of the Army of Northern Virginia had launched a massive attack
designed to roll up the entire left flank of the Union army. To the men of the
1st Minnesota, Longstreet's attack appeared on the verge of success.
III Corps infantrymen streamed back in confusion and disorganization
from their advanced positions. Hard on their heels came long, gray ranks of
Confederate infantrymen firing volleys, brandishing bayonets, shouting the
Rebel yell and waving battle flags as they advanced.*

*It was not the first time the Minnesotans had seen Confederate
infantry on the attack. At the outbreak of the American Civil War,
Minnesota earned the distinction of becoming the first State to offer volunteer troops to the federal government in order to preserve the Union. The 1st*

Minnesota assembled for duty at Fort Snelling, six miles outside of St. Paul. Three volunteer militia companies—the Minnesota Pioneer Guard from St. Paul, the St. Anthony Zouaves, and the Stillwater Guard—formed the basis of the new regiment. By April 29, 1861, the regiment of nearly 800 soldiers had completed its organization and was mustered into federal service for three years. The 1st Minnesota soon headed east and received its baptism of fire at the Union defeat at First Bull Run, where it was the last organized regiment to leave the battlefield. During early 1862, the Minnesotans gained valuable experience during the Army of the Potomac's first concerted effort to capture Richmond. In the last months of the year, they saw heavy fighting at the bloody stalemate at Antietam and the Union debacle at Fredericksburg. When Robert E. Lee's soldiers marched north into Maryland and Pennsylvania in the early summer of 1863, the 1st Minnesota moved with the Union Army in pursuit. By the late afternoon of the second day of the battle of Gettysburg, the 1st Minnesota was positioned at the very center of the Union line where Longstreet's attack threatened to break through.

Maj. Gen. Winfield S. Hancock, the commander of the Union II Corps, arrived on the scene of the crisis on horseback as the Minnesotans attempted to halt the retreat of their fellow soldiers. Hancock realized only one Union regiment was available to stem the Confederate tide. The southerners were apparently disorganized by their own success and had paused for a few moments to reorganize. The II Corps commander urgently needed more time to rush Union reinforcements to the threatened sector.

"What regiment is this?" Hancock asked, turning toward the Minnesotans. "First Minnesota!" replied Colonel William Colvill, the regimental commander.

"Colonel, do you see those colors?" Hancock asked, pointing to the Confederate battle flags some two hundred yards distant. When Colvill replied, Hancock barked his orders: "Then take them!" Stepping in front of his regiment, Colonel Colvill asked in a loud voice if all of the soldiers would go forward with him, and they shouted back that they were ready. Reduced in strength to only 262 men by casualties and detached companies, the Minnesotans had no time to reflect on the grim task before them as they formed into a line of battle.

"Forward, double quick!" Colvill shouted with his saber drawn high. With their National and regimental colors flying proudly and bayonets fixed, officers and men lunged forward, advancing in a line that extended nearly one hundred yards from end to end. The single attacking regiment soon attracted the attention of all the Confederate riflemen and artillery crews within sight. As the Midwesterners advanced, bullets and cannon shells buzzed and burst all about dropping men at a fearful rate.

The regimental colors went down three times, and each time courageous men grabbed the fallen flagstaff and pressed ahead. In the regiment's wake, nearly one hundred Minnesotans lay dead and wounded.

"Charge!" Colonel Colvill shouted as the regiment neared the Confederate lines. With leveled bayonets and wild cries, the Minnesotans rushed forward at a full run and collided with the southerners. A savage, close quarters fight ensued with both sides exchanging musket fire at point-blank range. Colonel Colvill went down severely wounded. For fifteen minutes, the 1st Minnesota held its position alone against overwhelming odds. As evening darkness settled across the battlefield, a number of Union regiments advanced to help extract the 1st Minnesota from its precarious situation. Under the cover of darkness and the protection of other regiments, the Minnesotans finally withdrew.

Once safe on Cemetery Ridge, the 1st Minnesota counted its losses. Of the 262 men who made the charge, 215 lay dead or wounded. Not a soldier was missing, and all forty-seven survivors were still with the colors. With the loss of 82 percent of its soldiers, the 1st Minnesota endured the highest percentage of casualties suffered by any Union regiment in a single engagement in all of the American Civil War. Still, the attack had not been in vain; the reckless assault had bought time for General Hancock to rush reinforcements to the threatened sector and avert a catastrophe. Afterwards, Hancock recalled of the charge of the 1st Minnesota: "No soldiers on any field, in this or any other country, ever displayed grander heroism... There is no more gallant deed recorded in history."

The 1st Minnesota's fearless attack at Gettysburg reflects only one aspect of the service militiamen provided throughout the 19th Century. Citizen-soldiers continued to serve their States as a local defense force in peacetime while fighting alongside Regulars during war. At the same time, the militia underwent profound changes. Political, social, and economic conditions resulted in the demise of the enrolled militia and fostered an increasing number of volunteer militia companies. Concurrently, an even deeper divide developed between Regulars and militiamen. After the War of 1812, the federal government preferred to raise volunteer units for foreign duty, and militiamen fought in many of the federal volunteer regiments that served in the Mexican War. At the outbreak of the American Civil War, volunteer militia companies formed the first fledgling units for the opposing armies, and throughout America's bloodiest conflict, militia units North and South performed important auxiliary functions.

Following the Civil War and Reconstruction, militiamen helped to settle the American West and became involved in bitter, long-running labor disputes. Post-bellum volunteer militia units placed increasing emphasis on military training rather than social functions, and militiamen sought improved representation and financial support by forming a national association. As the sectional crisis faded in memory, Regulars and citizen-soldiers pondered the possibilities of overseas service. Within the States, the continuous use of militia units for law enforcement prompted progressive citizen-soldiers to seek a new mission as the principle reserve force to the U.S. Army. As the 19th Century came to a close, Army and militia officers envisioned a closer working relationship between Regulars and citizen-soldiers.

The Jeffersonian Era

Following the passage of the Militia Act of 1792 and the Whiskey Rebellion, the States took some actions to place the militia on a more permanent footing. A common practice was to partition a State into militia "divisions" that were geographic recruiting districts rather than tactical organizations. In addition to the State AG, Governors appointed militia generals to oversee recruiting and training in each district. Although general officers received no pay, the positions carried genuine prestige and were often a stepping stone for ambitious leaders bent on becoming a Governor or congressman. The local company remained the backbone of the militia system. As in colonial times, towns in the North and counties in the South remained the basis of company organizations. Because more and more militiamen lived in an urban setting, the widespread ownership of weapons declined. States began to purchase weapons and to issue them from arsenals. Burdened by the cost of weapons procurement, the States charged the federal government with delinquency in supporting the militia.[1]

The election of Thomas Jefferson in 1800 as the third president brought about significant changes in military policy. An ardent Republican, Jefferson sought to roll back the great expansion of the central government that had occurred under the Federalists. In military affairs, the former Governor of Virginia was a strong supporter of the militia. In his inaugural address on March 4, 1801, Jefferson identified the militia as one of the "essential principles of our government." The key tenets of Jefferson's military policy were "the supremacy of the civil over the military authority" and "a well-disciplined militia—our best reliance in peace and for the first months of war, till Regulars may relieve them."[2]

Jefferson's defense policy evolved into a combination of Republican ideals mixed with hard realities. Persistent conflicts with the British on the high seas and along the Canadian border, disputes with Indians in the

Northwest Territory, wars of the French Revolution, and the rise of Napoleonic France made renewed armed conflict a near certainty. Jefferson forged defense plans that relied on a strong Navy, coastal defenses, the militia, and a small Regular Army. In the event of war, the Navy would protect America on the high seas and prevent the approach of enemy fleets. The nation constructed a substantial flotilla of small gunboats to protect its coastlines and built strong, masonry forts to defend its premier harbors. In the event of an enemy landing, local militia forces were to contain the invaders until Regulars arrived. Together, Regulars and militiamen would push the enemy back into the sea.[3]

Rather than eliminating the Regular Army, Jefferson set about to reduce its ranks, improve its professionalism and imbue its officers with Republican values. Congress obliged him in 1802 by cutting the Regulars from 4,051 to 2,873, a reduction that allowed the removal of officers whom Jefferson considered Federalist partisans. The same act founded the U.S. Military Academy at West Point, New York, a national educational asset intended to imbue young officers with a rigorous, scientific education and to lessen the influence of partisanship in the Regular Army. The States reacted to the founding of West Point by creating military schools of their own for the training of militia officers and the grooming of civic leaders. Norwich University in Vermont, the Virginia Military Institute, and The Citadel in South Carolina were among the most prominent State military academies.[4]

Jefferson's espousal of the militia as one of the country's defensive pillars prompted an appraisal of its preparedness. The War Department reported that the States had failed to comply with requirements to submit annual militia reports. Not until 1804 was it able to determine that 525,000 men were enrolled and organized into a hodgepodge of regiments and brigades. Proper weapons were not available to arm units adequately. While militiamen often performed ably as a local force to protect property or to enforce laws, it became clear that State soldiers were far from ready to perform as a coherent, national defense force. The militia did make one significant advance during the period that occurred literally under Jefferson's direct supervision. In 1803, Congress authorized a militia in the new District of Columbia and designated the president as commander in chief with the authority to appoint officers. Jefferson often presided over reviews and ceremonies, but wore civilian attire to emphasize civilian control over the military. The first permanent bridge over the Potomac River was constructed to facilitate the rapid assembly of the District's militia, originally consisting of companies in Georgetown, Maryland and Alexandria, Virginia that were on opposite banks of the river.[5]

Throughout his eight years in office, Jefferson pressed for militia reforms. States' righters in Congress thwarted or evaded recommendations to classify the State soldiery along age lines. In 1807, the *Chesapeake-Leopard* Affair, a violent conflict on the open seas between an American and a British warship, raised the specter of war. The following year, Congress again rejected substantive militia reforms but did approve an annual allotment of $200,000 for the purchase and distribution of weapons to the States on the basis of annual strength reports. At the going rate of $13 dollars per musket, the appropriation purchased approximately 15,000 new weapons each year.[6]

The War of 1812

In the decades following the Revolution, many Americans believed that England sought to humiliate and limit the growth of the United States. The main point of contention was on the high seas, where America attempted to retain its neutrality as a trading partner to the belligerents engaged in the Napoleonic Wars. English warships regularly stopped American vessels and impressed Yankee seamen into the British Navy. At the same time, British forts in lower Canada openly supported the Indians in the Northwest Territory. When economic and political initiatives failed to improve Anglo-American relations, Congress reluctantly declared war on Great Britain on June 18, 1812.

The War of 1812 revealed glaring inadequacies in the militia system and raised serious questions regarding the responsibilities the federal government and the States shared for the common defense. Before the outbreak of war, a successful commander in the New York militia had observed that the Regular Army was the sword of the republic and that the militia was its shield. Canada was the closest British possession vulnerable to American military and naval power, but both were pitifully small. With a Regular Army that numbered only 6,686 officers and men in 1812, military leaders concluded that the "sword of the republic" by itself was too small to mount major attacks against Canada and that offensives could only take place with substantial participation from the militia.[7]

From the beginning, the New England Governors seriously hampered the war effort. The region's economy depended heavily on trade with Great Britain, and as a political block, the New England States opposed the war and refused to support military operations. Governor John C. Smith of Connecticut maintained that British challenges on the high seas did not constitute an invasion, and since there was no need to enforce laws or to suppress insurrections, he declared President James Madison's call for militia forces as unconstitutional. The Governor of

Massachusetts made a similar argument, and both States refused to send militiamen off to war. In 1814, Connecticut and Massachusetts finally placed their militia into federal service, but only to guard their own coasts and with the agreement that the federal government would pay all expenses. The defiance of the New England States denied the country of some of its best organized militia units and greatly affected American strategy. Unable to mount an offensive from New England against Montreal or Quebec, the U.S. resorted to attacks against British forces around the Great Lakes. New England's reaction to an unpopular war demonstrated all of the weaknesses of divided federal and State control over the militia. When the president and the Governors disagreed on policy, the militia could not function as an effective national reserve.

Operations along the Canadian border revealed additional weaknesses in the militia system. From the beginning, relations between Regular Army and militia generals suffered from petty jealousies and an unwillingness to cooperate. Senior officers vied for command positions and authority in the field based on their date of rank rather than experience and demonstrated competence. Regular and militia generals alike refused to relinquish control of their troops for the sake of fostering better unity of effort and simplicity of command. Elderly generals who had gained their experience and formed fixed opinions as young Continental and militia officers in the Revolution harbored hard feelings toward one another throughout the War of 1812. Brig. Gen. Peter B. Porter of the New York militia summed up the strained relations between Regular and State general officers. "It is certain," General Porter declared, "that no militia general is to gain any military fame while united to a Regular force and commanded by their officers." When an American force surrendered to the British near Detroit in August 1812, the Regular Army commanding general blamed the war's first fiasco on the militia's ineptness, ill-discipline and insubordination.

Specific campaigns and battles revealed the weaknesses and strengths of Regulars and militiamen alike. On as many as half a dozen occasions, Ohio and New York militia units refused to cross into Canada to attack British positions. The New York militia's reputation suffered two black eyes in the summer of 1813 when citizen-soldiers failed to turn out in sufficient numbers to prevent British raiding parties from looting Plattsburgh and Buffalo. The incidents embarrassed militia advocates who had long argued that citizen-soldiers would fight to the death to defend home and hearth. However, under competent and aggressive leadership, militiamen performed creditably. William Henry Harrison, who had led a militia army to victory over the Indians at the battle of Tippecanoe in central Indiana in 1811, again arose as an effective militia leader. In September 1813, Harrison led a large, mixed force of 3,500 Regulars and militiamen into Ontario and smashed the British and their Indian allies on October 5th at the battle of the Thames River. Meanwhile, Army officers were busy proving that their fledgling force of Regulars could stand up to the British. In July 1814, Regular troops under Brig. Gen. Winfield Scott stood their ground against the Redcoats during the battle of Chippewa, supposedly prompting a surprised British commander to exclaim, "Those are Regulars, by God!"

With the end of the Napoleonic Wars, Great Britain transferred seasoned troops to America in 1814. On August 19th, 4,000 Redcoats landed on the western shores of Chesapeake Bay and marched on Washington, DC. A general alarm across Maryland, Virginia and the District of Columbia resulted in the concentration of an odd assortment of 5,000 militiamen and Regulars near Bladensburg, Maryland. In the ensuing battle on August 24th, a number of Army Regulars, Marines, and militiamen stood their ground until overrun, but a majority of the ill-trained militia units retreated with such ease that the action became known as the "Bladensburg Races." The British entered Washington and torched the Capitol Building, the White House, and a number of other public buildings.

The Redcoats experienced an altogether different reception when they attacked Baltimore two weeks later. Under determined leadership and with more time to prepare, Regulars and militiamen presented an effective defense. When British infantry landed north of Baltimore, militiamen blocked their advance from a formidable line of field fortifications. At the battle of North Point on September 13th, the Maryland militia turned back the invaders and inflicted considerable casualties including the death of the British commander, Maj. Gen. Robert Ross, the victor at Bladensburg. Meanwhile, a garrison of Regulars stubbornly manned Fort McHenry against a punishing British naval bombardment that went on for twenty-four hours. When Francis Scott Key saw the American flag still flying defiantly above Fort McHenry in the "dawn's early light" on September 14th, the panorama inspired him to jot down verses that eventually became the "Star Spangled Banner."

The militia's most dramatic display of bravery came at New Orleans under the command of Andrew Jackson. A combat veteran at the age of thirteen, "Old Hickory" established a well deserved reputation as the resourceful and iron-willed leader of the Tennessee militia. At the beginning of the War of 1812, the combative Jackson offered President Madison the freedom to employ the Tennessee militia "without Constitutional scruples of any boundaries." In March 1814, Jackson's militiamen delivered a devastating blow to the Creek Indians at the battle of

Maj. Gen. Andrew Jackson leads a largely militia army in an overwhelming victory over British invaders at the battle of New Orleans on January 8, 1815. (National Guard Education Foundation)

Horseshoe Bend in central Alabama. The victory imbued Jackson with a national reputation and resulted in his selection as a Regular Army major general responsible for defending the Gulf Coast region.

In a daring bid to capture New Orleans and possibly sever Louisiana from U.S. control, the British landed 5,300 troops under Maj. Gen. Sir Edward Pakenham just below New Orleans. To defend the Crescent City, Jackson cobbled together a diverse fighting force of 4,700 soldiers that included two regiments of Regulars, militiamen from Tennessee, Kentucky and Louisiana, aristocratic gentry and free Blacks from New Orleans, a band of Choctaw Indians, and pirates under Jean Lafitte. After a series of preliminary skirmishes against the Americans, Pakenham decided to carry out a direct frontal assault with massed infantry against Jackson's main defenses. Attacking in an early morning fog on January 8, 1815, the Redcoats made little headway against Jackson's strong earthworks. Sheltered behind bales of cotton, the Americans achieved a concentration of firepower that mowed down the orderly British ranks and killed Pakenham. In the end, the Redcoats suffered 2,400 casualties while Jackson lost about 70 soldiers. Ten days later the shattered remnant of the British Army embarked on transports and sailed away. Word soon arrived in Louisiana that the War of 1812 had ended on

December 24, 1814 with the Treaty of Ghent, a full two weeks before the battle of New Orleans.

Overall, the militia was crucial to the successful outcome of the war. However, critics pointed out that the militia still exhibited significant deficiencies more than twenty years after the implementation of the Constitution's militia clauses, the Militia and Calling Forth Acts of 1792, and individual State statutes. The most enduring legacy of the war for senior political leaders was the success of a few Governors in limiting militia participation and in the refusal of many citizen-soldiers to cross an international border. If the militia could not be depended upon to implement national policy, some leaders asked, might not a larger Regular Army better serve the common defense? On the battlefield, distinct highs and lows marked the militia's performance; for every Bladensburg there was a New Orleans. The key to the militia's successes was forceful leadership. William Henry Harrison and Andrew Jackson were two outstanding leaders whose reputations propelled them to national fame and eventually the presidency. The significance of the battle of New Orleans equaled that of Bunker Hill by adding to the ethos of the natural abilities and fighting spirit of the American citizen-soldier. In the popular mind, Jackson's lopsided victory reinforced the notion that American militiamen, hastily assembled and with scant training, could easily triumph over a better prepared enemy.

The Expansible Army Plan

Congress moved quickly after the War of 1812 to pare the military to acceptable levels. However, national pride over the second victory over Great Britain and good feelings regarding the performance of Regular troops motivated Congress to set the Army's peacetime strength at 10,000 officers and men. In the eyes of the fledgling U.S. Army, the victory of the Regulars at Chippewa–rather than the triumph of Jackson's militiamen at New Orleans–foreshadowed the future direction of defense planning.

The War of 1812 had revealed glaring financial irresponsibility and managerial incompetence in the War Department. In October 1817, President Monroe appointed John C. Calhoun, an ambitious congressman from South Carolina, as the nation's tenth secretary of war. He completed the organization of a General Staff system that had begun during the war by creating powerful bureaus responsible for the Army's quartermaster, medical, ordnance, and inspector general functions. In reality, the bureaus were a menagerie of experts that divided the Army's management into distinct compartments, bickered among themselves, and created a gulf between the general staff and field commanders. Calhoun was successful in getting Congress to recognize formally the position of Commanding General of the Army, although the relationships between subsequent commanding generals and the secretary of war and the commanders of the nation's military districts remained nebulous.[8]

Secretary Calhoun's most enduring legacy came in 1820 with the unveiling of a novel plan to retain an effective Regular Army in peacetime while reducing the nation's reliance on citizen-soldiers. The Panic of 1819 resulted in deep cuts in federal spending, and Congress directed Calhoun to slash the Army to 6,000 enlisted men. The secretary of war informed Congress that the War of 1812 contained enough examples of militia ineptitude that the Regular Army and not the enrolled militia should become the proper instrument for fighting wars. Calhoun advocated a peacetime "expansible" Army that could rapidly grow in wartime without diluting its capabilities. In peacetime, the Army would maintain a complete organization of companies and regiments with a full compliment of unit and staff officers but with reduced numbers of enlisted men. In wartime, the Army would quickly recruit and train young soldiers to fill the ranks of cadre units while experienced Regulars provided leadership, training, and staff planning. Calhoun proposed a peacetime Army of 6,316 expansible to 11,558 in wartime without adding a single officer or new unit. He argued that the expansible Army would eliminate the "confusion and disorder" of 1775 and 1812 and that at the "commencement of hostilities" the country would possess a Regular force "adequate to the emergencies." Congress rejected the creation of cadre units top-heavy with officers and a reduced reliance on the militia and scuttled the whole proposal. Legislators then cut the Army to 6,183 soldiers, eliminated a number of regiments and reduced the size of the officer corps.[9]

Despite its rejection, Calhoun's expansible Army plan was an important benchmark in military policy that developed a strong and enduring legacy. For the first time, the federal government had put forth a defense plan that repudiated the militia tradition and acknowledged the primacy of Regulars. Calhoun's proposal encouraged Regulars to view themselves, rather than the militia, as the focus of planning for future wars.

The Demise of the Enrolled Militia

Following the War of 1812, the enrolled militia entered a period of neglect and decline, and by the late 1840s, the entire system was all but defunct. The second victory over Great Britain and the continued elimination of serious Indian threats against western expansion caused most Americans to question the value of mandatory military service. The militia's uneven record in the war convinced a larger segment of society that the protection of the nation might rightly belong to professional soldiers. Despite the Militia Act of 1792 and the federal government's annual distribution of arms, the enrolled militia system simply became unmanageable. Increases in population from immigration and high birth rates resulted in a massive, theoretical militia enrollment that neither the federal government nor the States could adequately resource or administer. A congressional study in 1836 found that within two weeks of a declaration of war, nearly one million militiamen could be available for duty, a number far in excess of any national need that might arise. Ironically, the notion of universal, obligated service that was at the very heart of the enrolled militia concept finally produced a situation of near universal unreadiness.[10]

Broader political, social, and economic developments worked in combination to render the enrolled militia system ineffective. Jacksonian America was a country on the move. Old Hickory's populist movement gave a wider range of Americans a voice in politics, and men no longer interested in militia service shared their opinions with elected officials. The coming of the Industrial Revolution and the introduction of the steamship and the railroad as means of mass transit introduced social mobility and dislocation unlike anything the country had ever seen. Throughout the enrolled militia's ranks, shopkeepers and factory workers supplanted yeoman farmers as the typical citizen-soldier. As the country's labor force changed, the profit motive and higher wages became the driving forces in the private sector. Mercantilists, factory managers, and laborers viewed musters as a waste of time and energy, and the purchase of arms and equipment as an unnecessary burden.

A number of specific problems degraded the enrolled militia's effectiveness and social standing. In general, the States expanded the list of authorized exemptions from military duty available to the wealthy and professionals until the working class and the poor perceived militia service as their particular burden. Officers serving for short periods were exempt from further militia service for the rest of their lives, and the revolving roster of officers in many States damaged unit effectiveness and became the most visible abuse of authorized exemptions. Fines imposed for absences from musters and training days became the target of national outrage. Prosperous individuals with deep pockets often preferred to pay a fine rather than to appear at musters. For poorer Americans, an unpaid militia fine became a form of indebtedness to the State punishable by imprisonment. Progressive reformers seeking improvements in the prison system worked to abolish the incarceration of poor militiamen who could not pay fines. New Jersey in 1844 was the first State to abolish imprisonment for non-payment of militia fines, and Iowa, California, and Michigan followed suite by 1850.[11]

The failure of many State AGs to administer the system also hastened its demise. The position of AG was often the object of political patronage and bestowed upon men with little or no military experience. The compensation and recognition the States afforded the office ranged from the generous to the niggardly. In 1846, a visitor to Indiana was surprised to find that the office of the Hoosier State's senior soldier was located in the front room of the AG's private residence. State AGs and militia generals failed to insure that musters remained valuable training events. In many States, muster days started with the roll call and quickly degenerated into a daylong indulgence of heavy drinking, wild gambling, and crude profanity. The festive training days of the colonial militia had by the 19th Century become attended with the taint of social vices, and many citizens regarded militia musters as worthless and a source of immorality. The AGs struggled to submit proper reports of the enrolled militia's strength to the War Department. Starting in the late 1820s, slightly more than half of the States submitted annual reports, and thirty years later fewer than one in five reported strength numbers. By failing to report annual enrollments, States lost their portion of the federal government's annual allotment. In 1855, the distribution of the $200,000 yearly expenditure became based on the number of members each State had in Congress rather than upon militia muster rolls.[12]

In 1826, Secretary of War James Barbour undertook a systematic analysis of the enrolled militia with an aim toward implementing reforms. The Barbour Board, composed of five Regular Army and three militia generals, produced the most comprehensive review ever done of the 19th Century militia. The members concluded that the worst defect of the militia system was that it produced far more men than the States could possibly manage and train. Other deficiencies included a lack of serviceable weapons, insufficient numbers of qualified trainers, abuses of exemptions and the difficulties of forming effective units in thinly populated areas. To reverse the enrolled militia's decline, the Barbour Board recommended capping the militia's strength at 400,000 men and allocating quotas to the States based on population density. Other reforms included the creation of a national AG in the War Department to preside over militia affairs, requiring the States to form standard tactical units, the distribution of Army training manuals to all militia officers and the creation of ten-day, paid camps each year for officer instruction. Secretary Barbour forwarded his recommendations to Congress in 1827, but States' rights advocates did nothing to translate the plan into action. A second reform initiative in 1840 called for classifying the militia by age and recommended ordering citizen-soldiers to active duty for annual training during which they would receive full pay. Congress condemned the 1840 reform plan, stating that the Constitution made no provision for calling the militia into federal service for training and judging that the cost of paying militiamen a stipend for annual training was prohibitive.[13]

The creeping rot that afflicted the enrolled militia after the War of 1812 accelerated with each passing decade. In 1831, Delaware completely abolished mandatory service. Massachusetts eliminated compulsory service in 1840, while Indiana that same year classified its men by age and required only the youngest to attend musters and training. Maine, Ohio, and Vermont eliminated the enrolled militia in 1844, Connecticut and New York in 1846, Missouri in 1847 and New Hampshire in 1851. By the middle of the 1840s, the enrolled militia system had all but faded away into obsolescence.[14]

The Rise of the Volunteer Militia

As the enrolled militia system collapsed, an expanded network of volunteer militia companies emerged to infuse the concept of the citizen-soldier with renewed vigor. Volunteer militia companies were as old as the country itself. The first volunteer company formed in America was the Ancient and Honorable Artillery Company of Boston modeled on London's Honorable Artillery Company whose charter dated from 1537. After the leaders of the Massachusetts Bay colony were assured that the volunteer militia company posed no threat to civil liberties and would be subject to all laws, they chartered the Boston company in 1638. Other colonies chartered militia units of willing and often hand-picked volunteers that strove to remain distinct from the enrolled militia. The Governor's Foot and Horse Guard units in Connecticut and the First Corps of Cadets in Boston served as escort troops during official functions for their respective Governors. The First Troop, Philadelphia City Cavalry is perhaps the best example of an early volunteer company that accumulated a combat record with its service in the Revolution.[15]

Ironically, the same conditions in Jacksonian America that led to the demise of the enrolled militia fostered the growth of volunteer companies. An increasingly mobile society, the Industrial Revolution's new work practices, massive waves of immigration and the explosive growth of cities generated complex changes in America that prompted segments of the population to seek meaning, stability, and enjoyment through voluntary association with like-minded individuals. Volunteer militia companies sprang up as part of a broader social phenomenon among segments of society that because of class, profession, or ethnicity shared common interests in the face of the bewildering changes sweeping the country. Volunteer militiamen were a mostly conservative subset of society that

Table 1

**VOLUNTEER MILITIA COMPANIES FORMED PRIOR TO 1792
WITH CONTINUOUS SERVICE TO 1903**

UNIT	LOCATION	YEAR CHARTERED
Ancient and Honorable Artillery Company	Boston, MA	1638
Georgia Hussars	Savannah, GA	1736
Newport Artillery Company	Newport, RI	1741
1st Corps of Cadets	Boston, MA	1741
Charleston Light Dragoons	Charleston, SC	1753
1st Company, Governor's Foot Guard	Hartford, CT	1771
1st Troop, Philadelphia City Cavalry	Philadelphia, PA	1774
Kentish Guards	East Greenwich, RI	1774
United Train of Artillery	Providence, RI	1775
2nd Company, Governor's Foot Guard	New Haven, CT	1775
German Fusiliers	Charleston, SC	1775
Liberty Independent Troop	Walthonville, GA	1776
1st Company, Governor's Horse Guard	Hartford, CT	1778
Roxbury City Guard	Boston, MA	1784
2nd Corps of Cadets	Salem, MA	1785
8th Regiment of Infantry	New York, NY	1786
Chatham Artillery Company	Savannah, GA	1786
Richmond Light Infantry Blues	Richmond, VA	1789
Veteran Corps of Artillery	New York, NY	1790

(Source: War Department, *Report of the Military Secretary of the Army relative to The Militia of the United States,* June 30, 1906, 111–14.)

desired continuity rather than change and embraced the values of patriotism, duty, camaraderie, and honor rather than individualism and greed. Volunteer companies drew together those with an affinity for the military lifestyle and the pomp and circumstance of the parade route and the drill field. At the same time, militia officers viewed their leadership positions and activities as an avenue for political and social advancement, and many officers used their military titles long after they had left the militia.[16]

Volunteer militia companies all shared a number of common traits. New members required some form of sponsorship, and permission to join the unit was subject to the approval of existing members. By-laws governed membership requirements, the election of officers, unit organization, the wear of uniforms, the types of weaponry and equipment required and the frequency of social and military activities. Volunteer

The masthead of an enlistment certificate of the Newark, New Jersey "City Guard" from 1845. The uniforms and headgear were typical of the volunteer militia companies of the period. (Anne Brown Collection)

companies were largely self-sustaining; members normally paid dues and bore all of the expenses of uniforms, weapons, and accoutrements. The enrolled militia system included men wherever they dwelled, but the volunteer militia was concentrated mostly in urban centers. Enrolled militia musters usually occurred semiannually, but because volunteer companies were a source of camaraderie and hosted scheduled activities, unit musters occurred at least monthly or as often as one night per week. The frequency of unit meetings produced the tradition of State soldiers conducting drill periods on one night of the workweek. Increased unit activity resulted in a demand for adequate facilities, and volunteer companies sought public buildings suitable for meetings, social activities, and the storage of weapons and equipment. A few wealthy companies bought or constructed their own accommodations. For the first time, unit armories appeared in local communities.

Though volunteer companies touted their independence, distinct ties to the State governments and the enrolled militia existed. The States reserved the right to approve company charters as the means of asserting civilian control over all military organizations. The States granted volunteer militiamen with at least seven years of service an exemption from further duty in the enrolled militia. Specialized volunteer companies provided valuable augmentation to the enrolled militia's infantry fighting power. The States welcomed cavalry and artillery units because maintaining such organizations in the enrolled militia was difficult and expensive. The States often provided funds to defray the greater costs of purchasing and maintaining special weapons and equipment such as horses, cannons, saddles, and ammunition. As the elite troops of the armies of the day, grenadiers and light infantrymen formed the flank companies of regiments deployed in battle and assumed the position of honor at ceremonies and parades. Volunteer infantry companies organized as grenadiers and light infantry stressed that they did not belong to the undifferentiated masses of enrolled militia infantry and jealously protected their position of honor at public ceremonies. The Richmond Light Infantry Blues of Richmond, Virginia and the Washington Light Infantry of Charleston, South Carolina were typical of volunteer infantry units that emphasized their elite status.

Perhaps the most widely recognized characteristic of volunteer militia companies was martial ardor that found its expression in extravagant uniforms and dramatic unit names. With the Regular Army wearing dark blue, State soldiers often wore some shade of gray, and company names often hinted at the color and style of the uniform volunteers sported. Ethnicity often determined the type of dress, and companies of Irishmen in green jackets, Highlanders in kilts, Germans in hunting hats and Frenchmen in full, red trousers tramped down America's streets. For example, the Pioneer Rifles of Rochester, New York appeared at parades sporting a tall beaver hat, a green, swallowtail coat with large cuffs and a high collar, and white pants. Elite infantry units adopted uniforms and headgear—towering bearskin hats were a favorite—which accentuated their height and physical presence. One method of controlling unit membership was the extravagance of the uniform; the more exclusive the company, the more expensive the uniform. Titles of most units were descriptive, such as Rifles, Guards, and Cadets, while names like Invincibles, Avengers, and Terribles were intended to instill unit pride.

In addition to offering an outlet for patriotism, camaraderie, and social enjoyment, volunteer companies formed along occupational and ethnic lines. Skilled workers often banded together to emphasize their status in society. The Mechanic Phalanx of Lowell, Massachusetts, adorned in gray uniforms with yellow trimmings, is but one example. Volunteer companies proliferated among immigrants, especially the Germans and the Irish. The meeting halls and armories of immigrant companies allowed an environment that recreated their European roots. Gathered together in their militia company, immigrants could speak their native tongue without embarrassment, drink the spirits of the home country, and enjoy a congenial, familiar atmosphere. Immigrants considered membership in an American volunteer company as the soundest possible display of patriotism toward their adopted country. New York City included a rich variety of minority and ethnic units: the Napper Tandy Artillery (Irish), the Jefferson Riflemen (German), Gardes Lafayette (French), the Hannibal Guards (African-American), and the Empire Hussars (Jewish). By 1853, two-thirds of the 6,000 volunteer militiamen in New York City were foreign-born. Only New Orleans matched New York for its ethnic diversity and boasted of German Jaegers, Spanish Cazadores, French Lancers, and Creole Grenadiers. As a backlash to the rise of ethnic companies, native-born Americans formed their own exclusive units whose names and uniforms stressed the history and culture of the United States. For example, Milwaukee hosted two Irish companies, five German units and one native-born American outfit, the Milwaukee Light Guard.[17]

Volunteer companies fostered a sense of community through frequent social and philanthropic activities. Opportunities for fellowship, entertainment, and carousing were critical to maintaining membership and garnering the support of local communities. Among the more popular events were gala balls, where citizen-soldiers, resplendent in their distinctive uniforms, feasted and danced the night away with wives and sweethearts. The Washington Light Infantry of Charleston, South Carolina held an annual ball to honor the Washington's Birthday national holiday, and the gala of the Rock City Guards in Nashville, Tennessee was regarded as the highlight of the city's social season. Theatrical performances and concerts were popular social events and effective fundraisers. In addition, companies raised money for orphans and destitute families. When unit members died unexpectedly, other militiamen often became the guardians of the surviving children. Many companies acted as burial societies, securing plots for deceased members and conducting funerals with full military honors.

Volunteer companies were prominent at public ceremonies and celebrations. Citizen-soldiers marched and performed intricate drills to the amazement of onlookers. Companies frequently turned out at solemn occasions to honor the exploits of past militiamen. Boston and New York companies were present at the dedication of the Bunker Hill memorial in 1834, and South Carolina companies were on hand at the unveiling of a monument on the Cowpens battlefield in 1856. The nation's growing railroad system permitted frequent unit visits. In the South, Charleston, Columbia, Augusta and Savannah formed an axis for the routine exchange of unit members.

A volunteer unit was the first military organization in the United States to adopt the title "National Guard." The use of the name came about as the result of a visit to New York by the Marquis de Lafayette, the famous French hero of the American Revolution. Volunteer militiamen from the 2nd Battalion, 11th Regiment of Artillery comprised the honor guard for Lafayette. In observance of his visit on August 25, 1824, the battalion voted to rename itself the "Battalion of National Guards" in tribute to Lafayette's command of the Parisian militia, the *Garde Nationale*. (The battalion later became the famous 7th New York Regiment in 1847 and serves in the New York Army National Guard today as the 107th Support Group.)[18]

Despite the emphasis on social and ceremonial events, militiamen recognized that volunteer companies were primarily military organizations. The most common manifestation of military training was weekly drill periods in which citizen-soldiers practiced the intricate tactical maneuvers of the day. To acquire qualified instructors, companies often hired professional soldiers, veterans, and military retirees to serve as drillmasters. Militia officers frequently purchased military texts for their own studies. Parades and drill competitions provided an opportunity for companies to compare their relative strength and proficiency. Marksmanship training was a popular training event, especially when held as a competition between units. One of the most unusual competitive shoots occurred in 1843 as an artillery duel between the Alabama State Artillery of Mobile and the Native American Artillery of New Orleans. After each unit fired fifty rounds from their smoothbore, six-pound cannons at a target nearly 500 yards away, the Alabamans registered thirty-two hits to win the competition and a silver medal. Encampments that included groupings of volunteer companies were important training events that in many States eventually supplanted the enrolled militia's semiannual muster days. The typical encampment lasted a few days and included extensive drill periods and long road marches. Militiamen conducted parades and sham battles to the delight of large crowds of spectators.

Beyond social and training events, volunteer companies often responded to local crises. In the early 19th Century, police departments were organized in only the largest cities, and State police forces did not yet exist. Militiamen frequently served under the direction of sheriffs and

The "Boston National Lancers" in 1850. Volunteer militia companies were often organized as elite units of grenadiers, light infantry, artillery, and cavalry. (Anne Brown Collection)

marshals to enforce laws, act as posses, guard prisoners, and quell agitated mobs. Ethnic and religious violence, labor unrest, and abolitionist agitation created volatile conditions in many cities that precipitated rioting, and some volunteer companies gained extensive experience in controlling crowds. In the South, militia units continued with slave patrols. Virginia's volunteer companies played a major role in putting down the bloody Nat Turner's Revolt in 1831. Between 1834 and 1864, civil authorities in New York City called out the 7th New York Regiment on at least eighteen occasions to preserve the peace. The most sensational civil disturbance of the ante-bellum period was the Astor Place Riot of 1849 in New York. Sparked by an ethnic incident, an angry mob of 20,000 gathered outside the city opera house, and the mayor called out the 7th New York Regiment. Civil authorities finally authorized the militiamen to open fire, and they cleared the streets with volleys of musketry. Before the bloody affair ended, at least forty protesters were killed and wounded and 150 militiamen injured.[19]

The Mexican War

By the 1840s, many Americans believed that the United States should extend all the way from the Atlantic to the Pacific Ocean. The concept of "Manifest Destiny" advanced the popular notion that divine providence mandated the expansion of the country from coast-to-coast. However, Mexico included most of the western lands not acquired under the Louisiana Purchase and blocked America's westward expansion. A long simmering dispute between the United States and Mexico finally precipitated a major war. Citizen-soldiers of the Republic of Texas had gained independence from Mexico with bloody fighting at the Alamo and the battle of San Jacinto in the spring of 1836. Nearly a decade later, the U.S. offered statehood to Texas, and it was admitted to the Union as the twenty-eighth State in December 1845. Mexico, however, had never fully recognized Texan independence and broke diplomatic relations with the United States. By May 1846, a state of war existed between the two powers.

For the first time, the United States waged a war on foreign soil. The demise of the enrolled militia system and memories of citizen-soldiers refusing to cross the border and of a few States unwilling to support the War of 1812 prompted a major change in defense policy. While combinations of Regulars and militiamen had fought all previous wars, the administration of President James K. Polk relied for the largest part on volunteer regiments. In simplest terms, volunteer regiments were citizen-soldier units raised by the States for federal service. Unlike the militia, volunteer regiments did not exist in peacetime. However, militia traditions and laws hung heavy over the raising of volunteer units. The States assumed the responsibility for mobilizing volunteer regiments, volunteers elected their own company officers, and the Governors appointed more senior officers up to the rank of colonel. The Polk Administration levied troop requirements on the States, and eventually fifty-eight volunteer regiments and sixty-eight separate companies and battalions were raised. All together, the United States mobilized just short of 116,000 Regulars, volunteers, and militiamen. Of the total manpower effort, 75 percent—58 percent volunteers and 12 percent militiamen—were citizen-soldiers who served alongside Regular Army units.[20]

Despite the preponderance of volunteer units, the militia made significant contributions. At the outbreak of war, Texas and Louisiana provided 12,601 militiamen for immediate service, and many of these subsequently joined volunteer and Regular Army units as individuals. In many cases, the States first turned to volunteer militia companies to form their federal volunteer regiments. Nine volunteer militia companies in Georgia combined to create the 1st Georgia Regiment. The commander of the Little Rock Guards rallied nine other volunteer militia companies in Arkansas to form an Arkansas volunteer regiment. In Pittsburgh, the city's leading volunteer militia companies—the Dusquesne Grays, the

Jackson Blues and the Irish Greens—mustered into federal service to form the foundation of Pennsylvania's 2nd Regiment.[21]

Perhaps the best example of a federal volunteer regiment raised from State troops was the Mississippi Rifles. Commanded by Jefferson Davis and led by hard-fighting officers who were the sons of wealthy planters, the Mississippi Rifles established a combat record comparable to that of the best Regular Army regiments. Competent leadership, strict discipline, thorough training, modern weapons, and complete uniforms created a regiment that Army leaders cited for conspicuous gallantry and steadiness. At the battle of Buena Vista, where 90 percent of the American army was volunteer units, an unwavering performance by the Mississippi Rifles and two Indiana regiments, together with the superior fire of Regular Army artillery, broke the main Mexican attack. (Today the Mississippi Rifles still serve in the Mississippi Army National Guard as the 155th Infantry.)[22]

A number of the senior commanders in the Mexican War came from the militia, and President Polk appointed several militia generals to command large volunteer formations. Maj. Gen. William O. Butler from Kentucky, a veteran of the War of 1812, received command of the 1st Division of volunteers composed of regiments from Kentucky, Ohio, and Indiana. Maj. Gen. Robert Patterson, the senior militia general in Pennsylvania, took command of the 2nd Division of volunteers with regiments from Illinois, Georgia, Alabama, and Mississippi. Other militia brigadier generals effectively led brigades in the Mexican campaigns. Brig. Gen. John A. Quitman of Mississippi was perhaps the best militia brigade commander of the war.[23]

The successful outcome of the Mexican War had significant influences on the growth of the United States and its future military policy. At the cost of $100 million and the loss of 10,000 soldiers, the United States annexed about half of Mexico, a vast tract of land that eventually comprised the States of California, New Mexico, Arizona, Nevada, Colorado, and Utah. By 1848, America was a continental power stretching from sea to sea and ever closer to fulfilling its mandate of Manifest Destiny. In military policy, the Mexican War marked the debut of federal volunteer regiments as the best means of augmenting the Regular Army in wartime. Volunteer militia companies certainly hastened the raising of federal regiments, but for the first time, the United States relied on volunteers to augment the Regular Army rather than militiamen serving in pre-existing militia organizations. Volunteer regiments permitted the prosecution of the war without permanent increases in the size of the Regular Army. And to the delight of national political leaders, volunteer citizen-soldiers gladly returned to civilian society at the end of hostilities.

The victory in the Mexican War sparked renewed interest across the country in military affairs, and volunteer militia companies prospered. At the same time, a looming sectional crisis over States' rights and slavery heightened a sense of awareness regarding military preparedness. The militia's greatest advocate in the 1850s was Elmer Ellsworth. While a struggling law student in Chicago, Ellsworth eked out a living as a militia drillmaster. Though laboring in obscurity, the energetic Ellsworth was determined to make a name for himself as a militia leader. It was at this time that he met a Frenchman who had served with a Zouave regiment in the Crimea, and the soldier of fortune taught Ellsworth the intricate, peculiar commands and motions of Zouave drill routines. In 1859, Ellsworth was elected to the command of a volunteer militia company that he reorganized as the United States Zouave Cadets of Chicago. Ellsworth's men learned the rapid gymnastics-like movements of the Zouave drills, and adopted a picturesque costume complete with red cap, sash, and baggy trousers. The Zouave Cadets filled Chicago's streets with crowds anxious to watch their rapid, intricate drills. One Chicago newspaper described the drills as soldiers forming "figures of crosses, double crosses, squares and triangles, like the dissolving figures of the kaleidoscope."[24]

Ellsworth's fortunes changed dramatically when he gained employment as a legal clerk in the firm of Lincoln & Herndon in Springfield, Illinois. Abraham Lincoln and Ellsworth became friends and discussed possible militia reforms for Illinois. The Zouave leader also believed that the War Department needed a special bureau for militia affairs. In the summer of 1860, Ellsworth, now a colonel in the Illinois militia, gained national notoriety when the Zouave Cadets undertook a tour of twenty cities. At each stop, the Zouaves challenged the best local militia companies to a drill competition, and in cities across the Midwest and the Northeast, they dazzled crowds with drilling, marching, firing and wild bayonet exercises. Dozens of Zouave militia companies formed in the wake of the national tour. At the end of the excursion, Ellsworth returned to Illinois as the most renowned militiaman in the nation. In November, Abraham Lincoln was elected president. When he left for Washington early in 1861, Ellsworth accompanied Lincoln as a bodyguard. Neither could have imagined that both of them were destined to become national martyrs during the bloodiest war in American history.[25]

Civil War and Reconstruction, 1861–1877

On the crest of a bald hill outside Charlestown, Virginia at noon on December 2, 1859, a formation of nearly 1,500 militiamen surrounded a newly constructed gallows. On the platform stood the rabid abolitionist John Brown with the executioner's noose already tight around his neck. The Commonwealth of Virginia had found Brown guilty of treason for his deadly raid against the federal arsenal at Harpers Ferry and sentenced him to death by hanging. Fearful that radical abolitionists might attempt to rescue Brown on the day of his execution, Virginia's Governor had called out 1,500 militiamen to provide security. In the ranks of the Richmond Grays stood Private John Wilkes Booth, and for several minutes, the man destined to fire the last shot of the American Civil War studied the man who had fired the first shots in anger. Without warning, the executioner released the platform beneath John Brown, and the guerilla leader fell to his death. Afterwards, a jailer revealed the contents of a note Brown had slipped to him earlier that morning. "I, John Brown," the trembling handwriting said, "am now quite certain that the crimes of this guilty land will never be purged away but with blood…"[26]

John Brown's raid on the federal arsenal at Harpers Ferry was the first of a violent chain of events that finally caused the outbreak of the American Civil War. For nearly thirty years, the North and the South had drifted farther apart politically and socially on the issues of States' rights and slavery. Staunch abolitionists in the North believed that moral suasion and political action had failed to stem the spread of slavery and that violence was the only remaining remedy. On the night of October 16, 1859, Brown had led a band of eighteen men to seize the arsenal's weapons as the means to arm an anticipated slave uprising. Casualties occurred on both sides as Brown's raiders captured the facility. The next day, Virginia militia companies acting under the supervision of the town sheriff cornered Brown and a small number of followers in a stout, fire engine house. On the morning of October 18th, a platoon of U.S. Marines commanded by Colonel Robert E. Lee of the Regular Army stormed the engine house and took John Brown prisoner.

News of the raid hardened opposing views above and below the Mason-Dixon Line. Across the South, planters and politicians explained that northern radicals had intended all along to use force to limit the rights of the States, destroy slavery and threaten the southern way of life. Many southerners believed that John Brown's raid was only the opening blow in a larger, more violent contest. After Harpers Ferry, both sides anticipated war, and new militia companies sprang up all over the country that focused on preparedness rather than pageantry. The election of Abraham Lincoln in November 1860 on a platform that severely restricted the expansion of slavery deepened the nation's political divide. South Carolina responded to Lincoln's election by seceding from the Union, and by February 1861, six other southern States had left the Union and banded together to create the Confederate States of America. On April 12, 1861, Confederate troops fired on Fort Sumter in Charleston harbor. After the fort's surrender, four additional States joined the Confederacy, and the Confederate government, headed by President Jefferson Davis, established its capital in Richmond.

As America split in two, volunteer militia companies across the South were the primary agents of State governments in seizing control of federal forts, arsenals, customs houses, and mints. In Charleston, militiamen seized a federal arsenal and occupied fortifications that Union troops abandoned when they had evacuated to Fort Sumter. Georgia volunteer companies took Fort Pulaski at the mouth of the Savannah River, and Alabama State soldiers occupied the U.S. arsenal at Mount Vernon and two Union forts that controlled the entrance to Mobile Bay. In Florida and Louisiana, militia units captured the arsenals at Apalachicola and Baton Rouge, respectively. Virginia militiamen took control of the Norfolk Navy Yard, and in Arkansas, four militia companies forced federal troops to abandon Fort Smith without a fight.[27]

As the Union disintegrated, local leaders in the North hesitated to begin serious military preparations. Many hoped that war could be averted; others believed provocative actions might disrupt peace efforts. However, the blatant attack on Fort Sumter galvanized the North. On April 15th, President Lincoln invoked the Calling Forth Act of 1792 and ordered 75,000 militiamen into federal service for ninety days to put down an insurrection "too powerful to be suppressed by the ordinary course of judicial proceedings." The War Department apportioned troop quotas to the States, established mobilization sites and set May 20th as the final muster day for all units. The Governors of States that had not yet declared neutrality or joined the Confederacy exercised their executive powers and spurned Lincoln's call for troops. Kentucky's Governor replied: "Your dispatch is received. In answer, I say emphatically Kentucky will furnish no troops for the wicked purpose of subduing her sister Southern States."[28]

The top priority for the North was to secure its capital, and the first troops to provide for Washington's defense were thirty-eight militia companies from the District of Columbia. Five companies from Pennsylvania—the Ringgold Light Artillery of Reading; the Washington Artillery and the National Light Infantry of Pottsville; the Logan Guards of Lewiston; and the Allen Rifles of Allentown—were the first State troops to reach Washington. Massachusetts was the first State to forward a complete regiment to the capital. The 6th Regiment, Massachusetts Volunteer Militia reached Washington by rail on April 18th after fighting its way through a secessionist mob during a change of trains in Baltimore.[29]

Militiamen of the 7th New York Infantry outside of Washington, DC in 1861. The 7th New York was the first unit to adopt the title "National Guard," and the letters "NG" appeared on their uniforms and equipment during the Civil War. Note the "NG" sign at top center. (U.S. Army Military History Institute)

Throughout the spring of 1861 most northern States rushed regiments in various degrees of preparedness to Washington. Several regiments adopted the Zouave uniforms and drill methods that Elmer Ellsworth had promoted before the war. By early summer, thirty-five regiments consisting of 37,000 troops were encamped near the nation's capital. In northern Virginia, the Confederacy managed to concentrate an army of its own: thirty-two regiments numbering 33,000 troops. Volunteer militia companies formed the basis for a significant number of the regiments on both sides. While the two armies watched one another, an army of Ohio troops composed mostly of militiamen advanced into the rugged mountains of western Virginia. Unionist sentiment was strong in the region, and the Ohio soldiers cleared the region of southern troops. Consequently, West Virginia was admitted to the Union on June 19, 1863 as the thirty-fifth State.[30]

The concentration of Union troops around Washington produced the North's first national hero. When Elmer Ellsworth failed in a scheme to create and lead a new Militia Bureau in the War Department, he left Washington seeking a field command of his own. Ellsworth's national reputation permitted him to recruit quickly a Zouave regiment from New York. The 11th New York Volunteers entered federal service under Ellsworth's command and moved to Washington. On May 24, 1861, the 11th New York crossed into Virginia to occupy Alexandria. Colonel Ellsworth noticed a Confederate flag waving defiantly from the roof of a hotel in the heart of town. Accompanied by a detachment, the regimental commander hurried to the hotel, climbed to the roof and cut the flag down. The hotel's incensed proprietor, armed with a shotgun, confronted Ellsworth as he descended a staircase with his trophy. A point-blank blast from the shotgun killed Ellsworth instantly, and New York Zouaves shot and bayoneted the proprietor in return. As the first northern regimental commander killed in the Civil War, Ellsworth's death created a national sensation. A bereaved Abraham Lincoln hosted the funeral at the White House, and songs and poems across the nation celebrated Ellsworth's exploits. The 11th New York adopted the battle cry "Remember Ellsworth!" Throughout the country, Elmer Ellsworth's life and death personified the dedication and sacrifices of militiamen.[31]

By early summer, the buildup of Union forces around Washington prompted Lincoln's generals to consider an offensive. On July 21, 1861, northern troops attacked the southern army at the battle of First Bull Run. By any standard, the war's first major battle was a confused, amateur affair. The ranks of ante-bellum militiamen and raw volunteers displayed poor discipline, and officers demonstrated their inexperience in handling formations under fire. The convention of Union blue and Confederate gray uniforms did not yet exist, and the tendency of militia units to wear blue or gray without regard to regional affiliation resulted in friendly fire incidents. The small number of Regular Army units in the Union ranks performed not much better than green citizen-soldiers and did little to influence the outcome. What could have been an orderly retreat for the North turned into a rout as inexperienced soldiers panicked. Equally unseasoned southern troops were too exhausted and confused to exploit their victory.[32]

The defeat at First Bull Run shocked the North and prompted even greater efforts. Realizing that the small Regular Army and regiments based on volunteer militia companies were inadequate for a broader war, on July 25, 1861 President Lincoln called up 500,000 volunteers for up to three years of service. It was the first of a series of federal callups that eventually brought nearly 2.7 million men into the Union Army. Many of the militia-based regiments that had responded to the first callup after Fort Sumter immediately reformed as volunteer regiments. The War Department made the decision to keep the Regular Army together as a dependable reserve rather than to disperse its officers and men as training cadres for volunteer regiments, but the overwhelming number of volunteer regiments soon swallowed up the Regular Army. In the South, a similar pattern emerged as militia units and volunteers combined to create Confederate regiments. Many southern States formed their own troops for local duty, but as the war progressed, the Confederate government took control of these troops as well. In the end, the Civil War was fought by neither Regulars nor militiamen, but by the overwhelming numbers of volunteers who rallied to defend "Old Glory" and the "Stars and Bars."[33]

The exact number of Civil War regiments formed from ante-bellum militia units is almost impossible to determine, but usually the lower

U.S. Army Military History Institute

The American Civil War, 1861–1865
The Militia Presidents

Abraham Lincoln

Abraham Lincoln was born into pover-ty in a log cabin in Hodgenville, Kentucky in 1809. He moved with his family to Indiana in 1816 and finally to Illinois in 1830. Two years later, the Governor of Illinois called out the militia in a cam-paign against the Indians. The chieftain Black Hawk led the Sacs in a series of actions to reclaim territories they had given up by treaty. Young Abraham Lincoln joined a militia company and was elected captain. When it appeared that his unit would not see service, many of its members disbanded and went home. However, Lincoln volunteered as a private in a militia scout unit, sometimes called the "Independent Spy Battalion." Lincoln said later that no success gave him as much personal satisfaction as his time in the Illinois militia.

After the Black Hawk War, Lincoln successfully pursued law and politics and maintained an interest in militia affairs. He served with the Illinois legisla-ture in 1834–1841 and in the U.S. House of Representatives during 1847–1849. In 1860, Lincoln was elected the 16th president of the United States and became perhaps the most outstanding president in American history. Guided by great wisdom, sound judgement, and extraordinary common sense, Lincoln led the country through its darkest hours and was successful in preserving the Union and freeing the slaves. As commander in chief, Lincoln proved an adept strate-gist who realized that destroying the armies of the Confederacy was more impor-tant than capturing Richmond or seizing other strategic points.

On April 14, 1865, John Wilkes Booth, a former member of the Richmond Grays, became the most infamous militiaman of the 19th Century when he assas-sinated President Lincoln at Ford's Theater in Washington, DC. Booth broke into the presidential box during a play and shot the most prestigious citizen-sol-dier to ever serve in the Illinois militia. Booth jumped from the presidential box to the stage below, but as he leaped, he caught a spur on the flag of the Treasury Guards, a militia unit organized in the District of Columbia during the Civil War. Knocked off balance by the militia flag, Booth landed awkwardly on the stage and broke a bone in his ankle. The injury inadvertently caused by the militia flag hastened Booth's capture and death. The flag of the Treasury Guards still hangs in the presidential box at Ford's Theater and bears the tear caused by John Wilkes Booth's spur.

Jefferson Davis

Jefferson Davis dedicated much of his life to public service as a soldier-statesman with military experience as both a Regular Army officer and a leader of citizen-soldiers. Born in 1808 in Fairview, Kentucky, the Davis family eventually moved to Mississippi where they accumulated considerable wealth as planters. Young Jefferson Davis attended West Point, graduated in 1828, and served in the Northwest Territory as a lieutenant of dragoons before resigning his commission in 1835. For the next ten years, he concentrated on his plantation and State politics.

In 1845, Davis was elected to the U.S. House of Representatives but resigned his seat to command troops in the Mexican War. Returning to Mississippi, he led the citizen-soldiers of the Mississippi Rifles with distinction at the battles of Monterrey and Buena Vista. Davis' insistence on good order and discipline and the arming of his soldiers with the best rifled weapons available made the Mississippi Rifles one of the premier regiments of the Mexican War. The returning war hero was appointed as a U.S. senator in 1847, and during 1853–1857, Davis served effectively as Secretary of War. Davis returned to the Senate in 1857, but resigned his seat in January 1861 after Mississippi seceded from the Union. Immediately upon his return home, the Governor appointed Davis as commander of the Mississippi militia with the rank of major general.

The provisional government of the Confederate States of America selected Jefferson Davis as its president, and he was inaugurated at Montgomery, Alabama in February 1861. As president of the Confederacy, Davis encountered a bewildering array of political, economic, and military challenges. Though no one ever questioned Davis' moral and physical courage, an imperious temper, icy formality, and failing health eventually reduced his effectiveness. Despite his complete dedication, Davis never proved as politically able or publicly inspiring as his opponent, Abraham Lincoln.

As the Confederacy collapsed, Davis fled the southern capital at Richmond. On May 10, 1865, a Union cavalry patrol captured Davis at Irwinville, Georgia, and he was imprisoned at Fort Monroe, Virginia for two years on the charge of treason. Davis was released on bail in May 1867 after his physical and emotional health had deteriorated. He returned to Mississippi, refused to take the oath of allegiance to the United States, and eventually took up residence on the Gulf Coast at Biloxi. In 1881, Davis published *The Rise and Fall of the Confederate Government*. The Confederacy's only president died in 1889 and is buried in Hollywood Cemetery in Richmond.

numbered regiments in each State contained significant numbers of militiamen. In the North, the 69th New York was among the very best of the militia-based regiments that earned outstanding combat records. Irish immigrants had originally formed the 69th New York Regiment in October 1851. The regiment created two opportunities for the Irish—new immigrants publicly demonstrated their allegiance to the United States by participating in musters, and the regiment provided training to a cadre of young men who hoped to return home one day to fight for Irish independence. Immediately after Lincoln's call for 75,000 militia, the 69th deployed to Washington and was among the first Union regiments to occupy southern soil in Virginia. At First Bull Run, the Irish fought stubbornly but were eventually caught up in the northern retreat. The 69th New York fought in fourteen campaigns in the East as part of Brig. Gen. Thomas F. Meagher's famed Irish Brigade. The regiment's dash and gallantry during desperate assaults against Confederate defenses at the Bloody Lane at Antietam and Marye's Heights at Fredericksburg are indeed the stuff of military legend. It was Robert E. Lee who gave the 69th New York its colorful nickname. Upon learning once that the Irish were among the troops opposing his rebel infantry, Lee nodded and said, "Ah, yes...that fighting 69th ." Out of the approximately 2,000 regiments that served in the Union Army, the "Fighting 69th " ranked sixth in terms of soldiers killed. (The "Fighting 69th" still serves in the New York Army National Guard as the 69th Infantry.)[34]

The Washington Artillery from Louisiana was among the premier militia-based organizations in the Confederate Army and developed a reputation as one of the South's best artillery units. Originally formed in New Orleans in 1838 as a single battery, the Washington Artillery fought in the Mexican War and expanded into a full battalion at the outbreak of the Civil War. At First Bull Run, the Washington Artillery's batteries were in the thick of the heaviest fighting. On August 30, 1861, the Washington Artillery became the first American artillery unit to fire rounds in an air defense role. When Union balloonists went aloft for the first time in the Civil War to observe Confederate troop movements, the Washington Artillery's guns opened fire on the balloonists and forced them to the ground. Before the war ended, the Louisiana gunners participated in fourteen campaigns, and friends and foes alike developed a healthy respect for them. After one particularly sharp fight, the captured commander of a Union battery asked what southern guns had opposed him. Upon learning that it was the Louisianans, the northern officer growled: "Damn that Washington Artillery! I have been looking for it for three years and have found it at last!" The Louisianans stayed with Lee's army until the very end but refused to surrender. On the final day of the war at Appomattox Court House, the artillerymen evaded capture, destroyed their gun carriages, buried their bronze gun tubes in the woods and vanished into the surrounding hills. By ones and twos, the proud veterans made their way home to New Orleans. (The Washington Artillery serves today as the 141st Field Artillery of the Louisiana Army National Guard.)[35]

Ante-bellum militia units provided a wealth of military experience to the armies and often served as a training base. Early in the war the Hoosier State organized the "Indiana Legion," a militia command with the express purpose of providing rudimentary training to volunteers bound for federal regiments and militiamen remaining in State units. Prewar militiamen were prepared to drill and maneuver troops and often rose to high command and staff positions. New York's 7th Regiment provided six hundred officers to the Union Army. The Artillery Corps and the First Troop, City Cavalry of Philadelphia together provided nearly 250 officers. A number of militia officers rose to senior command. Frank Cheatham was Tennessee's senior militia general before the war, and he rose to the rank of lieutenant general and corps commander while amassing a reputation as one of the top division commanders in the

Militiamen of the Clinch Rifles formed Company A, 5th Georgia Infantry. The first pattern Confederate national flag is suspended from the tent pole, and a slave stands third from right. The photographic process of the day makes the "CR" for Clinch Rifles appear in reverse. (U.S. Army Military History Institute)

Confederate Army. The famous Confederate raider John Hunt Morgan was active in the ante-bellum Kentucky militia and in 1857 raised the Lexington Rifles. Phil Kearny, Lew Wallace, Alpheus Smith, Dan Butterfield, Alfred Terry, and Benjamin Butler were prominent Union generals with militia backgrounds.[36]

As in previous wars, conflicts and jealousies developed between Regulars and citizen-soldiers. Volunteer and militia officers were increasingly critical of the growing numbers of West Pointers in the Regular Army who allegedly arrayed themselves as a tightknit group against citizen-soldiers. The most outspoken critic of professional officers was John A. "Black Jack" Logan of Illinois. A citizen-soldier who eventually rose to temporary command of the Army of the Tennessee during the Atlanta campaign, General William T. Sherman refused to give Logan permanent army-level command. After the war, Logan became a vocal critic of professional officers and a staunch supporter of citizen-soldiers. In *The Volunteer Soldier of America*, Logan denounced West Pointers and other full-time soldiers as undemocratic, cliquish, and wasteful while citizen-soldiers remained the embodiment of America's native military genius.[37]

The State militia systems provided significant service throughout the war. Northern States furnished militia units that served independently or in conjunction with federal troops to hold forts, protect coastlines and the Canadian border, garrison the Indian frontier and guard Confederate prisoners. In performing these functions, the militia relieved federal troops for duty elsewhere. Militiamen also monitored subversive political activities, tracked down deserters and helped put down violent draft demonstrations. To ensure enough manpower for the war, Massachusetts once again instituted the enrolled militia in 1864 for men ages 18–24. Rhode Island, West Virginia, Ohio, and Indiana also instituted forms of compulsory militia service at various times. In 1861, Connecticut became the first State to adopt the title "National Guard" for its militia units, and the following year, the Empire State officially changed the designation of its militia forces to "The National Guard of the State of New York." Pennsylvania and Ohio raised State regiments for limited, local service that bore the title "National Guard" in their designations. In the South, militiamen manned coastal defenses, guarded northern prisoners and maintained aggressive patrols that tracked down runaway slaves and deserters. As Union troops advanced further into the South, militiamen more and more fought alongside the volunteer regiments of the Confederate Army.[38]

The States produced large numbers of militiamen on short notice in response to unexpected emergencies. When the Confederate Army invaded Kentucky in the fall of 1862, the Governor of Ohio declared a militia levee, and 15,000 militiamen rallied to defend Cincinnati. Further east, the Pennsylvania militia served on active duty for two weeks during the Antietam campaign. The summer of 1863 was a particularly busy time for northern militia units. In response to Lee's second invasion of the North, militiamen from Pennsylvania, New York and Rhode Island augmented the Army of the Potomac during the Gettysburg campaign. Ohio and Indiana militiamen turned out in large numbers to repel a raid north of the Ohio River by southern marauders under John Hunt Morgan.[39]

Because of the devastating effects of disease and the ghastly casualty rates of severe battles, the Civil War armies had a voracious appetite for manpower. Within a year of First Bull Run, both sides realized that the traditional approach of raising manpower by levying quotas against the States for volunteer and militia regiments was inadequate. Ironically, the Confederacy, based on the premise of States' rights, was the first to implement national conscription. In April 1862, the Confederacy enacted the first national draft law in American history. All white males ages 18–35 had to serve for three years and reenlistments were mandatory. By the summer of 1862, the North needed additional manpower, and the Militia Act of 1862 authorized a militia draft designed to stimulate recruiting in volunteer regiments. Less than a year later, the North resorted to full conscription when Congress passed the Enrollment Act of 1863. In reality, both sides enacted draft laws to spur recruiting and volunteerism; only 6 percent of Union and 20 percent of Confederate troops entered the military through conscription. Still, conscription was intensely unpopular, and anti-draft riots in Wisconsin, Pennsylvania, and New York required armed troops to restore order.[40]

In many ways, the key provisions of national draft legislation drew heavily from State militia laws. First and foremost, Union and Confederate laws embraced the ideal of universal military service that had started with the earliest American settlements. Colonial militia ordinances had allowed substitutes, exemptions, and the payment of commutation fines, and to varying degrees, Civil War conscription laws embraced all of these methods. At the same time, national draft laws represented an important, new change in military policy. Both Confederate and Union draft procedures largely ignored the States. Another significant change was the reliance on compulsory rather than voluntary enlistments as the basis for mobilization. While draft laws sought a more efficient use of manpower, they ignored the ties most citizens felt toward their States and local communities.[41]

Three weeks after Appomattox, the strength of the Union Army stood at just over one million men. Tired of four years of war, volunteer soldiers wanted to go home, and Congress obliged them by launching a massive demobilization. Within six months, nearly 800,000 citizen-soldiers were mustered out, and by August 1867, the Regular Army stood at 56,815 officers and men. Most of the Army deployed below the Mason-Dixon Line to become the government's executive agent for the occupation of the South while other units went west of the Mississippi River to deal with the Indian nations. The period of Reconstruction saw the readmission of the former Confederate States into the Union and necessary adjustments in southern society to permit the assimilation of freed blacks.[42]

The volunteer militia's lowest ebb occurred during 1865–1877. At first, the militia in the northern States all but ceased to exist. Exhausted by the bloodiest war in American history, men were not interested in voluntary military service. No threat seemed imminent, and the Regular Army appeared entirely capable of handling Indian affairs in the West and the occupation of the South without assistance from the militia. In the unlikely event of a serious threat, a vast reservoir of experienced veterans was available for military service. The States maintained their AG offices that were primarily responsible for organizing and storing Civil War records and for handling veterans' affairs. By one count, less than one-third of all the States maintained any semblance of a viable militia.[43]

In the South, however, the status and control of the militia was often central to Reconstruction policies. At first, southern States readmitted to the Union were free to reconstitute their militias. Confederate veterans dominated the postwar militias and were intent upon undermining Reconstruction policies, intimidating freed blacks and restraining Union occupation forces. Several southern States passed "Black Codes," laws designed to regulate the political, social, and economic rights of freed blacks. Southern militia units became the primary agents for enforcing the codes. Angered by southern actions, Congress passed civil rights legislation to negate the codes, and a rider to the Army Appropriations Act of 1867 disbanded the southern militias. White southerners refusing to bend to the forces of Reconstruction founded the Ku Klux Klan. Using nocturnal, hit-and-run guerilla tactics meant to instill terror, the Klan was determined to defeat Reconstruction and maintain control of the black population.[44]

In response to white terrorism, Congress allowed States readmitted to the Union to form militia units. The only criterion for militia membership was loyalty to the Union, and black militia units sprang up across the South. In 1866, the Regular Army had established four black regiments—the 9th and 10th Cavalry and the 24th and 25th Infantry—commanded by white officers. The creation of black militia units followed this trend except that they were free to elect black officers. In some States, African-American militia units played an important role in advancing Reconstruction policies and insuring black civil rights. South Carolina and Louisiana had black general officers in the early post-bellum period, and in 1870, Maj. Gen. Robert B. Elliott of South Carolina became the first African-American AG in the militia's history. The Governors of Arkansas, Tennessee, and North Carolina successfully used militia units to break the back of the Ku Klux Klan. In 1877, Reconstruction ended with the withdrawal of the Union Army from the South.[45]

Militiamen as Strikebreakers

Ten years after the Civil War, a semblance of National Guard organization appeared in most States. Perhaps nostalgic for the excitement and camaraderie of field duty, veterans banded together in volunteer militia units. Like their ante-bellum predecessors, militiamen sought a venue for the exercise of a military lifestyle and opportunities for self-improvement, recreation, and service to their community. By 1875, volunteer militia strength stood at 90,865 nationwide with more than half of the soldiers concentrated in the Northeast. Ten of the thirty-seven States in 1875 reported no organized militia forces.[46]

The Great Railroad Strike of 1877 thrust the militia back onto the national scene. Increased industrialization heightened tensions between ever larger companies and organized labor, especially among the growing railroads. After a decade of labor unrest and four years of economic depression, railroad employees launched violent protests in reaction to wage cuts. Workers shut down the Baltimore & Ohio Railroad in West Virginia in July 1877, and the strike spread spontaneously throughout the Northeast and Midwest, snarling rail traffic from St. Louis to Boston.[47]

Intent on restoring rail service and curbing violence, fifteen States called out approximately 45,000 militiamen. The militia's performance varied widely. Overall, citizen-soldiers remained loyal to their officers and civil authorities. In some cases, militiamen fired on strikers while in other instances they united with the workers. The failure of militiamen to control violence in West Virginia led to the commitment of federal troops. One thousand Regulars and 9,000 militiamen broke the strike in Pennsylvania, where it was the most violent and prolonged. Regulars also served in Maryland, Illinois, Indiana, and Missouri. Federal troops, police forces, and militiamen finally brought the situation under control by the first week in August. At least one hundred people lost their lives and hundreds more were injured.[48]

The Great Railroad Strike of 1877 served as a watershed event in the transformation of the State militias into the National Guard. In response to the violence, a number of States increased militia budgets and raised additional units. Pennsylvania increased its annual military budget to $200,000 and initiated a battery of reforms aimed at eliminating inefficiency and unqualified soldiers. New York boosted appropriations and placed a new emphasis on military readiness. The greatest changes occurred in the Midwest where a large number of new Guard units appeared with the backing of public and private monies. Two infantry regiments and a cavalry squadron were organized in Chicago and supported by an annual stipend of $100,000 from the Chicago Citizens' Association, an interest group of businessmen and industrialists. In Indiana, eleven new companies formed after the 1877 strike, and for the first time, Iowa created a separate military budget. State AGs entered into discussions regarding the relative efficiency of cavalry and artillery versus infantry in breaking up massed rioters. "There can be no question of the efficiency of the artillery of the National Guard in putting down riots," Pennsylvania's AG noted, "...a battery loaded with grape and canister has a most discouraging effect upon a body of rioters." Civil War veterans agreed that horses and cannon were most effective against massed protesters, though those units were vastly more expensive to equip, train, and maintain than infantry formations.[49]

The continued involvement of State troops in labor disputes throughout the 1880s and 1890s came to identify the National Guard as the protectors of big business. Guard leaders promoted the role of citizen-soldiers as strikebreakers in order to curry favor and financial support from elected officials. The industrial "robber barons" saw the Guard as the defenders of their established order and provided direct, private funding. On the other hand, organized labor branded the Guard as a tool of corporate capitalists and prohibited members of labor unions from serving as citizen-soldiers. Between 1865 and 1906, the Governors called out their troops 481 times; almost one-third of the calls stemmed from labor troubles.[50]

Concerns over the Regular Army's employment during Reconstruction and the strikes of 1877 resulted in benchmark legislation that forever altered the relationship between federal troops and civil authorities. The Posse Comitatus Act of 1878 prohibited the Army from aiding civil authorities unless ordered to do so by the president. The legislation prohibited the established practice of Regulars acting under the jurisdiction of U.S. marshals and judges. Army officers welcomed the change because they preferred to assert authority over civilians only when acting under presidential orders. On the other hand, the Posse Comitatus Act insured

The Chickasaw Guards of Memphis, Tennessee drilling in front of their armory in July 1881. Larger sized units and armory buildings differentiated militia organizations after the Civil War from their ante-bellum predecessors. (Anne Brown Collection)

that the Governors would continue to rely upon National Guard units for law enforcement. The law left citizen-soldiers free to enforce laws in the States unless the president ordered the Guard into active, federal service. The Posse Comitatus Act remains the key legislation governing the employment of Regular and National Guard soldiers during domestic emergencies.

Creation of the National Guard Association

The poor performance of some State units in 1877 resulted in the introduction in Congress of proposals for militia reform legislation. Citizen-soldiers were in a poor position to produce a reform bill of their own. While a number of States had their own militia associations at the time, no such national organization existed. Under the guiding leadership of an ex-Confederate, Maj. Gen. Dabney H. Maury, concerned militia leaders met for the first time in Richmond in 1878 to discuss militia reforms and the creation of a national lobbying group. The intent of the fledgling organization was to develop national positions on policy issues affecting the militia and to find remedies for nationwide militia problems. Unlike members of the Regular Army who eschewed political involvement, militia leaders believed that their unique status as both citizens and soldiers gave them an inalienable right to form opinions on military matters and to discuss them openly with their elected officials. Out of the original discussions in Richmond arose the National Guard Association (NGA), the nation's oldest and most successful military lobbying organization.[51]

The NGA held its first national conference in St. Louis in October 1879 at the armory of the 1st Missouri Infantry. The purpose of the NGA was to promote "military efficiency" in the militia and to develop national legislation for militia reform. Delegates from fourteen States sat on various panels that addressed a range of issues. Before the conference ended, participants elected a slate of NGA officers. Brig. Gen. George W. Wingate of New York became the NGA's first president, a position he held until 1890.[52]

Two issues dominated the first convention: achieving a substantial increase in the federal militia appropriation and consideration of the specifics of a militia reform bill. Since 1808, the annual federal militia allotment had remained at $200,000. The NGA believed that with the growth of the national population and the effects of inflation that Congress should increase the appropriation to $1 million and allow the States to use funds for items beyond weaponry. One delegate pointed out that the Regular Army of 26,000 officers and men cost the government $40 million each year, making the militia a rich return on the nation's investment. Proposed legislation intended to replace the Militia Act of 1792 included several key reforms. First and foremost, the National Guard was to supplant completely the old enrolled militia. (By 1879, many States had adopted the title "National Guard," but a formal name change at the national level was still nearly forty years in the future.) The National Guard was to consist of two groups: soldiers in organized units readily available for active duty, and a reserve force comprised of older citizen-soldiers subject to service only during the most severe emergencies. Other provisions called for mandatory annual encampments, the construction of rifle ranges for marksmanship training, and the assignment of Regular Army officers to senior staff positions in National Guard regiments and brigades.[53]

Militia officers travelling to Washington had difficulty convincing Congress of the need for reforms. A combination of apathy, antimilitarism and a devotion to States' rights prevented militia leaders from gaining approval for their bill. In a repeat of the political concerns of the 1780s, several Congressmen viewed the bill as an unnecessary intrusion

Company D, 1st Minnesota Infantry at the National Encampment in Washington, DC in May 1887. The descendants of the 1st Minnesota that gained fame for its charge at Gettysburg in 1863 won second place in the 1887 national drill competition. (John Listman Collection)

into State affairs. Finally, the NGA dropped the reform bill and concentrated its efforts on increasing militia funding. On this point, the Army lent its support. Increased appropriations for the militia meant that the Army could more quickly displace its aging inventories of weapons and equipment to the States and hasten the modernization of its own units. The NGA's lobbying efforts finally bore fruit in 1887 when Congress doubled the militia's annual allotment to $400,000.[54]

The Militia and Westward Expansion

The Louisiana Purchase in 1802 and the Treaty of Guadalupe-Hidalgo ending the Mexican War in 1848 gained for the United States the huge landmass that eventually constituted the States of the West and the Plains. As settlers pushed westward beyond the Mississippi River to carve new States and Territories from the wilderness, they formed militia groups. Citizen-soldiers provided protection against bandits and vigilantes, guarded prisoners, acted as posses, controlled riots in the cities, safeguarded officials and helped to settle disputes over ranch, water, and mining claims. A principle function of local militias was to provide security against Indian attacks and to launch reprisal raids. In August 1862, Minnesota citizen-soldiers put down a Sioux uprising that cost the lives of more than 600 whites. Perhaps the most bloodthirsty moment in the militia's history occurred in southeastern Colorado in November 1864 at the Sand Creek Massacre. The Third Regiment of Colorado Volunteer Cavalry, led by Colonel John M. Chivington, attacked a mixed settlement of Cheyennes and Arapahos. Many of the braves were away hunting, and Chivington's men destroyed the village, killing and mutilating nearly 150 Native Americans, most of who were women and children. The militiamen returned to Denver with one hundred scalps they displayed for public viewing. In New Mexico, Colonel Kit Carson used the militia to humble the Apaches. In 1868, a band of fifty-one militiamen suffered 55 percent losses while repelling a large Indian attack against Beecher's Island on the Arkansas River. After the 1860s, the Regular Army took up the primary burden of Indian fighting.[55]

On the Pacific coast, California created the most substantial militia forces in the West. Mexico ceded California to the United States in 1848, and two years later, it became the thirty-first State. California's first militia unit predated Statehood. Citizens organized the 1st California Guard in San Francisco in 1849 to subdue lawless gangs. At the ceremony marking California's admission to the Union, the 1st California Guard fired the necessary salutes. The unit drilled frequently at the Presidio of San Francisco, and in 1850, built the Military Hall as its own armory building. That same year, the legislature created the position of AG, divided the State into four militia districts and authorized the creation of volunteer militia companies. With the State's population and economic activity centered on San Francisco, Sacramento, and the gold mines of the Sierra Nevada, most militia companies formed in northern California. Within five years, the number of militia organizations had grown to thirty-four, and on the eve of the Civil War, "The Golden State" included seventy-four companies. Though no California regiments served in the Civil War's principle theaters, Californians volunteered as individuals for eastern regiments, formed regiments for duty in the West and joined local militia companies. At the end of the war, 164 militia companies existed. In 1866, the legislature changed the name of the militia to the "National Guard of the State of California" and directed all units to adopt the Regular Army's field uniform. After the Civil War, California maintained the largest State soldiery in the West. By 1885, California included 3,217 Guardsmen, and within ten years, strength had increased to 4,364 soldiers.[56]

Kansas developed the most respectable militia organization on the Plains. The establishment of the Kansas Territory in 1854 required the creation of a militia to enforce laws and deal with the Indians. After

Kansas entered the Union in 1861, militia units became embroiled in a deadly struggle to determine the State's ultimate fate as a free or slave-holding entity. The most intense fighting occurred along the Kansas-Missouri border where proslavery and abolitionist militia units engaged in a savage and protracted guerilla war. The 7th Kansas Cavalry became known as "The Jayhawkers," a term synonymous with indiscriminate destruction and looting. After the Civil War, the Kansas militia languished until the late 1870s when the State soldiery was revitalized by a dramatic increase in population, strike duty, and the action of veterans. In May 1879, ten volunteer militia companies combined to create the 1st Kansas Regiment, and within months, a second regiment was activated. Nearly two-thirds of all officers were Civil War veterans, and Kansas soldiers adopted the Army's field uniform. In 1880, Kansas created a State chapter of the NGA. The Militia Law of 1885 created a Military Board to administer units, provided funds for summer camp and armory rental, and renamed the militia as the "Kansas National Guard." By 1895, Kansas included 1,815 Guardsmen and was the largest Guard organization on the Plains.[57]

In the Southwest, the New Mexico Territory relied upon its Spanish *milicia* roots to develop a credible force of citizen-soldiers. The earliest militia forces came to New Mexico in April 1598 when Spanish adventurers first crossed the Rio Grande and took formal possession of the region. A system of citizen-soldiers—*Vecinos*—was in effect for the next two and a half centuries under Spanish rule. In 1846, U.S. troops occupied Santa Fe and established America's claim to New Mexico. The first territorial militia was organized that year, and in 1851, the legislature formally sanctioned the militia and created the position of AG. Under the command of the famous Indian scout, Colonel Kit Carson, the militia routed rival Indian tribes. During the Civil War, New Mexico fielded four militia regiments that fought successfully to retain New Mexico for the Union. At the battle of Glorietta Pass on March 28, 1862, a combined force of Union troops and New Mexico militia turned back an invading Confederate column and ended southern hopes for gaining control of the territory. In 1885, militia strength stood at nearly 1,500 soldiers, but territorial governors began to rely more on local law enforcement and less on citizen-soldiers to keep the peace. A decade later, the militia was down to 500 men, and the legislature renamed them the "New Mexico National Guard."[58]

The Rise of the National Guard

On April 30, 1889, New York City hosted elaborate ceremonies honoring the centennial of George Washington's first inauguration as president. More than a million astonished spectators watched as nearly 30,000 State soldiers paraded along New York's streets. The massed ranks of citizen-soldiers constituted the largest body of armed men assembled since the Civil War and the largest force of militiamen ever gathered in America. The parading units gave the appearance of a well armed, equipped, and disciplined force ready for immediate service. Perhaps more than any other event, the National Guard's participation at the centennial celebration demonstrated that the volunteer militia system that had flourished after the War of 1812 was fading away.[59]

The Guard's highly visible role in strikebreaking revived debates of the proper role of State soldiers in national military policy. Many Guardsmen disliked their role as industrial policemen and realized that in order to prosper they could not become identified solely as strikebreakers and the enemy of the working class. More and more, State soldiers eschewed their involvement in labor disputes and promoted themselves as an organized combat reserve of the Army. By the late 1890s, Guard spokesmen were strongly affirming their desire for a combat reserve role. Colonel James M. Rice of Illinois wrote that State soldiers would "be very much pained...to find that they were only organized to do police duty" and that service to the nation in wartime was the "pride and life of the National Guard." In a clever twist of public perceptions, Guardsmen presented themselves as the institutional embodiment of all citizen-soldiers, including the volunteers of the Civil War. But unlike volunteers called from the population at large, Guardsmen stressed that they were an organized, partially trained and equipped force available for duty at the outbreak of hostilities.[60]

The Guard's emerging vision of itself coincided with the Army's search for a new mission. The close of the American West and improved communications and advancing industrialization around the globe prompted the Army to consider overseas campaigning as its new *raison d'etre*. Army reformers believed that ultimately America would become involved in a war with one of the major European powers. In such a conflict, America would face an army manned by well-trained professionals and organized reserves. Progressive officers wanted the U.S. Army reorganized along European lines with a proficient general staff and a large, trained reserve force. In a war against a major adversary, America would not have the time to raise a volunteer-based, mass army after the outbreak of hostilities.[61]

One way the National Guard promoted itself as a national reserve was by taking on an appearance more like that of the Regular Army. The increase in the nation's population and the experience of the Civil War convinced citizen-soldiers to make regiments the basis of their post-bellum organizations rather than separate companies. Most States adopted the Regular Army's plain field uniform for normal duty and retained their extravagant uniforms for formal occasions. In 1871, New York Guardsmen had been instrumental in forming the National Rifle Association, and competitive marksmanship events became a hallmark of National Guard training. While Guard units still thrived as social organizations, they placed more emphasis on readiness.[62]

Pennsylvania citizen-soldiers became the personification of the Guard's new orientation. In 1879, the Keystone State eliminated its enrolled militia districts and reorganized itself into a single, tactical division with a headquarters and three brigades. Pennsylvania troops drilled one night per week, stood for periodic inspections and participated in an annual, six-day summer encampment. In 1884, the Pennsylvania division held its first encampment on the battlefield at Gettysburg. (By forming the nation's first organized division in peacetime in 1879, the U.S. Army officially recognizes what eventually became Pennsylvania's 28th Infantry Division as its oldest, permanently organized combat division.)[63]

Unlike the ante-bellum volunteer militia, the States supported the Guard with funding after 1877. Financial support was greatest in the industrialized and more populated States of the Northeast and Midwest. In general, the States recognized the sacrifices Guardsmen made by offering modest uniform allowances and stipends for attendance at summer camp. In 1895, State military budgets reached an aggregate of $2.7 million, far overshadowing the annual federal allocation of $400,000. Still, in the southern and western States with small military budgets, federal monies were significant in supporting Guard organizations struggling to survive. At the local level, officers and soldiers still contributed a great deal of the money needed to sustain their units.[64]

The bulk of State budgets went toward armory construction. State legislators welcomed the awarding of lucrative labor and construction contracts for the building of armories in their districts. In some cases, elite units with wealthy benefactors provided funding for the construction of their own armories. Across the nation, Guard units abandoned borrowed public facilities and rented space in private buildings and moved to new armory buildings. State and Guard officials agreed that armories had to be large enough to support a unit's administrative, training, and recreational activities. Armories were to have a distinct, military look, and architects adopted a "castellated" style that employed towers, turrets and parapets of heavy stone to make armories an imposing sight and a formidable defensive position. Soldiers and civilians alike believed that castellated armories constituted safe sanctuaries in urban centers from which Guardsmen would emerge to quell labor disturbances and urban rioting. Perhaps the most imposing and elaborate armory in the nation's history was the 7th New York's facility that was built with private funds and opened in 1879 to great fanfare.[65]

The mutual interest Army and Guard officers had in creating a trained, national reserve resulted in closer cooperation between the States and the War Department. The National Rifle Association sponsored competitive shooting events that pitted Guardsmen against Regulars. Beginning in 1880, the War Department detailed Regular officers to inspect Guard summer encampments whenever the States requested such assistance. Guardsmen and Regulars came into direct contact through the assignment of active duty officers to inspect and instruct State troops. By the late 1890s, nearly fifty Army officers were assigned full-time to the States, and during the summer training sea-

The National Guard armory in Worcester, Massachusetts, with its stone turrets and battlements, was typical of the castellated armories of the day. Dedicated in 1889, the building still serves as the National Guard Archives and Museum for the Bay State. (Massachusetts National Guard Archives and Museum)

son, many more were on temporary duty. Increased exposure to State soldiers convinced many Regulars that instructing the Guard should become one of their principle functions.[66]

However, the era was not one of complete harmony. Some Army reformers openly questioned the Guard's value as a viable reserve and stubbornly pushed for an expansion of Regular forces and the creation of a new, federally-controlled reserve. Many Regulars complained of the Guard's lack of discipline and skills and viewed the militia's tradition of electing company officers as detrimental to unit effectiveness. An attitude developed that Guard units deserved their own leaders in peacetime, but when called to active duty, trained professionals should lead them into battle. At the same time, many Guardsmen resented federal intrusion into their affairs. The States refused to reorganize their units to make them conform to Regular Army standards. In general, the Guard wanted the best of both worlds—federal aid without interference from the War

Citizen-soldiers of the "Tacoma Guard," Company C, 1st Infantry, of the Washington State National Guard during their summer encampment in July 1891. The use of federal uniforms and equipment reflects the National Guard's desire to become a combat reserve to the U.S. Army. (Washington State Historical Society)

Department. By the 1890s, progressive Guardsmen understood that to become an effective reserve force they would have to accept some degree of federal supervision.[67]

In 1895, the National Guard was well established across the country. Personnel strength stood at 115,699, making the Guard more than four times larger than the Regular Army. All forty-three States and three of the four Territories, Alaska excepted, maintained Guard units. African-Americans established a presence in the Guard, and between 1865 and 1914, at least twenty-two States and the District of Columbia at some time maintained black units that ranged in size from separate companies to complete regiments. The strongest States included New York, Pennsylvania, Massachusetts, Georgia, South Carolina, Illinois, Ohio, and California with more than 4,000 Guardsmen each. Only three States still used the term "militia." In terms of capabilities, the Guard included approximately 94,000 infantrymen, 5,500 artillerymen, and 7,000 cavalrymen. One observer calculated that the annual cost of maintaining one Regular was $1,000 while a Guardsman cost $24 annually, with the States and individual citizen-soldiers shouldering 80 percent of the financial burden.[68]

Conclusions

During the 19th Century, State soldiers underwent a metamorphosis that forever changed the militia. After the War of 1812, political, social, and economic conditions rendered the enrolled militia ineffective. In its place, volunteer militia companies arose that performed both social and military functions. The cataclysm of the Civil War swept the volunteer militia away, and it resurfaced only sporadically prior to 1877. Duty as strikebreakers returned the volunteer militia to the national scene. Citizen-soldiers tired of their role as industrial policemen, and as the 1800s came to a close, progressive State soldiers envisioned a new National Guard whose mission was to serve as the primary combat reserve of the U.S. Army.

Despite the demise of the enrolled militia, State soldiers still performed valuable service that was consistent with their constitutional mandate to "execute the Laws of the Union, suppress Insurrections and repel Invasions." In the War of 1812, militiamen provided the final victory at New Orleans that salvaged their reputation and begged comparisons with the battle of Bunker Hill. Militiamen guarded America's southern border and provided troops for volunteer regiments during the Mexican War. Militia regiments executed the opening moves of the Civil War and fought the first major battle at Bull Run. During the opening of the American West, militiamen dealt with Indians, protected settlements and provided valuable service to federal, territorial, and State officials. Beginning in 1877, State soldiers were involved in increasingly frequent and violent labor disputes between captains of industry and their workers.

Important policy changes profoundly affected defense plans. During the War of 1812 the refusal of key Governors to make their troops available for federal service and the unwillingness of certain militia units to invade Canada tarnished the militia's credibility as a reliable reserve force. Calhoun's Expansible Army Plan was the first proposal designed to create a Regular Army that did not require wartime augmentation from the militia. When America's first foreign war erupted, the War Department relied upon volunteers rather than militiamen to defeat Mexico, even though large numbers of State troops filled the ranks of volunteer regiments. The early crisis of the Civil War brought militiamen to the forefront again, but ultimately the North and the South relied upon volunteers and conscripts to man their armies. After the Civil War, the NGA appeared as a permanent lobbying organization to promote policies favorable to the Guard. The Posse Comitatus Act prohibited federal troops from engaging in law enforcement missions unless acting under presidential orders. With Regulars largely excluded from domestic missions, the militia became even more important in providing support to civil authorities during State emergencies.

In the 1890s, three separate groups were at work to create a more effective National Guard. The federal government had doubled its overall appropriation, and Army officers were available to inspect and train Guard units. The States supported citizen-soldiers with revised militia laws and increased funding that allowed the construction of armories, reimbursed individuals for uniforms and provided modest pay for summer encampments. Guard officers pressed for a new role as the Army's combat reserve while State soldiers still gave freely of their time, money, and efforts in order to maintain their units. The Militia Act of 1792 remained the enabling militia legislation between the States and the federal government, and until it was repealed or amended, efforts to improve the Guard's effectiveness would remain limited and incremental. In the end, the catalyst for reform did not come from the federal government, the States or serving Guardsmen, but from an unexpected, catastrophic explosion in Havana harbor that plunged the country into war.

Part II
The National Guard, 1898–1945

CHAPTER 4

The Birth of the Modern National Guard, 1898–1916

T he time is now near at hand when by Federal statute the organization, armament and discipline of the Organized Militia in the several States and Territories shall be the same as that prescribed for
the Regular Army of the United States.

> Senator Charles Dick,
> *National Guard* magazine,
> January, 1910

Introduction

Maj. Gen. John F. O'Ryan of the New York National Guard took great pride in the performance of his soldiers during the past few weeks. The United States and Mexico were on the brink of war, and in the summer of 1916, President Woodrow Wilson had ordered the National Guard to active duty to protect the nation's southwestern border. As commander of the National Guard's 6th Division, O'Ryan had supervised its rail movement from mobilization camps in the Empire State to cantonment areas in south Texas. During the long trek, Guardsmen had chalked "Get Villa!" and other patriotic slogans on the rail cars indicating that they were ready for a fight. From his headquarters near Laredo, General O'Ryan monitored the activities of the 6th Division's regiments deployed along the banks of the lower Rio Grande.

John O'Ryan marveled at the transformation that had occurred within the National Guard since he had enlisted as a private in Company G, 7th New York Infantry in 1897. After accepting a transfer to the artillery, he rose through the ranks to command his own battery in 1907. O'Ryan embraced the National Guard's new role as a combat reserve to the Regular Army. When he took command, he removed the billiard and ping-pong tables from the armory, told soldiers that weekly drill was mandatory and launched a strict training program. O'Ryan enjoyed the new summer maneuvers with the Regulars, and he became widely recognized for his aptitude in military matters. In 1912, the Governor of New York selected him to command one of the National Guard's new combat divisions. Two years later, O'Ryan was the first National Guard officer to graduate from the new Army War College.

Despite all of the changes, O'Ryan suspected even more challenges in the coming months. A grisly war of attrition raged in Europe, and if the United States became involved, New York's division would surely be sent to the fighting. The 6th Division had procured four machine guns, and troops spent their days under the hot Texas sun learning all they could about the weapons' devastating firepower. If called to fight in Europe, John F. O'Ryan was determined that his soldiers would be as ready as possible...

In the first two decades of the 20th Century, the United States exerted its authority more decisively beyond the borders of North America. New foreign policy interests in Latin America, the Caribbean, and the Pacific prompted the commitment of American armed forces overseas. At home, military reformers pressed for bolder, more robust defense policies. The Army faced the challenge of transforming itself from a force organized for domestic constabulary duty to one prepared for overseas campaigning. Both Regulars and citizen-soldiers needed capabilities commensurate with America's new status as an emerging world power. At the same time, a revolution in military technology occurred centered around the battleship, the airplane, and the internal combustion engine. Within the Army, improved weapons and equipment prompted changes in doctrine, organization, and tactics.

Military reforms of the early 20th Century forever altered the face of the citizen-soldier. The volunteer militia of the 19th Century, with deep roots in most States, gave way to a reformed National Guard with closer ties to the federal government. Benchmark legislation provided additional funding to Guardsmen, mandated tighter federal controls over State soldiers and established the National Guard's rightful place in U.S. military policy. The Guard changed fundamentally in terms of its funding, organization, training, and administration. By the end of the period, the National Guard was an active instrument of American foreign policy and a more effective combat reserve of the U.S. Army.

The Spanish-American War and the Philippine Insurrection

When the U.S.S. *Maine* exploded and sank in Havana harbor in Cuba on the morning of February 15, 1898, it ignited a long simmering conflict between Spain and the United States over Cuban independence. Americans blamed the explosion on Spanish sabotage, and war cries were heard across the country. Spain maintained a large army in Cuba in order to deter a growing independence movement. The actions of Spanish colonial authorities were often brutal, and sensational press reports about alleged atrocities outraged the American people. Congress declared war against Spain on April 22, 1898 with the goal of securing Cuban independence. By war's end, America was set upon the world stage as an imperial power with colonies in the Caribbean, the central Pacific, and the Far East.[1]

Within days, word arrived of Commodore George Dewey's quick and decisive naval victory over the Spanish fleet in Manila Bay in the Philippines, a key Spanish possession in the southwest Pacific. Dewey's victory on May 1st added more energy to the great wave of war excitement already running through the country. At the time, the Army numbered only 28,000 men, far too few to invade the major Spanish colonies in the Caribbean—Cuba and Puerto Rico—and to occupy the Philippines. President William McKinley called upon the States to raise 125,000 men for overseas service. As in the Civil War, the federal government called upon the Governors to raise volunteer regiments. Subsequent calls raised 58,000 more men, bringing the number of volunteers to 182,687.[2]

However, the presidential callup of April 22nd stipulated that all men filling the first volunteer units had to come from existing militia organizations. To negate concerns over the possible illegalities of militia service overseas, all State soldiers had to volunteer for foreign duty. With the popularity of the war, entire regiments of enthusiastic militiamen mustered into the Army for two years. A total of 194 militia units served during the period. Perhaps the most famous American unit of the war, the 1st U.S. Volunteer Cavalry, popularly known as the "Rough Riders," included one New Mexico National Guard cavalry squadron and two troops from the Arizona Guard. Theodore Roosevelt, a former New York Guardsman, was instrumental in raising the regiment and served as its lieutenant colonel. The Army in 1898 remained racially segregated, with African-American soldiers allowed to serve in only four regiments, and the militia followed this same pattern. Of the sixteen States with black commands, just eight offered up black units for service.[3]

By early May, troops quickly moved from their armories to induction camps at the State capitals. After completing preliminary mobilization procedures, the volunteer regiments boarded trains for hastily constructed training camps either in the South or near San Francisco, locations that allowed easy deployment to Cuba, Puerto Rico, and the Philippines. The major criteria used to select camp sites was railroad accessibility. Health concerns were not seriously considered, and troops arrived to find poor drinking water and unsanitary conditions. These factors led to the biggest killer of the war: disease. Far more American soldiers died from malaria, yellow fever, typhoid, and typhus than from bullets. For example, New York had 436 men die in service, only fifteen of whom were killed in combat.[4]

As training regimes began, a number of problems became apparent. Many of the militia officers lacked the qualifications and experience to properly train their soldiers. With help from Army advisors, most gained an acceptable level of competence, and talented men from the ranks replaced those who fell short. In training camps, militiamen spent almost all of their time drilling, marching, and learning the proper handling and care of their arms and equipment. Target practice and bayonet drills were regular activities. To toughen up the men, units conducted cross-country marches and field exercises. Within weeks, militiamen from all walks of life gained confidence in themselves and their leaders. The greatest problem facing enlisted men was the poor condition of their uniforms and equipment. Most States had adopted the Army blue fatigue uniform. However, the rapid increase of all units to wartime strength soon exhausted uniform stockpiles. Many men had to wait until they arrived at the camps to get their issues of clothing and equipment. The militia carried the obsolete .45 caliber Springfield rifle developed right after the Civil War. Ammunition for the .45 Springfield still used black powder that created puffs of gray smoke when fired and exposed soldiers' positions in combat. In contrast, the Regulars carried the more modern, magazine-fed Krag-Jorgensen rifle. While some militiamen deployed overseas with Krags, most carried their obsolete Springfields.[5]

By June, many of the regiments in the East coast camps were completely equipped, trained, and ready to go to Cuba. War plans called for the capture of Santiago (the base of the Spanish fleet) from the land side to compel the fleet to sail out and engage the much stronger American Navy. With the capture of Santiago, U.S. troops would then invest Havana and end Spanish rule. Most of the units identified to sail first were Regular Army commands of the newly organized U.S. V Corps, which included Guard units from the District of Columbia, Illinois, Ohio, Massachusetts, Michigan, and New York. These units massed at Tampa,

Florida to await transportation to Cuba. Due to the quickness of the mobilization, there was not enough shipping to carry the whole corps at once. Most of the vessels used were hired tramp freighters, often in poor condition and meant to carry goods, not soldiers and horses. So few horses could be taken that almost all of the cavalry ended up fighting dismounted. The first convoy sailed on June 14th and dropped anchor off Santiago on the 21st. Due to the shipping shortage only two State units, the 2nd Massachusetts and the 71st New York, sailed for Cuba with the V Corps.[6]

By June 24th, most of the men had been off-loaded while advance parties probed toward Santiago. An engagement occurred at Las Guasimas between U.S. cavalry and Spanish defenders. After a sharp fight the Spanish withdrew. American casualties included sixteen killed and fifty-two wounded Rough Riders. The Spanish then took up good defensive positions along a series of heights protecting Santiago, including Kettle and San Juan Hills. On July 1st, American troops assaulted the entrenched defenders. The attacks started at El Caney, a village with in-depth defenses. Among the assault troops was the 2nd Massachusetts Infantry. After a six hour fight, the Spanish withdrew, leaving eighty-one Americans dead, five of them militiamen. While the fight at El Caney continued, the battle to capture Kettle and San Juan Hills began. Teddy Roosevelt and the Rough Riders first charged up Kettle Hill and then against San Juan Hill, gaining fame for themselves. Among the first to reach the top of Kettle Hill were Guardsmen from two New Mexico cavalry troops. The cost was high; twenty Rough Riders died as did fifteen members of the 71st New York Infantry, the only other militia unit in the assault. After the capture of the heights, U.S. artillery bombarded Santiago harbor and compelled the Spanish fleet to sally forth, whereupon the U.S. Navy quickly destroyed it.[7]

Santiago surrendered on July 17th. While investing the city, Americans troops fell ill with yellow fever. Nearly 80 percent of the soldiers were sick, with many dying each day. To prevent further deaths, President McKinley ordered the newly-arrived VII Corps to garrison the city while the troops of the V Corps sailed to New York to recover their health. With the signing of a general armistice on August 12th, a number of militia regiments deployed to Havana to garrison the capital. They returned home after the peace treaty granting Cuban independence was ratified in March 1899.[8]

As the fighting ended in Cuba, the U.S. I Corps prepared to invade Puerto Rico. Most of the corps' units were from the militia, including eight of its ten infantry regiments, plus an artillery battalion composed of batteries from four States. The cavalry included units from New York and

Soldiers of the 2nd Wisconsin Volunteer Infantry enter Ponce, Puerto Rico on July 29, 1898. (Library of Congress)

Pennsylvania, and two militia engineer companies were among the corps' troops. On July 25th, the first elements landed on the southern part of the island, met no resistance and marched to the port of Ponce, Puerto Rico's second largest city. Two days later a direct landing was made at Ponce that encountered no enemy soldiers. These two forces linked up on July 31st. The next day a third landing occurred on the western portion of the island. According to plan, these groups moved cross-country toward the capital of San Juan, to besiege it from the land side while the Navy blockaded from the sea.[9]

The only significant engagement of the campaign occurred at a mountain pass named Coamo, on the line of march toward San Juan. Here the Spanish built six blockhouses to delay the American advance. Before the 2nd and 3rd Wisconsin Infantry launched their frontal attacks against the defenses, the 16th Pennsylvania Infantry succeeded in scaling the mountain on the Spanish right, coming down behind a startled enemy. As soon as the Pennsylvanians opened fire, the two Wisconsin units charged. The battle lasted less than two hours, resulting in one soldier killed and ten wounded. Following the general armistice of August 12th, the Americans quickly occupied San Juan. The Army immediately established permanent garrisons, with all of the militia units returning home by the end of 1898.[10]

With the campaigns in Cuba and Puerto Rico completed, only one theater of operations remained. The Philippines in the southwest Pacific were of particular strategic value to the United States. The McKinley Administration was intent on occupying the islands and establishing a permanent base there for the Navy in the Far East. The Philippine archipelago is composed of more than 1,000 islands, with the capital of Manila located on the large central island of Luzon. Before the war, the Filipinos had an independence movement directed against the Spanish authorities. General Emilo Aguinaldo commanded 15,000 guerilla fighters on Luzon who waged a hit-and-run war against the Spanish.[11]

In May 1898, the first of five convoys carrying the U.S. VIII Corps to the Philippines sailed from San Francisco. This increment consisted of 2,500 men, including the 1st California and 2nd Oregon Infantry plus two batteries of artillery. Part of the convoy was diverted to Guam, a Spanish colony, where Company A, 2nd Oregon landed with U.S. Marines to claim the island as an American territory. The main convoy arrived off Manila on June 30th and disembarked troops near Cavite, a peninsula seven miles south of the city. The soldiers quickly moved to the defensive lines near Manila and joined Aguinaldo's guerillas. There was great tension between the two forces, but they decided to act together. Reinforcements arrived before the end of July including the 1st Colorado, 1st Nebraska, 10th Pennsylvania, 1st Idaho, 1st North Dakota, and 13th Minnesota Infantry regiments and the 1st Battalion, 1st Wyoming Infantry. Added to these were two batteries of Utah artillery. With their arrival, the American force numbered more than 11,000 men and twenty-two field guns.[12]

The Americans were strong enough to take the city and desired no participation from Aguinaldo's forces. It was feared the guerillas might capture portions of the city and hold them against advancing U.S. troops. The Americans opened secret talks with the Spanish governor, reminding him of deadly reprisals against Spanish civilians if the guerillas joined in the attack. On August 11th, the governor agreed to surrender Manila to the Americans, but only after token resistance designed to preserve Spanish honor. The plan called for a preliminary naval bombardment and an American waterborne landing while other U.S. troops rushed the city's land defenses. To prepare for the assault, the 1st California and 10th Pennsylvania Infantry moved into trenches occupied by Aguinaldo's men without incident. The guerillas were to be kept out of the city.[13]

Aguinaldo was warned not to interfere in the coming action. On the morning of August 13th, the Navy opened fire against the fortress protecting the old portion of the capital. No Spanish guns replied, and the Americans soon ceased fire. As planned, the 2nd Oregon rowed ashore to surround and occupy the governor's palace and government buildings to prevent any guerillas from entering. The land assault met little resistance until troops reached the city's center. Some Spaniards fired on the advancing militiamen who quickly overcame the resistance. Manila was soon under American control at a cost of six killed and ninety-two wounded. Unknown to anyone, the belligerents had signed an armistice ending the war the day before the attack.[14]

Over the next months, an uneasy alliance developed between U.S. authorities and Aguinaldo as the Spanish withdrew and the new American colonial government was established. During this time, the last two VIII Corps convoys arrived with heavy militia reinforcements: the 51st Iowa, 20th Kansas, 1st Montana, 1st South Dakota, 1st Tennessee, and 1st Washington Infantry, plus a battery of artillery from Wyoming and 1st Troop, Nevada Cavalry. Many of these units occupied the outer ring of defenses around Manila. After months of stalemate, Aguinaldo's forces finally launched coordinated attacks on several American outposts on the night of February 5, 1899. The insurgents hit positions held by the 10th Pennsylvania and 1st Nebraska. Militiamen repelled these attacks with few casualties. Soon other U.S. forces joined the defenders, and by morning the rebels broke off their assaults. Then the militiamen went on the attack, taking many insurgent positions. By day's end, fifty-nine Americans were dead and 278 wounded. More than 600 guerillas were killed.[15]

Over the next few weeks the Americans and Filipinos took turns launching hit-and-run raids against each other, resulting in increased losses on both sides. On March 25th, the Americans went on the offensive. Their plan was to capture the rebel capital at Malolos, sixty miles north of Manila. While there were several sharp engagements, the main cause of losses for the Americans was the hot, humid climate. Many more soldiers lost their lives from sunstroke than from combat. After a grueling six-day advance, the Americans captured the smoldering ruins of Malolos. The rebels had fallen back to their new capital at San Isidro.[16]

In mid-April, the Americans advanced toward San Isidro. During this march, twenty soldiers made National Guard history by earning the Medal of Honor. The first three medals were awarded to members of the 20th Kansas. Colonel Frederick Funston and two men braved intense enemy fire to swim a river with a guide rope that was used to pull rafts loaded with troops across in the face of the enemy. Once enough men were across, Funston led them in a charge, quickly overrunning the position and capturing twelve cannon. Soon after, a group of volunteers drawn from the 1st North Dakota and 2nd Oregon became the vanguard of the column, leading the advance under the command of a local

A skirmish line of the 2nd Oregon Volunteer Infantry in the Philippines in 1898. Three members of the regiment were among the twenty Guardsmen awarded the Medal of Honor in the Philippines. (National Archives)

American civilian, William Young. Known as "Young's Scouts" they first stormed across a burning bridge under intense enemy fire, saving it for the American advance. Later they were surrounded and cut off in a small village. During several hours of desperate fighting, Young's Scouts repelled numerous enemy assaults. When finally relieved, every man was wounded at least once. All thirteen survivors were awarded the Medal of Honor, and four additional State soldiers earned the Medal of Honor during the campaign.[17]

At home, operations in the Philippines generated sharp debates. Many Americans did not favor involvement in the Philippines, and they demanded that citizen-soldiers come home. The men had enlisted to fight for Cuban independence, not to subdue the Philippines. The Army decided to organize four new regiments known as the "Federal Volunteer Force" for use exclusively in the Philippines. By offering a $500 bonus to any man willing to enlist for two years, the Army managed to fill the ranks with former militiamen. The remaining State soldiers moved back to Manila to await shipment home. By August 1899, all militia units arrived back in their States, where enthusiastic crowds greeted them. In all, the militia had made the occupation of Puerto Rico and the capture of the Philippines possible, adding greatly to American gains during the war.[18]

The Root Reforms

Although the United States was victorious in the Spanish-American War, inefficiency, waste, and scandal characterized the mobilization and the logistical support of field forces. Newspaper reporters investigated the mobilization thoroughly and presented their readers with graphic illustrations of poor planning and outright incompetence. Filthy, disease-infested mobilization camps, huge transportation jams at major rail yards and port facilities, and allegations that troops received embalmed and maggot-ridden beef rations—later proven untrue—were among the most egregious deficiencies. A presidential commission investigated the mobilization, found that most problems were due to poor leadership and excessive paperwork rather than malfeasance, and recommended major changes within the War Department.[19]

On August 1, 1899, President McKinley appointed Elihu Root as the new secretary of war. A celebrated Wall Street lawyer, Root was intimately familiar with corporate reorganization and international law. McKinley wanted a secretary of war who could handle the complexities of administering America's new overseas possessions while at the same time reorganizing and modernizing the War Department. In Elihu Root, the president found a public servant capable of both. Root proved himself as a competent administrator and an effective reformer who led the Army into a new era.[20]

The new secretary of war instinctively understood that America's emerging role in foreign policy required a larger and more capable Regular Army backed by effective reserves. Root held forth the "fundamental proposition" that "the real object of having an army is to prepare for war." The Army and the militia would have to make a huge, cultural shift from their more recent roles of frontier constabulary and strike-breakers to an effective instrument for overseas service. The Spanish-American War thus created an opportunity for progressive Regular and Guard officers who had sought closer cooperation since 1877. The old ways of doing business, that included a division of authority between the secretary of war and the commanding general, the near independent authority of the various bureau chiefs, and the iron grip of bureaucratic red tape that existed during peacetime, were no longer acceptable.

The first target of Root's reformist agenda was the Army's school system. Just after the Spanish-American War, one-third of Regular Army officers possessed no formal military education whatsoever, and Root set out to create a more professional officer corps with the intellectual and technical skills to administer the new colonies and to serve in overseas campaigns. On November 27, 1901, the War Department announced a reorganization that brought integration and order to the military education system. Every post of any significant size formed an officers' school of instruction. Officers demonstrating notable skills and potential for increased responsibilities went on to advanced schools at Army posts designated as the home of the various arms and services. Many of these schools predated Root's tenure, and prominent among them were the Infantry and Cavalry School at Fort Leavenworth, the Coast Artillery School at Fort Monroe, and the Engineer and Medical Schools near Washington, DC.

At the apex of the new schools system sat an embryonic Army War College, first established in the nation's capital. Root intended for the War College to train the Army's best officers while directing the military's intellectual activities, gathering information related to policy matters and devising plans and alternatives for the War Department's consideration. Originally consisting of only five senior officers, the War College nevertheless made credible studies of the daunting tasks of organizing and equipping field armies as large as 250,000 soldiers. From its humble beginnings, the War College flourished over time and finally established itself as the Army's premier educational institution.

Root also enacted a permanent reorganization and expansion of the Regular Army. Victories in a recent war, the ongoing guerilla uprising in the Philippines and the specter of future overseas commitments paved the way for a larger Army. In February 1901, Congress authorized an expansion from twenty-five to thirty infantry regiments, and for the first time, regiments were organized into three battalions comprised of three companies each. Cavalry regiments grew from ten to fifteen. The Army's artillery forces were entirely reorganized into two factions; field artillery and coast artillery. The field artillery consisted of thirty batteries, while the coast artillery's 126 companies manned the country's coastal defenses. Three engineer battalions became a standing part of the Army. Not counting indigenous forces in the new territories—a regiment of Filipino scouts and a Puerto Rico regiment—the Army's new authorized strength stood at 88,619 officers and men. This new girth stood in stark contrast to the Army's size of around 27,000 during the 1880s and 1890s.

A task more daunting than educational reform or organizational expansion was Root's drive to create a modern general staff system. Drawing upon his legal and business background, Root concluded that the War Department lacked the strong leadership that America's new status as a rising world power required. "Our system," he observed, "makes no adequate provision for the directing brain which every army must have, to work successfully." Because no precedent for such a controlling authority existed in America, Root turned to the study of Europe's armies. The acknowledged paradigm of military efficiency at the time was Germany's Great General Staff which had quickly mobilized a massive and victorious army during the Franco-Prussian War of 1870–1871. Root realized that directly grafting the methods of the Prussian Army onto American society would not work. Still, the German General Staff had several characteristics worthy of emulation. A new American General Staff would be the Army's central planning body and prove its worth by preparing war plans for all possible contingencies. His concept for a general staff developed over time and often encountered substantial opposition from the Army's own commanding general, Nelson A. Miles.

The General Staff Act of 1903 converted Root's vision into a reality. The legislation authorized the creation of a General Staff Corps limited to forty-five officers assigned to the War Department. The commanding general's position was abolished and replaced with an Army chief of staff whose main duties were to supervise the new staff and to serve as the principal military advisor to the secretary of war. Officers were to rotate periodically between field and staff assignments in order to gain a broad base of military experience. The act officially sanctioned the Army War College and reaffirmed its importance. The law gave only supervisory and coordinating authority over the War Department's various offices and bureaus, and outright opposition to the new General Staff was not uncommon. Even with limited powers, the new staff made significant gains in improving officer education, field maneuvers, intelligence gathering, and mobilization planning. Army deployments to the Caribbean and Central America in 1906, 1911, and 1913 went much smoother than the mobilization of 1898.

The Root reforms eventually had a profound affect on both Regulars and citizen-soldiers. In coming decades, the National Guard benefited from the creation of the General Staff and the improvements in Army schools. The reforms firmly established Elihu Root as one of the most significant and influential secretaries of war in American history. In addition, Root had an abiding interest and an important role in developing new policies that affected the militia. However, many of the principles and attitudes affecting militia reform after the Spanish-American War came from a man that Elihu Root and most of the American officer corps had never met.

The Influence of Emory Upton

The Army's progressive reformers after the Spanish-American War drew most of their inspiration from the writings of Emory Upton. An 1861 graduate of West Point, Upton proved a remarkable combat leader during the Civil War, rising to the rank of brevet major general by war's end. After commanding a Regular artillery battery and serving on a division staff, he became the colonel of the 121st New York Infantry in October 1862. Upton's most famous moment of the war came on May 10, 1864 during the brutal battle of Spotsylvania. A heavy assault column of twelve regiments under his command successfully breached the Confederate salient known as the Mule Shoe. Though unable to exploit the success, Upton's assault on the southern works was widely recognized for its novel tactics and daring execution. Two days later, he was promoted to brigadier general. After recovering from a wound received in September 1864, Upton led a Union cavalry division until the end of the war and achieved the rank of brevet major general just short of his twenty-sixth birthday.[21]

Upton's most immediate influence on the Army came after the Civil War when he became an earnest and articulate advocate for organizational change and policy reform. With the blessing of General Sherman,

Upton revised the Army's infantry, cavalry and artillery tactics to reflect lessons learned during the Civil War. Upton's new infantry tactics replaced the volley firing, linear formations of the 19th Century with open order, fire and maneuver tactics that placed a premium on the individual soldier's initiative and marksmanship. In various forms, Upton's tactical system has endured throughout the 20th Century.[22]

During 1875–1876, Upton went on a global tour to observe the armies of other world powers and to bring home recommendations for reforms. Upton published his findings in 1877 as *The Armies of Asia and Europe*, in which he advocated a system of officers' schools and an Army general staff based on the German model. In addition, he pressed hard for sweeping policy reforms that reduced the nation's reliance on

Maj. Gen. Emory Upton in 1865. His writings challenged the contributions of the American citizen-soldier tradition and argued that a professional army was the only proper foundation for national defense. (U.S. Army Military History Institute)

citizen-soldiers and expanded and strengthened the Regular Army while freeing it from what Upton considered meddlesome civilian control. Though his tactical and organizational changes took hold quickly throughout the Army, as a policy reformer, Upton clearly failed. Discouraged by the apparent rejection of some of his best ideas for policy reform, possibly despondent over his wife's death and in failing health, on March 14, 1881 Upton penned his resignation from the Army in his private quarters at the Presidio of San Francisco. Moments later, he picked up a service revolver and put a bullet through his head. The suicide horrified the Army and added to Upton's prestige as a dedicated reformer.[23]

Upton's most significant and enduring contributions to American military policy appeared in *The Military Policy of the United States*, an unpublished manuscript at the time of his death. In it, Upton focused on civil-military relations, the checkered battlefield performance of citizen-soldiers, and the waste and amateurism that he believed cast a dark cloud over America's military history. He was the first to advance the notion that the U.S. Army should consist of three components—Regulars, volunteers, and the militia—with the militia relegated to a minor, domestic role. Upton believed that a variant of the reserve systems used by European armies was suitable for the United States. Instead of State soldiers acting as the Army's primary combat reserve, America needed a robust national reserve under direct, federal control to support a larger Regular Army led by professional officers. The call for a federal reserve was not far removed from Calhoun's Expansible Army Plan. Upton disdained political influence in military affairs and believed that officers should be apolitical and loyal only to the president and the Constitution. Conversely, politicians should be denied access into the officer corps by means of cronyism and political patronage.[24]

Upton saved his cruelest cuts of all for the militia. He argued that one of the chief weaknesses in the nation's defense was an excess expenditure of money and lives that resulted from a reliance on an ineffective militia system. Based on his own Civil War experience, Upton scorned the employment of militia troops led by officers utterly ignorant of the art of war. The power of the Governors and the AGs was an "intrusion" into the nation's military affairs, and Upton lamented the power of the States in the appointment of officers. He rejected outright the proposals in Washington's "Sentiments" and the Knox Plan of 1790 for making the militia a more reliable, reserve force. Emphasizing the failures of militia troops at Bladensburg and Bull Run, Upton ignored the successes at Bunker Hill, Bennington, Saratoga, Cowpens, and New Orleans. Upton stated flatly that if the Union army at Gettysburg had been comprised of only militiamen that Robert E. Lee's troops would have prevailed with Washington, DC captured and the federal government "hopelessly destroyed." Short of promoting the militia's outright elimination, Upton argued that the militia should restrict itself to domestic missions and receive no federal financial support. In Upton's world, the militia's roles were limited to State service and occasionally assisting the Army and the new federal reserve in enforcing the nation's laws, suppressing rebellions, and repelling invasions.[25]

Upton's philosophies were well known throughout the officer corps, but not until twenty years after his death did they appeared in a final, published format. Reformers brought Upton's unpublished manuscript to the attention of Elihu Root who directed that it be printed and disseminated. In fact, many of Upton's greatest ideas—the creation of a general staff, improved military education and the three battalion system for regiments—came to fruition during Root's tenure. Though he admired Upton's writings, the reform-minded secretary of war realized that Upton was naive when it came to the realities of national politics and the formulation of policy. To Root, Upton wrote "from a purely military point of view" and failed "to appreciate difficulties arising from our form of government" and the force of public opinion "with which civil government has necessarily to deal in its direction" of the military. Regardless of such shortcomings, Upton's disdain for the militia and the machinations of partisan politics were assimilated into the collective consciousness of the American officer corps. The full-time professionals who adopted Upton's dour views on State soldiers became known as "Uptonians," and they became a powerful influence in military planning for the remainder of the 20th Century.[26]

The Militia Act of 1903

Elihu Root had managed to expand the Army considerably, but pleas for additional increases in the number of Regular troops fell on deaf ears. Congress viewed a larger Army as too expensive, too militaristic and inconsistent with America's long political tradition. Denied huge increases in the Regular Army, the War Department still lacked sound plans for raising a mass, national Army for a possible war against one of the European powers. At first, Root endorsed an Uptonian view that eschewed the employment of the militia. Instead of fighting, the militia would serve as a training base for a larger Army, perform home defense duties during peacetime and provide willing volunteers during a national crisis. However, two key developments finally convinced the secretary of war that the militia was a viable, credible military force he could no longer ignore.[27]

Perhaps more than any other factor, the militia's achievements in the Spanish-American War put citizen-soldiers in high standing with the American people. Militia volunteers had formed the bulk of the forces sent to Puerto Rico and the Philippines. In fact, without the militia volunteers who agreed to remain in the southwest Pacific, the Army would have been hard-pressed to put down the Filipino insurrection. Militiamen felt they had done their full share while suffering the abuses of a poorly organized mobilization. They had endured disease-ridden camps, improper uniforms, and poor food while carrying antiquated weapons into battle.[28]

After the war, militiamen across the country hastily reconstituted their units. Most militia organizations that had entered federal service as volunteer regiments had returned home by late 1898. Military reorganization in the States was at the grass roots without any direction from the War Department. For example, Vermont's 1st Infantry came home after the war, quickly reoccupied its vacant armories and reclaimed its title as the 1st Infantry Regiment, Vermont National Guard. Texas reorganized the bulk of its units into two infantry brigades that were better manned than comparable brigades in the Regular Army. New York, the largest militia State with an aggregate strength of 13,869 soldiers, organized itself into a balanced force of infantry, artillery, cavalry, engineer, and signal units. Nevada claimed the smallest number of citizen-soldiers while mustering two infantry companies. By 1903, the total strength of the militia organized in the forty-five States stood at 116,542 officers and men. All served without promise of federal pay; most still remitted unit dues and provided their own uniforms.[29]

Elihu Root's reforms convinced the NGA and militia leaders that the time had finally come to press for legislation that would fundamentally redefine the State soldiery and its ties to the federal government. The conduct of the Spanish-American War and the closing of the American West convinced senior National Guard leaders that their real value at the dawn of the 20th Century was as a federal reserve to the Army. While the National Guard would certainly continue to meet the needs of the Governors, its best future was to become an indispensable adjunct of the Regular Army. The time had come to replace the Militia Act of 1792 and to position the National Guard in America's first line of defense. For their service, National Guard soldiers were to receive federal funding and personal pay instead of continuing the traditional practice of providing for themselves. National Guard units properly trained and equipped were to constitute a low cost alternative to a larger, standing Army.[30]

By 1903, Elihu Root recognized the need for a trained reserve and took affirmative steps in that direction. With Root's endorsement, the

Senator Charles W. F. Dick:
Father of the Modern National Guard

Charles William Frederick Dick enjoyed a long life of public service dedicated to the National Guard and the nation. He was born in Akron, Ohio in November 1858 where he attended public schools and studied law. In 1894, Dick opened his own law practice and became active in politics.

Charles Dick's military career began in 1885 when he volunteered in Company B, Eighth Regiment, Ohio Infantry. One year later, he became the Company B commander. Over the next fourteen years, Dick rose to the rank of lieutenant colonel, and in 1898, he served with the Eighth Ohio in Cuba.

National Guard Education Foundation

After the Spanish-American War, Dick was elected to the U.S. House of Representatives in November 1898. In March 1904, he was elected to the U.S. Senate and served there until losing a reelection bid in 1911. It was during his years as a member of Congress that Dick championed the 1903 Dick Act and its 1908 amendments. During Dick's service in Congress, his military career flourished. In 1900, he became the commander of the Ohio Division, National Guard, with the rank of major general. In 1902, he was elected president of the NGA and held that position for seven years.

After leaving the Senate in 1911, Dick resumed his law practice. He ran for the U.S. Senate in 1922 but lost the election. Charles Dick lived long enough to see his labors bear great fruit during the massive National Guard mobilizations for World Wars I and II. He died in Akron, Ohio on March 13, 1945 at age eighty-six and is buried in Glendale Cemetery.

NGA successfully lobbied Congress to increase the Guard's annual appropriation in 1900 from $400,000 to $1 million. Root put forward his own version of a militia reform bill as a platform for debate toward final legislation that Congress could support. The NGA was fully prepared with militia legislation of its own. Root frequently conferred with Congressional and NGA leaders on the legislative proposal. On Capitol Hill, Representative Charles Dick from Ohio, a longtime member of the Ohio Guard, Spanish-American War veteran, and Chairman of the House Militia Affairs Committee, championed the final bill. Due to the careful cultivation of support by Secretary Root, Congressman Dick, the NGA, and State soldiers, the legislation moved through Congress without significant opposition and became law on January 21, 1903.[31]

The Militia Act of 1903 was benchmark legislation that repealed the antiquated Militia Act of 1792 and converted the volunteer militia into the National Guard. In simplest terms, Guard units received increased funding and equipment, and in return, they were to conform to federal standards for training and organization within five years. The law recognized two classes of militia; the Organized Militia (National Guard) under joint federal-State control and the Reserve Militia, the mass of 18–45 year old males otherwise available for military service. The Dick Act required Guardsmen to attend twenty-four drill periods per year and five days of summer camp. For the first time, Guardsmen received pay for summer camp but not for drill periods. The law called for Guard units to conduct maneuvers with the Army and to receive training assistance and formal inspections from Regulars. The Guard was subject to federal callups for nine months, though its service was restricted to within U.S. borders. The participation of Guard members in national callups was no longer discretionary; any soldier not reporting to his armory during a federal mobilization was subject to court martial.[32]

It is hard to overstate the significance of the Dick Act for the National Guard. The practices of the volunteer militia as a self-supporting and largely independent entity gave way to a new military force with significant federal funding and subject to the administrative controls of the War Department. The days of the ill defined relationship between the federal government and the militia were gone. For the first time, the States and the AGs had a formal relationship with the War Department. While the Dick Act was a new beginning for the Guard, in many ways it was the end of a twenty-six year crusade by the NGA and progressive Guard leaders. Since the beginning of labor disputes in 1877 and the founding of the NGA two years later, Guardsmen had sought recognition as a viable, federal reserve to the Regular Army. The Dick Act, with its provisions for a better trained and equipped National Guard, partially fulfilled the vision of reform minded Guardsmen.

At the same time, the Dick Act had it limitations. While the legislation addressed the internal workings and administration of the Guard, it made little mention of the National Guard's intended roles and missions, nor did it clarify the specific nature of the relationship between the Guard and the Regular Army. Charles Dick and the NGA included important provisions that allowed Guard troops to be called up for as long as nine months while remaining together as distinct units under the leadership of Guard officers. This stopgap measure was designed to prevent an initial, short-term callup of the Guard followed by the widespread dissolution of its units, the dismissal of State officers, and the complete assimilation of Guardsmen into the Army as individuals. (In addition, the strategic thinking of the period held that future wars would be short, lasting not longer than one year.) As military policy, the Dick Act did not provide adequate means for raising a massed, citizen-soldier Army for overseas campaigns. The mechanism for providing for such an Army would not materialize for another thirteen years.

A New National Guard Takes Shape

The passage of the Dick Act set in motion a number of developments that caused a gradual transformation of the National Guard. At first, the activities of Guard units were little affected, but over time, units reorganized and began to comply with federal oversight. Additional resources resulted in better weapons, equipment and facilities, and Guardsmen embraced their new role as an important, ready adjunct to the Army. The most dramatic and immediate affect on the Guard came in the form of federal financial aid. Starting in 1900, the Guard received an annual, federal appropriation of $1 million. A provision of the Dick Act allowed a one-time additional disbursement of $2 million in 1903. Under pressure from the NGA and the States, Congress doubled the annual appropriation to $2 million in 1906. Two years later, the NGA gained a separate $2 million annual disbursement that rose the total amount of annual federal aid to $4 million. By 1908, Congress had increased the amount of annual federal expenditures to the National Guard nearly tenfold from what they had been just a decade earlier. Federal funding following the Dick Act was particularly generous considering the fact that the U.S. government had expended only $22 million on the militia during the entire 1800s.[33]

Increased appropriations improved the preparedness of Guard units and greatly augmented State military budgets. Federal monies were allocated to the States on the basis of one hundred Guard enlisted men per congressional district. Federal funds allowed the States to draw standard Army weapons, uniforms, and equipment and to requisition supplies and other property. Federal appropriations were no longer restricted to the issue of weapons, clothing, and camp equipment. States used federal dollars to fund training camps, usually the largest item in their military budgets. Money from the War Department covered transportation, subsistence, and pay for soldiers attending summer camp.[34]

Federal monies proved invaluable to States with small military budgets and bolstered the Guard budgets in richer States. At the time of the Dick Act's passage, eighteen States and Territories received half or more of their combined military budgets from Washington. Massachusetts, New York, New Jersey, and Ohio provided the lion's share of monies for their own units, while Arkansas, Nevada, and Oklahoma depended almost exclusively on federal monies. State military budgets roughly doubled during 1903–1913 but this was not enough to keep pace with the flow of increased federal appropriations. By 1913, federal dollars accounted for half or more of the combined military budgets of twenty-eight States.[35]

Ironically, efforts to increase the Guard's effectiveness initially resulted in a loss of personnel. Four years after the Dick Act, manpower fell below the levels of 1903. Federal inspections and the new emphasis on military readiness drove some men from the ranks and made recruiting more difficult. New Jersey's AG, Wilbur F. Sandler, Jr., noted that federal oversight "greatly retarded recruiting." Guardsmen who viewed summer encampments as part vacation and part social outing resented War Department intruders. Junior officers especially felt the burden of increased regulations and higher standards, and many AGs reported that fewer men demonstrated an interest in becoming officers. In the South, the States used federal regulations as a bludgeon to eliminate nearly 8,000 black Guardsmen during a period of strained race relations. By 1906, several States in the South had disbanded black units to prevent them from receiving federal monies. Afterwards, only the District of Columbia and five other States maintained black units.[36]

Table 2
NATIONAL GUARD STRENGTH, 1903–1916

YEAR	TOTAL	YEAR	TOTAL
1903	116,547	1910	119,660
1904	115,110	1911	117,988
1905	111,057	1912	121,852
1906	105,693	1913	120,802
1907	105,213	1914	128,043
1908	110,941	1915	129,398
1909	118,926	1916	132,194

(Source: Militia Bureau, *Annual Report*, 1916.)

For many in the Guard, the antidote to personnel losses was pay beyond the summer camp allowance contained in the Dick Act. In fact, several States recognized the new demands on soldiers by instituting compensation schedules of their own. Utah offered troops $1.50 per drill period, and Massachusetts paid a flat, annual rate of $32 while other States offered much less. Starting in 1910, the NGA launched a sustained lobbying effort for drill pay. If the federal government wanted increased efficiency and more reliable service from soldiers, the association argued, then it should have to pay. Guard leaders reasoned that drill pay was little more than compensation for past national service. Drill pay became a major point of contention between the Guard and the War Department. Federal officials had no objections to drill pay as long as the Guard submitted to even more stringent controls, a proposition that Guard leaders refused to accept. A major impasse developed that was not resolved until 1916.[37]

The increased flow of weapons, equipment, and property to the States generated the need for more and better armories. Federal regulations mandated new, stringent requirements for properly storing arms and equipment and accounting for government property even though armory construction remained a State responsibility. To comply with federal guidelines, an armory construction boom started in the Northeast and swept across most of the country. Between 1905 and 1915, Massachusetts spent $3.2 million to put nearly all of its units in State-owned armories. New York launched a similar building program, with Pennsylvania and Connecticut not far behind. In the Midwest, Ohio and Illinois initiated armory construction efforts, while on the West coast Washington and California led the way. States not building armories allocated annual grants for the rent of suitable facilities. The southern States, still recovering from the economic devastation of the Civil War and Reconstruction, allocated few funds for armories. In Arkansas and Mississippi, no funds were available. Where State monies were wanting, local governments, private benefactors, and soldiers' ingenuity made up the difference. Clinging to the practices of the old volunteer militia, Guardsmen rented their armories to community groups for special events and organized dinners, dances, theatricals, and military demonstrations as fundraisers. The Indiana Guard still allowed dues paying businessmen to use armories as gentlemen's clubs and gymnasiums.[38]

Starting in the early 1900s, National Guard armories took on a new look. Castellated armories that included floor space appropriate for social clubs gave way to more contemporary designs that advanced military training and the storage and maintenance of weapons and equipment. Armory floor space was divided along functional lines; one portion of the armory contained a main entrance with administrative offices, classrooms, and an arms room while the other included large drill halls or stables. In the major cities of the Northeast and the Midwest where a single, large armory might house an entire regiment, ample space was needed for training, especially during inclement weather. Spacious drill halls with huge vaulted ceilings supported by large steel trusses provided enough room for an entire regiment to practice close order drill. Baltimore's 5th Regiment armory was one of many built early in the 20th Century with a large drill hall.[39]

The southern and western States lacking adequate military construction budgets used innovative management techniques to build and sustain armory facilities. In Virginia, the new Richmond Light Infantry Blues armory built in 1910 included ground-floor public markets that generated revenues to support both the unit and the building. Throughout the South, sparse construction budgets allowed for only modest armories, and the use of rented space abounded. In the West, Guard units met in the upper floors of commercial buildings, fair ground exhibition halls, and fraternal halls. Unable to build large drill halls, units took advantage of the warmer climates of the South and West to train and drill outdoors on established parade grounds.[40]

For the average Guard soldier, the most visible demonstration of the Guard's new status was joint exercises with the Regular Army. Guard units began a challenging transition from semiprivate organizations based on fellowship and recreation to public institutions dedicated to training and

An infantry company of the Arkansas National Guard at mess during annual training at Fort Riley, Kansas in August 1906. The nation's mature railroad system allowed National Guard units to journey to Regular Army installations for summer training. (U.S. Army Military History Institute)

military preparedness. Starting in 1904, joint maneuvers were held each year until 1916. In 1904, over 25,000 Guardsmen and 10,000 Regulars participated in the first joint maneuvers at American Lake, Washington, Altascadero, California and Manassas, Virginia. The massing of nearly 26,000 Guardsmen and Regulars in northern Virginia resulted in the greatest military maneuvers since the Civil War. Regular officers supported the exercises by serving as umpires, observers, and instructors and by performing required staff work. *The New York Times* noted that the exercises were a "necessary complement for the Militia, and indeed for the Regular Army." By 1912, over 125,000 Guardsmen and Regulars went to combined annual encampments. Large maneuvers proved too expensive and their tactical scenarios unrealistic, so smaller encampments became more common. The States sent a portion of their units to federal maneuvers biannually while the balance of the units attended State encampments at local training areas.[41]

The joint maneuvers and summer encampments mandated by the Dick Act benefited both Regulars and Guardsmen. All officers profited from the experience of leading and supporting large numbers of troops. In contrast to sterile classroom map exercises, commanders had to cope with the specific challenges of maneuvering major formations while logisticians responded to the feeding, transport, and supply of a substantial field force. Professional soldiers imparted their expertise to citizen-soldiers while becoming more comfortable with the Guard. It was not uncommon for Regular officers to work with the same Guard units over a long period or to serve as instructors during State encampments.[42]

Guard officers attempted to take advantage of the rejuvenated Army schools system, but the results were mixed. Guard officers received the best training at local Army posts and at branch schools. In 1912, the War Department reported that over 3,000 National Guard officers attended "camps of instruction" and that another seventy-six received resident training at the Army's branch and specialty schools. Attendance and student performance at the more demanding schools at Fort Leavenworth and the Army War College were disappointing. Most Guard officers could not afford to take a year away from their jobs to attend full-time schooling, while others failed to pass admissions tests. Those few who did attend complained of a blatant prejudice against citizen-soldiers among the instructors. In turn, Regulars lamented the lack of military knowledge displayed by Guard officers. The most noteworthy student of the period was John F. O'Ryan of New York, the first Guard officer to graduate from the Army War College. A lawyer by training, O'Ryan's first love was the military, and he went on to a stellar career as an outstanding combat leader during World War I.[43]

Perhaps the best cooperation between Regulars and Guardsmen occurred during the manning of America's coastal defenses. The new overseas possessions acquired during the Spanish-American War placed a greater burden on the Army's limited coastal defense resources. In 1907, the Army admitted that it needed additional forces to man the increased number of coastal defenses overseas and at home. Congress soon passed legislation authorizing the National Guard to serve in the Coast Artillery. The War Department specified that Regular Coast Artillery units would man all overseas defenses and half of the fortifications in the United States while Guard units assumed responsibility for the remaining defenses. In Massachusetts, Connecticut, and New York, Guard units had prior experience in manning coastal defenses and were the first Guardsmen to man fortifications around Boston and New York harbors. Twelve other States created Coast Artillery companies. Regular Army instructors provided training and certified new units as ready for duty. Once proficient, Guard companies took over the manning and maintenance of defenses and maintained close ties with the nearest Regular Coast Artillery unit. By 1912, the Guard had created 126 Coast Artillery companies with a total strength of 8,186 soldiers that manned fortifications along the East, West, and Gulf coasts.[44]

The Dick Act became law eleven months prior to the Wright Brothers' historic first flight at Kitty Hawk, North Carolina, and the National Guard took an avid interest in the harnessing of powered flight for military purposes. New York's 1st Signal Company had experimented with balloons since 1908, and it was natural for the Empire State to take the lead in heavier-than-air flight. The first Guard aviator went aloft in 1911, when Beckwith Havens of New York took to the skies in an early Curtis aircraft. The New York National Guard activated the 1st Aero Company in 1915, and the following year, formed a second aviation company in Buffalo. At the same time, Guard aviators in California, Ohio, and Michigan made progress in organizing flying units and obtaining pilot ratings. On May 22, 1912, Lt. Col. Charles B. Winder of Ohio became the first Guard officer to obtain a reserve military aviator rating.[45]

The Militia Act of 1908

The years following the 1903 Dick Act demonstrated important internal changes within the Guard. At the same time, officials in the War Department and senior officers in the Regular Army opined that a heavy reliance on the National Guard might jeopardize national security. The Dick Act had authorized Guard service for only nine months and restricted its employment to within U.S. borders. Emory Upton's sentiments against the militia cast a long shadow over War Department thinking that maintained national security could not safely depend upon forces with a dual allegiance to the States and the federal government. To the Uptonians, State powers inherent in the National Guard system restricted federal authority. Might not the Governors inhibit the raising and employment of State troops as they had done in 1812 and 1861? Instead, hardliners pressed for a large federal reserve rather than a more capable National Guard.[46]

Determined that the National Guard was to become indispensable and integral to the nation's defense, Guard advocates sought important legislative changes designed to mute the Uptonians. Charles Dick, now an Ohio Senator, sponsored a revised Militia Act that became law on May 27, 1908. The president was given full authority to call out the Guard during national emergencies. The Militia Act of 1908 removed limits on the Guard's length of service and geographic employment. In return, Congress directed that the National Guard would be called to active duty before the raising of any volunteer units. The time allowed for Guard units to conform to Army standards was extended for an additional two years.[47]

Another important development came with the creation of the Division of Militia Affairs (DMA), the precursor of the modern National Guard Bureau (NGB). Since the passage of the 1903 act, administrative duties related to the National Guard had been spread among the Army's bureaus. In February 1908, the DMA came into existence to oversee administrative duties related to the National Guard's "armament, equipment, discipline and organization." Other functions included oversight of field exercises and mobilization planning. Lt. Col. Erasmus M. Weaver, a Regular Army Coast Artillery officer, was appointed the first chief of the DMA and given a staff of fourteen clerks. Like many Guard units in the States, the DMA sought shelter in a leased facility. The National Guard's first federal offices were located on the third floor of an office building at the corner of 18th and G Streets in northwest Washington, DC. Originally organized as an office under the direct charge of the Secretary of War, in 1910 the DMA became the responsibility of the Army chief of staff, and the following year, Congress elevated the chief of the DMA to flag rank. Brig. Gen. Albert L. Mills, an old cavalry Regular who had received the Medal of Honor in the Spanish-American War and served as the Superintendent of West Point, became the first general officer on the Army Staff responsible for Guard affairs. Under Mills's supervision, the DMA grew and expanded its influence with the War Department and the States.[48]

Assured somewhat by the Militia Act of 1908 that the Guard would be available for service beyond America's borders, the War Department began an historic realignment of the nation's military command structure. The U.S. military had always used geographic districts for peacetime command and administration, but the arrangement had little to do with organizing forces into a major field army. By creating new military regions responsible for the training of designated Regular and National Guard forces, the War Department hoped to create in peacetime the basic framework for a large field army. New plans called for the consolidation of small Army garrisons across the country into larger, more centralized posts for ease of training and administration. A second reform that raised the hackles of many old soldiers was the substitution of the regiment with the division as the Army's major tactical headquarters. The outcome of field exercises in 1911 emphasized the need for change; it took the Regulars more than ninety days to concentrate 13,000 troops at San Antonio, Texas and to organize them into a patchwork divisional configuration.[49]

In some respects, the National Guard was ahead of the Regulars in forming combat divisions. As early as 1879, Pennsylvania had organized its units into a division rich in infantry but short of support troops. In the same fashion, New York formed a division in 1908 with its headquarters at Albany. In 1910, the War Department published orders for the creation of the Army's first units composed of both Regular and Guard troops. Plans called for the creation of three composite divisions stationed between Maine and New York with a desired troop composition each of 25 percent Regulars and 75 percent National Guard. However, within two years, the War Department scuttled the plan. Renewed thinking held that divisions manned by Regulars alone would be more ready and could deploy faster. However, the 1910 proposal was the beginning of force structure actions regarding mixed Regular and Guard units that would continue on and off again for the remainder of the century.[50]

The War Department's publication in 1912 of *The Organization of the Land Forces of the United States* broke important, new ground in defense planning. The War Department rejected the notion of an expansible peacetime Army in favor of a standing force ready for combat. The plan called for the organization of the Regular Army into three infantry divisions and one cavalry division "ready for immediate use as an expeditionary force." In a major war, Regular divisions would deploy and fight while divisions of National Guard and volunteers mobilized. The plan divided the United States into four military departments—Eastern, Southern, Central, and Western—with each department responsible for the organization of one Regular division and a full complement of support troops. For the first time, the Army specified the division's main components: three infantry brigades, a field artillery brigade, a cavalry regiment, and support troops that included engineer, signal, medical, and supply units. The National Guard was to organize its 139 infantry regiments into sixteen divisions under the supervision of the new military departments. Other provisions called for the raising of additional divisions of volunteers. In the end, the new policy outlined a three-tiered force: Regular divisions ready for immediate deployment, National Guard divisions prepared to reinforce the Regulars, and an army of volunteers "organized under prearranged plans" for use when additional forces were required.[51]

However, the creation of Guard divisions across the country was easier said than done. The DMA organized the entire Guard into twelve division districts, each responsible for forming a division. Arrayed from east to west and numbered 5–16, the districts ranged in size from one to seven States. (The Army retained the designations 1–4 for the four active divisions aligned with the new military departments.) Unity of command allowed New York (6th Division) and Pennsylvania (7th Division) to make good progress in creating true tactical divisions, but both States lacked artillery, cavalry, and support troops. The multi-State districts made little headway toward organizing divisions because no single authority was appointed to coordinate the effort. The Militia Acts required existing Guard units to conform to Army standards, but the War Department could not compel the States to create specific types of units. When told to raise artillery and cavalry units, the States replied that equipping, training, and quartering such units was too expensive. Except in New York and Pennsylvania, the Guard divisions existed largely on paper.[52]

The War Department influenced other aspects of State planning. In 1912, the DMA established the first outlines for State headquarters. The AG was authorized the rank of brigadier general and was authorized a staff of twelve to seventy-five officers depending upon the extent of State forces. The War Department, in coordination with the States, established the first peacetime mobilization stations. States had always created impromptu mobilization camps during wartime, but new plans established predetermined rallying points for established Guard units even before they entered federal service. The main purpose for units moving to mobilization stations was to complete their issue of weapons, equipment, and uniforms; training was to occur at other sites. Each State designated one primary mobilization site, and most selected the State capital, a Regular Army post, or a prominent training camp. The AGs developed mobilization plans, but they were little more than an extension of the same procedures used in getting units to summer camp.[53]

The Continental Army Plan

Even with the Guard's continued development, the Army General Staff did not yet consider State soldiers as a viable federal reserve. The deeply ingrained philosophies of Emory Upton, negative reports from Army inspectors on Guard preparedness and increased concerns with overseas threats convinced the Army that a full-fledged federal reserve was indispensable. Political turmoil in Mexico raised concerns over U.S. interests in Latin America. Across the Atlantic, Germany and France had completed the enlargement of their standing and reserve forces that gave the two countries armies of 1.75 million and 1.5 million men, respectively. How was a tiny American Army of approximately 200,000 Regulars and Guardsmen ever to compete with the armies of Europe? To the War Department, the Army had to create a large pool of trained reservists under direct federal control instead of a more robust National Guard.[54]

In fact, the Army had already begun the process. Rightly concerned over its lack of physicians during the Spanish-American War, the Army sought legislation to create a reserve corps of medical officers it could mobilize during an emergency. Congressional action on April 23, 1908 created the Medical Reserve Corps, the first group of citizen-soldiers placed under the Army's direct supervision in peacetime. Within weeks, the Medical Reserve Corps included 160 physicians, and by 1916, the corps had grown to 1,903 officers, four times the number of physicians on active duty. The creation of the Medical Reserve Corps put the Guard on notice as to the Army's intentions to create an even broader, federal reserve.[55]

Even as late as 1912, serious questions lingered over the legality of National Guard service overseas. Secretary of War Henry L. Stimson asked Army Judge Advocate General Enoch H. Crowder to study the issue. Crowder found that the Guard was bound in its operations by the specific language of the Constitution and was not a substitute for a federal reserve force. He also opined that Congress had erred in the Militia Act of 1908 by authorizing the Guard's use abroad.[56]

Secretary Stimson forwarded Crowder's findings to the Department of Justice for a formal legal opinion. On February 12, 1912, U.S. Attorney General George W. Wickersham rendered an opinion that was potentially devastating to the Guard. Wickersham followed a strict interpretation of the Constitution and ruled that the federal government was forbidden from employing the National Guard for purposes beyond those enumerated in the Constitution's militia clauses. The attorney general declared that provisions of the Militia Act of 1908 authorizing the Guard's overseas service were unconstitutional, and furthermore, that the Guard could not serve as part of an army of occupation on foreign soil "under conditions short of actual warfare." The Wickersham decision meant that the federal government could not order State troops overseas as long as they retained their status in the National Guard. In the War Department, the attorney general's ruling destroyed the Guard's value as a viable federal reserve.[57]

According to one prominent National Guard historian, the Wickersham decision gave the Guard "a severe jolt." Guard veterans who had fought overseas in the Spanish-American War must have scoffed at the decision. To some senior leaders, the ruling put the Guard's legal status back to where it had been prior to the Dick Act. Others rightly declared that the time had come to secure a full and final legislative solution to the problems posed by the Guard's dual status as both State and federal troops. The ruling set the stage for bitter confrontations between the War Department and the National Guard during 1912–1916, an historic nadir in Army-Guard relations.[58]

The Wickersham decision galvanized the National Guard leadership. Since the Spanish-American War, an internal schism had divided the NGA over the question of the Guard's federal role. The AGs in the industrial Northeast and Midwest stressed the Guard's domestic role in law enforcement. A competing group of AGs from the Plains States and the South, who benefited more directly from increased federal funding, identified their splinter group as the "Interstate National Guard Association" and argued stridently for the Guard as a combat reserve. Under the leadership of Charles Dick, who served as NGA President during 1902–1909, the schism narrowed. In 1911, a new, stronger organization emerged from the discord and adopted the name "The National Guard Association of the United States" (NGAUS). Another primary interest group soon formed. Brig. Gen. Charles I. Martin of Kansas engineered the creation of "The Adjutants General Association of the United States" (AGAUS). The AGs had been active during 1912 to gain drill pay for soldiers and to negate the Wickersham decision, and the creation of AGAUS gave additional impetus to their efforts. Henceforth, AGAUS would help in developing the best plans and policies for the Guard and work with NGAUS in securing favorable legislation.[59]

Another challenge to the Guard came in 1913 with the rising tide of the Preparedness Movement. With the increasing likelihood of American intervention in crises abroad, the Preparedness Movement advocated universal military training (UMT) for all able-bodied young men as well as reserve officer training. The movement's principle public advocates were former President Teddy Roosevelt and Army Chief of Staff Leonard Wood. An ambitious, outspoken maverick who served as chief of staff during 1910–1914, Wood envisioned a large, wartime Army composed almost entirely of volunteers and conscripts. In Wood's mind, the National Guard's proper role was as a domestic security force. His most enduring contribution to the Preparedness Movement was the creation of summer training camps for college students and civic-minded business and professional men. The most publicized of the summer encampments came in 1915 in Plattsburg, New York. With war raging in Europe, the training camps became increasingly popular; in the summer of 1916, 10,000 volunteers attended ten different camps across the country.[60]

Legal decisions against the Guard's use overseas, rising public awareness regarding military preparedness and the unending desire among full-time professionals for a standing, federal reserve found their ultimate expression in the War Department's *Statement of a Proper Military Policy for the United States*. Published in 1915 and prepared under the leadership of Secretary of War Lindley M. Garrison, the new policy became known as the "Continental Army Plan" because it provided a blueprint for a million-man national army. At its heart, the plan advocated an American Army of 500,000 troops comprised of 121,000 Regulars and 379,000 reservists with two years of prior service in the active Army. An additional pool of 500,000 trained reservists was to give added depth to the field army.[61]

As military policy, the Continental Army Plan all but ignored the 129,398 Guardsmen serving in 1915. The plan fully endorsed the Wickersham decision and declared that "no force can be considered a portion of our first line" whose training, manning, and equipping were not fully subject to federal authority. Accordingly, the Guard's wartime service was restricted to manning coastal defenses and guarding key strategic points and lines of communications within the United States. Adding insult to injury, the War Department called for the repeal of the provisions of the Militia Acts of 1903 and 1908 that required the full mobilization of Guardsmen prior to the callup of volunteers. Perhaps as a foil to deflect certain outrage, the plan recommended an increase in the Guard's annual appropriation from $6.6 to $10 million. Many in the Guard considered the War Department's newfound generosity as little more than a cynical effort toward a buy off.[62]

The National Defense Act of 1916

The unveiling of the Continental Army Plan came at a time of increasing international tensions. Starting in August 1914, Americans had soberly watched the unfolding nightmare of trench warfare in Western Europe as the major powers struggled for Continental domination. In Mexico, a major political revolution was underway, and President Woodrow Wilson sent U.S. forces to occupy Veracruz as a forceful sign of America's hostility toward a dictatorial government. Calls for intervention in the European war reached a fever pitch when a German U-boat sank the British liner *Lusitania* on May 7, 1915, killing 1,000 British and 128 American civilians. Problems abroad and credible promises of drill pay promoted Guard recruiting, starting in 1914. Within two years, the Guard included 132,914 soldiers, an all time high for peacetime strength.

International tensions caused growing political and social divides within the country. The Wilson Administration preached nonintervention in the European war while advocating democratic ideals, international law, and the rational cooperation of nations. President Wilson repeatedly assured the American people that intervention in Europe was unnecessary, and even as late as 1916, he responded with anger to newspaper reports that the War Department was preparing contingency plans for a war against Germany. On the other hand, many Americans believed that war was inevitable and accused the Wilson Administration of pacifism and neglect in defense matters. The Preparedness Movement was the popular counterbalance to the belief that the President was soft on defense. To assure the country that his administration did have a blueprint for national defense, Wilson encouraged the development of the Continental Army Plan.

However, the plan's public release ignited a serious political firestorm. The president's supporters felt betrayed that the War Department had developed a specific plan for the raising of a million-man Army while the administration preached nonintervention. Wilson's detractors claimed that the Continental Army Plan proved that the president intended all along to send troops to fight in the trenches. Guard advocates pointed out the folly of a plan that ignored the country's only available reserve fighting force. The greatest opposition developed on Capitol Hill, where Representative James Hay, the Chairman of the powerful House Military Affairs Committee, led the campaign against Secretary Garrison and the War Department. (Charles Dick had left the Senate in 1911.) To Congressman Hay, the Continental Army Plan gave too much power to the federal government, reduced the role of the States in national defense and denigrated the National Guard. Congress balked at the costs of doubling the size of the active Army and questioned the military's ability to recruit the large numbers of men needed for the federal reserve. Chairman Hay informed the president that the Continental Army Plan did not have sufficient congressional support and that new legislation more friendly to the National Guard was needed.

President Wilson withdrew his support for the War Department's plan, and in protest, Secretary of War Garrison resigned.[63]

The political imbroglio over the Continental Army Plan resulted in the most comprehensive defense legislation the U.S. Congress had yet passed. On June 3, 1916, Congress stepped into the void caused by the scuttling of the Continental Army Plan and the resignation of Secretary Garrison to approve a sweeping reorganization of the Army. The National Defense Act of 1916 called for a composite Army of Regulars, Guardsmen, and Army Reservists with the potential to compete against Europe's mass armies. The Regular Army's peacetime strength was increased to 175,000 soldiers and authorized a wartime strength of 286,000. The National Guard would comprise the Army's principle trained reserve. Its maximum strength was set at 435,800 soldiers based on an allocation of 800 Guardsmen for each member of Congress. To assuage concerns in the States and in the War Department, Congress increased Guard funding and approved tighter federal controls over the States. Legislators acknowledged the need for a federal reserve. Summer civilian training camps and student military training on college campuses were to continue and become permanent with the creation of the Officers' Reserve Corps (ORC) and the Reserve Officer Training Corps (ROTC). An Enlisted Reserve Corps (ERC) was to serve as a repository for reserve enlisted talent in a number of combat support specialties.[64]

The National Defense Act of 1916 established remedies for many of the problems the Guard had encountered since the passage of the Dick Act. Congress quashed the controversy over the legality of Guard service overseas by stipulating that during a national emergency Guardsmen would be drafted into the Army as individuals and then serve in their State units as part of the Regular Army. To facilitate such a transition, all Guardsmen would take an enlistment oath to obey the president and to defend the U.S. Constitution. The DMA was elevated to a new status as the Militia Bureau on the Army General Staff. Guard officers were authorized to serve in the Militia Bureau, and Lt. Col. Frank M. Rumbold of Missouri became the first Guard officer assigned to the Militia Bureau. The Secretary of War was empowered to withdraw funding from States not complying with federal regulations. The States surrendered to increased federal control in order to receive additional funding, and the term "National Guard" became the official designation for all organized militia forces. Congress addressed the Army's frustrations in managing the Guard's force structure by giving it the authority to prescribe the numbers and types of State units. NGAUS and AGAUS won a major victory over drill pay; soldiers were to receive full pay for attending forty-eight drill periods and fifteen days of field training each year. To account for the increased flow of money, weapons and equipment to the Guard, each State was to appoint a "property and disbursing officer" responsible for the accountability of federal property and funds.[65]

The Mexican Border Crisis

The National Defense Act of 1916 became law concurrent with a growing international crisis south of the border. Tensions between Washington and Mexico City had increased steadily, and by early 1916, a civil war raged within Mexico. Hoping to solidify his position as a dominant Mexican warlord, Francisco "Pancho" Villa conducted a cross-border raid against Columbus, New Mexico on the night of March 9, 1916, killing seventeen Americans. In response, President Wilson ordered a large punitive expedition into northern Mexico to track down the bandits. The Army assembled a strike column of 10,000 Regulars under the command of Brig. Gen. John J. "Black Jack" Pershing that soon splashed across the Rio Grande into Mexico.

With the bulk of the active forces in the Southwest absent, border towns feared additional Mexican raids. The Governors of Texas, New Mexico, and Arizona expressed grave concerns over the security of their citizens. On May 9th, the president ordered those Governors to deploy Guardsmen for border protection, and two days later, 5,260 State troops headed for the border. Meanwhile, with hostile terrain and an elusive enemy frustrating its efforts, Pershing's expedition pushed further into Mexico. On June 16th, the Mexican government warned Pershing to advance no further. Fearing a growing crisis, President Wilson ordered a partial callup of the National Guard on June 18th. Only fifteen days after the passage of the National Defense Act of 1916, the National Guard responded to its first call to active federal service in the 20th Century. For the first time, the War Department activated Guardsmen by specific type of unit rather than sending numerical quotas to each State. The response was swift. The first unit to reach the border was the 1st Illinois Infantry, enduring a grueling, 48-hour train ride from Springfield to arrive in San Antonio on the evening of June 30th. The hauling capacity of America's mature railroad network allowed a rapid buildup. The Connecticut Guard endured the longest movement—2,916 rail miles from Hartford to Houston. On July 4th, nearly 25,000 Guardsmen observed Independence Day at camps in Texas. By August 31st, 111,954 Guard troops were in close proximity to the border, including the two divisions from New York and Pennsylvania. To add to the logistical accomplishment, the railroads hauled the 60,000 horses and mules required to support Guard cavalry, artillery, and supply units. The mobilization included one important

Rhode Island cavalrymen load their horses aboard a train for deployment to the Mexican border in June 1916. (National Archives)

milestone—New York's 1st Aero Company was the first Guard flying unit to be called to active duty though it did not serve on the border.[66]

Despite the rapid buildup, there were significant problems. More than anything else, too many unfit soldiers filled the ranks. The States had been lax in enforcing physical standards; more than 10,000 soldiers failed physical examinations and were discharged. Commanders had not strongly enough impressed upon soldiers that their service was no longer voluntary and that enlistments had the full force of a legal, binding contract. As a result, thousands of Guardsmen requested discharges upon mobilization. The States approved more than 6,000 hardship discharges before the War Department forced a curtailment. The Guard's force structure still contained too many infantry units, and other types of combat and non-combat units were not available to form division-like formations in the Southwest. Those units not mobilized consisted mostly of coast artillery and excess infantry. In one case, an infantry unit voluntarily converted to cavalry to qualify for border duty. The Richmond Light Infantry Blues became the 1st Squadron, Virginia Cavalry. They traded in their rifles for pistols and sabers, underwent elementary cavalry training, and deployed to Texas without mounts.[67]

The utilization of mobilization camps remained the callup's most controversial aspect. The growing crisis prompted the War Department to send Guardsmen directly to the border, bypassing most State facilities and negating pre-mobilization planning. Preparations that should have occurred at mobilization camps were postponed until units arrived in the southwest where the Army had done next to nothing to prepare for the Guard's arrival. In many cases, Guardsmen built their own cantonments from scratch. Poor facilities, intense heat, and dusty winds added to soldiers' frustrations. As Guardsmen discerned that security duty was their primary mission rather than combat below the Rio Grande, grumbling and loud protests became common. In all, 158,664 Guardsmen saw duty. Regular Army reports on the Guard's performance were mixed. Guard commanders certainly made mistakes regarding personnel matters, but many deficiencies were due to poor planning by the General Staff. At least one War Department observer took a broader view of the Guard's efforts. "When one considers the number of men moved and distances they were moved," wrote a young Major Douglas MacArthur, "the recent mobilization...was the best job of its kind done by any country."[68]

Though far from perfect, the mobilization was a political and military success and a vast improvement over the incompetence and bungling

New York's 1st Aero Company became the first National Guard flying unit ordered to active duty when it was mobilized in 1916 for the Mexican Border Crisis. (National Archives)

of 1898. No Guard unit saw combat, but citizen-soldiers provided valuable protection to U.S. borders and constituted a ready reserve while Pershing's column operated directly against the Mexicans. Guardsmen fulfilled their intended role as the Army's primary combat reserve instead of the federal volunteers favored by the Uptonians. The States became familiar with the complexities of moving great numbers of troops, and the AGs learned the value of recruiting soldiers who met fitness standards and understood the obligations of their enlistment. Senior commanders received experience in handling large troop formations while soldiers benefited from training and physical conditioning. Still, significant improvements were needed in training, manpower, and equipment.

By the early spring of 1917, the crisis had passed and the Guard started to return home. Across the country, local communities enthusiastically welcomed the troops. In Richmond, the long-suffering 1st Virginia Cavalry experienced a gala reception at its downtown armory on Sunday, March 18, 1917. But the troopers had little time to bask in their accomplishments; eighteen days later the United States declared war on Germany.

Conclusions

The years 1898–1916 were a period of significant transformation for the National Guard. Guardsmen began and ended the period with calls to active federal service. In the sun-kissed Caribbean, the cities and jungles of the Philippines, and along the hot, dusty southwestern border, the National Guard conducted important military operations that effectively supported American foreign policy. In the process, a new National Guard replaced the volunteer militia.

The National Defense Act of 1916 was the final destination in a near forty-year journey of change that had begun during the labor disputes of 1877. The arguments of NGAUS, AGAUS, and congressional leaders promoting the Guard's use as the primary provider of reserve combat forces to the Army prevailed over those in the War Department hoping to restrict State soldiers to domestic defense. Legal support for the traditional practice of raising federal volunteer regiments was greatly diminished. Though the Guard had found a permanent place in the defense establishment, whether or not the Regular Army and the National Guard alone could produce a major American field army remained a serious question. The creation of the ORC, the ERC, and ROTC in 1916 indicated that individual reservists and even conscripts would be required to create a citizen army capable of competing with the European powers. Despite the important legislative benchmark achieved in 1916, verbal dueling between Guardsmen and Uptonians over the merits of State soldiers continued unabated. Federal funding had improved the Guard, but adequate time for training beyond basic soldier skills was still lacking.

By the end of the Mexican border mobilization, the Guard's internal workings had changed significantly. The Guard embraced the new missions of military aviation and coast artillery. While enlistment in Guard units remained on a voluntary basis, participation at summer camps and drill periods was no longer discretionary. Federal service during national emergencies was compulsory, and soldiers received individual pay for drill periods and summer camp. Increased federal funding produced a better trained and equipped force. In return for the infusion of federal monies, the Guard surrendered much of its autonomy. For the first time, the AGs had a formal relationship with the War Department. The Guard became subject to federal inspections, agreed to new qualifications for officer selection and conformed to Army standards for unit organization. Joint maneuvers and inspections may have produced animosity between the States and the War Department, but they had benefits as well. Regulars observed the capabilities and limitations of citizen-soldiers while Guardsmen learned the art and practice of war from professionals.

However, much in the Guard remained the same. The Governors retained final authority over the commissioning, promotion, and assignment of officers. The Guard endured as a volunteer organization with unit commanders responsible for the recruiting and retention of qualified soldiers. Guard members still attended drill periods one night each week where training focused on the teaching of basic, individual soldier skills rather than unit maneuvers. Units retained close ties with local communities. Uniforms, insignia, and unit designations reflected local, regional, and State pride. Unit organization and force structure in many cases mirrored the desires and interests of the AGs and senior commanders rather than the needs of the War Department. More work was needed to shape the Guard into a national fighting force of combat divisions, and the Mexican border callup indicated that the States and the War Department lacked detailed mobilization plans.

At the beginning of 1917, U.S. involvement in the war in Europe was all but certain. What was not so foreseeable was the critical role the National Guard would eventually play during two World Wars fought on bloody battlefields in Europe and in the Pacific.

CHAPTER 5

The National Guard In The World Wars, 1917–1945

If American citizen armies, extemporized after the outbreak of war,
could do as well as the citizen armies of Grant and Lee, what might
they not do if organized and trained in time of peace?

Brig. Gen. John McAuley Palmer

Introduction

Fifteen minutes after sunrise on June 6, 1944, the landing craft carrying soldiers of the 29th Infantry Division deployed into their final assault
formations off the coast of France. Still 4,000 yards offshore, the coxswains
pointed their vessels squarely at the beach ahead and gunned the engines.
In a ragged line one and one-half miles long, the twenty-four boats carrying
the 116th Infantry's four assault companies headed for the beach. Off to the
east, the assault craft carrying the first wave of the 1st Infantry Division
also headed for the hostile shore. As the bobbing craft plowed toward the
beach, the land ahead and the ocean all around shook with the ferocity of
the Allied bombardment. The battleships "Texas" and "Arkansas," with
their supporting cruisers and destroyers, blazed away at the German
defenses. Not far away special landing craft fitted with multiple rocket
launchers let loose with a torrent of missiles that rained down on the bluffs
and beaches. Out in front of the infantry landing craft, heavier vessels
deposited tanks onto the beach that added the noise and firepower of their
cannons and machine guns to the crescendo.

From inside the landing craft, the Virginia Guardsmen of the 116th
Infantry attempted to identify the prominent features of the Normandy
coastline they had studied so intently on maps and models. As the vessels

moved closer to shore, the soldiers could make out the white sands of Omaha Beach and the green grass of the tall bluffs beyond. Each boat carried a thirty-one man assault team commanded by an officer. Different soldiers carried rifles, automatic weapons, bazookas, light mortars, demolitions, and a flamethrower. Besides their weapons, the troops carried enough to sustain them for two days of combat—ammunition, food, life vests, and gas masks. In all, each man was burdened with nearly sixty pounds of gear and supplies. The landing craft were so filled that everyone had to stand; the men in the center of the boat could see little more than the backs of their buddies. Inside the vessels some men prayed and others cursed, but most were too frightened and miserable to say anything. Soaked to the bone by frigid seawater and suffering from seasickness, the men stoically endured the nearly fifteen-minute, final approach to the beach. The Virginia Guardsmen traced their heritage to the Stonewall Brigade of the Civil War, and they were about to add to their proud traditions by enduring fighting just as bloody and ferocious as anything their forefathers had faced at Gettysburg in 1863 or in the Meuse-Argonne in 1918.

With a sudden jolt, the assault craft ran aground. The front ramps dropped forward onto the beach, and the soldiers rushed ahead. From defensive positions along the beach and bluffs, German small arms, machine guns, mortars, and artillery opened up with a vengeance. Enemy bullets tore at the landing craft, and killed and wounded GIs fell face forward onto the sand. On the right side of Omaha Beach, Company A was nearly destroyed. One landing craft swamped and sank before it hit the beach, and a German shell scored a direct hit on another, killing every man on board. Before the day was over, Company A's home community of Bedford, Virginia would lose nineteen of its native sons to enemy action. At other locations, the infantry struggled across the beach seeking cover behind German beach obstacles. Finally, a number of men dashed through the deadly fire toward the protection of a sea wall at the base of the cliffs. Across the entire landing zone, small unit leaders struggled to get their men out of the water, across the beach and inland. Capt. Lawrence Madill, the Company E commander, moved boldly among the beach obstacles shouting for his men to move off the beach. Enemy fire inflicted a serious shoulder wound that nearly tore Madill's left arm from his torso, but he kept moving among his troops. Finally, a burst of machine gun fire knocked him to the ground. As he lay dying on Omaha Beach, Captain Madill cried, "Senior noncom, take the men off the beach!" By the end of the day, the 116th Infantry was off the beach and inland. The cost of victory was high; one-third of the regiment— about 1,000 soldiers—were killed and wounded. The shallow toehold the 116th Infantry helped to create on D-Day eventually enabled a powerful Allied army to launch a series of major offensives directly into the heart of Nazi Germany.

Dramatic events such as the Normandy invasion thrust the United States onto the center stage of world affairs between 1917 and 1945. In World War I, the country mobilized a vast amount of men and material in order to fight its first coalition war since the American Revolution. U.S. military power in France helped guarantee the defeat of Imperial Germany and placed America in the role of erstwhile peace negotiator. During the interwar years, an uneasy quiet settled over Europe, the pall of economic depression gripped the globe and isolationism became a potent political force in America. The events of 1941 drew the United States into an even larger and more destructive war against totalitarian regimes in Europe and Asia. By the end of World War II, American forces stood victorious among the cooling ashes of Berlin and Tokyo, and America found itself without a serious, international competitor.

The National Guard played a key role in the events of the World Wars and the interwar period. The Guard's trained personnel and standing units permitted the United States to project substantial combat power quickly onto the Western Front in 1918. Between the World Wars, the Guard more firmly established itself as a permanent component of the common defense and was a source of social stability amidst the suffering and dislocation of the Great Depression. The Guard's participation in the national mobilization of 1940–1941 helped to prepare America for even greater exertions. During World War II, Guard soldiers and airmen enabled vigorous American ripostes to the aggression of Nazi Germany, Imperial Japan, and Fascist Italy. By 1945, the National Guard had contributed greatly to the concentration of U.S. combat power in Europe and the Pacific during the most destructive war in human history.

America Goes to War

On the evening of April 2, 1917, President Woodrow Wilson addressed an emergency, joint session of Congress to ask for a declaration of war against Imperial Germany. The drama of the moment filled the air; a troop of mounted cavalry escorted the president from the White House to Capitol Hill, and when the commander in chief entered the chamber of the House of Representatives, nearly every legislator was holding or wearing a tiny American flag. In a somber, succinct address, the president reviewed the international situation and established the nation's idealistic war aims. In Wilson's words, America would fight to make the world "safe for democracy." At the end of the speech the legislators gave the president a standing ovation, and four days later they declared war on Germany.[1]

War came at the United States with the certainty and sureness of a German torpedo slicing straight through the cold, churning waters of the North Atlantic. After the sinking of the *Lusitania* in May 1915, war fever in America reached new heights until the German High Command promised to suspend its campaign of unrestricted submarine warfare. In the spring of 1917, Germany decided to risk U.S. intervention in the war by unleashing the U-boat menace once again in a final gamble to knock Great Britain out of the war. Woodrow Wilson responded by breaking off diplomatic relations with Berlin. With an executive order, the president authorized the arming of U.S. merchant shipping. American diplomats acknowledged the existence of the Zimmerman telegram, a secret diplomatic cable from Berlin to Mexico City, in which Germany sought a military alliance with Mexico against the United States. In the middle of March 1917, German U-boats sank three American merchant ships, and the president decided to ask Congress for a declaration of war.[2]

While a national consensus existed for going to war, there was little agreement as to the extent and type of the nation's commitment. Many Americans assumed that sending troops to France was unnecessary and that destroying the U-boat menace and supplying the Allies with food, supplies, and munitions would be enough to tip the scales against Germany. British and French diplomatic missions to Washington, DC in late April 1917 delivered a blunt message: America must send troops directly to the Western Front to bolster the Allied armies. The British High Command recommended that U.S. troops move immediately to Europe and fight as individual replacements in British and French divisions, a proposal that turned stomachs in the War Department. The French delegation, headed by the hero of the battle of the Marne in 1914, Marshal Joseph Joffre, pressed for the commitment of a U.S. combat division. During a May 2nd meeting with Marshal Joffre, President Wilson pledged to dispatch an American division to France within the month. Before long, the War Department concluded that the best means of fulfilling the country's diplomatic and military objectives was to commit the American Expeditionary Forces (AEF) directly into the trenches. To command the AEF, the president selected the stern and taciturn "Black Jack" Pershing who was a new national hero for leading the Army's punitive expedition into Mexico during the previous year.[3]

For various social, political, and economic reasons, the president and the War Department decided even before the declaration of war that conscription was the most effective technique for raising a national army. The most compelling argument in favor of the draft was economic; conscription was the most efficient method of raising a mass army without disrupting the economy, especially in agriculture and in those sectors dedicated to wartime production. At the president's direction, the War Department composed a conscription bill that repaired the defects of the Civil War draft system. The Selective Service Act of 1917 prohibited enlistment bounties and the hiring of substitutes but authorized deferments on the grounds of dependency or essential work in industry and agriculture. A Selective Service System composed of some 4,600 local draft boards staffed by civilian volunteers made final decisions on the induction or deferment of particular individuals. After an intense debate, a final draft bill passed Congress, and President Wilson signed it into law on May 18, 1917. With a stroke of the president's pen, the techniques used since colonial times for creating volunteer armies based on State quotas died a quiet death. The Selective Service Act of 1917 was the first effort at gearing all of the manpower of the U.S. not already serving in the Regular Army, the National Guard, and the Organized Reserves into a coordinated pool of obligated manpower directed toward a single, national purpose.[4]

Intense prewar concerns in the War Department regarding the manning of a large Army stood in stark contrast to a near total neglect of industrial mobilization planning. American industry had provided the Allied armies in Europe with some munitions, weapons, and equipment, but the industrial base was woefully unprepared to entirely clothe, arm, equip, and sustain a large field army. The need to get troops to the Western Front quickly before the Allied armies collapsed outpaced the ability of the government and corporate leaders to retool the industrial base. In the end, Regulars, Guardsmen, Reservists, and draftees went to war armed largely with weaponry of foreign manufacture.[5]

The Mobilization of 1917

On July 20, 1917, young men all across America focused their attention on a hearing room of the Senate Office Building on Capitol Hill. At the appointed hour, Secretary of War Newton D. Baker donned a blindfold, reached into a large glass jar filled with capsules and randomly selected number 258. Six weeks prior, on June 5th, nearly 9.5 million men ages 21–30 had complied with the Selective Service Act by registering for the draft. The number in Secretary Baker's hand corresponded to a number assigned to a draft registrant in each of the nation's local draft board areas. Throughout the remainder of the day, the random drawing continued until enough numbers were chosen to meet the demands of the initial draft call. The Governors were responsible for implementing the draft law, and they delegated the authority to their AGs and State military headquarters. The primary responsibility of the AGs was to oversee the establishment of district and local draft boards, to provide administrative and medical support as needed and to facilitate successful public relations.[6]

In the War Department, decisions for utilizing the nation's manpower moved forward rapidly. By necessity, the soldiers in any major field force would come from three sources: Regulars, Guardsmen, and draftees. In general, Army Reservists served as individual officer replacements, physicians, and in other skilled specialties. The Army would continue the creation of combat divisions on active duty and in the Guard while draftees were to serve in new divisions designated as "National Army." Months would pass before draftees could be converted into soldiers, and America's initial response came from Regulars and Guardsmen. On April 1, 1917, the Regular Army numbered 127,588 officers and enlisted men. To meet President Wilson's pledge of sending a division to Europe, the Army hastily assembled a reinforced regiment for shipment to France. On July 4, 1917, one battalion of the U.S. 16th Infantry paraded through the streets of Paris, the first contingent of Pershing's AEF to arrive in France. Later that day at a welcoming

A Washington State National Guard recruiting station seeks volunteers in the days following America's entry into World War I. The sign reads: "General Pershing says all young men should be encouraged to join a unit either of the National Guard or of the Organized Reserves. The most appropriate place for such first service is in the National Guard." (Washington State Historical Society)

ceremony, an American officer uttered the immortal phrase, "Lafayette, we are here!"[7]

While draftees waited for their numbers to come up and the Army rushed to establish a presence in France, the National Guard worked diligently to build the backbone of a major field army. At the declaration of war on April 6th, 66,694 Guardsmen were still on active duty from the Mexican border mobilization. Most of these Guardsmen would remain away from their homes and jobs until the middle of 1919. Included in the group were some units previously released from active duty and then recalled as war approached. Within days after the declaration of war, the War Department dispersed serving Guard units across the country to protect key transportation hubs, industrial facilities, and utilities against German saboteurs and sympathizers.[8]

In the States, recruiting became the top priority. The national crisis cleared the way for increasing the Guard's strength to nearly 435,800 men, the maximum amount allowed by the National Defense Act of 1916. The Guard's local roots and talk of an impending draft spurred volunteerism. Guard commanders struck a chord with prospective recruits by pointing out that those joining the Guard would serve with friends and families from local communities rather than fighting with total strangers in draftee units. The argument worked; between April and July 1917 the Guard recruited approximately 200,000 new soldiers and nearly doubled its size. Intent on avoiding the confusion over obligatory service that had occurred during the Mexican Border callup, commanders stressed that men were legally bound to report for duty. Captain Fred Ellis of Company D, 2d Kansas Infantry told recruits that future calls would mean "business" and those failing to report would be tried for desertion.[9]

On July 15, 1917, President Wilson ordered the Guard to active federal service for the second time in as many years. To ease the administrative and logistical burdens of mustering nearly 400,000 troops all at once, the War Department mobilized the Guard in two increments. The initial presidential callup affected the Guard in eleven States, and on July 25th the remainder of the Guard received mobilization orders. On August 5th, President Wilson exercised the authority granted by the National Defense Act of 1916 and the Selective Service Act of 1917 to draft the National Guard into federal service as individuals. The commander in chief did this to clarify the federal government's powers over the State soldiery. By drafting the entire National Guard into the Army, the government removed any lingering questions pertaining to the Guard's geographic employment and time of service. Once drafted, State soldiers ceased to have any legal connection with the National Guard and instead became individual members of the U.S. Army. For the duration of the war,

Guardsmen strove to retain their distinctive character derived from State and local roots but did so with only mixed results.[10]

With the Guard's tremendous expansion, the War Department built on its prewar force structure planning to increase the number of Guard divisions from twelve to sixteen. On May 5, 1917, the Militia Bureau sent to the States details enumerating the composition of the sixteen divisions by State and type of unit. At the time, only New York and Pennsylvania had fully organized divisions, and Ohio's 11th Division lacked only one artillery regiment.[11]

Converting nearly 400,000 Guardsmen into a combat-ready force proved to be a formidable task. Draftee divisions would not be formed for several months, but Guardsmen were ready to begin training immediately. No training camps with permanent facilities were available, but the Army did have enough tentage to create sixteen canvas cantonments in the South and Southwest, one for each of the Guard divisions. The division commanders understood the necessity for the expedient. State troops were better organized and prepared than raw draftees to sustain themselves while living in tents, and most Guardsmen expected to be in France before the full onset of winter. Between August and October, the Guard's sixteen divisions moved by rail to an equal number of tent cities spread along a large arc that extended westward through the southern and southwestern States from Charlotte, North Carolina to Palo Alto, California. Texas contained three camps, more than any other State, and Waco, Houston, and Fort Worth became the temporary homes of the 13th, 14th, and 15th Divisions, respectively, that were formed from Guardsmen from the Plains States.[12]

Guard commanders hoping to focus entirely on training at the new cantonments received a rude surprise shortly after their arrival. The War Department's announcement of a major reorganization of all divisions threw training plans into chaos. After consultation with the Allies, General Pershing concluded that the existing structure of the Army's divisions could not generate the sustained combat power needed for trench warfare. Instead, Pershing favored a larger "square" division consisting of four infantry regiments organized into two brigades. In addition to the infantry, the square division included two artillery regiments, an engineer regiment, a signal battalion, and supply and medical units for a total strength of 28,061 soldiers.[13]

The immediate result of converting Guard divisions to the square configuration was confusion and frustration. The greatest challenge was converting infantry and cavalry units to support troops, a process the Militia Bureau described as "fraught with considerable difficulty." Resentment ran high in proud infantry regiments broken up to create other types of combat and support units. A major in Pennsylvania's 30th Infantry went to his quarters and wept after discovering his proud regiment was selected for "mutilation." Two hundred enlisted men from Oklahoma's 1st Infantry went absent without leave in protest upon learning their regiment was to become support troops for the Texas division. At the direction of the Militia Bureau, the entire Utah Guard in 1916 had converted from infantry and artillery units to a cavalry regiment. Then in June 1917, the Militia Bureau ordered Utah to switch all of its cavalry to artillery. In Virginia, the Richmond Light Infantry Blues, who had converted from infantry to cavalry in order to serve on the Mexican border, received orders to become an artillery unit. At one camp, Guard cavalrymen held a mock funeral to bury their distinctive uniforms before converting to another type of unit.[14]

Another blow to the Guard's pride came with the mandatory redesignation and renumbering of all units. In the Army's mind, the AEF in France was to become a single, integrated whole with no differentiation between Regular, Guard, and National Army divisions. Toward this end, the Army set aside numbers 1–25 for Regular divisions and 26–75 for Guard divisions. Draftee divisions had numerical designations beginning with 76. The National Guard divisions numbered 5th–20th became the Army's 26th–41st Divisions. In the same manner, the two brigades in each square division took on sequential numerical designations. The 26th Division included the 51st and 52nd Brigades while the new 41st Division's brigades were numbered 81st and 82nd. A regimental numbering system replaced all State and local unit identifications. Regiments of all arms as well as separate battalions and companies received numerical designations from 101–300 that ran sequentially throughout the Guard's force structure. The 6th Massachusetts Infantry, whose origins dated back to the earliest enrolled militia units in the Massachusetts Bay Colony, was broken up to provide troops to the new 101st, 102nd, and 104th Infantry. New York's famous "Fighting 69th" became the 165th Infantry. Guardsmen countered the impersonal numbering system by devising unit slogans and nicknames that reflected State and local ties. For example, Ohio's 37th Division adapted the nickname "Buckeye" while the 30th Division, with troops from Tennessee and the Carolinas, became "Old Hickory" in honor of Andrew Jackson.[15]

The reorganization of the Guard into square divisions resulted in surplus units in a majority of the States. In the War Department, Major Douglas MacArthur seized upon the opportunity to propose the creation of a combat unit singularly unique in Guard history. MacArthur argued for the creation of an additional Guard division drawn from the surplus units. In MacArthur's own words, such a division would cover America "like a rainbow" and diffuse competition among the States for gaining the honor of sending the first Guardsmen to France. Secretary Baker approved the proposal and promoted MacArthur to lieutenant colonel, assigning him as the new division's acting chief of staff. The Chief of the Militia Bureau, Maj. Gen. William A. Mann of the Regular Army, left his post to become the commander of the newly designated 42nd "Rainbow" Division, a move that outraged many Guard generals who considered themselves qualified for the position. By late August 1917, troops from twenty-six States and the District of Columbia were assembled at Camp Mills near Mineola, New York, where training began in earnest.[16]

The utilization of black Guardsmen was far different from their white counterparts and yielded the eighteenth Guard division to serve in the war. At first, the Militia Bureau delayed the callup of black units, but finally ordered them to active duty with the proviso that they would serve only within their own State. The Army's policy of racial segregation prohibited black troops from serving in the Guard divisions. At the time, the Guard's African-American combat units included the 15th New York and 8th Illinois Infantry as well as a number of separate battalions and companies of infantry in five other States and the District of Columbia. Unlike units in the Regular Army, most African-American Guard units had their own black officers. Over time, black Guard units received orders to move to mobilization camps. The Militia Bureau proposed the formation of an African-American separate brigade composed of three infantry regiments, but Secretary of War Baker approved the creation of a provisional black division composed of three regiments of Guardsmen and a regiment of black draftees. The 15th New York became the 369th Infantry, the 8th Illinois the 370th Infantry, and the other black Guard units were consolidated to form the 372nd Infantry. The 371st Infantry, all black draftees, formed the fourth regiment. Heightened racial tensions at black training camps in the South hastened the creation of the new division. On January 5, 1918, the 93rd Division (Provisional) formed at Camp Stuart near Newport News, Virginia. The 93rd Division lacked any units other than its four infantry regiments, but it soon received orders to board shipping for France.[17]

Life in the training camps often exposed Guardsmen to a variety of unfamiliar professional and social attitudes. At Camp MacArthur in Waco, Texas, local residents tried to convince the Wisconsin and Michigan men of the 32nd Division that "damn Yankee" was really one word. Despite the obvious regional differences, a great affection soon developed between the soldiers and the Texans. Hard feelings that lingered from the Civil War led to a huge brawl between the old 4th Alabama and 69th New York at the 42nd Division's training camp on

Long Island. The Army assigned Regular officers to Guard units whenever State officers were found physically unfit, lacking in military knowledge or deficient in leadership. Guardsmen deeply resented this intrusion into what was considered their own internal affairs. An infusion of ORC officers and draftees was required to bring the Guard divisions to full strength, and State soldiers remained suspicious of outsiders. The assignment of two Jewish lieutenants from the North to the 2nd South Carolina concerned Palmetto State soldiers. Similarly, Guard enlisted men looked askance at new draftees assigned to their squads and platoons. An Army hierarchy formed quickly in the training camps that endured throughout World War I; Regulars looked down on Guardsmen who in turn scorned the green draftees.[18]

The extent and effectiveness of training varied widely. On Long Island, the Rainbow Division implemented a training regime that emphasized unit cohesion, physical fitness, and basic combat skills even though most of the troops lacked uniforms and shoes. In general, noncommissioned officers trained their soldiers while officers huddled together to master the details of tactics and staff work. The 32nd Division held an officers' school each evening while brigade, regimental, and battalion commanders attended classes on combat operations taught personally by the division commander. Shortages of weapons and equipment hampered training in every division. Artillerymen of the 33rd Division trained with dummy, wooden guns for the first weeks, and two months passed before "Prairie" Division machine gunners received their weapons. At Camp Wadsworth in Spartanburg, South Carolina, New York's 27th Division reached a high level of training that included tactical maneuvers during live fire exercises. The 32nd Division constructed an elaborate system of trenches to train assault teams in the tactics of trench warfare. In the fall of 1917, the 36th Division at Camp Bowie near Fort Worth, Texas welcomed a contingent of British and French officers who passed on lessons learned from the Western Front.[19]

One unintended consequence of the 1917 mobilization was to leave the States without troops for domestic emergencies, a circumstance neither the Militia Acts of 1903 and 1908 nor the National Defense Act of 1916 had addressed. Two expedients emerged, one from the federal government and the other from the States, to provide troops for domestic missions. The War Department authorized the creation of "United States Guards" to provide security at key installations and sites in order to free up all Regular and Guard troops for training and overseas service. The United States Guards fell under the administrative control of the Militia Bureau, but operated under the command of the Army's geographic departments. This force eventually grew to 26,284 troops organized into forty-eight separate battalions with soldiers coming from those men not qualified for the draft or overseas duty. The United States Guards provided security at shipyards, rail hubs, arsenals, and federal installations in thirty-two States before their dissolution at war's end.[20]

With their National Guard units on active duty, the Governors moved to create their own State forces. Organizations varied greatly from established infantry companies serving under the AG to county posses under the local sheriff. In all, twenty-seven States organized some type of State Guards with an approximate strength of 79,000. State Guard units maintained National Guard armories, responded to natural disasters, supported local law enforcement, kept watch on possible saboteurs, and monitored the activities of various social and labor groups suspected of sympathizing with the Germans and the Bolsheviks.[21]

The Guard Goes "Over There!"

On June 13, 1917 General Pershing and a small staff arrived in France to begin planning for the commitment of U.S. troops to the Western Front. Pershing soon made several policy decisions that established the broad parameters of American conduct during the entire war. Despite intense pressure from the Allies, Pershing remained adamant that American doughboys would not be amalgamated into the Allied armies and would charge into battle only under American commanders. Pershing resisted the temptation to throw his troops into action prematurely and insisted that they receive thorough training in offensive operations before going up against the German Army. Logistical factors largely determined that the AEF would take shape in the Lorraine province southeast of Paris. A relatively quiet sector, the AEF would complete its training in Lorraine, occupy a wide sector of the front below Paris and then launch a series of offensives to

Soldiers of the 26th Division wait to board shipping for France on September 25, 1917. (Massachusetts National Guard Archives and Museum)

convince the German High Command that it could not win the war. Pershing's staff estimated that ultimately the AEF would require as many as one hundred divisions and that it would not be ready for offensive operations until 1919.[22]

While Pershing's staff developed their plans, the first elements of the AEF arrived in France. The new 1st Division could claim it was the first to France, but the National Guard was fast on its heels. In perhaps the most unique unit movement in National Guard history, the 26th "Yankee" Division declined to move to its designated training camp in North Carolina and instead deployed directly to France. Maj. Gen. Clarence R. Edwards, a Regular assigned to command the division, made a series of unilateral agreements with port authorities in New York City and Montreal. The 26th Division, consisting of Guardsmen from the six New England States, completed its reorganization into a square division while still at State mobilization camps and moved directly to ports of embarkation. By the time a surprised War Department learned of the clandestine movement, the flow of troops was too far along to halt. The 26th Division headquarters arrived in France on October 28th. Close behind came the 42nd Division. In mid-October, the poorly clad soldiers of the Rainbow Division received heavy, knee length woolen overcoats, a sure sign they were headed overseas. By November 1st, lead elements of the 42d Division were in France. After rigorous training regimes, both divisions took control of their own trench lines in February 1918. Soon afterwards, a large German trench raid bloodied the Yankee Division, making it the first Guard division to see action. The 41st Division reached France in December 1917, and the 32nd Division arrived in February 1918, bringing the total of National Guard divisions overseas to five, including the provisional 93rd Division. After an extended training period, the 32nd Division occupied forward trench lines in May 1918.[23]

If Pershing and the Allies had plans for ending the war on favorable terms, so too did the enemy. In autumn of 1917, the war turned badly for the Allies. An Austro-German army smashed the Italians at Caporetto, and the Bolshevik Revolution knocked Russia out of the war. Once faced with a three-front war, the German High Command focused all of its resources on the Western Front. The German generals knew the Americans were headed to France, and they developed plans for huge offensives to win the war before the AEF could bring its weight to bear. On March 21, 1918, the German Army launched its "Peace Offensive" against the British north of Paris and against French divisions below the capital. The Allied lines strained but held. The crisis prompted two changes in Allied planning. Pershing agreed to release a limited number of American units to assist the hard-pressed Allies, and the British committed additional shipping to expedite the flow of doughboys to France. Between May and July 1918, the War Department shipped more than 800,000 soldiers to Europe, the better part of twenty-one divisions. Included in the movement were eight National Guard divisions—the 27th, 28th, 29th, 30th, 33rd, 35th, 36th, and 37th—bringing the total number of Guard divisions in France to thirteen. Before the end of the war, the last five Guard divisions were in France, raising the National Guard's total contribution to the AEF to eighteen divisions.[24]

True to his promise, Pershing released American divisions to go to the aid of the Allies. U.S. divisions had trained in Allied rear areas in order to make themselves readily available as an emergency reserve. North of Paris, the 27th, 30th, and 33rd Divisions trained in the British sector. In late summer, the 27th and 30th Divisions deployed to the front and played an important role in successful British counterattacks along the Somme River. In the French sector south of Paris, the 26th and 28th Divisions fought dogged defensive battles along the Marne River that repulsed numerous German attacks. In a coordinated, massed Franco-American counterattack starting on July 18, 1918, four National Guard divisions—the 26th, 28th, 32nd, and 42nd—pushed the enemy back from the Marne and put the German Army on the defensive for the remainder of the war.[25]

The National Guard regiment with arguably the best combat record in the war was the 369th Infantry. After arriving in France, the AEF parceled out the 93rd Division's African-American regiments to shore up the French Army. The 369th was assigned to the French 16th Division on March 8, 1918 and over the next eight months earned the title "Hell Fighters" for its determined and daring performance on the battlefield. When the armistice came on November 11, 1918, the 369th was the American unit closest to the German border. Six days later, the Hell Fighters became the first Allied troops to reach the Rhine River since the beginning of the war. The 369th served in combat for 191 days, longer than any other U.S. regiment, and during that time it never lost a prisoner or a trench line to enemy action. On December 13, 1918, the French government recognized the Hell Fighters with the award of the coveted Croix de Guerre. On February 17, 1919, the 369th Infantry returned to New York City and marched up Fifth Avenue toward Harlem in a welcome home parade. At the head of the proud regiment waved the flag of the 15th New York.[26]

Though no National Guard aviation unit went to war, Guard flyers made important contributions. At the beginning of the war, approximately one hundred qualified Guard pilots were available for service. Colonel Raynal C. Bolling, the original commander of New York's 1st

Table 3
NATIONAL GUARD DIVISIONS IN WORLD WAR I

DIV	STATES	HQs IN FRANCE	CASUALTIES
26	CT, MA, ME, NH, RI, VT	Oct 1917	13,664
27	NY	May 1918	8,334
28	PA	May 1918	14,139
29	NJ, VA, MD, DE, DC	Jun 1918	5,570
30	NC, SC, TN	May 1918	8,415
31	GA, AL, FL	Oct 1918	Depot Div
32	MI, WI	Feb 1918	13,261
33	IL	May 1918	6,864
34	MN, IA, NE	Oct 1918	Depot Div
35	MO, KS	May 1918	7,296
36	TX, OK	Jul 1918	2,584
37	OH	Jun 1918	5,387
38	IN, KY, WV	Oct 1918	Depot Div
39	LA, MS, AR	Aug 1918	Depot Div
40	CA, NV, UT, CO, AZ, NM	Aug 1918	Depot Div
41	WA, OR, MT, WY	Dec 1917	Depot Div
42	26 States and DC	Nov 1917	14,683
93	NY, IL, OH, DC, MD, TN, MA	Dec 1917	3,534

Total casualties = 103,731

(Source: American Battle Monuments Commission, *American Armies and Battlefields in Europe*, 515–17; and Jim Dan Hill, *The Minute Man in Peace and War*, 285.)

Aero Company, helped to establish training centers in Europe for American fliers. Other Guard officers filled important aviation staff positions. Four Guardsmen became aces during aerial combat. 2nd Lt. Erwin B. Bleckley, a Kansas artilleryman who volunteered for duty as an aerial observer, became the first Guard aviator to receive the Medal of Honor when German ground fire downed his aircraft during a desperate mission over the Argonne Forest.[27]

Once in France, Guardsmen suffered another blow to their identity as State soldiers. On July 13, 1918, the Army issued General Order No. 73 stating that "this country has but one Army," the Army of the United States. Henceforth, there was to be no distinction between Regulars, Guardsmen, Reservists, and draftees. The order directed Guardsmen to remove all distinctive State or National Guard markings and to replace them with Regular Army insignia. At the same time, the Army instituted the wear of new division patches on the left shoulder of each field uniform, though most patches were not actually worn until near the end of the war or until after the armistice. The creation of division patches presented Guardsmen with an opportunity to put their heritage on display daily. Every division patch contained letters or symbols indicative of State ties. The 26th Division developed a shoulder patch that contained the letters Y and D as a constant reminder of the Yankee Division's roots in New England. Pennsylvania's 28th Division adapted a red keystone as its shoulder patch. The 40th and 41st Division patches included images of the sun that reflected the healthy lifestyle and weather of the West coast. Perhaps the most unique patch came from New York's 27th Division. The curved letters N and Y stood for New York, and arrayed behind them were the stars of the constellation Orion, a visual pun that paid tribute to the division's beloved commander, John F. O'Ryan.[28]

Not all Guard divisions saw combat. With all Allied shipping dedicated to bringing new units to France, Pershing decided that for every two divisions fighting on the line, another division had to provide replacements. The AEF designated two Regular, six National Guard, and five National Army divisions as "Depot Divisions." These divisions principally provided individual replacements to combat units and served as a training base. The 31st, 34th, 38th, 39th, 40th, and 41st Divisions served for the entire war as depot divisions. Individual Guardsmen shipped to France with depot divisions eventually fought in other Regular, National Guard, or National Army divisions as replacements. The improvised replacement system shattered the expectations of Guardsmen desiring to serve with soldiers from their own units and communities. However, the emergency of the moment and the craven bloodlust of the trenches rendered other alternatives impractical.[29]

The Army's habit of relieving Guard leaders and replacing them with Regular officers generated deep resentment among State soldiers. Many Guardsmen believed that removals were not done on the grounds of improving combat readiness but to provide Regular officers opportunities for promotion and fame. The process began in the stateside training camps and continued in France. Eleven Guard generals who had been considered fit for service on the Mexican border were immediately declared physically unfit for overseas service. In 1917, 12,115 Guard officers entered active duty, and within one year, 1,480 were sent home or reclassified. Guard soldiers often considered junior officer replacements from the ORC as less experienced and capable than their former leaders.[30]

In France, General Pershing set a stern and disciplined tone for the Army and was intolerant of officer incompetence. The number of officers relieved, whether Regulars, Guardsmen, or Reservists, ran extremely high. Combat officers losing their posts were often reassigned to support units, and it is no coincidence that the AEF's supply system performed poorly. Emotions over the relief of Guard officers ran high, especially regarding the leadership of the divisions. Regulars usually filled three of the four senior command positions in a division. Guard officers filled secondary assignments on the division staffs while Regulars served in the principle positions. Guardsmen noted the regularity with which the Army relieved their senior commanders just prior to major operations. Brig. Gen. Charles I. Martin of Kansas, the founder of AGAUS, lost his position as commander of the 70th Brigade, 35th Division on the eve of the Meuse-Argonne offensive. Martin was popular with his soldiers, and afterwards the 35th Division historian lamented that "more of us would have come out of the Argonne with [Martin] in command of the 70th Brigade." General O'Ryan of the 27th Division was the youngest division commander in the entire AEF and the only Guard division commander to remain in command for the entire war.[31]

Battery C, 130th Field Artillery, 35th Division prepares to open fire in September 1918. The 130th was organized from the 1st Regiment, Field Artillery of the Kansas National Guard. (National Archives)

By the late summer of 1918 the German Army was permanently on the defensive, and with the continuous buildup of American doughboys, Pershing was finally able to implement his plan for ending the war. During September 12–16th, the AEF reduced the St. Mihiel salient. In a classic pincer movement, American divisions attacked the salient's northern and southern faces. In the northern sector, the Yankee Division distinguished itself by punching through German defenses, running roughshod throughout the enemy's rear area and gaining contact with the U.S. 1st Division far ahead of schedule. The main American effort began in the difficult Meuse-Argonne sector on September 26th. Pershing's ultimate objective was to reach Sedan on the Meuse River, a vital railroad link in the German supply lines. Nearly 600,000 Americans backed by 4,000 guns bulled their way forward against a determined enemy in the largest military operation yet seen in American history. Eight National Guard divisions played a vital role during the difficult, bloody advance. The 29th Division in particular earned a reputation as an outstanding fighting unit. By November 6th, American troops threatened Sedan, and four days later the AEF opened a mass offensive that ruptured German defenses along the entire Meuse River. Forced with disaster on the Western front and the defection of its remaining allies, the Germans accepted armistice terms. On November 11, 1918, exhausted American doughboys climbed from their muddy trenches, lit warming fires and reflected on the high cost of their victory. In 200 days of combat, 50,280 men had been killed and over 200,000 wounded.[32]

If America's participation in the war effort meant victory for the Allies, the National Guard contributed significantly to that end. Throughout World War I, the Guard fought in America's first line of defense. The 433,478 Guardsmen who served represented a modest percentage of the 2.8 million soldiers who eventually wore the Army uniform, but the Guard's contribution was much more significant than the numbers indicate. The standing Guard divisions allowed the United States to respond rapidly and decisively after the declaration of war. Without the divisions, America's initial response would have been timid with little impact on either Allied or enemy morale. Guard combat units filled the lapse in time and capabilities between the early deployment of Regulars and the delayed flow of draftees. In all probability, the absence of the Guard divisions would have seriously postponed Pershing's 1918 offensives and greatly prolonged the war.

On the Western Front, the Guard divisions distinguished themselves in combat. Of the forty-three American divisions sent to France, eighteen of them—about 40 percent of the entire AEF—were National Guard. The Guard divisions accumulated a total number of days in combat that exceeded that of either Regular or National Army divisions. The Yankee Division had the dubious distinction of accumulating 205 days in combat, more than any other Guard division. Guard divisions suffered a total of 103,721 killed and wounded—approximately 43 percent of American casualties—and nearly the equivalent manpower of the entire National Guard in 1903. Pennsylvania's 28th Division suffered the most losses with 14,139 killed and wounded. As Guardsmen fell in alarming numbers, thousands of draftees filled the depleted ranks thereby diluting the distinctive character of each Guard division.[33]

In battle, Guardsmen proved themselves the equivalent to Regulars, Reservists, draftees, and Allied soldiers and demonstrated their superiority over the Germans. The Guard's performance fully vindicated the improvements in training, manning, and equipping that had occurred since the 1903 Dick Act and refuted the notions of Regulars who believed that Guardsmen were only capable of limited, domestic missions. Guard soldiers in the 30th Division received twelve Medals of Honor, more than any other division in the AEF. Perhaps the best tribute to Guardsmen came from their adversary. The German High Command considered eight American divisions especially effective; six of those were National

Officers of the 372nd Infantry call the roll dockside prior to their men boarding ships to return home after World War I. The 372nd, composed of African-American units from six States, was one of three all-black National Guard regiments in the 93rd Division during World War I. (National Archives)

Guard. An incisive assessment of Guardsmen in battle came from one of their Regular Army leaders, Col. John "Gatling Gun" Parker, who commanded the 102nd Infantry in the 26th Division. On February 28, 1918, a large German trench raid hit the 102nd Infantry's defensive positions and was repulsed only after the most savage fighting. Awed by the determination and esprit of his Guard troops, Colonel Parker wrote afterwards: "The American militiaman, when he is properly led, is the finest soldier who ever wore shoe leather."[34]

The Influence of John McAuley Palmer

If Emory Upton's dim views of the militia influenced defense planners before World War I, the more positive attitudes of John McAuley Palmer toward citizen-soldiers helped to shape policy after the war. A Regular Army officer from the West Point Class of 1892, Palmer's early career reflected the changing nature of service in the Army at the turn of the century. An infantryman, he served in various assignments in Cuba, the Philippines, and China. Palmer felt the influence of the Root reforms when he attended the School of the Line and the new Staff College at Fort Leavenworth in 1908. In Kansas, Palmer struck up a close personal friendship with Lieutenant George C. Marshall that endured for decades. When the Army assembled its first peacetime division in Texas in 1911, Palmer served as a brigade adjutant. The following year, he worked in the War College Division of the Army General Staff and authored the War Department's *Organization of the Land Forces of the United States*. With the outbreak of war, Palmer became the head of the AEF's operations section in France until incapacitated by a nervous breakdown. Following his recovery, he commanded the 58th Brigade of the 29th Division during the last three months of the war.[35]

Palmer's views on citizen-soldiers took shape even before he entered West Point. His grandfather, Maj. Gen. John McAuley Palmer, was a citizen-soldier who rose through the ranks to corps command in the western theater during the Civil War. The elder Palmer held a distinct bias against the narrow professional views of Regular Army officers and believed that positions of military leadership should remain open to able civilians. General Palmer told his grandson that if left only to professional officers the military might evolve into a privileged "samurai" caste entirely inconsistent with American ideals. The younger Palmer's own observations in subsequent years reinforced a favorable opinion of citizen-soldiers. He formed a positive view of the National Guard during the 1909 joint maneuvers held in Missouri, and during World War I, Palmer was impressed by the competence and leadership of

Colonel Milton A. Reckord of Maryland who commanded the 115th Infantry in the 58th Brigade.[36]

In numerous staff reports and magazine articles before World War I, Palmer argued that the "most important military problem" facing the country was to devise the most effective means for preparing "great armies of citizen soldiers" to meet the demands of modern war. Armies possessed dynamic and political aspects. An army's dynamic characteristic was simply its ability to project and generate combat power while political traits included social attitudes and political and military traditions. Sound solutions to the challenges of raising a modern, mass army could not ignore either aspect. At the heart of Palmer's ideas was the notion that a small, Regular Army formed on the expansible army concept was no longer appropriate for the Industrial Age. He argued that taxpayers would never support a Regular force large enough to serve as the mainstay for a major field army. On the other hand, a small Regular Army incapable of rapid expansion would prove inadequate during a national emergency. Palmer realized that a vast pool of individual, trained reservists, like that favored by advocates of UMT and the Preparedness Movement, could not easily provide the organized units required. The solution was to build a reliable, organized citizen reserve and provide it with additional training after mobilization. Palmer considered the National Guard vital to the country's defense while recognizing the role of the Army Reservist as well.[37]

The philosophies of Emory Upton and John McAuley Palmer stood in stark contrast. Upton used military history, and the Civil War in particular, to advocate manpower policies that eschewed the militia, called for a larger Regular Army and relied heavily upon volunteers. Palmer drew from the militia tradition to support the idea of a trained and ready National Guard that was an organized reserve to a smaller Regular Army organized for overseas campaigning and occupation duty. While Upton advocated the formation of an army of volunteers created after the outbreak of war, Palmer promoted the creation and training of organized citizen-soldier units in peacetime. Upton abhorred political influence in military affairs and cautioned the officer corps to remain politically aloof. Palmer recognized the inherent, positive role politics played in democratic military institutions and believed officers had the responsibility to educate and inform the nation's elected leaders. Palmer's policies combined history and current events to recommend defense plans suitable for the new demands of Industrial Age warfare. Upton's advocates failed to realize that changes in American society and foreign policy rendered anachronistic most of the Civil War general's policy reform initiatives. War Department policies prior to World War I that attempted to organize

Regular and National Guard units into a standing force signaled an end to a reliance on the expansible army concept, and the Selective Service Act of 1917 forever demolished the system of volunteers. How little Upton's disciples understood the changing world around them became readily apparent in the months following World War I.

The National Defense Act of 1920

Entire National Guard units had entered federal service in 1917 with great fanfare, but at the end of the war Guardsmen returned home as individuals. Once Guard soldiers were drafted into federal service in August 1917, the Army's bureaucratic personnel system treated each man as an individual without regard to prewar unit or State affiliation. Units returned from France to demobilization camps across the country, and Guardsmen returned home with individual discharge papers in hand free of any federal or State obligations. In most large cities and local communities, Guard units reformed on their own to participate in parades and welcoming home ceremonies. Once back in civilian life, Guardsmen received little information on the future of the National Guard or the status of their old units.[38]

At the annual NGAUS convention in Richmond in November 1918, the chief of the Militia Bureau delivered an ominous message about the Guard's future. Speaking only four days after the armistice, Brig. Gen. John S. Heavey, a Regular general officer, told NGAUS members not to claim too much credit for the victory in Europe. Though the Guard had thrown itself entirely into the war effort, Heavey pointed out that Guard troops comprised only about 10 percent of the Army's total strength. The bureau chief ended his speech by announcing that the Army would be better served in future wars by a wholly federal reserve without State ties. A hushed audience allowed the pronouncements to pass without comment from the convention hall floor.[39]

General Heavey's remarks merely reflected the sentiments of the Uptonians in the War Department and on the General Staff. They hoped to ignore or diminish the Guard's contributions during the war and to resume the prewar legislative bid for the creation of a large, standing Army and an organized federal reserve sustained by UMT. In January 1919, the War Department forwarded to Congress a proposal for the postwar military establishment. The plan called for a standing force of 500,000 Regulars backed by a vast reservoir of 500,000 trained reservists and made no mention of the National Guard. In essence, the proposed bill flatly rejected the key provisions of the National Defense Act of 1916 and was little more than a warmed over version of the 1915

Continental Army Plan. On Capitol Hill, yet another War Department proposal appeared too militaristic and expensive. One congressman labeled the plan "an outrage," and another declared that he had had "a bellyful of the damned Army."[40]

The development of a sound military policy fell to Senator James W. Wadsworth of New York, a former Guardsman and chairman of the Senate Military Affairs Committee. During hearings throughout 1919, Wadsworth's committee heard from various experts. The most impressive Guard leader to testify was New York's John O'Ryan, who pressed for the Guard's full involvement in national defense but proposed to turn the Guard into a predominantly federal force organized under the Constitution's Army clauses. Wadsworth's panel also heard from General Pershing, who acknowledged the friction between Regulars and Guardsmen. After complimenting the Guard's excellent service during the war, Pershing declared, "The National Guard never received the wholehearted support of the Regular Army during the World War. There was always more or less a prejudice against them…"[41]

The most remarkable testimony came on October 9, 1919 from Col. John McAuley Palmer of the Army's War Plans Division. Already a recognized expert on Army organization, Palmer articulately analyzed all aspects of the pending legislation before Congress and put forth his own opinions based on his extensive reading, writing, and firsthand experiences. Palmer argued that a small Regular Army backed by a large, organized citizen reserve sustained by UMT was most consistent with American military tradition and capable of meeting the country's expanded defense needs. The citizen reserve would be organized regionally into divisions, and the charter members would be those Guardsmen and draftees with recent combat experience. New recruits would enter the reserves through UMT. Impressed with Palmer's knowledge and candor, Senator Wadsworth asked for his reassignment as an advisor to the Military Affairs Committee. In the end, Palmer was deeply involved with the writing of new legislation.[42]

NGAUS and AGAUS exerted their influence on Capitol Hill as well. With its members on active duty, NGAUS was largely dormant during World War I, but starting in 1919 the association revitalized. Lt. Col. Bennett C. Clark of Missouri was elected president, an officer widely known for his extreme views favoring the Guard. Clark soon declared that the aim of NGAUS was "to build up the National Guard and smash the Regular Army." Many Guardsmen harbored resentment against the Army for the way it had treated them during the war, but such hyperbole drew protests from many senior association members and generated negative comments in the press. Behind the heated rhetoric, NGAUS took a largely defensive stance and desired an affirmation of the Guard's status as defined in the National Defense Act of 1916. The association was not opposed to the ORC as a coexisting, volunteer agency as long as the Army did not use it as a subterfuge to reduce or eliminate the Guard. AGAUS sought solutions to specific problems. As a group, they wanted a stronger voice in the formulation of federal regulations governing the Guard. Additional Guard officers should serve in the Militia Bureau, and the AGs maintained that the bureau chief should be a Guard general officer.[43]

In its final form, the National Defense Act of 1920 created a multi-tiered force with varying degrees of readiness. Congress firmly rejected the notion of a large, Regular Army backed by an immense pool of trained reserves created through UMT. Instead, it favored a smaller, active force reinforced by standing units of the National Guard and individuals of the Organized Reserves. Congress created the "Army of the United States" to consist of the Regular Army, the National Guard "while in the service of the United States" and the Organized Reserves. The active Army was authorized 298,000 soldiers and assigned the missions of defending overseas possessions, expeditionary duty, and border protection. The Defense Act authorized the postwar reorganization of the National Guard, designated the Guard as the primary Federal reserve force and set its strength at a maximum of 435,000 soldiers. The Organized Reserves would provide a pool of officers in wartime and man nine Reserve Divisions to absorb and train conscripts during national emergencies.[44]

Key provisions addressed specific Guard concerns. To ensure that the Army would never again discharge Guardsmen as individuals, the law specified that in the future Guardsmen released from active service would revert to their status as State soldiers. To better represent the Guard's interests in the War Department, the chief of the Militia Bureau would be a National Guard major general appointed by the president to a four-year term. Maj. Gen. George C. Rickards of Pennsylvania became the first Guard general officer to serve as chief of the Militia Bureau. The number of Guard officers to serve in the Militia Bureau was increased. In addition, the law stipulated that Guard officers would serve on the General Staff and established a committee of senior Guard leaders to review and recommend policies affecting the entire National Guard.[45]

The Interwar Years

Prior to the passage of the National Defense Act of 1920, a bewildering set of issues thwarted the National Guard's reorganization. Without clear guidance from the War Department, the States moved slowly to reform units. Most Governors were willing to await the outcome of defense debates in Washington before expending scarce resources on the Guard. Hostility from labor unions and a generation of young men appalled by the horrors of trench warfare made recruiting difficult. The press was full of reports of Guard veterans with grievances toward the Army. In some locations, State Guard forces hoped to usurp the National Guard and retain possession of armories.[46]

Several States clearly understood the importance of having a peace-time force for domestic disturbances and natural disasters. By the summer of 1919, the States reported the organization of 37,210 troops into National Guard units. A year later, Guard strength stood at 56,090 soldiers in thirty-four States. In the absence of guidance from the War Department, Guard units grew from the ground up without supervision from higher command levels. Company-sized units of infantry and cavalry were normal with troop strength ranging from 50–100 soldiers. The passage of the National Defense Act of 1920 removed all ambiguity regarding the future, and a recruiting boom resulted. In less than two years, manpower nearly tripled to an all time high of 159,658 soldiers. By the summer of 1922, all States except Nevada had organized Guard units, and twenty States had completed the organization of all units authorized.[47]

The 1920 Act directed the peacetime organization of the Army into corps areas. In August 1920, the War Department divided the country into nine corps areas, with each corps to contain one Regular, two National Guard, and three Reserve divisions giving the Army a total of fifty-four divisions. The priority for manning, equipping and training within the Guard went to the new, eighteen divisions, two separate infantry regiments in Hawaii and Puerto Rico and a Coast Artillery corps of 11,600 soldiers. The eighteen divisions reverted to the unit nicknames and designations adopted during World War I with the divisional numbers 26–38 and 40–45 but excluding the 42nd and 93rd Divisions. In 1922, the Guard received authority to raise four cavalry divisions numbered 21–24. Guard historians worked to integrate the lineage and honors of old historic units into modern designations. For example, the Bay State's 181st and 182nd Infantry traced their heritage all the way back to the Massachusetts North Regiment of 1636. Units adopted distinctive regimental crests and shoulder patches that emphasized local ties and long traditions of service. For the first time, the War Department issued standard divisional and brigade flags, regimental colors, and company guidons to Guard units. By 1927, the organization of all units assigned to the eighteen infantry divisions was 85 percent complete while the cavalry divisions still lacked one-third of their units.[48]

The growth of the Guard presented new management challenges to the AGs and the Militia Bureau. To improve the management of the officer corps, the Militia Bureau in 1922 began publication of the *National Guard Register* that contained a summary of every Guard officer's service record. The National Defense Act of 1920 had authorized 435,800 Guardsmen, but congressional appropriations never allowed Guard strength to rise much above 180,000 throughout the 1920s. AGs managed their units in terms of numbers of troop spaces authorized versus the actual manning levels allowed by appropriations. To enhance recruiting, the States dispersed units as broadly as possible and placed armories in a maximum number of communities. For the first time, the AGs split company-sized units between towns. By 1922, the Guard had formed 2,200 units in 1,250 towns and cities. The States decided it was better to have a maximum number of organized units partially filled than fewer units at full strength. The manpower experience of the recent war hung heavy over management decisions; the AGs assumed that upon mobilization new Guard recruits or draftees would fill their understrength units. Still, the Militia Bureau established hard rules for managing the force. Units of less than fifty soldiers were to be organized and manned exactly the same as Regular outfits. No armory was to house less than fifty soldiers. For units of more than fifty soldiers, the Militia Bureau established manning levels of 65–80 percent. Guard organizations throughout the country ranged in size from single armories of fifty men scattered across the Plains to 13,000 Guardsmen concentrated in New York City.[49]

New types of units and weapons reflected the changing nature of modern warfare. The first tanks appeared in the Guard, with one tank company assigned to each infantry division. The 34th Division's tank company from Duluth, Minnesota became the Guard's first armor unit on May 25, 1920. Tank unit activations increased steadily until the Guard armor force included eighteen tank companies. The Guard received motor vehicles from World War I stocks, but by 1933 old sedans and transports were falling apart. New trucks appeared that afforded Guard units increased training opportunities. Reliable wheeled transport allowed units to use training areas that were formerly inaccessible because of the time and distances of foot marches. During the summer, National Guard wheeled convoys headed to annual training became an enduring image on America's highways. Throughout the entire interwar period, the horse still served many units. The Army chief of artillery managed to motorize most of the Guard's horse-drawn artillery regiments, but these units did not disappear until 1941. As late as 1940, half of Guard cavalrymen were on horseback, and the cavalry was not fully mechanized until April 1942.[50]

The most dramatic advances in technology occurred with the activation of flying units. A large number of Air Service pilots, crewmen, and support personnel left the Army after World War I, and the National Guard was eager to take advantage of their special skills. The organization of each Army division called for an observation squadron for air reconnaissance missions. The first aviation unit after World War I to receive federal recognition occurred in January 1921 when Minnesota's 109th Observation Squadron became part of the 34th Division. Within months, Maryland and Indiana had organized their own divisional aviation units. By 1930, eighteen National Guard observation squadrons were on duty. The most dramatic accomplishment of any Guard aviator came on May 20, 1927 when Captain Charles A. Lindbergh of Missouri's 110th Observation Squadron became the first pilot to fly solo across the hazardous North Atlantic. For his incredible passage between New York and Paris, Lindbergh received the Medal of Honor.[51]

Combat experience from World War I prompted Guard commanders to make dramatic changes in training. They placed emphasis on getting troops out of sterile classrooms and into the field for firsthand experience. Marksmanship training dominated weekly drill periods for enlisted men while officers held command post exercises. During summer encampments, commanders stressed live fire exercises, force-on-force maneuvers and terrain walks. Five Guard divisions managed to assemble and train as entire units during the summer of 1928. The Regular Army struggled to provide barely half of the officers and senior sergeant instructors required because of its own budget and manning constraints. In 1927 the Army initiated a new, innovative, and cost saving instruction technique; correspondence courses. Within six years, two-thirds of Guard officers were enrolled in some type of correspondence course.[52]

The stock market crash of October 29, 1929 set in motion an economic calamity that affected all Americans. Social dislocation and unemployment spread rapidly; by the summer of 1932, nearly one-third of the American work force was idle. National Guard service provided badly needed income. An unemployed worker who was a private in the Guard earned $75 a year by attending armory drills and summer camp. The lure of pay created a surge in volunteerism. For the first time, many units had waiting lists of men wanting to volunteer. At the lowest point of the Great Depression in 1932, National Guard strength stood at an historic, peacetime high of 187,413 soldiers. Attendance at both armory drill and summer camp exceeded 90 percent during 1932–1933. In 1934, Congress reduced the number of paid drills from 48 to 36 as a cost savings measure. Many Guard units continued a full regime of weekly drills, calling the unpaid assemblies "free drills." Despite the reduction in pay, drill attendance stood at 91.5 percent. The chief of the Militia Bureau reported that it no longer took "any particular effort" to maintain strength. On the contrary, the challenge was to restrict manpower to within "the limits permitted by appropriations."[53]

Table 4
NATIONAL GUARD STRENGTH, 1919–1940

YEAR	TOTAL	YEAR	TOTAL
1919	37,210	1930	182,715
1920	56,106	1931	187,386
1921	113,640	1932	187,413
1922	159,658	1933	185,925
1923	160,598	1934	184,791
1924	176,332	1935	185,915
1925	177,525	1936	189,174
1926	174,969	1937	192,161
1927	181,142	1938	197,188
1928	181,221	1939	199,491
1929	176,988	1940	242,402

(Source: Militia Bureau and National Guard Bureau, *Annual Reports*, 1919–1940.)

The National Guard helped the nation endure the Great Depression's rigors in other ways. Armory construction and camp improvements performed by the Works Progress Administration constituted the first federal dollars expended on Guard facilities in the States. Government contracts to vehicle and weapons producers stimulated the economy. As a public institution, the Guard provided stability and refuge to families and communities whose social and economic well-being were threatened. With little money available for entertainment, townspeople went to local armories for free social activities that included dances, concerts, parades, marksmanship contests, and athletic events. A number of Guard cavalry units opened their armories to make horse back riding available for families on Sundays. For a period, social activities overshadowed military preparedness, and some of the romantic uniforms of the old, volunteer militia reappeared during parades and ceremonies.

The Guard earned a reputation during the Great Depression as a reliable instrument of State power in enforcing laws. On several occasions, Guard units became involved in bitter labor disputes. During the San Francisco longshoremen's strike of July 1934, the California Guard restored order after rioting killed and injured nearly twenty-five policemen and bystanders. During violent protests by steel workers in Ohio, several Guardsmen were killed, and Ohio Guard flying units dropped tear gas from the air to disperse angry crowds.[54]

An important amendment to previous National Guard legislation came in 1933. Since the passage of the Dick Act thirty years prior, the Guard's dual nature—its role as both a State and federal force—had confused and confounded many soldiers and legislators alike. Under the leadership of Milton Reckord, NGAUS and Guard supporters drafted and passed into law an amendment to the National Defense Act of 1916 that defined and institutionalized the Guard's unique status. The legislation established the "National Guard of the United States" as a permanent "reserve component" of the Army consisting of federally recognized

National Guard Education Foundation

Maj. Gen. Milton A. Reckord: Service to State and Nation

Milton Atchison Reckord was an experienced veteran of two forms of combat: as a talented military leader during two World Wars and as a shrewd lobbyist in Washington, DC. He left a deep imprint on American military policy during a distinguished military career to Maryland and the nation that spanned sixty-four years.

"Milt" Reckord joined the Maryland National Guard as a private in 1901. Within two years, he was elected to company command, and in 1916 saw duty on the Mexican Border. In World War I, he commanded the 115th Infantry, 29th Division, as well as two different brigades in the division.

In 1920, General Reckord was appointed the AG of Maryland, a position he held for an unprecedented forty-five years. He mobilized Guard opinion in favor of the National Defense Act of 1920 and served as NGAUS president, 1923–1925. Reckord was the author of the 1933 legislation giving Guardsmen a permanent status as both State and federal troops. General Reckord commanded the 29th Division from 1934–1941, and during World War II, he served as the Provost Marshal of the European Theater. In 1945, he helped lay the groundwork for the establishment of the postwar National Guard.

After his retirement in 1965, Reckord maintained an interest in Guard affairs. He was the first recipient of the NGAUS Distinguished Service Medal and a life member of the NGAUS Executive Council. He died in Baltimore in September 1975 at the age of ninety-five and is buried in Fallston, Maryland.

National Guard units. At the same time, the law identified the "National Guard of the several States" consisting of the voluntary members of the State militias that served under the Governors. In simplest terms, the "National Guard of the United States" pertained to the Guard's federal role as a deployable asset of the Army, while the "National Guard of the several States" recognized the role of Guardsmen on State active duty. Henceforth, officers would take a dual oath to both the nation and their State. The legislation also changed the name of the Militia Bureau to the National Guard Bureau (NGB).[55]

The same year that Milton Reckord championed new legislation, Adolf Hitler became the chancellor of Germany at the head of the National Socialist Party. Soon after the Nazis came to power, they rearmed the German military. Hitler's inflammatory rhetoric that promoted a 1,000-year Third Reich based on racial purity and military power caused alarm in Europe. Eventually, the European powers launched rearmament

The last mounted color guard of Virginia's 111th Field Artillery in 1933. By the late 1930s, the National Guard's field artillery units had traded their horses for trucks. (Virginia National Guard Historical Collection)

programs of their own while keeping a wary eye on the Nazis. The disturbing developments in Europe and Asia created favorable conditions for General Douglas MacArthur, the new Army chief of staff, to argue for much needed increases in defense spending. Throughout his tenure, MacArthur stressed the Army's deficiencies in personnel and materiel while presiding over the development of plans for manpower and industrial mobilization.

MacArthur's appeals resulted in limited but important increases in defense spending. For the first time in nearly twenty years, Regular and Guard units held joint maneuvers during 1935. Starting that same year, Congress increased appropriations that allowed the Guard to add manpower at an annual rate of 5,000 soldiers. By early 1940, Guard strength stood at over 200,000 troops. Personnel increases allowed the Guard divisions to complete their unit organization even though actual manning levels remained below full strength. At the same time, the Guard created hundreds of combat and support units that would serve at the corps and army level in wartime. As a percentage of the U.S. armed forces, the Guard's twenty-two infantry and cavalry divisions and separate units represented a substantial portion of America's combat capability on the eve of World War II.[56]

The Mobilization of 1940–1941

In the late 1930s, diplomatic and military events in Europe and Asia set the stage for a second global conflict. Between 1936–1939, Hitler occupied the Rhineland, annexed Austria and seized control of the Sudetenland. The Italians extended their African empire into Ethiopia, and the Germans and Italians supported fascists in the Spanish Civil War. In the Far East, the Japanese invaded China and inflicted brutal atrocities upon the Chinese people. Militarists in Tokyo spoke of expansion throughout Southeast Asia to create an economic sphere to support Imperial Japan's ambitions. The leaders of Western Europe appeased Hitler, prompting the German *Fuehrer* to accelerate his plans of conquest and expansion. On September 1, 1939, Hitler's legions attacked Poland and started World War II. The stage was set for an epic struggle that ultimately pitted the Axis powers of Germany, Italy, and Japan against the Allied countries of Great Britain, the Soviet Union, and the United States.

Ironically, one of the men most responsible for the ultimate Axis defeat came to power the very day World War II started. On September 1, 1939, Gen. George C. Marshall was sworn in as the fifteenth Army chief of staff. A Pershing protege, Marshall brought to the job long years of experience and a widely recognized reputation for superior intellect and character. Marshall had a healthy respect for citizen-soldiers based on his service as a senior staff officer in World War I and during assignments with the National Guard in the interwar years. Considering the state of America's defenses in 1939, Marshall had to muster all of his considerable skills and talents to meet the impending crisis.

At the beginning of World War II, the U.S. Army was ranked the 17th largest in the world with only 190,000 Regulars, just behind the Rumanian Army. More than a quarter of the active Army's manpower occupied the overseas possessions, and the 140,000 soldiers in the U.S. were scattered among 130 posts that housed battalion-sized units. The Army's nine divisions existed mostly on paper. Only the 1st, 2nd, and 3rd Infantry Divisions had even a semblance of divisional organization, and the other six divisions were in reality small brigades. The 1st and 2nd Cavalry divisions numbered only 1,200 soldiers each. In most respects, the Army of 1939 closely resembled the AEF of World War I in its organization and equipment. The infantryman remained the core of the Army's combat capability. Because of the isolationism and austere military budgets of the interwar years, the Army had done little to promote military aviation or mechanized warfare.[57]

The ORC was perhaps in better shape than the Regular Army given its limited goals. Like the National Guard, the ORC organized in earnest after the passage of the National Defense Act of 1920. A large number of World War I veterans joined the ORC, and its strength stood at 68,232 by the summer of 1921. In June 1923 the Army General Staff created the Reserve Officers' Section to "handle questions pertaining to the Reserves." During the interwar years, students commissioned from ROTC constituted the bulk of ORC membership. The ORC manned the officer positions in twenty-seven infantry and six cavalry divisions at approximately 80 percent strength. Officers attended drills and enjoyed periods of active duty on an intermittent basis. An opportunity came during the Great Depression with the ORC's management of the Civilian Conservation Corps, a Federal public works program. The total number of ORC members to work with the corps was in excess of 30,000. By 1939, the number of active ORC officers had grown to 104,575.[58]

The outbreak of war in Europe spurred new measures to increase the Army's readiness. On September 8, 1939, President Franklin D. Roosevelt declared a national emergency and directed increases in the Regular Army and the National Guard by presidential executive order. The Regular Army was authorized an increase of 17,000 to a strength of 227,000 soldiers. The Guard was directed to expand its ranks by 43,000 to an aggregate strength of 235,000. Nearly three-quarters of the growth was intended to bring the Guard's eighteen infantry divisions to full strength.

In addition, annual armory drills increased from 48 to 60 and summer encampments expanded from 15 to 21 days. Between June 1939 and June 1940, the Guard added nearly 40,000 men, and manpower in the summer of 1940 stood at a peacetime, historic high of 242,402 soldiers.[59]

Hitler's military machine achieved a string of dazzling victories in 1940 that shocked the world. In a series of lightning strikes in April, German troops occupied Denmark and Norway. On May 10, 1940, Germany unleashed a blitzkrieg against Western Europe. The Lowlands countries surrendered quickly, and German troops forced the evacuation of the British from Dunkirk. In a series of rapid thrusts, German troops swept into France, occupied Paris and destroyed the French Army. On June 22nd, Hitler accepted the surrender of a humiliated France. Soon afterwards, the German *Luftwaffe* opened an air campaign against Great Britain. In less than three months, most of Western Europe except England had fallen under the Nazi boot, and an invasion of the British Isles appeared imminent.

German aggression drew an unusually sharp response from the United States. Even before France's final capitulation in late June, Congress authorized a full expansion of the Regular Army to 280,000 troops. Meanwhile, a national debate ensued over the callup of the Guard and the implementation of a peacetime draft. Before ordering the National Guard to active duty short of a declaration of war, President Roosevelt wanted Congress to provide additional funding for the Guard and to authorize its use beyond U.S. borders. Prominent civilian leaders pressed for conscription as the best means of preparing the country for war and transmitting American resolve to the Axis powers. On August 27, 1940, Congress passed a joint resolution authorizing the president to order the National Guard and the Reserves to active duty for twelve months but restricting their employment to the Western hemisphere. Three weeks later, Congress passed the Selective Training and Service Act of 1940, and on September 16th President Roosevelt signed into law America's first peacetime draft.[60]

Even before the National Guard entered active duty, certain provisions of the draft law profoundly affected Guard manpower. Because Guardsmen and draftees were to enter active service in peacetime, the War Department decided that the same induction standards should apply to both groups. The Selective Service Act called for the drafting of men over age 21 without dependents who did not hold critical jobs in agriculture or war production. NGB issued similar implementing instructions for discharges to the States on July 23rd. Over the ensuing months a mass exodus took place. Guardsmen with good jobs knew that enlisted pay would not suffice to support their families. Nearly 51,000 Guard enlisted men—20 percent of the total—received dependency separations. The Guard released another 4,906 underage soldiers who had enlisted without parental consent. In an incredible dint of effort, the Guard, in only a few weeks, recruited enough volunteers to make up for the huge losses. In the twelve months following June 1940, the Guard released another 40,000 troops for defense and agriculture related jobs. Though the Guard did manage to maintain its overall strength, the loss in experienced soldiers was severe and imposed on units the huge task of providing initial training to large numbers of new recruits.[61]

On August 31st, President Roosevelt signed an executive order initiating the Guard mobilization of 1940. The first increment of 63,346 soldiers ordered to active duty on September 16th included the 30th, 41st, 44th, and 45th Divisions, eighteen Coast Artillery regiments, and four observation squadrons. The entire mobilization eventually comprised twenty-five increments over thirteen months with the last callup occurring on October 6, 1941. The phased mobilization was intended to allow the smooth assimilation of Guardsmen onto active duty, but the rapid and simultaneous inflow of Regulars, Guardsmen, Reservists, and draftees into the Army created chaos.[62]

Guardsmen reporting to their armories in the fall of 1940 encountered various degrees of confusion. To ease logistical burdens, commanders told soldiers to eat breakfast at home each morning until units moved to training camps. In most instances, a chronic shortage of uniforms and shoes forced new unit members to report each day in civilian clothes. The uniforms that were available were a mixed, ill-fitting lot, mostly dating from World War I. Newly promoted sergeants spent their time learning their duties and drilling fresh recruits. When not training, soldiers prepared for movement by filling out required forms, undergoing physical examinations and manning work details.[63]

When the Guard divisions reported to their training camps in late 1940, few sites were ready. At Fort Dix, New Jersey the 44th Division found barracks for only 1,500 of its nearly 11,000 soldiers, and 200 carpenters labored to construct 2,700 wooden tent pads. The 45th Division's designated training site was so ill prepared that the Army switched it to Fort Sill. Throughout the winter, "Thunderbird" Division soldiers lived in harsh, cold conditions under tents. Private Bill Mauldin of Arizona's 120th Quartermaster Regiment indulged his love of drawing to portray the dismal conditions in Oklahoma. Before the end of the war, Mauldin's cartoon characters "Willy and Joe" would become the most beloved GIs of World War II. All of the divisions had similar experiences with inadequate training sites. On March 5, 1941, Illinois' 33rd Division was the last Guard division to enter active duty.[64]

As in 1917, significant problems hampered post-mobilization training. The most serious deficiencies were shortages of weapons and equipment. In some cases, units surrendered precious equipment for shipment to the hard-pressed Allies under the Lend Lease Program. Turbulence in unit organization and personnel turnover disrupted training plans. The Guard's four cavalry divisions were immediately converted into artillery, antitank, and mechanized cavalry units. Another 500 units converted to other types of organization. On average, each Guard division required an infusion of 6,000 draftees to bring it to full strength, and the influx of untrained soldiers kept training focused on individual soldier skills rather than unit maneuvers. Organizations often had to surrender their most experienced personnel to form the nucleus for new draftee divisions. Guard leaders chafed at critical Army inspectors who pointed out training deficiencies but seemed unable or unwilling to provide assistance.[65]

The Guard and Army collided head-on over officer assignments, promotions, and dismissals. The focal point for the Guard's frustrations became Lt. Gen. Leslie J. McNair. As commander of the Army Ground Forces, McNair was responsible for all Army training in the United States. A long serving Regular, McNair was an avowed Uptonian who made no secret of his disdain for the Guard and citizen-soldiers in general. After visiting the 30th Division early in the mobilization, McNair characterized the Guard's leadership as "the blind leading the blind." In 1944, McNair complained to General Marshall that Guard generals were unprofessional and "not competent to exercise the command appropriate to their rank." Just before his untimely death by friendly fire in Normandy in July 1944, McNair wrote that in his opinion the National Guard had contributed little to national defense.[66]

The most contentious personnel issue centered on the relief of the Guard's division commanders. Of the eighteen division commanders assigned in 1940, only two went on to lead their troops in combat. The main reasons for relief were age and infirmities; seven commanders were age sixty or older. Recent scholarship has put new light on the controversy by comparing the fate of Regular and Guard division commanders in 1940. Much like the Guard generals, few of the original fourteen Regular division commanders survived the mobilization. None took their divisions into battle, and only three went on to higher command. Four of the Guard's division commanders had been in command for ten or more years, and the common denominator among Regular and Guard commanders was the military's stagnant, peacetime seniority system that permitted the eldest generals to retain command. In fact, of the original thirty-two division commanders, only Maj. Gen. Robert S. Beightler, the commander of Ohio's 37th Division, remained in command for the entire war. In retrospect, it appears that the fate of the original group of Guard division commanders was not much different from their active duty counterparts.[67]

By the spring of 1941, conditions had improved in the mobilization camps and unit training began in earnest. However, troop morale suffered because of an uncertain future. Guardsmen, Reservists, and draftees had entered active duty for twelve months to defend the western hemisphere, and Axis ambitions appeared satisfied for the moment. Unless another international crisis loomed, citizen-soldiers expected to head home starting in the fall and most wanted to make family and employment arrangements toward that end. Congress reserved the right to extend conscription and the reserve callup, but the political debates dragged on inconclusively. Citizen-soldiers exercised their perceived right of self-expression and wrote their elected representatives urging a quick solution to the impasse. Throughout the Army, disgruntled troops scrawled the acronym "OHIO"—Over the Hill In October—on barracks walls and on the sides of vehicles, signifying that the first troops ordered to active duty wanted to head home in the fall. In May 1941, the Chief, NGB (CNGB) cited national security needs to recommend the Guard's indefinite retention on active duty. One month later the War Department took the same position. On June 22, 1941 Hitler attacked Russia, and an expansion of the European crisis seemed all but certain. After an intense

Missouri Guardsmen of the 203rd Coast Artillery prepare to open fire at a target drone during the 1941 Louisiana Maneuvers. (National Archives)

debate, Congress passed a six-month extension of the reserve component mobilization and conscription on August 12, 1941 by only one vote in the House of Representatives. The Guard would remain on active duty until April 1942.[68]

With all uncertainties removed regarding the availability of troops, the Army launched the largest peacetime training exercises in the nation's history. The maneuvers of the fall of 1941 involved nearly half a million soldiers and riveted the nation's attention. The Guard divisions fully participated in the maneuvers in Louisiana, Tennessee, California, and the Carolinas. The ranks most remembered the primitive living conditions and the embarrassing shortages of weapons and equipment. Guardsmen used stove pipes to simulate cannons and mortars, carried sticks and brooms for rifles and pretended that pine logs were machine guns. Trucks and jeeps with signs marked "TANK" simulated enemy armored vehicles, and low flying aircraft dropped sacks of flour instead of bombs. Despite the obvious deficiencies, the maneuvers provided valuable training for staffs and commanders, revealed unfit leaders and identified rising stars ready for more senior commands.[69]

Unfortunately, the renewal of the draft and the Guard mobilization by only a single vote in Congress sent a strong signal to Japanese militarists in Tokyo. Bent on expansion in the Pacific, they believed the United States would be an easy opponent; Americans apparently did not want war and had no stomach for suffering large casualties. One swift, powerful blow would surely send the Yankees reeling. On Thanksgiving Day 1941, as America enjoyed a traditional holiday meal, the Imperial Japanese Navy set sail from northern Japan, steaming east toward Hawaii under a shroud of secrecy to deliver an audacious, surprise attack against the American fleet at Pearl Harbor.

The Opening Shots of World War II

"AIR RAID, PEARL HARBOR. THIS IS NOT A DRILL!" This short, dramatic message from Hawaii on the morning of December 7, 1941 plunged the United States into World War II. The next day, President Roosevelt proclaimed December 7th as "a date which will live in infamy," and Congress declared war on Japan. In response, Germany and Italy promptly declared war on the United States. With all of the major participants finally engaged, World War II escalated to new levels of fury and destruction.

Even as Congress declared war on Japan, National Guardsmen were already in combat. On October 15, 1940, the Hawaii National Guard's 298th and 299th Infantry entered active duty at Schofield Barracks on

Oahu; the 298th was assigned to the Regular Army's 25th Infantry Division and the 298th to the 24th Infantry Division. A month later, California's 251st Coast Artillery arrived in Hawaii from Los Angeles, the first Guard unit to leave the U.S. for overseas duty in World War II. When the Japanese attacked Pearl Harbor, the 298th and 299th Infantry and the 251st Coast Artillery took part in the defense of Oahu and fired the National Guard's first shots of World War II.[70]

On December 7, 1941, Guardsmen were already on duty in the Philippines. The month before, three Guard units with troops from seven States arrived in the Philippines to bolster the island defenses. The largest was New Mexico's 200th Coast Artillery consisting of 1,800 men, many of them Hispanic. During the 1940 mobilization, the Army had consolidated the tank companies assigned to each Guard division into four composite tank battalions. The 192nd Tank Battalion, with troops from Wisconsin, Illinois, Ohio, and Kentucky, and the 194th Tank Battalion, consisting of companies from Minnesota and California with a sprinkling of Guardsmen from Missouri, added their firepower to the Philippine defenses. The 200th Coast Artillery valiantly defended against Japanese aerial attacks at Clark Field on December 8th. During the battle, the New Mexicans fired the first shots in defense of the Philippines and suffered a number of casualties while downing five enemy planes. The Japanese Army invaded the Philippines, backing the Americans and Filipinos onto the Bataan Peninsula and the island fortress of Corregidor. Cut off from supplies and reinforcements, the defenders held on for four months. Throughout the defensive battles, Guard units fought stubbornly. Finally, with their backs to the sea and low on all commodities except courage, the "Battling Bastards of Bataan" surrendered on April 9, 1942. The defenders suffered through the horrors of the Bataan "Death March" and went on to endure over three years of deprivations and brutality in Japanese prisoner of war camps.[71]

The Japanese attack on Pearl Harbor set into motion a chain of events that resulted in the National Guard's "Lost Battalion" of World War II. On December 7, 1941, the 2-131st Field Artillery of the Texas National Guard was aboard a ship in the south Pacific and headed to reinforce the American garrison in the Philippines. Because of the Japanese invasion of the Philippines, the ship diverted first to Australia and then to Java in the Dutch East Indies where the battalion was to provide fire support to Dutch, British, and Australian defenders. The Japanese soon invaded Java and the Dutch surrendered after token resistance; the entire 2-131st Field Artillery was taken prisoner. For the next three years, Texas Guardsmen worked as slave laborers in Japan and throughout Southeast Asia, including the construction of the infamous Burma-Siam railroad.

Altogether, 163 Guardsmen died in captivity before they were liberated. Because no one heard from the unit for three years, the 2-131st became known as the Guard's "Lost Battalion."[72]

While fighting raged in the Philippines, Guardsmen at home reorganized for combat. Hitler's blitzkrieg victories convinced the Army of the effectiveness of maneuver warfare and prompted the abandonment of the square infantry division as the primary combat formation. Earlier in 1941, the Army had created a "triangular division" based on the employment of three infantry regiments, and active duty divisions converted to the new design. Stripped of all unnecessary combat and support units, the smaller triangular division was designed for agility and responsiveness on the fluid battlefields of mechanized warfare. After Pearl Harbor, the Army directed the Guard divisions to convert from the square to the triangular configuration. The end result of the reorganization was to release eighteen separate infantry regiments for duty elsewhere. Guard leaders viewed the detachment of eighteen regiments as yet another effort to degrade the National Guard's size and autonomy. A few of the separate regiments went on to fight with Regular or draftee divisions, but most assumed security missions at various locations worldwide. At the same time, the Army officially recognized the existence of different types of divisions within the Army and added branch identifications to each division's official title.[73]

The outbreak of war precipitated other changes in the States and at NGB. The Guard mobilization left the Governors without troops, and as in World War I, the States created State Guard forces. Throughout the war, State Guards performed disaster relief, aid to civil authorities and security missions. Overall control of the State Guards fell to NGB, and at their peak strength in June 1943, the State Guards numbered 170,403 troops in forty-four States. With all National Guard units on active duty during the war, NGB's authority was greatly diminished. In March 1942, NGB ceased to exist as a special staff and came under the authority of the Army's Adjutant General. Before the end of the war, the NGB staff was reduced to forty-nine civilian workers who served as a subordinate agency of the Personnel Division of the Army Service Forces.[74]

A Japanese whirlwind overran Southeast Asia and the central Pacific in early 1942. The miraculous victory at Midway in May 1942 gave the United States the strategic initiative, but the Japanese continued to occupy key terrain. Japanese forces in New Guinea and in the Solomon Islands threatened Australia and the sea routes linking Australia and Hawaii. National Guard infantry was at the center of early American victories on Guadalcanal and in New Guinea. Three infantry regiments—the 132nd (Illinois), 164th (North Dakota), and the 182nd (Massachusetts)—made available by the triangular division conversion were rushed to New Caledonia in March 1942. The three regiments formed the basis for the activation of the "Americal" Division on May 27, 1942, the nineteenth Guard division to serve in World War II. ("Americal" is an abbreviation of "America" and "New Caledonia.") The 164th Infantry deployed to Guadalcanal in October to reinforce the U.S. Marines. The North Dakotans became the first Army troops to go on the offensive in World War II. The remainder of the division soon arrived on the island and played a major role in the Japanese defeat. For its actions on Guadalcanal, the Americal Division became the only Army division to be awarded the Navy Presidential Unit Citation. In the last stages of the Guadalcanal campaign, Ohio's 37th Division entered the fight and saw action in April 1943.[75]

The 32nd Division from Wisconsin and Michigan was set to deploy to Europe when it received orders to head for the port of embarkation at San Francisco. By May 1942, the "Red Arrow" Division was in Australia, and before the end of the summer it was in New Guinea fighting along-side the Australians. General MacArthur ordered the 32nd Division to take Buna, a critical Japanese enclave on the northern tip of New Guinea. In one of the most grueling campaigns of the war, Guardsmen attacked heavily defended Japanese pillboxes in the thick, sweltering jungles. Short on supplies, troops ate half rations and suffered through bouts of malaria. The Americans absorbed crippling losses but finally captured Buna in January 1943. The 41st Division, manned by Guardsmen from the Pacific Northwest, relieved the 32nd Division on New Guinea, and the Red Arrow division returned to Australia for rest and refit.

The War in Europe

Though American naval and ground forces in the Pacific were bat-tling the Japanese with positive results, the priority for operations shifted to Europe. In consultation with the Allies, the Roosevelt Administration determined that Nazi Germany posed a more serious threat than Japan and adopted a national strategy of "Germany First." Initially, General Marshall and the Joint Chiefs of Staff (JCS) advocated a direct attack against Nazi-occupied Western Europe across the English Channel from bases in Great Britain. However, it soon became evident that American troops were not yet ready for such an ambitious undertaking. President Roosevelt insisted that American troops engage the Germans before the end of 1942 and decided to support Allied operations in the Mediterranean. For American troops, the road to Berlin would begin in the sands of North Africa.

During 1942–1943, Guardsmen were in the thick of the fighting in the Mediterranean. The 34th Infantry Division was the first American combat division to deploy overseas following Pearl Harbor. The "Red Bull" Division sailed to Ireland in February 1942 to train for the invasion of Western Europe. Reflecting Allied strategic decisions, the 34th Division was reassigned to the landing forces for Operation TORCH, the invasion of North Africa. On November 8, 1942, the 34th Division made an assault landing on the Algerian coast, and with other U.S. divisions, fought its way across the sands and mountains of Tunisia against Germany's *Afrika Korps.* The enemy surrendered in May 1943, with the 34th Division suffering 4,200 casualties. The 45th Division had its baptism of fire on June 8, 1943 during the amphibious invasion of Sicily. In twenty-two days of continuous combat, the Thunderbird Division covered more ground than any other Army division. The 36th Division from Texas became the third Guard division to see action in the Mediterranean when it landed at Salerno on the Italian peninsula on September 9, 1943. Stiff enemy resistance nearly doomed the landing, and the 45th Division quickly deployed into the Salerno beachhead to strengthen the Allied defenses. The invaders finally captured Naples and began a slow, bloody advance up the Italian peninsula against rugged, mountainous terrain, abysmal weather, and a determined enemy. The 34th, 36th, and 45th Divisions participated in every major campaign in Italy, including the assault of the German Winter Line, the bloody crossing of the Rapido River, desperate fighting at Anzio and the liberation of Rome on June 5, 1944. To increase pressure on Nazi forces, the Allies landed in southern France on August 15th. Both the 36th and 45th Divisions splashed ashore in the French Riviera, were at the forefront of the offensive up the Rhone River valley, fought their way through to the German frontier and helped to overrun Germany in the spring of 1945. Meanwhile, the 34th Division continued fighting in northern Italy until German forces surrendered there on May 2, 1945.

On June 6, 1944, Allied land, sea, and air forces invaded Western Europe in the largest amphibious assault of all time. After airborne landings and preparatory bombardments by air and naval forces, Allied ground troops assaulted five separate invasion beaches in Normandy. The most difficult fighting occurred on Omaha Beach where elements of the 1st and 29th Infantry Divisions landed abreast. German defenses, high bluffs, and rough seas made the assault precarious. By the end of the day, the divisions had a viable toehold on the French coastline. The 29th Division went on to accumulate an impressive combat record in Europe, though at a high cost. Veterans grimly recalled that in reality three separate 29th Divisions existed during the war—one on the front lines, one in the hospital, and one in the cemetery.

The 28th Infantry Division marches triumphantly down the Champs Elysees to mark the liberation of Paris on August 29, 1944. (National Archives)

Five other National Guard divisions proved their mettle in Europe. The 30th Division arrived in Normandy ten days after D-Day and went on to a stellar combat career. At the battle of Mortain the Old Hickory Division blunted a strong German counterattack intended to thwart the American breakout from Normandy and in the fall of 1944 was one of the first American divisions to breach the vaunted Siegfried Line. The 35th Division received its baptism of fire in Normandy while helping to capture the vital road junction at St. Lo in July 1944. After Lt. Gen. George S. Patton's dash across France, the "Santa Fe" Division liberated the city of Nancy, took part in the American offensive following the battle of the Bulge and ended the war on the banks of the Elbe River. The 28th Division stumbled badly during the ill-fated attack against the small town of Schmidt in the Huertgen Forest. Because of punishing casualties, veterans referred to the division's red, keystone shoulder patch as "the bloody bucket." After a period of rest and retraining, the 28th Division redeemed its reputation during a series of stubborn defensive battles in the opening days of the Bulge. The 26th Division entered combat in Lorraine in the late summer of 1944 and led the advance to capture the fortress complex at Metz. In December, the Yankee Division participated in Patton's attack to relieve the hard-pressed defenders at Bastogne. The 26th Division drove across Germany the following spring, captured Linz,

Austria and ended the war in Czechoslovakia. The 44th Division did not arrive in Europe until October 1944 and fought in the difficult Vosges Mountains. In the last months of the war, the "Four by Four" Division breached the Siegfried Line, captured Mannheim and ended the war in Austria. All together, the nine National Guard divisions serving in Europe suffered losses of 125,630.[76]

Of the nearly seventy American divisions that fought in Europe, the 45th Division compiled a combat record perhaps second to none. The Thunderbird Division endured 511 days in combat in Sicily, Italy, France, and Germany and conducted three amphibious assault landings. After observing the division in action in Sicily, General Patton declared: "Born at sea, baptized in blood, your fame shall never die." One of the Guard's most distinguished soldiers from World War II came from the 45th Division. Raymond S. McLain had joined the Oklahoma National Guard in 1912 and was a veteran of the Mexican Border mobilization and World War I. By 1940, he was a brigadier general and commander of the 45th Division artillery. In the Mediterranean campaigns, he was noted for conspicuous bravery in Sicily and at Salerno. After D-Day, McLain took command of the troubled 90th Infantry Division in France and transformed it into an effective fighting unit. In October 1944, McLain became the commander of the U.S. XIX Corps and the first citizen-soldier corps commander since the Civil War. By war's end, the 45th Division had captured 103,000 enemy soldiers and suffered a total of 62,563 casualties. Eight soldiers received the Medal of Honor. In April 1945, the Thunderbird Division had the dubious distinction of liberating the infamous Nazi death camp at Dachau. When it occupied Munich at the end of the war, the division's ranks included soldiers from forty-one States, yet the leadership was still predominantly National Guard, except for the most senior positions.[77]

Compared to World War I, black Guardsmen saw little combat in World War II. The War Department failed to address racial inequality in the military and supported policies of segregation and discrimination. Cognizant of racial injustice, African-American Guardsmen fought constantly for victory at home and abroad. Black units that had served with distinction in 1917–1918 were mostly converted to artillery and engineer units. New York's 369th Infantry became the 369th Antiaircraft Gun Battalion that garrisoned Hawaii and ended the war as part of the occupation forces on Okinawa. The only black Guard units to see combat were the 1698th and 1699th Engineer Battalions (Combat) that were formed from Illinois' 370th Infantry and saw action in Europe near the end of the war. Only the 372nd Infantry retained its original organization throughout the war while performing guard and security mission in the New York

City area. In early 1945, the 372nd shipped out to Schofield Barracks and became part of Hawaii's garrison until January 1946.[78]

National Guard flying units contributed to the war effort. After Pearl Harbor, Guardsmen flew anti-submarine patrols along both coasts. The Army Air Forces were desperately short of trained pilot instructors, and eight National Guard squadrons spent the entire war in stateside training camps. Three of the first observation squadrons to depart the U.S. were the 111th (Texas), 122nd (Louisiana), and the 154th (Arkansas). They sailed for the Mediterranean as part of the 68th Observation Group and took part in the invasion of North Africa. Other squadrons that saw early combat were Michigan's 107th Observation Squadron and the 109th from Minnesota. Redesignated as tactical reconnaissance squadrons, the two units flew photo-reconnaissance missions for the Normandy invasion planners. In July 1944, the 107th became the first U.S. Army Air Forces unit to operate from French soil.[79]

The War in the Pacific

While Allied operations in Europe focused ultimately on the invasion of Western Europe and the occupation of Nazi Germany, American strategy in the Pacific sought to isolate Japan geographically as a prelude to the invasion of its home islands. After the initial operations on Guadalcanal and New Guinea in 1942, the availability of Navy and Marine forces insured that the United States would maintain pressure against Japan even while implementing a "Germany First" strategy. The main objective of all operations was to strangle Japan's economy and make the home islands vulnerable to direct attack by occupying a triangle formed by Formosa, China, and the Philippines. A strategy finally emerged that employed dual offensives directed westward across the Pacific's vast reaches. In the Southwest Pacific, Douglas MacArthur would command U.S. and Australian divisions, with supporting air and naval forces, in attacks aimed at recapturing the Philippines. In the Central Pacific, Admiral Chester W. Nimitz would attack with considerable naval forces as well as Marine and Army divisions. Nimitz's goals were to destroy the Japanese Navy, capture island airfields that would allow the strategic air bombardment of Japan and place ground forces within reach of the home islands.

Throughout the Pacific campaigns the National Guard contributed ten divisions that played an important role in Japan's final defeat. New York's 27th Infantry Division was the only Guard outfit to support Nimitz's Central Pacific drive, but its combat role had several significant outcomes. Sent to Hawaii in March 1942, the 27th Division formed

Table 5
NATIONAL GUARD DIVISIONS IN WORLD WAR II

DIV	STATES	THEATER	NICKNAME
26	MA	Europe	Yankee
27	NY	Pacific	Empire
28	PA	Europe	Keystone
29	VA, MD, DC	Europe	Blue and Gray
30	NC, SC, TN	Europe	Old Hickory
31	FL, AL, LA, MS	Pacific	Dixie
32	MI, WI	Pacific	Red Arrow
33	IL	Pacific	Prairie
34	ND, SD, MN, IA	Europe	Red Bull
35	KS, MO, NE	Europe	Santa Fe
36	TX	Europe	Texas
37	OH	Pacific	Buckeye
38	IN, KY, WV	Pacific	Cyclone
40	CA, UT, NV	Pacific	Sunshine
41	OR, WA, ID MT, WY	Pacific	Sunset
43	CT, ME, VT, RI	Pacific	Winged Victory
44	NJ, NY	Europe	Four by Four
45	OK, AZ, CO, NM	Europe	Thunderbird
Americal	IL, MA, ND	Pacific	Americal

(Source: Adapted from Headquarters, Department of the Army, 50th Anniversary of World War II Commemoration Committee, Fact Sheet, "The National Guard in World War II," 1.)

regimental combat teams that participated in Nimitz's opening blows. While the Marine Corps attacked Tarawa in November 1943, the 27th Division seized nearby Makin Island after three days of combat. Only three months later, the 27th captured Eniwetok in the Marshall Islands. In both instances, Marine commanders criticized the Army's cautious tactics and complained of poor leadership and inadequate training in the 27th Division.

The Army-Marine confrontation came to a head during fighting on Saipan in the Marianas Islands in June 1944. Dissatisfied with the 27th Division's conduct during some of the most vicious fighting yet encountered in the island campaigns, the Marine Corps general in overall command of the invasion force relieved the 27th's commander, a Regular Army general. The relief initiated bitter recriminations between marines and soldiers that had repercussions far beyond Saipan's shores. The incident poisoned Army and Marine Corps relations for the remainder of the war and fueled interservice rivalry afterwards. After Saipan, the 27th Division participated in the bloody capture of Okinawa and was preparing for the invasion of Japan when the war ended. The division suffered 6,800 battle casualties, but its most enduring legacy from the war occurred on Saipan. The roots of the uneasy rivalry that has existed between the Army and the Marine Corps since World War II can be traced to the relief of the 27th Division's commander on Saipan.[80]

Nine Guard divisions played a key role in MacArthur's Southwest Pacific campaigns that traversed the mountainous jungles of New Guinea and liberated the Philippines. During the last half of 1943, the 37th, 40th, 43rd, and Americal Divisions fought in the Solomon Islands. Fighting raged in New Georgia and Bougainville, and the 40th Division played a vital role in eliminating the Japanese bastion at Rabaul. Starting in early 1944, MacArthur conducted a brilliant air, land, and sea offensive along the northern coast of New Guinea. Superior mobility allowed American forces either to bypass completely enemy strongpoints or to concentrate overwhelming combat power against isolated Japanese defenses. The 31st, 33rd, 41st, and 43rd Divisions saw action at Aitape, Hollandia, Wakde, and Biak, sometimes hitting together and other times striking singly against more distant targets. By September 1944, the 31st Division had occupied Morotai, and MacArthur's forces were well toward Singapore and the southern tip of the Philippines.[81]

With the Navy's successes in the Central Pacific, MacArthur received permission to carry out his return to the Philippines. In November 1944, the 32nd and Americal Divisions landed on Leyte followed not long afterwards by the 31st and 41st Divisions. After the Leyte invasion, MacArthur planned major attacks on Luzon and Mindanao. The 31st and 41st Divisions landed on Mindanao in early 1945, and the 40th Division soon joined them. By late summer, American forces had entirely surrounded the last defenders on the island. Four Guard divisions—the 32nd, 37th, 40th, and 43rd—were in the vanguard of MacArthur's main blow against Luzon. The offensive slashed through Luzon's low lands to capture Manila in the Army's most difficult urban fighting of the entire war. Meanwhile, the 38th Division landed on the Bataan Peninsula and recaptured Corregidor. Facing defeat, the Japanese withdrew into northern Luzon for a characteristic last stand. The 33rd and 37th Divisions plunged northward into the tropical mountains to defeat the Japanese and complete the conquest of the Philippines.[82]

Seven National Guard observation squadrons fought in the Pacific. Two squadrons, the 106th (Alabama) and the 110th (Missouri), fought in the southwestern Pacific theatre. The 106th flew from Henderson Field on Guadalcanal in July 1943. The 110th flew reconnaissance missions out

Under heavy enemy machine gun fire, men of the 41st Infantry Division crouch low in a bomb crater on Jolo Island in the Philippines, April 1945. (National Archives)

of New Guinea, the Philippines, and Okinawa. Five National Guard squadrons saw action in the China-Burma-India Theater, performing photo-reconnaissance missions over Burma's mountainous jungles and flying observation, light transport, and evacuation missions for British, Chinese, and American troops.[83]

The ten Guard divisions in the Pacific bore a significant portion of the burden of Army operations while suffering 48,521 casualties. Combat losses and disease depleted the numbers of Guardsmen in the ranks, but many of the divisions retained a Guard flavor in terms of leadership style and command positions. General Beightler commanded Ohio's 37th Division for all of World War II and retained Guard officers as the chief of staff and division artillery commander. In addition, the 37th Division's principle staff officers were Guardsmen, and most infantry regiments had Guard commanders. Compared to outfits in Europe where casualties were significantly higher, Guard divisions in the Pacific better retained their State and regional identities.[84]

Preparations for the invasion of Japan came to an abrupt halt after the atomic bombings of Hiroshima and Nagasaki. World War II ended with Japanese surrender ceremonies aboard the battleship *Missouri* in Tokyo Bay on September 2, 1945. Though the troops thought only of returning home, several Guard divisions remained in Japan on occupation duty. The 40th Division went to Korea to assist in the repatriation of Japanese prisoners. In April 1946, the "Sunshine" Division was the last Guard division released from active duty. At the end of the war, Secretary of War Robert P. Patterson summed up the Guard's service:

> The National Guard took to the field 18 infantry divisions, 300,000 men. Those State troops doubled the strength of the Army at once, and their presence in the field gave the country a sense that it had passed the lowest ebb of its weakness...Nine of those divisions crossed the Atlantic to Europe and Africa and nine went to the far reaches of the Pacific. The soldiers of the Guard fought in every action in which the Army participated from Bataan to Okinawa. They made a brilliant record on every fighting front. They proved once more the value of the trained citizen-soldier.[85]

Perhaps more than any other event, the homecoming of New Mexico's 200th Coast Artillery reflected the service and sacrifices of Guardsmen during World war II. The 200th had proudly gone off to war, fought bravely on the Bataan Peninsula and endured three horrid years in Japanese prison camps. In mid-1945, a hospital train carried the frail, gaunt survivors from Phoenix to Albuquerque. During a brief stop at Gallup, New Mexico, those men well enough stepped from the train, dropped to their knees and kissed New Mexico's white sands. Most went on to long convalescent stays at Bruns General Hospital in Santa Fe. On November 13, 1945—"Bataan Day" in New Mexico—the regiment's survivors gathered to celebrate Catholic mass in historic St. Francis Cathedral in downtown Santa Fe. As the service progressed, the regiment's veterans and the families of men killed in the Pacific filled the cathedral with prayers for the souls of those Guardsmen who did not return from World War II.[86]

Conclusions

National Guard units were integral to America's victories in the World Wars. In both conflicts, the Guard divisions were a ready, standing force that deployed soon after the outbreak of hostilities. Without them, America's initial ground response might have taken years instead of months. In total numbers, the clear burden of the fighting in the World Wars fell upon draftees, but the Guard's real contribution was in buying precious time for draftee units to form and train. The 26th and 42nd

Divisions deployed quickly to France in World War I, and the 34th and 32nd Divisions were among the first divisions to go to Europe and the Pacific in World War II. The divisions brought with them experienced officers and enlisted men who often helped to organize other units. Guard divisions bore their share of the fighting, leading the way or battling alongside Regular and draftee divisions. Guardsmen quickly adapted to new technologies including tanks, airplanes, machine guns, rapid-fire artillery, and wheeled vehicles. The divisions' leaders proved they were capable of fighting and coordinating combined arms forces during tough fighting in the Meuse-Argonne, Normandy, and the Philippines.

The Army's handling of Guardsmen during both major mobilizations generated a lingering, institutional bias among State soldiers against Regulars. More than anything else, the Army's release of Guardsmen as individual soldiers rather than units after World War I signaled the deep institutional divide that still existed between the Army and the National Guard. Another epicenter of controversy was the relief and reassignment of Guard officers in favor of Regulars. Clearly, some Guard officers encountered blatant bias from Regulars like General McNair, but at the same time, too many Guard officers were unqualified for command due to advanced age, physical infirmities, poor leadership skills, and a lack of knowledge. At the same time, a number of talented Guard officers, such as General O'Ryan in World War I and Generals McLain and Beightler in World War II, showed that they were equal if not superior to many of their counterparts on active duty. Guardsmen resented the Army's efforts to amalgamate them with active forces during extended active duty. State soldiers complied with the letter of Army regulations in the redesignation of long serving units but retained their identity through the wear of distinctive shoulder patches and insignia. Overall, Guard units tried to retain a distinct style of leadership and administration that reflected prewar State and local ties.

Legislation during the interwar years gained the Guard a permanent place in the defense establishment. The National Defense Act of 1920 settled planning and manpower differences that had dogged Army-Guard relations since 1903 and became one of the most enduring and significant pieces of military legislation in the 20th Century. Congress embraced the idea that to guarantee the readiness of the Army for war, its organization must be established in peace. The Regular Army would be the professional component for a larger, national force of Guardsmen and Reservists and not a cadre or skeleton to be expanded in war. As military policy, the ideas of John McAuley Palmer won out over those of Emory Upton. The act ended the Uptonian notion that large wartime forces should consist of masses of individual, federal reservists led by professional soldiers. In a similar fashion, national conscription during the World Wars forever demolished the concept of volunteer units raised by the States for federal service. The National Guard became the Army's sole, standing combat reserve, and additional legislation in 1933 further clarified the Guard's status in war and peace while strengthening its position in policy matters.

In many ways, the interwar years were the National Guard's Gilded Age. Isolationism, economic hardships, and a paucity of defense dollars made security issues a low priority for most Americans. A new National Guard used the hiatus to dig its roots deeply into local communities and the States. Largely based on the Guard's World War I combat record, citizens came to regard it as a serious, modern military force. The social image of the volunteer militia quickly faded in the public mind. Stability in force structure permitted units to concentrate on training and providing services to their local communities. For the first time in the Guard's history, units maintained waiting lists for men desiring to join, a phenomenon that would not occur again until the 1960s.

Guardsmen came home at the end of World War II knowing that they had helped to secure freedom throughout the world while greatly elevating America's status as a world power. Yet, no one was certain of the shape of the postwar world. The mushroom clouds over Hiroshima and Nagasaki signaled that a new age was at hand, but lingering tensions between democracy and communism suggested that many animosities had survived the war intact. If the World Wars were any indicator, Guardsmen knew they would be square in the middle of any new dangers that emerged.

Part III
The Army National Guard, 1946–2000

CHAPTER 6

The Early Cold War, 1946–1970

W̲e know that the country cannot support a standing Regular Army of sufficient size to perform all essential missions in the early stages of a war of the future. Thus, the existence of trained National Guard units in an adequate state of readiness is vitally essential to the success of our whole program.

Maj. Gen. Manton S. Eddy,
War Department Information Chief,
October 1947

Introduction

Sergeant Herbert R. Temple, Jr. stood in the darkness with other soldiers at the railing of the dilapidated troop transport "Private Joe P. Martinez" awaiting orders to go over the side. Dressed in a long, woolen olive drab overcoat and a helmet, Temple carried a full field pack, extra ammunition, and a rifle. Moments before, the ship had glided into the South Korean port of Inchon loaded with infantry replacements desperately needed on the front lines. In the middle of the night, the port facilities and the entire town were blacked out for protection. The only illumination came from intermittent bursts of orange light low on the distant horizon, the muzzle flashes of American artillery shelling North Korean and Chinese positions. Finally orders came, and the soldiers clambered over the ship's railing, working their way slowly down cargo nets onto the deck of a waiting barge. When the loading was complete, the barge pulled away from the transport and headed for Inchon's docks. Moments later, the replacements stepped onto Korean soil for the first time.

Three years earlier Herbert Temple had been a teenager growing up in post-war Los Angeles when a friend encouraged him to volunteer in the

California National Guard. On June 2, 1947, he enlisted in Headquarters Company, 160th Infantry which was reforming after World War II. A proud Guard infantry regiment with a long history of service, the 160th cherished its motto, "Los Angeles' Own." At first, the young Temple took his military duties casually, but his attitude changed when he was promoted and assigned as the unit supply sergeant. More and more, he spent his free time working at the armory and was finally hired as a full-time unit caretaker. With the outbreak of war in Korea, Sergeant Temple mobilized with California's 40th Infantry Division in September 1950. At first, he was assigned to supply duties in the installation headquarters at Camp Cooke, the 40th Division's mobilization station. Weeks later, Temple received orders assigning him as an individual infantry replacement in Korea. Sergeant Temple had never attended either individual basic or infantry advanced training and only possessed the rudimentary infantry skills he had learned in the California Guard. He made the Pacific passage to Japan on a decrepit freighter and was assigned to the replacement depot of the 25th Infantry Division. After additional training, a group of replacements boarded the "Private Joe P. Martinez" for passage to Korea.

Standing in the pitch black on the dock at Inchon, Sergeant Temple and the others learned to their dismay that they were no longer assigned to the 25th Division. Days before, the 24th Infantry Division had taken heavy casualties and was in dire need of replacements. In the darkness, the heavily burdened soldiers trudged to a waiting train for shipment north to the 24th Division. Sergeant Temple served with Company B, 5th Regimental Combat Team, first as a rifleman and then as a squad leader. During weeks of combat, Herb Temple honed his fighting and survival skills despite serious bouts of malaria and frostbite. At one point, the Army learned that the California Guardsman had not received formal infantry training and offered a new assignment, but Sergeant Temple declined to leave his comrades in Company B. Finally, the 5th Regimental Combat Team pulled off the front lines for much needed rest and refit. While leaving the mountains of Korea, Sergeant Temple vowed to himself that if he was ever in a position of influence that he would do everything possible to ensure that other Guardsmen would never again go into combat without adequate preparation. A simple promise made in Korea turned into a lifelong commitment that motivated Sergeant Temple for decades until he was appointed as CNGB with the rank of lieutenant general in the mid-1980s.

At the dawn of the Nuclear Age, Americans speculated on the new international order emerging from the ashes of World War II. Despite the decisive victories in Europe and Asia, an age of peace seemed improbable. In retrospect, postwar concerns over the world's future were more than justified. No sooner had World War II ended than the U.S. found itself ensnared in a global, ideological struggle with the Soviet Union, China, and their surrogates. Communist challenges came fast and furious. In 1948, the Russians invaded Czechoslovakia and blockaded the land routes to Berlin, forcing the Allies to supply the city with a massive, sustained airlift. The following year, the Soviets exploded their own atomic bomb, and communists took control of the Chinese mainland.

Military planners found few precedents upon which to build a viable, national security strategy for the Cold War. For more than 150 years, the United States had anchored its security on two solid pillars: the defensive barriers of the oceans and the mobilization of mass, citizen-soldier armies. New, nuclear bombers and heightened tensions between East and West negated America's sole reliance on oceanic defenses and large, mobilized armies. The U.S. adapted a strategy of containment against communist expansion along a vaguely defined perimeter that ran through central Europe and Asia. America and its allies fostered the United Nations (UN) for collective security, and at the same time, created regional, defensive alliances all along the length of the global perimeter. Forward deployed land, sea, and air forces guarded the line, backed by long-range, nuclear bombers capable of striking the Soviet homeland. The Army maintained a strong constabulary force in central Europe and an even larger occupation force in Japan. While the anticipated uses of nuclear weapons dominated military thinking, missiles, jet aircraft, helicopters, and other modern weapons changed the face of conventional warfare.

The early challenges of the Cold War prompted the creation of a more modern and ready Army National Guard (ARNG). In the early years of the Cold War, the ARNG fought in two Asian wars, played a key role in defending America against nuclear attack and helped to maintain domestic law and order during periods of social unrest. At the same time, it became a more professional and capable organization by greatly improving training, readiness, and deployability.

Plans for the Postwar Guard

In many ways, the National Guard's status following World War II was determined even before the war began. As Army chief of staff, General Marshall held views and established principles favorable toward the Guard. Marshall was determined to avoid the bitter animosities that had marred Army-Guard relations during and after World War I. Marshall had developed his attitudes toward the Guard during intermittent duty as an inspector and instructor of State soldiers before World War I and throughout the interwar period. A long, close friendship with John

McAuley Palmer enhanced the future chief of staff's broad understanding of citizen-soldiers' strengths and weaknesses. Marshall's last tour with the Guard occurred during 1933–36 when he served as chief of staff of Illinois' 33rd Division. Only three years after leaving the Illinois Guard as a newly promoted brigadier general, Marshall was a full general and Army chief of staff. During World War II, Marshall recognized the Guard's shortcomings but rejected the extreme, anti-Guard views of General McNair and others. He understood that to depend upon citizen-soldiers was to accept in advance a less than ideal level of military preparedness but at a cost acceptable to taxpayers. Marshall favored a prominent position for the Guard in the postwar military establishment based on the National Guard's long tradition of service and its contributions during World War II. To avoid the bickering among Congress, the War Department, and the States that had occurred after World War I, Marshall laid the groundwork for the post-World War II Guard even before the war was won.[1]

Marshall turned to his old friend John McAuley Palmer for help in forging specific plans and policies for the postwar military. Palmer had retired in 1926 as a brigadier general after thirty-seven years of military service. Retreating to the mountains of New Hampshire, Palmer had spent most of his time with his family and indulged himself in writing. In retirement he held fast to his favorable views on citizen-soldiers and became more passionate regarding the need for peacetime UMT. In 1941, the synthesis of Palmer's beliefs appeared in his book *America in Arms*. Because peacetime conscription had already started in 1940, Palmer's advocacy for UMT and the role of the citizen-soldier struck a chord with the public in general and senior military leaders in particular. The CNGB, Maj. Gen. John F. Williams, purchased fifty copies for distribution to selected AGs and Guard division commanders. Subsequently, General Williams invited Palmer to Washington to advise Guard leaders on future defense planning. General Marshall was in the same line of thinking as the CNGB but went one step further. The chief of staff recalled Palmer to active duty and arranged an office for him in a study room in the Library of Congress, an environment conducive to contemplation and free of the War Department's daily turmoil.[2]

Preliminary staff work toward a future defense establishment came to a sudden halt with the attack on Pearl Harbor. Burdened down with the war effort, the Army staff suspended all work on postwar organizations. In March 1942, the War Department rejected the Guard's request to form an Army-Guard planning committee. From observation posts in Washington, DC and around the country, senior Guard officers grew alarmed from 1943 on over the Guard's uncertain future. Their concerns were many. The relief of Guard officers and the random reassignment of infantry regiments freed up by the conversion to the triangular division design smacked of the Army's heavy-handed methods of 1917–1918. The reduction and reassignment of the NGB staff as a subordinate office of the Army Service Forces was interpreted as a sign of things to come. The War Department had raised the ire of Guardsmen by largely excluding Guard representation on key staff groups. The Uptonian views expressed by General McNair were well known, and Guardsmen feared that without fair representation, similar negative sentiments would dominate staff thinking. For Guardsmen wanting to discuss their concerns with a War Department representative, their only recourse was to meet informally with John McAuley Palmer in the Library of Congress building.[3]

Guard leaders remaining in the U.S. agreed that NGAUS should be the focal point for efforts to restore the postwar Guard. In April 1943, a small conference of influential Guard leaders met in Harrisburg, Pennsylvania. Though the conference numbered only sixty-five attendees, it was one of the most significant meetings in National Guard history. The attendees bestowed the presidency of NGAUS upon Maj. Gen. Ellard A. Walsh, the AG of Minnesota who had served in the National Guard since 1905. Walsh had commanded the 34th Division when it entered active federal service in February 1941, but chronic ulcers forced him from command, and he had returned to Minnesota.[4]

Small in stature but vigorous in action, Walsh seemed particularly suited to become the Guard's principal advocate. He held strong opinions in favor of the merits and abilities of Guard soldiers and against those wanting to dismantle the Guard. Based on his own military career of over thirty-five years, Walsh believed the War Department had never overlooked an opportunity "to destroy the National Guard." With great energy and focus, Walsh never missed an opportunity to write or to speak on the Guard's behalf. Walsh's position on the Guard's proper standing after the war was simple; citizen-soldiers who had fought valiantly in Europe and Asia should have full representation in the postwar Army. To make his voice heard in the larger, more bureaucratic Washington, D.C. that resulted from the war effort, Walsh realized that NGAUS needed significant enhancement. With only limited association funds available, he used personal money to place a small, full-time staff in a more presentable NGAUS headquarters in an office building in downtown Washington. A major NGAUS transformation had begun that would continue under Walsh's leadership for fourteen years.[5]

Despite the heavy burdens of coordinating a global war, General Marshall remained keenly aware of the importance of having a blueprint for a postwar military even before hostilities ended. Less than ninety days

Maj. Gen. Ellard A. Walsh
Father of the Modern NGAUS

Ellard A. Walsh was born in Canada in October 1887, and his family moved to Minneapolis, Minnesota while he was still a child. His military career began in 1905 when he enlisted in the 1st Minnesota Infantry. For the next fifty-two years, Walsh served in National Guard leadership positions ranging from squad leader to division commander, Minnesota AG, and president of NGAUS.

Ellard Walsh served in the 1st Minnesota as a first sergeant during the Mexican Border Crisis of 1916, returned home for a month and entered active duty again in April 1917 for World War I. He received an officer's commission in the 135th

National Guard Education Foundation

Infantry and served with the 34th Division in France. After the war, he remained active in the Minnesota Guard, and by 1924 he served as the Assistant AG and chief of staff of the 34th Division. In 1927, Walsh was promoted to brigadier general and appointed as Minnesota's AG, a position he held for forty-two years. His most lasting contribution to the Minnesota National Guard was the acquisition and development of Camp Ripley, a legacy that remains to this day.

After he became AG of Minnesota, Walsh developed into an even stronger advocate of the National Guard, and he served a two-year term as president of NGAUS starting in 1928. In July 1940, he was promoted to major general, became the commander of the 34th Division, and entered active duty with the division in February 1941. However, chronic ulcers disqualified him from command, and he returned to Minnesota and his post as AG. With the entire National Guard on active duty for World War II, Ellard Walsh took an active role in promoting the Guard's long-term interests. In 1943, he was reelected as president of NGAUS, a position he held for fourteen years. Walsh provided the leadership that transferred NGAUS into a premier lobbying organization in Washington, DC with a full-time staff, an imposing headquarters building, and a monthly magazine. He was an articulate, tireless advocate who worked with Congress and the Defense Department to insure that the National Guard retained a prominent role in the nation's defense after World War II and in the early years of the Cold War. In addition to putting NGAUS on a more sure footing, he considered a federal armory building program and military retirement for long serving Guardsmen as his greatest legacies.

Walsh retired from public life in 1957 and returned to Minnesota to spend more time with his family and his hobby of gardening. He died in August 1975 at the age of eighty-seven. Today, the "Walsh-Reckord Hall of States" in the National Guard Memorial in Washington, DC stands as a permanent monument to his tireless efforts in promoting NGAUS and the National Guard.

after Ellard Walsh was elected president of NGAUS, Marshall created a unique War Department staff called the "Special Planning Division." The group became the forum for National Guard leaders and the Army staff to address their various concerns. John McAuley Palmer served as the Special Planning Division's primary advisor and elder statesman. The staff's first achievement occurred in August 1944 with the publication of War Department Circular No. 347 that established the principles for a postwar military establishment. The staff rejected a large standing army that concentrated military planning and policy in a small caste of professional soldiers. Such an army had no place "among the institutions of a modern, democratic state," and the circular boldly reminded its readers that insular, professional armies had thrived in Nazi Germany and Imperial Japan. Instead, the staff favored a mix of Regulars and citizen-soldiers as the basis for the postwar Army.[6] The circular's entries regarding a citizen-soldier army are worth quoting at length:

> The second type of military institution through which the national manpower can be developed is based upon the conception of a professional peace establishment (no larger than necessary to meet normal peacetime requirements) to be reinforced in time of emergency by organized units drawn from a citizen army reserve, effectively organized for this purpose in time of peace; with full opportunity for competent citizen soldiers to acquire practical experience through temporary active service and to rise by successive steps to any rank for which they can definitely qualify; and with specific facilities for such practical experience, qualification, and advancement definitely organized as essential and predominating characteristics of the peace establishment...
>
> And finally, as all of our great wars have been fought in the main by citizen armies, the proposal for an organized citizen army reserve in time of peace is merely a proposal for perfecting a traditional national institution to meet modern requirements which no longer permit extemporization after the outbreak of war. This is the type of army which President Washington proposed to the first Congress as one of the essential foundations of the new American Republic...
>
> Details of military organization change with changes in weapons, modes of transportation, and international relations. But the type of our military institutions was determined in the beginning by the form of our government and has not changed since Washington's Administration. It will therefore be made the basis for all plans for a post-war peace establishment.[7]

Authored by John McAuley Palmer and issued over the signature of George C. Marshall, the policy achieved the chief of staff's objectives regarding Army-Guard relations. The end of World War II would not precipitate a huge, public showdown between Congress, the War Department, the Army and the National Guard over military policy.

Armed with approved principles for a postwar Army, the Special Planning Division went to work to hammer out a viable plan. General Walsh became a critical participant in the deliberations. General Reckord returned to Washington from his wartime duties as the Provost Marshal of the European Theater to help the Army and NGAUS develop a work-

Brig. Gen. John McAuley Palmer, 1945. (Library of Congress)

able plan. Unfortunately, implementation of peacetime conscription and the huge growth of the wartime Army infused the group with unrealistic expectations for the future. Key planning assumptions included a huge, postwar Army and UMT. NGAUS encouraged UMT, viewing it as the best means to infuse Guard units with personnel already trained in the ever increasing, complex tasks of modern warfare.[8]

As a final result of discussions between NGAUS and the Army leadership, the War Department in October 1945 issued a directive that specified the Guard's purpose, mission, and force structure. The National Guard would be "an integral part and a first line Reserve component" of the military. The directive fully acknowledged the Guard's dual nature and clearly identified federal and State missions. The War Department authorized an initial strength of 425,000 enlisted soldiers for NGB to allocate to the States based on the available male population ages 18–35. Unit manning levels were set at 80 percent. Each State was to receive sufficient units for disaster relief and support to civil authorities. The first priority for the rebuilding of the Guard was the activation of eighteen divisions. Second and third priorities were to regimental combat teams (RCT) and antiaircraft artillery (AAA) battalions. Fourth priority for activation was non-divisional combat units and other support units. The

War Department specified that all units of regimental size and below would be stationed within the same State.[9]

Army Demobilization

The greatest victory in U.S. military history resulted in the country's most rapid demobilization. After four years of war, GIs were anxious to come home, and Congress was even more anxious to remove them from the payrolls. Demobilization occurred at a dizzying pace. At the end of World War II, the Army's strength stood at a whopping 8.3 million soldiers and airmen. All together, the Army included eighty-nine combat divisions. By the summer of 1948, the Army's strength had dropped to little more than 550,000 soldiers, and only ten divisions remained on active duty.[10]

The postwar Army was underfunded and stretched far beyond its capabilities. In response to communist threats, the principle mission of the Army's ten active divisions was the occupation of central Europe and the Far East. The 1st Infantry Division, backed up by three armored cavalry regiments (ACRs), garrisoned Germany and Austria. Four under-strength divisions were stationed in Japan, and in all cases except the 1st Division in Germany, all of the Army's major combat units were severely below strength. In Japan, several combat battalions were unmanned with their weapons, vehicles, and equipment placed in storage. To make matters worse, the day-to-day demands of rebuilding and maintaining order in war ravaged countries made unit training nearly impossible.[11]

Instead of returning entire units home from overseas after World War II, the Army implemented a system of individual rotation based on the accumulation of points for the length and types of duty each soldier had performed. Veterans with the highest point totals were consolidated into units for early shipment home. As happened at the end of World War I, Guardsmen left active duty with individual discharge papers in hand. Guardsmen returning home in 1945 had been in active, continuous service since the mobilization of 1940, and their State enlistments had expired. Legally, the Army could not have returned Guard units to the States because prewar Guardsmen were free of any obligation to serve and draftees filled the ranks of many units. Until the War Department and NGB determined the allocation of units to the States, the Army retained the colors of Guard units that had served during the war.[12]

The National Guard Rebuilds, 1946–1947

Assuming that Congress would pass some sort of UMT legislation and not dramatically slash defense budgets, the War Department drafted plans for a peacetime Army of 1.4 million men. The National Guard received authorization for nearly 655,000 personnel, though based on demographics, the NGB staff estimated only 425,000 enlisted men would volunteer for service. Bolstered by the efforts of NGAUS and guided by new War Department policies, the NGB staff began the difficult tasks of defining the Guard's postwar organization and allocating units to the States. Plans called for the National Guard to include twenty-five infantry divisions, two armored divisions, twenty-one RCTs, and hundreds of other separate companies and battalions.[13]

The first postwar National Guard unit, the 120th Fighter Squadron from Colorado, received federal recognition on June 30, 1946. Thereafter, the Guard's reorganization was rapid and widespread. By the end of the first year of reconstitution, personnel strength stood at 97,526 soldiers organized into 2,615 units. Nearly two-thirds of volunteers were World War II veterans. Unlike after World War I when the Guard reconstituted from the bottom up, the advance planning by the War Department allowed the establishment of major commands followed by the organization of subordinate units. Officers seeking positions in new units often discovered that enough billets were not available commensurate with the rank they had attained during the war. Many took reductions in rank to serve in the Guard. As a result, a dedicated cadre of combat experienced officers emerged to lead the Guard for nearly twenty years.[14]

Early recruiting efforts reflected the Guard's strong ties with communities and among family members. In Batavia, New York, the commander of Battery B, 72nd AAA Gun Battalion must have set an all time recruiting record. Over a four day period he completed his battery's organization by enlisting 117 officers and men. (There was a great irony here—Batavia was Emory Upton's hometown.) In Chicago, the five Plum brothers, who together had seventeen years of combat experience in World War II, enlisted in Company H, 129th Infantry to form the core of the unit's noncommissioned officer leadership. In New Mexico, eleven pairs of father-sons enlisted in a single antiaircraft battalion. In Pennsylvania, the Provost Marshal of the 28th Infantry Division proudly enlisted his nephew and two sons-in-law in the 28th Military Police Company. At the armory of Headquarters Company, 1/117th Infantry in Henderson, Tennessee, the five Orr brothers arrived on the first night of post-World War II drill to volunteer in the Tennessee Guard. And in Baltimore, Maryland, Mrs. George Bailey lined up her five sons in the family parlor for uniform inspection before they went off to drill with Company D, 175th Infantry of the 29th Infantry Division.[15]

Veterans' Day 1946 was a particularly significant day in the Guard's history. On November 11, 1946 the Army returned to the States the guidons and battle flags of National Guard units that had fought in World War II. In huge, military ceremonies and galas held in forty-five States, Hawaii, and Puerto Rico, the National Guard's revered battle flags passed from active Army color guards into the waiting hands of Guardsmen. Officials held colorful and impressive parades around the State capitols as radio stations broadcast the ceremonies. At Arlington National Cemetery, President Harry S Truman laid a memorial wreath at the Tomb of the Unknown Soldier, and in comments afterwards, marked the day's significance:

> It is my pleasure this morning symbolically
> to hand back the colors of the National Guard in the
> various states. It gives me a great deal of pleasure
> to do that. I was a National Guardsman myself in
> the First World War...
> I return these colors to the National Guard.
> I hope they will use them to train young men in
> the interests of peace and the welfare of the country.
> And I am sure they will do just that.[16]

The Armed Forces Reorganize

The many incidents of interservice rivalry during World War II and the new demands of the Cold War prompted a major reorganization of America's defense establishment. Senior civilian and military leaders wanted increased cooperation between the armed services to counter a growing communist threat. The National Security Act of 1947 created a National Military Establishment in the Executive Branch. At the Pentagon, the position of Secretary of Defense (SECDEF) was created to coordinate the efforts of the armed forces. Three military departments—Army, Navy, and the newly created Air Force—were established with their own service secretaries and staffs. Subsequent legislation in 1949 renamed the National Military Establishment to the Department of Defense (DOD), strengthened the powers of the SECDEF and created the new position of Chairman, JCS (CJCS). In that same year, the U.S. banded with the European powers to form the North Atlantic Treaty Organization (NATO), a collective security arrangement to deter Soviet aggression against western Europe.[17]

The National Security Act of 1947 had an immediate and dramatic impact on the National Guard. With the creation of a new Air Force, the legislation charged NGB to become the channel of communications between the Department of the Air Force and the States on all matters pertaining to the Air National Guard. Prior to 1947, the coordination of air activities had been the responsibility of an "Aviation Group" in NGB. On October 1, 1948, the modern NGB headquarters came into being. CNGB retained several staff sections to coordinate legislative concerns, public affairs, the budget, and other administrative functions. Army and Air Divisions, both under the direction of National Guard major generals, handled matters for their respective services. The first chief of the Army Division was Maj. Gen. Raymond H. Fleming, a thirty-two year Guard veteran who had served continuously as Louisiana's AG since 1928. To maintain positive control over the expanding ARNG, Fleming had a staff of several dozen civilians and forty-one officers—a mix of Regular, Guard, and ORC—organized into staff groups responsible for organization and training, budget, personnel, plans, and logistics.[18]

While the Truman Administration reorganized the country's defense establishment, Congress addressed peacetime manpower. As World War II drew to a close, the War Department stated its support for UMT, arguing that the National Guard and the Organized Reserves together had not met wartime manpower requirements. President Truman and a number of congressmen endorsed UMT in principle, but specific proposals floundered. In Congress, legislators paid more attention to unification matters, frowned upon the projected costs of peacetime UMT and more and more came to favor a continuation of the draft rather than creating a new program. Tired of more than fifteen years of Depression and global war, the American people wanted to enjoy peace and prosperity without further obligations to the government. Indeed, many Americans believed the era of industrialized, mass armies was over; conventional air power and the atomic bomb would surely decide the outcome of future wars. UMT eventually died from neglect on Capitol Hill, and Congress extended the Selective Service Act of 1940 through March 1947. However, the Berlin airlift prompted a revival of the draft, and in June 1948, a new selective service act went into effect calling for the drafting of all males 19–26 years of age. A number of exemptions were allowed, including those who were veterans or already members of the Guard or reserves.[19]

Like the Guard, the Army's Organized Reserves had to rebuild from the ground up. By January 1946, more than half of the Reserve officers who had served in World War II had accepted commissions in the ORC. Two years after the war, ORC strength stood at 274,839 officers. The War Department authorized the activation of nearly 6,800 officer cadre units with only fifty-nine units manned at full strength. Recruitment for the ERC went much better than during the interwar years. By June 1948, ERC strength stood at 467,608 soldiers. However, the lack of positions for enlisted men in Reserve cadre units prompted the War Department to assign Reserve soldiers to a huge manpower pool. The amorphous manpower reservoir very nearly resembled Emory Upton's recommendation for organizing a federal reserve, but the pool's effectiveness during wartime remained uncertain.[20]

Late in 1947, the first SECDEF, James Forrestal, chartered a special board to examine the best use of the country's reserve forces. The recent unification of the armed forces prompted inquiries from several quarters regarding the amalgamation of the National Guard and the Reserves. ORC leaders argued that there was no longer any need for federally supported State troops and that the merging of the Guard and Reserves would produce military and fiscal efficiencies. Headed by Gordon Gray, the assistant secretary of the army, the board concluded that the National Guard system, with its dual federal and State allegiances, was not adequate for the needs of the Cold War. In addition, board members discerned that the more tightly controlled units in the Organized Reserve might be more prepared for national crises than Guardsmen. As a result, the Gray Board recommended the merging of the National Guard and the Reserves into a force directly under federal control with the name "National Guard of the United States." Senior Guard leaders and NGAUS fought the proposal with all of their energy. Ellard Walsh labeled the Gray Board findings as "just another effort over a long period of time by the War Department and the Regular establishment to supplant the National Guard system with a Federal Reserve or Militia." In the end, NGAUS successfully appealed to Congress who quickly dismissed the Gray Board's findings.[21]

Final Growth of the ARNG, 1948–1950

Under the supervision of a reinvigorated NGB headquarters and the AGs, the ARNG continued to expand and develop. In 1948, the ARNG experienced its greatest increases ever in personnel and units. By 1948, 288,427 Army Guardsmen were organized into 4,646 federally recognized units. In the summer of that year, units conducted large-scale field training for the first time since the mobilization of 1940. As reorganization and training continued at a steady clip, units drew equipment from excess World War II stocks or received equipment NGB had purchased from the Army's technical services. Within two years, the ARNG reached a peak strength of nearly 325,000 soldiers. Twenty-one States and Hawaii had completed their reorganizations by 1950. Forty-two States founded their own military academies where 3,000 officer candidates were in training. The organization of twenty-seven divisions and twenty RCTs was complete, and seven new ACRs were in the process of forming. During summer field exercises in 1950, all of the ARNG divisions trained as complete units. In addition, 14,551 civilian employees supported the ARNG throughout the States in positions as clerks, accountants, and caretakers at armories, training sites, and maintenance shops.[22]

During postwar reorganization, the greatest impediment to rebuilding the ARNG—other than recruitment—was a lack of adequate facilities. Most of the armories and buildings that had housed the Guard prior to World War II were unable to accommodate greater numbers of more modern combat units. At the local level, ARNG leaders improvised to provide roofs over their units. Soldiers moved into the attics and cellars of courthouses, schools, and other public buildings. In one town, a persuasive Guard officer convinced a local banker to secure his unit's ammunition in the local bank vault. The infusion of tanks, half-tracks and trucks required storage and maintenance facilities that were beyond the ability of the States to provide. In Hastings, Nebraska, Capt. Francis S. Greenlief did not have enough room to park the 2 1/2 ton trucks assigned to his Company G, 134th Infantry. The future CNGB took the trucks home and parked them in front of his house even though their weight eventually damaged his driveway.[23]

In 1950, Congress enacted legislation that called for federal assistance for new armory construction for all reserve components. For the Guard, the States had to contribute 25 percent of construction costs, provide the necessary real estate, equipment, and furnishings and defray all maintenance and operations costs. In addition, Congress authorized the SECDEF to allocate funds to the States for the expansion and repair of the ARNG's 2,316 existing armories. Despite the legislators' good intentions, two years passed before Congress appropriated money for new armories.[24]

A new wave of armory construction began in 1952 that had a profound affect on the ARNG. With an appropriation of $16 million, new brick, steel and glass armories based on standard, approved designs for single and multiple units began to appear across the country. The first, postwar armory was completed in Arizona in 1952, and by the end of the following year, sixty-six additional armories were under construction. The new armories were a radical departure from previous experience; large, vaulted drill halls and castellated designs became a sign of the past. Guardsmen no longer looked upon armories as places for unit meetings or social events. While armories did continue to support community activities, they increasingly became fully equipped training centers. The postwar Guard was no longer primarily an infantry force, and new training regimes addressed the increasingly complex training requirements of mechanized and support forces. Tank turret trainers, sub-caliber devices for mortars and bazookas and a wide range of training aides appeared on drill floors. Builders installed power connectors that provided electric power to radios for use during civil emergencies and command post exercises.[25]

While the States worked to rebuild their units, NGAUS focused on obtaining a new, significant benefit for all Guardsmen: military retirement. Ellard Walsh and Milton Reckord combined their legislative skills to get a National Guard retirement provision enacted into law on June 29, 1948. The law established a modest system of retirement benefits for Guardsmen who had served for twenty years and had reached sixty years of age. A point system was created to establish eligibility based on years of service. Retiree pay was calculated and capped at 75 percent using the annual base pay of the highest grade held. The law gave all Guardsmen retirement credit for service dating back to the 1916 Mexican Border mobilization, and in 1953, Congress amended the law to include all Guard service since 1903.[26]

The Korean War, 1950–1953

On the morning of June 25, 1950, America awoke to the shocking news that a 90,000-man North Korean army had launched a sudden, massive invasion against South Korea. Americans compared North Korea's actions to the surprise attack on Pearl Harbor and wondered how the fighting on the Korean peninsula would change their lives. Within days, President Truman announced his intention to commit American land, sea, and air forces as part of a broader UN effort to blunt the communist attack. The U.S. 24th Infantry Division immediately sent reinforcements from Japan to assist the hard pressed South Korean Army in stopping the communists. Unfortunately, the 24th Division was unprepared for battle. Its earliest combat actions resulted in the division commander's capture and the ruin of "Task Force Smith," a name that in U.S. military annals has become synonymous with defeat due to unpreparedness. Despite their best efforts, the South Koreans and U.S. reinforcements were unable to stop the communists. By late summer, American and South Korean units, now under the overall UN command of Douglas MacArthur, were backed into a defensive perimeter surrounding the port city of Pusan at the southern tip of the Korean peninsula.

The magnitude of the crisis in Korea, coupled with the determination of the UN and President Truman to punish communist aggression, resulted in a broadening of the war effort. Within a month of the North Korean attack, it was clear that additional forces were needed. In an address to the nation on July 19th, President Truman announced a partial mobilization of Guardsmen and Reservists for twenty-one months. Three days later, NGB received notice that many of the ARNG's 325,000 soldiers would be mobilized, and the first units called to active, federal service reported to their armories on August 14th. In a reflection of the anxiety of the period, NGAUS canceled its annual conference scheduled for late September in Houston.[27]

As Guardsmen prepared for deployment, the Korean crisis depleted their resources. Because active Army units needed additional space and facilities to prepare individual replacements and units for deployment to Korea, the ARNG was denied or given only limited access to eight major training sites. The heaviest burden was the transfer of equipment to units headed for Asia. In the summer of 1950, the ARNG possessed only 46 percent of its authorized equipment, but the need for weapons, vehicles, and equipment in Korea overrode all other considerations. The Guard turned over 748 tanks, 5,595 tactical vehicles, and 95 light aircraft. Within the year, the ARNG had surrendered nearly one-quarter of its equipment, prompting CNGB to report that equipment transfers resulted in "training limitations" for Guard units attempting to prepare for service in Korea.[28]

In August and September 1950, thousands of Army Guardsmen reported for active duty. The lion's share of soldiers came from four infantry divisions; the 28th (Pennsylvania), the 40th (California), the 43rd (Connecticut, Rhode Island, and Vermont), and the 45th (Oklahoma). In addition, hundreds of separate combat, combat support, and combat service support units were mobilized. By the summer of 1951, nearly 110,000 ARNG soldiers in 1,457 units were on active duty.[29]

A significant number of ARNG units deployed very quickly to Korea. The 936th Field Artillery Battalion from Arkansas was the first ARNG unit to enter combat in Korea. Armed with towed, 155-mm. howitzers, the battalion entered active duty on August 21, 1950 and transferred to Camp Carson, Colorado for five months of training. The Arkansans embarked from California and arrived at Pusan on February 10, 1951. The 936th Field Artillery fired its first round against the Communists on March 29th while supporting the U.S. 7th Infantry Division during the counterattack to restore the 38th Parallel. In 100 days of heavy fire support to the U.S. I Corps, the Arkansas artillerymen fired a staggering 50,000 rounds, approximately one-third of the shells they had fired during 500 days of combat in World War II.[30]

Though the early crisis in Korea required a large and immediate response, it was evident to senior civilian and military leaders that a total, national mobilization was not necessary. This attitude was particularly prevalent after the stunning reversal of fortunes in Korea following MacArthur's successful landing at Inchon on September 15th. In a matter of days, the North Koreans were in headlong retreat, the bitter defeats of late summer faded in memory, and the most optimistic soldiers believed the war would be over by year's end. In November 1950, NGAUS held the position that the fighting in Korea was essentially the responsibility of active forces which "might necessitate" the call up of "certain elements" of the ARNG and other reserve components. General Walsh argued that full mobilization might affect the economy, and he feared that too many ARNG units would be mobilized only to sit in their armories for extended periods. However, the Chinese Communist counterattack in late 1950 and the headlong retreat of UN forces back below the 38th Parallel created an international crisis. On December 15th, President Truman declared a national emergency, and China's entry into the war changed the expectation that ARNG units would not go overseas.[31]

A nation accustomed to full mobilizations and clear cut, absolute objectives during two World Wars now fought a war under the spectrum of the nuclear umbrella that was to be limited in scope, duration, and outcome. As an alternative to full manpower mobilization, planners settled on a personnel rotation policy based on the use of Regulars, Guardsmen, Army Reservists, and draftees as individual replacements. In simplest terms, the Army maintained a rather constant group of units in Korea through which it rotated combatants and support personnel. All together, the United States sustained eight fighting divisions in Korea—seven Army and one Marine—with the ARNG providing two of the Army's seven divisions. Though a controversial policy, the reasons for rotating soldiers were compelling. The army wanted to avoid the chronic combat exhaustion casualties suffered during World War II by limiting a soldier's time in battle. A strong desire existed to spread the burden of fighting among all available manpower and to minimize the burden placed on World War II veterans. An elaborate point system developed that determined a soldier's eligibility for rotation home from Korea, though the service of most Guardsmen on active duty was determined by the president's call up of twenty-one months that was extended to twenty-four months in July 1951.[32]

The effects of the limited mobilization and rotation policies on the ARNG were immediate and widespread. Guard leaders reluctantly adjusted to partial mobilization. In April 1951, the AGs argued for a phased mobilization of the entire ARNG so units could better plan and prepare for mobilization and deployment. They also demanded unit integrity; ARNG units were to be mobilized and returned to the States without being broken up. However, the Army's rotation policy carried the day. From the very beginning of the mobilization, large numbers of units lost

A 155-mm. howitzer from Arkansas' 937th Field Artillery lights up the cold, Korean night during a fire mission on February 21, 1951. (National Archives)

over half of their most experienced officer and enlisted leaders for quick deployment to Korea. As a result, a significant number of Guardsmen served in Korea as individual replacements. Wholesale stripping of units severely tested morale among Guardsmen who had been promised they would serve and fight with men from their own communities. Army training evaluators angered senior ARNG leaders by declaring stripped units unready for combat.[33]

ARNG units called up for Korea fulfilled three important missions. First, Guard units deployed to Korea served in combat, combat support, and combat service support roles. A second, important mission of the ARNG was to bolster NATO. Constabulary forces in Germany had been drained of personnel for Korea, and it fell to Guardsmen to deter against a feared Soviet attack in central Europe. Similarly, the Army's strategic reserve in the U.S. had been depleted, and mobilized ARNG units replenished the strategic reserve while acting as training and replacement depots for individual soldiers going to and from Korea.

The service of the eight ARNG divisions illustrates the missions Guardsmen performed. The 40th and 45th Divisions were selected for service in Korea, and after extensive post-mobilization training in the continental United States (CONUS) and Japan, entered combat in early 1952. The 28th and 43rd Divisions went to Europe in the fall of 1951, taking up defensive positions in central and southern Germany. Four more infantry divisions were called out in January 1952 to support the strategic reserve; the 31st (Alabama and Mississippi), the 37th (Ohio), the 44th (Illinois), and the 47th (Minnesota and North Dakota). The 31st Division remained on active duty at Fort Jackson, South Carolina while the 37th Division went to Fort Polk, Louisiana and the 47th Division trained at Camp Rucker in Alabama. In anticipation of possible service in Korea, the 44th Division deployed to California for post-mobilization training.[34]

The service of California's 40th Division was not much different from the experiences of most ARNG units. On August 1, 1950, the "Sunshine" Division received notification that it was to be ordered to active duty. The 40th Division was among the first divisions called for several reasons. The Army leadership desired to mobilize major ARNG combat units from across the nation, and with the 28th and 43rd Divisions coming from the East coast and the 45th Division from the heartland, it became necessary to call up a western combat unit. Of the divisions available in the West, the 40th Division in southern California had the highest readiness. The division also had recent service in Korea. After the Japanese surrender in 1945, it had assumed occupation duties in Korea and did not return to the United States until April 1946, the last Guard division to leave active duty in World War II.[35]

On August 22, 1950, an advance party of 185 officers and enlisted men from the 40th Division entered active service and began preparations for mobilizing the entire division. On September 1st, the division received orders to mobilize, and by the end of the day, 9,461 Guardsmen had reported to their armories. This still left the division more than 9,000 men short of its authorized wartime strength of 18,600. As the rank and file moved through in-processing stations at their armories, plans unfolded to move the entire division to its post-mobilization training site at Camp Cooke, 130 miles up the coast from Los Angeles and the present-day location of Vandenburg Air Force Base. Camp Cooke had been abandoned after 1946 and reflected the neglect of the military after World War II. Though the wood plank barracks were dirty but livable, thieves had stripped the buildings of all telephone lines and plumbing fixtures that had to be replaced.[36]

After the division consolidated at Camp Cooke, it began a twenty-eight week training program. Unfortunately, training had just started when the division lost many of its World War II veterans, who shipped out immediately to Korea as individual replacements. At about the same time, hundreds of new soldiers—nearly all draftees with no training whatsoever—arrived at Camp Cooke to bring the division to full strength. Between October 1950 and February 1951, 14,273 recruits joined the division. Once again, the division was stripped of experienced soldiers for duty in Korea. The constant flow of men entering and leaving caused severe training problems. All new draftees had to receive basic training as well as schooling in their combat specialties. The 40th Division was compelled to run several basic and advanced individual training cycles instead of division exercises. Though the number of prewar Guardsmen in the division had diminished, enough remained to give it a distinct California, citizen-soldier identity.[37]

In March 1951, the 40th Division shipped out for Japan and its new home at a training site near Yokohama in the shadow of Mt. Fuji. With the initial training of it new soldiers completed, the Sunshine Division concentrated solely on preparing for war. For the first time, the division trained as a single unit. The infantry practiced offensive and defensive maneuvers as well as amphibious landings and cold weather training. The division artillery, which had only limited training at Camp Cooke, spent many days and nights in live fire training. By the close of 1951, the Army rated the division ready for combat.[38]

In dire need of manpower to support the war of attrition taking place in the mountains and along the ridgelines of central Korea, the 160th Infantry received orders to move to Korea immediately and to begin the relief of the 24th Division. By January 12, 1952, the 160th Infantry was in Korea, and two days later, the regiment occupied bunkers and trenches manned by soldiers of the 24th Division. Within a week, the 40th Division suffered its first battle death when mortar shell fragments killed Sergeant First Class Kenneth Kaiser, a Guardsman from Los Angeles. The division's main body soon followed the 160th to Korea, landing at Inchon on February 4th. Each unit quickly moved to the front by truck, and within eleven days, the Sunshine Division had completed the relief of the 24th Division without incident. Much to the chagrin of the California Guardsmen, they had left their heavy weapons and equipment behind in Japan to fall in on the 24th Division's battle worn vehicles and weapons.[39]

The 40th Division quickly took up the routines of trench warfare. The men occupied bunkers and trenches situated along the crests of ridgelines. Occasionally, engagements broke out along the lines as Americans, Chinese, and North Koreans fought to gain a slight advantage in their sector. Artillery duels were common and often resulted in significant casualties on both sides. The infantry mounted frequent trench raids in an effort to bag prisoners for questioning. The soldiers manned their positions during long days and bitter nights of sub-zero temperature and were rotated to the rear on a regular basis for hot food, showers, and a comfortable rest.[40]

In less than a month, the first group of Guardsmen became eligible for rotation back to the United States and discharge from active duty. In twenty-one months, the division members had mobilized and trained for war only to find them ready to return home. On March 15, 1952, nearly 5,400 Guardsmen were still in the division, and nearly 400 of them departed before the end of the month, their service in the Korean War finished. Over the next three months, all of the Guardsmen who did not voluntarily extend their tours returned home. A few Guard volunteers stayed with the division through tough fighting until the end of the war and the division's inactivation in June 1954.[41]

Individual Guardsmen returning home from active duty often discovered they did not have a State unit to join. The Army and NGB agreed to expand the organization of ARNG units on active duty to permit the retention of Guardsmen returning home. The ARNG activated new units in each State that carried the same designation as Guard units on active duty but added the suffix "NGUS" to designate the redundant State units. This unorthodox solution permitted a Guardsman from the 28th Division returning home from Germany to join a unit of the 28th Division (NGUS) at his home armory in Pennsylvania. All together, the ARNG created 1,384 NGUS units that accommodated returning Guardsmen and at the same time provided forces to meet the needs of the Governors. Over time, all Guardsmen returned home, and ARNG units were released from federal control and returned to the States. By 1955, the ARNG had inactivated all of its NGUS units.[42]

Though peace negotiations between communist and UN forces had started at Panmunjon in November 1951, the war of attrition dragged on until the signing of an armistice in July 1953. The opposing sides ceased fire and held their positions with loaded weapons, creating the conditions of an uneasy peace that have not changed significantly since the signing of the armistice. In 1954, six of the eight ARNG Divisions were released from active duty, and the ARNG's involvement in the war ended in February 1956 when the last four units on active duty returned to State control. By the end of the war, 138,600 Army Guardsmen organized into 1,698 units of company or detachment size—approximately 33 percent of the ARNG—had answered the call to arms.[43]

The Korean mobilization remains one of the ARNG's most significant achievements after World War II. Despite problems caused by partial mobilization and individual soldier rotation, the ARNG performed several key functions. Guard units provided the means for rapid expansion of the Army to a larger, wartime posture. ARNG units served around the globe, from the defense of NATO to combat operations in Korea. Four ARNG divisions remained in strategic reserve, acting as a training base and an insurance policy against further communist aggression. In addition, the Guardsmen who did not serve on active duty remained a ready reserve of untapped manpower available for both domestic and overseas employment. However, the continuation of the peacetime draft after World War II provided the bulk of the manpower for the Korean War and reduced the Army's reliance on the ARNG as an important combat reserve. Near the end of the war, Army Chief of Staff General J. Lawton Collins wrote to the Governors expressing his "heartfelt gratitude" for the "magnificent service" of ARNG units and stating that Guardsmen had added "another brilliant chapter" to their long history.[44]

Important Developments After Korea

The most significant, strategic result of the Korean War was to strengthen America's defenses for the long-term prosecution of the Cold War. Reversing the neglect of conventional ground forces that had occurred after World War II, the Army saw improvements in all of its components. While the active Army expanded to fifteen divisions, the ARNG increased its strength to nearly 405,000 soldiers by 1956. Combat in Korea and increasing concerns over a Soviet blitzkrieg in Europe convinced the Army to add heavier units to its force structure. The ARNG activated nine ACRs and converted four infantry divisions to armored divisions, giving it a mix of twenty-one infantry and six armored divisions. The helicopter had proven its worth in Korea, and in April 1953, the first ARNG helicopter was issued to the Alabama Guard. In subsequent years, the numbers of helicopters in the ARNG increased, though a lack of pilots and maintenance personnel constrained the growth of aviation units.[45]

The Korean War mobilization led to renewed congressional interest in the reserve components and to the passage of the Armed Forces Reserve Act of 1952. The legislation's overall intent was to consolidate many of the existing laws regarding the reserve components and to establish in greater detail the composition, responsibilities, and regulations of the Guard and reserves. The law formally specified the seven categories of reserve component forces with the ARNG placed in the highest order of precedence. The ORC and the ERC were discontinued, and the Army's Organized Reserves were renamed the U.S. Army Reserve (USAR). Congress established three levels of reserves: Ready, Standby, and Retired. The Ready Reserve consisted of all units and individuals liable for active service in case of war or a national emergency while Standby and Retired Reserve members were subject to involuntary recall only by Congressional action.[46]

After the Korean War, Congress set out to organize and consolidate all laws pertaining to the branches of the federal government. In August 1956, Congress created Title 10, U.S. Code to contain all laws pertaining to federal military forces. Title 10 legislation included all laws governing the employment and administration of the Regular Army, those ARNG soldiers serving in a full-time, federal status and all Guardsmen ordered to active duty during national emergencies. Later that same year, Congress created Title 32, U.S. Code that consolidated all laws governing the administration and regulations of the National Guard while in State service. The chapters of Title 32 addressed topics including organization, personnel, training, service, supply, and procurement. Since 1956, Regulars and citizen-soldiers have recognized Title 10 as the federal government's responsibilities toward active duty forces while Title 32 pertains to State obligations in the national defense.[47]

Several important changes within the ARNG resulted in a training renaissance. The Korean mobilization highlighted the shortfall of an Army practice that had endured for nearly 200 years—unit basic training for recruits. The need for combat units manned with fully trained soldiers who could respond immediately to Cold War crises prompted the active Army to initiate a system of centralized basic training for all soldiers. Legislation passed in 1955 required Guardsmen and Reservists to attend basic training on active Army installations. For the first time, individual Guardsmen entered active duty for extended training periods. In 1956, 4,400 Guardsmen attended an eight-week basic training program while another 3,600 Guardsmen received advanced, individual training.[48]

Free of the burden of imbuing new soldiers with fundamental skills, ARNG leaders sought larger blocks of time that would allow them to conduct unit training. In September 1955, CNGB authorized the substitution of two paid, four-hour assemblies conducted on a single calendar day for two, regular two-hour armory drill assemblies. Subsistence funds were made available to feed Guardsmen during the new eight-hour drill periods. Many units used multiple drills to increase the limited number of available training hours. For the first time, Guardsmen drilled on the weekends rather than during the traditional, week-night periods. By the end of 1958, 16 percent of the ARNG drilled on weekends, though NGB did not mandate weekend drill until 1966. For the first time, the American people began to refer to Guardsmen as "weekend warriors."[49]

With more time to train, ARNG units honed their skills at the squad and platoon level. In the parlance of the day, Guardsmen referred to collective training as "unit basic training." Aware that the ARNG was free from the burden for individual basic training and had more hours available for training, the Army altered the ARNG's training goals. In

October 1958, the Army declared that the focus of ARNG training would be at the unit level, "starting at squads or comparable unit" and progressing to "larger units." Thus, over a three-year period, the ARNG's training plans changed from two-hour drill periods on week nights that focused on individual soldier skills to extended, weekend drill periods aimed at unit training.[50]

In October 1957, an era of National Guard leadership came to an end with the retirement of Ellard Walsh as NGAUS president. Before his departure, Walsh put into motion the construction of a new National Guard Memorial Building at One Massachusetts Avenue in Washington, DC that was dedicated two years later in ceremonies presided over by former President Truman. The closing minutes of the NGAUS General Conference in Louisville, Kentucky on October 4, 1957 were particularly memorable. While the attendees expected to see General Walsh retire that day, they were not ready for the sensational news that rocked the entire Western world that morning: the Soviets had put the first space satellite into orbit. The launch of Sputnik and the end of Walsh's NGAUS presidency marked the beginning of an era of increased missions and high technology for the ARNG.[51]

Missile Age Minutemen

Before the outbreak of the Korean War, the Truman Administration had undertaken a comprehensive review of America's defense strategy. An outcome of the process was the recognition of growing Soviet nuclear capabilities. The administration believed that by 1954 the Russians would possess a substantial, long-range bomber fleet capable of delivering a widespread nuclear attack against America's centers of population and industry. Suddenly, the defense of the American homeland became a top priority.

The Air Force created the Air Defense Command in 1951 to develop an integrated defensive system of interceptors, antiaircraft artillery, missiles, and radar early warning. As a counterpart to Air Defense Command, the Army Air Defense Command (ARADCOM) became responsible for the placement and functioning of antiaircraft sites around strategic locations throughout CONUS. ARADCOM's plan called for the perimeter defense of the northeastern U.S. and a point defense of key areas in the Midwest and on the West coast. The defense zones integrated short and long-range air defense weapons and antici-pated the use of missile technology still in development. ARADCOM designated the antiaircraft battalions assigned to its air defense plans as the "Special Security Force."[52]

By May 1953, all ARNG AAA battalions mobilized for the Korean War were released from active duty to prepare for the CONUS defense mission. Battalions were authorized to recruit 100 percent of their officers and 75 percent of their enlisted strength in anticipation of joining the Special Security Force. ARADCOM plans called for the employment of ninety ARNG AAA battalions in CONUS. In 1954, the 340th AAA Gun Battalion (120-mm.) of the District of Columbia ARNG took up a firing position outside of Washington, the first ARNG unit to participate in CONUS defense. Within a year, fifty ARNG AAA batteries were deployed, and 105 ARNG AAA batteries eventually served in the Special Security Force.[53]

The CONUS air defense mission was a major change for the ARNG. For the first time, units in a State status were assigned a full-time, federal mission. In an arrangement worked out by ARADCOM, ARNG air defense units were instantly ordered to active duty whenever an enemy air threat appeared. To meet the requirements for round-the-clock preparedness, fifteen Guard technicians manned each battery-sized site on a full-time basis. Upon alert, all members of the unit reported directly to their battle stations from homes and work places. Not since the colonial minutemen had Guardsmen been called upon to make such a sudden transition from peace to war.[54]

New missile technology radically altered the ARNG's role in the Special Security Force. In May 1954, the Army fielded the first NIKE missile battery at Fort Meade, Maryland. Named for the winged, Greek goddess of victory, NIKE was a radar controlled, antiaircraft rocket designed to protect large areas from bomber attack. The NIKE-AJAX missile, with a range of twenty-five miles and a ceiling of 70,000 feet, carried a high explosive fragmentation warhead. While active Army gun batteries trained to convert to NIKE-AJAX, ARNG AAA battalions assumed their defensive roles.[55]

California's 720th Missile Battalion became the ARNG's first NIKE-AJAX unit in June 1957. Stationed at Long Beach, the battalion's mission was the area defense of Navy facilities and aircraft production plants. After an extensive training period of nearly a year, the 720th became operational on September 14, 1958. To man its four NIKE-AJAX sites full-time, the battalion relied upon 191 technicians. The 720th's commander, Lt. Col. Julian A. Phillipson, was a typical Guard officer of the period. Phillipson had enlisted in the California Guard in 1933 and entered active duty as a first lieutenant during the mobilization of 1940. During World War II, he fought in the Pacific and rejoined the California Guard in 1947 where he served in a number of command and staff positions. Command of the 720th Missile Battalion was Phillipson's third battalion command.[56]

Sergeant Earl Pritchard inspects a NIKE-AJAX missile in 1964 at one of the missile sites manned by the Virginia ARNG. (Virginia National Guard Historical Collection)

The success of the 720th Missile Battalion in manning its NIKE-AJAX sites set the precedent for an extension of the ARNG's participation in the missile defense program. By 1961, eighty-two ARNG NIKE-AJAX batteries were operational in fifteen States. At the program's peak in 1962, 17,000 Guardsmen—including some 4,936 technicians—manned missile sites. As early as 1958, the Army began to replace NIKE-AJAX with the NIKE-HERCULES, a missile of increased speed, range, ceiling, and payload. In 1962, the first ARNG air defense units received the NIKE-HERCULES in Hawaii where the missile's increased capabilities seemed ideal for the protection of the high concentration of U.S. military facilities on Oahu. By 1964, the NIKE-AJAX was retired, fully replaced by the NIKE-HERCULES. Under pressure to provide soldiers for an escalating military presence in Southeast Asia, the Army handed more and more missile sites over to the ARNG. At the peak of the NIKE-HERCULES program, Army Guardsmen manned forty-eight of the 112 NIKE-HERCULES sites defending CONUS.[57]

By the early 1970s, changes in the strategic situation resulted in the elimination of the NIKE-HERCULES program. Intelligence estimates in the late 1960s put less emphasis on the significance of Soviet bombers.

Instead, the Soviets were developing intercontinental ballistic missiles and threatening to take the lead in the construction and deployment of heavy missiles. Rather than relying further on missile defense for protection, the U.S. decided to deploy its own heavy missiles that could survive a surprise nuclear attack and still inflict enormous damage on the Soviets. American planners believed that "mutual assured destruction" could protect their cities just as effectively as defensive missile sites. In August 1973, DOD announced the end of the NIKE-HERCULES program. On September 14, 1974—sixteen years to the day after the 702nd Missile Battalion had gone operational—the ARNG retired the colors of all its NIKE missile units during impressive ceremonies at Fort Indiantown Gap, Pennsylvania.[58]

The ARNG's long-term success in the missile defense of CONUS established several important precedents for the Guard's role in future defense programs. First, Guardsmen established themselves as a readily accessible asset, fully capable of participating in the first line of defense against the nation's most dangerous threats. As such, Guardsmen shared federal responsibility with active forces for the execution of a key component of the nation's military strategy. Second, Guardsmen proved themselves of quickly and confidently mastering high technology weaponry. ARNG air defenders at NIKE-AJAX and NIKE-HERCULES sites debunked the myth that citizen-soldiers could not master the intricacies of new, computer age weapons. Third, Guard participation in the missile defense program resulted in significant manpower and dollar savings for the active Army. At a time when the Army was attempting to maintain an active force of fifteen divisions, ARNG missile units each year yielded an annual cost savings of $11.9 million and enough personnel spaces to man nearly two combat brigades.[59]

The Pentomic Era

While missile technology prompted the ARNG's role in homeland defense, the emergence of new, nuclear technology affected the Guard's mission, force structure, and training. In the aftermath of the Korean War, the Eisenhower Administration adopted a national security strategy based on "massive retaliation." Hoping to avoid another bloody and indecisive war like Korea, President Dwight D. Eisenhower vowed to employ nuclear weapons in any crisis that threatened U.S. security.

However, advances in nuclear weapons quickly altered the massive retaliation policy. By the late 1950s, a new generation of smaller nuclear weapons was available that possessed sufficient firepower to influence the outcome of large battles or entire campaigns. The Army viewed tactical nuclear weapons as the ideal, economical response to a conventional, Soviet blitzkrieg. While the threat of massive retaliation with strategic, nuclear weapons lacked credibility in many circles, the prosecution of a large ground war with tactical nuclear weapons seemed all too possible. Looking for a way to participate in nuclear warfare on an equal footing with the Air Force and the Navy, the Army eagerly took up the cause of tactical nuclear warfare and fielded a whole range of delivery systems including missiles, heavy artillery, and even mortars.

The expected demands of the tactical nuclear battlefield resulted in the most massive Army reorganization in twenty years. The triangular division, that had been the Army's workhorse in World War II and Korea, gave way to a new "pentomic" division. Army planners believed that in the chaos and confusion of a nuclear battlefield, divisions would fight independently and respond to threats from any direction. The linear battlefield became an anachronism. On the attack, pentomic divisions were to exploit gaps in the enemy's lines created by nuclear firepower, and on the defensive, the division would fight from a huge, circular battle position. At each level of divisional organization, units existed in groups of five, a recurrence that led to the designation "pentomic." Companies consisted of five platoons, five companies made up a "battle group," and each division had five battle groups. A pentomic battle group was smaller than a traditional infantry regiment but much larger than a single battalion.[60]

The active Army converted its infantry and airborne divisions to the pentomic design in 1956–1957, and the ARNG followed suite a year later. By October 1959, the Guard had completed a massive reorganization of its twenty-one infantry and six armored divisions. The transition complete, the ARNG considered itself "light, mobile, hard-hitting and ready to fight on nuclear or conventional battlefields." Concurrent with the pentomic reorganization, the ARNG followed the Army's lead in the historical redesignation of units with the implementation of the Combat Arms Regimental System. Though the ARNG did lose the traditional designations of some of its oldest units, the Guard retained the lineage and honors of its oldest regiments while active Army units traced their history to individual battalions.[61]

As an outgrowth of its emphasis on tactical nuclear warfare, the Army created the Special Forces (SF). Originally intended to operate amidst the confusion of the nuclear battlefield, SF units quickly became identified with the task of supporting native peoples. In late 1959, SF units entered the ARNG's troop structure. By the summer of 1960, 1,000 SF Guardsmen were in detachments in five different States, and the Army authorized the creation of four ARNG SF Groups. The mission of the SF was to infiltrate hostile areas and to arm and organize the indigenous peoples for guerrilla warfare.[62]

With the Army facing the real possibility of fighting wars in Europe and Asia, planners began to allocate forces to specific theaters. Before World War II, the War Department had developed broad plans based on possible conflicts with particular foreign powers, but not until the late 1950s were Army units designated to enter combat in a specific theater. Based on the system of America's diplomatic, defensive alliances created after World War II, the Army identified four potential fighting fronts; Europe, Southeast Asia, the Middle East, and Korea. With Army divisions already stationed in Europe and Korea, the divisions in CONUS received the missions of reinforcing forward-deployed divisions or entering the Middle East or Southeast Asia to defend America's interests.

For the first time, ARNG units received critical missions in support of the overseas theaters. Top priority ARNG units were assigned to the Army's Strategic Reserve Force (STRAF), an active duty corps that was to deploy overseas quickly in an emergency. Without its Guard units, the STRAF was incomplete. Army planners admitted that the ARNG "rounded out" the STRAF, and for the first time, "round out" became part of the language of Army force structure. Six ARNG divisions formed a priority, army-sized force available for overseas service. The remaining units constituted a strategic reserve to facilitate full national mobilization.[63]

The ARNG developed training plans to better support possible deployment timelines. All units were to attain a sufficient training level so they would be combat ready with only a minimum of training after mobilization. At NGB, training experts determined that a pentomic division battle group would be ready for overseas service following a thirty-six week training program. The program's first sixteen weeks were dedicated to a soldier's basic and individual training followed by ten weeks of rudimentary unit training. After mobilization, ARNG units would require an additional ten weeks of field exercises and maneuvers prior to commitment to battle. Thus, the ARNG concluded that its divisions could be ready for combat within thirty-six weeks and that non-divisional units would "require less time."[64]

The Struggle Against Segregation

New developments within American society in the late 1950s and early 1960s had a profound affect on the ARNG. The civil rights movement gathered momentum as blacks sought equality at the ballot box and strove to tear down the barriers of segregation throughout America. In 1954, the U.S. Supreme Court ruled that separate schools for the races were unconstitutional and ordered schools across the nation to integrate.

The first use of National Guard troops to enforce integration occurred at Clinton, Tennessee in September 1956. The Ku Klux Klan rallied at Clinton to enforce the segregation of a local school, and Tennessee's Governor decided to enforce integration laws and deter violence with the intimidating presence of an ARNG tank company. Under the personal supervision of the Tennessee AG, the overwhelming show of force by a fully armed tank company had the desired affect, and black children attended the local school without incident. To the north, the Governor of Kentucky turned out the ARNG to enforce integration at schools in the towns of Sturgis and Clay in western Kentucky. Some violence did erupt at Sturgis that resulted in minor injuries, but once again, the ARNG proved an effective instrument in providing support to State law enforcement authorities.[65]

The National Guard found itself in the middle of a much more serious racial incident during the integration of the public school system in Little Rock, Arkansas in 1957. Governor Orville Faubus of Arkansas was a staunch segregationist and decided to use the National Guard to block the integration of schools in the State's capital. On September 2, 1957, Governor Faubus stood in the front door of Central High School in Little Rock and called out the Arkansas ARNG to enforce segregation. Faubus informed Arkansans that he intended to use the National Guard to maintain law and order by preventing the violence that he believed would surely come with school integration.[66]

From the White House, President Eisenhower watched the growing racial crisis in Arkansas with increased alarm. After much deliberation, the president decided that integration laws would be enforced, even at the point of the bayonet. Eisenhower trumped Governor Faubus' use of the Arkansas ARNG as a segregationist force by ordering the entire Arkansas National Guard into active federal service on September 24, 1957. The president bypassed the Governor's office, sending the mobilization order directly to the Arkansas AG. Presented with orders straight from the federal commander in chief, the Arkansas National Guard responded by disregarding further directions from Governor Faubus. Angered by Eisenhower's move, Faubus referred to his own Arkansas National Guard as "occupation troops."[67]

Concurrent with federalizing the National Guard, the president dispatched a battalion of the 101st Airborne Division from Fort Campbell, Kentucky to Little Rock. From a staging area at Camp Robinson in North Little Rock, the paratroopers and nearly 1,800 Arkansas Guardsmen moved to Central High School. For nearly a month, a joint task force of Regular and ARNG soldiers maintained peace while enforcing school integration. All the while, the balance of the 8,504 officers and enlisted men in the Arkansas National Guard remained on full alert at their armories and air facilities. In November, with the main crisis passed, federal troops returned to Fort Campbell, and the Arkansas Guard began to demobilize. At Central High School, Guardsmen remained to provide personal security for the nine black students in attendance. A large detachment of Army Guardsmen remained on active duty at the school throughout the entire year until commencement exercises in May 1958.[68]

The ARNG's most publicized involvement with school integration came six years later at the University of Alabama at Tuscaloosa. Governor George Wallace, a staunch segregationist, hoped to use racial issues to propel him onto the national political scene. In the early summer of 1963, Wallace announced that he intended to defy the court ordered integration of Alabama's universities by refusing to admit blacks. On Sunday, June 9th, Wallace ordered 700 Guardsmen to report to armories in the Tuscaloosa area to make them readily available "to maintain law and order" on the University of Alabama campus. Governor Wallace publicly declared that he would personally "stand in the school house door" to prevent the enrollment of blacks. Two days later, the confrontation came to a head. On the morning of June 11, 1963, senior Department of Justice officials escorted black students to the university administration building where Governor Wallace himself refused them entry.[69]

President John F. Kennedy's response was swift and dramatic. An immediate presidential executive order federalized the entire Alabama National Guard with the purpose of assisting Department of Justice officials in maintaining order, quelling civil disturbances and enforcing court ordered integration. Later that same afternoon, federal officials in Tuscaloosa decided to enforce the court's orders with the full backing of the Alabama ARNG. Around 3:00 p.m. on June 11th, a force of one hundred Alabama Guardsmen from Companies A and B of the 20th SF Group escorted federal officials and black students onto the campus. Wearing steel helmets and carrying rifles with fixed bayonets, the SF soldiers made a strong impression. At the head of the column walked Brig. Gen. Henry V. Graham, the assistant division commander of the 31st Infantry Division. General Graham was a twenty-six year Alabama ARNG veteran with active service in both World War II and Korea and had served as the Alabama AG from 1959–1963 when he reverted to one-star rank to serve as the second-in-command of the Dixie Division. Under the intense scrutiny of network television cameras, General Graham led the Department of Justice officials and the black students up the stairs of the administration building where Governor Wallace stood waiting. Graham saluted the Governor and asked him to step aside. Wallace returned the salute and asked for permission to make a short statement. Graham granted the Governor's request, and after reading a statement in which he vowed to continue the fight against integration, Wallace left the campus.[70]

Throughout the civil rights struggles of the 1950s and 1960s, the use of ARNG units in civil disturbances proved effective. The improvements in National Guard training and equipping that occurred after Korea made the ARNG an effective and reliable instrument that did not question federal control, even at the local level. During the civil rights crises in the South, there were additional political advantages in removing Guardsmen from State control and using them rather than Regulars to enforce federal integration laws.

Integration in the ARNG

On July 26, 1948, President Truman signed Executive Order No. 9981, directing the integration of America's armed forces. The order declared that "equality of treatment and opportunity" would exist for all service members without regard to "race, color, religion or national origin" and established a presidential committee to oversee service integration. Despite President Truman's historic order, integration occurred slowly. When the Army's 24th Infantry Regiment went to Korea two years after the integration order, it fought as an all-black unit led by mostly white officers. Regular Army field artillery, engineer, and military police units also went to Korea fully segregated. Three all-black ARNG transportation units from Maryland and the District of Columbia deployed to Korea, the last fully segregated Guard units ever to enter active, federal service. While both units integrated in Korea with the receipt of replacements, they segregated once again after returning home.[71]

A small number of States did integrate their units, but overall the ARNG made little progress toward integration throughout the 1950s. Since the president's integration order only referred to federal units, most Guardsmen argued the order did not apply to them. While the active Army utilized a diverse pool of draftees to integrate its units, the tradition of voluntary recruitment in the Guard restricted progress toward full integration. Meanwhile, serving black Guardsmen in selected States continued their tradition of service. In several locations, demographics caused segregated ARNG units. Spanish-speaking natives filled entire units in Puerto Rico, and a similar situation existed in Hawaii. In Alaska, the Eskimo Scouts consisted of native enlisted men led by white officers. Still, some States had fully integrated units. In the Southwest, Native Americans, Hispanics, and Asians had served in integrated ARNG units since before World War II.

The Civil Rights Act of 1964 and the ARNG's national exposure during race riots and anti-war protests during the Vietnam era prompted integration. In 1965, CNGB declared that federal recognition could be withdrawn from National Guard units denying an individual membership or promotion on the grounds of race, color, religion, or national origin. The following year, NGB issued the first regulations dealing with integration and established a staff section to address equal opportunity and civil rights issues. Slowly, States began to recruit blacks actively. New Jersey and New York conducted aggressive recruiting campaigns for minorities with modest results. In the South, many States repealed "white only" militia laws that were still on the books from Reconstruction in order to recruit African-Americans. By the mid-1960s, the ARNG in the southern States had only a small, minority representation.[72]

Table 6
ARNG STRENGTH, 1947–1970

1947	87,421	1959	399,427
1948	288,427	1960	401,765
1949	315,042	1961	393,807
1950	324,761	1962	360,970*
1951	226,636*	1963	361,080*
1952	215,341*	1964	381,546
1953	255,522*	1965	378,985
1954	318,006*	1966	420,924
1955	357,542	1967	418,074
1956	404,403	1968	389,182*
1957	422,178	1969	388,954*
1958	394,329	1970	409,192

(Source: National Guard Bureau, *Annual Reports*, 1947–1970.)
*ARNG troops ordered to active duty are normally not included with annual Guard troop strengths and instead are counted along with Regular Army strength figures. Reduced strength levels for the designated years reflect the ARNG mobilizations for Korea, Berlin, and Vietnam.

Though a variety of minorities had always served in the ARNG, the role of women did not begin until the late 1950s. No women had served in the Guard before World War II, and females were not authorized to serve in the postwar period. However, the Regular Army did retain the Women's Army Corps after the war, and job openings in many non-medical fields became available to women on active duty. Increasing numbers of women joined the USAR to serve in support positions, but because the ARNG remained mostly a combat organization, few positions were available that allowed female service.[73]

Starting in the early 1950's, NGB allowed the Air National Guard to use female augmentees from the Air Force Reserve to work in medical units. The policy allowed female officers to work and train in military medical facilities, but did not permit women to mobilize and deploy with their National Guard units. To improve the Guard's medical readiness, women would have to serve directly in units. In May 1956, NGAUS endorsed legislation allowing female nurses and women in medical specialties to join the ARNG.[74]

While waiting for the approval of pending legislation, several States granted commissions to nurse officers. In the summer of 1956, Congress passed a law permitting female officers in the National Guard. The first ARNG woman granted federal recognition was 1st Lt. Sylvia Marie St. Charles Law. Appointed in a temporary federal recognition status on January 21, 1957, she joined Alabama's 190th Evacuation Hospital in Birmingham. After completing the Army's six-week military orientation course at Fort Sam Houston, Texas—the first Guardswoman to do so— Lieutenant Law returned to her unit and received federal recognition.[75]

Over the next few years, a small but growing number of women entered the ARNG. In 1957, eleven female nurses served, though 468 available positions existed in hospital units. Three years later, only fifty-six women served out of a total ARNG strength of 401,765 personnel. During the Berlin Crisis in October 1961, seventeen female nurses mobilized and became the first Guardswomen ever ordered to active duty. Through the 1960s, the jobs open to females were in officer positions, and no enlisted women served. But the status of Guardswomen changed under the influence of the civil rights and women's movements. On November 8, 1967, Congress finally passed legislation that allowed enlistment women to serve in the National Guard. After four years of planning for the introduction of women, CNGB announced in September 1971 that prior service enlisted women could join the ARNG, and the authority to enlist female recruits without previous military experience came in May 1972.[76]

The Berlin Crisis

The Kennedy Administration entered office in January 1961 with a new vision for America's national defense. Rejecting Eisenhower's policy of massive retaliation, President Kennedy favored a new strategy of "flexible response." The young president wanted a military capable of responding to a whole host of threats, ranging from nuclear to guerrilla warfare. Kennedy favored a broader use of conventional forces, especially the Army's new SF units that were to lead efforts at defeating communist "wars of national liberation" threatening Southeast Asia.

In the summer of 1961, flexible response was put to a severe test. Soviet Premier Nikita Khrushchev announced the end of the European powers' established rights to occupy portions of Berlin and threatened the city's complete isolation. As a shocked world looked on, the Soviets constructed a solid wall of steel, concrete, and barbed wire that divided east and west Berlin. In an instant, Berlin became the focal point where U.S. commitments to NATO and Soviet ambitions met in open confrontation. On July 25, 1961, Kennedy addressed the nation, outlining the nature of the Berlin crisis, putting the U.S. military on high alert and asking for authority to mobilize the National Guard and the reserves. A rapid buildup of conventional forces was intended to demonstrate U.S. resolve and to cool Soviet ambitions. In lieu of a declaration of national emergency, on July 31st Congress passed a joint resolution authorizing the callup of 250,000 Guardsmen and reservists for twelve months.[77]

Within two weeks, Army planners and the NGB staff had drawn up a list of prospective units for mobilization, and on August 25th, NGB alerted 107 ARNG units for mobilization. A week later, four ARNG divisions were placed on accelerated training schedules to increase their combat readiness. On September 19th, DOD published an even more expansive alert order. Units on alert status used precious time to complete physical exams, update personnel records and to prepare vehicles and equipment for movement to mobilization stations.[78]

During the first two weeks of October 1961, 44,371 ARNG soldiers from thirty-nine States and the District of Columbia entered active duty. Three major combat units contained the lion's share of troops; the 32nd Infantry Division (Wisconsin), the 49th Armored Division (Texas) and the 150th Armored Cavalry (West Virginia). In addition, 264 non-divisional units were mobilized. The 32nd Division quickly moved from Wisconsin to its mobilization station at Fort Lewis, Washington, while the 49th Armored Division began post-mobilization training at Fort Hood, Texas. The mission of the two ARNG divisions was to replace two active divisions in the CONUS strategic reserve—the 4th Infantry and the 2nd Armored—should they deploy to bolster the five Army divisions already in Europe. The 32nd and 49th Divisions launched into an ambitious eight-week training program that included exercises for all levels of organization. Active Army inspectors declared the two divisions combat ready only four months after mobilization. During the spring and summer of 1962, all mobilized ARNG units continued to train and to provide support to other ARNG and USAR units engaged in annual training.[79]

Despite the apparent success of the Berlin mobilization, a number of significant problems dogged the buildup. The personnel problems of

Tracked vehicles of the 150th Armored Cavalry, West Virginia ARNG, participate in amphibious training at Fort Miles, Delaware in May 1962 during the Berlin Crisis. (National Guard Education Foundation)

the Korean mobilization from a decade earlier reappeared. Though the 32nd and 49th Divisions reported to their mobilization stations with nearly 100 percent of their authorized strength, manpower levels were far short of wartime requirements. The 32nd Division required 3,850 fillers and the 49th Division an additional 5,500 troops to reach full strength. Like the Korean mobilization, a large percentage of fillers were individual Army Reservists not in a paid drill status. These 28,000 Reservists complained long and hard that they had been called before hundreds of thousands of Guardsmen and Reservists in paid, drilling units. The complaints fell on fertile ground, resulting in broad press coverage and congressional hearings. The mobilization revealed great shortages of equipment in the ARNG. Logisticians withdrew over 10,500 items of equipment from the States to support mobilized units. Many Guardsmen questioned the validity of the callup, feeling that stateside duty alone did not justify major disruptions in their professional and personal lives. The following year, ARNG retention and NGAUS membership suffered.[80]

American resolve finally convinced the Soviets to back down in Berlin, and ARNG units returned home during the summer of 1962. Despite acknowledged problems, Secretary of the Army Elvis J. Stahr, Jr.

called the mobilization "the most efficient in the history of the country," and NGB declared it "the most successful ever conducted." Though no ARNG unit deployed overseas, the mobilization achieved its desired results. For the first time in American history, a reserve component mobilization was used as a political instrument to deter war. And in the event deterrence had failed, ARNG divisions were immediately available for combat. Guard units achieved combat readiness in a relatively short time and successfully bolstered the nation's strategic reserve. However, a series of important reforms soon completely overshadowed the ARNG's contributions during the Berlin Crisis.[81]

The McNamara Reforms

From his office in the Pentagon, President Kennedy's new secretary of defense, Robert S. McNamara, had watched the Berlin mobilization with deep concern. Though acknowledging the sacrifices and service of individual Guardsmen and reservists, McNamara was not satisfied with the callup's overall results. To implement flexible response with its heavy reliance on conventional forces, McNamara knew that increases in the efficiency and readiness of both Regular and reserve component forces were needed. Relying upon his background as a statistical analyst, Harvard Business School graduate, and senior corporate executive, McNamara embarked upon a program of reforms that changed the ARNG in ways not seen since World War I.

While McNamara and his systems analysts—the advisors known as the "Whiz Kids"—pondered alternatives for improving the military's readiness, the Army underwent a profound change. To the Army's relief, the era of massive retaliation and pentomic divisions came to an end. Looking to fight the conventional battles implicit in the strategy of flexible response, the Army reverted to a more traditional, divisional organization. The pentomic design gave way to the new "Reorganization Objectives Army Division," or more simply, the ROAD division. In many ways, the ROAD division concept resembled the former triangular division except that three brigades rather than three regiments formed the division's backbone. The brigade organization allowed tactical flexibility for the creation of combined arms task forces to meet the demands of specific situations and missions. The Army began conversion to the ROAD design in the early 1960s. In a prodigious effort, the ARNG's twenty-three infantry and armored divisions completed the ROAD reorganization between January and May 1963. The ROAD structure proved sound, and with only minimal, incremental changes, continues to serve the Army.[82]

The Berlin crisis had revealed several personnel and equipping shortcomings that Secretary McNamara set out to repair. By the end of 1962, the active Army's strength had increased to more than one million soldiers organized into sixteen divisions. A growing defense budget permitted increases in stocks of supplies, equipment and ammunition. McNamara realized the need for greater strategic mobility and implemented an aggressive acquisition program for new, long-range aircraft capable of transporting large numbers of troops and light equipment to trouble spots anywhere in the world. For the first time, the U.S. prepositioned heavy equipment in Europe for use by units airlifted to help defend NATO in a crisis and established floating stocks aboard ships anchored in the Far East.[83]

McNamara's modernization program resulted in many ARNG enhancements. In the early 1960s, a flood of new equipment entered units. The Guard modernized to the M48 tank, the M113 Armored Personnel Carrier, the M109 self-propelled howitzer, the M60 machine gun and the M14 rifle. Bolstered by improvements in training and modernization, Guard capabilities increased. In 1960, a Utah ARNG field artillery battalion flew to Puerto Rico for annual training aboard Air Guard transports, the first time Guardsmen had deployed to an overseas training location. Four years later, over 10,000 ARNG soldiers flew on Air Guard transports from CONUS to overseas sites for annual training. In May 1964, two ARNG armored brigades participated in major exercises with active Army units in the California desert, the first time since World War II that such training had occurred.[84]

As McNamara's Whiz Kids took a firmer hold on the Pentagon, DOD and the Army increased their needs for statistical information. New, quantitative management methods required a more rapid collection and analysis of accurate data. In short order, the ARNG entered the computer age. In 1958, the ARNG had implemented a crude system of manual punch card operations under a contract awarded to the growing IBM Corporation. The first punch cards allowed the receipt and transfer of a host of personnel reports with the promise of eliminating the writing or typing of reports at unit level and the manual compilation of data at State headquarters. By 1963, newer automatic data processing equipment was at work at NGB and in the States. Two years later, the growing ARNG computer facility moved from the Pentagon to a new National Guard Computer Center located in the Nassif Building in Arlington, Virginia.[85]

Secretary McNamara sought to increase reserve component readiness through drastic force structure reductions. Since 1946, the ARNG had retained a force structure of 655,000 while maintaining an actual strength of approximately 350,000 soldiers. Consequently, ARNG units recruited and manned at 100 percent of their authorized strength remained far short of their required, wartime strength. The imbalance between force structure and manning became most evident during the Korean and Berlin mobilizations when Guard units needed significant infusions of Guard recruits, Army Reservists, and draftees to bring them to wartime strength. By reducing the number of ARNG units, McNamara aimed to bring the ARNG's force structure more in line with its authorized manpower levels. The first round of unit inactivations came in May 1963. The ARNG lost four infantry divisions: the 34th (Iowa and Nebraska), the 35th (Kansas and Missouri), the 43rd (Connecticut, Rhode Island, and Vermont), and the 51st (South Carolina and Florida). In return, the ARNG activated four, new separate infantry brigades. By 1964, the ARNG included a wide array of combat units; seventeen infantry divisions, six armored divisions, seven separate brigades and seven ACRs.[86]

On December 12, 1964, McNamara shocked the defense establishment by unveiling a bold, sweeping plan to increase reserve readiness. Taking the exact opposite stance of the Gray Board in 1948, the SECDEF announced he intended to merge the USAR into the ARNG while carrying out additional, significant reforms. The Army Reserve would lose all of its units and consist only of individuals, while the ARNG inactivated fifteen more divisions. McNamara argued that in terms of management and practice, America's dual, military reserve system was too cumbersome and expensive. To implement flexible response, the U.S. no longer needed large numbers of reserve component soldiers for a mass mobilization, but a smaller reserve force of more ready, efficient, and responsive units.[87]

McNamara's merger plan faced bitter opposition. Proponents for and against the ARNG-USAR merger expressed their concerns during tense congressional hearings. Congressman challenged the SECDEF's authority in unilaterally announcing and implementing such a drastic plan. Both Guard and Reserve leaders believed turmoil in the reserve components was not desirable in light of the buildup in Vietnam. NGAUS, AGAUS, and NGB supported the merger despite the difficulties that would come with the acceptance of USAR soldiers and proposed Guard force structure cuts. The USAR and the Reserve Officer's Association exercised a new level of organization and influence on Capitol Hill against the merger. Uniting the ARNG and the USAR proved too divisive, and Congress expressly forbade the merger with language in the Defense Appropriations Act of 1966.[88]

Undaunted by congressional opposition, McNamara initiated deep cuts in the Guard and the Army Reserve. On June 2, 1967, the SECDEF announced a major realignment of ARNG and USAR units. All combat and combat support units would transfer to the Guard, while the USAR would contain only combat service support units. At the heart of McNamara's plan for the ARNG was the inactivation of fifteen divisions and the creation of a like number of separate brigades. In the aggregate, the ARNG faced a reduction of 1,000 units and 18,500 personnel authorizations. Though concerned over the strain the massive reorganization would impose on the Guard, NGAUS, NGB and the AGs understood that a smaller, better prepared ARNG was in the national interest. In light of the civil disturbances of the early 1960s, the Governors demanded the retention of enough military police, medical, aviation, and logistics units to provide their States with the resources to respond adequately to natural disasters and civil unrest. At the same time, DOD authorized significant increases in the State headquarters to offset command and control losses resulting from the elimination of fifteen division headquarters.[89]

Between December 1967 and June 1968, the ARNG quickly implemented the most sweeping reorganization in its history. When it was all over, the Guard retained only eight divisions: the 26th Infantry (Massachusetts and Connecticut); the 28th Infantry (Pennsylvania, Maryland, and Virginia); the 30th Mechanized Infantry (North Carolina, South Carolina, and Georgia); the 38th Infantry (Indiana and Pennsylvania); the 42d Infantry (New York, Michigan, and Ohio); the 47th Infantry (Minnesota, Iowa, and Illinois); the 30th Armored (Alabama and Mississippi); and the 50th Armored (New York, New Jersey, and Vermont). In addition, the ARNG included eighteen separate brigades, four ACRs, and two SF Groups. True to its promise, DOD assigned each ARNG unit to a specific war plan and provided the resources needed to maintain readiness. Unfortunately, Guardsmen had little time to adjust to their reorganization. Escalating levels of violence in the rice paddies of Vietnam and on America's streets and college campuses soon placed new, difficult demands on all Guardsmen.[90]

The Vietnam War

Since the French defeat in Indochina and the splitting of Vietnam along the 17th Parallel in 1954, the U.S. had actively supported the survival of a free South Vietnam. However, the communists in North Vietnam were determined to reunite their country. In 1960, the North Vietnamese commenced operations to conquer the opposition leadership in Saigon along with their American patrons. The campaign took on two forms; conventional attacks by units of the North Vietnamese Army and guerilla operations by the Viet Cong. Like Truman in Korea, President Kennedy took a stand against communist expansion. Military advisors moved to South Vietnam, and by 1963, 16,000 Americans were active throughout the country. After Kennedy's assassination and a coup in Saigon in November 1963, the North Vietnamese and the Viet Cong stepped up operations in hope of scoring a quick victory.[91]

President Lyndon B. Johnson inherited a war for which he had little enthusiasm. Unwilling to hand the communists an easy victory, Johnson reaffirmed American backing for South Vietnam. After North Vietnamese gunboats attacked U.S. vessels in early August 1964, Congress passed the Gulf of Tonkin Resolution, giving Johnson the authority "to take all necessary steps, including the use of armed force" to defend South Vietnam. The president deployed American air power to Vietnam that bombed the Viet Cong, the North Vietnamese, and their supply lines. In response, the Viet Cong mounted strong raids against air bases in the south, and their attacks prompted a major escalation of the war.[92]

In 1965, the U.S. committed 20,000 Army and Marine combat troops to South Vietnam to prop up the government and defend military installations. Against the recommendations of his top advisors, Johnson refused to mobilize the National Guard and the Reserves. While the president wanted to resist aggression, he had no desire to provoke a major war in Southeast Asia. Calling out the National Guard and Reserves, Johnson argued, might prompt the Soviets and the Chinese to enter the fighting. In the end, the president decided not to disrupt American society with a major mobilization; he would prosecute the war with expanded active forces and draftees. Throughout 1966 and 1967, DOD pressed for a reserve callup to bolster NATO and the weakened U.S. strategic reserve, but the White House remained adamant against a National Guard and reserve mobilization.[93]

As an alternative to a reserve component callup, DOD announced in September 1965 the creation of the Selected Reserve Force (SRF), a 150,000-man composite force of ARNG and USAR units. The SRF's mission was to provide additional, ready forces to offset the deployment of active Army units to Vietnam and to act as a strategic hedge against threats in Korea, Europe, and elsewhere. The Army established high readiness goals for the SRF; units were to mobilize within seven days of alert at 93 percent strength and to deploy overseas with a minimum of post-mobilization training. The ARNG provided nearly 120,000 combat and combat support troops to the SRF in three composite infantry divisions, six separate brigades and an ACR.[94]

Bolstered by huge increases in training and recruiting budgets, ARNG SRF units worked mightily to improve readiness. Training long hours during extended drill periods, Guardsmen in the SRF proudly called themselves the "Super Ready Force" and believed they were preparing for eventual deployment to Vietnam. By July 1966, 88 percent of Guard SRF units had passed readiness tests qualifying them for mobilization only seven days after initial alert. Senior ARNG leaders believed the SRF's divisions would be combat ready only eight weeks after mobilization. To sustain their high readiness, ARNG leaders consciously diverted resources from lower priority organizations to units designated for early deployment. Many States transferred their best soldiers and equipment into SRF units. Low priority units provided training and evaluation support to the SRF while their own training suffered. For the first time, Guardsmen grumbled about two sets of units; the "haves" and the "have nots."[95]

Despite the widely recognized success of the SRF, DOD terminated the program in September 1969. The rising demand for resources to support the Vietnam War precluded the continued funding of SRF readiness. At the same time, the control of widespread race riots and antiwar demonstrations diverted more and more of the Guard's attention away from normal training. Four years after it began, DOD believed that the strategic uncertainties that had called for the SRF's creation no longer existed. Still, the SRF had increased reserve component readiness and provided a ready, strategic reserve during the peak years of involvement in Vietnam.[96]

Denied the opportunity to serve in Vietnam with their units, individual Guardsmen volunteered for overseas service. In the war's early years, approximately 2,000 ARNG soldiers fought in Vietnam, half of them officers. In all, the group provided distinguished service, and twenty-three were killed in action. Major Homer L. Pease of Johnson City, Tennessee personified the service and dedication of Guardsmen. An adolescent at the beginning of World War II, Pease lied about his age to fight as a paratrooper in the 101st Airborne Division. By age sixteen, Pease had earned two Bronze Stars, two Purple Hearts, the Senior Parachute Badge and the Combat Infantryman's Badge. Joining the Tennessee Guard after the war, Pease earned his officer's commission and volunteered to go to Vietnam where he was awarded the Silver Star and a third Purple Heart. Homer Pease died in the Mekong Delta on November 16, 1966 while battling against a massive Viet Cong attack that wiped out his entire unit with the exception of one sole survivor. Nearly 200 ARNG aviators volunteered for Vietnam and received high praise for their daring and skill. Warrant Officer Jerome Daly was perhaps the ARNG's most illustrious aviator in Vietnam. Daly earned his wings in 1958 as a member of the Pennsylvania Guard and volunteered for two tours of duty in Vietnam. Flying nearly 5,000 total hours, Daly logged over 2,000 hours as a gunship helicopter pilot. In a remarkable combat career, Daly was awarded the Distinguished Service Cross, two Silver stars, three Distinguished Flying Crosses, two Purple Hearts, and seventy Air Medals. In 1967, the Army Aviation Association of America honored Daly as the "Army Aviator of the Year."[97]

The decision to fight the war with draftees had a profound affect on ARNG manpower, and by the end of the war, many Americans considered the Guard a haven for draft dodgers. The Selective Service Act of 1967 contained numerous educational and professional deferments and exclusions that permitted young men to avoid the draft. A popular exclusion was membership in the reserves. Anyone entering the ARNG could avoid the draft but had to serve for six years in a drill status. As the war dragged on, young men increasingly sought ARNG service. Unit recruiters maintained long waiting lists of eager volunteers, and commanders closely managed unit vacancies. The ARNG's end strength skyrocketed, reaching a peak strength of 466,000. To curb the Guard's growth, a strength ceiling of 400,000 was imposed in 1968, and CNGB suspended the enlistment of all individuals without prior military service.[98]

The reserve component draft exclusion created bitter feelings among many long serving Guardsmen who were already disappointed that their units had not been mobilized. Their displeasure turned to dismay when units began to fill with young men openly opposed to America's involvement in Vietnam. Many professional Guardsmen who had trained and sacrificed to defend their country became disgusted as more and more men with a strong desire to avoid active military service filled their units. On the other hand, a NGAUS survey in 1970 revealed that men seeking to avoid the draft did so largely for expedient reasons rather than antiwar sentiments. To the new Guardsmen, joining the ARNG fulfilled their military obligation with the least interference to their personal lives.[99]

Unexpected events in early 1968 finally prompted a reserve mobilization. On January 23rd, the North Koreans seized the USS *Pueblo* and imprisoned its crew. Only eight days later, the North Vietnamese and the Viet Cong launched the Tet Offensive, a massive effort to defeat American and South Vietnamese forces. The strength, intensity and duration of the Tet Offensive surprised American commanders. Though U.S. forces finally turned the offensive back with heavy losses to the enemy, it became necessary to rush additional troops to Vietnam. Concerns over the *Pueblo* incident, the Tet Offensive, possible Soviet action in Berlin and the weakened U.S. strategic reserve convinced President Johnson to mobilize the reserves. On April 11th, the president issued an executive order calling to active duty 24,500 National Guardsmen and reservists.[100]

On May 13, 1968, 13,633 Guardsmen from seventeen States reported to their armories for active duty. To augment the forces in Vietnam as well as the CONUS reserve, the ARNG mobilized a balanced force of thirty-four combat, combat support, and combat service support units. Two ARNG brigades were ordered to active duty. The 29th Infantry Brigade in Hawaii, reinforced by an infantry battalion from the USAR, consolidated at Schofield Barracks on Oahu for post-mobilization training. The 69th Infantry Brigade from Kansas, bolstered by Iowa's 2-133rd Infantry, reported to Fort Carson, Colorado. California's 1st Squadron, 18th Cavalry also mobilized and reported for duty at Fort Lewis, Washington. Twenty-two combat support and nine combat service support units quickly deployed to various Army posts for extended duty or for pre-deployment training.[101]

Of the Guardsmen mobilized, 2,729 soldiers in eight units went to Vietnam. After three months of stateside training, Alabama's 650th Medical Detachment was the first ARNG unit to reach Vietnam, arriving on August 27, 1968. The following week, Idaho's 116th Combat Engineer Battalion arrived to begin a year's tour of duty constructing defenses and maintaining important supply routes. The first ARNG combat unit in Vietnam was New Hampshire's 3-197th Field Artillery armed with 155-mm. towed howitzers. The only ARNG ground maneuver unit sent to Vietnam was Company D (Ranger), 151st Infantry from Indiana. A special unit with nearly every member parachute and jungle warfare qualified, the Rangers reached Vietnam in November 1968. Operating from a base camp they named "Camp Atterbury East," the Rangers conducted extensive patrolling and reconnaissance missions. By the end of their tour, 65 percent of the Indiana Rangers were awarded the Combat Infantryman's Badge. In addition to the eight units deployed to Vietnam, another 4,000 soldiers from the 29th and 69th Brigades served as individual replacements.

Two members of Company D, 151st Infantry (Ranger), Indiana ARNG on patrol in South Vietnam on January 23, 1969. (National Guard Education Foundation)

Army leaders in Vietnam recognized the enthusiasm and esprit of Guardsmen whom they considered more mature, experienced, and better educated than the typical draftee. The ARNG's most unfortunate moment in South Vietnam occurred on June 19, 1969 when Viet Cong sappers launched a massive attack against an American fire base. Battery C, 2-138th Field Artillery of the Kentucky ARNG helped to defeat the enemy attack but suffered heavy losses. Bardstown, Kentucky was shocked to learn that thirteen of its ARNG native sons had been killed and wounded in the attack.[102]

On December 12, 1969, the last mobilized Guardsman returned home. All together, over 9,000 Guardsmen served in Vietnam, either in units or as individual volunteers and replacements. The smooth mobilization and quick deployment to Vietnam vindicated the McNamara reforms and proved that if properly manned and equipped, ARNG units could serve overseas shortly after mobilization. The ARNG's Vietnam veterans performed another important service for the Guard. From their ranks developed a group of seasoned officers at the State and national level who would become the ARNG's senior leadership during the century's last two decades.[103]

Domestic Strife, 1965–1970

During the Vietnam War, America coped with violence on two fronts. While Regulars chased an elusive enemy in South Vietnam, the ARNG engaged in the difficult and divisive task of controlling riots in American cities and on college campuses. While the reasons for social discontent were complex, two key issues prompted widespread civil disturbances. The civil rights activism of nonviolence championed by Martin Luther King, Jr. faced a challenge from militant black leaders who advocated violence and forceful self-defense as agents of change, a position that caused increasing concerns among the white population. At the same time, society grew disillusioned with the Vietnam War. College students and young Americans subject to the draft became the shock troops of the antiwar movement that reached its peak in 1970. The National Guard was the only organization in each State with sufficient manpower and equipment to assist local law enforcement in riot control.

The first major civil disturbance in an American city since World War II took place in the Watts section of Los Angeles in August 1965. On the evening of August 11th, a confrontation between the California Highway Patrol and two black youths sparked widespread rioting. The following day, city and State law enforcement agencies attempted to stop the rioting, but elected officials realized they needed the National Guard.

Guardsmen of California's 40th Armored Division direct traffic away from the riot-torn area of Watts, Los Angeles in the summer of 1965. (National Guard Education Foundation)

By noon on August 13th, California Guardsmen from the 40th Armored Division were in Watts. A quick deployment of troops was possible because the division was ready for movement to Camp Roberts for summer training. As the violence escalated, Guardsmen occupied roadblocks, confronted angry crowds, and provided protection to firefighters. To augment the 40th Armored's efforts, the California Air Guard airlifted 5,200 Guardsmen from the 49th Infantry Division from northern California to Los Angeles. Over the following week, rioting killed 35 people, injured 1,000, and another 4,000 were arrested. Fires and looters damaged or destroyed nearly 1,000 businesses, and property losses were put at $200 million. By the time it was all over on August 22nd, 13,393 Guardsmen had seen duty in Watts. The police chief of Los Angeles later told reporters: "Guardsmen can hold their heads just a little higher today for a job well done."[104]

Another major challenge to civil authority in Detroit in July 1967 required the involvement of Regular and National Guard troops. A police raid on a black nightclub in the early morning hours of July 23rd sparked widespread rioting that quickly escalated out of control. By evening the next day, 8,000 Guardsmen from the 46th Infantry Division who had been at summer training at Camp Grayling were in Detroit. The Guard's quick deployment was possible due to detailed, prior planning by the Michigan ARNG and Detroit law enforcement. Looting, arson, and vandalism spread and intensified even though over 10,000 Guardsmen were on duty. Casualties from sniper gunfire prompted Guardsmen to load their rifles and shoot back. Finally, Michigan's Governor appealed for federal troops, and President Johnson ordered 5,000 paratroopers from the 101st and 82nd Airborne Divisions to Detroit. The paratroopers took charge of one half of the riot zone while the Michigan ARNG retained control over the remainder. The overwhelming show of force restored order by the end of the month. The final tally of the Detroit riot was shocking: 42 dead, 1,000 injured, 3,700 under arrest and $500 million in property damage.[105]

Disturbed by the race riots, President Johnson appointed a National Advisory Commission on Civil Disorders headed by Governor Otto Kerner of Illinois. The Kerner Commission studied the genesis of race riots and made recommendations for eliminating the causes of unrest and improving riot control training and preparations by law enforcement, the Army, and the National Guard. While the Guard's performance had usually pleased Governors and local officials, the Kerner Commission took a more critical view. The panel recommended that Guardsmen receive additional riot control training and special equipment. The commission questioned the individual performance of a number of Guard officers on riot duty and pushed for a comprehensive review of officer selection standards. The image of a largely white National Guard confronting black rioters caught the Kerner Commission's attention, and it encouraged increased black participation in the ARNG.[106]

The Kerner Commission's findings were not lost on the active Army or the ARNG. A flurry of directives emanated from the Pentagon to the States. Beginning in August 1967, every Guardsman participated in a vigorous, thirty-two hour training program on crowd control and urban combat. Officers received instruction on proper decision-making techniques during riots. Forty States that included large cities developed civil disturbance plans. Many States adjusted annual training schedules to insure that large units would always be available for riot duty. Guard officers held conferences and training exercises with elected officials and law enforcement agencies. ARNG units received a wide array of new equipment; searchlights, emergency radios, bull horns, nightsticks, body armor, and face shields. Special weapons issued included shotguns and the new M79 grenade launcher capable of lofting tear gas projectiles.[107]

Fortunately, riot training occurred just before a particularly violent year. In 1968, nearly 105,000 Guardsmen were committed on seventy-seven different occasions to riot duty in twenty-nine States and the District of Columbia. The worst civil disturbances occurred in April 1968 in the aftermath of Martin Luther King, Jr.'s assassination. To help control riots in Detroit, Washington, Chicago, and Baltimore, 25,000 Guardsmen were called to active federal service. During 1969 and 1970, race riots and antiwar demonstrations continued, but their frequency and intensity waned. More importantly, Guardsmen on State active duty controlled riots without assistance from Regulars. Senior Guard leaders believed that the lack of federal intervention was testimony to the ARNG's riot control preparations and experience.[108]

Perhaps the most unfortunate moment in modern ARNG history came at Kent State University in Ohio on May 4, 1970. The previous month, President Richard M. Nixon had ordered the invasion of Cambodia, a move many Americans believed was an unnecessary expansion of the Vietnam War. Violent antiwar protests erupted on college campuses. In Ohio, rioting caused by the Cambodian incursion capped the end of an especially violent month. Racial incidents, antiwar protests and a wildcat truckers strike had prompted the Governor to put nearly the entire Ohio ARNG on State active duty. A fierce antiwar protest broke out at Kent, Ohio on Saturday night, May 2nd, when students burned the ROTC building on the Kent State University campus.

The following day was relatively quiet as 1,400 Guardsmen converged on Kent State and coordinated their efforts with local law enforcement. When classes resumed on the morning of Monday, May 4th, students gathered at mid-morning to chant antiwar slogans. Before long, 2,500 students shouted obscenities and insults at the Guardsmen. Afraid that the situation could get out of control, the police ordered the large crowd to disperse or face arrest. The students pelted police with rocks, and orders were given for the Guardsmen to disperse the crowd.[109]

At noon, 115 Guardsmen from Companies A and B, 1-145th Infantry and Troop G, 107th Armored Cavalry donned gas masks and deployed into formation. While most soldiers carried M-1 rifles with fixed bayonets, others carried shotguns and tear gas launchers. The advancing soldiers pushed the rioters back with bayonets and strong doses of tear gas. In response, the students hurled rocks, bricks, and bottles that inflicted dozens of injuries. Just as they were about to disperse the crowd, the soldiers ran out of tear gas. Sensing the Guardsmen's helplessness and confusion, the protesters intensified their attacks. Afraid for their lives and angered by the students' actions, approximately thirty Guardsmen opened fire. In only thirteen seconds, a fusillade of nearly sixty bullets swept across the campus, killing four protesters and wounding nine others. Afterwards, the soldiers slowly withdrew, and the crowd dispersed. The Guardsmen looked after their wounded; nearly sixty had suffered severe cuts and bruises. The president of Kent State University closed the campus and ordered all students to leave.[110]

Ohio ARNG soldiers confront antiwar protesters on the campus of Kent State University, May 4, 1970. After fifty Guardsmen were injured by rocks and other projectiles, they opened fire, killing four students and wounding nine others. (Kent State University Archives)

By May 8th, calm returned, and the Guardsmen went home. The shooting resulted in a number of federal, State and private investigations. In 1973, the federal government indicted eight Guardsmen for violating the students' civil rights, but the charges were eventually dropped. In the end, no Guardsmen were ever convicted for the Kent State shootings, and no students were charged for the injuries that they had inflicted.[111]

Perhaps in retribution for the Kent State shootings, violence came to the NGAUS headquarters building in Washington, DC. In the early morning hours of Sunday, May 10th, vandals placed a twenty-pound satchel charge of black powder against the building's marble and glass outer walls. Though no one was injured, a huge explosion did considerable harm, shattering seventy glass doors and windows. Flying glass damaged several marble and stainless steel plaques and tore holes in the numerous State flags on display.[112]

Conclusions

In the early decades of the Cold War, the ARNG proved itself as a consistent, reliable instrument of national power. On three occasions,

Guardsmen mobilized in response to communist threats. The ARNG divisions provided valuable service during the Korean War by fighting in Asia, supporting the defense of NATO and bolstering the U.S. strategic reserve. A lesser number of Guardsmen performed similar functions during the Vietnam War. For the first time, Guardsmen mobilized to help deter war during the 1961 Berlin Crisis. A select group of Guardsmen trained in the use of the latest high-technology weaponry participated in a key aspect of America's defense strategy for nearly twenty years. The NIKE missile program remains the ARNG's longest, sustained effort in the direct defense of the American homeland. Domestically, the ARNG acted in concert with civil authorities to implement the nation's laws and to maintain order. Despite personal views they may have held on integration and Vietnam, Guardsmen remained loyal to their government during the turbulent 1960s.

While the basic concept of citizen-soldiers serving both State and nation remained intact after World War II, nearly every other aspect of National Guard service changed. The federal government provided additional resources for training, equipment, pay, and armories, and in return, the ARNG became more ready and deployable. The substitution of extended, weekend drill periods in place of frequent, week night drill and mandatory, initial training for all soldiers changed the face of the Guard. No longer simply the basis for all-out mobilization, ARNG units focused exclusively on preparedness for overseas campaigning while building stronger, closer ties with the active Army. Realistic field exercises replaced armory classroom instruction, and by the mid-1960s, the ARNG manned its units at 70 percent of wartime strength or higher. The cumulative affect of reforms and improvements on the individual soldier was significant. Guardsmen began to view their service as a career instead of a leisure or social activity and believed that lifelong involvement in ARNG activities constituted valuable service to the nation.

The ARNG's transformation took place against the backdrop of turbulent times. In 1948 and 1964, the National Guard avoided two concerted attempts at amalgamation with the USAR. The Army's frustration in finding a larger, more viable mission in the Nuclear Age prompted the ARNG into major reorganizations to the pentomic and then to the ROAD division design. In the 1960s, the ARNG went through a major downsizing but came out for the better. The McNamara force reductions foreshadowed another, more painful cut in ARNG forces that was to come thirty years later.

The ARNG ended the early years of the Cold War with its historical reputation intact. The American people continued to rely on Guardsmen for national defense and for assistance during natural disasters and domestic disturbances. At the same time, important concerns remained. The ARNG continued as a largely white, male institution despite the nation's move toward racial integration. Questions lingered over the Guard's role in domestic disturbances, and perceptions persisted that it was a haven for draft dodgers. Still, the National Guard avoided the severe crisis of confidence and the loss of public approval that shook the Regular Army following Vietnam. As the 1970s began, whether or not the ARNG could sustain the great advances made in readiness and training since World War II remained an open question.

CHAPTER 7

The Era of Total Force Policy, 1970–1990

We have to make our reliance on the Guard and the Reserves real. No longer will the lyrics be any good. If we make it real in the eyes of the reserve components, then it will be real for the country.

General Creighton W. Abrams, Jr.

Introduction

Plumes of thick, black diesel exhaust shot skyward from the smokestacks of ARNG D-8 bulldozers as they strained to break the red earth of Panama. Working in sweltering heat and stifling humidity, Guard engineers from Louisiana's 225th Engineer Group skillfully employed their bulldozers to cut down a hill and fill in a valley to create a viable roadbed. Road graders moved back and forth methodically, kicking up thick clouds of red dust as they leveled the road surface. Engineer dump trucks came and went continuously, delivering gravel from distant rock quarries that would make the new road weatherproof year-round. While the Guard engineers labored, soldiers from the Panama Defense Force provided local security and often worked alongside the Americans to learn critical engineering skills. Throughout the early spring of 1984, ARNG engineers labored to complete the construction of an improved road network on the Azuero Peninsula in central Panama.

The Louisiana engineers lived in a nearby base camp where other Guard soldiers from Puerto Rico and Florida staffed a mess hall and a dispensary and operated laundry and bath facilities. The base camp's remote location in the jungles of Panama made communications and transportation difficult. A daily helicopter shuttle between the base camp and an Army installation near Panama City that brought supplies, rations, and spare parts was the only routine contact with the outside world. A high technology, satellite communications system allowed the ARNG soldiers who were deployed for their annual training to make long distance phone calls back to their families. When the nearly 400 Guard soldiers assembled for their evening meal at the base camp, their ranks reflected the ever increasing presence of blacks, women, and Hispanics in the ARNG. An occasional movie was available for evening entertainment, but the day's work was sufficiently strenuous and the heat so oppressive and exhausting that most soldiers turned in for the night not long after sundown. Before their exertions were completed weeks later, Guard engineers from the 225th Group had blazed a nine-mile trail through the steep hills and deep ravines of the Panamanian countryside.

Seventy years earlier, the War Department and the Army had questioned the legality of any National Guard service beyond America's shores. By the early 1980s, ARNG units routinely deployed overseas during annual training periods to participate in exercises and to provide assistance to America's allies. In 1984, the Army had authorized the ARNG to undertake road building operations in Panama as part of a broader effort to provide military assistance to Central American governments. The first phase of the project was the completion of a stretch of road on the Azuero Peninsula meant to join the agricultural region with Panama's established road network and commercial areas.

After the close of the winter rainy season in 1984, ARNG engineers from Louisiana, Missouri, Wisconsin, and North Carolina returned to Panama early the next year to add another seventeen miles of gravel highway to the Azuero Peninsula. All together, ARNG engineers completed twelve bridges along the twenty-six mile span of highway. On May 17, 1985, the president of Panama officiated a ribbon cutting ceremony to celebrate the opening of the longest bridge that measured 360 feet. Near the bridge, the Panamanian government placed a permanent, roadside plaque honoring the ARNG's work. Afterwards, Lt. Col. Charles Partin of Louisiana's 527th Engineer Battalion recalled: "The training in that country has been invaluable...It's the best training I've ever been through with the Guard."

The commitment of ARNG troops to Central America in the 1980s was only one manifestation of the resurgence of the U.S. military following the bitter experience of the Vietnam War. Though direct American involvement in Southeast Asia ended with the signing of the Paris Peace Accords in 1973, the lingering effects of the Vietnam War were widespread and persistent. In American foreign policy, retrenchment followed defeat. The Nixon Doctrine declared that the U.S. would honor its direct commitments to NATO, Japan, and Korea, but all other allies should expect only American air support, technical assistance, and weapons shipments while facing a crisis. Before his resignation in 1974, President Nixon initiated an era of détente that allowed for a broader accommodation with the Soviet Union and Red China. At the same time, cuts in military spending, the end of the draft and discipline problems further weakened the U.S. military. To compensate for dwindling manpower and materiel, the Defense Department announced the Total Force Policy, a move designed to better integrate reserve units with their active duty counterparts.

American disarray and retrenchment encouraged communist boldness. While the U.S. military bled in Vietnam, the Soviet Union had modernized its nuclear and conventional forces. Armed with new tanks, artillery, and aircraft, the Soviet Army's threat against Central Europe appeared more credible than ever. In the Middle East and Africa, the Soviets stretched their diplomatic and military muscle. In late 1979, two events marked the highpoint of American trouble in the Middle East: the capture of over 200 American hostages by Islamic fundamentalists in Iran and the Soviet invasion of Afghanistan. Closer to home, trouble festered in the Caribbean and Central America as Cuba took a more aggressive role in supporting insurgencies.

In the 1980s, America reasserted its world influence under the leadership of President Ronald W. Reagan. Communist provocation around the globe demanded a vigorous response. Aided by increased defense spending, the armed forces modernized and solved their personnel problems. Increasing their presence around the world, American forces saw action in Lebanon, Libya, Grenada, and Panama. In the end, the Soviet Union collapsed, and the most serious threat to U.S. national security after the Cold War occurred in the Middle East, not in Europe.

For the ARNG, the twenty years following the Vietnam War was a period of decline and resurgence. In 1970, the ARNG was adequately prepared to perform its role in a large, deliberate mobilization followed by eventual commitment to a war zone. Twenty years later, the ARNG was a combat ready, reserve force immediately available for deployment to hot spots around the globe. Improvements in training, equipment, and personnel gave the ARNG the wherewithal to participate fully in the nation's first line of defense. Still, manning the Guard with sufficient numbers of quality troops proved a daunting task. The Total Force Policy established closer ties than ever before between the Regular Army and the ARNG. At the same time, force modernization proved difficult, and

Guard soldiers found themselves training on older, less capable equipment. But ten years after Vietnam, the ARNG turned an important corner. In a buildup reminiscent of the military revival following the Korean War, the Guard expanded its ranks and received the resources necessary to improve readiness. Fully integrated into the Army's war plans, Guardsmen prepared to fight a war in Europe while participating in training exercises and support missions around the globe.

The Army After Vietnam

Immediately following its withdrawal from Vietnam, the U.S. Army entered a period of self-analysis and renewal. The problems of ill discipline, drug abuse, and racial tensions that appeared during the last year of the Vietnam War soon engulfed the entire Army. In Europe, senior commanders lamented that discipline problems had rendered the once proud U.S. Seventh Army nearly combat ineffective. The commandant of the Command and General Staff College at Fort Leavenworth, Kansas publicly admitted that the Army "faces serious problems of manpower, morale, strategy and leadership." Under the influence of its new chief of staff, General Creighton W. Abrams, Jr., the Army in 1972 began a concerted effort to repair the institutional damage inflicted by the Vietnam War.[1]

The first priority for Creighton Abrams was to identify the Army's post-Vietnam missions. After examining the nation's most likely security threats, the Army concluded that a mechanized war in Europe and a light infantry war elsewhere were the two most probable challenges. Even though a major war against the Soviets in Central Europe seemed unlikely, such a conflict represented the greatest challenge to U.S. national security. Striving to move beyond the specter of Vietnam, the Army focused on the defense of Europe as its major mission in the 1970s.[2]

In 1976, new Army doctrine outlined the concepts for defending NATO against the Soviets. The Army's challenge was to fight and win the first battle of the next war by employing aggressive, defensive tactics that destroyed the enemy with maneuver and firepower. Facing vastly superior numbers, Americans were expected to fight outnumbered and win. Army strategists believed NATO could triumph in a short, violent and decisive war without having to resort to nuclear weapons. The 1973 Yom Kippur War seemed to verify the Army's assumptions about future warfare. In a brief but bloody war, the Israeli victory demonstrated the effectiveness of new, more lethal weapons and the need for highly trained armies of Regulars and citizen-soldiers capable of conducting combined arms warfare. The Yom Kippur War convinced U.S. planners that future reserve component mobilizations would have to be more rapid than ever before.[3]

Developing a strategy for the defense of Europe was easier than providing badly needed manpower and equipment. During Vietnam, the Army had done little modernization while the Soviets had substantially strengthened their forces. The Yom Kippur War warned of the need for new weapons and equipment. Despite a dwindling defense budget, the Army forged ahead with plans aimed at developing a wide range of new, more capable weapons systems. But new weapons and equipment programs would not bear fruit for nearly a decade, and in the meantime, older and less capable hardware remained in soldiers' hands.

The familiar pattern of rapid demobilization following a major war began even before the Army had withdrawn from Vietnam. At the height of the war in 1968, the Regular Army had grown to nearly 1.6 million soldiers organized into sixteen divisions. As the Army started its slow withdrawal from Vietnam in 1969, difficult personnel and unit cuts ensued. The Army inactivated three divisions, and many Vietnam veterans left the service. By the time of the Bicentennial of the American Revolution in 1976, budget cuts had reduced the Army by half. Only 775,000 soldiers remained on active duty in thirteen divisions posted in CONUS, Europe, Hawaii, and Korea. To make matters worse, the Army had to grapple with serious challenges posed by the end of the peacetime draft.[4]

The All-Volunteer Force

The end of conscription that had run almost continuously since 1940 came as a direct consequence of the nation's bitter experience in Vietnam. During the presidential campaign of 1968, Richard Nixon indicated that terminating selective service was part of his overall plan to end the Vietnam War. The draft had become inextricably connected with the war effort and the object of sharp antiwar protests. In order for the country to pull free from the Vietnam debacle and heal its deep, internal wounds, the draft would have to go. After his election victory in November 1968, President Nixon moved quickly to fulfill his campaign promise.

On March 27, 1969, Nixon established the Advisory Commission on the All-Volunteer Armed Force and appointed Thomas S. Gates, Jr., a former SECDEF, to head the effort. The Gates Commission was not to consider the merits of retaining or eliminating the draft. Its mission was "to develop a comprehensive plan for eliminating conscription and moving toward an all-volunteer armed force." After eleven months of intense study and analysis, the Gates Commission reported its findings to the president on February 6, 1970. However necessary conscription had been during World War II and the Cold War's early years, the Vietnam draft had been a "costly, inequitable, and divisive procedure for recruiting men." The commission concluded that an all-volunteer military was both feasible and desirable. The panel endorsed three major initiatives to implement the all-volunteer force: a doubling of base pay for all enlisted personnel in the first two years of service, comprehensive improvements in the living conditions and lifestyle of service members and the establishment of a stand-by draft system. To the surprise of many, the Gates Commission recommended July 1, 1971 as the date to end the draft and to initiate the all-volunteer military.[5]

At the Pentagon, senior civilian and military leaders did not share the Gates Commission's optimism. Military planners believed that recruiting enough quality people in the correct military specialties would be nearly impossible. Surely, they argued, an all-volunteer force would jeopardize national security and prove too expensive. A fear existed in the Pentagon and on Capitol Hill that the American people would consider well paid, all-volunteer soldiers as little more than mercenaries. Still, realizing that an all-volunteer force was all but inevitable, the Army initiated programs to ease the transition from the draft to volunteerism. The Army increased its recruiting force, started family and bachelor housing construction projects and increased educational benefits and opportunities. To the horror of many veterans and retirees, the Army abolished reveille and retreat formations, curbed the use of soldiers for work details, relaxed long established haircut and grooming standards, permitted single soldiers to decorate their living quarters and allowed beer in the barracks.[6]

The winding down of the Vietnam War, reduced draft quotas, and public discussions on the end of selective service curbed the desire for membership in the Army Guard. By 1970, the ARNG included 409,412 soldiers formed into eight divisions, four ACRs, eighteen combat brigades and hundreds of support units. Lists of men waiting to join the Guard quickly diminished and finally disappeared. In January 1970, NGAUS came out strongly against the end of the draft, arguing that the National Guard could not maintain its forces "at anything approaching their current size and state of readiness by purely voluntary means, even with additional rewards and incentives." At the same time, NGAUS prepared reports and conducted seminars to assist senior Guard commanders in the transition to an all-volunteer force.[7]

The National Guard leadership enacted new recruiting programs in anticipation of the end of the draft. During 1970, the ARNG initiated a "Try One in the Guard" recruiting campaign to attract trained and experienced veterans. It provided prior service soldiers an opportunity to evaluate Guard membership for one year without a lengthy commitment. Additionally, the ARNG offered soldiers approaching the end of their six-year commitment a one-year extension to allow them additional time to make a final decision on choosing the Guard as a long-term career. Commanders put renewed emphasis on acquiring and retaining experienced soldiers because the cost of training a new recruit was the same as retaining three experienced soldiers.[8]

Following World War II, young men had often sought service in the ARNG rather than subjecting themselves to the draft and active military service. In many respects, the ARNG no longer possessed the recruiting skills and practices that had been prevalent before 1940. With the end of the draft looming and former incentives for Guard service about to evaporate, the ARNG developed its own skilled and dedicated recruiting force. A select group of noncommissioned officers with distinguished careers qualified for recruiting duty after attending lengthy schooling. NGB produced an array of recruiting materials that included pamphlets, brochures, posters, and special radio and television advertising. By the end of 1972, the ARNG had 6,000 trained recruiters, the equivalent of two full-time recruiters for each company-sized unit. In addition to recruiting efforts in armories and local communities, ARNG recruiters manned offices on thirty Army installations hoping to sign up soldiers leaving active duty.[9]

Despite the Gates Commission's recommendation to terminate the draft in 1971, DOD and congressional leaders convinced the Nixon Administration to extend the draft for two additional years. They argued successfully for additional time to implement new legislation and programs to ease the transition to a "zero draft" environment. The last draftee entered the Army in December 1972, and after a nearly continuous stint of thirty-three years, selective service terminated on July 1, 1973. Within six months, ARNG strength tumbled to just below 388,000, and senior Guard leaders feared that the permanent crippling of the ARNG was at hand. However, innovative recruiting efforts by a professional recruiting force and increased benefits packages for volunteers helped to stem the tide. In 1977, the ARNG's personnel strength fell to 355,721, the lowest level since the end of the Korean War. The greatest crisis ever in ARNG peacetime manpower came that same year when the termination of service by Vietnam era Guardsmen resulted in the mass exodus of 104,000 soldiers. At the same time, commanders released large numbers of soldiers due to unsatisfactory performance. A concerted recruiting campaign sustained personnel numbers, but the worst was yet to come; ARNG strength bottomed out in 1979 at 346,974 soldiers.[10]

Table 7
ARNG STRENGTH, 1971–1990

1971	402,175	1981	390,659
1972	387,539	1982	409,238
1973	385,600	1983	417,178
1974	410,682	1984	434,702
1975	401,981	1985	440,778
1976	375,706	1986	446,872
1977	363,777	1987	451,858
1978	347,340	1988	455,182
1979	346,974	1989	456,960
1980	368,254	1990	444,224*

(Source: National Guard Bureau, *Annual Reports* and *Reviews*, 1971–1990.)
*Decline in troop strength for 1990 reflects Guard soldiers initially ordered to active duty for the Persian Gulf War.

The ARNG could not have maintained an acceptable manning level throughout the 1970s without the increased participation of minorities. Though the Guard's roles in enforcing racial integration and controlling riots had exposed a lack of minorities in the ranks, widespread service by African-Americans and women began only with the end of the draft. The impact of new black Guardsmen was particularly significant. In July 1971, 4,961 black soldiers comprised just over 1 percent of the ARNG. Though legislators had removed legal barriers to minority participation in all States, more was needed to bring blacks into uniform. In September 1971 at the annual NGAUS Conference in Honolulu, CNGB announced a major initiative on African-American recruiting. Maj. Gen. Francis S. Greenlief challenged National Guard commanders to double their black ranks within a year. In addition, the Guard established the long-term goal of having every unit reflect the racial composition of its local community. Within a year, the number of blacks in the ARNG increased to 7,680, and only five years later, 46,696 blacks comprised over 12 percent of the ARNG. The procurement of African-American officers lagged, but the growth of black leadership did make progress. In 1972, Brig. Gen. Cunningham Bryant became the first African-American to receive federal recognition as an ARNG general officer when he became the commanding general of the District of Columbia National Guard.[11]

In addition to African-Americans, increasing numbers of women filled the ARNG's ranks. Previous legislation had authorized the service of enlisted women in the National Guard, but the recruiting of female soldiers did not begin in earnest until May 1972. An internal ARNG study

Guard soldiers of the 1-104th Infantry, 26th Infantry Division paddle across a lake during training exercises at Fort Drum, New York in 1977. Not until the 1970s did the ARNG include significant minority participation. (National Guard Education Foundation)

concluded that female soldiers could serve in 37 percent of the Guard's authorized positions. In 1972, only fifty-six officers and enlisted women were in the ARNG, but within a year, the number of females had increased nearly tenfold to 518. Women made important advances in the early years. In August 1974, the first female warrant officer was appointed, and a year later, the first female ARNG aviator earned her flight wings. NGB established an informal goal of recruiting up to 20,000 women into the ARNG, and within three years of the end of the draft, over 11,000 females were on duty.[12]

Total Force Policy

In the early 1970s, the convergence of three significant trends— force reductions, public demands for smaller defense budgets, and the end of the draft—prompted a major change in U.S. defense policy. To fill the void in active forces caused by drastic cuts in resources, the Pentagon turned to the Guard and Reserves. In August 1970, Defense Secretary Melvin R. Laird espoused a "Total Force" concept that called for the reserves to bear more of the direct burden for national defense. In the absence of the draft, Laird called for the reserve components to become the "initial and primary source" for reinforcing Regulars in any emergency "requiring a rapid and substantial expansion of the active forces." The Guard would resume its traditional role of providing ready combat units while the USAR furnished support units and augmented the Army's training installations. The SECDEF ordered the service staffs to apply the Total Force concept "in all aspects of planning, programming, manning and equipping" the reserve components. Despite Laird's guidance, the application of the Total Force concept across the services was inconsistent and uneven.[13]

It fell to one of Melvin Laird's successors, James R. Schlesinger, to convert the Total Force concept into more specific plans and programs. With a forceful memorandum issued on August 22, 1973, Secretary Schlesinger promulgated the "Total Force Policy." Total Force was no longer only a concept; the services were to integrate their active and reserve forces "into a homogeneous whole." Schlesinger emphasized that the Guard and the Reserves were the initial, primary, and sole augmentation to active forces. While he acknowledged that the services had made progress in reserve component integration, Schlesinger declared that reserve units had not yet achieved the readiness standards required for wartime contingencies. The SECDEF directed the Army and the other services to provide the resources necessary to improve reserve component readiness.[14]

The Total Force Policy's implications for the relationship between the Regular Army and the ARNG were profound. Overall, the policy called for an equal partnership between the Army and the Guard. Without the draft, the Army would once again have to rely heavily on the ARNG to provide additional, immediate combat power. Because of force structure reductions and the end of conscription, the Army would require a significant portion of the ARNG in order to fight a major war in Europe or to respond to large emergencies elsewhere. The Total Force Policy required major institutional and cultural changes in the Regular Army and the ARNG unlike any that generation of soldiers had ever experienced.[15]

In order to be an effective combat reserve, ARNG units had to mobilize on short notice, deploy overseas quickly, and enter combat with only a minimum of additional training. The Total Force Policy prompted a number of initiatives to improve ARNG readiness and to increase integration between Regulars and Guardsmen. In 1970, the Army arrayed Guard units on master priority lists that established the allocation of resources to all Army units consistent with wartime planning. At the same time, the management of manpower and equipment intensified. The

ARNG became part of an Army centralized computer system that closely monitored personnel and equipment authorizations in every battalion and separate company. The organization of National Guard units had conformed to standard Army designs since 1916, but computer technology in the early 1970s permitted an improved system of monitoring and managing ARNG resources at the national and State levels. Aided by the power of computers that matched unit equipment inventories against equipment shortages throughout the entire ARNG, logisticians improved readiness by redistributing weapons, vehicles, and critical equipment items. Within a year, the Guard had achieved its highest equipment readiness in history; nearly 75 percent of high priority combat battalions had the essential equipment required for early deployment. The measurement of Guard combat readiness took on a completely new meaning as well. The first submission of formal ARNG readiness reports to the Army began in October 1973. For the first time, senior military leaders scrutinized quantitative readiness data on the Guard. The ARNG developed streamlined deployment procedures that allowed its units to meet stringent deployment timelines, and in 1975, Guard commanders participated in the Army's first, post-Vietnam mobilization exercises.[16]

The Total Force Policy increased training opportunities between active duty and Guard units. As early as 1970, a new Army Affiliation Program linked independent ARNG battalions with active Army divisions for training support. During annual summer training, affiliated ARNG battalions trained with Regulars from designated Army divisions. Units established a year-round program of training visits and coordinated administrative and logistical procedures, but the Affiliation Program stopped short of establishing a direct command relationship between ARNG battalions and Army division commanders. Overall, the Affiliation Program was a great success, and the belief that closer ties to the Regular Army increased Guard readiness set the stage for the program's expansion. Over the next five years, thirty-six ARNG battalions formed affiliations with active units, creating perhaps the closest peacetime ties that had ever before existed between Regular and Guard units. By 1976, eighty-nine ARNG combat battalions had affiliations with active units.[17]

The Roundout Program

The full implementation of the Total Force Policy and the ascension of General Abrams to the post of Army chief of staff created conditions for the beginning of the Army's Roundout Program. The Total Force Policy called for increased utilization of the National Guard, a notion that Abrams embraced. In forty years of military service, Abrams had developed a healthy respect for citizen-soldiers. As one of the Army's premier tank battalion commanders in World War II, Abrams had learned that American citizen-soldiers had the courage to fight and the ability to master the challenges of armored warfare. During the years of racial strife in the 1960s, Abrams had often served as the Army chief of staff's personal representative during ARNG mobilizations, an assignment that brought him into close contact with ARNG leaders and units during difficult circumstances. Abrams developed a great deal of respect for Guardsmen, and as the overall commander of ground forces in Vietnam, he believed the failure to mobilize the Guard and the Reserves at the beginning of the war had been a crucial error.[18]

After becoming chief of staff in October 1972, Abrams set out to revitalize a tired and demoralized Army. He advocated an expansion of the active Army from thirteen to sixteen divisions, a move designed to restore the Army's prestige while providing the combat power needed to meet post-Vietnam, global commitments. DOD agreed to the activation of three new divisions, but required that the new commands had to come from existing Army assets and not from increases in personnel levels. The outcome of the Vietnam War had convinced Abrams that the Army should never again go to war without the full support of the American people. In his mind, the direct link between the active Army and the American people ran through the ARNG and the USAR. Faced with the challenges of increasing the number of active Army divisions while at the same time strengthening the Army's ties to the American people, Abrams's staff came up with a novel solution; the ARNG Roundout brigade.[19]

Building on the successes of the Affiliation Program, Roundout brigades would be permanently assigned to active duty divisions for training and become a permanent and integral portion of the division's structure. In peacetime, selected Army divisions were to have only two combat brigades, and upon mobilization, the addition of a Roundout brigade would bring a division to its full configuration. Roundout brigades were to deploy and fight as a division's third combat maneuver brigade. The Roundout brigade's peacetime commander, an ARNG brigadier general, would act as an assistant division commander in war. In addition, the Army assigned a number of active divisions a separate ARNG combat battalion to provide the tenth ground maneuver unit each division required. By reducing the standing size of selected active divisions, the Army would gain a portion of the manpower needed to create three new divisions.

The Army's first Roundout was the 29th Infantry Brigade in Hawaii. Upon redeployment from Vietnam, the 25th Infantry Division at

Schofield Barracks had inactivated one brigade, and the Army's Pacific Command asked to integrate the 29th Brigade into the "Tropical Lightning" Division. By 1973, the ARNG had reconfigured the Hawaii brigade to function as an organic element of the 25th Division. CNGB reported that the new relationship was "most encouraging" and promised "new avenues" for shared training opportunities.[20]

The Roundout experiment in Hawaii went well, and by the summer of 1976, the Army had added Roundout brigades to its three newly activated divisions. In 1975, the Louisiana ARNG's 256th Infantry Brigade became the Roundout to the 5th Infantry Division (Mechanized) at Fort Polk, while Georgia's 48th Infantry Brigade (Mechanized) joined the 24th Infantry Division (Mechanized) at Fort Stewart, Georgia. The following year, Oregon's 41st Infantry Brigade became the Roundout to the 7th Infantry Division at Fort Ord, California. By 1977, the 256th Brigade had converted to mechanized infantry, and the ARNG had restructured all three brigades to make them an integral part of their parent divisions.[21]

Equipping the new Roundout units challenged Army and ARNG logisticians. Equipment incompatibility between active and ARNG battalions had caused training restrictions in the Affiliation Program, and the Army did not want to repeat the mistake with the Roundout units. A concerted effort began to equip the Roundout brigades with the same weapons systems and equipment as their active duty divisions. The M60 tank, new anti-tank missile systems, and modern radios and wheeled vehicles went to the Roundouts. At the same time, Guard logisticians redirected excess vehicles and equipment to Roundout battalions. However, Roundout modernization soon slowed because of competing demands and the lack of an acquisition program for ARNG equipment. To keep the Guard's readiness reporting levels high, the Army designated older equipment as authorized substitutes for more modern items. ARNG commanders believed that liberal substitutions masked readiness problems and that the Army had given them new missions and responsibilities but not the equipment necessary to get the job done. Out of frustration, some Guardsmen referred to the Total Force Policy as the "Total Farce."[22]

The Roundout Program achieved many of the positive results that General Abrams had intended. The close ties between active divisions and Roundout brigades increased ARNG readiness and gave Guardsmen a new sense of purpose. In making the Roundout brigades organic to active divisions, the Army was able to generate the manpower required to raise three new divisions and to place sixteen divisions on active duty once again. As designed, the Roundout program achieved one of Creighton Abrams' most important goals. Linking the Roundout brigades to several active divisions ensured that the Army could never again go to war without a significant National Guard mobilization, an action that would require the full backing of the American people and the consent of Congress. Unfortunately, Abrams did not live to witness the full benefits of the Roundout Program; he succumbed to cancer in September 1974, the only Army chief of staff ever to die on active duty.[23]

Overseas Training and Mobilization Preparedness

Under the Total Force Policy, the requirement for Guard and Reserve forces to deploy quickly to NATO and other regions prompted the Army to increase ARNG participation in overseas training. Prior to the Vietnam War, Guardsmen had trained at sites in Hawaii, Alaska, and Puerto Rico, and in the early 1970s, small groups of ARNG linguists and SF teams had deployed worldwide. The Army's focus on the defense of Europe insured that most ARNG overseas training would take place in the NATO region. At first, overseas training consisted of foreign exchange programs with other NATO reserve forces and ARNG participation in major exercises. In both instances, units deployed outside the U.S. during normal annual training periods.[24]

The first foreign exchange program occurred between the Minnesota ARNG and the Norwegian Home Guard in 1972. A platoon from the 47th Infantry Division traveled to Norway for annual training while a force of Norwegians trained at Camp Ripley, Minnesota. The exchange's success produced a longstanding relationship between Norwegians and Minnesotans. Other States began exchange programs with NATO forces. In 1977, one rifle company each from New York's 42nd Infantry Division and Massachusetts's 26th Infantry Division traveled to South Wales for annual training with the British Territorial Army. Meanwhile, other ARNG units trained overseas outside the NATO region. Hawaii infantrymen flew to Australia for training, Puerto Rican Guardsmen hacked their way through Panamanian jungles, and detachments from the 19th SF Group deployed to Korea. In 1976, 2,400 Guardsmen participated in overseas training exercises.[25]

ARNG participation in major exercises focused largely on the defense of Central Europe. Beginning in the mid-1970s, senior command and staff officers from ARNG high priority units regularly visited Army units and potential battlefields in Europe. The tours familiarized Guardsmen with the tactical and logistical plans of active units in Europe and allowed Guard commanders to study the terrain of their designated defensive sectors. The real thrust of European training became the annual Return of Forces to Germany (REFORGER) exercises in which Regular

A Guardsman from the 42nd Infantry Division receives instruction on British communications equipment from a member of the 5th Battalion (Territorial), Royal Anglican Regiment. Overseas exchange programs increased the ARNG's integration with the Regular Army and NATO forces in the 1970s. (National Guard Education Foundation)

and ARNG units flew to Europe, drew equipment from pre-positioned stocks, and participated in large maneuvers. REFORGER exercises trained ARNG leaders in mobilization and deployment procedures under realistic and stressful conditions and familiarized all soldiers with NATO operations. In 1980, fourteen ARNG units participated in REFORGER, including South Carolina's 3-178th Field Artillery, the first, complete ARNG battalion to deploy directly from home armories to West Germany. That same year, 6,500 Guardsmen in seventy-three units deployed overseas for training.[26]

One of the Army's most beneficial Total Force initiatives began in 1979 with the CAPSTONE Program. The Army identified all units required to fulfill wartime missions in the overseas theaters and to support full mobilization in CONUS and then aligned ARNG units with an appropriate Army headquarters. For ARNG commanders at all levels, their CAPSTONE alignment provided the basis for the development of training and planning associations with an active duty unit they would serve with in wartime. The CAPSTONE Program produced important results. First, ARNG units received a valid, wartime mission. Second, small unit commanders were able to direct their training toward a specific, tangible mission. For most Guardsmen, the CAPSTONE Program allowed detailed preparations for a defensive, mechanized war in Europe. But starting in 1980, several ARNG units received notice of their CAPSTONE alignment to the newly formed Rapid Deployment Force, a major joint headquarters responsible for U.S. military operations in Southwest Asia. For the first time, Guardsmen prepared for a war in the Middle East, a prospect that must have seemed remote at the time.[27]

In conjunction with the CAPSTONE Program, the Army developed detailed mobilization schedules for the overseas theaters. ARNG units appeared on classified deployment schedules for the first time in 1979. The schedules provided ARNG commanders with detailed, specific time-lines that outlined the days required for mobilization, deployment from ports of embarkation, drawing of equipment from pre-positioned stocks, and the expected date of availability for combat. Airlift and sealift were planned to quickly move CONUS based Regular and ARNG divisions to Europe to help defeat a Soviet offensive. With deployment dates that followed shortly after mobilization, Guard commanders made every effort to conduct realistic training toward the survival and early success of their units in a European war.[28]

The new emphasis on short deployment schedules caused a reap-praisal of the role of the States in a large, federal mobilization. A major reorganization of the State headquarters commenced in 1978 that placed more emphasis on the mobilization function of the AGs. The AGs received more resources that allowed them to control and to support mobilized ARNG units moving from local armories to federal mobiliza-tion stations or ports of embarkation. In 1980, mobilization exercises in various States evaluated the capabilities and effectiveness of the State headquarters to act as a mobilization asset.[29]

Other Important Developments in the 1970s

A long-term, political legacy of the Vietnam War came with the enactment of the War Powers Act of 1973. Concerned that an excess of presidential power might one day plunge the country into another bloody, unpopular war, the law required congressional approval of troop deployments abroad in combat situations within sixty days of commitment. The act sparked an ongoing debate over the exercise of presidential power during national emergencies. Concerned it had overly restricted the president's power to react quickly in a major crisis, Congress passed a new statute in 1976 giving the president authority to callup a limited number of Guardsmen and Reservists for short periods without congressional approval. In it final form, Section 673b authorized the mobilization of 200,000 National Guard and Reserve personnel for up to 180 days.[30]

The era of Total Force Policy brought a number of important changes to the NGB command structure. In 1970, an adjustment of responsibilities and offices between the NGB staff and the Army and Air Divisions occurred. A new organization emerged consisting of a joint NGB headquarters with separate Army and Air National Guard

Directorates. The major general responsible for the operations of the ARNG Directorate was designated as the Director, ARNG (DARNG). Increased reliance on the Guard brought more responsibility to the position of CNGB, and in 1978, DOD elevated the position to three stars, the same rank held by the principle general officers on the Army and Air Force Staffs. Lt. Gen. LaVern E. Weber, the former AG of Oklahoma, was the first CNGB to wear the new rank. (Another Oklahoman, Raymond S. McLain, had been the first Guardsman ever promoted to lieutenant general in June 1945.) The National Guard expanded across the country as well, adding new jurisdictions in the U.S. Virgin Islands in 1973 and in Guam in 1981.[31]

The States believed their full-time technician force needed more training, and NGB searched for a suitable site for a new, centrally located, national training facility. Arkansas agreed to provide the land and partial funding for construction, and in 1975 the National Guard Professional Education Center opened at Camp Robinson in North Little Rock, remaining under the direct control of NGB. Within two years, the Professional Education Center became the central training facility for technicians with living accommodations for 240 students. In subsequent years, the center grew in size and prominence to become the ARNG's most important instructional and conference facility, serving both full-time and traditional Guardsmen.[32]

The inactivation of many Regular Army aviation units after Vietnam resulted in the creation of a robust ARNG aviation force. Helicopters, pilots, and aviation units too expensive to retain on active duty found a natural home in the Guard. In 1971 alone, a total of 320 helicopters flowed into the Guard, including the UH-1 "Huey," the AH-1 "Cobra," and the CH-54 "Flying Crane," and the ARNG aircraft inventory jumped to 1,218 airframes. Officer and warrant officer pilots leaving active duty who wanted to maintain their flight certification flocked to the Guard. In 1972, the number of ARNG aviators surged from 2,826 to 3,617, and the Guard's aircraft inventory expanded dramatically to 1,542 helicopters and 166 fixed wing aircraft. A separate staff group became necessary to manage aviation assets, and in 1974, an Aviation Division appeared in the ARNG Directorate. In addition to managing pilots and aircraft, the division supervised safety, training, and maintenance programs. By 1980, nearly 30 percent of the Army's total aviation assets were in the ARNG.[33]

A second, organized group of Guardsmen added their voice to the public discussion of Guard issues in 1972 with the creation of the Enlisted Association of the National Guard of the United States (EANGUS). Two years earlier, a group of National Guard senior enlisted soldiers and airmen had met in South Dakota to create an organization that they hoped would make the National Guard a more influential arm of national defense by improving the status, welfare, and professionalism of the enlisted ranks. EANGUS received its charter as a national organization in 1972, established a headquarters in Alexandria, Virginia and eventually published an association magazine. In conjunction with NGAUS, EANGUS pushed legislation to increase the pay and benefits of enlisted soldiers and airmen while advocating better equipment, weapons, and facilities for all Guardsmen. Though serious proposals have been made to merge NGAUS and EANGUS, the two organizations remain separate advocates for the National Guard's well being.[34]

The decade of the 1970s saw the loss of the National Guard's most visible supporters and the rise of its newest advocate. In December 1972, President Truman passed away. Since his entry into the Missouri National Guard in 1905, Truman had been a keen supporter of the National Guard and of citizen-soldiers. In an irony of history, the National Guard lost two of its principal advocates within days of one another. Ellard Walsh died at age eighty-eight on August 31,1975, and less than a week later, Milton Reckord passed away in Baltimore at the venerable age of ninety-one. But the National Guard did not have to wait long for a new champion. Congressman G.V. "Sonny" Montgomery of Mississippi became the Guard's staunchest advocate on Capitol Hill.[35]

The Reagan Buildup

President Ronald Reagan entered office in January 1981 promising to restore national power and prestige to a country that had suffered significant social, political, economic, and military setbacks during the 1970s. Reagan came to power riding the crest of a conservative movement that emphasized increased defense spending, reductions in wasteful and unnecessary domestic programs, and tax cuts. Concerned over Soviet advances in the Middle East, Africa, and Central America, the Reagan Administration was determined to square off against the Soviets. In numerous speeches, Reagan spoke of an "evil empire" that was the "focus of evil in the modern world."[36]

Secretary of Defense Caspar Weinberger presided over the nation's largest, peacetime military buildup. For his CJCS, President Reagan selected Army General John W. Vessey, Jr., a former Guardsman. General Vessey had enlisted in the Minnesota National Guard in May 1939 and was ordered to active duty in February 1941. He had served with the 34th Infantry Division throughout the campaigns in the Mediterranean and was a first sergeant when he received a battlefield commission on May 6, 1944 at the Anzio beachhead in Italy. Spending during the Reagan

Buildup even exceeded expenditures during the Korean and Vietnam Wars. In its first five years in office, the Reagan Administration spent nearly $1 trillion on defense, an amount that almost equaled the combined defense budgets under Presidents Nixon, Ford, and Carter. The Pentagon's budget doubled in five years, from $143.9 billion in 1980 to $294.7 billion in 1985. The clear bulk of the surge in defense spending went to the modernization and expansion of a whole range of large nuclear programs including the MX missile, the Trident submarine and the resurrection of the B-1 bomber. The balance of buildup dollars went to the military services' personnel, operations, and modernization accounts. On March 23, 1983, President Reagan surprised the nation with the announcement of his intention to develop and deploy a comprehensive defense against strategic nuclear missiles. Dubbed "Star Wars" by the media, Secretary Weinberger organized various missile defense programs into the Strategic Defense Initiative that became the most distinctive and innovative defense program of the Reagan years.[37]

The Reagan Buildup began at a time when the U.S. military had deteriorated badly as a result of the turbulent and austere 1970s. The debacle at "Desert One" in Iran in April 1980, in which a raid to free American hostages in Tehran unravelled in its early stages, highlighted the need for renewal and reform in the military. The Army chief of staff, General Edward C. Meyer, spoke of a "hollow Army" in which inadequate logistical and support units backed up undermanned combat formations. The Army manned divisions in CONUS at low levels to ensure that forward deployed units had a full complement of soldiers. In 1981, General Meyer told Congress that fully two-thirds of the Army's logistical capabilities were in the reserve components and that the Regular Army could not sustain itself without Guardsmen and Reservists who would certainly see early service in both large and small contingencies. The invasion of Grenada in October 1983 reflected improvements in combat forces but revealed some of the same shortcomings in intelligence, communications, and joint service planning that had doomed the Iranian rescue mission.[38]

Despite its apparent shortcomings, President Reagan called on the Army to implement a new national security strategy that went far beyond the defense of Western Europe. The Reagan Administration advocated a comprehensive strategy for meeting head-on the "evil empire's" multiple threats. In addition to the continued defense of NATO, the Army was expected to counter and defeat communist threats in the Middle East, Africa, and Central America. To enhance America's global reach, DOD created the U.S. Central Command in January 1983. From its headquarters at MacDill Air Force base in Tampa, Florida, Central Command had responsibility for U.S. joint operations in the Middle East. Army planners retooled their strategic thinking and soon developed a new strategic paradigm that described a "spectrum of conflict" ranging from high-intensity to low-intensity warfare. Nuclear warfare and large conventional battles posed the most serious threats while low-intensity conflict consisted of guerilla operations. The Army's strategic thinking shifted from a single focus on the defense of Western Europe to countering a broader range of threats. Military leaders began to develop the doctrine, forces, and weapons required to conduct operations along the entire spectrum of conflict.[39]

The Army's new doctrine for warfare in the 1980s became known as AirLand Battle. Two new concepts were key: the attack of enemy forces in depth and the synchronization of maximum combat power from all the military services into a coordinated, joint effort. To train armor and mechanized units in the tactics of AirLand Battle, the Army established the National Training Center (NTC) at Fort Irwin, California in 1983. Formerly an ARNG training installation, the Guard had returned Fort Irwin to the Army's control in 1981. The arid, open spaces of the Mojave Desert permitted heavy combat battalions to train in realistic tactical situations against a highly proficient opposing force using Soviet style weapons and equipment. Sophisticated laser equipment, computer monitoring systems and massive live-fire exercises gave soldiers a "near combat" experience. By 1985, as many as twenty-eight tank and mechanized infantry battalions trained each year at the NTC.[40]

Changes in the Army's force structure occurred concurrently with the advent of new doctrine and tactics. A series of studies called "Army 86" examined the best ways to capitalize on new technology and weapons. Significant structural changes occurred in the Army's heavy divisions, corps and at levels above the corps. The Army's senior leadership determined that insufficient forces were available to meet communist threats across the entire spectrum of conflict. Prior emphasis on fighting the Soviet blitzkrieg in Europe had prevented the creation of lighter forces to confront communist insurgencies elsewhere. Under the leadership of Army Chief of Staff General John A. Wickham, Jr., the Army bolstered its SF and infantry units. Two new light infantry divisions brought the total number of divisions on active duty to eighteen. The 10th Mountain Division (Light) became active at Fort Drum, New York in 1985 and the following year the 6th Infantry Division (Light) was created at Fort Richardson, Alaska. The light infantry divisions were austere, air-transportable organizations capable of early commitment to threatening situations at the lower end of the spectrum of conflict.[41]

By the late 1980s, the fruits of the Reagan Buildup were evident throughout the Army. A whole host of modernization programs initiated in the 1970s came to fruition and provided the means for implementing AirLand Battle. Increased defense spending accelerated the fielding and development of five, key weapons systems: the M-1 Abrams tank; the M-2 Bradley Fighting Vehicle; the AH-64 Apache attack helicopter; the UH-60 Blackhawk utility helicopter; and the Patriot air defense system. Guided by the tenets of AirLand Battle, Army units trained on sophisticated, high-technology weaponry aided by training devices based on lasers and computer chips that added greater realism to field exercises. Significant changes in force structure permitted the maximum use of more destructive weapons systems requiring fewer numbers of operators. To meet the challenge of low-intensity conflict, SF and light infantrymen were available for rapid air transport to the world's hot spots. The U.S. military's swift and successful invasion of Panama in December 1989 demonstrated the efficacy of the Army's internal reforms and improvements in joint operations made during the 1980s.[42]

The ARNG and the Reagan Buildup

During the Reagan years, the ARNG had a firm supporter in John O. Marsh, Jr., the Secretary of the Army. He had enlisted in the Army as a private during World War II, received an officer's commission in 1945, and served with American occupation forces in Germany from 1945–1947. In 1951, Marsh joined the Virginia ARNG, and for the next twenty-five years, served in various positions with the 116th Infantry, the 29th Division and State headquarters. Starting in 1963, he served four terms in the U.S. House of Representatives. While in Congress, Marsh served a thirty-day, voluntary tour of active duty in Vietnam as a major. After his service in the House, he was appointed to high positions in the Executive Branch, culminating in August 1974 with his appointment as Counselor with cabinet rank to President Gerald R. Ford. In January 1981, Marsh took the oath as Secretary of the Army. He instituted the concept of annual themes based on traditional, military values to motivate and inspire soldiers as the Army sought to heal the wounds of Vietnam and the austere 1970s. Marsh encouraged expansion and improvements in the ARNG during the Reagan Buildup. When he retired as Secretary of the Army in August 1989, Marsh's tenure was the longest of any Secretary of the Army or Secretary of War in American history.[43]

The most important gains in the ARNG during the Reagan years came in manpower. From a low of 346,974 Guardsmen in 1979, ARNG strength grew steadily throughout the 1980s. Increased recruiting

Congressman G.V. "Sonny" Montgomery National Guard Soldier and Statesman

Congressman G. V. "Sonny" Montgomery stands as one of the National Guard's most important advocates in the second half of the 20th Century. During World War II, he served as a lieutenant in the 12th Armored Division in Europe.

After the war, he returned home to Mississippi and joined the National Guard. Montgomery was mobilized with the 31st Infantry Division for the Korean War and remained on active duty until 1952. After the Korean War, Sonny Montgomery was elected to the Mississippi legislature and served there for ten years. He had his first national exposure in 1962 while commanding a detachment of Mississippi Guardsmen ordered to safeguard Martin Luther King, Jr.'s "Freedom Ride" to Jackson, Mississippi. He retired from the Mississippi Guard with the State rank of major general.

National Guard Education Foundation

In 1966, Sonny Montgomery was elected to the U.S. House of Representatives where he became a principal advocate for personnel in the all-volunteer military. In the early 1980s, he sponsored a new G.I. Bill that gave service members important enlistment and education benefits. Tens of thousands of Guard men and women eventually took advantage of the program. In 1987, Congress formalized the Montgomery G.I. Bill. The same year, he sponsored the Montgomery Amendment, a key piece of legislation that supported overseas training for Guardsmen and paved the way for the U.S. Supreme Court's 1990 Perpich Decision. During the Persian Gulf War, Congressman Montgomery was a key supporter for the mobilization and deployment of ARNG combat units.

Sonny Montgomery retired from Congress in 1996 after thirty years of distinguished service. The impressive Montgomery Room in the National Guard Memorial in Washington, DC is a fitting tribute to this outstanding soldier-statesman. Because of his long-term advocacy for National Guard issues, Sonny Montgomery stands as one of the most important Guard legislators since the end of World War II.

budgets, more generous incentive programs, flexible enlistment options, and a thoroughly professional recruiting force promoted volunteerism. Recruiters and commanders agreed that a more favorable recruiting climate existed due to society's improved views on the military and a nationwide resurgence in patriotism. A centerpiece of the recruiting effort was the Montgomery G.I. Bill that became law in 1987 after a three-year test program. Sponsored by Sonny Montgomery and named in his honor, the bill provided partial college funding to high school graduates who enlisted in the military for six years and successfully completed their initial active duty training. Congressman Montgomery insisted that the benefits package should apply to the reserve components as well, and by the end of the decade, nearly 58,000 Guardsmen had utilized the Montgomery G.I. Bill. ARNG strength levels grew until reaching an historic, peacetime high in 1989 of 456,960 soldiers. Never before had so many Guardsmen filled the ranks. Across the country, Guardsmen discussed the possibility of the ARNG growing to 500,000 soldiers.[44]

The increasing presence of minorities explains much of the Guard's growth. At the close of the 1980s, the ARNG's minority strength stood at 111,973 soldiers, nearly one-quarter of the force. African-American participation doubled during the Reagan years, and by 1989, 75,000 black Guardsmen comprised over 16 percent of the force. Female membership grew precipitously early in the decade but reached a plateau in 1985. In an organization composed largely of combat units in which females were not authorized to serve, women faced limited opportunities for assignments and promotions. Positions for women eventually opened in more fields including vehicle operators, helicopter crew chiefs, and staff positions in field artillery units. By 1989, nearly 30,000 female soldiers comprised over 6 percent of the ARNG.[45]

Though barred by law from serving in direct combat positions, by the 1980s women served in most ARNG combat support roles. Members of the Support Battalion, 116th Infantry Brigade of the Virginia ARNG prepare for training in the early 1980s. (Virginia National Guard Historical Collection)

Two innovative personnel programs began during the manpower increases of the 1980s. The Key Personnel Upgrade Program provided selected Guard officers and enlisted soldiers in leadership positions the opportunity to train closely with an active duty counterpart during field training and command post exercises. Guardsmen learned improved military skills that added to the readiness of their units. From modest beginnings in 1981, the program grew steadily, and by 1987, over 7,500 Guardsmen on active duty for training participated in fourteen major exercises in thirteen different countries while another 2,900 accompanied Regular units to the NTC. The ARNG placed experienced officers, warrant officers and enlisted soldiers on active, Federal service starting in 1981 under the Active Guard/Reserve (AGR) Program. Full-time AGR soldiers with experience, expertise, and knowledge of ARNG programs and policies served as advisors, coordinators, and staff officers in the Pentagon and at major Army installations throughout CONUS and overseas. By 1986, 1,266 AGRs were serving at Army installations worldwide.[46]

With the growth in ARNG manpower came an increase in units. The greatest boon to the Guard's force structure came with the addition of two new divisions. To add depth to the strategic reserve of combat heavy

Secretary of the Army John O. Marsh, Jr., Army Chief of Staff Gen. John A. Wickham, Jr. and Chief of the National Guard Bureau Lt. Gen. Emmett H. Walker, Jr. preside over the activation ceremony of the 29th Infantry Division (Light) at Fort Belvoir, Virginia on September 30, 1985. (Virginia National Guard Historical Collection)

forces, the ARNG reactivated the 35th Infantry Division (Mechanized) in ceremonies at Fort Leavenworth, Kansas on August 25, 1984. The Santa Fe Division drew its units from five states: Kansas, Nebraska, Kentucky, Colorado, and Missouri. As part of General Wickham's initiative to increase the number of light infantry forces, the ARNG received authority to raise a light infantry division. On September 30, 1985, the 29th Infantry Division (Light) was restored to the ARNG's force structure during ceremonies at Fort Belvoir, Virginia. The "Blue and Gray" Division remained true to its World War II heritage by drawing its units from Virginia and Maryland and by reviving its distinctive shoulder patch and traditional nickname. The addition of the 35th and 29th Divisions gave the ARNG a total of ten combat divisions.[47]

The Reagan Buildup also saw significant increases in the Roundout Program as the Army placed greater reliance on ARNG combat units. In 1984, Mississippi's 155th Armored Brigade became a Roundout to the 1st Cavalry Division at Fort Hood. Two years later, the ARNG assigned New York's 27th Infantry Brigade as Roundout to the new 10th Mountain Division. Independent ARNG tank and mechanized infantry battalions from Minnesota, North Carolina, Alabama, and Texas became separate Roundout battalions to active, heavy divisions in CONUS. In 1989, Alaska's 6-297 Infantry Battalion (Light) became part of the 6th Infantry Division (Light) at Fort Richardson. The following year, the Army asked the ARNG for a group of units to Roundout the 4th Infantry Division (Mechanized) at Fort Carson, Colorado. The newly organized 116th Cavalry Brigade, with units in Idaho, Oregon, and Nevada, and North Carolina's 2-120th Infantry became the last units to achieve Roundout status under the Total Force Policy. The Roundout Program flourished in the 1980s. The Commanding General of the 5th Infantry Division stated in 1987 that he would take Louisiana's 256th Brigade to war "tomorrow, if necessary." At Fort Stewart, then Maj. Gen. H. Norman Schwarzkopf said of the Georgia ARNG's 48th Brigade: "Roundout is a fact of life...I expect them to fight alongside us...They are, in fact, combat ready."[48]

With President Reagan's increased defense budgets, the ARNG's equipment posture improved significantly, both in quantity and quality. The Army initiated a new equipping policy that changed the face of the ARNG; Roundout units would receive the same, new modern equipment as their active divisions. The first M-1 tanks appeared in the ARNG in 1983, going to North Carolina's 1-252 Armor, a separate Roundout battalion to the 2d Armored Division. In 1985 alone, Roundout units received 180 M-1 Abrams tanks, sixty-four M-2 Bradley Fighting Vehicles, advanced artillery computers and radars, and large numbers of new, light tactical vehicles and heavy trucks. The steady flow of new equipment into

Roundout brigades made displaced equipment available to upgrade the weapons and equipment of lower priority units.[49]

The combined efforts of NGAUS, EANGUS, and AGAUS raised concerns in Congress over ARNG equipping. Starting in 1983, Congress authorized funding in a Dedicated Procurement Program (DPP) for the specific purchase of National Guard weapons and equipment. The first year's funding of $113.9 million went toward the purchase of heavy trucks, tracked vehicles, radios, and aircraft. DPP funding increased throughout the Reagan years, reaching a level of $248 million by 1989. An equipping record was set in 1988 when the ARNG received a total of $2.7 billion in new, displaced and refurbished equipment. By the end of the decade, the Apache and Blackhawk helicopters and the multiple launch rocket system (MLRS) had been added to the inventory. Commanders believed that the ARNG was finally eliminating the equipment shortfalls that had dogged their units since the early 1970s.[50]

Increased participation in overseas deployments became the foundation of ARNG training in the 1980s. The ARNG's role in REFORGER increased each year. In 1981, Indiana's 2-152d Infantry was the first ARNG maneuver unit to go to REFORGER. Two years later, the 1-198th Armor from Mississippi's 155th Armored Brigade deployed with the 1st Cavalry Division to Germany, drew prepositioned equipment and conducted extensive maneuvers. The Guard's greatest participation in REFORGER occurred in 1986 when the entire 32d Infantry Brigade (Mechanized) from Wisconsin deployed to Germany with all of its equipment and personnel. North Carolina's 30th Infantry Brigade (Mechanized) deployed a task force to Italy in 1983 for NATO exercises, the first time a Guard unit had shipped its equipment overseas for training. Starting in 1980, the U.S. began BRIGHT STAR exercises, the biennial deployment of forces to Egypt and the Sudan. Two years later, the first Guardsmen went to the Middle East for training and felt the sand, heat, and wind of the Egyptian desert. In the Pacific, Guardsmen deployed to Korea on TEAM SPIRIT, an annual exercise designed to test America's response to the sudden outbreak of war in Asia. An infantry task force from California's 40th Division deployed to Korea in 1986 as part of TEAM SPIRIT, marking the Sunshine Division's first return since the end of the Korean War.[51]

ARNG soldiers experienced the best training during tough, realistic exercises at the NTC. The first Guard combat unit to train at Fort Irwin was a Roundout battalion, Georgia's 1-108th Armor, that went to the NTC with the 24th Infantry Division in September 1983. The following spring another Roundout battalion, Minnesota's 2-136th Infantry, went to the NTC with Regulars from the 1st Infantry Division. Private First Class

Daren Wickline, a member of the 2-136th Infantry and a farmer from Verges, Minnesota, summed up the attitudes of Guardsmen training at Fort Irwin: "It was as close as you can get to real combat without actually being shot at." In 1985, 2,700 Guardsmen in five Roundout battalions went to the NTC with their parent divisions. Later that year, the ARNG Directorate published a training schedule that required all Roundout units to rotate through Fort Irwin once every three years. In August 1987, Louisiana's 256th Brigade became the first ARNG unit to act as the controlling headquarters during an NTC rotation. Dozens of ARNG support units received valuable training at Fort Irwin while providing logistical, maintenance, and transportation services to field exercises and the installation.[52]

The Perpich Lawsuit

Beginning in 1983, the ARNG participated in extensive training and humanitarian support missions in Central America. Under the auspices of the U.S. Southern Command, ARNG engineers began a series of road building and repair exercises in Panama in conjunction with active Army units and the Panama Defense Force. In 1984, a combined task force of Puerto Rico, Florida, and Louisiana Guardsmen as well as U.S. Army and Panamanian soldiers constructed a nine-mile gravel road in the interior of Panama.[53]

Training exercises in Central America soon changed dramatically in size and scope. The road building program, dubbed *Fuertes Caminos* or "Blazing Trails," became larger and more ambitious. Between January and May 1985, battalions of Guard, Regular, and Panamanian engineers repaired and constructed another seventeen-mile section of road on the western coast of the Azuero Peninsula, 150 miles from the Panama Canal. In addition to engineer activities, the 10,000 Guardsmen who deployed to Panama in 1985 repaired school buildings, distributed clothing and supplies, and provided medical assistance. ARNG medical units from North Carolina and Illinois deployed to Honduras and Ecuador to train and to provide health care. ARNG combat units also headed to Central America. A Texas armored task force trained with the Honduran Army and conducted anti-armor exercises only three miles from Nicaragua's border. At the same time, Illinois' 2-132d Field Artillery worked with the Hondurans to organize several joint, live fire exercises.[54]

Political leaders opposed to the Reagan Administration's policy of confrontation with the Soviet Union and its surrogates raised eyebrows at the use of ARNG troops in Central America. Though the Pentagon argued that the deployments trained Guardsmen to perform difficult

Engineers construct a bridge in Central America in the 1980s as part of the ARNG's deployments to the region. (National Guard Education Foundation)

engineering feats in mountains and jungles and provided humanitarian aid to important allies in the region, several Governors objected. Opponents believed that the Guard's presence was little more than a thinly veiled threat of American power against authoritarian regimes in Central America, especially against the *Sandinistas* in Nicaragua. These Governors threatened to withhold their consent to Guardsmen training in the region. Hoping to avert a showdown over the deployments, Congressman Sonny Montgomery attached an important amendment to the 1986 Defense Authorization Act. The "Montgomery Amendment" declared that the consent of a Governor to call Guardsmen to active duty training might not be withheld with regard to active duty outside the United States "because of any objection to the location, purpose, type or schedule of such active duty."[55]

A three-year court battle over the rights of the Governors to deny their consent to overseas National Guard training soon ensued. After Minnesota Guardsmen returned from training in Central America in early 1987, Governor Rudy Perpich of Minnesota and six other Governors filed suit against DOD. Perpich argued that the Montgomery Amendment was unconstitutional and that the Governors had the authority to withhold consent to peacetime Guard training conducted overseas. After a series of decisions and appeals within the 8th U.S.

Circuit Court, the full court in June 1989 upheld the Montgomery Amendment and decided that the Constitution did not require gubernatorial consent for National Guard training. Governor Perpich appealed the decision to the U.S. Supreme Court who rendered a final ruling on June 11, 1990. The court decided that the Montgomery Amendment was constitutional and that the authority of the States to train the militia did not limit the Army's authority to train personnel on federal active duty as reserves of the Army. However, the court did recognize the power of the Governors to withhold consent to National Guard active duty training whenever a State had an immediate need for the Guard's presence during an emergency.[56]

The End of the Cold War

The stage was set for dramatic changes in the international order when Mikhail Gorbachev came to power in the Soviet Union in 1985. A visionary and a progressive, Gorbachev realized the Soviet Union had forfeited its economic power and influence in order to build a massive military machine. In Gorbachev's mind, the cost of maintaining and modernizing the Soviet military had become prohibitive, and he set the Soviet Union on a new course of reform and renewal. A lessening of tensions between East and West ensued as the Soviets turned away from international adventures to concentrate on domestic social and economic reforms. At the same time, centralized control over the Soviet Empire weakened.

President George H. W. Bush entered office in January 1989, and in his inaugural address, he spoke of a "new breeze of freedom" blowing around the world. By the end of 1989, the breeze had swelled into a tremendous hurricane that swept away most visages of the Cold War. The greatest changes came in eastern Europe where countries threw off the yokes of communism and Soviet control. The most dramatic developments came in October and early November when the East German government collapsed and the Berlin Wall fell. By the end of the year, a violent revolution in Romania and free elections in Czechoslovakia had ushered in new governments. To the delight of New Year's revelers ringing in a new decade on January 1, 1990, the protracted Cold War was finally over.

In the United States, cuts in the growth of defense spending had started as early as 1987, but relief over the end of the Cold War produced quick calls for even deeper cuts. The American people and many in Congress anticipated a "peace dividend," the expected savings from defense cutbacks. President Bush's Defense Secretary, Richard Cheney, ordered the military services to formulate plans for cutting $180 billion from the Pentagon's multi-year budget. Despite the president's warnings that the world situation still posed significant threats, public opinion demanded reductions in defense and increased spending for social programs. In public opinion polls in 1990, defense ranked last on the public's list of the ten most important spending priorities. Bowing to public pressure, the Bush Administration made plans for a 25 percent reduction in military forces across the board.[57]

The post-Cold War demobilization began with a vengeance. Planned cuts in Army forces were deep and widespread. Secretary Cheney recommended that the number of Army divisions be reduced from twenty-eight to eighteen by 1995 with commensurate cuts in Regular, ARNG, USAR and Army civilian personnel. The Army developed and set in motion an extensive plan dubbed "Quicksilver" that outlined an orderly progression of budget and personnel cuts throughout the 1990s. DOD directed the Army to lose 20,000 active duty soldiers in 1990 alone, thus bringing the Regular Army down to 744,169 soldiers, the lowest manning level since before the Korean War. To save money, the Army cancelled REFORGER for the first time since its inception in 1966.[58]

Even before budget cuts developed as a serious threat, the National Guard addressed readiness problems that appeared in the late 1980s by implementing the largest unit reorganizations since 1968. ARNG units concentrated in the Northeast had difficulty meeting required manning levels. The demographic recruiting pool of available young men and women had shifted from the Northeast to the "Sunbelt," a vaguely defined tier of southern and southwestern States enjoying economic prosperity that stretched from the Carolinas, through the Deep South, across Texas and into Arizona. The 26th Infantry Division (Massachusetts and Connecticut) and the 50th Armored Division (New Jersey and Vermont) had particular problems in maintaining strength. In 1988, the ARNG transferred a brigade of the 50th Armored Division from Vermont to Texas, inactivated a brigade of the 26th Division in Massachusetts and realigned the brigades of both divisions in an effort to improve their personnel posture. Concerned that further cuts in the Northeast might be needed, NGB developed a plan for eliminating the majority of the 50th and 26th Divisions and integrating the remaining units into a single, more robust division stationed in the Northeast.[59]

After reaching an all time, historic peak of 456,980 soldiers in 1989, the Guard braced for personnel cuts. In January 1990, the Army notified the ARNG that a cut of 10,000 soldiers over the next nine months was required to meet budget targets. For the first time since 1970, recruiters abandoned the practice of unconstrained growth and targeted their efforts on only the very best recruits. At the same time, ARNG commanders improved readiness by selectively retaining only their best soldiers. The ARNG Directorate assigned reduced strength targets to each State that had to be met by September 30, 1990. However, disturbing news suddenly interrupted deliberations in the Pentagon over defense cuts. On August 2, 1990, the Iraqi Army invaded the tiny kingdom of Kuwait at the head of the Persian Gulf. Within days, Iraqi soldiers took up positions from which they could threaten the world's main petroleum reserves just across the border in Saudi Arabia.[60]

Conclusions

The era of Total Force Policy caused the significant transformation of the ARNG from a strategic reserve, mobilization force to a combat ready organization focused on early deployment. Prior to 1970, the Guard had been adequately prepared to carry out its role in large, deliberate mobilizations followed by eventual deployment to a war zone. By the end of the Reagan Buildup, the ARNG was a combat-ready reserve force immediately available for deployment to hot spots around the globe. Improvements in training, equipment, and personnel gave the Guard the wherewithal to participate fully in the nation's first line of defense.

A key result of the Total Force Policy was the development of closer, more functional ties between the Regular Army and the ARNG. The Roundout Program built the strongest possible ties between Regulars and citizen-soldiers. The Army's equipping policies put Roundout units on an equal footing with their parent, active divisions. Training opportunities at the NTC placed active and Roundout battalions together in the toughest, most realistic training exercises possible. The CAPSTONE Program imparted Guardsmen with a renewed sense of purpose by giving them a clearly defined, wartime mission and direct ties to active units they would serve beside in a future conflict. Overseas training exercises built confidence as Guardsmen demonstrated time after time their ability to quickly muster and deploy combat ready units.

The Total Force Policy's success in improving the overall capabilities of the active Army and the ARNG were readily apparent by the end of the 1980s. Still, Regulars and Guardsmen had not yet demonstrated the effectiveness of their newly acquired relationships and capabilities in war. The ultimate test of the Total Force Policy was to come in the sands of Southwest Asia.

CHAPTER 8

The Persian Gulf War, 1990–1991

T his victory belongs...to the Regulars, to the Reserves, to the National Guard. This victory belongs to the finest fighting force this nation has ever known in its history.

President George Bush, Address to Congress, March 6, 1991

Introduction

Sergeant First Class Palmer Burchstead emerged from the dark, cavernous interior of the huge C-141 transport and stepped out onto the bright, hot tarmac of the Riyadh airport on the afternoon of August 9, 1990. Moments later, Sergeant First Class Timothy Hester joined Burchstead outside the large transport. On their hips were 9-mm. pistols, and attached to their web gear were full magazines of pistol ammunition. Not knowing what lay ahead on the ground in Saudi Arabia, the soldiers on board the C-141 had broken open ammunition boxes and distributed the pistol rounds before landing in Riyadh. The two Guardsmen were relieved to be free of the C-141s confined spaces after a long, grueling flight from Atlanta, Georgia with only a short refueling stop in Spain. Less than forty-eight hours earlier, they had received orders to report immediately to Third Army Headquarters at Fort McPherson, Georgia for rapid deployment to Saudi Arabia. The two men were a long way from home; their normal duty station was the armory of Headquarters Company, 228th Signal Brigade in Spartanburg, South Carolina where both served as full-time AGRs.

Before long, ninety-four soldiers from Headquarters, U.S. Third Army stood on the tarmac and watched as the C-141 crew and Saudi stevedores off-loaded pallets of cargo from the transport. On board the airplane was one of the 228th Signal Brigade's single channel tactical satellite sets. The following day, Sergeants Burchstead and Hester used their high technology communications equipment to establish a direct line from the Saudi Defense Ministry in Riyadh to Third Army Headquarters at Fort McPherson. A few days later, the South Carolina Guardsmen deployed north to King Khalid Military City where their satellite communications set eventually became part of the most elaborate and advanced communications system ever deployed in a theater of war.

What Sergeants Burchstead and Hester did not know on the afternoon of August 9, 1990 is that they were the first soldiers of an eventual deployment of over 37,000 Army Guardsmen to Saudi Arabia. By the conclusion of Operation Desert Storm on February 28, 1991, Guard combat, combat support, and combat service support units had seen extensive service in the Persian Gulf. Overall, more than 62,000 ARNG soldiers participated in Operation Desert Shield, the largest National Guard mobilization since the Korean War. In addition to the troops deployed to Southwest Asia, another 25,000 Guardsmen trained and provided support in Europe and CONUS. In all respects, Operations Desert Shield and Desert Storm tested the effectiveness of the Total Force Policy and the improvements in the Army and the ARNG made during the 1980s.

The ARNG in 1990

By nearly all measures, the ARNG in the summer of 1990 had never been in better shape. At the beginning of the year, Guard strength in organized units stood at an all time high of 456,960 soldiers. The ranks reflected the recruiting policies and environment that had emerged since the end of the draft in 1973. Nearly one-quarter of the ARNG consisted of minorities. Black soldiers numbered 71,334, or 16 percent of the force, while 31,456 female soldiers comprised 7 percent of the ARNG. A combined total of 54,621 full-time AGRs and military technicians manned the fifty-four State and Territorial headquarters, nearly 2,500 armories, scores of training and maintenance sites and represented the Guard at major Army commands world-wide.[1]

While the ARNG was primarily a combat force, it included a large segment of the Army's total combat support and combat service support units. In Washington, DC, the ARNG Directorate acted as the central, controlling headquarters for the allocation and distribution of Guard resources. Maj. Gen. Donald Burdick, a Georgia Guardsman, served as DARNG. In the States, the majority of Guardsmen manned the ARNG's major combat units that included 10 divisions, 6 Roundout brigades, 14 separate brigades, 2 ACRs, and 2 SF Groups. In addition, the Guard contained 39 brigade-level headquarters that controlled a wide range of combat, combat support, and combat service support units.

In terms of operations and readiness, the ARNG was at peak proficiency. By the end of the first half of 1990, thousands of Guardsmen had trained in hundreds of different exercises both in CONUS and overseas. During the year, 25,000 ARNG soldiers had responded to emergencies in thirty-eight States by providing support to civil authorities during 6 civil disturbances, 77 natural disasters and over 200 relief missions. In addition, an average of 2,400 Guardsmen per day actively supported law enforcement agencies in counter-drug operations. As for its ability to go to war, General Burdick reported that the ARNG's readiness "has never been better." Even in terms of equipment, the Guard's traditional impediment to readiness, the ARNG was in great condition. Receipt of equipment from Army procurement and the DPP Program drove equipment levels to 75 percent of wartime needs, the highest in the Guard's history. Overall, nearly 92 percent of all units had the minimum, essential equipment required to go to war. Still, the Guard remained critically short of wheeled vehicles, radios, and high technology test sets and repair equipment in many combat support units.

Despite the ARNG's overall excellent condition, a number of deep concerns clouded its future. Budget cuts had already curtailed some training exercises, and the cancellation of other training events was all but certain. Guard commanders feared that shrinking defense budgets would inevitably reverse positive trends in personnel and equipment readiness. With the Cold War over, opinions in Congress and DOD were divided over the proper role, size, and missions of the reserve components. Early in 1990, the Army directed the ARNG to plan for force structure cuts as large as 76,000 soldiers by 1995. However, concerns over long-term problems faded in early August when the U.S. military suddenly focused its attention on the very real prospects of a major war in the Middle East.

The Road to War

Prior to Iraq's invasion of Kuwait in August 1990, Southwest Asia had been in turmoil for more than a decade. In 1979, Islamic fundamentalists had overthrown the government of Iran and captured American hostages. Later in the year, the Soviet Army invaded Afghanistan, starting a brutal, protracted war in which Afghan freedom fighters eventually forced a Soviet withdrawal. In 1980, a bloody war of attrition broke out between Iran and Iraq that dragged on for eight years and included the use of chemical weapons. Near the end of the decade, Iran sought to exert its influence in the region by attacking oil tankers in the Persian Gulf shipping lanes with anti-ship missiles. The U.S. Navy and other European powers increased their presence in the Persian Gulf.[2]

The American response to turmoil in Southwest Asia had been swift but not decisive. In the aftermath of the Iranian revolution and the invasion of Afghanistan, President Jimmy Carter announced a new policy for Southwest Asia. The Carter Doctrine declared any invasion in the region to be a threat to America's vital national interests. The U.S. created the Rapid Deployment Joint Task Force, a headquarters responsible for military planning in the Persian Gulf region. In January 1983, the Rapid Deployment Force became the U.S. Central Command, America's sixth major headquarters responsible for overseas operations. Unlike the other overseas theaters, Central Command had no troops stationed in its area of responsibility. The Arab nations were willing to accept U.S. equipment and training assistance but balked at a permanent American presence on their soil. General H. Norman Schwarzkopf became the Central Command commander on November 23, 1988 and began to study likely options for the use of American power in the Persian Gulf. During 1990, Schwarzkopf's staff conducted an extensive planning exercise in which Central Command reacted to a major invasion of Saudi Arabia by the large armored formations of the Iraqi Army.

Central Command's concerns over Iraqi aggression were based on recent developments emanating from Baghdad. Saddam Hussein sought to fill the power vacuum created in the Persian Gulf region after the collapse of the Soviet Union. By increasing his hold on neighboring oil fields and attacking Kuwait, the Iraqi dictator hoped to become the region's undisputed leader and to relieve his country's debts by raising the price of crude oil. After several threats against Kuwait, the Iraqi Army launched its offensive before dawn on August 2, 1990. Over 100,000 troops and 1,000 tanks overran Kuwait's meager border defenses and advanced on Kuwait City. Within forty-eight hours, Saddam's forces had occupied the entire country. In the following days, Iraqi reinforcements poured into Kuwait to tighten their hold on the country and to take up threatening positions along the Saudi border.

In Washington, DC, President George Bush and his national security advisors monitored the developments at the head of the Persian Gulf with deep concern. After consultations with senior U.S. defense officials, King Fahd of Saudi Arabia requested American assistance in defending his realm. On August 7th, Central Command set into motion Operation Desert Shield, the massive buildup of Allied combat power in the Persian

Gulf. The next day, President Bush publicly announced the commitment of U.S. ground troops to Saudi Arabia. Paratroopers from the 82d Airborne Division departed Fort Bragg immediately, and within seven days, nearly 5,000 soldiers and all of their equipment were on the ground and ready to fight. By August 24th, all of the 82d Airborne's parachute battalions had deployed to Southwest Asia.

To support the lightly armed paratroopers positioned in the desert, Central Command issued orders for the rapid deployment of the 101st Airborne and 24th Infantry Divisions. The 101st began deployment from Fort Campbell, Kentucky by strategic airlift on August 17th, and by the end of the month, half of the division was in defensive positions in Saudi Arabia. By early September, two heavy brigades from the 24th Division were moving into forward positions in northern Saudi Arabia. By September 14th, the 197th Infantry Brigade (Mechanized) from Fort Benning, Georgia had arrived in the desert to fight as the "Victory" Division's third brigade. The 24th Division's Roundout unit, Georgia's 48th Brigade, remained in CONUS awaiting mobilization orders.

The rapid buildup of Allied forces in Saudi Arabia and Saddam Hussein's reinforcement of his army in southern Kuwait and Iraq made a quick resolution to the escalating crisis unlikely. To prepare for a protracted military campaign, Central Command planners recognized the need for an adequate logistical base in Saudi Arabia capable of sustaining and supporting a large, fighting force. The lack of host nation support in the desert exacerbated the acute need for additional support units. Before long, Central Command realized that the creation of a much needed logistical system would be impossible without the immediate callup of ARNG and USAR units.

Operation Desert Shield

On the same day the 82nd Airborne started its deployment to Saudi Arabia, the ARNG Directorate began preparations for a major mobilization. A twenty-four hour a day operations center opened to coordinate mobilization efforts and to act as an information center for the ARNG Directorate and the AGs. On August 7th, the Army requested Guard volunteers for active duty. Of foremost concern was Arabic- speaking linguists. The ARNG identified fifty-three qualified personnel, and thirteen Arabic linguists from Utah's 142nd Military Intelligence Battalion volunteered immediately. The remainder of the Arabic-speaking Guardsmen entered active duty with their units. Other specialties in immediate demand included military lawyers, chaplains, and aviation support personnel. By September 4th, 171 Guard volunteers were on active duty serving in a variety of operational, training, and support positions. By war's end, over 1,200 volunteers had contributed to the effort.[3]

The Bush Administration chose to take an incremental approach to the reserve component callup. The president refused to institute a partial mobilization, which would allow up to one million National Guard and Reserve personnel to serve for as long as two years. Instead, the White House used the 1976 mobilization authority contained in Section 673b, Title 10, U.S. Code that permitted the mobilization of 200,000 reserve component personnel for ninety days, renewable for a second ninety days. Any extension of service beyond the initial 180 days required congressional approval. Under the parameters of Section 673b, DOD had created a predetermined list of 200,000 Guardsmen and Reservists by type unit from all services for immediate callup. With President Bush's decision on August 8th to send U.S. forces to Saudi Arabia, the Army released its portion of the 200,000 list to the ARNG. Staff divisions within the ARNG Directorate analyzed the list to determine which specific units were best prepared for active duty.[4]

While the ARNG prepared to mobilize selected units, it took action to keep others ready for callup. The ARNG Directorate ordered units scheduled for inactivation due to planned force structure cuts to take no further actions until the Army better determined the complete requirements for Desert Shield. Other organizations slated for conversion, often to a different branch requiring retraining of personnel and turning in old equipment for new, were maintained in their existing configuration. Along with the Army, the ARNG implemented a "Stop Loss" personnel policy that prevented all soldiers from voluntarily leaving the service. DOD cancelled several training exercises to make more strategic airlift available for moving troops and equipment to the Persian Gulf and redirected training funds to cover the mounting costs of Desert Shield. On September 5th, the Army cancelled the scheduled NTC rotation of Tennessee's 278th Armored Cavalry to allow an active unit to train at Fort Irwin.[5]

On August 22nd, President Bush signed Executive Order No. 12727 authorizing DOD to commence the reserve component mobilization. In addition to Central Command's urgent requests for Guard and Reserve units, citizen-soldiers were needed at other locations worldwide to replace Regulars heading to the Persian Gulf. However, Secretary Cheney's message of August 23rd to the JCS and the military departments specified that the ARNG was to provide only combat support and combat service support units. No authority was granted for mobilizing ARNG combat units. On August 24th, CNGB sent an alert order notifying selected States of the first sixty-nine ARNG units identified for mobilization. As in previous major mobilizations, units were federalized in increments to insure an orderly transition to active duty. The first nineteen units, consisting of 482 personnel from thirteen States, were ordered to active duty on August 27th. For the first time since March 1970, when soldiers of the 42nd Infantry Division had been mobilized to react to a postal workers strike in New York, Guardsmen entered active duty. Ironically, a coin toss determined which organization received the honor of being the first ARNG unit called to active duty. Two mobilization orders arrived simultaneously at the operations center of the Alabama ARNG in the early morning hours of August 27th. Realizing the significance of the occasion, the officers on duty flipped a coin to determine which unit they would notify first. Thus, Alabama's 1241st Adjutant General Company (Postal) received the first call to duty followed by the 1207th Quartermaster Detachment (Water Purification).[6]

Before the Persian Gulf crisis ended, 62,411 Guardsmen in 398 units saw active service. Soldiers from forty-eight States, the District of Columbia, Guam, and Puerto Rico were called to active duty in thirty-six different increments. In the early stages of Desert Shield, 129 units mobilized between August 27th and November 17th. As the prospects for war increased, the buildup accelerated. The largest increment occurred on November 21st, when sixty units were mobilized. Between November 21st and the opening of hostilities on January 17, 1991, another 233 units were ordered to active duty. Units ranged in size from three-man military history detachments to the 863-man 3-141st Infantry (Mechanized) from Texas. A full 97 percent of the units activated met or exceeded Army deployment standards. Guardsmen moved promptly from home armories to mobilization stations to overseas duty. Over a quarter of all units left CONUS within twenty days of callup; two-thirds deployed within forty-five days.[7]

Despite doubts by some in the press and in the Army, all of the Guard soldiers called reported for duty, and 94 percent were immediately available for overseas service. Of the 6 percent rejected, most lacked required training or had medical conditions ranging from pregnancy to heart problems. Large numbers of Guardsmen with dental problems caused serious concerns. Dentists identified nearly 14,000 soldiers as requiring dental work in the next thirteen months; however, only two Guardsmen were rejected for deployment due to dental problems.[8]

Starting with the first ARNG units mobilized, a fairly uniform set of activities that soldiers had practiced during mobilization exercises took place at home armories. Soldiers checked their personnel records, updated wills, and reviewed important pay documents. Commanders insured soldiers had all of their personal equipment and identified

Delaware's 736th Supply and Service Battalion processes through a mobilization station during Desert Shield prior to deploying to the Persian Gulf in December 1990. (National Guard Bureau)

Guardsmen with problems that might prohibit them from serving on active duty. Troops packed unit equipment for overseas shipment. While at home station, Guard spouses and families learned firsthand of their rights and benefits from Family Support officers dispatched from State headquarters. Each State had one or more Family Support officers to assist family members in coordinating pay and medical benefits, and they gave aid to the families of active duty and USAR service members as well. Desert Shield marked the first use of Family Support officers, and they proved a quick remedy in most cases. In addition, military lawyers and chaplains addressed family problems. Despite the best efforts, pay problems and family issues dogged the mobilization. In many cases, Guard and Regular Army administrative systems did not integrate well, and spouses often had difficulty resolving pay and medical issues.[9]

After a short stay of three to five days at home armories, Guardsmen moved to designated mobilization stations. Soldiers and equipment most often traveled by military convoy, and many Guardsmen headed to mobilization stations aboard leased commercial buses. As in past mobilizations, Guard units received rousing farewells from their local communities. State and local leaders organized elaborate farewell ceremonies in many towns that drew extensive regional and national media coverage. On the day of departure, large crowds of well-wishers lined the streets and stood along the major highways and interstates heading toward mobilization stations. All cheered, some cried, and many waved American flags and sported yellow ribbons to show their support.

Mobilization stations were usually active duty installations with all of the necessary training and support facilities required to certify individual soldiers and units as ready for overseas deployment. Soldiers qualified on personal and crew served weapons, conducted chemical warfare training and took physical fitness tests. A series of physical and dental exams identified soldiers with treatable medical problems before they deployed to remote desert locations. A great deal of time was spent preparing vehicles and equipment for movement to ports of embarkation and shipment overseas. Most vehicles bound for Saudi Arabia were camouflaged with desert sand paint. Small units with only light equipment stayed only a few days at mobilization stations. Other units waiting for their heavy vehicles and equipment to reach Saudi Arabia by ship remained at mobilization stations for up to a month. When troops departed for overseas duty assignments, they usually flew from civilian or military airfields closest to their mobilization station. Guardsmen boarded military or leased civilian aircraft for long flights to new duty stations in either Europe or Saudi Arabia.[10]

Some units in the early increments reached their mobilization stations to find that the Army had made few preparations for their arrival. The speed and size of the mobilization caught some posts unprepared. Despite plans that had been drawn up to support large mobilizations during the Cold War, many installations did not have adequate housing, bedding, and dining facilities. In part, the shortages were due to reduced civilian work forces caused by budget cuts of the late 1980s. Insufficient transportation to move Guardsmen from barracks to ranges and training areas was a serious problem. While ARNG units normally used their own organic wheeled transport to support training, vehicles were often unavailable because they were already enroute overseas. Most posts solved the problem by hiring civilian buses. Two significant supply problems persisted throughout Desert Shield. Many posts lacked the stocks of rifle and machine gun ammunition needed to qualify soldiers on their weapons. The Army rushed some additional ammunition to needy posts, but most stockpiles of ammunition were already on their way to Saudi Arabia to support training or to constitute an ammunition reserve for a ground campaign. Shortages of the desert pattern, camouflaged battle dress uniform never eased. Soldiers in the first ARNG units mobilized received at least one or two sets of desert uniforms and one pair of desert boots. However, troops in later increments served in the desert wearing their normal, forest green camouflaged uniforms. Fortunately, the Army had solved most problems by early November, just in time for the largest troop callups.[11]

The scope of Desert Shield changed dramatically on November 5th when President Bush signed Executive Order No. 12733 authorizing the mobilization of Guard and Reserve combat units for possible use in a ground offensive to eject the Iraqis from Kuwait. Throughout the autumn, diplomatic efforts to compel Saddam Hussein to withdraw had failed, and by early November, it was clear that the Iraqi Army had no intention of leaving Kuwait. In fact, the Iraqis were busy constructing a vast network of defensive positions along the Saudi border. Senior military commanders informed President Bush that American and Allied troops could not sit in the desert indefinitely. The Guard and Reserve units federalized in August were already near the midpoint of the 180 days of service allowed under Section 673b, and any further service would require congressional action. President Bush believed the only way to increase pressure on Saddam Hussein was to place a military force into Saudi Arabia capable of credible, offensive action. Guardsmen entering active duty after November 5th realized they might soon be involved in a shooting war. Between November 21–30th, a total of ninety-nine ARNG units entered active federal service, including most of the elements of three Roundout brigades.[12]

Colorado's 1158th Transportation Detachment (Movement Control) arrived in Saudi Arabia on September 9th, the first of 297 ARNG units that eventually served in the theater. Other early deploying Guardsmen soon followed, dispersing across the desert to perform missions as diverse as logistics, transportation, traffic control, water purification, and military police. Kentucky's 217th Quartermaster Detachment (Water Purification) landed on October 9th, and after some quick refresher training, was assigned to a forward logistics base where it supplied potable water until returning home in May 1991. Virginia's Headquarters, 1030th Engineer Battalion moved to Khobar Towers near Dhahran. The towers were a large apartment complex that served as a permanent barracks for several thousand troops and provided additional, temporary billeting for units awaiting the arrival of equipment by ship. The 1030th kept the facilities working, seeing that mess halls were properly run and providing all of the other amenities necessary to make living conditions as comfortable as possible for transient troops.[13]

Guardsmen arriving in the Persian Gulf region entered a strange environment with alien customs and traditions. Saudi Arabia holds the holiest sites in the Muslim world, and the government feared an Arab backlash against the introduction of western influences. One of the earliest problems involved the role of women in uniform. Saudi heritage holds women to the traditional roles of wife and mother, requiring women to appear in public covered from head to toe except for their eyes and hands. Saudi soldiers were shocked to observe American women in positions of authority, working in tee shirts with their arms bared and giving orders to men. To prevent a cultural clash, the Army quickly established a policy that women in camp could work in their tee shirts, but off-post they had to wear headgear and shirts with long sleeves rolled down at all times. Other problems centered on the display of the American flag and

Soldiers of the Maryland ARNG arrive in Saudi Arabia on a commercial airliner during Desert Shield in 1990. (National Guard Bureau)

religious articles. The flying of the U.S. flag was initially restricted to American compounds in the major cities, but as the threat of war grew closer, the Saudis permitted American units to display their flags in the border areas. Many ARNG units carried State flags, and Guardsmen proudly displayed their State colors in the Saudi desert for all to see. Under Saudi pressure, the outward display of the Bible was forbidden, even though private reading of the Scriptures was not prohibited. Christian and Jewish church services were allowed, but could only be held in American camps away from the public scrutiny of the Saudi people. Living conditions for Guardsmen ranged from air-conditioned quarters in the cities to tents in the wind swept desert. But for most Guard troops, their home in Saudi Arabia was a tent. Fine, grainy sand filled and caked their clothing, equipment, and personal possessions. Though expecting blistering heat and dryness, the chilly, wet Arabian winter and cold, desert nights surprised most Americans. As the Allied buildup continued into December and January, low clouds and scattered, cold rains dominated the weather pattern.[14]

During Desert Shield, the nation's attention remained focused on events in the Persian Gulf and the continuing buildup of Allied forces.

Little notice was given to those 101 ARNG units that remained in CONUS or deployed to Europe to replace active forces rushing to Saudi Arabia. Sixteen ARNG units, ranging in size from engineer battalions to medical detachments, went to Europe to perform a variety of support missions. Of particular note was the service of Florida's 108th Public Affairs Detachment. Sent to Turkey, the detachment performed public affairs functions during the post-Desert Storm Allied effort to feed Kurdish refugees in northern Iraq. The 3,378 Guardsmen who deployed to Europe provided valuable but largely unrecognized service for the war effort.[15]

Eighty-five Guard units that remained in CONUS contained a cross section of specialties, including medical, transportation, aviation, and military police. These support units served on active duty posts performing duties usually done by Regulars. In many cases, Guardsmen assisted with the mobilization of other ARNG and USAR units. Of the 21,185 mobilized Guardsmen who remained in CONUS during the war, nearly 13,000 were assigned to three Roundout brigades.[16]

The ARNG Roundout Brigades

After the presidential callup of National Guardsmen and Reservists on August 22nd, Operation Desert Shield intensified greatly. While the Navy, Air Force, and Marine Corps received authority to activate combat troops, Secretary Cheney restricted the Army reserve component mobilization to only combat support and combat service support troops. In the early weeks of Desert Shield, Army divisions deploying to Saudi Arabia went without their assigned Roundout brigades. The 24th Division had already deployed without Georgia's 48th Brigade. In early September, the 1st Cavalry Division at Fort Hood, Texas shipped out to the Persian Gulf with a brigade from the 2d Armored Division in lieu of Mississippi's 155th Armored Brigade. For nearly three months, the two Roundout brigades remained at home awaiting orders.[17]

Over time, DOD and the Army offered four reasons for not mobilizing the Roundout brigades. First, the immediate objective of Desert Shield was to deter and defend against a possible Iraqi attack. Facing a real threat in Saudi Arabia, the Army believed only active component units were capable of rapidly deploying and facing immediate combat. Second, General Schwarzkopf had requested two full-strength heavy divisions in early August. With little time available for the Roundout brigades to join their parent divisions, the Army had substituted two active duty brigades. Third, the Central Command request for heavy forces had come on August 6th, sixteen days before President Bush authorized a reserve component callup. The Army maintained that even if they had wanted to deploy the Roundout brigades, no authority existed. Finally, the Section 673b mobilization statute allowed Guardsmen to remain on active duty for a maximum of 180 days. The Army refused to acknowledge that one of the purposes of Section 673b was to provide for a transition to a national mobilization and insisted that the six-month utilization period precluded the effective use of Roundout brigades. By the time the two brigades could complete their training and deploy, the Army argued, Guardsmen would either face demobilization or require congressional approval to extend their service.[18]

By early September, members of Congress, CNGB, and NGAUS were extremely concerned over the Roundout brigades. On September 6th, Congressman Les Aspin, the powerful chairman of the House Armed Services Committee, Congressman Sonny Montgomery, and two other committee members sent Secretary Cheney a sharp, candid letter criticizing the Pentagon's handling of the brigades. The congressmen wrote that while Capitol Hill had clearly demonstrated its support of the Total Force Policy, DOD's commitment was "far less clear," and they urged the SECDEF to reconsider the decision not to mobilize the brigades. Secretary Cheney replied that his senior military advisors had not recommended the brigades' mobilization and that only Congress could remove the 180-day callup limitation imposed by Section 673b. Still, Congressman Montgomery kept up the pressure with speeches on the House floor and a series of letters to President Bush and the Pentagon. In Saudi Arabia, General Schwarzkopf told CNGB, Lt. Gen. John B. Conaway, that activating the brigades was an issue "for the politicians back in Washington to figure out" and that what he really needed was more ARNG support units. On October 31st, the senior leadership of NGAUS met with Secretary Cheney and made an emotional appeal for an immediate, brigade callup. The Defense Secretary explained the reasons why the brigades had not been mobilized and indicated he had not ruled out their eventual use.[19]

The fate of the Roundout brigades changed in early November with the president's decision to double the size of American forces in the Persian Gulf. At a press conference on November 8th, Secretary Cheney and General Colin L. Powell, chairman of the JCS, announced the mobilization of three Roundout brigades. General Powell stated that the brigades would undergo extensive training to ensure they were fully combat ready, including a rotation at the NTC. In addition to the 48th and 155th Brigades, Louisiana's 256th Infantry Brigade (Mechanized), the Roundout unit to the 5th Infantry Division (Mechanized) at Fort Polk, Louisiana, would be called to active duty along with the separate

Roundout battalions of the 24th Infantry, 1st Cavalry, and 5th Infantry Divisions. All units would be alerted on November 15th and called to active duty within weeks.[20]

Three factors combined to convince Secretary Cheney and General Powell to mobilize the Roundout units. First, when the military mission in the Persian Gulf changed from defensive to offensive, the Pentagon needed to increase the number of combat troops available to reinforce Central Command in the event of a protracted ground war. Second, Desert Shield had severely depleted the U.S. strategic reserve, and third, the Roundout brigades were needed in case a second regional crisis developed that required U.S. ground troops. Congressional action also relieved concerns over the 180-day limit on reserve component availability. The 1991 Defense Appropriations Act contained language authorizing the president to order reserve component combat units to active duty for up to 360 days. When President Bush signed the bill into law on November 5th, limits on reserve component usage were all but eliminated.[21]

In November 1990, Georgia's 48th Brigade included nearly 4,000 Guardsmen under the command of Brig. Gen. William A. Holland. The brigade had undergone extensive training in recent years. During 1986–1988, the 48th had modernized to the M-1 Abrams and the M-2 Bradley. For years, command post exercises and training with the 24th Division took place on a regular basis. Since 1983, elements of the 48th had participated in four training rotations at the NTC. The most recent rotation had occurred in July 1990, only four months prior to mobilization. The commander at the NTC, then-Brig. Gen. Wesley Clarke, who would go on to become Supreme Allied Commander in Europe and leader of NATO's war against Yugoslavia in 1999, declared that the Georgians had performed "as well or better than most active component units that have come through."[22]

During the early stages of Desert Shield, the 48th Brigade anticipated mobilization by identifying personnel and equipment shortages and preparing detailed, post-mobilization training plans. All tracked vehicles and heavy equipment were transported to Fort Stewart. South Carolina's 1-263rd Armor served as the 24th Division's separate Roundout battalion. The South Carolina battalion established direct communications with the Georgia brigade to coordinate mobilization and training. By the time of the callup, the 48th Brigade had coordinated extensive preparations for mobilization with Fort Stewart and other major Army headquarters at Fort McPherson and Fort Gillem in Georgia. With the 24th Division already in the Gulf, the Pentagon directed Headquarters, Second Army at Fort Gillem to oversee the mobilization and training of the 48th Brigade.

Upon receipt of the mobilization order on November 30th, soldiers moved immediately to armories in Georgia and South Carolina. In anticipation of the mobilization, most Guardsmen had their administrative and personal affairs in good order. In staggered intervals during December 2–4th, the brigade's units headed for Fort Stewart after emotional farewells in their local communities. By sundown on December 4th, the 48th Brigade and the 1-263rd Armor were at their mobilization station. From December 5–23rd, an intense training regime ensued that included tank and artillery gunnery, small arms qualification, dismounted infantry drills, and specialized individual training for support troops. Persistent rains and fog reduced range availability, so Bradley crews traveled to Fort Benning for live fire training. Medical screening disqualified a significant number of soldiers for overseas duty, especially among the full-time AGR force. Training at Fort Stewart identified several, critical problems. Soldiers were not knowledgeable regarding vehicle and equipment maintenance. While most Guardsmen could perform basic soldiering tasks, too many junior officers and sergeants lacked adequate leadership skills. Officers on the brigade and battalion staffs displayed insufficient knowledge of the difficult tasks of coordinating combined arms operations.

After a four-day Christmas pass, the 48th Brigade deployed to Fort Irwin. While junior officers supervised the movement to California and the draw of training equipment, brigade and battalion staff officers attended an eight day course at Fort Leavenworth, Kansas designed to teach critical, battlefield coordination skills. While Guard officers believed the training was valuable, the Fort Leavenworth period initiated friction between the brigade's leadership and Regulars. Some Guard officers believed instructors were attempting to identify staff members for elimination. The Army insisted that the brigade abandon its standing operating procedures that had worked well with the 24th Division and adopt new, unfamiliar practices. The directed change in operating procedures created confusion, generated resentment, and broke down staff cohesion.

On January 5th, the staff officers rejoined the troops at Fort Irwin, and the brigade deployed to the desert to begin the longest NTC rotation ever recorded. Initial training focused on individual soldier skills and then advanced to crew, section, squad, and platoon training. In many cases, platoons needed refresher training because of personnel turnover and the addition of new soldiers. Tankers, mechanized infantrymen, and artillery soldiers fired extensive gunnery exercises. The brigade staff received tactical instruction and learned new techniques for the more rapid preparation and dissemination of improved operations orders. By late January, the 48th Brigade began maneuver exercises in the Mojave Desert. An interesting aspect of training was the attack of simulated Iraqi defenses. The Georgians experimented with mine plows and mine rollers designed to eliminate minefields and worked their way through tank traps and deep ditches searching for the best tactics and techniques to use against Iraqi obstacles. The Army forwarded the lessons learned to Saudi Arabia where American heavy forces were preparing to attack real Iraqi defenses. During the last two weeks of February, the 48th Brigade conducted several maneuver exercises against the NTC's opposing force. For the first time at Fort Irwin, a brigade headquarters maneuvered three combined arms task forces in the open desert. On February 28th, the same day the ground war ended, Army leaders certified the 48th Brigade as combat ready and prepared for deployment.

Despite the value of NTC training, a number of problems dogged the brigade. Poor leadership skills among junior officers and sergeants held back many small units. Too often, promising junior leaders were thrust into positions of greater responsibility for which they were not prepared. At the top, the brigade's leadership changed when General Holland was recalled to Georgia and replaced by the brigade's second-in-command, Colonel James D. Davis. Over time, the brigade's leadership and staff proficiency improved. Many Guardsmen thought an excess of active duty trainers smothered their units, subverted the chain of command, and often gave contradictory and conflicting training assistance. Vehicle maintenance was a particular Achilles heel. The NTC staff admitted the equipment issued to the brigade was worn and torn. Still, vehicle operators and crews showed little aptitude for preventive maintenance, and unit maintenance sections failed to adequately perform vehicle repairs.

On November 30th, Louisiana's 256th Infantry Brigade and Alabama's 2-152nd Armor were called to active duty to join the 5th Infantry Division. Within days, Louisiana and Alabama Guardsmen had closed on their mobilization station at Fort Polk where the 5th Division was to oversee their training. On December 7th, the Roundout units to the 1st Cavalry Division, Mississippi's 155th Armored Brigade and the 3-141st Infantry (Mechanized) from Texas, were mobilized. The 155th and the 3-141st reported to their mobilization station at Fort Hood. Because the 1st Cavalry Division had already deployed to the Persian Gulf, the Army assigned the 4th Infantry Division (Mechanized) at Fort Carson, Colorado as the parent division responsible for training the Mississippians and Texans.[23]

For several weeks, both brigades remained at their mobilization stations conducting individual and small unit training. By late January, the

256th and 155th Brigades had concentrated at Fort Hood for large-scale maneuvers and live fire exercises. The 256th's infantrymen underwent modernization training from older vehicles to the M2 Bradley. On February 3rd, fifty-three soldiers from the 256th Brigade went absent without leave from Fort Hood to protest poor training and living conditions. All but one of the soldiers voluntarily returned from Shreveport, Louisiana to Fort Hood where they received non-judicial punishment.[24]

Operation Desert Storm

Western diplomatic efforts to avert war in the Persian Gulf continued into the late fall of 1990. Allied demands toward Saddam Hussein remained constant: withdraw the Iraqi army from Kuwait and allow the return of the emirate's legitimate leaders. On November 29th, the UN Security Council passed Resolution 678, authorizing the Allied coalition to use "all necessary means" to eject the Iraqi army from Kuwait and setting January 15, 1991 as the deadline for Iraq to comply with Allied demands. Still, Saddam Hussein refused to budge. On January 9th, the U.S. secretary of state met with the Iraqi foreign minister in Geneva, Switzerland in last-ditch talks to avert war. After nearly seven hours, the discussions collapsed. On January 12th, after three days of somber, eloquent debate, the U.S. Congress passed a joint resolution authorizing the use of military force. The January 15th deadline passed without any reaction from Saddam Hussein. The world watched and waited for the Allied response.[25]

Allied air forces fired the opening shots of Operation Desert Storm with raids against downtown Baghdad and other key military sites throughout Iraq in the early morning hours of January 17th. Over the next six weeks, the Allies conducted a relentless bombing campaign designed to gain air superiority, degrade enemy air defenses, destroy Scud missile sites, and wear down Iraqi ground forces. As the air war progressed, pilots turned their attention more and more to the attack of enemy armor and artillery units arrayed against Allied troops. Meanwhile, diplomatic efforts sought to avert what many feared would be a costly and destructive ground war. When Saddam Hussein displayed continued intransigence, President Bush reacted with a final ultimatum. Speaking from the White House lawn on February 22nd, the president told the world that Iraqi forces had until twelve noon the next day to withdraw or be attacked. During the next twenty-four hours, the Iraqi army did not move.

Before dawn on February 24th, American ground forces launched General Schwarzkopf's "Hail Mary" play, a huge turning movement against the right flank of Saddam Hussein's troops designed to liberate Kuwait and destroy the Iraqi army. The gigantic offensive reflected the many reforms and improvements in the Army that had occurred since the Vietnam War. Using high technology weapons and equipment, motivated troops who had experienced tough, realistic training at the NTC and in Europe routed the Iraqis. Compared with past American wars, the first battle of the Persian Gulf War was a resounding success. In many places, tired and demoralized enemy soldiers surrendered en masse. In one hundred hours of mobile warfare, Allied ground forces routed the Iraqis and freed Kuwait. American air power and heavy ground forces eventually engaged and destroyed Iraq's elite, mechanized units. On February 28th, Allied leaders declared a cease-fire, and negotiations for a final peace settlement ensued.

When Allied airmen fired the opening shots of Desert Storm on January 17th, more than 23,000 ARNG soldiers in 201 units were on duty in Saudi Arabia. The next day, President Bush declared a partial mobilization and invoked his authority to mobilize nearly one million reservists for two years. The opening of hostilities accelerated the deployment of Guardsmen. After January 17th, another fifty-six ARNG units were mobilized. When a cease-fire came six weeks later, the number of Guard personnel in the war zone had increased to more than 37,000 soldiers in 296 units. Eventually, sixty units commanded by either ARNG colonels or lieutenant colonels served in the Gulf. Two field artillery brigades—Arkansas's 142nd and Tennessee's 196th—were the only ARNG combat troops to see action. Nine other brigade and group headquarters and twelve hospitals deployed. Throughout the theater of operations, a balanced force of thirty battalions ranging from field artillery to quartermaster provided a diverse range of combat, combat support, and combat service support capabilities. Desert Storm Guardsmen saw action in all respects. In fact, the credit for the first American unit to breech the Iraqi defensive zone went to Tennessee's 212th Engineer Company.[26]

The service of Arkansas's 142nd Field Artillery Brigade best illustrates the performance of ARNG combat units. On the afternoon of November 15th, Col. Charles Linch, the commander of the 142nd Brigade, received the unit's alert order for mobilization at the brigade headquarters in Fayetteville, Arkansas. The 142nd Brigade's wartime mission was to provide command and control for field artillery battalions in support of assigned missions from a corps artillery headquarters. Subordinate to the 142nd Brigade were two Arkansas artillery battalions, the 1-142nd Field Artillery headquartered in Harrison and the 2-142nd Field Artillery stationed in Fort Smith. At the same time, another alert order went to the ARNG's only MLRS battalion, the 1-158th Field

Artillery (MLRS) in Lawton, Oklahoma. Only five MLRS artillery battalions were in the entire Army at the time, and Central Command insisted on having all MLRS battalions deployed to Saudi Arabia. The 1-158th Artillery became the third battalion assigned to the 142nd Brigade. The Arkansas and Oklahoma artillery units had a long history of distinguished service. Arkansas's 1-142nd Field Artillery traced its origins back to 1893 and had seen service in the Mexican Border crisis and in both World Wars. Ironically, the 1-142nd had been the first ARNG artillery unit to enter combat in Korea under its previous designation as the 936th Field Artillery. The 1-158th Field Artillery had been in the Oklahoma Guard since 1920 and fought in World War II and Korea with the 45th Division.[27]

On the late afternoon of November 15th, all full-time support personnel reported to their armories in Arkansas and Oklahoma. By the next day, 10 percent of all unit personnel were on duty to begin preparations for movement to the brigade's mobilization station at Fort Sill, Oklahoma. Six days later, the brigade received its mobilization orders, and all Guardsmen reported to their armories. For three days, armories in Arkansas and Oklahoma hummed with activity. Artillerymen checked their personnel records while commanders reassigned soldiers into the most pressing unit vacancies. Troops maintained, inventoried, and uploaded both personal and unit equipment. On November 24th, the 142nd Brigade and its three subordinate battalions departed their armories by commercial bus and military convoy. By day's end, the entire brigade had closed on Fort Sill.

Initial mobilizations steps went smoothly because Fort Sill had already processed many units heading to the Gulf. III Corps Artillery Headquarters at Fort Sill took a particular interest in supporting the 142nd Brigade and in helping the Guardsmen to acquire critical shortages of equipment. Administrative processing and training in common soldier skills consumed the first days, but an even larger training and equipping challenge soon confronted the artillerymen. The 142nd Brigade did not have automated artillery computers and communications equipment and had to rely on slower, manual computations and voice radio communications. In Saudi Arabia, the 142nd would face the near impossible task of interfacing with other artillery commands possessing more sophisticated equipment. In an intense, whirlwind training program, the brigade modernized to new artillery computers and radios. Assisted by III Corps trainers and civilian contractors, Guardsmen went through classroom training and two, rigorous field exercises. In less than a month, the Arkansans mastered skills normally taught in thirteen weeks. Meanwhile, other soldiers prepared the brigade's guns and equipment for shipment overseas. By December 15th, all howitzers and heavy equipment had departed Fort Sill by rail for ports of embarkation.

Meanwhile, the 1-158th Artillery prepared for deployment. The battalion had reported to Fort Sill with only 80 percent of its required personnel. The addition of 39 ARNG volunteers and the assignment of 54 Regulars brought the battalion to near its full strength of 463 soldiers. Training sessions stressed artillery skills, first aid, and chemical defense. During sixty hours of continuous painting operations, the battalion covered 253 pieces of rolling stock with desert sand camouflage paint. After little more than two weeks at Fort Sill, the 1-158th loaded its vehicles and equipment on rail cars. A long freight train pulled out of Fort Sill on December 9th, heading for the port of Galveston, Texas where the rocket launchers sat for more than a month awaiting shipment.

Impatient with the slow sealift of MLRS assets, Central Command ordered the immediate, aerial deployment of one battery from the 1-158th. On January 21st, the nine launchers, support vehicles, equipment, and 122 soldiers of Battery A flew on five C-5A Galaxies from Ellington Field near Houston, Texas directly to King Khalid Military City in Saudi Arabia. The Guardsmen arrived in the early morning hours of January 23rd, after completing the longest, direct deployment in history of an ARNG unit from CONUS to a theater of war. Battery A deployed north toward the Kuwaiti border and prepared to assist in the launching of artillery raids prior to the beginning of the ground campaign. On February 16th, Battery A became the first ARNG unit to fire on Iraqi forces. The MLRS launchers let fly with ninety-eight rockets that delivered over 63,000 explosive bomblets against six enemy targets. Over the next four days, the battery launched another 119 rockets. On the receiving end, Iraqi soldiers referred to the devastating hail of MLRS bomblets as "steel rain."

While Battery A was making history, the balance of the 1-158th Artillery was arriving in the desert and moving into firing positions. By February 16th, the remainder of the 1-158th had flown to Saudi Arabia, and its equipment had arrived in port. In a prodigious effort, the Oklahoma Guardsmen deployed north toward the Saudi-Kuwaiti border and took up firing positions only four days after their equipment had arrived in country. On February 22d, Batteries B and C fired sixty-seven rockets against Iraqi positions.

On January 15th, the 142nd Brigade headquarters arrived in Saudi Arabia and prepared for the arrival of its subordinate battalions. The 142nd's initial mission was to support the U.S. 1st Infantry Division's attack on the Iraqi defensive zone. Unfortunately, the 8-in. howitzers of the 1st and 2nd Battalions, 142nd Artillery did not arrive until

A self-propelled howitzer of the 142nd Field Artillery Brigade from Arkansas moves into Iraq during the ground attack phase of Desert Storm in 1991. The inscription on the gun tube—It's Personal—expresses the artillerymen's sentiments about the conflict. (National Guard Education Foundation)

February 19th due to shipping delays. Within seventy-two hours of receiving their howitzers, the battalions had deployed 314 miles north and taken up firing positions. On February 22nd, the entire 142d Brigade opened up in a vigorous artillery preparation.

In the early morning hours of February 24th, the 1st Division advanced against the Iraqis after the 142nd delivered a punishing thirty-minute artillery bombardment consisting of both cannon and missile fire. Troops from the "Big Red One" rolled through the enemy defenses largely unopposed. VII Corps then assigned the Arkansas self-propelled battalions and Battery A, 1-158th to support the British 1st Armoured Division during its advance into Kuwait. Meanwhile, the balance of the 1-158th stayed with the 1st Division until reassigned to support the 2d Armored Cavalry. The 100-hour war was one dizzying, nonstop period of movement and fire missions for the 142nd Brigade. In one unusual incident, fifty-five Iraqi prisoners surrendered to an officer in the 1-158th . By the end of the fighting, the brigade had fired over 1,000 rounds of 8-in. and MLRS munitions. Continuous fire support to the 1st Division, 2d Armored Cavalry, and British 1st Armoured Division undoubtedly reduced Allied casualties. After the war, the British division commander commended the 142nd Brigade for its "timely and accurate fire" that "contributed significantly" to light casualties and the division's "swift and crushing victory." The commander of the 1-158th Artillery, Lt. Col. Larry Haub, proudly proclaimed after the war that his troops had "never missed a start point, a fire mission, or a release point."[28]

Iowa's 1133rd Transportation Company demonstrated the tremendous capabilities of ARNG combat support units. On September 19th, Capt. Daniel A. Thorsen received orders to mobilize his company. Eight days later, all soldiers reported to their armory in Mason City. In three days of intense activity, troops inventoried and packed equipment, performed vehicle maintenance, filled out required paperwork and tended to last minute personal matters. The 1133rd had recently returned from an overseas deployment to Korea and was well prepared for wartime service. The soldiers of the 1133rd were the descendants of a proud militia heritage. In August 1862, they had first formed in Mason City as Company B, 32nd Iowa Volunteer Infantry and saw combat in the Civil War's western theater. For nearly 150 years, the company had maintained a National Guard presence in Mason City under various unit configurations and had served in the Spanish-American War, the Mexican Border Crisis and with the 34th Division in World Wars I and II.[29]

Soldiers from the 1776th Military Police Company of the Michigan ARNG prepare to receive Iraqi prisoners of war during Desert Storm. (National Guard Education Foundation)

Just after noon on September 30th, the 162 soldiers and sixty-four wheeled vehicles of the 1133rd Transportation Company departed Mason City to the cheers of over 10,000 well-wishers. The convoy headed east across the American heartland toward its mobilization station at Fort McCoy, Wisconsin. Army inspectors at Fort McCoy declared the 1133rd at the highest possible state of readiness and ready for immediate deployment. By October 11th, all vehicles were painted desert sand and loaded on rail cars for transportation to the port of embarkation at Bayonne, New Jersey. At Fort McCoy, the 1133rd learned it would operate in Saudi Arabia under control of the 68th Transportation Battalion, an active Army headquarters controlling two Regular, four ARNG, and two USAR transportation units.

On November 13th, the 1133rd arrived at Dhahran airport in Saudi Arabia after an exhausting trip from Volk Field, Wisconsin aboard two C-141 transports. Three days later its trucks and trailers arrived in country, and the company began long haul transport missions of ammunition and medical supplies from the port of Damman. During Desert Shield, the 1133rd continued trailer transfer and over-the-road long haul of supplies and equipment from rear area supply points to forward deployed units and supply points. On Thanksgiving Day, the soldiers enjoyed a traditional Thanksgiving meal and received a visit from President and Mrs. Bush who spent the holiday with American troops. On December 19th, the 1133rd began operations from a temporary motor pool in the Saudi desert, and for the next 148 days, all personnel lived in tents or slept in the open. After New Years, signs of impending war were everywhere. Soldiers mounted machine guns on their vehicles, and nerve agent pills were distributed. The day after the opening of the air war, the company received anthrax shots. On January 20th, an Iraqi Scud missile exploded in the air above one of the company's trailer transfer points. In early February, the Iowa Guardsmen deployed further north near the Kuwaiti border where ammunition distribution continued at a rapid pace.

In the first forty-eight hours of the ground war, the 1133rd hauled priority ammunition loads until receiving orders for a new, unexpected mission. On February 27th, the company reported to a pickup site near the Kuwaiti border to begin the transport of Iraqi prisoners from a forward prisoner collection point to a holding area in the rear. Guards were supposed to be on hand to escort the prisoners, but none were available. Nearly 4,000 Iraqi prisoners stood in the open desert awaiting orders. The lack of guards did not deter the 1133rd. The Iowans trained their M-16s and M-60 machine guns on the prisoners while crowding them onto trucks and trailers. The company successfully transported the Iraqis to the rear while providing the security force.

The end of the ground war presented new challenges to the 1133rd. On March 1st, the company became part of a large relief effort to transport badly needed humanitarian supplies to Kuwait City. The trucks moved north in convoy over heavily bombed roads littered with unexploded ordnance. Thick, black smoke and heavy fumes from burning oil wells filled the air. In Kuwait City, the inhabitants wildly greeted the 1133rd as liberators. For ten days, the company hauled food, water, fire fighting equipment, and other necessities through Kuwait City and ventured north into Iraq to deliver humanitarian supplies to a Red Cross refugee camp. On March 12th, Captain Thorsen wrote to the AG of Iowa that his company had logged nearly 200 missions while carrying 72,026 tons of material over a distance of 1.3 million miles. Two days later, the 1133rd was told to return to Saudi Arabia for administrative hauling missions.

Duty by Guardsmen assigned to combat service support units is personified in the service of Idaho's 148th Public Affairs Detachment (PAD). The 148th was a thirteen-member unit designed to provide military journalistic skills and media relations to an army corps or division. The Idaho PAD had a long history of overseas experience with deployments to Germany and Panama. In February 1990, the 148th underwent three weeks of annual training in Germany while supporting its CAPSTONE unit, the 3rd Armored Division.[30]

The 148th PAD, commanded by Capt. Kim P. Wortham, was activated on December 7th. The days following mobilization involved a flurry of administrative activity and cross leveling of personnel and equipment. The unit had one vacancy and two members were unavailable because they had not yet attended required training. Staff Sergeant Gail Seaman volunteered to leave his slot in the 116th Cavalry Brigade to return to the 148th PAD for duty. Specialist Edgar Morrison, a newspaper copy editor who had already moved to a new civilian job in South Carolina but had not yet left the Idaho Guard, returned to Boise for duty.

On December 12th, the 148th PAD, with a complement of twelve soldiers, reported to its mobilization station at Fort Lewis, Washington. The PAD was declared fully ready for overseas duty even though two members were medically disqualified for deployment. Meanwhile, the 3rd Armored Division in Germany was beginning its deployment to Saudi Arabia and had requested that the 148th serve as their PAD. The good relations that had developed between the 148th and the division during exercises ten months earlier had prompted the request. Before leaving Fort Lewis, the Idaho Guardsmen learned that they would support the "Spearhead" Division in the coming weeks.

A team of the 103rd Public Affairs Detachment from the Montana ARNG raises the Montana State flag inside Iraq thirty minutes after the cease fire on February 28, 1991. Throughout the Persian Gulf War, ARNG units flew their State flags in the Arabian Desert for the first time. (National Guard Education Foundation)

The 148th PAD arrived at Dhahran airport on January 12th and was taken to temporary living quarters in dilapidated warehouses near the Dhahran port facilities. To their great surprise, the Idaho soldiers discovered thousands of soldiers from the 3rd Armored Division jammed into the warehouses awaiting the arrival of vehicles and heavy equipment from Europe. The next day, the 148th joined the 3rd Armored Division headquarters. The short stay in Dhahran saw several tense moments. On the first night of Desert Storm, loudspeakers announced a Scud alert, and the entire division donned chemical suits and protective masks against an attack that never came. The next night, the 148th witnessed the first combat launch of a Patriot missile that intercepted an incoming Scud at low altitude. The burning debris from the Scud landed only blocks away.

By the end of January, the 3rd Armored Division started to deploy to positions near the Kuwaiti border. The Idaho Guardsmen watched as column after column of tanks, personnel carriers, and other heavy equipment and vehicles assembled in the desert. Operating out of two large tents located near the main division command post, the 148th escorted reporters and published a weekly division newsletter, the "Saudi

Spearhead." To accomplish this, the 148th transported their stories and photographs by vehicle to Dhahran twelve hours away. In Dhahran, a rear detachment of the 148th produced a camera ready layout of the newsletter's pages that were then flown to Germany for printing. Stacks of the newsletter were flown back to Saudi Arabia for eventual distribution in the field. By the time of the ground war, the 148th had established excellent working relations with the division staff, and nearly a dozen civilian journalists had moved in with the Guardsmen.

With the beginning of the ground war, the 148th accompanied the 3rd Armored Division into the largest American tank battles since World War II. Journalists from *Time, ABC News, AFRN* radio, the *Wall Street Journal* and other media organizations filmed and reported on the war assisted by the 148th PAD. After the cease-fire, the PAD escorted the media into refugee camps in occupied Iraq. To create a record of the division's service in Desert Storm, the 148th wrote, designed, and published a special, twenty-four page commemorative edition of "Spearhead Magazine." During the war, the 148th gained the distinction as the most forward deployed PAD in the theater and the only PAD to publish a wartime, divisional newsletter. On May 16th, the 148th returned to Fort Lewis and left active duty five days later.

Redeployment and Demobilization

Even before Desert Storm was over, the Army began preparations to smooth the return of troops and equipment. On Feb 1st, the Army issued guidelines for mobilization stations to use in outprocessing units and returning them to State control. Soon after the end of the ground war, ARNG units began to demobilize. Outprocessing at mobilization stations usually required four or five days, but some units required more than a week. Each soldier underwent a physical examination to document service incurred problems. Officers and sergeants received efficiency reports reflecting their wartime service, and at separation, all Guardsmen received important documents giving them credit for retirement points and future benefits. Guardsmen were advised of their reemployment rights and the availability of family assistance programs to help in the transition back to civilian life. On July 23rd, the 119th Medical Company from Lakeland, Florida was the last ARNG unit to leave active duty.[31]

After returning to their home armories, Guardsmen began to recover fully from the war effort. Many units initially returned without their vehicles and equipment that had been loaded on ships for the long journey to the United States. Some units received their equipment in a few weeks, while others received it several months later. In some cases, equipment never returned or was damaged in transit. Desert Storm units resumed weekend drill within the first month of their return. However, few conducted annual training in 1991 in order to save money and to ease employers' concerns over losing workers for an additional, extended period.[32]

With Desert Storm over, the Roundout brigades demobilized. On March 2d, the 48th Brigade began to turn in its training equipment at Fort Irwin and to redeploy back to Georgia. The majority of the brigade reached Fort Stewart by March 11th, and four days later, the last Guardsman departed the NTC. The brigade retained 10 percent of its key personnel on active duty to assist with demobilization and to write after action reports. By April 10th, the entire brigade was back under State control. On March 11th, the 155th Brigade reached the NTC and began a two-week training rotation. The 256th and the 155th Brigades went on to complete their post-mobilization training regimes and were released from active duty by May 14, 1991[33]

The ARNG's combat battalions initially remained in Saudi Arabia to assist in the enforcement of an uneasy armistice, but eventually they started for home. On May 14th, Arkansas's 142nd Brigade departed Saudi Arabia by commercial airliner, landing at Altus Air Force Base, Oklahoma at 0100 hours the following morning. The soldiers expected little in the

Infantrymen of the 3-141st Infantry, Texas ARNG, train in the dust and heat of Fort Hood, Texas during Desert Shield. The battalion was assigned to Mississippi's 155th Armored Brigade during the callup for the Persian Gulf War. (National Guard Education Foundation)

way of a welcome because of the early hour. However, as they made the sixty-mile journey to Fort Sill by commercial bus, hundreds of fellow Guardsmen and family members stood along the route cheering and waving flags in the darkness. At Fort Sill, a large crowd of 6,000 people turned out at 2 o'clock in the morning to greet the brigade.[34]

A number of ARNG support units stayed in the Persian Gulf after the cease-fire to assist with humanitarian efforts and to transfer equipment and supplies. Iowa's 1133rd Transportation Company remained in the Persian Gulf for nearly four more months, redistributing ammunition from forward caches to more secure holding areas. Special missions included a second relief effort to Kuwait City and the transport of Air Force ordnance from Saudi Arabia to Bahrain. After a week spent preparing its vehicles and equipment for shipment home, the 1133rd departed Dhahran airport on June 7th and received a rousing welcome at Volk Field, Wisconsin. Over 10,000 people turned out in Mason City, Iowa on June 12th to welcome the 1133rd back to its home armory. In all, the 1133rd served a whopping 261 days on active duty. During 207 days of operations in the Persian Gulf, the Iowans hauled 112,000 tons of material over 2.1 million miles throughout four different Arabic countries.[35]

On May 20–21st, the ARNG Directorate conducted an extensive debriefing in Alexandria, Virginia with brigade and battalion commanders from Desert Storm. All agreed that the high levels of manning and equipping that resulted from the Total Force Policy and the Reagan Buildup contributed to the great success in mobilizing and deploying their units. The CAPSTONE Program received high praise. Even though CAPSTONE relations had been developed with Army units in Europe in anticipation of a Soviet blitzkrieg, the working relationships facilitated smooth operations in the unfamiliar and challenging Saudi desert. Commanders unanimously agreed that overseas deployment training was a key ingredient to their success. Experience gained during mobilization exercises, deployments, and realistic, overseas training exercises paid great dividends. Commanders praised the Key Personnel Upgrade Program for providing officers and sergeants with increased tactical and technical knowledge. A common complaint was that several Army installations slowed the mobilization by repeating many of the administrative tasks previously completed at home armories.[36]

As in all wars, victory came with a price. All together, thirty-four Guardsmen gave their lives during Desert Shield and Desert Storm. Eighteen died in Southwest Asia, though none died as a result of direct enemy action. Common causes of death included vehicle accidents, aircraft crashes, and heart attacks. For the first time, ARNG women died in wartime; of the thirty-four soldiers who perished, eight were female.[37]

New York's 719th Transportation Company marches up Broadway during New York City's Persian Gulf War Victory Parade on June 10, 1991. (National Guard Bureau)

The country experienced an outpouring of patriotism after the Persian Gulf victory. After units returned home, victory parades occurred in large cities and small towns across the nation. Pride, gratitude, and humility filled the hearts of Guardsmen marching in victory parades. For ARNG Vietnam veterans who had served in Desert Storm, the parades and ceremonies were a much delayed welcome home from Southeast Asia. On June 8th, Guardsmen marched down Constitution Avenue in Washington, DC as part of a huge National Victory Celebration. A long parade of troops and vehicles from all the services passed in review before President Bush and Desert Storm's most senior military commanders.

Conclusions

In almost all respects, the Persian Gulf War was a resounding success for the ARNG. Desert Shield marked the thirteenth federal callup in National Guard history and the eighth time Guardsmen had been ordered to active duty in the 20th Century. All together, 62,411 ARNG soldiers in 398 units answered the call to arms. Not since the Korean War forty years earlier had so many Guardsmen served on active duty. In the Persian Gulf, 37,484 ARNG soldiers in 297 units performed valuable combat, combat support, and combat service support missions. The Guardsmen who deployed to Europe or remained in the U.S. provided important support and security capabilities, received valuable training, and constituted a ready reserve. All Guardsmen reported for duty, and only those who were not available for medical reasons or a lack of required training did not serve. The wisdom of the Total Force Policy was vindicated, and the investments in personnel and equipment made during the Reagan Buildup generated a quick military victory with a minimal loss of life.

A number of broad, crucial lessons emerged from Desert Storm. Of greatest significance, the ARNG mobilization helped to generate widespread, sustained public support for the war. In this respect, Creighton Abrams' vision was vindicated; the National Guard callup helped cement the bond between the American people and the armed forces in wartime. The ARNG proved its units could deploy and carry out their assigned missions with little advance notice. Rapid, organized unit movements were a particular Guard strength. The greatest impediments to Guard deployments were not shortages of training, personnel or equipment, but the lack of available sealift. Guardsmen displayed a mastery of complicated, high technology equipment ranging from advanced communication devices and tactical computers to the revolutionary Global Positioning System that made land navigation possible in the open desert. For the first time, ARNG female soldiers proved their worth while performing worldwide, wartime missions. The State headquarters performed valuable service by assisting units with rapid mobilizations and quick movements to federal mobilization stations.

At the same time, Desert Shield identified a number of areas for remedial action. While the States were at the forefront of providing support and assistance to deploying soldiers and their families, it was clear that a larger, more coordinated and comprehensive Family Support Program was needed. The mobilization surfaced new problems associated with child custody, dual military parenting and related issues that had come with the inception of the all-volunteer military. National Guardsmen required additional health and dental care and medical screening. Too many soldiers who met standards for recruiting and retention were not medically qualified for deployment. At mobilization stations, electronic computer programs conflicted with paper forms and records. Poor administration slowed the mobilization process by creating extra work, frustrating soldiers and their families, and distracting leaders from command responsibilities.

The performance of the Roundout brigades revealed several positive aspects about the Roundout concept and the Total Force Policy. Upon mobilization, the 48th Brigade was a modernized unit fully structured to complete the organization of its parent division and manned by trained soldiers that met established readiness standards. The fact that the 48th Brigade existed in such a high state of readiness testified to the effectiveness of the Total Force Policy and the Reagan Buildup. Compared to previous National Guard mobilizations, the Roundout brigades achieved deployment readiness standards in record time. Only ninety-one days after mobilization, the Army declared the 48th ready for deployment, and the 155th and 256th Brigades were near the end of their training when Desert Storm ended. Though they did not deploy, the brigades constituted a ready reserve in the event of a longer war in the Gulf or the outbreak of a second, unexpected regional crisis.

A closer look at the 48th Brigade's training regime reveals a unit that was more ready than many believe. Of the ninety-one days between mobilization and the declaration of combat readiness, seventy-six days were fully dedicated to training. Administration and unit movements consumed the remaining days. Out of seventy-six training days, thirty were devoted to attacks against Iraqi defenses, the same training conducted by active divisions in Saudi Arabia. Consequently, the 48th Brigade required forty-six days to achieve established readiness standards for training. The brigade estimated before the callup that it would require a maximum of forty-two days of additional training after mobilization. Considering the brigade had not counted on training without support from the 24th Division, its pre-Desert Shield training estimate very closely approximated the actual training program that unfolded at Fort Stewart and the NTC.[38]

The mobilization revealed significant weaknesses in Roundout planning. First, a number of conflicting perceptions existed throughout DOD, the Army, the National Guard and on Capitol Hill regarding missions and readiness. Many believed Roundout brigades should be ready for immediate deployment with their parent divisions and require little or no training after mobilization. Others held the more accurate view that the brigades were never intended to deploy immediately with their divisions and would require additional training. Second, specific mobilization plans prepared before Desert Shield proved nearly worthless. Even with war looming and time running short, the Army imposed new, post-mobilization training plans and unique readiness standards for deployment. The changes forced Guardsmen to adjust to new operating procedures and a lengthy, unscheduled rotation at the NTC. In its rush to assist the brigades, the Army may have done too much; to help train the 13,000 Guardsmen in the three brigades, the Army committed nearly 9,000 troops. The poor relations that developed between some Guard leaders and Army trainers smacked of the bitterness generated during previous mobilizations.[39]

For the first time in modern history, the Army prosecuted a major war without using a single National Guard ground maneuver unit. Of all the services, only the Army experienced major difficulties in integrating its combat reserve components during Desert Storm. The reasons for the delay in calling out the brigades left lingering doubts in the ARNG and on Capitol Hill as to the Army's motives. NGAUS argued that several Regular units less well trained, manned, and equipped than the 48th Brigade had gone to Saudi Arabia. If the 180-day limit imposed by Section 673b prevented the use of Roundout brigades, it did not keep the Army from sending over 200 ARNG support units to Saudi Arabia during Desert Shield. The media raised the specter that the Army believed the brigades would fail and cause a military setback reminiscent of Task Force Smith in the Korean War. Others suspected that successful ARNG combat units would threaten the existence of active combat forces during the post–Cold War demobilization. In the end, the Roundout brigades would have better served the nation with a more timely callup, deployment to the Persian Gulf, training in the Saudi desert, and combat with their parent divisions.

In the end, the wisest assessment of the 48th Brigade's service came from its own commander. Soon after returning to Georgia, Col. James D. Davis told his troops:

> Even though we were denied the opportunity to join forces overseas, we made a significant contribution to the overall war effort...It doesn't matter that we didn't get a chance to fight. We won our own victory at the NTC. Sixty days in the harshest environment of America at a constant, non-stop pace challenged our stamina. Never once did we falter. The strength of this brigade, from start to finish, has been your attitude, your grit and your physical courage.[40]

American military history repeated itself after Desert Storm as the armed forces returned home to face steep force reductions. For the ARNG, the 1990s would prove to be one of the most difficult and contentious periods in its long history.

CHAPTER 9

A New World Order, 1991–2000

T oday, a generation raised in the shadows of the Cold War assumes new responsibilities in a world warmed by the sunshine of freedom but threatened still by ancient hatreds and new plagues.

President William J. Clinton,
Inaugural Address, January 1993

Introduction

Capt. Michael E. Patterson walked in full battle gear along the cold, wind-swept roadway of a long, concrete bridge spanning the Sava River on the border between Croatia and Bosnia. Moments before, Company C, 3-116th Infantry of the Virginia ARNG had assumed responsibility for guarding the Sava River bridge from the U.S. Army's 10th Mountain Division. A platoon of heavily armed Guardsmen occupied defensive positions on the bridge while the company's other platoons remained in reserve nearby. Captain Patterson was pleased with his company's perform-ance; the transfer of responsibility had taken place without incident. On November 1, 1997, Company C, 3-116th Infantry became the first ARNG ground maneuver unit to go in harm's way since the Indiana Rangers had fought in Vietnam in 1968.

Charlie Company was an ocean away from its armory in Leesburg, Virginia. The bridge defense mission was a small portion of a much larger effort, Operation Joint Guard, the NATO peacekeeping initiative to bring peace and stability to the war-torn, former Yugoslavia. After mobilization on September 3, 1997, the company had deployed to Fort Polk, Louisiana for extensive training before heading to Europe. Since October 22nd, the company had completed final preparations at the main NATO staging area in Tazar, Hungary before moving to the Sava River bridge on November 1st.

The first day of duty was not without its tense moments, as buses filled with Croatian pilgrims crossed into Bosnia to visit the gravesites of deceased relatives in observance of All Saint's Day. A hostile crowd of Serbs protested the crossings at the Bosnian end of the bridge. Several busloads of pilgrims crossed the bridge without incident, but sporadic gunfire was heard on the far side of the bridge. Before the day was over, Captain Patterson coordinated the efforts of American attack helicopters and Norwegian mechanized infantrymen sent to bolster the bridge's defenses. Before sundown the vehicles returned with frightened passengers; angry Serbs had shattered the windows on at least two buses. The show of force by the disciplined, heavily-armed Guardsmen had helped to maintain order throughout a tense, difficult day. Afterwards, Captain Patterson remembered the company's first day of guard duty on the Sava River bridge as one of its most successful.

The peacekeeping mission of Company C, 3-116th Infantry is but one example of the manner in which the ARNG adapted in the 1990s to the New World Order, the complex and fragmented international environment that emerged following the Cold War. Three key developments dominated activities throughout the decade: the lessons learned from the Persian Gulf War, post-Cold War force structure reductions, and the determination of the Guard's new roles and missions within the framework of a new, evolving American defense strategy.

The lessons of Desert Storm sparked a number of new initiatives and caused controversial changes in the Army's implementation of critical aspects of the Total Force Policy. The deep military cuts first articulated in the months preceding Desert Storm finally came to pass when the ARNG underwent the most painful unit and personnel reductions in its history. At the same time, the Pentagon struggled to define a new national security strategy. Confounded by the New World Order, deep budget and personnel reductions, and a revolution in military affairs wrought by the computer and the microchip, the nation's civilian and uniformed military leaders labored to develop a coherent military strategy that utilized a smaller, balanced force of Regulars, Guardsmen, and Reservists. In a span of less than seven years, DOD conducted no less than four major defense reviews. As the 1990s ended, the Guard emerged as an integral part of the nation's defense while striving to retain its traditional role as the Army's primary combat reserve.

The Search for a New Strategy

Ironically, the basis for American strategic thinking that emerged after the Persian Gulf War was first articulated on the very day Saddam

Hussein invaded Kuwait. In a speech in Aspen, Colorado on August 2, 1990, President Bush announced the "Base Force," the new shape of America's armed forces and a new strategy for national defense that marked the end of America's forty-year reliance on the strategy of containment. The plan's principal architect and advocate was General Colin Powell, the CJCS. General Powell defined the Base Force as the minimum troop levels required among all of the uniformed services that still allowed the U.S. to maintain its superpower status and to meet worldwide responsibilities. The Base Force shifted away from a strategy concentrated solely on defeating the Soviet Union to one focused on lesser, known threats and the retention of sufficient forces to maintain critical military capabilities. He envisioned four basic missions for the military; the ongoing defense of NATO, the preservation of peace in the Pacific, the creation of a CONUS-based contingency force capable of rapidly deploying to overseas trouble spots, and continued nuclear deterrence.[1]

The Army soon articulated a new strategic vision that conformed to the Base Force. With the Soviet Union gone, the Army's principle missions were to deter or defeat aggression, maintain America's global influence, promote regional stability, staunch the flow of illicit drugs into the United States, and combat terrorism. Throughout the Cold War, the Army had maintained a large, forward defense along the containment perimeter. Now it planned for a much smaller overseas presence backed by mobile forces based in CONUS. The new strategy placed a premium on the ability to project combat forces rapidly from CONUS or from other forward deployed locations in Europe and Asia. A CONUS-based contingency corps capable of rapid deployment to overseas trouble spots and made up of more than five Regular Army divisions became central to strategic planning.[2]

Like General Powell and the Army leadership, the ARNG searched for its proper role in the New World Order following the Persian Gulf War. NGAUS and AGAUS collaborated in an examination of new Guard roles and missions for the 1990s and into the 21st Century. In their analysis, senior leaders emphasized the worth of the Guard's traditional federal and State missions. In November 1992, the Guard leadership identified four enduring missions. The National Guard should remain the nation's primary federal reserve, maintain combat forces in the first line of defense, and continue its role as the nation's primary domestic disaster response force. In addition, the Guard was to engage in domestic missions that contributed to the "social and moral fabric of the nation."[3]

The Aftermath of Desert Storm

Despite early initiatives to reshape the nation's defenses, the first real changes to the ARNG occurred as a direct result of lessons from the Persian Gulf War. Two Army reforms struck directly at programs that had been at the heart of the Total Force Policy for nearly twenty years. The Roundout Program was perhaps the ARNG's most visible casualty following Desert Storm. The precedent of not deploying the 48th and 155th Brigades to the Persian Gulf with their parent divisions and the Army's new emphasis on force projection from CONUS generated the new concept of "Roundup" brigades. The five divisions in the new contingency corps would be composed entirely of active troops in order to facilitate rapid deployment and the invasion of a hostile war zone. Reinforcements for subsequent operations would come from a fourth, ARNG Roundup brigade assigned to each heavy division. By 1992, the 24th Infantry and 1st Cavalry Divisions had three active brigades, and the 48th and 155th Brigades were assigned as Roundups, respectively. At the same time, the Army retained five other Roundout brigade and active division pairings that had existed prior to Desert Storm. Still, many Guardsmen saw the reduced role of the 48th and 155th Brigades as the first step in the eventual elimination of the Roundout Program and as the means for the active Army to protect more of its combat units from expected force cuts.[4]

The shift from forward deployed divisions to a CONUS-based force caused a major restructuring of the successful CAPSTONE Program in which each ARNG unit had a direct, wartime assignment to a Regular Army organization. In August 1992, the Army determined that major changes in the CAPSTONE Program were necessary. The prospect of multiple, regional wars and the smaller number of available support units due to downsizing prompted the Army to assign ARNG combat support and combat service support units to more than one overseas command. The CAPSTONE Program that had laid the foundation for much of the ARNG's success in the Persian Gulf War vanished in short order. The new WARTRACE Program stressed training relationships between active and Guard units instead of strict, wartime alignments. Over time, Guard commanders lost the advantages of focusing training and deployment activities on a single, specific theater and were forced to plan for multiple contingencies.[5]

The reserve component callup for Desert Shield convinced Pentagon planners that the presidential 180-day mobilization limit for Guardsmen and Reservists imposed by Section 673b was too restrictive. An initial mobilization of 90 days followed by a second 90-day period before Congress granted authority for extended active duty inhibited long range planning and created unnecessary confusion among citizen-soldiers and their families. Longer mobilization periods were needed in the 1990s in light of the mounting number of overseas humanitarian and peacekeeping missions. In October 1994, DOD convinced Congress to amend Section 673b to permit a reserve component, presidential callup of 270 days.[6]

Despite the ARNG's successes in Desert Storm, Congress implemented modest reforms to improve the Guard's overall readiness. Members of the House Armed Services Committee composed legislation that addressed a number of concerns. Overall, the bill's provisions were designed to enhance Guard deployability, improve the Regular Army's capacity to measure Guard readiness, make ARNG units more compatible with active forces, facilitate the development of Guard leaders, and improve the Guard's medical preparedness. In its final form, the "Army National Guard Combat Readiness Reform Act of 1992" became Title XI of the 1993 Defense Authorization Act. Overall, Title XI contained eighteen sections that outlined specific measures to improve Guard readiness. Nine initiatives were designed to increase Guard deployability by enhancing leadership skills and improving personnel, medical, and dental programs. A key provision sought to increase the level of military experience. By September 1997, 65 percent of the Guard's officers and one-half of its enlisted soldiers were to have had prior, active service of not less than two years. The Army was given the latitude to review officer promotions and to enforce stricter noncommissioned officer education requirements. Congress ordered more frequent medical screening and dental checkups to avoid deployment problems that had surfaced during Desert Shield. Title XI specified changes to the Army's readiness reporting system that permitted a more detailed and accurate portrayal of a unit's readiness posture. Other key provisions were designed to minimize the Guard's post-mobilization training by increasing the Army's oversight and involvement in peacetime training. As many as 5,000 Regulars would be assigned to Guard units with the aim of improving readiness. Lastly, the Army was to create compatible personnel, supply, maintenance, and financial administrative systems across all Army components by 1997.[7]

While Pentagon staffs worked to implement Title XI's administrative changes, the Army revamped ARNG training. A new readiness enhancement program called "Bold Shift" complied with Title XI initiatives by seeking to increase reserve component readiness and facilitating more positive interactions between Regulars and the Guard. Desert Shield had revealed weaknesses in the chain of command of several ARNG units, and Bold Shift included new initiatives for improving the training of commanders, staffs, and small unit leaders. A key objective was to enable

The crew of an M2 Bradley Fighting Vehicle engages a target with their 25-mm. cannon at Yakima Training Center, Washington. (National Guard Bureau)

ARNG combat brigades to be ready for deployment in a shorter time period than the three Roundout brigades had required during Desert Storm. The Army assigned 1,300 Regulars to Bold Shift training evaluation teams and as advisors to the Roundout and Roundup brigades.[8]

Unit training was the aspect of Bold Shift that most affected Guardsmen. Before the Persian Gulf War, ARNG units sought to train at the highest level organized, but the Bold Shift training philosophy was to train Guard units to a higher standard at the lowest levels of organization. New training plans targeted the skills of individual soldiers, crews, squads, and platoons. Training exercises focused primarily on gunnery skills for vehicle crews in tank and mechanized infantry battalions and platoon level maneuvers for all combat arms. Platoon exercises were conducted during "lanes training" in which Guardsmen maneuvered through a predetermined training site while reacting to various tactical scenarios. A "crawl-walk-run" training philosophy emphasized the mastery of simpler, basic skills before advancing to more demanding tasks. Regular Army advisors closely monitored training and facilitated a detailed discussion and critique after each training session. In addition, active duty personnel organized training sites and provided logistical support to allow Guard units to concentrate solely on training. Bold Shift also established the operational readiness evaluation, an inspection and training exercise that took stock of a Guard unit's readiness and its ability to deploy quickly.[9]

The Army's rationale for emphasizing training at the lowest levels caused considerable concern in the ARNG. To the Army, Desert Shield had demonstrated that the three Roundout brigades were not immediately prepared for combat. ARNG soldiers, crews, and platoons may have performed well, but the Army believed brigade and battalions staffs were inadequately trained. Regulars maintained that the complex tasks of coordinating the combat arms into an integrated combined arms team on a fast paced, high technology battlefield was beyond the ability of Guard officers with limited time for training. By emphasizing small unit training in peacetime, the Army hoped to maximize the amount of training time available after mobilization to permit Guardsmen to master the difficulties of combined arms warfare.

Many Guardsmen interpreted the Army's arguments and new training strategy as a cynical ploy to discredit their major combat units at a time when massive force structure reductions were the hot topic at the Pentagon. By maligning the ARNG's combat brigades and divisions, Guardsmen believed that the active Army was building the case for eliminating a peer competitor while retaining more of its own divisions on active duty. Guard commanders did not understand why the new training strategy focused on the small unit level—where soldiers' jobs were the least complex and personnel turnover was the highest—instead of on higher staffs where tasks were more complicated and personnel stability more pronounced. Some suspected that by restricting Guard training to the small unit level, the Army was anticipating the wholesale stripping of Guard organizations for replacements in a national emergency as had occurred during the opening stages of the Korean War. At the same time, many Guard commanders welcomed Bold Shift's emphasis on providing training support. Burdened by stressful personnel reductions and widespread unit reorganizations, many States were relieved to be free of the mundane tasks of preparing training plans and organizing training sites.

Within three years, the Army reported near full compliance with most of Title XI's provisions. However, personnel readiness still posed a significant challenge. The elimination of medical units and facilities during the post-Cold War drawdown made periodic medical and dental screening throughout the Guard impossible. In the end, medical resources were primarily focused on Guardsmen in early deploying units. Acquiring sufficient numbers of former active duty personnel to raise the experience level throughout the ARNG proved difficult. The accession of commissioned officers above the grade of captain, warrant officers, and enlisted personnel above the grade of sergeant became the priority. Soldiers leaving active duty during the drawdown were often attracted to the Guard, but as the pace of personnel cuts slowed, this source of manpower evaporated.[10]

Project Standard Bearer

In response to the flurry of post-Desert Storm reforms, the ARNG Directorate established Project Standard Bearer on November 1, 1991. The project's purpose was to develop, coordinate, and institutionalize policies and programs to ensure high priority Guard units were ready and fully capable of early deployment. In addition, Project Standard Bearer controlled many aspects of the Guard's involvement in Title XI and Bold Shift. The original focus of Standard Bearer's attention was the Roundout and Roundup brigades, but the project eventually included a large pool of combat support and combat service support units.[11]

Standard Bearer initiated important personnel and equipment policies that resulted in the shifting of declining resources to high priority units. Standard Bearer required high priority units to maintain a 95 percent manning level of fully trained soldiers, and innovative recruiting and retention policies supported robust manning. By 1993, new recruits signing up in early deploying units received a $2,000 enlistment bonus. Standard Bearer units were required to have 100 percent of their equipment instead of the lesser equipping levels normally acceptable for deployment. Vehicles, weapons, and equipment from inactivating Regular and ARNG units filled armories and motor pools as logisticians further adjusted national equipment inventories to fill high priority units. In the States, Guardsmen in low priority units watched helplessly as increasingly scarce personnel and equipment resources migrated toward Standard Bearer units. Across the nation, Guardsmen once again complained of the "haves" and the "have nots," the perceived disparity on resources between high and low priority units.[12]

After Desert Storm, the Army organized its total inventory of support units to better sustain combat brigades and divisions deploying from CONUS. Desert Shield had taught planners the huge logistical demands of supporting a regional contingency, especially where weather and terrain were difficult and host nation support lacking. The Army developed the Contingency Force Pool to support the early deployment of the contingency corps and the movement of reinforcements. A key function of Project Standard Bearer was the selection and management of the Guard's portion of new contingency force support units. The ARNG at first provided 192 combat support and combat service support units, but

Mr. Thomas A. Hill
A Lifetime of Guard Service

(Thomas A. Hill)

Thomas A. Hill has proven over a lifetime of distinguished service that the functioning of the National Guard depends very much upon its civilian work force. He has been a civilian employee of NGB from the earliest days of the Cold War and has served in the ARNG Directorate during every national emergency since the Korean War.

Tommy Hill was born in Wilkes-Barre, Pennsylvania in 1919. After graduating from high school he eventually worked for the Department of the Interior in Washington, DC. In 1940, he took a position with the War Department but soon left to enlist in the Army. Mr. Hill got his first experience with the National Guard when he was assigned to the 29th Infantry Division. Here he observed the close-knit ties that abound in Guard units. Immediately after Pearl Harbor, his regiment moved to Washington to provide security around federal buildings. In April 1942, he was assigned to the War Department where he served for the remainder of the war.

In July 1946, Tommy Hill accepted civilian employment with the Army in the Pentagon. NGB officers were so impressed with his expertise and enthusiasm that they offered him a job. His first day at work with the ARNG was October 1, 1948, the same day the NGB staff was split into Army and Air National Guard components. After more than fifty years of continuous service, Mr. Hill still guides training activities. While he has supervised a number of projects, he is proudest of the role he played in establishing State Officer Candidate Schools. In 1950, only four States had their own commissioning programs, and by the early 1960s, each State had its own school. Tommy Hill also contributed to the success of overseas training exercises by developing goals and guidelines used to make the deployments a more rewarding experience for ARNG soldiers.

In addition, to his formal duties, Tommy Hill has been friend and mentor to generations of Guard officers and civilian employees, and has served as advisor and confidant to senior NGB leaders. No other person has served longer or made greater contributions to the ARNG Directorate.

its complete commitment finally tallied 389 units. Initially, only 84 percent of selected units met the Army's readiness standards for deployment, but Standard Bearer initiatives eventually allowed 97 percent of units to become mission ready. By 1993, the readiness of the ARNG's contingency force support units exceeded that of those in the Regular Army or the USAR. Throughout the 1990s, the readiness of contingency force units remained a top ARNG priority.[13]

The Counter-Drug War

In the face of budget cuts at the end of the Cold War, senior military leaders were eager to consider alternative missions to increase the military's value in the eyes of American taxpayers. At the end of the 1980s, Americans were deeply troubled over mounting crime and social ills attributed to increased drug usage and the massive flow of illicit narcotics into the country. President Bush declared a "war on drugs," appointed a national "Drug Czar" and ordered DOD to bring its full weight to bear against the drug epidemic. At first, the Pentagon was a reluctant warrior. Military leaders were concerned over the restrictions of the Posse Comitatus Act of 1878 that prohibited Regulars from arresting drug offenders. Many commanders argued that full-time, counter-drug operations would divert their units from the primary mission of combat readiness. However, political and social pressures that favored the military's involvement in the drug war finally prevailed.

In reality, the Guard was already on the drug war's front lines. As early as 1977, the Hawaii Guard had operated with State law enforcement officials to detect and eradicate marijuana fields. Four States reported ARNG counter-drug missions in 1983, and by 1988, thirty-two States had committed 4,042 Guardsmen to 456 counter-drug missions. With President Bush's declaration of a war on drugs, it was natural for the National Guard to become DOD's primary agency in providing domestic support to law enforcement agencies. The AGs and Guard commanders developed arrangements to accommodate the constraints of posse comitatus. No Guardsmen were to participate directly in making arrests or confiscating property but could provide direct support to police activities.[14]

In 1989, Congress appropriated $300 million for the Pentagon's drug war; $40 million was specifically earmarked for the Guard. Several congressional provisos came with the funding. Each State was to develop drug interdiction plans for the use of ARNG soldiers and equipment subject to approval by DOD. Counter-drug operations were not to interfere with normal unit training, and no more than 4,000 Guard soldiers nationwide could participate at one time. To comply with the Posse Comitatus Act, only Guardsmen on State active duty would assist law enforcement. NGB established a Counter-Drug Directorate to provide guidance to the States, to manage a budget, and to perform long-range planning. Each State appointed a senior officer to coordinate Guard efforts with law enforcement agencies.[15]

In 1990, the ARNG's counter-drug activities increased dramatically. During the peak marijuana eradication season, as many as 2,400

Guardsmen were on duty on any given day. All together, Guard troops participated in over 5,000 missions across the nation, including aerial and ground reconnaissance and surveillance and the inspection of commercial cargo at land border entry points, seaports, and international airports. Other support missions included the transport of law enforcement personnel and contraband, equipment loans and the use of high technology communications equipment, radar, night vision devices, and thermal imaging sights. In 1990 alone, Guard troops supported operations that resulted in 1,318 arrests, the eradication of 6.7 million marijuana plants, confiscation of $18 million in drug money, and the seizure of 34,000 pounds of cocaine.[16]

The peak year for National Guard counter-drug activities was 1993. Congress dedicated $260 million in counter-drug funding to the Guard. To facilitate planning, DOD issued a list of sixteen standard missions the States could perform ranging from surveillance and interdiction to border crossing inspections. The States astride the major drug routes leading from Mexico, the Caribbean, and Latin America into the country— Florida, Texas, New Mexico, Arizona, and California—were at the forefront of the counter-drug war. The ARNG Aviation Division organized special reconnaissance and interdiction flying units to support law enforcement agencies, and in 1993, ARNG aviators flew 46,000 hours during counter-drug missions. In 1993 alone, Guardsmen assisted law enforcement in arresting 69,000 drug traffickers and seizing caches of drugs with a total, estimated street value of $150 billion. The Guard's successes prompted the conclusion that the inflow of drugs could be interrupted when adequate resources were available and effectively employed.[17]

Throughout the remainder of the 1990s, the level of ARNG counter-drug activity remained nearly constant. Congressional funding averaged just over $200 million each year. Guard troops remained fully engaged in reconnaissance and surveillance and performed search and seizure missions at border crossings. New activities included the construction and improvement of roads along the southwestern border to assist the U.S. Border Patrol. Guardsmen became fully involved with drug demand reduction educational programs in their local communities. The ARNG instituted it own aggressive substance abuse program that used random, surprise drug testing to insure that soldiers remained drug free.[18]

The Drawdown of 1992–1997

President Bush's Base Force speech on August 2, 1990 outlined steep cuts in the armed forces to accompany the change in the nation's military strategy. The president called for cuts of up to 25 percent in the military, with active forces declining from 2.1 to 1.6 million. President Bush assured the audience that reserves would still be important but "in new ways." The need for a massive, national mobilization was diminished, argued the president, and adjustments in the "size, structure and readiness of our reserve forces" were necessary.[19]

The Base Force outlined steep reductions in Army forces. At its post-Vietnam peak, the Army included eighteen Regular and ten Guard divisions organized into five corps. The Base Force demanded that the Army's divisions be reduced by the mid-1990s to a total of twenty divisions in four corps. The number of active divisions was to fall from eighteen down to twelve, and ARNG divisions would decline from ten to eight. The Army "strongly believed" that twenty divisions was the "minimum force" required to meet the commitments inherent in the national defense.[20]

The Base Force's implications for the ARNG were ominous. Expected cuts would eliminate the gains made during the Reagan Buildup and then some. Before the end of 1990, the Army directed the ARNG to plan for cuts of up to 137,000 troop billets. After Desert Storm, NGAUS and AGAUS reacted to planned Army Guard cuts by calling for the maintenance of the ARNG at a strength of 420,000 soldiers. At the same time, the Guard built a consensus in the States and on Capitol Hill against widespread Guard reductions.[21]

Despite strong opposition to DOD's plans, the Guard had already started to reduce troop levels. Before the Persian Gulf War, the ARNG Directorate had reduced troop strength in the Northeast where shifting demographics no longer supported recruiting efforts. The ARNG's three divisions in the Northeast—the 42d Infantry (New York), the 26th Infantry (Massachusetts and Connecticut), and the 50th Armored (New Jersey and Vermont)—lagged in unit manning. A brigade of the 50th Armored was transferred from Vermont to Texas in 1988. A broader plan known as the "3 into 1" soon emerged that broke up two of the divisions, inactivated or restationed weak units and merged all remaining commands into a single division. To comply with Base Force cuts, the headquarters of the 26th and 50th Divisions were eliminated in 1993 and subordinate units either inactivated or reassigned. The 42d Division, with subordinate units from surrounding States, remained the only existing ARNG division between New York and Maine.[22]

Much of the planning and execution of ARNG cuts occurred under the leadership of Maj. Gen. Raymond F. Rees, the new DARNG. A West Pointer and Vietnam veteran, General Rees came to the Pentagon from his post as the AG of Oregon. The Guard leadership in Washington, DC believed that significant cuts were inevitable and established criteria for unit reductions. Combat brigades with high readiness would be retained while organizations unable to maintain personnel strength would go. While General Rees sought to spread the pain of unit reductions equitably across the States, several powerful congressional delegations engineered minor cuts in their own districts. During 1991–1995, the ARNG was forced to cut over 70,000 citizen-soldiers. Unlike the McNamara reductions of the late 1960s that trimmed Guard troop authorizations, the post-Cold War cuts forced the outright elimination of units and personnel. In most States, unit reductions caused the near endless shuffling of remaining units and personnel among existing armories. For example, the elimination of the 30th Armored Brigade in western Tennessee forced the reorganization or relocation of nearly every unit in the Tennessee ARNG.[23]

Table 8
ARNG STRENGTH, 1991–2000

YEAR	STRENGTH	PERSONNEL CHANGES
1991	446,121	
1992	426,528	-19,593
1993	409,919	-16,609
1994	396,928	-12,991
1995	374,930	-21,998
1996	369,976	- 4,954
1997	370,046	+ 70
1998	362,459	- 7,587
1999	357,469	- 4,990
2000	353,045	- 4,424
		Total = -93,076

(Source: National Guard Bureau, *Annual Review*, 1991–2000.)

One benefit of military downsizing was an increased flow of modern equipment to the ARNG. All types of vehicles, weapons, and equipment from Army divisions inactivating in Europe returned stateside for redistribution to active, Guard, and Reserve units. In 1992, the ARNG opened six maintenance sites across the country where all types of equipment returning from Europe went for inspection, repair, refurbishment, and eventual redistribution. By the time the program terminated in 1998, Guard technicians had repaired and redistributed 6,948 vehicles and 11,850 items of equipment valued at $2.6 billion. Overall, the flow of excess equipment from Regular units to the ARNG, and the reallocation of Guard equipment inventories from inactivating to remaining units, greatly improved the Guard's equipment readiness posture. By the end of the 1990s, the ARNG's equipment readiness was at near peak levels.[24]

Even as inactivating Guard units folded their colors, wrangling over the aggregate amount of ARNG reductions continued. However, by the end of 1993, the Army reached a preliminary consensus over the draw-down's final extent. In a series of meetings known as "off-sites" because of their location in Washington, DC at various places outside the Pentagon, senior leaders from the active Army, the Guard, and the Reserves agreed on force structure and manning levels for the remainder of the decade. To create wide support and acceptance for the decisions reached, repre-sentatives from NGAUS, the Association of the United States Army, and the Reserve Officers' Association attended the sessions as well. Off-site negotiations were the product of the Army's self-interests. By 1993, many members of Congress had voiced their frustrations over the Army's inability to resolve contentious issues and insisted that it was time for the Army to settle its own internal problems rather than using Capitol Hill as an arbitration forum.[25]

Maj. Gen. John R. D'Araujo, Jr., the acting CNGB and the new DARNG, established the Guard's goals for the off-sites. A proud infantry-man, General D'Araujo was a Vietnam veteran, the former commander of Hawaii's 29th Infantry Brigade and an experienced Pentagon insider. His principle objective was to retain 367,000 Guardsmen on the rolls through the year 2000. The Army had threatened to decimate ARNG flying units, and General D'Araujo was determined to save the Guard's critical heli-copter assets and SF units. Last, he hoped to establish a precedent for insuring that Guard leaders were included in all Pentagon decision making forums affecting the Guard.[26]

The Regulars and the Army Reserve had their own goals. The active Army saw the opportunity to achieve reductions in the USAR and the ARNG, though not to the lower levels it desired. With reserve component reductions identified for the next several years, the Army could make bet-ter choices as to the number of troops and units to be retained on active duty. The Army Reserve wanted to refocus efforts on its primary role as a provider of combat support and combat service support assets and divest itself of unwanted combat units.[27]

In October 1993, the Pentagon announced the results of the "Off-Site Agreement" during a televised press conference. The off-site's final form gave much needed stability to the Guard's future. Reserve compo-nent troop levels were to fall to a total of 575,000 troops by 1999 and remain constant. The ARNG was allocated 367,000 soldiers and the USAR 208,000. The Guard would provide the Army's reserve combat forces while retaining an overall balanced force of combat, combat support, and combat service support units. The USAR was to surrender nearly all of its aviation and SF units to the ARNG, and in return, would receive many Guard support units. In all, the two reserve components agreed to swap nearly 12,000 troop billets.[28]

The migration of units began in 1994 when the ARNG assumed responsibility for all reserve component SF Groups. A total of twenty-two combat and twenty-eight aviation units went from the USAR to the ARNG, and the Guard transferred 128 support units to the Reserves. By 1997, the ARNG had implemented the provisions of the Off-Site Agreement. In the end, the ARNG retained its traditional posture as a balanced force that provided the nation's reserve, ground combat power.[29]

A major exception to the many contentious issues surrounding the drawdown was the migration of a large amount of the Army's field artillery to the Guard. Desert Storm's 100-hour war and the artillery bombardments that preceded it convinced the Army's senior leaders of the necessity of retaining as much artillery as possible in the smaller, post-Cold War Army. But budget realities made it readily apparent that the retention of non-divisional artillery units on active duty was not affordable. A consensus developed in the artillery community that the Guard

Post-Cold War downsizing resulted in additional ARNG artillery units. Three M-109 self-propelled howitzers from the New Jersey ARNG in action during annual training. (National Guard Bureau)

was fully capable of assuming the support, general support, and general support reinforcing artillery missions. The performance of ARNG artillery battalions in Korea, Vietnam, and Desert Storm bore witness to the Guard's artillery proficiency. Starting in 1995, the migration of nearly all of the Army's non-divisional artillery into the ARNG commenced. In addition to retaining units identified for inactivation, the number of Guard artillery battalions actually grew, including two brigades that migrated from the USAR. By the time the realignment of artillery force structure was complete, approximately 70 percent of the Army's entire artillery assets were at home in the Guard.[30]

The bulk of the ARNG's force structure and personnel reductions were over by 1997. By any measure, the post-Cold War drawdown had been devastating. The ARNG lost 90,000 troops, shrinking from an all-time, historic high of 457,000 soldiers in 1989 down to 367,000 personnel. The Guard lost the equivalent of two divisions and eleven combat brigades. Still, due to intense lobbying efforts in Washington and across the country, the Guard lost 64,000 authorized billets as opposed to the original, proposed cuts of 137,000. General Colin Powell later observed:

> Cutting the National Guard and the Reserves was even harder than base closings...When we tried to cut back to sensible levels, however, we had our heads handed to us by the National Guard and Reserve associations and their congressional supporters. We were threatening part-time jobs, armories and money going into communities. We managed some reductions, but could still save much more money on the Guard and Reserves without hurting national security.[31]

However, the Guard's success in avoiding or delaying cuts had its disadvantages. While saving units and soldiers' careers, the extended drawdown challenged morale, hampered the recruitment and retention of quality personnel, and reduced opportunities for military education and promotions.

The Bottom-Up Review

General Powell's strategic vision had provided the basis for defense planning starting in August 1990, but changing world events and the presidential election of 1992 resulted in the Base Force's hasty demise. In little more than three years, historic events forever changed the international order. The Soviet Union completely collapsed, Germany reunified, democracy took hold in Eastern Europe and Central America, and an Allied coalition successfully reversed Iraqi aggression. In 1992, Governor William J. Clinton of Arkansas challenged George Bush for the presidency. Regarding defense matters, Clinton pledged his support of reserve forces and the restructuring of military forces for a new era while promising additional cuts of billions of dollars from the defense budget along with 200,000 more active duty personnel.

The Defense Department's first, comprehensive critique of American strategy in the post-Cold War era came in September 1993 with the release of the "Bottom-Up Review" (BUR). Though General Powell remained on duty at the Pentagon, the BUR was clearly the product of the Clinton Administration's new SECDEF, former Congressman Les Aspin. As the chairman of the House Armed Services Committee, Aspin had been a frequent, active critic of the Pentagon who took very seriously Congress' constitutional responsibility for raising and maintaining the armed forces. Though a brilliant intellect, Aspin lacked the managerial and executive skills required to run the Pentagon. After a short, stormy tenure, Aspin resigned as SECDEF in February 1994 over the controversial conduct of American peacekeeping operations in Somalia.

The BUR displaced the Base Force and provided a new focus for defense planning. With the threat from the Soviet Union gone, the BUR recognized four new dangers. First, the threat from the use and proliferation of nuclear, biological, and chemical weapons remained constant. A range of regional dangers persisted, from aggression by regional powers against their neighbors to internal conflicts prompted by ancient religious and ethnic animosities. The possible failure of democratic reforms in the former Soviet Union, Eastern Europe, and elsewhere posed a danger to U.S. interests. Finally, America had to build a strong, competitive, and growing economy to reduce economic dangers that might threaten national security.[32]

As the future basis for defense planning, the BUR declared that the U.S. had to field forces sufficient to fight and win "two nearly simultaneous regional conflicts." North Korea and Iraq posed the most likely regional threats. The forces necessary to fight two wars were smaller than those contained in the Base Force. Overall, the armed forces would lose another 160,000 personnel, with the Army shrinking further from 12 to 10 active duty divisions. The BUR assumed Regulars alone could win one regional conflict, but ARNG combat brigades were required as reinforcements in order to deter or fight a second regional war. Aspin's plan called for Guard combat units to be "better trained, more capable and more ready" than ever before. However, the BUR remained vague regarding the overall size of the ARNG. In a press briefing on September 1, 1993,

Secretary Aspin announced the ARNG was to contribute 15 "enhanced readiness brigades" to the national defense while the number of ARNG "division equivalents" was to shrink from eight to something more than five. In the end, the BUR recommended that the ARNG should contain "about 37 brigades."[33]

In one fell swoop, the BUR eliminated the last remnants of the ARNG Roundout Program that had formed a key link between the ARNG and the Regular Army. Many Guard leaders saw the end of the Roundout Program as the logical but unfortunate conclusion to the Army's handling of the 48th, 155th, and 256th Brigades during the Persian Gulf War. Disappointment over the elimination of the Roundout Program was compounded by the BUR's lack of details regarding the composition and missions of the new Enhanced Brigades (EB). Indeed, Les Aspin's unveiling of the EBs surprised the ARNG Directorate in Washington, DC.[34]

If the BUR ended the Roundout Program, subsequent action by the Pentagon in 1994 partly reaffirmed the ARNG's historical role as the principle combat reserve of the Army. The Army authorized the retention of fifteen EBs and established the parameters for their employment. The EBs were to be organized and provided with the resources in order to train, mobilize, and deploy to a war zone within ninety days of mobiliza-

An M1 Abrams main battle tank from one of the ARNG's Enhanced Brigades, South Carolina's 218th Brigade, prepares for action at the NTC. (National Guard Bureau)

tion. To fulfill the term "enhanced," the brigades were to receive priority for manning, modernization, and training resources over the ARNG's other major combat units.[35]

The ARNG moved to select its fifteen EBs based on the criteria of readiness, modernization, manning, location, and past relationships with Army divisions. The first brigades selected were the former Roundout and Roundup brigades. Seven additional brigades and the ARNG's only ACR filled out the remaining openings. In a mimic of the Roundout Program, a flow of new equipment, weapons, and vehicles into the EBs insured their compatibility with active divisions. The ARNG set optimum readiness goals for the brigades. By the end of 1999, all EBs were to achieve the highest readiness posture possible and be capable of deployment within ninety days of mobilization.[36]

Table 9
THE ARNG's FIFTEEN ENHANCED BRIGADES

27th Infantry (NY)	53rd Infantry (FL)
29th Infantry (HI, CA, OR)	76th Infantry (IN)
30th Mechanized (NC)	81st Mechanized (WA)
39th Infantry (AR)	155th Armored (MS)
41st Infantry (OR)	218th Mechanized (SC)
45th Infantry (OK)	256th Mechanized (LA)
48th Mechanized (GA)	278th Armored Cav. Regt. (TN)
116th Cavalry (ID, OR, MT, WY)	

(Source: National Guard Bureau, *Annual Review*, 1994.)

Less than two years after the release of the BUR, General John M. Shalikashvili, General Powell's successor as CJCS, outlined the specific details of America's new military strategy. Shalikashvili advocated a plan of flexible and selective engagement to promote stability and thwart aggression around the globe. In addition to retaining their traditional missions of deterring and fighting wars, America's armed forces would undertake the new mission of "peacetime engagement." In short, peacetime engagement included a broad range of "non-combat" activities that demonstrated American commitment, improved collective security, promoted democratic ideals, relieved human suffering, and enhanced regional stability. To implement Shalikashvili's vision, the U.S. military was to establish direct military-to-military contacts with foreign armies, continue participation in counterdrug and counterterrorism programs, conduct humanitarian relief operations, and take a more active role in international peacekeeping.[37]

In reality, Shalikashvili's strategy advocated many programs in which the ARNG was already fully engaged, including the counter-drug war and regional assistance to Central America. Dr. William J. Perry, the Clinton Administration's new SECDEF after Les Aspin's departure, was a great advocate of peacetime engagement and direct, military-to-military contacts. The National Guard's involvement with other foreign military institutions, a trend that had started in the 1970s, expanded greatly. Lt. Gen. Edward D. Baca, the former AG of New Mexico and the first Guard general officer appointed directly from the position of State AG to CNGB, came to the Pentagon in 1994 and advocated increased involvement with foreign armies through the National Guard's State Partnership Program. By 1996, the ARNG in twenty-one States had created formal partnerships with an equal number of Central and Eastern European countries. To the military institutions of Europe's new democracies, Guardsmen personified the desired ideal of a military force subject to civil authority. Guardsmen instructed their counterparts on the best ways to respond to civil emergencies and natural disasters, and European military leaders listened to advice on the methods of establishing reliable reserve forces, recruiting quality soldiers, and coordinating activities with full-time forces.[38]

Guardsmen as Peacekeepers

Even before General Shalikashvili's declaration of the strategy of peacetime engagement in 1995, Guardsmen had participated in peacekeeping operations. In December 1992, U.S. forces went to Somalia on the horn of Africa on a massive, humanitarian relief effort against starvation that quickly turned into a peacekeeping mission between warring clans. Before it was all over, U.S. ground forces became engaged in a series of intense firefights on the streets of Mogadishu, the Somali capital. American casualties generated congressional opposition that finally led to a withdrawal by May 1994. The ARNG became involved at the close of the Somali effort when special training teams deployed to Africa to instruct UN peacekeepers on the operation of older weapons systems, including the M-60 series tank and the AH-1 attack helicopter. Guard aviation specialists also assisted in the shrink wrapping of helicopters for shipment home.[39]

The ARNG's first significant involvement in peacekeeping occurred much closer to home. In 1994, the Clinton Administration moved to restore the legitimacy of the president of Haiti who had been overthrown

Missouri Guard soldiers from the 1107th Aviation Classification Repair Activity shrink wrap an AH-1 Cobra attack helicopter in Haiti before shipment back to the United States. (National Guard Bureau)

in a coup. A large, joint U.S. task force assembled off the coast of Haiti ready for an armed invasion. Fortunately, last minute negotiations by Clinton Administration peace envoys averted a conflict. American forces stormed into Haiti without firing a shot and deployed into rural and urban areas to restore order to a country wracked by anarchy.

For the first time since the Persian Gulf War, the president exercised his authority to order Guard and Reserve soldiers to active duty. Hoping to minimize the effects of the callup on citizen-soldiers and their communities, the Pentagon directed that units be filled with volunteers before soldiers were involuntarily called. At the same time, the ARNG was eager to demonstrate that its units were entirely available and capable of deployment, even during a period of continued downsizing. Three ARNG military police companies, all completely filled with volunteers, served at CONUS Army posts performing the missions of Regular military policemen who had shipped out to Haiti. The Puerto Rico ARNG supported the Haiti mission by providing Camp Santiago as a training site for Caribbean coalition forces and other multi-national peacekeepers preparing for duty in Haiti. As the effort increased in size and duration, Guardsmen finally deployed to the Caribbean. Starting in February 1995,

Guard soldiers from the 19th and 20th SF Groups and several aviation units served in Haiti. Guard aviators flew helicopter transport and observation missions while aviation support troops performed maintenance, air traffic control, and aircraft shrink wrap functions. SF citizen-soldiers served alongside their active duty counterparts, providing peace and security to the Haitian people.[40]

With declining numbers of units and personnel on active duty, the Army explored the use of Guardsmen and Reservists to meet global peacekeeping obligations. As part of the Camp David Peace Accords of 1979, the U.S. had maintained a peacekeeping battalion along the Israeli-Egyptian border in the Sinai Desert since 1982. Over thirty infantry battalions had rotated through the Sinai on six-month peacekeeping tours designated as the Multinational Force and Observers (MFO-Sinai). The Army's new peacekeeping concept called for a composite battalion of Regular, Guard, and Reserve soldiers to go to the Sinai for six months. Reserve component soldiers would serve in a volunteer status, and the 29th Infantry Division assumed the responsibility for recruiting the nearly 400 Guard volunteers required.[41]

Starting in February 1994, the composite unit formed and began training at Fort Bragg, North Carolina. The Army designated the

The composite MFO-Sinai peacekeeping battalion on parade at Fort Bragg, North Carolina prior to deployment. (National Guard Bureau)

battalion as the 4-505th Parachute Infantry, and it formally activated on November 4th. Over 70 percent of the MFO-Sinai battalion consisted of Guardsmen. In the end, 401 Guardsmen from twenty-four States participated. The 4-505th Infantry served in the Sinai January–July 1995. Overall, the composite battalion was a genuine success largely due to extensive pre-deployment training and the effective blending of Regulars and citizen-soldiers. The MFO-Sinai battalion's training regime eventually became a model for other Army units to emulate while preparing for peacekeeping duty. The 4-505th Infantry proved that ARNG peacekeepers were an effective means for the Army to meet its expanding peacekeeping commitments.[42]

Missions to Haiti and the Sinai foreshadowed the expanded use of Guard peacekeepers in the war torn Balkans. After the collapse of communism and the demise of the Soviet Empire, the multi-ethnic Republic of Yugoslavia dissolved. In June 1991, Slovenia and Croatia declared their independence from Yugoslavia, and months later Bosnia-Herzegovina and Macedonia seceded as well. In Belgrade, Serbian President Slobodan Milosevic was determined to impose his will on the seceding states through force of arms. Milosevic resolved to retain control over traditionally Serbian territory in the new, independent states while carving out a larger, united Serbia in the Balkans.

Brutal conflict fed by ancient racial, religious, and ethnic hatreds erupted in Bosnia and Croatia. The world watched in horror as Serb forces encircled the Bosnian capital of Sarajevo and subjected the civilian population to shelling and small arms fire. In order to gain complete control of certain areas, the Serbs employed "ethnic cleansing," the deliberate removal or elimination of the native Croat and Bosnian populations. World opinion, fueled by graphic media images that conjured up parallels between Serbian actions and Nazi atrocities during World War II, demanded an end to the fighting. The Clinton Administration exercised its political and military influence to get the warring factions to the peace table. On November 11, 1995, the belligerents finally agreed to a resolution of territorial disputes and initialed the Dayton Peace Accords that ended the fighting. The signing of a formal peace treaty occurred in Paris on December 14, 1995.

A key aspect of the Dayton Peace Accords was the use of UN peacekeepers to oversee the enforcement of treaty provisions. Almost immediately, American heavy forces from Germany moved to staging areas in Hungary and deployed into Bosnia and Croatia. The UN supervised implementation of the Dayton Accords was expected to last for twelve months. The extent of the Balkan commitment and the deep cuts that had occurred in active forces since Desert Storm prompted the use of citizen-soldier peacekeepers. President Clinton ordered Guardsmen and Reservists to the Balkans for as long as 270 days, the maximum extent allowed under the revised presidential callup authority. In all, the Pentagon activated nearly 8,200 citizen-soldiers from all services, and the Army received authority to callup 7,800 reserve component soldiers. Beginning on December 14, 1995, the ARNG mobilized 2,087 troops in fifty-three different units from twenty-eight States. The majority of troops were in eight military police and two maintenance companies as well as nine public affairs detachments. The first units arrived in Europe as early as December 24th and prepared to stay on active duty for a full 270 days. Guard peacekeepers in Europe during 1996 served at duty stations in Germany, Hungary, Croatia, and Bosnia.[43]

To no one's surprise, the Balkan peacekeeping effort extended into 1997 as the mission changed from treaty implementation to stability operations. The constant engagement of Regular Army forces in the Balkans required an even larger commitment of Guard soldiers to Europe. During 1997, 3,482 ARNG soldiers from forty-two States deployed to Europe, and their peacekeeping effort included several unique aspects. In August, sixty-five Guard aviators journeyed to Macedonia to lend support to active Army peacekeepers stationed on the Macedonian-Serbian border. In September, Company C, 3-116th Infantry from the Virginia ARNG mobilized and began training for a bridge security mission at the

Bundled up against the winter cold, ARNG peacekeepers go on patrol in the Balkans in December 1997. (Michael J. Kacmarcik)

town of Slavonski Brod on the Sava River between Croatia and Bosnia. The infantrymen eventually deployed to Europe and assumed responsibility for guarding the Sava River bridge on November 1st. In April 1998, Company C successfully completed its mission and returned home to a rousing welcome in Leesburg, Virginia. One unit serving in Germany in 1997—Oregon's 41st Personnel Services Company—had deployed directly from Oregon to Europe. All reserve component units had previously moved to mobilization stations at either Fort Benning, Georgia or Fort Dix, New Jersey. However, NGB asked for and received permission to mobilize and deploy one unit under the control of a State headquarters. The home station mobilization of the 41st Personnel Services Company from Salem, Oregon proved that a State headquarters could serve as an effective mobilization platform while saving precious time and relieving the Army of a portion of its mobilization responsibilities. In subsequent callups for peacekeeping, home station mobilizations became routine.[44]

The last two years of the 1990s saw the ARNG's sustained commitment to peacekeeping operations in both the Balkans and the Persian Gulf. In 1998, nearly 2,000 Guardsmen served in Bosnia. An additional 200 Guard aviators deployed to Kuwait to assist Allied forces in keeping an eye on Saddam Hussein. Peacekeeping efforts continued in 1999 with 865 Guard soldiers serving in Bosnia. Building on the success of Company C, 3-116th Infantry in Bosnia, the ARNG deployed four infantry companies—three from Arkansas' 39th Brigade and one from Oregon's 41st Brigade—to the Persian Gulf. The infantrymen served as the security force for Army Patriot air defense batteries stationed in Kuwait and Saudi Arabia. ARNG attack and utility helicopter units also deployed to the Gulf. Between 1994 and 1999, approximately 13,400 Guardsmen served in Haiti, the Sinai, the Balkans, and the Persian Gulf as peacekeepers, and world events all but insured that Guardsmen would remain fully engaged as global peacekeepers.[45]

Increased Domestic Missions

A near continuous string of natural disasters and domestic emergencies in the 1990s kept the ARNG busy providing military support to civil authorities. While the Guard had always responded to domestic crises, the difficulties of the 1990s had unique aspects. A number of disasters were so remarkable for their size and intensity that, in some cases, they required a regional ARNG response rather than action by a single State. Additionally, a string of terrorist acts increased the ARNG's role in combating domestic terrorism and set the stage for the Guard's increased involvement in defending the American people at home.

The Guard's first major challenge in domestic responses came in Los Angeles in April 1992 during the most violent and widespread urban rioting in America since the late 1960s. Racial tensions increased during the trial of several Los Angeles policemen charged with the roadside beating of African-American motorist Rodney King. When the jury rendered an acquittal in the case on April 29th, south central Los Angeles erupted. Governor Pete Wilson called out 10,336 California Guardsmen who performed valuable service in restoring order. Before the Guardsmen withdrew on May 10th, fifty-three people were dead and property loss was estimated at more than $800 million. Unlike the Watts riots of 1965 when less than 1 percent of the ARNG consisted of minorities, Guard units included a cross section of minority soldiers that reflected the racial diversity of southern California, a factor that many believed increased the Guard's effectiveness in dealing with the citizenry.[46]

Just four months later, the Florida National Guard found itself confronting one of America's most serious natural disasters. On August 23, 1992, Hurricane Andrew tore across the southern tip of the Florida peninsula causing the most extensive property damage of any storm in U.S. history. Guardsmen on State active duty rushed in after the storm passed, and eventually 6,000 ARNG soldiers did important work in restoring order and preventing looting. The Regular Army deployed 20,000 troops to the region to provide shelter, medical care, food, and water. The Army wanted to federalize the Florida Guard to simplify the command structure and to increase the efficiency of federal operations. However, Guardsmen were performing important law enforcement work, and an order to active federal service would have invoked the Posse Comitatus Act and prevented Guardsmen from arresting lawbreakers. In the end, Florida Governor Lawton Chiles and CNGB won the argument, and Florida Guardsmen remained under State control until the recovery from the hurricane was complete.[47]

Unusual weather conditions produced the Great Flood of 1993, the most severe flooding along the upper Mississippi River in the past 500 years. Before the waters subsided, a huge, inland lake flooded much of the upper Midwest, inundating farmlands and either sweeping away or threatening hundreds of communities. The Great Flood resulted in the mobilization of nearly 8,400 Guard troops from the midwestern States bordering the Mississippi. Whether piling sandbags to reinforce levees or purifying a town's drinking water, the presence of Guard soldiers had a significant, positive impact on flood ravaged areas. One effect of the large natural disasters of 1992–1993 was the creation of a nationwide network of interstate compacts between the States. The agreements allowed for the employment of Guards troops across State lines for mutual aid and support, and the Guard was given the legal authority to provide regional responses to acute disasters, whether natural or manmade.[48]

Domestic terrorism emerged in the 1990s as a real threat to America's internal security. The first dose of domestic terrorism occurred in February 1993 when Islamic fundamentalists exploded a powerful truck bomb at the World Trade Center complex in lower Manhattan. At the same time, a white supremacist movement emerged in America that scorned gun control laws and expressed contempt for federal law enforcement agencies and various international organizations. Heavily armed, radical elements organized themselves into scattered "militia" groups that emphasized weapons handling, military tactics, and survival techniques. On April 19, 1993, a sensational, fiery assault by federal law enforcement agencies against the compound of the Branch Davidian religious cult in Waco, Texas became a symbolic rallying cry for radical groups opposed to the federal government.

Two years to the day after the Waco assault, America experienced its worst act of domestic terrorism conceived and executed by a white militant with links to a militia group. On April 19, 1995, a truck bomb exploded outside of the Alfred P. Murrah Federal Building in downtown Oklahoma City. A huge blast collapsed nearly half of the building, injuring over 400 and killing 168. Within hours, the Oklahoma National Guard was fully engaged. Military policemen cordoned off the area around the building while other Guard soldiers provided medical assistance and special equipment. Guard chaplains and family support officers helped grief stricken families cope with their losses. Staff Sergeant George Dugan, a member of the 445th Military Police Company from McAlester, Oklahoma, summed up a common sentiment: "I served in both Vietnam and Desert Storm, but neither compares to this destruction. We fought half a world away to stop things like this, and now it hits home right here in Oklahoma City." Before it was all over, the Oklahoma National Guard had participated in every aspect of the rescue and recovery effort.[49]

The following year, security for the 1996 Summer Olympic Games in Atlanta was unusually tight. To provide broad assistance and to deter further acts of terrorism, over 13,000 National Guard personnel from forty-seven States supported the Centennial Olympic Games. Despite heightened security, a pipe bomb exploded during an evening concert killing one bystander and wounding several others. The Olympic bombing was another reminder of America's vulnerability to domestic terrorism.[50]

In response to the rising terrorist threat, Congress passed legislation in 1996 charging DOD with the new mission of domestic antiterrorism. Of particular concern was the ability to respond quickly to terrorist acts employing chemical, biological, and explosive weapons of mass destruction against the civilian population. The National Guard was to support State and local organizations in the early stages of a catastrophic terrorist attack. With a wide variety of communications and logistics capabilities and trained personnel in each State and Territory, the ARNG was particularly well suited for the terrorist response mission. In nearly half the States, the AG was the primary executive for emergency management. A key component of the counter-terrorist mission was the creation near America's major metropolitan areas of highly specialized ARNG Civil Support Teams that included chemical reconnaissance and decontamination capabilities.[51]

The ARNG in the Information Age

Perhaps the most significant trend affecting American society throughout the 1990s was the emergence of new computer and information management technologies. Americans spoke of the demise of the Industrial Age with its assembly lines and smokestack factories in favor of a new, computer based Information Age that ushered in improved communications and promoted electronic commerce. The personal computer, improved telecommunications equipment, and the Internet changed the way Americans worked and lived. In military circles, discussions about future warfare focused on an alleged "revolution in military affairs" wrought by the harnessing of computer power to warfare's myriad tasks. The influence of technological advances on field forces and military administration was not restricted to active forces. New technologies improved ARNG training and allowed NGB to more effectively fulfill its mission as the channel of communication between the States and DOD.

The first technological improvement to have a widespread affect on the National Guard was the Reserve Component Automation System (RCAS). First proposed in 1988, the purpose of RCAS was to fully computerize mobilization planning and unit administration for both the ARNG and the USAR. The many administrative problems identified during Desert Shield highlighted the need for more compatible computer systems throughout the Army. Full fielding of RCAS hardware and software commenced in 1997 and is scheduled for completion by 2002. In its final configuration, RCAS is to be a fully automated information system that provides timely and accurate information for mobilization planning and improved administration. RCAS will ultimately link over 10,500 ARNG and USAR units at over 4,000 sites in the fifty-four States and Territories as well as Europe and the Far East. RCAS has enabled ARNG peacekeepers in Bosnia to communicate directly with their States and has quickened more effective responses to domestic emergencies.[52]

A major step forward in the ARNG's harnessing of information technology occurred on April 22, 1993 with the opening of the new ARNG Readiness Center at Arlington Hall, Virginia. In addition to consolidating most ARNG functions in the Washington, DC area under one roof, the Readiness Center serves as the high technology platform for all ARNG information systems. The modern building houses six mainframe computers and a network control center that manages the ARNG's local area network, electronic mail, and data processing functions. The Arlington Hall complex serves as the nexus for fiber-optic cable communications and contains a state of the art video teleconferencing center with the ability to network with any other fiber-optic based facility in the world.[53]

New technology has had a dramatic affect on ARNG training. Technological innovations have reduced the costs of increasingly expensive training and live fire exercises and made maximum use of limited training time. Guard soldiers have benefited from a wide variety of new simulators ranging from computer-driven conduct of fire trainers for tank and helicopter crews to command post exercises based on sophisticated software programs. A major step forward in harnessing new technology was the creation of the ARNG Distance Learning Network that brought soldiers and instructors together through the power of fiber-optic cable. The advanced network allowed a shift from traditional classroom

The Army National Guard Readiness Center in Arlington, Virginia. (National Guard Bureau)

instruction conducted at a centralized location to the high technology distribution of quality instruction via fiber-optic cable that is accessible to troops in their local armories. By the end of the 1990s, the ARNG possessed one of the most advanced distance learning networks in the entire country.[54]

A Rift Over Roles and Missions

The stresses and strains of the military drawdown of the 1990s eventually caused the most serious deterioration in Army-Guard relations since the mobilization of 1940–1941. Disputes between the Regular Army and the ARNG were the natural byproduct of intense competition for scarce resources. Despite the successes of the 1993 Off-Site Agreement, the smooth migration of Regular field artillery units to the Guard, and the respected performance of ARNG peacekeepers, wrangling over the final size and assigned missions of the post-Cold War ARNG all but unhinged the Total Force Policy. Any stability gained from the Off-Site proved short-lived; as it turned out, the agreement was only the first in a series of related steps to further reduce the Guard. Beginning in 1995, Army-Guard relations sank to dangerous lows before improving at the end of the decade.

Significant disagreements stemmed from plans and policies regarding the ARNG's fifteen EBs and eight divisions. Guardsmen believed that in a period of sustained force cuts and declining defense budgets that the Army viewed the ARNG as a peer competitor rather than a partner. To protect the number of its divisions remaining on active duty, Guardsmen believed the Army promoted the elimination of the ARNG's major combat units. The Army's treatment of the three Roundout brigades during the Persian Gulf War provided the basis for Guard leaders to question the Army's motives. Despite the BUR's guidelines for utilizing the EBs, the Army was slow to assign them to war plans, and even after the improvements of the Bold Shift Program, the Army questioned the brigades' ability to be ready for deployment within ninety days. Guard senior commanders chafed at this barb against their units, especially when the Army had declared the 48th Brigade combat ready ninety-one days after mobilization during Desert Storm, well before the Bold Shift Program had come into being. During 1991–1996, no ARNG brigades were permitted to train at the NTC, an exclusionary policy that convinced Guard commanders of the Army's bias against ARNG combat brigades and deepened the growing divide between Regulars and Guardsmen.[55]

The Army ignored any suggestions for employing the Guard divisions, insisting they were little more than Cold War relics. Training resources for the divisions were constantly reduced. General Gordon R. Sullivan, the Army chief of staff, told the House Armed Services Committee early in 1992 that the Army "cannot train [ARNG] divisions to fight in less that 365 days." In light of the various short war scenarios that formed the basis for most defense planning, the Army was implying that the Guard divisions would be irrelevant in future conflicts. Furthermore, General Sullivan's pronouncement of "365 days" to train a Guard division became a near mantra in the Pentagon, though the empirical evidence supporting the assertion was sparse.[56]

Other factors contributed to the growing divide. In Washington, NGAUS and NGB leaders were routinely excluded from crucial decision making forums. In the States, a divisive "us and them" mentality often developed between Guardsmen and Regular Army advisers. Guard leaders maintained that full-time soldiers did not understand the unique difficulties of citizen-soldiers and often expected too much. Army advisers countered that Guard commanders did not understand Army training procedures and were not objective in their readiness evaluations.[57]

Certain findings of DOD's Commission on Roles and Missions in May 1995 confirmed the Army's suspicions about the relevance of ARNG fighting units. The commission confirmed that the Army questioned the readiness of the EBs and recommended policy changes and the commitment of additional resources to improve EB readiness. However, the commission stated that the eight Guard divisions "are not needed for the current national security strategy" and advocated their elimination or reorganization. The Army maintained that a shortage of 60,000 support troops existed to implement the BUR's "nearly simultaneous" two war strategy. All together, the Guard divisions included approximately 110,000 personnel spaces. The Commission on Roles and Missions recommended that the Army convert 60,000 troop billets in the Guard divisions to support units and eliminate the remaining 50,000 positions.[58]

The commission's recommendations left Guard leaders breathless. The 26th and 50th Divisions had already been eliminated earlier in the decade, and the outright loss of the remaining eight divisions was unthinkable. Still, two separate views emerged on the need for the ARNG to provide more support units. One group clung fast to the Guard's traditional role as the Army's primary combat reserve. The Guard divisions were needed as a strategic reserve, to respond to domestic emergencies, and to provide forces for extended peacekeeping operations. Reduced training budgets for divisional units and the Army's need for more support troops were interpreted as ploys to eliminate the Guard divisions. Others argued for the continued relevance of the ARNG in defense planning by converting a portion of the divisions to support units. Both sides agreed that the ARNG could not be relegated to the marginal role of a home constabulary called out only for natural disasters and domestic emergencies.[59]

In the end, Guard senior leaders decided to provide more support units and formed the ARNG Division Redesign Study to examine the conversion of low priority, divisional combat units to more critical support forces. The group concluded that up to twelve combat brigades—the equivalent of four divisions—were available for conversion. The Army approved the plan in May 1996, but the $5 billion needed to implement the conversions was slow to appear. In December 1998, the ARNG identified combat brigades from California, Nebraska, and Indiana as the first three to convert to support units starting in 2001.[60]

In 1997, the Defense Department conducted the congressionally mandated Quadrennial Defense Review (QDR), the fourth comprehensive analysis of defense planning since the end of the Cold War. The QDR, under the leadership of Defense Secretary William S. Cohen, built upon previous reviews to examine America's defense needs through 2015. While endorsing the basic strategy of fighting two "nearly simultaneous" regional conflicts, the QDR offered a broader strategic vision. DOD outlined three tenets of American strategy; to shape the strategic environment in accordance with U.S. interests, to respond to a full spectrum of threats, and to prepare for future dangers. American forces were to exploit the advantages of new computer technology to dominate the battlefield. At the same time, the services were to find the resources to continue important modernization initiatives even as more and more defense dollars were diverted to peacekeeping operations.[61]

The QDR's findings regarding the Army and the ARNG set off a storm of controversy that eventually beat a path to the White House. The Army was to retain ten divisions on active duty while absorbing losses of an additional 15,000 soldiers. At the same time, the ARNG and the USAR were to lose 45,000 more troops. The QDR reaffirmed the role of the fifteen EBs as outlined in the BUR but stopped short of endorsing the elimination of ARNG divisions. Instead, the QDR recognized combat support, strategic reserve, and domestic missions for the divisions while still mandating the elimination of thousands of Guard personnel slots.[62]

Hopeful that the drawdown of the 1990s was finally behind them, the Guard's senior leaders were chagrined with the QDR's recommendations for additional cuts. In Washington, the Guard's primary response came from a new DARNG, Maj. Gen. William A. Navas, Jr. A Vietnam veteran and Puerto Rico Guardsman, General Navas had been instrumental in creating the successful *Fuertes Caminos* program in Central America in the 1980s and became DARNG after serving nearly ten years in various senior staff assignments within NGB and DOD. He was disturbed that while the ARNG had been allowed to participate in some aspects of the Army's QDR staffing process it had been completely excluded from any meaningful role in the Army's actual decision making process. Furthermore, he suspected that the Army intended to use resources garnered from reserve component cuts to fund its own modernization programs. NGAUS had warned that without Guard participation, the QDR results might be "extremely detrimental" and "possibly disastrous" for the Guard. Five former CNGBs wrote to Secretary Cohen asking that Guard officers be included in QDR study groups. Congressman Sonny Montgomery had retired in 1996, and Guard leaders suspected that the Army sensed an opportunity to cut the ARNG further while its influence on Capitol Hill was weakened.[63]

A showdown between the Guard and the active Army occurred at Oklahoma City on May 2, 1997 when senior Army generals announced the details of proposed QDR cuts at an annual meeting of AGAUS. The vice chief of staff of the Army informed the assembled AGs that the Defense Department had directed Guard cuts of 67,000 troops. The AGs objected vehemently, arguing that neither DOD nor the Army had provided rationale or justification for such large and disproportionate cuts and demanded a meeting with Secretary Cohen. Furthermore, the AGs suspected that the real impetus for the recommended cuts had come from the Army's senior leadership and not from DOD. Perhaps not fully aware of the consequences of their own words, the Army's representatives insisted that the AGs "go through their chain of command" and avoid a meeting with the Defense Secretary. The AGs returned home, reported to their civilian leaders, and within a week, a letter went to President Clinton signed by a large number of Governors inquiring as to why DOD was making questionable decisions without proper analysis and consultation with the Guard.[64]

The result of the AGs' protests was another off-site meeting between senior Guard and Army leaders at Fort McNair in Washington, DC during June 2–4, 1997. The CNGB, Lt. Gen. Baca, and the DARNG, Maj. Gen. Navas, represented the Guard during negotiations to determine force cuts among the Regular Army, the ARNG, and the USAR. Maj. Gen. Ronald O. Harrison, the AG of Florida, and Maj. Gen. Richard C. Alexander, the AG of Ohio, represented the interests of the States. (General Harrison would eventually serve as NGAUS president and General Alexander as the full-time, executive director of the association.) The main issue was the allocation of 45,000 troop losses among the two reserve components. The Army proposed that 38,000 cuts come from the ARNG and 7,000 from the USAR. Regular and Army Reserve generals

The National Guard Memorial at One Massachusetts Avenue in downtown Washington, DC serves as NGAUS headquarters. (National Guard Education Foundation)

argued that the USAR had absorbed disproportionate cuts and divested itself of irrelevant units in the 1993 Off-Site Agreement; now it was time for the ARNG to do the same. After tough and tense negotiations, the participants reached a compromise. Between 1997 and 2000, the USAR would surrender 3,000 troop spaces and the ARNG 17,000. Army planning processes that considered programs for the years beyond 2001 would determine the disposition of the remaining 25,000 troop reductions between the Guard and the Reserves. By 2000, the ARNG honored the QDR off-site agreement by trimming an additional 17,000 troop spaces from its force structure without inactivating any large units and by sharing the burden among the States and Territories.[65]

The ARNG in 2000

At the very end of the 20th Century, the ARNG consisted of 353,045 soldiers assigned to fifteen EBs, eight divisions, two separate brigades, two SF Groups, one Scout Group and hundreds of combat support and combat service support units. The EBs and contingency force support units remained the ARNG's highest priority units. In sharp contrast to previous periods, the ARNG had a high level of experience in the ranks; nearly 60 percent of Guard soldiers had prior service in the Regular

Army. Of the entire force, minority participation stood at 25.9 percent. Black troops represented nearly 16 percent of the ARNG while women comprised just under 10 percent and Hispanics 7 percent. Significant gains occurred in the 1990s in minority representation among the Guard's senior leadership. By the end of the decade, six AGs were either black or Hispanic, and in 1997, the National Guard received its first female AG when the Vermont legislature selected Air National Guard Maj. Gen. Martha T. Rainville as the State's AG. Lt. Gen. Baca served as the first Hispanic CNGB during 1994–1998, and in August 1998, Lt. Gen. Russell C. Davis, an Air National Guard general officer and the former commanding general of the District of Columbia National Guard, became the first black general officer to serve as CNGB.[66]

Despite the ARNG's important contributions to national defense in the 1990s, it finished the decade a much smaller force. Out of a total defense appropriation of $280.9 billion in 2000, ARNG funding was only $7 billion, representing less than 10 percent of the Army's entire budget and only 2.5 percent of DOD's. In force structure and manning, the ARNG was much smaller than before the Persian Gulf War. Authorized troop positions declined from 477,000 in 1989 down to 388,000, a loss of nearly 19 percent. Cuts in actual troop strength were even greater. From an all time high manpower level of 457,000 in 1989, the ARNG lost 107,000 personnel by 2000, a reduction of over 23 percent. Because of increasing concerns over declining military readiness, DOD announced in December 1999 that the 25,000 reserve component troop reductions remaining from the QDR would be deferred.[67]

The ARNG remains vital to U.S. peacekeeping efforts around the globe. A total of 2,652 Guardsmen performed peacekeeping missions in Bosnia and Southwest Asia during 2000. Several hundred Guard soldiers also deployed into Kosovo in the aftermath of NATO's bombing campaign against Serbia and Serb forces in Kosovo. The most significant development occurred on March 7th when the 49th Armored Division Headquarters from Texas assumed command responsibilities for the American sector in Bosnia. The 49th Armored Division was the first ARNG division headquarters to deploy to Europe on an operational mission in nearly fifty years. Not since the Korean War, when the 28th and 43rd Divisions deployed to West Germany, had a Guard division seen service in Europe. Pentagon planners have scheduled the deployment of additional ARNG combat forces to the Balkans by the end of 2002.[68]

At the beginning of a new millennium, the ARNG Directorate in Washington, DC continues its work under the leadership of Lt. Gen. Roger C. Schultz. An Iowa Guardsman, General Schultz became the first DARNG to wear three stars with his promotion to lieutenant general on

June 13, 2001. The increase in rank was intended to make the position of DARNG commensurate with the principle general officer staff positions on the Army Staff and to give the ARNG improved access to Army deliberations. Across the nation, the ARNG is engaged in a number of other important missions. The EBs and high priority support units focus their planning and training on possible participation in two "nearly simultaneous" regional conflicts. Guard soldiers continue to participate in the counter-drug war and perform valuable service in the States during emergencies. The Guard's role in defending the American people against terrorist attacks employing weapons of mass destruction continues to increase.[69]

For the most part, Army-ARNG relations appear to be improving. The Guard plans to convert as many as nine additional combat brigades to support structure by 2012 in order to meet the Army's need for more support units. In 1999, the Army activated two "Integrated Divisions" that placed six EBs under the training and readiness oversight of two Regular Army headquarters. The "Division Teaming" concept has created direct training affiliations between four ARNG and four active duty divisions. The creation of composite support units, consisting of Regulars, Guardsmen, and Reservists, has brought the Army's components into closer harmony. In 1996, a command exchange program began when a Regular officer took command of a Guard artillery battalion. The initiative proved mutually beneficial, and in January 2000, an ARNG armor officer assumed command of an active duty tank battalion.[70]

Beyond the 1990s, the ARNG's service to the nation and the States will remain vital. However, the ARNG's future contributions to the common defense can only be fully understood within the context of a broader analysis of the National Guard's development and service during the past 400 years.

CHAPTER 10

The National Guard in Review

Sound military institutions are organic growths and not structures. A sound national defense system is not like a tower of brick and stone that can be built *de novo* on the surface of the ground. It is, rather, like a living tree with roots deep in the political tradition and history of a nation. It is the province of the military statesman, not to invent something new, but to improve a living thing that already exists.

Brig. Gen. John McAuley Palmer

The National Guard's Core Characteristics

Since the creation of the first militia regiments in 1636, the National Guard has been a continuous and substantial presence in the American defense establishment. Borrowing from John McAuley Palmer's metaphor that likens military institutions to living organisms, today's ARNG stands as the oldest and most mature living tree among the country's military organizations. The physical components of a strong, flourishing tree aptly correspond to the ARNG's past, present, and future. The roots of the organization dig deep into American history, providing an immovable anchor and drawing nourishment from the Guard's long traditions, values, and service. The trunk represents the current generation of Guard soldiers who provide steady, reliable service and protect the main body of the organization by responding resolutely to various challenges. Outstretched limbs that shoot skyward seeking sunlight and nourishment, all the while buffeted by the winds of change, are symbolic of the ARNG's journey toward a hopeful future.

An awareness of the National Guard's core characteristics is necessary for a thorough understanding and appreciation of the full significance of the Guard's important role in history. First and foremost, the National Guard has almost always relied upon volunteer citizen-soldiers to fill its ranks. Only the enrolled militia derived its membership from mandatory service. Since the 1840s, when volunteer militia companies became widespread, citizen-soldiers have offered freely of their time and service. Throughout the Guard's history, motivated citizen-soldiers have volunteered for many of the same reasons—the fondness of a military lifestyle, opportunities for self-improvement and adventure, a sense of camaraderie and friendship, family traditions, and the satisfaction of genuine service to their local community, State and nation. In all probability, if today's ARNG men and women had the opportunity to mingle with the minutemen of Lexington and Concord, both groups might be surprised at the common values of duty, patriotism, and selfless service shared among them.

ARNG members are volunteer citizen-soldiers who covet their rights as citizens as much as they do their responsibilities as soldiers. As citizens, they exercise the right to share views on defense matters with the American people and their elected representatives. In contrast, Regulars accept restraints on their full right of citizenship in order to honor the sacred tradition of civilian control over the military. As soldiers, Guard men and women willingly sacrifice a portion of their work and personal lives to participate in the training required to learn and hone soldier skills. The early militiaman was a symbol of public virtue, a citizen-soldier willing to lay aside private concerns in times of public need and to risk all, even his life, for the general welfare. Militia service demonstrated a commitment to the community and to the maintenance and protection of social order and values. Today, the men and women of the ARNG cling just as proudly to their status as citizen-soldiers as did the early militia.

Civic and military leaders desiring to better understand the fundamental reasons for the ARNG's existence have no further to look than the U.S. Constitution. Article I, Section 8 authorizes the militia "to execute the Laws of the Union, suppress Insurrections and repel Invasions." Since 1789, all efforts to maintain and employ the militia, the National Guard and the ARNG have related directly to the three missions mandated in the Constitution. Starting with the Militia Act of 1903, key legislation, executive orders, and court rulings throughout the 20th Century have allowed the National Guard to mobilize in a timely manner and deploy anywhere in the world in support of the nation's military strategy. Short of war, the president's current executive authority to mobilize Guard soldiers for up to 270 days assures their full participation in Army operations world-wide.

From the time of the earliest English settlements, American citizen-soldiers have engaged in local and national defense matters. The colonial militia protected local settlements and formed units for more ambitious military ventures. Since the ratification of the Constitution, the National Guard has enjoyed a formal, dual status as a federal and a State force. As a federal force, the Guard provides ready, trained units as an integral part of America's field forces. In its State role, the Guard protects life and property and preserves peace, order, and public safety under the direction of State and federal authorities. In times of peace, the Governors serve as the commanders in chief of their respective National Guards. ARNG soldiers ordered to active duty during national emergencies serve under the federal chain of command that ultimately ends with the president. The dual nature of the ARNG has always been and still remains one of its fundamental pillars.

The Guard's Greatest Contributions

As America's oldest military institution, the National Guard has contributed to the nation's defense by consistently providing additional troops and units during national crises. Early Spanish troops and *milicias* in Puerto Rico, Florida, and New Mexico were the first to introduce European military systems to North America. However, it was the English militia system that took root and ultimately determined the shape of the country's policies and practices regarding citizen-soldiers. During the colonial period, militiamen acted as a local defense force to protect new settlements against Indian attacks. When a state of war existed between whites and Native Americans, the militia conducted reprisal raids. Local militiamen formed the basis of colonial provincial units organized for sustained offensive operations against the French and Spanish. By protecting settlements in the New World, the militia guaranteed the successful English colonization of North America.

The enrolled militia played a central role in the winning of the American Revolution and in the establishment of the United States. The militia in New England opened the war with the fights at Lexington, Concord, and Bunker Hill. Afterwards, militiamen provided the troops for the creation of the Continental Army, and State troops from the various Continental lines sustained the Army throughout eight years of war. The militia excelled at turning out large numbers of troops on short notice, a characteristic that successfully foiled British plans at Boston and Saratoga. Militiamen provide vital augmentation to the Continental Army at crucial periods and formed the bulk of the American forces in the bloody, southern campaigns. In addition to the opening blows in New

England, Saratoga, Bennington, Cowpens, and King's Mountain were important militia victories. Militia outposts and raiding parties constantly nipped at the heels of the British Army. By controlling the populations and the countryside, the militia sustained support for the Patriot cause and dampened Loyalist sentiments. The militia's greatest contribution was its part in the winning of the American Revolution. Perhaps no other group of American citizen-soldiers has achieved so much by continuing to fight under the most arduous circumstances.

Throughout the 19th Century, the militia continuously performed a wide range of functions. As Americans moved west, citizen-soldiers provided security to settlers, first beyond the Appalachians and then into the vast expanses west of the Mississippi. Despite its mixed performance in the War of 1812, the militia helped to put to rest once and for all the question of resurgent British influence over America. Militiamen provided the basis for many of the volunteer regiments that fought the Mexican and Civil Wars. In 1861, volunteer militia companies were the first to take up arms for the North and the South and largely fought the Civil War's first major battle at Bull Run. State soldiers rallied at crucial times during America's bloodiest war to defend their home territories. Starting in 1877, militiamen performed long-term service as strikebreakers, distasteful duty that caused many State soldiers to seek a new role as the primary combat reserve of the Army. During the Spanish-American War, State soldiers formed the bulk of the troops sent to Puerto Rico and the Philippines. The performance of militiamen in the Caribbean and the southwest Pacific made a convincing argument that State soldiers could participate effectively in extended, overseas campaigning.

In the first half of the 20th Century, the National Guard provided large numbers of troop units for bloody battles fought in Europe and the Pacific. Even before the World Wars, Guardsmen manned the nation's coastal defenses and in 1916 protected American interests during a serious confrontation with Mexico. After America's entry into World War I, Guard units deployed to Western Europe to help support the exhausted Allies. Eighteen Guard divisions constituted a significant portion of the AEF's combat power in France, and in savage operations around Paris, at St. Mihiel, and in the Meuse-Argonne, Guardsmen helped to convince Germany's war lords that they could not win the war. Guard units deeply embedded in America's local communities provided social stability during the Great Depression and helped the country to endure severe economic deprivations. During World War II, Guardsmen in nineteen divisions and countless numbers of separate combat, combat support, and combat service support units saw action in every major campaign. Guard units bore a high share of the burden of the initial, bloody fighting in the Philippines, New Guinea, North Africa, and Sicily and fought on to total victory in Europe and the Pacific.

The ARNG participated to varying degrees in all of the armed conflicts of the Cold War and helped to prevent the outbreak of a third, global war. During the Korean War, Guardsmen fought in Korea, bolstered NATO's defenses in Europe, and enhanced the Army's strategic reserve in CONUS. During the Berlin Crisis, President Kennedy mobilized Guardsmen as a political signal to the Soviets of U.S. resolve. Missile Age minutemen manned air defense sites to detect and intercept possible attacks by Soviet bombers against the American homeland. Individual Guard volunteers served in Vietnam during the war's early years, and the Johnson Administration called up a limited number of ARNG units after the *Pueblo* crisis and the Tet Offensive in 1968. As the war raged in Southeast Asia, Guardsmen controlled race and antiwar riots in many of America's major cities. In a period akin to the militia's long involvement with labor strife starting in 1877, the ARNG served extensively as a domestic law enforcement agency between 1957 and 1970. Starting with the mobilization of the Arkansas National Guard in 1957 and ending with the tragic Kent State shootings in 1970, Guardsmen enforced integration laws, controlled race riots, and endured the abuses of anti-war protesters for nearly fifteen years. In the 1980s, a revitalized ARNG with more modern weapons and equipment and the highest personnel levels in its history trained to defeat a Soviet blitzkrieg in Central Europe. At the same time, Guard support units maintained an important presence that promoted democracy in Central America.

The fall of the Berlin Wall in 1989 and the collapse of the Soviet Union three years later ended the Cold War and ushered in an era of international relations rife with complexities and uncertainties. During the Persian Gulf War, ARNG units served in Southwest Asia, reinforced Europe, and strengthened the nation's strategic reserve against surprises elsewhere around the globe. A new, national security strategy of peacetime engagement required the Army to deploy troops to global trouble spots, and Guard soldiers served as peacekeepers in Haiti, Somalia, and in the Sinai Desert. Starting in 1996, Guard units deployed to the Balkans to support UN efforts to bring peace to one of the world's most conflicted regions. Since then, the ARNG has greatly expanded its peacekeeping commitment to the Balkans, deploying troops into war torn Kosovo and acting as the Army's controlling headquarters in the region. At the same time, Guardsmen participated fully in the recoveries from the largest domestic calamities of the 1990s: Hurricane Andrew, the midwestern floods, and the Oklahoma City bombing. As the 20th Century comes to a close, the ARNG maintains peacekeepers in the Balkans and in Southwest

Asia, trains to keep its combat and support units ready for unexpected emergencies, and is increasing its ability to protect the American people against attacks from weapons of mass destruction.

The National Guard's Transformation

Since the nation's earliest beginnings, citizen-soldiers have displayed an innate ability to adapt to constantly changing circumstances while providing meaningful capabilities to America's defense needs. For nearly 400 years, State soldiers have successfully responded to the dynamic social, political, and economic conditions that fashion and shape American society. The constant evolution of defense policy and steady advances in the technology and methods of warfare have always prompted Guard soldiers to implement a bewildering array of changes in unit organization, weapons, equipment, logistics, administration, and training.

The early militia system served as both a training base and a reservoir of manpower and required the service of all available, white males ages 16–60. The typical militiaman was a yeoman farmer tilling the soil in an effort to eke out a living for himself and his family. The local company was the militia's organizational foundation, and the company commander served as the chief recruiting officer and provided the most vital leadership. Citizen-soldiers elected their company officers while the Governors appointed more senior officers up to the rank of colonel. The central focus of militia training was to produce an armed, equipped, and trained individual for local defense. Rudimentary training occurred during periodic, local musters. On less frequent training days, battalions and even regiments assembled to practice the battle tactics of the day. Village commons and designated training fields outside of towns served as muster sites and training facilities in the days before local armories and Army training centers.

During combat operations, militiamen adapted their tactics to the terrain of the New World and to the capabilities of Native Americans and European competitors. Originally armed with mostly blade weapons, the enrolled militia quickly adopted flintlock muskets when they appeared. The militia was a local defense force, and in an agrarian society, citizen-soldiers were able to mount only limited offensive operations timed around the annual planting and harvesting cycles. As the population grew and the economy became more complex, men were available either through volunteerism or a militia draft, and the colonies mounted more extended operations against competing European powers. Militiamen joining provincial units may have received additional training from more experienced leaders before embarking on an expedition. The New

England militia army that captured the French bastion at Louisbourg in 1745 personified the militia's ability to generate offensive power when needed. Massachusetts citizen-soldiers at Lexington and Concord in April 1775 represented the zenith of the militia as a local defense force.

The evolution of the early militia into the modern ARNG has occurred during three major periods of transformation. The first major evolution was the decline of the enrolled militia and the rise of the volunteer militia. The Industrial Revolution and Jacksonian democracy created major social, political, and economic shifts that the enrolled militia was unable to withstand. As longstanding threats from Native Americans and other European powers diminished, urban laborers viewed militia service as burdensome and unnecessary. The States proved either unwilling or unable to manage effectively the large numbers of enrolled militiamen that compulsory service produced. By the 1840s, volunteer militia companies had replaced the enrolled militia as an effective military force. Instead of being compelled to participate in musters and training, volunteer militiamen shared a fondness for a military lifestyle and an interest in service to their local community. Groups that shared common values and social status bonded together in militia companies for enjoyment and camaraderie as much as military service. Just as in the enrolled militia, the company was the backbone of the volunteer militia, and members elected their officers. Volunteer militiamen distanced themselves from the undifferentiated masses of the last remnants of the enrolled militia by forming specialized units such as grenadiers, light infantry, cavalry, and artillery. Companies adopted extravagant uniforms and inspirational names that stressed their martial ardor. City dwellers replaced the yeoman farmer as the typical militiaman, and companies were located largely in urban centers. With only limited assistance from the federal and State governments, militiamen paid dues, provided their own uniforms and equipment, and hosted fundraising events to garner the necessary resources to sustain their units. Because volunteer companies were recreational and social outlets as much as military organizations, units met frequently to plan events, and the practice of militiamen gathering at a central location one night per week became commonplace. For the first time, militiamen sought suitable housing in public buildings or rented floor space in private facilities to store weapons and equipment and to hold meetings. Units conducted training and participated in limited exercises, but the focus of training remained on the individual citizen-soldier. The greatest contribution of volunteer militia companies was to provide the basis for the volunteer regiments of the Civil War.

In the last decades of the 19th Century, the volunteer militia transformed itself into the National Guard. Tired of repeated service as a strikebreaking force, State soldiers sought a new identity as the Army's recognized combat reserve. The creation of NGAUS in 1879 helped State soldiers to acquire the funding and legislation needed to become an effective reserve. The basic tactical organization of the National Guard changed from the local company to regiments, brigades and even divisions, and the Guard remained a largely infantry force. Armories in urban centers and smaller towns served as storage facilities and training centers and were symbolic of the Guard's presence in local communities. Though the Guard was organized into larger tactical units and had adequate facilities, the focus of training was still on the individual soldier. Guardsmen trained one night per week on individual soldier skills, and rudimentary, small unit training occurred only at annual summer encampments. The Army and the Guard acknowledged that State units would need much additional training after mobilization to make them ready for battle. The Militia Act of 1903 replaced the Militia Act of 1792 and marked the beginning of the National Guard as a formal, federal reserve. The National Defense Acts of 1916 and 1920 specifically established the National Guard as the Army's primary combat reserve and further clarified the relationship between the States and the War Department. The National Guard proved its worth in the World Wars by providing combat divisions that greatly expanded the Army's fighting power.

The early decades of the Cold War witnessed the dramatic transformation of the National Guard into the modern ARNG. With the dawn of the Nuclear Age and the threat of worldwide communism, sufficient time was no longer available to provide Guard units additional training after mobilization. The new challenge for the ARNG was to create units capable of deploying immediately to the world's hotspots without undertaking extensive, additional training. The focus of peacetime training shifted from individual soldiers to entire units. To create large blocks of time for unit training, the ARNG discontinued week night drill periods and implemented weekend training. Recruits attended active duty basic training, relieving local units of the burden of imparting fundamental skills to new Guardsmen. A massive infusion of the latest weapons and equipment changed the ARNG from a largely infantry force to a modern combined arms team with adequate logistical support. For the first time, federal monies were available to fund armory construction. Large, consolidated maintenance and repair facilities appeared to support fleets of airframes and tracked and wheeled vehicles. Overseas training exercises imparted valuable deployment skills, brought ARNG and Regular units into closer contact, and allowed Guardsmen to become intimately familiar with potential combat zones. An historic change occurred in the 1970s with the introduction of greater numbers of minority soldiers. The inclusion of more minorities and females allowed the ARNG to weather the declines in manpower that occurred after the Vietnam War and reflected the greater participation of minorities throughout American society. The Reagan Buildup further increased the lethality and staying power of Guard units with an infusion of modern tanks, infantry fighting vehicles, self-propelled and missile artillery, helicopters, radios, and fleets of wheeled vehicles. The quick deployment and full participation of Guard units in the Persian Gulf War clearly demonstrated the ARNG's new, modern capabilities.

Armories have always been a powerful symbol of the National Guard's presence in local communities, and the design and construction of armories says much about the Guard's transformation through the centuries. For the early militia, village commons and training fields adjacent to local communities served as muster sites and training grounds. As the volunteer militia developed in urban locations, militiamen took up part-time residence in public facilities and private buildings. Starting in 1877, large, masonry armories appeared across the nation that identified the fledgling National Guard as an organization dedicated to protecting the nation and the social order. Castellated armories were as much social clubs as military installations and reflected the Guard's martial and social nature. In the early 20th Century, the appearance of large, vaulted armories with cavernous drill halls used to train battalions and entire regiments reflected the growing emphasis on military preparedness. After World War II, armories of brick, steel, and glass were built with an emphasis on military administration and efficiency. At the same time, the mechanization of warfare resulted in the addition of concrete pads and motor pools for the storage of vehicles needed to support weekend training. Centralized vehicle maintenance and repair facilities became an important component of each State's Guard infrastructure. In the Information Age, the computer has once again transformed the local armory. Classrooms filled with computer terminals and special rooms for video-teleconferences are linked by distance learning capabilities that ease unit administration, improve command and control, promote the use of training simulators, and invite the use of more advanced software.

Two distinct cycles of change that had a profound influence on the creation of the modern ARNG merit closer scrutiny. Starting with the Militia Act of 1903 and ending with the National Defense Act of 1916, the Guard's internal dynamics and relations with the federal government changed fundamentally. The National Guard received federal funds and in return surrendered much of the autonomy that States' righters had jealously protected since the ratification of the Constitution. The AGs for the first time had a formal relationship with the War Department and were responsible for submitting periodic reports and implementing new personnel and training standards. Guardsmen accepted the assistance and occasional intrusion of Regular Army inspectors and trainers and complied with federal standards for the commissioning of officers and the recruitment of enlisted volunteers. The organization of regiments, brigades, and divisions diminished the influence of company commanders and inserted additional command layers between the local armory and the AG's office. At the same time, company commanders bore the brunt of a host of new burdens caused by the implementation of federal standards for equipment accountability, recruitment, and training. The National Guard's acceptance of federal controls in return for funding and legal recognition of its status as the Army's combat reserve constitute an historic change in the relationship between State soldiers and the federal government.

The two decades following the Korean War represented a second cycle of change that created the modern ARNG. State soldiers accepted further levels of federal control in return for additional funding that provided retirement benefits, recruiting incentives, modern armories, new facilities, and improved weapons and equipment. For the first time, the Army integrated ARNG units into comprehensive war plans for specific overseas theaters. The Roundout Program, overseas training, and the CAPSTONE Program brought Regulars and Guardsmen into closer harmony. The ARNG willingly made the shift from individual to unit training and increasingly submitted to controls emanating from the Pentagon. In the late 1960s, the Guard leadership acquiesced to the massive force structure reductions imposed by Secretary McNamara that greatly reduced the number of combat divisions and created a large pool of separate brigades. The cuts improved the ARNG's readiness by reducing personnel authorizations more in line with actual strength levels. However, the McNamara drawdown served as a stark reminder that the driving force in National Guard interests was shifting dramatically from Capitol Hill and the State houses to the Pentagon. The advent of recruiting incentives in the late 1970s had a more subtle but no less significant influence on Guard membership. While payments for college education undoubtedly helped the ARNG to recruit quality soldiers, the incentives brought men and women into the Guard for other than traditional reasons.

The first decade following the end of the Cold War indicates that dynamic forces are at work that might propel the ARNG into yet another historic cycle of change. A possibility exists that the ARNG might lose its enduring mission as the Army's primary combat reserve and place more emphasis on support units. A legacy of Desert Storm was the Army's willingness to integrate the ARNG's support units into plans and contingency operations but to denigrate the value of its combat units. The continuous defense policy revisions that occurred throughout the 1990s placed a higher premium on support units rather than combat formations. When large defense cuts came, the ARNG was forced to reduce its combat brigades. In addition, the strategy of peacetime engagement has required the extended presence of American peacekeepers at various points around the globe. A new challenge for the ARNG will be to determine whether or not it is capable of sustaining operational deployments in peacetime for extended periods. New social, technological, and strategic conditions are affecting the ARNG as well. The increase in minority populations assures that the Guard's ranks will become even more diverse. Information Age technology that promotes distance learning and high-speed communications on the battlefield and in armories is causing a revolution in tactics and administration and prompting Guard soldiers to master novel computer skills. The possibility of new threats from terrorist groups and rogue nations armed with weapons of mass destruction might compel the Guard to shift more time and resources away from its traditional combat role and into programs designed to protect the American people on their own soil.

Regulars and Guardsmen

Since the creation of the Continental Army in 1775, the American military has relied upon a dual system of Regulars and citizen-soldiers. Federal and State troops have argued back and forth for centuries regarding the relative merits each brings to the common defense. For the most part, relations between the Army and the National Guard have seen alternating periods of mutual support and mutual competition. During the worst times, Regulars have argued for a much smaller National Guard with only diminished, domestic roles. During the best relations, professionals and citizen-soldiers have worked closely together in peace and war. Regulars have too often clung to false hopes that the American people will support a large, standing Army in peacetime or permit the creation of an extensive, federal reserve under the Army's direct control. Resources expended on State soldiers, Regulars have argued, would be better invested in full-time forces or a wholly federal reserve force. These persistent arguments reveal an officer corps that has never fully comprehended a fundamental truth; a system of citizen-soldiers inevitably contains military inefficiencies but prompts the broader participation of the American people in national defense. On the other hand, Guard leaders have often overstated the abilities of citizen-soldiers, especially at the beginning of a war. Guard commanders are slow to admit that citizen-soldiers with only thirty-nine days of training available each year require additional training to place them on more equal footing with Regulars who operate and train year-round. In addition, Guardsmen can be overly sensitive to valid criticisms of inadequate discipline, training, and leadership in their units.

Distinct attitudes and policies have determined the working relationship between Regulars and Guardsmen at various times. Friction between Regulars and citizen-soldiers predates the founding of the American Army and first occurred with the posting of the British Army to North America. British officers developed a loathing for colonial provincial troops during the French and Indian War but failed to realize that militiamen in provincial units did not represent the best of the enrolled militia. The British Army's misplaced contempt for the Yankee militia created a false confidence that helped the minutemen to prevail at Lexington and Concord and for the New England militia to inflict huge casualties on the Redcoats at Bunker Hill. Within weeks of the creation of the Continental Army, animosities that had existed between Redcoats and militiamen quickly took root in the relations between Continentals and State soldiers. Throughout the Revolution, George Washington's often quoted condemnations of the militia were not so much aimed at the institution itself but at the militia's inability to suddenly transform itself in the middle of a war from a local defense force into a coherent, national reserve. Following the Revolution, the mixed performance of militia units in the Northwest Territory fueled Federalist arguments for a larger, standing Army.

Policies in the nation's early years more sharply defined the delineation between Regulars and citizen-soldiers. Washington's "Sentiments" advocated militia reforms and increased federal controls to make State units more uniform and reliable as a coherent national reserve. The Constitution codified a dual system of Regulars and State soldiers. In the minds of States' rights advocates, the militia was to act as a counterbalance against federal power and possible abuses from a strong, standing Army. The Second Amendment, guaranteeing the right of citizens to bear arms, was largely a mechanism to guarantee the existence of an armed citizenry for militia service. In 1790, Secretary of War Henry Knox put forth a plan for the classification of the militia by age group. In pressing for militia reforms, the federal government indicated that the enrolled militia was not a viable combat reserve, a notion that found support among advocates of a standing Army. The Militia Act of 1792 further established the militia as integral to the national defense and codified its administration and organization for more than a century. In 1802, the founding of West Point led to the creation of a cadre of professional, trained officers whose personal fortunes were inextricably linked to those of the Regular Army. After the War of 1812, Secretary of War Calhoun's Expansible Army Plan placed the focus of planning for war on Regulars rather than militiamen. Calhoun hoped to create a standing Army of cadre units that would quickly reach its wartime potential with the infusion of eager men joining the ranks in the opening stages of a national emergency. Influential political leaders and State soldiers countered each initiative aimed at reforming or diminishing the militia by pointing to the past, credible performances of citizen-soldiers and refusing to surrender the rights of the States to maintain and train militia units.

Bickering between Regular Army and militia generals during the War of 1812 highlighted institutional biases and hinted at the early decay of the enrolled militia. Starting with the Mexican and Civil Wars, volunteers supplanted the militia as the principle means of raising large field forces. During the Civil War, senior volunteer soldiers echoed the militia's earlier charges of bias on the part of Regular officers who openly criticized the inefficiency and ill discipline of volunteer regiments. Progressive Regulars and Guardsmen explored the possibilities of closer cooperation after the Civil War in anticipation of conflict with the European powers.

The Spanish-American War thrust the United States onto the world stage, and the need for a larger, peacetime Army backed by trained reserves was no longer rhetoric but a stark reality. The performance of citizen-soldiers in Puerto Rico and the Philippines paved the way for the passage of the 1903 Dick Act that established the National Guard as a credible, national reserve. Guardsmen learned to comply with new federal standards for training, education, and unit organization but bristled at those wanting to reduce the Guard's importance or to diminish its State ties. Many Regulars believed the Guard was not up to the task and began to espouse the effectiveness of a national reserve separate from State troops and directly under the Army's control. The writings of Emory Upton condemned the militia system as wasteful and riddled with political influence and became the philosophical basis Regulars used in attempts to reduce the Guard to a purely State constabulary. While State soldiers promoted the capabilities of their units, the National Guard was unable to provide all of the special skills that a larger and more complex Army required. In 1908, the Medical Reserve Corps became the Army's first, federally controlled reserve force and marked the earliest beginnings of the USAR.

Throughout the 1910s, Army-Guard relations sank to an historic nadir as Regulars made repeated attempts to reduce the National Guard to little more than a State defense force. The Wickersham Decision of 1912 and the Continental Army Plan of 1915 were the most deliberate efforts to destroy the Guard's value as a viable, federal reserve. Increasing international tensions with Europe and Mexico compelled Congress to exercise its constitutional powers and intervene in the Army-Guard feud. The National Defense Act of 1916 created an integrated Army of Regulars, Guardsmen, and Reservists and established the Guard as the Army's principle combat reserve. Guardsmen in World War I resented a massive Army reorganization that stripped units of their traditional designations and bristled at the Army's tendency to replace their commanders with Regular officers. Despite the National Guard's vital contributions in World War I, the Army used its enormous size and prestige at the end of the war to advance yet another plan for eliminating State soldiers. The arguments of John McAuley Palmer who believed in a regionally based, citizen reserve won out over those of Emory Upton, and Congress favored the nation's continued reliance on citizen-soldiers. The National Defense Act of 1920 rejected the notion of a large, Regular Army backed by an immense pool of trained reserves in favor of a smaller Army reinforced by National Guard units and individual officers in the ORC.

Throughout the 1920s and 1930s, the Regular Army and the National Guard coexisted in relative harmony. Apathy, parsimonious defense budgets, and economic depression caused Regulars and Guardsmen to concentrate on maintaining their respective forces rather than seeking an advantage over one another. The approach of World War II and the mobilization of 1940 brought the Army and the National Guard back into conflict. In general, Regulars lamented the unpreparedness of State units entering active duty and the inadequacies of the Guard's senior leadership. The widespread relief of Guard general officers caused the most serious rift in Army-Guard relations since the end of World War I. In reality, the Guard's seniority system permitted too many generals past their prime to retain their posts as division commanders in peacetime. General George C. Marshall represented the views of moderates in the Army who valued the tradition of America's citizen-soldiers while admitting that Guardsmen needed significant, additional training before entering combat. General McNair personified the Army's remaining Uptonians who decried the National Guard as an organization riddled with waste and incompetence that added little to national defense. While many State units were not ready for the challenges of World War II's fluid battlefields, a number of Guard commanders distinguished themselves in Europe and the Pacific. Robert Beightler and

Raymond McLain were among the Guard generals who proved equal to their Regular Army peers and superior to Axis opponents.

The onset of the Cold War resulted in fundamental changes in the historic Army-ARNG relationship. The threat of warfare with the Soviet Union and other communist regimes after World War II prompted the continuation of the draft and the maintenance of a large, standing Army. Sustained by a fresh flow of draftees, the Army's peacetime strength remained at unprecedented, high levels. Draftees came to replace the National Guard as the *de facto* combat reserve of the Army. Guardsmen fought in Korea but not in numbers comparable to that of the World Wars. The Vietnam War in particular had a corrosive affect on Army-Guard relations. Because Guardsmen were not mobilized until 1968, and then in only small numbers, the Vietnam War was the first in American history fought without significant involvement from State soldiers. Unlike the World Wars and Korea, Regulars did not have the opportunity to serve beside Guardsmen in combat. Instead, many Army officers and the American people at large came to view the ARNG as militarily ineffective and as a haven for draft dodgers. The ARNG's role in controlling race and anti-war riots during the 1960s identified it as a domestic constabulary, further diminishing its reputation as a combat reserve. The decision not to send the ARNG to Vietnam in significant numbers prompted Regular officers to focus more inwardly on the problems and policies of the active Army and fostered a growing ignorance regarding the Guard's capabilities and characteristics.

The end of the Vietnam War, the cessation of the draft and the implementation of the volunteer Army forced Regulars and Guardsmen to attempt reconciliation. Both institutions closed ranks against the threat of world communism and worked to repair internal damage caused by volatile race relations, poor discipline, and widespread drug use. A major purpose of the Total Force Policy was to wean the Army from its reliance on draftees and to once again create a dependency on the National Guard as its primary combat reserve. However, more than thirty years of the draft and the trauma of the Vietnam War made reconciliation slow and only partially successful. Because of the bitter Vietnam experience, General Abrams was determined to structure the active Army so it could never again go to war without the full support of the American people. The Roundout Program made ARNG combat brigades the vital link between the American people and the Army. The generation of senior Army leaders that included Generals Creighton Abrams and John Vessey had served with Guardsmen in World War II and Korea and knew citizen-soldiers could fight. However, younger Regular officers who had little firsthand experience with the ARNG in combat or otherwise shared the public's poor perception of State soldiers and questioned the Guard's effectiveness as a combat reserve. Once again, many of Emory Upton's historical criticisms emerged. A new generation of Regular officers often failed to understand the Army's responsibility in training Guard units and did not comprehend the significance of the National Guard's dual nature as a federal and State force. An attitude developed among Regulars that time and money expended on the ARNG would be better used to sustain the largest peacetime Army in American history.

The robust defense budgets of the Reagan Buildup allowed the Army and the ARNG to repair much of the damage of the Vietnam War, guaranteed the success of the volunteer Army, and fostered better intraservice relations. The Roundout Program flourished, and ARNG units widened their participation in overseas training events and debuted at the NTC. Guardsmen became engrossed in planning and training for the defense of Europe. In the event of a Soviet attack, the Army was to rely heavily on early deploying ARNG combat divisions to reinforce NATO's Central Region. By the late 1980s, the Army and the ARNG had reached peak strength levels and enjoyed the best working relations since World War II. For a short span of years, the ARNG seemed to have resumed its historical position as the Army's primary combat reserve.

The Persian Gulf War created a serious rift in Army-Guard relations. While active duty and Guard support units worked extremely well together in Saudi Arabia, a lack of conviction on the part of DOD and the Army to mobilize selected Roundout brigades seriously upset Army-Guard relations. For many Guardsmen, the slowness in ordering the brigades to active duty and the unwillingness to deploy them overseas constituted a serious breach of the Army's faith in the ARNG. Instead of deploying to the Gulf for combat operations, the three Roundout brigades remained stateside to train at Fort Hood and the NTC. With no ARNG combat maneuver brigades in Southwest Asia, Desert Storm became the first and only war in American history fought without National Guard ground maneuver units.

The end of the Cold War and sharp reductions in the armed forces made the 1990s the most contentious period in Army-Guard relations since the 1910s. The Persian Gulf War simply delayed deep cuts of 25 percent in defense spending that were announced well before Saddam Hussein invaded Kuwait. The depth of the losses set the Army and the ARNG's senior leadership at cross-purposes as both struggled to avoid severe losses in units and manpower. At first, the Army argued that active forces and the Guard had similarly benefited during the Reagan Buildup and that both should experience proportional declines. However, as the actual depth of the losses became painfully apparent, some Army leaders viewed the Guard as a peer competitor for dwindling resources. A generation of leaders that only knew the large, standing Army of the Cold War and carried negative stereotypes of the ARNG from the Vietnam years advocated deep cuts in the Guard as the best means of garnering defense dollars to avoid losses in active duty forces. The Army's handling of the Roundout brigades during Desert Storm created an atmosphere of distrust and suspicion within the ARNG toward the Army's motives. Subsequent Army decisions to eliminate the Roundout Program, the labeling of large parts of the ARNG's combat force structure as irrelevant, and suggestions that ARNG divisions could not be ready for combat in less than a year further deepened the divide. The Army's senior leaders appeared willing to accept the risks of going it alone in a new and uncertain world by maintaining a large standing force free of support from ARNG combat reserves.

In the end, defense cuts were large enough to impose huge reductions in the Army and the ARNG not seen since the 1970s. The number of active duty combat divisions plummeted from eighteen to ten. For the first time ever, the ARNG leadership and the AGs made tough decisions to eliminate selected units and to release soldiers from Guard service. The National Defense Acts of 1916 and 1920 had imposed finality on War Department bickering in the 1910s, but a lack of political resolve and interest at the end of the Cold War failed to produce defining legislation that addressed vexing strategic and policy questions regarding the roles and missions of the Army and the Guard. Instead, Congress and DOD embarked upon a series of alphabet soup studies—the BUR, QDR, and others—that failed to generate a binding consensus on major issues and provided only temporary solutions to long-term, perplexing questions.

The strategy of peacetime engagement in the latter half of the 1990s has had the unintended consequence of bringing the Army and the Guard once again into closer accord. For the first time since the Korean War, Regulars and citizen-soldiers have worked together well during extended overseas operations in the Caribbean, the Middle East, and in the Balkans. New initiatives such as the Integrated Divisions and command exchange programs are once again creating familiarity between Regular and Guard soldiers. The high number of prior service personnel now serving in the ARNG gives States soldiers increased credibility in the eyes of the Army. Anecdotal evidence suggests that a new generation of Army officers that has worked closely with the ARNG during Desert Storm and in peacekeeping operations is developing a more positive view of citizen-soldiers.

Army and National Guard Integration

Since 1775, Regulars and citizen-soldiers have combined their efforts during national emergencies. State soldiers have time and time again successfully augmented and expanded the capabilities of standing forces or have made their employment unnecessary. For the most part, the Army and the National Guard have laid aside their policy differences during actual operations, especially during overseas campaigns, and Guardsmen have often formed an important part of the defenses assigned to protect the American homeland.

Militiamen and Continentals were the first to combine efforts during the American Revolution. While Continentals for the most part stood up in open battle against British Regulars, militia units supported the Patriot population, battled Loyalist militia and harassed Redcoat outposts. Outstanding commanders like Nathaniel Greene and Daniel Morgan learned the best techniques of combining the complementary skills of Continentals and militiamen. After the Revolution, the pattern of complementary employment continued. In 1794, the militia rallied under President Washington to suppress the Whiskey Rebellion while most of the embryonic Regular Army was deployed against the Indians in the Northwest Territory

During the War of 1812, the militia added significantly to the nation's combat power, albeit with mixed results. The British repulse at Baltimore in 1814, with militia fighting from field fortifications while Regulars defended the thick, masonry walls at Fort McHenry, is a particular example of integrated Army operations. In 1846, militiamen hurried to defend the southwestern border and to join volunteer regiments that made possible the successful campaigns of the Mexican War. At the outbreak of the Civil War, militia companies executed the opening moves by the North and South, fought with Regular units at First Bull Run, and went on to form volunteer regiments on both sides. Militiamen and Regulars often pooled their resources or divided responsibilities to provide security for settlers moving beyond the Appalachians and then into the West. After 1877, Regulars and State soldiers combined efforts during nearly twenty years of continuous labor strife.

The Spanish-American War fostered a new era of Army-Guard integration. Faced with the operational and logistical challenges of conducting a war on opposite sides of the globe, the Army implemented a policy of shared responsibilities. While Regulars focused on the main prize in Cuba, Guardsmen constituted the bulk of the troops sent to Puerto Rico and the Philippines. Without State troops, neither the occupation of the Philippines nor the suppression of the Philippine Insurrection would not have occurred. Stretched beyond its normal capabilities by requirements to garrison new overseas possessions, the Army relied on the National Guard for homeland defense. For more than thirty years, Guard coast artillerymen successfully defended the majority of the East, West, and Gulf coasts from attack, thereby freeing Regulars to defend strategic points in the Caribbean and the Pacific. It was no coincidence that the first head of the DMA in 1908 was a Regular Army coast artillery officer, Col. Erasmus Weaver. After leaving his position with the militia's fledgling federal headquarters, Weaver was promoted to brigadier general and became Chief of the Coast Artillery Corps.

During the Mexican Border callup, Guard units defended the line of the Rio Grande and allowed the Army to concentrate its forces for a punitive expedition into northern Mexico. In the opening months of the World Wars, Guard combat divisions rushed overseas in equal numbers with Regular divisions until the nation could raise even larger citizen-soldier armies. On distant battlefields, Regular and Guard combat units fought in tandem to generate quantities of combat power the enemy could not withstand. The efforts of the 1st and 26th Divisions in reducing the St. Mihiel salient in September 1918 and the coordinated landing by the 1st and 29th Infantry Divisions on Omaha Beach on June 6, 1944 are the best examples of Regulars and Guardsmen working closely together in battle.

The onset of the Cold War demanded even closer integration between professionals and citizen-soldiers. With a large portion of the Army posted overseas to man a defensive perimeter intended to contain the spread of communism, the ARNG served as a ready reserve force. During the Korean War, Guardsmen fought alongside Regulars in the Far East, augmented Army units defending Europe, and strengthened the CONUS strategic reserve. The practice of Guardsmen serving in a war zone, reinforcing other forward deployed active duty units, and augmenting the strategic reserve became a familiar pattern during Cold War conflicts. The threat of Soviet nuclear bombers attacking America's centers of population and industry drew the ARNG into the NIKE Missile Program. In one of the very best examples of Army-ARNG integration, Guardsmen manned missile sites to defend the American homeland against possible nuclear attacks for more than twenty years. While U.S. combat units deployed to Vietnam starting in 1965, selected Guard units participated in the SRF, a ready reserve capable of responding to unexpected threats and quickly expanding the Army's capabilities. In many respects, the Vietnam War was fought on two fronts; the rice paddies of Southeast Asia and the streets of America. While Regulars and draftees fought and died in Vietnam, the ARNG attempted to keep the peace in America's major cities.

The era of Total Force Policy increased the number of Army-ARNG initiatives. Roundout brigades trained on a continuous basis with their parent divisions. Overseas training programs allowed Guardsmen to deploy to the NATO region and to the Pacific to coordinate logistics and to train with active duty units. The CAPSTONE Program matched Army and Guard organizations on contingency war plans and fostered direct contacts between units. Throughout the Reagan Buildup, Army and Guard commands worked together closely to prepare and train for the defense of Europe. In Central America, DOD effectively used the ARNG to expand America's influence.

The Persian Gulf War represented a double-edged sword in Army-ARNG integration. The Army lauded the work of ARNG support units and artillery brigades sent to the Gulf. Without the stellar support of ARNG and USAR support units, the Army could not have sustained itself or fought in the hostile Arabian Desert. Instead of deploying to the Gulf for combat, three mobilized Roundout brigades remained stateside to train at Fort Hood and the NTC. The Army's decision not to deploy the Roundout brigades to Saudi Arabia stands in stark contrast to the integration other armed services implemented with their reserve component combat units.

As the Regular Army shrank after the Cold War, the ARNG made packages of support units available whose mission was to sustain active duty combat troops in the opening weeks of a conflict. At the same time, ARNG units and personnel meshed well with other Army and DOD assets in the war on drugs. The peacekeeping operations of the 1990s helped to restore operational integration between the Army and the ARNG. Guard peacekeepers have served alongside active duty soldiers in Somalia, Haiti and the Sinai Desert. ARNG infantry companies in Kuwait guarded pre-positioned equipment and air defense sites. Starting in 1996, ARNG units maintained a constant and substantial presence during UN peacekeeping efforts in the Balkans. ARNG responsibilities in the Balkans increased in 2000 when the 49th Armored Division from Texas served as the region's controlling headquarters.

The Army and the National Guard have had considerable success in integrating whole units into larger organizations. After the Spanish-American War, Guard coast artillery units operated smoothly as part of the Army's Coast Artillery Corps. Army plans in the late 1910s called for the first joining of Regular and Guard brigades into Integrated Divisions though the plan was never fully implemented. In the interwar years, Guard divisions fit well into Army corps areas established in CONUS. In the Cold War's early decades, ARNG NIKE missile units were an integral component of the ARADCOM. After Vietnam, the Roundout brigades and even separate Roundout battalions became an integral part of active duty divisions. In the 1990s, selected EBs have successfully joined under the control of active Army headquarters to create Integrated Divisions. However, the Army and the ARNG must insure that the policies, plans, and procedures for the mobilization and deployment of the EBs is well understood throughout Congress and DOD. In this way, the Army can avoid the confusion over expectations that clouded the mobilization and training of the Roundout brigades during the Persian Gulf War.

In contrast to the successful integration of entire units, the Army and the Guard have not favored the use of cadre and other reduced strength units. Organizations structured to increase to full strength upon mobilization have never been popular or numerous nor have they existed for extended periods. In general, Congress has been reluctant to tolerate incomplete organizations heavy with officers and noncommissioned officers whose readiness in peacetime cannot be adequately measured. Instead, U.S. defense policy has preferred complete, standing units ready for deployment on short notice. The idea of partially structured units that increase to full strength in emergencies has endured since Calhoun's Expansible Army Plan of the 1820s but has never taken full root in defense planning and likely never will.

A number of patterns emerge from the experience of Army-Guard integration. As a general rule, whenever a clear danger is capable of threatening the American homeland, the National Guard shares in the defensive role. Initially, the Army carries the main onus of homeland defense, but as new threats emerge or conditions change, the Army determines that additional resources are required. At this time, the ARNG assumes responsibility for a portion of the mission. Eventually, the Army's priorities and attentions are drawn toward new threats, and citizen-soldiers assume the responsibility for nearly all of the original effort. In due time, the perceived threat recedes, and the Army terminates the program in order to pursue new priorities. Such was the overall pattern of Army-Guard integration during the coast artillery defense of America's shores and the NIKE Missile Program. The final outcome of the ARNG's participation in the drug war remains in the future. The life cycle of CONUS defensive missions may also apply to the Army's overseas presence. Since 1996, the ARNG has assumed more of the peacekeeping burden in the Balkans as the Army concentrates on transforming itself for future warfare. Experience suggests that Guard soldiers will comprise the majority of the last remnant of Balkan peacekeepers whenever America withdraws from the region. Only in Central America has the ARNG consistently served as the dominant exercise participant.

National Guard Mobilizations and Preparedness

Supporters and critics of National Guardsmen have always expressed an interest in two aspects of their performance. First, will Guardsmen show up in a crisis? And secondly, assuming that State soldiers successfully mobilize, will they be ready? The history of the National Guard indicates that the nation can always count on State soldiers stepping forward in a national emergency. However, the readiness of units at the earliest stages of a crisis usually reflects the degrees of funding, leadership, training, and manning provided in peacetime. Since 1636, the readiness of the National Guard has been measured largely by the preparedness of its major combat units.

Since the earliest times, the States have acted as the nation's mobilization base, and the AGs have maintained a central role in the mobilization and deployment of Guardsmen, volunteers, and draftees. In the colonial period, the separate colonies supported the enrolled militia for local defense, formed provincial units for extended operations and sometimes combined their units into broader, regional efforts. During the Revolution, the thirteen colonies provided troops to the Continental Army while maintaining the enrolled militia. After the ratification of the Constitution, the common method of raising armies was for the federal government to levy troop quotas against the States. Once the States received the numbers of troops the government required, the Governors and the AGs were free to conduct the mobilization. In the War of 1812, the States provide portions of the enrolled militia for operations against the British. Militiamen formed the basis of many regiments that fought in the Mexican and Civil Wars, and the States raised large numbers of purely volunteer regiments for both conflicts. In the Spanish-American War, Guardsmen filled the ranks of volunteer regiments before new volunteers were accepted for federal service.

Between 1903 and 1917, military reforms altered most of the aspects of Guard mobilizations. The War Department's increased management over the number and types of State units ended mobilizations based on troop quotas alone. The Mexican Border mobilization of 1916 was the first time the War Department issued mobilization orders to specific units instead of quotas to the States for round numbers of soldiers. With better knowledge of State units, the War Department was able to pick and choose the outfits that deployed to the border. The Guard was still largely an infantry force, and a significant number of excess infantry units remained at home or were compelled to convert to new types of units before deploying. The War Department and the States had created a series of mobilization camps, and though these were not widely used in

1916, a precedent was established for Guard units to report to mobilization stations upon entering active duty. Supplies and facilities were not available to accommodate all Guardsmen at once, and the Army devised a system of calling out Guard units in a controlled fashion by specific increments. For the first time, Guardsmen had to meet medical standards for service and underwent thorough physical examinations. The significant numbers of Guardsmen declared unfit for duty in 1916 and in subsequent mobilizations reflected lax adherence to recruiting standards, changing mobilization standards, poor records keeping, and a tendency to allow limited numbers of unqualified Guardsmen to remain in uniform for various reasons. In 1917, conscription became the main method for raising manpower. Though the federal government initiated conscription, the administration of local draft and medical boards became the responsibility of the Governors and the AGs.

Throughout the wars of the 20th Century, Guardsmen have served proudly. At the beginning of World War I, Guardsmen were formed into eighteen combat divisions that served in France. The National Guard mobilization of 1940 helped America to prepare for even greater exertions after Pearl Harbor. Starting in 1942, a total of nineteen Guard divisions entered combat. During the Korean War, eight Guard divisions and hundreds of support units served in Korea, Europe and in CONUS. Two mobilized divisions and one ACR were a symbol of America's political resolve during the Berlin Crisis. In 1968, a smaller number of Guard units entered active duty including two combat brigades that provided thousands of troops for service in Vietnam even though the brigades remained stateside. The Indiana Rangers were the only ARNG ground maneuver unit to fight in Southeast Asia. During the Persian Gulf War, over 65,000 Guard men and women served in Southwest Asia, Europe, and CONUS. Support units and Guard artillery brigades deployed to Saudi Arabia helped to prosecute the war, but three Roundout brigades busied themselves with stateside training. After the Cold War, a steady stream of unit ARNG mobilizations has sustained American peacekeeping efforts around the globe.

The pattern of National Guard mobilizations in the 20th Century raises questions regarding the ARNG's future as the Army's primary combat reserve. Between 1917 and 1990, the number of Guard combat units ordered to active duty during national emergencies has steadily declined. The onset of limited conflicts during the Cold War and the infusion of draftees reduced the Army's need for support from Guard combat formations. Between 1973 and 1989, American diplomacy and military preparedness successfully deterred a major war with the Soviet Union and China. When war broke out in the Middle East in 1990, the latent power of the Army's heavy combat divisions intended for a major war in Europe was enough to achieve victory without significant augmentation from ARNG combat units. For the first time since 1775, the U.S. Army conducted a major campaign without the presence of a single National Guard ground maneuver unit. Throughout the 1990s, the Army has largely depended upon ARNG support units to sustain peacekeeping efforts. In 1997, the ARNG sent its first ground maneuver unit in harm's way since the Vietnam War, and the Army has planned the deployment of portions of Guard brigades and divisions to the Balkans in coming years. Overall, as the 20th Century progressed, the Army has depended more and more upon smaller Guard support organizations rather than major combat units.

National conscription has had a profound influence on the employment of Guard soldiers. In the 20th Century, conscription has been in effect for every national emergency except two; the Mexican Border Crisis and the Persian Gulf War. In both 1916 and 1990, the National Guard played a vital role. Starting in 1917, draftees supplanted militiamen and volunteers as the main source of military manpower. During the World Wars, the National Guard's major combat units formed a vital link between the Regular Army and the untapped resources of the American people. The Guard divisions that deployed overseas in late 1917 and after Pearl Harbor bought the precious time required to convert draftee manpower into additional combat divisions. With the continuation of the draft in peacetime, the Guard's physical and psychological value as a bridging mechanism between the Army and the people diminished. Instead of retaining its historic position as the Army's primary combat reserve, draftees pushed the Guard to second place. Conscription allowed the U.S. to fight in Korea and especially Vietnam without a full reserve component mobilization. Fortunately, Saddam Hussein's ineptness as a strategist prompted him to prosecute a war at a time when Regulars and Guardsmen were at their zenith of power from the Reagan Buildup and were able to achieve the nation's objectives without an infusion of draftee manpower. Surely, in the absence of renewed conscription, the Regular Army will not be able to go it alone in the next major regional conflict. The ability of a much smaller, post-Cold War Army to fight a major regional contingency successfully without the support of major ARNG combat and support units seems unlikely.

The mobilization of State soldiers depends not only on their willingness to serve, but on the legality of their service. Various laws and legal opinions have restricted and advanced the service of State troops. In colonial times, the Governors jealously protected their power to call out the militia and were generally unwilling to surrender operational control of their militia units to other colonies. The Calling Forth Act of 1792 granted presidential authority to order the militia into federal service, and two years later, the Whiskey Rebellion established an important precedent for the president's use of the militia in maintaining domestic order. The New England Governors disrupted plans for the War of 1812 by refusing to allow their militiamen to enter active duty. In the opening months of the Civil War, Governors of States declaring neutrality refused to respond to Lincoln's call for militiamen to put down the rebellion. Following Reconstruction and the Great Railroad Strike of 1877, the Posse Comitatus Act restricted the authority of the Regular Army to act as a domestic police force, leaving State soldiers as the only instrument available to the Governors to deal with large emergencies.

After the Spanish-American War, the War Department questioned the legality of National Guard service beyond America's borders, but the National Defense Act of 1916 permitted the federal government free use of the Guard for overseas campaigning. A number of southern Governors attempted to use their soldiers to continue segregation during the early civil rights struggles of the 1950s and 1960s, but several presidents successfully employed the Guard to enforce integration and civil rights legislation. A special mobilization compact allowed Guardsmen manning NIKE missile sites to enter active duty instantly whenever enemy aircraft appeared on their radar screens. During the 1980s, a number of Governors opposed the deployment of Guard soldiers to Central America. In its 1990 Perpich Decision, the U.S. Supreme Court decided that the States did not have the authority to limit the Army's ability to train citizen-soldiers as federal reserves. The War Powers Act of 1973 curbed presidential powers to commit American troops overseas without congressional approval. In subsequent years, Congress allowed the president limited authority to commit troops in the early weeks of a crisis. The presidential callup authority allowed the Bush Administration to conduct Operation Desert Shield well before Congress voted to authorize the use of force in Desert Storm. Additional presidential callups have allowed the extended deployment of Guard peacekeepers in the Balkans.

The National Guard has always operated in an environment of constrained resources, and a practice of tiered resourcing has helped to maintain higher readiness. Tiered resourcing refers to the strategy of allocating additional, scarce resources to improve the readiness of a select group of units identified for early deployment or immediate action. Units that benefit from tiered resourcing are usually intended to respond to those threats that pose the greatest dangers to the military or possess the ability to attack the American homeland. The earliest example of tiered resourcing was the Massachusetts minutemen who before Lexington and

Concord received priority for the receipt of ammunition and equipment and were required to participate in additional musters. George Washington's "Sentiments" recommended the classification of the enrolled militia by age, with the youngest militiamen organized for immediate use and older citizen-soldiers filling a reserve role. The Knox Plan of 1790 was the first time the War Department recommended tiered resourcing in the militia by concentrating scarce monies and limited time on the youngest and most energetic citizen-soldiers. Classification of the militia by age was proposed several times throughout the 19th Century, but the States successfully challenged all attempts at reforms. The coast artillery defense mission was the first example of tiered resourcing in the 20th Century when Guard coast artillery units received priority for manning, training, and ammunition. The Cold War created immediate threats that America had never before experienced, and the ARNG consistently utilized tiered resourcing throughout the era. The NIKE Missile Program created a subset of ARNG units that required additional resources so that they could respond instantly to air attacks against CONUS. During Vietnam, Guard SRF units received additional resources that improved their readiness and made them more effective as a strategic reserve. The Total Force Policy resulted in the designation of Roundout brigades that became the focal point of Guard readiness. Roundout brigades received modern weapons and equipment that made them compatible with their parent, active duty divisions. After the Persian Gulf War, the ARNG directed additional resources to high priority combat support and combat service support units that were subject to early deployment in a national emergency. Similarly, the ARNG EBs received priority for additional resources to prepare them for possible employment in near simultaneous regional wars in the Persian Gulf and the Far East.

Major mobilizations have often exposed National Guard units to periods of chaos and confusion. The U.S. Army has a marked propensity to reorganize at the beginning of wars. In 1917, the Army mobilized the Guard divisions and immediately reorganized them into the square division design for trench warfare. In addition, all Guard units lost their traditional, State designations and were numbered using a national system. Both events were major distractions from training. The relief of a significant number of senior commanders early in World War II disrupted unit cohesion. After Pearl Harbor, the Army converted National Guard divisions to the triangular configuration, a move that once again disrupted training and resulted in a number of regiments serving far afield from other Guard units. Guard divisions mobilized in the Korean War surrendered large numbers of personnel and quantities of equipment for immediate action in the Far East. Guardsmen resented the fact that Army inspectors criticized them as not ready for battle after they had willingly given up large amounts of precious resources. The Berlin Crisis taught the Army that Guardsmen must be gainfully employed once they are ordered to active duty. Mobilized citizen-soldiers complained that overseas duty was preferable to stateside training and that service only in CONUS did not justify major disruptions in their professional and personal lives. During the Persian Gulf War, the Army imposed major changes in the 48th Brigade's operational and logistical procedures that afforded commanders and staffs little time to learn new practices and placed them at a disadvantage.

Service in local communities generates unit cohesion and creates close bonds between Guardsmen and the American people. However, a system of regionally based units can produce unfortunate circumstances in wartime. Whenever a citizen-soldier unit suffers heavy casualties, a disproportionate share of the losses can fall on a single community. On April 19, 1775, Lexington, Massachusetts suffered ten killed out of a total of fifty militiamen who died on that fateful day. In World War II, Bedford, Virginia lost nineteen of its native sons from Company A, 116th Infantry during the D-Day landing on Omaha Beach. During the mobilization for the Korean War, an unfortunate railroad disaster resulted in the deaths of over thirty Guardsmen from Wilkes-Barre, Pennsylvania. On June 19, 1969, a Viet Cong sapper attack against an American fire base resulted in heavy casualties, and Bardstown, Kentucky mourned the loss of five men killed and eight wounded from Battery C, 2-138th Field Artillery. Subsequent generations in these same communities have embraced Guard service, and no locality in America has ever rejected the presence of a Guard unit in its midst because it was unwilling to pay the often heavy price of freedom.

National Guard readiness is strongly tied to leadership. While State and federal governments can provide resources to create reliable units, the critical element of leadership is unregulated and must come from the Guard's own ranks. Ever since Captain John Smith's service as a militia leader at Jamestown in 1607, competent, assertive leadership has been essential to the success of citizen-soldier units. The resolute, determined leadership of Colonel William Prescott in defending the militia redoubt on the Charlestown Peninsula made Bunker Hill one of America's most famous battles. William Henry Harrison's gift of persuasion and Andrew Jackson's iron-willed determination inspired militiamen in the War of 1812. The leadership of Jefferson Davis made the Mississippi Rifles one of the premier volunteer regiments of the Mexican War. Elmer Ellsworth's violent death at the opening of the Civil War inspired northern soldiers. General Dabney Maury provided the leadership that resulted in the creation of NGAUS, and Senator Charles Dick was a Guard leader in peace and war whose legislative abilities made an indelible stamp on citizen-soldiers. Competent division commanders like John O'Ryan in World War I and Robert Beightler and Raymond McLain in World War II were role models of inspirational leadership. After World War II, Generals Ellard Walsh and Milton Reckord were the foremost champions of ARNG soldiers. At the height of the Cold War, Congressman Sonny Montgomery emerged as a great advocate of citizen-soldiers on Capitol Hill.

An unfounded criticism of citizen-soldiers is that they are slow to adapt to the new technologies of warfare. Only professionals, the argument goes, have the time and expertise to learn the intricacies of new weapons and tactics. However, successive generations of citizen-soldiers have demonstrated their ability to master new technologies from the musket to the microprocessor without degrading their readiness. The earliest militiamen advanced from blade to gunpowder weapons while discarding the linear tactics of European warfare and employing stealthy raids and ambushes against Native Americans. In the 19th Century, militiamen adjusted to changes in tactics wrought by rifled weapons and became marksmanship experts. During World War I, Guardsmen embraced the great military advances of the day; the machine gun, the tank, and the airplane. Citizen-soldiers mastered the tactics and logistics of employing a combined arms team of infantry, armor, and artillery in combat. Guard flyers quickly embraced military aviation that laid the foundation for the creation of the Air National Guard and led to the placement of a substantial, modern helicopter fleet in the ARNG. The introduction of the military truck increased the numbers and capabilities of Guard transport and logistics units. In World War II, Guardsmen again mastered new weapons and tactics. Vast advances in military technology during the Cold War were not a deterrent to ARNG readiness. Guard soldiers mastered a range of skills, from operating and maintaining huge fleets of tracked and wheeled vehicles to manning the sophisticated radar and communications systems at NIKE missile sites. By the end of the Cold War, Guard soldiers routinely operated the Army's most sophisticated weapons systems including the M-1 tank, the Apache helicopter, and the MLRS artillery system. In 2000, a new generation of ARNG men and women is embracing rapid changes in information technologies that are revolutionizing training and administration.

Towards the 21st Century

The end of the 20th Century marks a convenient stopping point for the ARNG to pause and consider its accomplishments and evolutions since 1636. After nearly 400 years of continuous service, the National Guard still does best what it has done from the beginning—to bring the capabilities of trained and ready citizen-soldiers to bear in times of national emergencies.

In the year 2100, historians will look back and evaluate the ARNG's greatest contributions of the past century. If past is prelude, they will find unchanged many of the characteristics that have defined the Guard since its first regimental muster in colonial Massachusetts. Guard men and women will come forward to serve as volunteers in America's first line of defense. The ARNG will continue as a force with dual allegiances to the States and the federal government. At the same time, Guard soldiers in local communities will form a critical bridge between the American people and the federal government and the Army. Guard missions will find their origins in the Constitution, and citizen-soldiers will still mobilize "to execute the Laws of the Union, suppress Insurrections and repel Invasions." Feuds between Regulars and Guardsmen will ebb and flow, but in the face of national challenges they will combine efforts during emergencies and cooperate in plans designed to protect the American people from attack. A broad host of participants that have determined past defense policies—Congress, the Governors, DOD, the Army, NGB, NGAUS, AGAUS, and EANGUS—will collectively determine the ARNG's proper place in the common defense. The ARNG will most likely continue to use some form of tiered resourcing to improve its overall readiness while some portion of the Guard is assigned to provide security for the American homeland.

While the National Guard clings dearly to its core characteristics, it is an organization unafraid of change and will undoubtedly evolve in the coming decades. At the beginning of the 21st Century, strong winds of change are blowing that will surely steer the ARNG in new directions. The continuing transformation from the Industrial Age to the Information Age will produce new threats and forms of warfare that will affect the Guard's force structure and training. Future generations of Guard soldiers will master technologies and techniques that would have befuddled their forebears. Technology might change the whole face of training with drill periods becoming more fragmented rather than centralized. Such a shift in training techniques would be comparable to the change that occurred when the Guard instituted weekend drill in order to facilitate unit training at the beginning of the Cold War. The increased participation of minorities in American society will introduce greater social and ethnic diversity among citizen-soldiers. New educational and work habits may change the entire face of recruiting and retention and alter the demographic base available for service.

The most serious and challenging role for the ARNG in the coming century will most likely be full participation in a major, regional war. With smaller active duty and reserve forces and little prospects for a return to national conscription, ARNG manpower will be especially critical in the next war. The Guard's high priority support units, field artillery and attack helicopter battalions, and EBs will be the first exposed to hostile action. Other units will be ordered to active duty to relieve Army units for service in the theater of war and to bolster the strategic reserve in CONUS. Depending upon the severity of the crisis, the stripping of ARNG units of personnel and equipment for immediate overseas service might once again occur. The Guard's role in the early stages of the next regional conflict may not be too dissimilar from its functions at the beginning of the World Wars and the Korean War.

While defense rhetoric at the end of the 20th Century often espouses a return to the concept of America as a militia nation, real progress has been slow. A major inhibitor to the creation and implementation of the concept has been a disturbing lack of knowledge as to what exactly constitutes a militia nation. Political and military leaders alike would benefit from a better understanding of the concept. Like the Clausewitzian trinity of war, the militia nation demands the involvement of the American people, the government, and the armed forces. The American people have the responsibility to choose qualified leaders who establish sound defense policies, provide the necessary resources, and retain ultimate control over the military. A standing Army properly sized to meet immediate needs and to protect the nation's vital interests during the opening stages of a national emergency is a crucial portion of the militia nation's military capabilities. All units not required on active duty must be placed in the reserves. Historically, America has been unwilling to pay the price of maintaining large, standing forces in order to provide an iron-clad guarantee against all unforeseen risks. The additional forces America requires to impose its will on a stubborn enemy come from a ready, citizen-soldier reserve such as the ARNG. The American people through the centuries have understood that even though reserve forces are not always as militarily effective as Regulars in the opening stages of a war, they nevertheless reflect the willingness of American society to go to war and are a more cost effective method of providing for the common defense. The citizen-soldier units of a militia nation are geographically based and serve under their own leadership, which has the opportunity to rise to command levels commensurate with their demonstrated abilities. In the event finite numbers of Regulars and Guardsmen prove inadequate for protecting the nation's vital interests, the American people must be prepared to participate directly in the nation's defense through volunteerism or conscription.

However, a change in social attitudes since the end of the draft in 1973 is problematic for all American soldiers. For centuries the predominating emotion of the American people toward standing armies was fear. In the last thirty years, ignorance has replaced fear as the prevailing emotion regarding defense matters. From the founding of the republic, an informed citizenry has been a critical component of the common defense. The absence of knowledge and interest regarding military affairs constitutes a major cultural challenge for the Army and the ARNG as more and more Americans, including elected officials, have less and less firsthand knowledge of the military. In coming decades, the Army and the National Guard must work together to educate the public on defense matters. The ARNG must not lose focus of its vital role as a presence in local communities and as a bridging mechanism between Regulars and American society. Concerned soldiers point to the reinstatement of the draft as the best means of restoring diminished ties to the American people. However, advocating a return to the draft is too simplistic a solution, especially since the American people have not demonstrated a propensity toward public service, military or otherwise.

At the end of the 21st Century, scholars and soldiers will undoubtedly take stock of the military organizations that provide for the common defense. In studying the evolutions and growth of the military, pundits will perhaps find themselves agreeing with John McAuley Palmer's belief that military organizations are living organisms akin to strong trees rather than fixed structures. If the past is any indicator, the stand of healthy trees providing for the common defense one hundred years from now will contain one that is particularly strong and vibrant. Upon the thick bark of that tree's rugged trunk will appear the inscription: "Civilian in Peace, Soldier in War…I AM THE GUARD."

Glossary

AAA	Antiaircraft Artillery
ACR	Armored Cavalry Regiment
AEF	American Expeditionary Forces
AG	Adjutant General
AGAUS	Adjutants General Association of the United States
AGR	Active Guard/Reserve
ARADCOM	Army Air Defense Command
ARNG	Army National Guard
ARNGRC	Army National Guard Readiness Center
BUR	Bottom-Up Review
CJCS	Chairman, Joint Chiefs of Staff
CNGB	Chief, National Guard Bureau
CONUS	Continental United States
DARNG	Director, Army National Guard
DMA	Division of Militia Affairs
DOD	Department of Defense
DPP	Dedicated Procurement Program
EANGUS	Enlisted Association of the National Guard of the United States
EB	Enhanced Brigade
ERC	Enlisted Reserve Corps
JCS	Joint Chiefs of Staff
MLRS	Multiple Launch Rocket System
NATO	North Atlantic Treaty Organization
NGB	National Guard Bureau
NGA	National Guard Association
NGAUS	National Guard Association of the United States
NGUS	National Guard of the United States
NTC	National Training Center
OCS	Officer Candidate School
OR	Organized Reserves
ORC	Officers' Reserve Corps
PAD	Public Affairs Detachment

QDR	Quadrennial Defense Review
RCAS	Reserve Component Automation System
REFORGER	Return of Forces to Germany
ROAD	Reorganization Objectives Army Division
ROTC	Reserve Officer Training Corps
SECDEF	Secretary of Defense
SF	Special Forces
SRF	Selected Reserve Force
STRAF	Strategic Reserve Force
UMT	Universal Military Training
UN	United Nations
USAR	United States Army Reserve

Appendix 1
Chiefs of the National Guard Bureau

Col. Erasmus M. Weaver	1908–1911
Brig. Gen. Robert K. Evans	1911–1912
Maj. Gen. Albert L. Mills	1912–1916
Maj. Gen. William A. Mann	1916–1917
Maj. Gen. Jessie McI. Carter	1917–1918
Brig. Gen. John C. Heavey (Acting)	1918–1919
Maj. Gen. Jessie McI. Carter	1919–1921
Maj. Gen. George C. Rickards	1921–1925
Maj. Gen. Creed C. Hammond	1925–1929
Col. Ernest R. Redmond (Acting)	1929–1929
Maj. Gen. William G. Everson	1929–1931
Maj. Gen. George E. Leach	1931–1935
Col. Harold J. Weiler (Acting)	1935–1936
Col. John F. Williams (Acting)	1936–1936
Maj. Gen. Albert Blanding	1936–1940
Maj. Gen. John F. Williams	1940–1946
Maj. Gen. Butler B. Miltonberger	1946–1947
Maj. Gen. Kenneth F. Cramer	1947–1950
Maj. Gen. Raymond H. Fleming	1950–1953
Maj. Gen. Earl T. Ricks (Acting)	1953–1953
Maj. Gen. Edgar C. Erickson	1953–1959
Maj. Gen. Donald W. McGowan	1959–1963
Maj. Gen. Winston P. Wilson*	1963–1971
Maj. Gen. Francis S. Greenlief	1971–1974
Lt. Gen. LaVern E. Weber	1974–1982
Lt. Gen. Emmett H. Walker, Jr.	1982–1986
Lt. Gen. Herbert R. Temple, Jr.	1986–1990
Lt. Gen. John B. Conaway*	1990–1993
Maj. Gen. Philip G. Killey (Acting)*	1993–1994
Maj. Gen. Raymond F. Rees (Acting)	1994–1994
Maj. Gen. John R. D'Araujo, Jr. (Acting)	1994–1994
Lt. Gen. Edward D. Baca	1994–1998
Lt. Gen. Russell C. Davis*	1998–Present

*CNGBs appointed from the Air National Guard

Appendix 2
Directors of the Army National Guard

Maj. Gen. Raymond H. Fleming	1948–1950
Maj. Gen. William H. Abendroth	1951–1955
Maj. Gen. Donald W. McGowan	1955–1959
Maj. Gen. Clayton P. Kerr	1959–1962
Brig. Gen. Francis S. Greenlief	1962–1963
Brig. Gen. Charles L. Southward	1964–1967
Brig. Gen. Leonard C. Ward	1968–1970
Maj. Gen. Francis S. Greenlief	1970–1971
Maj. Gen. LaVern E. Weber	1971–1974
Maj. Gen. Charles A. Ott, Jr.	1974–1978
Maj. Gen. Emmett H. Walker, Jr.	1978–1982
Maj. Gen. Herbert R. Temple, Jr.	1982–1986
Maj. Gen. Donald Burdick	1986–1991
Maj. Gen. Raymond F. Rees	1991–1992
Maj. Gen. John R. D'Araujo, Jr.	1993–1995
Maj. Gen. William A. Navas, Jr.	1995–1998
Lt. Gen. Roger C. Schultz	1998–Present

Notes

Chapter 1

The Colonial Militia, 1636–1775

1. Martin W. Andresen, *The New England Colonial Militia and Its English Heritage, 1620–1675* (Fort Leavenworth, KS: Master of Military Art and Science Thesis, 1979), Ch. 1 passim. Precious little scholarship has been done on the earliest origins of the militia prior to the settlement of North America. The cited reference is one of the best summaries available, and all materials on the militia's English origins are drawn from this source unless otherwise noted.

2. John Shy, "Armed Force in Colonial America," in Kenneth J. Hagan and William R. Roberts, *Against All Enemies: Interpretations of American Military History from Colonial Times to the Present* (New York: Greenwood Press, 1986), 5; and Douglas E. Leach, *Arms for Empire: A Military History of the British Colonies in North America, 1607–1763* (New York: Macmillan, 1973), 1–2.

3. National Guard Education Foundation Library, Puerto Rico Territory File, "The Puerto Rico National Guard," n.d., 1–3.

4. Robert Hawk, *Florida's Army* (Englewood, FL: Pineapple Press, 1986), 13–20.

5. Shy, 6–7.

6. William L. Shea, *The Virginia Militia in the Seventeenth Century* (Baton Rouge, LA: Louisiana State University Press, 1983), Ch. 1 passim. All material on the early Virginia militia is from the cited source unless otherwise noted.

7. Darrett B. Rutman, "A Militant New World, 1607–1640" (Ph.D. diss., University of Virginia, 1959), 80–95.

8. Ibid.

9. Leach, 2–3.

10. Shea, 25–35.

11. William L Shea, "The First American Militia," *Military Affairs,* February 1982, 15–18.

12. Andresen, Ch. 2, passim. All material on the Plymouth militia is from the cited source unless otherwise noted.

13. Ibid., 37

14. Ibid., 38.

15. Ibid., 51–52; and Robert K. Wright, "Massachusetts Military Roots: A Study Prepared for the Chief, National Guard Bureau," (Washington, DC: National Guard Bureau, Historical Services Division, 1986), 2–3.

16. Andresen, 55–61; and Wright, 2–3.

17. *Records of Massachusetts, I,* 186–87; David R. Millar, "The Militia, the Army and Independency in Colonial Massachusetts" (Ph.D. diss., Cornell University, 1967), 41–42; and Wright, 8–9.

18. Leach, 45–46.

19. John R. Galvin, *The Minute Men: The First Fight, Myths and Realities of the American*

Revolution (Washington, DC: Brassey's, 1996), 10–11.

20. National Guard Education Foundation Library, Connecticut State File, "History of the Connecticut National Guard," n.d., passim; Robert W. Kinney, *The Citizen Soldier: A Brief History of the National Guard of Rhode Island*, Rhode Island National Guard, March 1977, 1; and NGB Historical Services Division, Information Paper, "Historical Sketch of the New Hampshire National Guard," n.d., xi–xii.

21. Leach, 59–66.

22. Ibid.

23. The Army and Air National Guard and Naval Militia Association of the State of New York, "Minute Men of the Empire State," September 1957, 6–7; and New Jersey Department of Defense, Information Office, "Three Centuries of Service," June 1977, 1.

24. Joseph M. Balkoski, *The Maryland National Guard: A History of Maryland's Military Forces, 1634–1991* (Baltimore, MD: Maryland National Guard, 1991), 3; and Donn Devine, *The Delaware National Guard: A Historical Sketch* (Wilmington, DE: The Adjutant General's Office, State of Delaware, 1968), 6–8.

25. Jean Martin Flynn, *The Militia in Antebellum South Carolina Society* (Spartanburg, SC: The Reprint Company, 1991), 31–33.

26. James M. Johnson, *Militiamen, Rangers and Redcoats: The Military in Georgia, 1754–1776* (Macon, GA: Mercer University Press, 1992), 159–63.

27. Allan R. Millett and Peter Maslowski, *For the Common Defense: A Military History of the United States of America* (New York: The Free Press, 1984), 4–9.

28. Ibid.

29. Leach, 224–41.

30. Charles Johnson, Jr. *African American Soldiers in the National Guard: Recruitment and Deployment during Peacetime and War* (Westport, CT: Greenwood Press, 1992), 1–3.

31. Millett and Maslowski, 36–45. All material on the French and Indian War is from the cited reference unless otherwise noted.

32. Samuel J. Newland, *The Pennsylvania Militia: The Early Years, 1669–1792* (Annville, PA: Department of Military and Veterans Affairs, 1997), 70–83.

33. Frederick P. Todd, "Our National Guard," *Military Affairs*, Summer 1941, 75–76.

34. Don Higginbotham, *The War of American Independence: Military Attitudes, Policies and Practice, 1763–1789* (Bloomington, IN: Indiana University Press, 1971), 46.

35. David Hackett Fischer, *Paul Revere's Ride* (New York: Oxford University Press, 1994), 51.

36. Galvin, Chs. 7–8 passim.

37. Ibid.

38. Galvin, 59–62; and Higginbotham, 47–48.

39. Galvin, 55.

40. Fischer, 43–65.

41. Ibid.

42. Ibid.

43. Ibid., 75–77.

44. Ibid.

45. Fischer, 174–260; and Galvin, Chs. 13–26 passim. The best modern accounts of the battle of Lexington and Concord are found in Fischer and Galvin. All material on the battle of Lexington and Concord is from the cited sources unless otherwise noted.

46. Fischer, 254, 320–21.

CHAPTER 2

Revolution and Early Nationhood, 1775–1794

1. John Adams to Abbe de Mably, in Charles Francis Adams, ed., *Works of John Adams*, 5: 494.

2. John R. Elting, *The Battle of Bunker's Hill* (Monmouth Beach, NJ: Philip Freneau Press, 1975), 10–13.

3. Ibid.

4. Martin K. Gordon, *Imprint on the Nation: Stories Reflecting the National Guard's Impact on a Changing Nation* (Manhattan, KS: Sunflower University Press, 1983), 55.

5. Higginbotham, 68–70.

6. Elting, 19–21.

7. Higginbotham, 71–73.

8. Elting, 29–30.

9. Ibid., 30–37.

10. Ibid., 37–39.

11. Ibid.

12. Higginbotham, 83.

13. Maurice Matloff, ed., *American Military History* (Washington, DC: U.S. Army, Office of the Chief of Military History, 1969), 46–49.

14. Higginbotham, 94.

15. Ibid., 98–99.

16. Ibid., 104–05.

17. Ibid.; Robert K. Wright, Jr., *The Continental Army* (Washington, DC: U.S. Army, Center of Military History, 1983), 51–56; and Matloff, 55.

18. Millett and Maslowski, 51–53.

19. James B. Deerin, *The Militia in the Revolutionary War* (Washington, DC: The Historical Society of the Militia and National Guard, 1976), 14–19.

20. Ibid.

21. Ibid.

22. Ibid., 22; Russell F. Weigley, *History of the United States Army* (New York: Macmillan, 1967), 36; and Matloff, 65.

23. George Washington to the President of Congress, December 20, 1776, in Fitzpatrick, ed., *Writings of George Washington*, 4:403.

24. Don Higginbotham, "The American Militia: A Traditional Institution with Revolutionary Responsibilities," in *Reconsiderations on the Revolutionary War: Selected Essays*, ed. Don Higginbotham (Westport, CT: Greenwood Press, 1978), 98–99; and Deerin, 23–24.

25. Deerin, 25.

26. Matloff, 75–79.

27. Ibid.

28. Deerin, 26.

29. Matloff, 78–79.

30. Millett and Maslowski, 53; and Deerin, 19–21.

31. Matloff, 87.

32. Deerin, 21, 29–30.

33. Matloff, 90–93.

34. Ibid.

35. Ibid.; and Higginbotham, "American Militia," 99.

36. Gordon, 5; and Higginbotham, "American Militia," 98. Another excellent summary of the militia in the American Revolution is John Shy, "The Military Conflict Considered

as a Revolutionary War" in *A People Numerous and Armed: Reflections on the Military Struggle for Independence* (New York: Oxford University Press, 1976), Ch. 9.

37. Richard H. Kohn, *Eagle and Sword: The Federalists and the Creation of the Military Establishment in America, 1783–1802* (New York: The Free Press, 1975), 86, 77.

38. Ibid., 83, 87.

39. Millett and Maslowski, 84–85.

40. George Washington, Memorandum, "Sentiments on a Peace Establishment," to Lt. Col. Alexander Hamilton, Chairman of Congressional Committee, May 2, 1783, passim.

41. Ibid.

42. Kohn, 74–75; and Millett and Maslowski, 87.

43. Kohn, 79.

44. John K. Mahon, *History of the Militia and National Guard* (New York: Macmillan, 1983), 49.

45. Kohn, 128–133.

46. Ibid.

47. 2nd Congress, Session I, "An Act more effectually to provide for the National Defence by establishing an Uniform Militia throughout the United States," May 8, 1792, passim; and Mahon, 51–53.

48. 2nd Congress, Session I, "An Act to provide for calling forth the Militia to execute the laws of the Union, suppress insurrections and repel invasions," May 2, 1792, passim; and Mahon, 53.

49. Mahon, 53–54.

50. Francis Paul Prucha, *The Sword of the Republic: The United States Army on the Frontier, 1783–1846* (Lincoln, NE: University of Nebraska Press, 1969), 4–6.

51. Ibid., 20–21.

52. Ibid., 22–27.

53. Ibid., 28–38.

54. Ibid., 43–49.

55. Kohn, 157–70.

56. Ibid.

57. Ibid.; and Mahon, 54.

Chapter 3

The Volunteer Militia, 1795–1878

1. John K. Mahon, *The American Militia: Decade of Decision, 1789–1800* (Gainesville, FL: University of Florida Press, 1960), 32–46.

2. Albert E. Bergh, ed., *The Writings of Thomas Jefferson*, 3 vols. (Washington, DC: The Thomas Jefferson Memorial Association, 1907), 3:317–24.

3. Millett and Maslowski, 99–102.

4. Ibid.

5. Mahon, *Militia and National Guard*, 63–64; and Martin K. Gordon, "The Militia of the District of Columbia, 1790–1815" (Ph.D. diss., George Washington University, 1975), 100–05.

6. C. Edward Skeen, *Citizen Soldiers in the War of 1812* (Lexington, KY: University Press of Kentucky, 1999), 10–12.

7. Mahon, *Militia and National Guard*, 67–77. All material on the War of 1812 is from the cited reference unless otherwise noted.

8. Weigley, 134–43.

9. Ibid.; and Millett and Maslowski, 121–22.

10. Mahon, *Militia and National Guard*, 80.

11. William H. Riker, *Soldiers of the States* (New York: Arno Press, 1979), 28–29; and Lena London, "The Militia Fine, 1830–1860," *Military Affairs*, Fall 1951, 118–29.

12. Paul Tincher Smith, "Militia of the United States from 1846 to 1860," *Indiana Magazine of History*, 1919, 24; London, 120; and Riker, 24–26.

13. John K. Mahon, "A Board of Officers Considers the Condition of the Militia in 1826," *Military Affairs*, Summer 1951, 106–15; and London, 124–25.

14. Mahon, *Militia and National Guard*, 83.

15. Kenneth O. McCreedy, "Palladium of Liberty: The American Militia System, 1815–1861" (Ph.D. diss., University of California, Berkeley, 1991), 269–71; Millett and Maslowski, 7–8; and Rutman, 732–33.

16. Marcus Cunliffe, *Soldiers & Civilians: The Martial Spirit in America, 1775–1865* (New York: The Free Press, 1973), Ch. 7, passim; and McCreedy, Ch. 11, passim. The volunteer militia companies of the 19th Century still lack a comprehensive, analytical treatment. The two chapters from Cunliffe and McCreedy are the best secondary sources currently available. All information on the rise of the volunteer militia companies is from the cited references unless otherwise noted.

17. Gordon, *Imprint on the Nation*, 53.

18. *National Guard Almanac, 2000* (Falls Church, VA: Uniformed Services Almanac, Inc., 2000), 139–40.

19. Todd, 82–86.

20. Jim Dan Hill, *The Minute Man in Peace and War: A History of the National Guard* (Harrisburg, PA: Stackpole Books, 1964), 19–24; and Marvin A. Kreidberg and Merton G. Henry, *History of Military Mobilization in the United States Army* (Washington, DC: U.S. Army, Department of the Army Pamphlet No. 20–212, 1955), 62–78.

21. McCreedy, 355–56.

22. Todd, 84; and McCreedy, 360.

23. McCreedy, 358–59.

24. Cunliffe, 241–47.

25. Ibid.

26. Burke Davis, *They Called Him Stonewall* (New York: Holt, Rinehart and Winston, 1968), 3–8.

27. McCreedy, 371–72.

28. James M. McPherson, *Ordeal by Fire: The Civil War and Reconstruction* (New York: Alfred A. Knopf, 1982), 149; and Kreidberg and Henry, 93.

29. McCreedy, 392–93; and Jim Dan Hill, "Those Civil War Regiments," *National Guardsman*, April 1961, 2–5, 28.

30. McCreedy, 401–08; and Mahon, *Militia and National Guard*, 101.

31. Cunliffe, 246–47; and Gordon, *Imprint on the Nation*, 9.

32. McCreedy, 402; and Cunliffe, 3–15.

33. Kreidberg and Henry, 90–97.

34. William F. S. Root, *The 69th Regiment in Peace and War* (New York: Blanchard Press, 1905), 9–17; and National Guard Education Foundation, New York State file, Kenneth H. Powers, "The Fighting Sixty-Ninth of New York: Its History, Heraldry, Traditions and Customs," n.d., 1.

35. Louisiana Civil War Centennial Commission, *The Washington Artillery* (New Orleans: Office of the Adjutant General, Louisiana, 1961), 1–6.

36. Ezra J. Warner, *Generals in Gray* (Baton Rouge, LA: Louisiana State University Press, 1959), 47–48, 220–21; McCreedy, 402–03; and Cunliffe, 20–22, 235–41.

37. Ibid.

38. Robert S. Chamberlain, "The Northern State Militia," *Civil War History*, June 1958, 107–09; and *National Guard*, September 1980, 48.

39. Mahon, *Militia and National Guard,* 101–02.

40. Millett and Maslowski, 196–201.

41. Ibid.

42. Hill, *Minute Man,* 100–01.

43. Riker, 44–47.

44. McPherson, 564–65; and Johnson, 12–13.

45. Ibid.; and John W. Listman, Jr., "Not to be Denied," *National Guard,* February 2001, 14–19.

46. Jerry Cooper, *The Rise of the National Guard: The Evolution of the American Militia, 1865–1920* (Lincoln, NE: University of Nebraska Press, 1997), 21–31.

47. McPherson, 586–88; and Cooper, 49.

48. Ibid.; and Riker, 47–48.

49. Cooper, 50–51; and Riker, 51–52.

50. Mahon, *Militia and National Guard,* 116–18; Riker, 51–55; and Cooper, 52–60.

51. Hill, *Minute Man,* 320–23.

52. Ibid.

53. National Guard Association, *Proceedings,* 1st Annual Conference, St. Louis, MO, October 1879, 8–12; and Hill, *Minute Man,* 323.

54. Martha Derthick, *The National Guard In Politics* (Cambridge, MA: Harvard University Press, 1965) 21–22; and Cooper, 87.

55. Mahon, *Militia and National Guard,* 119.

56. Frederic P. Todd, *American Military Equipage, 1851–1872.* 3 vols. (Westbrook, CT: Company of Military Historians, 1978), 2:655–59; *California National Guard's 150th Anniversary* (Sacramento, CA: Office of the Adjutant General, California National Guard, 1999), 9–12; and Cooper, 36.

57. Brian Dexter Fowles, *A Guard in Peace and War: The History of the Kansas National Guard, 1854–1987* (Manhattan, KS: Sunflower University Press, 1989), Chaps. 1–3, passim; and Cooper, 35.

58. NGB Historical Services Division, Information Paper, "New Mexico," n.d., 1–2; and Cooper, 36–37.

59. Francis V. Greene, "The New National Guard," *Century Magazine,* February 1892, 483–98.

60. Cooper, 88–95.

61. Ibid.

62. Cooper, 87–88; and Greene, 493–94.

63. Ibid.

64. Cooper, 39–43.

65. Dianna Everett, *Historic National Guard Armories: A Brief, Illustrated Review of the Past Two Centuries* (Washington, DC: National Guard Bureau, Historical Services Division, n.d.), 14–22.

66. Cooper, 89–97.

67. Ibid.

68. Greene, 483–98; Cooper, 30–31; and Listman, 14–19.

CHAPTER 4

The Birth of the Modern National Guard, 1898–1916

1. Hill, *Minute Man,* 151–153.

2. Frank Friedel, *The Splendid Little War* (New York: Dell Publishing, 1962), 19–26; Hill, 154–158; and Adjutant General of the Army, *Statistical Exhibit of the Strength of Volunteer Forces Called Into service During the War With Spain With Losses From All Causes* (Washington,

DC: U.S. Government Printing Office, 1899), passim.

3. Hill, *Minute Man,*154–158; Adjutant General of the Army, *Statistical,* passim; and Department of the Army, Lineage and Honors Certificate, "200th Air Defense Artillery (First New Mexico)"; and NGB Historical Services, Information Paper, "Historical Sketch of the Arizona National Guard," n.d., 18–19.

4. Hill, *Minute Man,* 160–163; and Adjutant General of the Army, *Statistical,* passim.

5. Hill, *Minute Man,* 160–164.

6. Adjutant General of the Army, *Correspondence Relating to the War With Spain, Including the Insurrection in the Philippine Islands and the China Relief Expedition, April 15, 1898 to July 30, 1902,* 2 Volumes (Washington, DC: U.S. Government Printing Office, 1902; reprint, Washington, DC: U.S. Government Printing Office, 1993) I: 37–64.

7. Freidel, 56–61, 72–94; Adjutant General of the Army, *Correspondence,* I: 84–105; and Hill, 167–168.

8. Hill, *Minute Man,* 168–169.

9. Ibid.; and Adjutant General of the Army, *Correspondence,* I: 147–165.

10. Hill, *Minute Man,* 162–185.

11. Ibid.; and Adjutant General of the Army, *Correspondence,* II: 236–278.

12. Ibid.; and Douglas R. Hartman, *Nebraska's Militia: The History of the Army and Air National Guard, 1854–1991* (Virginia Beach, VA: The Donning Company, 1994), 62–63.

13. Adjutant General of the Army, *Correspondence,* II: 278–310

14. Ibid.

15. Ibid., II: 310–341; and Hartman, 66–71.

16. Ibid.

17. Committee On Veterans' Affairs, United States Senate, *Medal of Honor Recipients, 1863–1978* (Washington, DC: U.S. Government Printing Office, 1979), twenty individual citations in Philippine Insurrection section; *National Guardsman,* April 1953, 2–4; and *National Guardsman,* November 1960, 14–15, 30.

18. Adjutant General of the Army, *Correspondence,* II: 417–432.

19. Millet and Maslowski, 285–286.

20. Ibid., 309–310; and Weigley, 313–320. All information related to the Root Reforms is from the cited references unless otherwise noted.

21. Ezra J. Warner, *Generals In Blue* (Baton Rouge, LA: Louisiana State University Press, 1992), 519–520.

22. Stephen E. Ambrose, *Upton and the Army* (Baton Rouge, LA: Louisiana State University Press, 1964), 56–63.

23. Ibid., 98–111, 147–150.

24. Ibid., 122–123.

25. Emory Upton, *The Military Policy of the United States* (Washington, DC: U.S. War Department, 1907), xiii–xv.

26. Ibid., iv.

27. Hill, *Minute Man,* 180–184.

28. Ibid., 179–180.

29. Ibid., 184–186.

30. Cooper, 108–09.

31. Ibid.

32. Fifty-fifth Congress, 1901–1902, "An Act to Promote the Efficiency of the Militia, and for other Purposes," Public Law No. 33, January 21, 1903.

33. Cooper, 109–111.

34. Ibid.

35. Cooper, 130–133.

36. Derthick, 29–32; Johnson, *African Americans,* 77–78; and Cooper 134–141.

37. Ibid.

38. Ibid., 135–136.

39. Everett, 14–26.

40. Ibid.

41. *National Guard*, November 1992, 16–20; and Timothy K. Nenninger, "The Army Enters the Twentieth Century, 1904–1917," in Kenneth J. Hagan and William R. Roberts *Against All Enemies: Interpretations of American Military History from Colonial Times to the Present* (New York: Greenwood Press, 1986), 220–222.

42. Ibid.

43. Report of the Secretary of War, 1912, 27; and Nenninger, 220.

44. War Department, *Annual Report*, 1912, "Report of the Chief of Coast Artillery," 975–977; and Division of Militia Affairs, *Annual Report*, 1908, 25–27. (Reports of the Division of Militia Affairs are hereafter cited as "DMA, *Annual Report*" followed by the appropriate year and page entry.)

45. Charles J. Gross, *Prelude to the Total Force: The Air National Guard: 1943–1969* (Washington, D.C.: U.S. Air Force, Office of Air Force History, 1985), 1–2.

46. Mahon, *Militia and National Guard*, 142.

47. War Department, General Orders No. 99, "Reprint of the Militia Act of May 27, 1908 to Amend the Militia Act of 1903," June 11, 1908.

48. DMA, *Annual Report*, 1908, 5–7; Julius Rothstein, *The History of the National Guard Bureau* (Arlington, VA: National Guard Bureau, n.d.), 1–2; and Hill, *Minute Man*, 209–210.

49. Weigley, 333–334.

50. DMA, *Annual Report*, 1910, 15–20.

51. War Department, *Annual Report*, 1912, Appendix A, "Report on the Organization of the Land Forces of the United States," 87, 108, 114, 123–125; and Weigley, 339–341.

52. DMA, *Annual Report*, 1913, 197–211; DMA, *Annual Report*, 1914, 199–201; and DMA, *Annual Report*, 1915, 8–9.

53. DMA, *Annual Report*, 1912, 32–34; and Militia Bureau, *Report on the Mobilization of the Organized Militia and the National Guard of the United States*, 1916, 21–35.

54. Weigley, 335–336.

55. James T. Currie and Richard B. Crossland, *Twice the Citizen: A History of the United State Army Reserve, 1908–1995* (Washington, DC: Office of the Chief, Army Reserve, Department of the Army Pamphlet No. 140–14, 1997), 17–19.

56. Cooper, 114.

57. Ibid.; and U.S. Attorney General George W. Wickersham to Secretary of War Henry L. Stimson, Memorandum, February 17, 1912, 1–4.

58. Hill, *Minute Man*, 205.

59. Bruce Jacobs, "The Adjutants General Association: Origins, 1912–1923," January 14, 1978, 1–5; *National Guard*, September 1988, 57; and Hill, 327–329.

60. Weigley, 342–344; and Millett and Maslowski, 323–324.

61. War Department, *Annual Report*, 1915, 133–135.

62. Ibid.; and Hill, *Minute Man*, 220.

63. Weigley, 344–350.

64. Ibid.

65. Ibid.; Militia Bureau, *Mobilization of the Organized Militia*, "Extracts from the National Defense Act," 156–169; and Militia Bureau, *Annual Report*, 1916, 45, 57–58. Reports of the Militia Bureau are hereafter cited as "MB, *Annual Report*" followed by the appropriate year and page entry.

66. Militia Bureau, *Mobilization of the Organized Militia*, 12, 65, 156.

67. Ibid.155; and Hill, *Minute Man*, 234–237.

68. Hill, *Minute Man*, 237–243.

CHAPTER 5

The National Guard in the World Wars, 1917–1945

1. Edward M. Coffman, *The War to End All Wars: The American Military Experience in World War I* (Madison, WI: University of Wisconsin Press, 1986), 6–8.

2. Ibid.

3. Ibid., 8–9, 42–43

4. John Whiteclay Chambers II, *To Raise an Army: The Draft Comes to Modern America* (New York: The Free Press, 1987), Chs. 5 and 6 passim; and Hill, *Minute Man*, 258.

5. Millett and Maslowski, 333–37.

6. Coffman, 28–29; and Kreidberg and Henry, 256.

7. Ibid., 3–4, 18.

8. Hill, *Minute Man*, 261–63.

9. Mahon, *Militia and National Guard*, 154–57; and Cooper, 168.

10. Ibid.; and MB, *Annual Report*, 1917, Appendix C.

11. MB, *Annual Report*, 1917, 8–10.

12. Ibid.; and Hill, *Minute Man*, 257–58.

13. Weigley, 385–86.

14. Cooper, 168–71; and Coffman, 65.

15. Hill, *Minute Man*, 265–67; and MB, *Annual Report*, 1918, Appendix A. (Appendix A of the MB's 1918 report is a detailed listing of all unit redesignations and an indispensable source for those interested in tracing the lineage and honors of specific National Guard units.)

16. James J. Cooke, *The Rainbow Division in the Great War, 1917–1919* (Westport, CT: Praeger, 1994), 1–5; Hill, 269; and MB, *Annual Report*, 1918, 9–10.

17. Johnson, *African Americans*, 97–104; and MB, *Annual Report*, 1918, 10.

18. Joint War History Commission of Michigan and Wisconsin, *The 32nd Division in the World War, 1917–1919* (Madison, WI: Wisconsin War History Commission, 1920), 30–32; Coffman, 84; and Cooper, 169.

19. Kenny Franks, *Citizen Soldiers: Oklahoma's National Guard* (Norman, OK: University of Oklahoma Press, 1984), 23–26; Cooke, 13, 18; and Coffman, 66–68.

20. MB, *Annual Report*, 1919, 18–21.

21. Ibid.; and Barry M. Stentiford, *The State Militia in the Twentieth Century* (Ph.D. diss., University of Alabama, 1998), Ch. 2, passim.

22. Allan R. Millett, "Over Where? The AEF and the American Strategy for Victory, 1917–1918" in Kenneth J. Hagan and William R. Roberts *Against All Enemies: Interpretations of American Military History from Colonial Times to the Present* (New York: Greenwood Press, 1986), 235–39.

23. Elbridge Colby, "The National Guard of the United States," unpublished manuscript, n.d., VII-22 thru VII-23; Hill, 269–72; Cooke, 18–19; and Mahon, 159–60. (The Colby manuscript is in possession of the National Guard Education Foundation Library in Washington, D.C.)

24. Millett, "Over Where?", 239–43; and Mahon, *Militia and National Guard*, 159–60.

25. Colby, VII-23 thru VII-24.

26. Johnson, 108–111.

27. Charles J. Gross, *The Air National Guard: A Short History* (Washington, D.C.: NGB Historical Services Division, 1994), 7–9.

28. Mahon, *Militia and National Guard*, 161.

29. Hill, *Minute Man*, 280–83.

30. Mahon, *Militia and National Guard*, 162–64.

31. Ibid.; and Hill, *Minute Man,* 265, 269, 275, 296.

32. Colby, VII-24 thru VII-28; and Millett and Maslowski, 354–58.

33. Mahon, *Militia and National Guard,* 159–60; and Hill, *Minute Man,* 285–84.

34. Colby, VII-28; and Col. John H. Parker, Commander, 102nd Infantry, Letter to General J. G. Harbord, March 16, 1918 located in the holdings of the National Guard Bureau Historical Services Division.

35. I.B. Holley, Jr., *General John M. Palmer, Citizen Soldiers, and the Army of a Democracy* (Westport, CT: Greenwood Press, 1982), 182–87, 195–99, 202–06, 274, 304, 364.

36. Ibid., 31, 187, 370.

37. Ibid., 203; and War Department, *Annual Report,* 1912, 77–78.

38. Hill, *Minute Man,* 298–300.

39. Stentiford, 107–13.

40. Millett and Maslowski, 366.

41. Holley, 432–33, 456; and Hill, *Minute Man,* 305.

42. Holley, 430–39.

43. Ibid., 423–25; and Hill, *Minute Man,* 293, 307.

44. Sixty-sixth Congress, Public Law 66–242, June 4, 1920, Chapter I, passim.

45. Ibid.

46. MB, *Annual Report,* 1920, 5.

47. Ibid., 5–8, 26; and MB, *Annual Report,* 1922, 5.

48. MB, *Annual Report,* 1921, 13; MB, *Annual Report,* 1922, 5; MB, *Annual Report,* 1927, 18; and Colby, IX–3.

49. MB, *Annual Report,* 1921, 9; MB, *Annual Report,* 1922, 5; and MB, *Annual Report,* 1925, 11.

50. MB, *Annual Report,* 1921, 16; National Guard Bureau, *Annual Report,* 1936, 1; National Guard Bureau, *Annual Report,* 1941, 11–13; and Colby, IX–17 thru IX–20. (Reports of the National Guard Bureau are hereafter cited as "NGB, *Annual Report*" followed by the appropriate year and page entry.)

51. Gross, *Short History,* 8–10.

52. Colby, IX–11 thru IX–17.

53. MB, *Annual Report,* 1931, 1; MB, *Annual Report,* 1932, 1; and Colby, IX–14.

54. Mahon, *Militia and National Guard,* 176–77.

55. Mahon, *Militia and National Guard* ,174–75; and NGB, *Annual Report,* 1935, 6.

56. Colby, IX–3, IX–8.

57. Weigley, 419.

58. Currie and Crossland, Ch. 3, passim.

59. Kreidberg and Henry, 555; and NGB, *Annual Report,* 1941, 1, 4, 14–15.

60. Kreidberg and Henry, 575–80.

61. NGB, *Annual Report,* 1941, 15–19.

62. Presidential Executive Order No. 8530, August 31, 1940.

63. W. D. McGlasson, "Mobilization, 1940," *National Guard,* September 1980, 10–21.

64. Ibid.

65. Ibid.; and Colby, X–9.

66. Bruce Jacobs, *Tensions Between the National Guard and the Regular Army* (Washington, DC: Historical Society of the Militia and National Guard, 1990), 1–12.

67. Ibid.

68. NGB, *Annual Report,* 1941, 29–31; and Earl Rickard, "The Crowded Foxhole: Citizen Soldiers and Regulars From World War I to Pearl Harbor," unpublished ms., 1999, Ch. 5, passim.

69. Hill, *Minute Man,* 430–33.

70. Headquarters, Department of the Army, 50th Anniversary of World War II Commemoration Committee, Fact Sheet, "The National Guard in World War II," n.d., 1; Shelby L. Stanton, *Order of Battle, U.S. Army, World War II* (Novato, CA: Praeger, 1984), 240,

471; and National Guard Bureau, Historical Services Division, Information Paper, "The National Guard at the Time of Pearl Harbor, 7 December 1941," September 17, 1991, 1.

71. *Lest We Forget...New Mexico's National Guard Heroes on Bataan, 1941–42* (Washington, DC: Historical Society of the Militia and National Guard, 1992), 1–10; and Stanton, 299, 467.

72. Office of the Adjutant General of Texas, Department Historian, Information Paper, "The Lost Battalion," November 11, 2000.

73. Mahon, *Militia and National Guard*,185; and NGB, *Annual Report*, 1942, 51–52.

74. Mahon, *Militia and National Guard*, 186; Rothstein, *National Guard Bureau*, 5–6; and NGB, *Annual Report*, 1946, 5, 38–40.

75. NGB, *Annual Report*, 1946, 26; and Stanton, 184–85. (Shelby Stanton's magnificent *Order of Battle* is the definitive overview of American ground units in World War II, including the National Guard. Unless otherwise noted, the details of National Guard divisional operations are from the appropriate entries in *Order of Battle*.)

76. NGB, *Annual Report*, 1946, 31–32.

77. Colby, X–16; Franks, 70, 113, 139; and *National Guard*, March 1987, 22–24.

78. Johnson, 156–57; Stanton, 254; and *National Guard*, February 2001, 19.

79. Gross, *Short History*, 10.

80. Allan R. Millett, *Semper Fidelis: The History of the United States Marine Corps* (New York: The Free Press, 1980), 413; and NGB, *Annual Report*, 1946, 32.

81. Colby, X–20 thru X–22.

82. Ibid.

83. Gross, *Short History*, 10.

84. Colby, X–22; and NGB, *Annual Report*, 1946, 31–32.

85. Hill, *Minute Man*, 480–81.

86. Dorothy Cave, *Beyond Courage: One Regiment Against Japan, 1941–45* (Las Cruces, NM: Yucca Tree Press, 1992), 390.

CHAPTER 6

The Early Cold War, 1946–1970

1. Holley, 622–23.

2. Ibid., 541, 618–20.

3. Holley, 623; and Hill, *Minute Man*, 489–92.

4. Hill, *Minute Man*, 342–45; and *National Guardsman*, October 1975, 25, 27.

5. Ibid.; Holley, 653; and Derthick, 69–71.

6. Holley, 631, 659–60; Hill, *Minute Man*, 492–97; and War Department, Circular No. 347, 25 August 1944.

7. Ibid.

8. Holley, 679, 686; and NGB, *Annual Report*, 1946, 62–67.

9. NGB, *Annual Report*, 1946, Appendix O.

10. Weigley, 569.

11. Hill, *Minute Man*, 501–02.

12. Ibid., 483–85.

13. NGB, *Annual Report*, 1946, 61, 71 and Appendix P.

14. Hill, *Minute Man*, 497–98.

15. *National Guardsman*, March 1947, 10; *National Guardsman*, May 1948, 28; *National Guardsman*, March 1949, 28; *National Guardsman*, April 1949, 30; and *National Guardsman*, May 1952, 28.

16. NGB, *Annual Report,* 1947, 9–10.

17. Millett and Maslowski, 480–82.

18. NGB, *Annual Report,* 1949, 2.

19. Weigley, 500–01; and NGB, *Annual Report,* 1948, 10.

20. Currie and Crossland, 83–90.

21. Mahon, *Militia and National Guard,* 201–02; and Currie and Crossland, 90–91.

22. NGB, *Annual Report,* 1948, 2, 31–32; NGB, *Annual Report,* 1950, 1, 7–9; and Mahon, 221.

23. NGB, *Annual Report,* 1951, 17–20; and Maj. Gen. Francis S. Greenlief (Ret.), Interview by Lt. Col. Franklin D. Simmons, Jr., Senior Officers Oral History Program, Program 82–C (Carlisle Barracks, PA: U.S. Army Military History Institute, 1982), 118.

24. Ibid.

25. NGB, *Annual Report,* 1952, 10; and NGB, *Annual Report,* 1953, 19.

26. *National Guardsman,* July 1948, 4–5; and *National Guardsman,* February 1953, 1.

27. NGB, *Annual Report,* 1951, 1, 11–12.

28. Ibid., 22.

29. Ibid., 11–12.

30. *National Guardsman,* September 1951, 16–17.

31. *National Guardsman,* November 1951, 30–33.

32. *National Guardsman,* January 1952, 8; and *National Guardsman,* March 1952, 2–6.

33. *National Guardsman,* April 1951, 2; and *National Guardsman,* September 1951, 1,8.

34. NGB, *Annual Report,* 1952, 9.

35. William Berebitsky, *A Very Long Weekend: The Army National Guard in Korea, 1950–1953* (Shippensburg, PA: White Mane Publishing, 1996), 176–77.

36. Ibid., 180–88; and McGlasson Papers, "Summary of the 40th Infantry Division in Korea," 1–3. (The McGlasson Papers were written and compiled by Capt. Wilford F. McGlasson who served as the Public Relations Officer of the 40th Infantry Division in 1950. He stayed with the division through its training and deployment to Korea in 1952. McGlasson forwarded news reports to southern California newspapers throughout the mobilization, keeping the homefront informed as to the California Guard's activities. The papers are located in the National Guard Education Foundation Library.)

37. Ibid

38. Berebitsky, 194–208; and McGlasson Papers, 1–3.

39. Berebitsky, 208–13; and McGlasson Papers, 1–3.

40. Berebitsky, 214–16; and McGlasson Papers, 1–3.

41. Berebitsky, 216–36; and McGlasson Papers, 1–3.

42. NGB, *Annual Report,* 1953, 2–3, 10.

43. NGB, *Annual Report,* 1954, 10; and NGB, *Annual Report,* 1956, 15.

44. *National Guardsman,* February 1953, 10.

45. NGB, *Annual Report,* 1956, 15.

46. Weigley, 530; and Currie and Crossland, 100–01.

47. Title 10, U.S. Code, Chapter 1041, paragraph 1, August 10, 1956; and U.S. Congress, Public Law 85–861, Title 32, U.S. Code, 1956.

48. NGB, *Annual Report,* 1956, 24.

49. NGB, *Annual Report,* 1956, 3; and NGB, *Annual Report,* 1958, 338.

50. NGB, *Annual Report,* 1958, 338.

51. *National Guardsman,* October 1975, 27.

52. Millett and Maslowski, 495.

53. AEROMK, *Nike Quick Look III,* Fort Worth, TX, June 1990, 1–4; and *National Guardsman,* April 1952, 10.

54. NGB, *Annual Report,* 1954, 10.

55. *Nike Quick Look III,* 1–4.

56. National Guard Education Foundation Library, Information Paper, "Facts on the 720th Missile Battalion," n.d., 1–2.

57. *National Guardsman*, November 1974, 2–8.

58. Ibid.

59. Timothy Osato, *Militia Missilemen: The Army National Guard in Air Defense, 1951–1967* (Ent Air Force Base, CO: U.S. Army Air Defense Command, 1968), 99.

60. A. J. Bacevich, *The Pentomic Era: The U.S. Army Between Korea and Vietnam* (Washington, DC: National Defense University Press, 1986), Ch. 5, passim.

61. NGB, *Annual Report*, 1960, 6–9.

62. NGB, *Annual Report*, 1960, 33–34.

63. NGB, *Annual Report*, 1960, 12.

64. Ibid, 35.

65. Mahon, *Militia and National Guard*, 224–26.

66. Ibid.

67. Ibid.; and NGB, *Annual Report*, 1958, 28.

68. Mahon, *Militia and National Guard*, 225–26.

69. *National Guardsman*, August 1963, 9–10.

70. Ibid.

71. Presidential Executive Order No. 9981, July 26, 1948; and Berebitsky, 27.

72. NGB, *Annual Report*, 1965, 61–62; and NGB, *Annual Report*, 1967, 14.

73. Bettie J. Morden, *The Women's Army Corps, 1945–1978* (Washington, DC: U.S. Army, Center of Military History, 1990), 292–296.

74. *National Guardsman*, July 1956, 6.

75. NGB, *Annual Report*, 1956, 5; and Personnel Record of First Lieutenant Sylvia Law; *National Guardsman*, March, 1957, 6. (Portions of Lieutenant Law's personnel records were made available from the Historical Records Branch, Adjutant General's Office, Alabama National Guard.)

76. NGB, *Annual Report*, 1957, 26; NGB, *Annual Report*, 1960, 28, 32; NGB, *Annual Report*, 1962, 47; NGB, *Annual Report*, 1968, 46; NGB, *Annual Report*, 1972, 25, 29; and Morden, 292.

77. NGB, *Annual Report*, 1962, 9–13.

78. Ibid.

79. Ibid.; and Hill, *Minute Man*, 548.

80. Mahon, *Militia and National Guard*, 229; and John D. Stuckey and Joseph H. Pistorius, "Mobilization of the Army National Guard and the Army Reserve: Historical Perspective and Vietnam War" (Carlisle Barracks, PA: U.S. Army War College, Strategic Studies Institute, September 1984), 18–25.

81. Ibid.; and NGB, *Annual Report*, 1962, 10.

82. NGB, *Annual Report*, 1963, 27.

83. Weigley, 538.

84. NGB, *Annual Report*, 1960, 24; and NGB, *Annual Report*, 1964, 21.

85. NGB, *Annual Report*, 1958, 35; and NGB, *Annual Report*, 1965, 15.

86. NGB, *Annual Report*, 1963, 6, 38; and NGB, *Annual Report*, 1964, 31.

87. Mahon, *Militia and National Guard*, 231–35.

88. Ibid.

89. NGB, *Annual Report*, 1968, 1, 3, 27–34.

90. Ibid.

91. Millett and Maslowski, 544–50.

92. Ibid.

93. Stuckey and Pistorius, 41–48.

94. *National Guardsman*, September 1969, 12–21; *National Guardsman*, September 1966, 3–11; and Stuckey and Pistorius, 29.

95. Ibid.

96. Ibid.

97. *National Guardsman,* March 1968, 22–27.

98. NGB, *Annual Report,* 1968, 29.

99. *National Guardsman,* July 1970, 26.

100. Stuckey and Pistorius, 58–63, 67.

101. NGB, *Annual Report,* 1968, 10.

102. NGB, *Annual Report,* 1969, 2; Stuckey and Pistorius, 77–79; and Headquarters, 2–138th Field Artillery, "Operational Report–Lessons Learned , Period ending 31 July 1969."

103. NGB, *Annual Report,* 1970, 2, 9.

104. NGB, *Annual Report,* 1968, 17; *National Guardsman,* October 1965, 8–13, 40; and Higham, 101–09.

105. *National Guardsman,* September 1967, 6–7, 40; and Higham, 187–202.

106. *National Guardsman,* April 1968, 12–19, 40.

107. NGB, *Annual Report,* 1968, 13–17.

108. Ibid.; NGB, *Annual Report,* 1969, 20; and NGB, *Annual Report,* 1970, 3.

109. James A. Michener, *Kent State: What Happened and Why* (Greenwich, CT: Fawcett Crest Books, 1971), 294–98; and *National Guardsman,* June 1970, 3–4.

110. Adjutant General of Ohio, After Action Report, "Kent State University, 2–8 May 1970," 6; Krause vs Rhodes Exhibits; Michener, 296–97, 305; and *National Guardsman,* June 1970, 3. (The exhibits cited in "Krause vs Rhodes" are taken from evidence contained in the court transcripts of "Arthur Krause, et al. Plaintiff vs James A. Rhodes, et al., Defendants, Case No. C 70–544, United States District Court, Northern District of Ohio, Eastern Division, 1974.)

111. Adjutant General of Ohio, After Action Report, "Kent State University, 2–8 May 1970," 5; and Stang, "American Opinion" June 1974, 1–21.

112. *National Guardsman,* June 1970, 8.

CHAPTER 7

The Era of Total Force Policy, 1970–1990

1. Major Robert A. Doughty, *The Evolution of US Army Tactical Doctrine, 1946–76* (Fort Leavenworth, KS: Combat Studies Institute, August 1979), 40–46 ; and General Bruce Palmer, Jr., *The 25-Year War: America's Military Role in Vietnam* (New York: Touchstone Books, 1984), 170.

2. Doughty, 40–46.

3. Ibid.

4. Weigley, 568–69.

5. *U.S. President's Commission On An All-Volunteer Armed Force* (Washington, D.C.: Government Printing Office, February 1970), vii, 8–10.

6. Gus C. Lee and Geoffrey Y. Parker, *Ending the Draft-The Story of the All Volunteer Force* (Alexandria, VA: Human Resources Research Organization, April 1977), 50–74.

7. *National Guardsman,* January 1970, 10; *National Guardsman,* April 1973, 1; and NGB, *Annual Report,* 1970, 7.

8. NGB, *Annual Report,* 1970, 21.

9. NGB, *Annual Report,* 1972, 28–29.

10. NGB, *Annual Report,* 1972, 26; NGB, *Annual Review,* 1977, 22; and NGB, *Annual Review,*

1979, 1. (Starting in 1976, the name of the NGB *Annual Report* was revised to the NGB *Annual Review*; all subsequent references to NGB's annual summary of activities reflects this name change. Also note that the NGB summary for 1976 included the period known as "Transition Quarter." The Transition Quarter represented the federal government's change of the beginning of the fiscal year from July 1st to October 1st starting in 1976.)

11. NGB, *Annual Report*, 1972, 3; NGB, *Annual Report*, 1973, 3; and NGB, *Annual Review*, 1976 and Transition Quarter, 31.

12. NGB, *Annual Report*, 1972, 25, 29; NGB, *Annual Report*, 1973, 3; NGB, *Annual Report*, 1975, 29; and NGB, *Annual Review*, 1976 and Transition Quarter, 31.

13. Robert W. Sennewald and James D. Blundell, *The Active and Reserve Components: Partners in the Total Army*, (Arlington, VA: Association of the United States Army, December 1989), 9–10.

14. Secretary of Defense, "Readiness of the Selected Reserve," Memorandum, August 23, 1973.

15. Sennewald and Blundell, *Active and Reserve Components*, 9–10.

16. NGB, *Annual Report*, 1970, 33–34; NGB, *Annual Report*, 1974, 127, 142; NGB, *Annual Report*, 1975, 35, 39; and NGB, *Annual Review*, 1976 and Transition Quarter, 13, 42.

17. Greenlief interview, 203–05. Assistant Secretary of Defense for Manpower and Reserve Affairs, *The Guard and Reserve in the Total Force*, June 1975, 2; and *National Guardsman*, October 1970, 12–17.

18. National Guard Association of the United States, "The Abrams Doctrine: Then, Now and in the Future" Symposium Proceedings, July 16, 1993, 8–9.

19. Lewis Sorley, *Thunderbolt: General Creighton Abrams and the Army of His Times* (New York: Simon & Schuster, 1992), 360–366.

20. NGB, *Annual Report*, 1973, 3.

21. NGB, *Annual Report*, 1975, 2; and NGB, *Annual Review*, 1976 and Transition Quarter, 1.

22. Greenlief interview, 306.

23. Sorley, 375.

24. *National Guardsman*, December 1977, 22–24.

25. Ibid.

26. NGB, *Annual Review*, 1980, 34–39.

27. *National Guard*, July 1983, 1.

28. NGB, *Annual Review*, 1979, 44.

29. Ibid.; and NGB, *Annual Review*, 1980, 1.

30. Stephen M. Duncan, *Citizen Warriors: America's National Guard and Reserve Forces and the Politics of National Security* (Novato, CA: Presidio Press, 1977), 6.

31. NGB, *Annual Report*, 1970, 14; NGB, *Annual Report*, 1973, 10; NGB, *Annual Review*, 1979, 4; and NGB, *Annual Review*, 1981, 1.

32. *National Guard*, June 1985, 10.

33. NGB, *Annual Report*, 1971, 3; NGB, *Annual Report*, 1972, 36; and NGB, *Annual Report*, 1974, 145.

34. Enlisted Association of the National Guard of the United States, Fact Sheet, n.d., 1.

35. Mahon, *Militia and National Guard*, 257.

36. Daniel Wirls, *Buildup: The Politics of Defense in the Reagan Era* (Ithaca, NY: Cornell University Press, 1992), 31–41.

37. Ibid.

38. Department of the Army, "The Posture of the Army and Department of the Army Budget Estimates for Fiscal Year 1982," 4; and Robert H. Scales, Jr., *Certain Victory: The U.S. Army in the Gulf War* (Washington, DC: Brassey's, 1997), 29–31.

39. Wirls, 40–43.

40. Harry G. Summers, Jr., *On Strategy II: A Critical Analysis of the Gulf War* (New York:

Dell Publishing, 1992), 142; and Department of the Army, "The Posture of the Army and Department of the Army Budget Estimates for Fiscal Year 1986," 15, 51.

41. Department of the Army, "Posture Statement, 1986," 17–20.

42. Wirls, 42–43.

43. Office, Chief of Public Affairs, United States Army, Biography, John O. Marsh, Jr., 1981; and National Guard Education Foundation Library, Biographical File, John O. Marsh, Jr.

44. NGB, *Annual Review*, 1981, 1; and NGB, *Annual Review*, 1989, 23, 25.

45. NGB, *Annual Review*, 1989, 23.

46. NGB, *Annual Review*, 1981, 1; NGB, *Annual Review*, 1982, 47; NGB, *Annual Review*, 1986, 32; and NGB, *Annual Review*, 1987, 24.

47. NGB, *Annual Review*, 1984, 18, 23; and NGB, *Annual Review*, 1985, 19, 26.

48. NGB, *Annual Review*, 1984, 18; NGB, *Annual Review*, 1986, 22; NGB, *Annual Review*, 1989, 26; NGB, *Annual Review*, 1990, 26; *FY 1988 Department of Defense Appropriations Hearings*, I: 340; and *National Guard*, May 1991, 12.

49. NGB, *Annual Review*, 1985, 29, 35.

50. NGB, *Annual Review*, 1983, 30; NGB, *Annual Review*, 1988, 37, 41; and NGB, *Annual Review*, 1989, 31, 39.

51. NGB, *Annual Review*, 1981, 1; NGB, *Annual Review*, 1983, 16; and NGB, *Annual Review*, 1986, 16; and *National Guard*, November 1985, 20–27.

52. NGB, *Annual Review*, 1983, 16; NGB, *Annual Review*, 1984, 18; *National Guard*, January, 1986, 29; and *National Guard*, February, 1988, 24–29.

53. NGB, *Annual Review*, 1984, 24.

54. NGB, *Annual Review*, 1985, 30–31.

55. National Guard Association of the United States, "On Writ Of Certiorari To The United States Court of Appeals For The Eighth Circuit, Rudy Perpich, Governor of Minnesota, et al., Petitioners v. Department of Defense, et al., Respondents, In the Supreme Court of the United States, October Term, 1989, No. 89–542," 8.

56. NGB, *Annual Review*, 1990, 8; Supreme Court Decision , No. 89–542, "Rudy Perpich, Governor of Minnesota, et al., v. Department of Defense, et al., June 11, 1990"; and National Guard Association of the United States, Fact Sheet, "Court Upholds Montgomery Amendment," n.d., 1–2.

57. Wirls, 220–223.

58. Ibid.; and Department of the Army, "Posture Statement, 1991," Appendix X.

59. *National Guard*, April 1988, 34–38.

60. NGB, *Annual Review*, 1990, 20.

CHAPTER 8

The Persian Gulf War, 1990–1991

1. NGB, *Annual Review*, 1990, passim. Unless otherwise noted, all background information pertaining to the ARNG's status in 1990 is from the cited reference.

2. Scales, *Certain Victory*, Chapter 2, passim. Unless otherwise noted, all background information on the Persian Gulf War and the beginning of Operation Desert Shield is from the cited reference.

3. NGB-AAR, *Army National Guard After Action Report, Operation Desert Shield, Operation Desert Storm, 2 August 1990 – 28 February 1991* (Arlington, VA: Army National Guard, June 28, 1991), 2, 116, 126, 132 and 135 (hereafter cited as *ARNG Desert Storm After Action Report*); and ARNG Operations and Training Division, Emergency Operations Center,

Daily Log, 12 August 1990.

4. Emergency Operations Center, Daily Log, 10 August; and Office of the Assistant Secretary of Defense for Reserve Affairs, *Operation Desert Shield/Desert Storm Milestones*, n.d.

5. Emergency Operations Center, Daily Log, 14 August; *ARNG Desert Storm After Action Report*, 121, 133; and Headquarters, Department of the Army, Message, August 24, 1990, "Suspension of Voluntary Separation of Officer and Enlisted Personnel (STOP LOSS) for Reserve and National Guard."

6. *ARNG Desert Storm After Action Report*, 125–127; Lineage and Honors Certificate, Headquarters and Headquarters Company, 42nd Infantry Division, 1980; and Lt. Gen. John B. Conaway (Ret.) with Jeff Nelligan, *Call Out the Guard* (Paducah, KY: Turner Publishing, 1997), 168.

7. NGB-AAR, Memorandum, "ARNG Unit Federalization Dates," May 30, 1991; and *ARNG Desert Storm After Action Report*, 1–5.

8. *ARNG Desert Storm After Action Report*, 6, 17, 69.

9. Department of Defense, *What Now? A Guide for Reserve Component Families*, September 1990; and Desert Shield/Desert Storm Experiences Questionnaire (hereafter Questionnaires), 1073rd Maintenance Company, Michigan ARNG. NGB Historical Services Division distributed questionnaires to each mobilized Guard unit for completion and return. The completed forms are held in the offices of the NGB Historical Services Division.

10. *ARNG Desert Storm After Action Report*, 69; and Questionnaires, passim.

11. *ARNG Desert Storm After Action Report*, 82–85.

12. Presidential Executive Order No. 12733, November 13, 1991; and *ARNG Desert Storm After Action Report*, 149.

13. *ARNG Desert Storm After Action Report*, 134; After Action Report, 217th Quartermaster Detachment, Kentucky ARNG; and After Action Report, 1030th Engineer Battalion, Virginia ARNG, on file with Command Historian, Virginia ARNG.

14. Department of the Army, *A Soldier's Guide to Saudi Arabia*, November 1990, 18, 22.

15. NGB-AAR, Information Paper, "ARNG Units Assigned to U.S. Army, Europe During Operation Desert Shield and Desert Storm," November 14, 1991.

16. *ARNG Desert Storm After Action Report*, Table 181.

17. Scales, 53, 131.

18. Congressional Research Service, *The Army's Roundout Concept After the Persian Gulf War*, October 22, 1991, 9–10; and Department of Defense, *Conduct of the Persian Gulf Conflict*, July 1991, 11–1 thru 11–5.

19. Letter, House Armed Services Committee Members to Secretary of Defense, September 6, 1990; Conaway, 172; and Duncan, 62–63, 67–69.

20. *National Guard*, May 1991, 13–14.

21. Congressional Research Service, *Roundout Concept*, 12.

22. "After Action Report, 48th Infantry Brigade (Mechanized)," June 25 1991, 1–16, E–1 thru E–15; "The 48th Brigade, A Chronology from Invasion to Demobilization," *National Guard*, May 1991, 12–15; Congressional Research Service, *Roundout Concept*, 1–25; and United States General Accounting Office, Report to the Secretary of the Army, *Peacetime Training Did Not Adequately Prepare Combat Brigades for Gulf War*, September 1991, 1–30. Unless otherwise noted, the narrative of the 48th Brigade is from the cited references.

23. *ARNG Desert Storm After Action Report*, 6–7; and U.S. Army, Forces Command, Message, "Roundout Brigade Mobilization," November 21, 1990.

24. NGB-AAR, Information Paper, "Absent Without Leave Incident, 256th Infantry Brigade (Mechanized), LA ARNG," October 28, 1991; and *National Guard*, "48th Brigade Chronology," May 1991, 15.

25. U.S. News and World Report, *Triumph Without Victory* (New York: Random House, 1992), 197–207, and Appendix A, 429–430.

26. *ARNG Desert Storm After Action Report*, 1–3.

27. Questionnaire, 142d Field Artillery Brigade, n.d., 1–4; *After Action Review*, 2–142d Field Artillery, 21 October 1991; Demobilization Report, Operation Desert Shield/Storm, Headquarters, 142d Field Artillery Brigade, 20 June 1991; *National Guard*, "Oklahoma's 1–158th Field Artillery Engages the Enemy," August 1991, 32–36; *100 Hours with Light TACFIRE*, Maj. Russell Graves and Capt. Richard Needham, 142d Field Artillery Brigade; and Desert Shield/Storm unit narrative, 1–158th Field Artillery (MLRS), n.d. Unless otherwise noted, the narrative of the 142d Field Artillery Brigade and its subordinate units is from the cited references.

28. Maj. Gen. R. A. Smith, Commander, 1st U.K. Armoured Division, Letter to Colonel Charles Linch, Commander, 142d Field Artillery Brigade, March 9, 1991; and NGB-AAR, Information Paper, "Oklahoma ARNG Success Stories: Operations Desert Shield and Desert Storm," 3.

29. Staff Sergeant Carl P. Jungbluth, Jr. and Specialist Michelle L. Rhodes, *History of the 1133rd Transportation Company, Mobilization and Deployment for Operation Desert Shield –Operation Desert Storm, September 1990-June 1991*, n.d., 19–34. Unless otherwise noted, the narrative of the 1133rd Transportation Company is from the cited reference.

30. Orlan J. Svingen, ed., *The History of the Idaho National Guard* (Boise, ID; Idaho National Guard, 1995), 180–185; NGB-AAR, Information Paper, "Idaho Army National Guard Success Stories: Operation Desert Shield and Desert Storm," August 8, 1991, 1–2; and NGB-ARG, Information Paper, "Idaho Army National Guard Success Stories: Operations Desert Shield and Desert Storm," March 17, 1992, 1. Unless otherwise noted, the narrative of the 148th Public Affairs Detachment is from the cited references.

31. U.S. Army, Forces Command, "Demobilization Plan" February 1, 1991, 9–10; Questionnaires, passim; and *ARNG Desert Storm After Action Report*, 190.

32. Questionnaires, passim.

33. "After Action Report, 48th Infantry Brigade," 14–16; *National Guard*, May 1991, 15; and *ARNG Desert Storm After Action Report*, 186–87.

34. Desert Shield/Storm narrative, 1–158th Field Artillery (MLRS), 11.

35. Jungbluth and Rhodes, 27–31.

36. *ARNG Desert Storm After Action Report*, 26–27.

37. Historical Survey, "ARNG Casualties During Desert Shield/Desert Storm," November 1998. In the files of the NGB Historical Services Division.

38. Colonel D. Allen Youngman, *Citizen-Soldiers, Combat and the Future: America's Army at War With Itself* (Washington, DC: American Defense Coalition, March 1998), 15.

39. General Accounting Office, *Peacetime Training*, 27.

40. Georgia National Guard, *48th Brigade, Mojave Patriot*, April 24, 1991, 9.

CHAPTER 9

A New World Order, 1991–2000

1. Colin L. Powell and Joseph E. Persico, *My American Journey* (New York: Random House, 1995), 451.

2. *Army Posture Statement*, 1994, 7.

3. NGAUS and AGAUS, *Roles and Missions of the National Guard*, November 1992, 6.

4. *Army*, "The Mission and the Base Force," October 1992, 50–61.

5. NGB, *Annual Review*, 1993, 39–40.

6. U.S. Congress, Public Law 103-337, October 5, 1994.

7. U.S. Congress, Public Law 102–484, National Defense Authorization Act of Fiscal Year 1993, Title XI, "Army Guard Combat Reform Initiative"; and *Army Posture Statement*, 1995, 2; Headquarters, Department of the Army, DAMO-TRR, "Title XI, FY93 Defense Authorization Act, Army National Guard Combat Readiness Reform Act," Information Briefing, n.d.

8. *Army*, "The Mission and the Base Force," October 1992, 50–61; RAND, Arroyo Center, *Training Readiness in the Army Reserve Components*, 1994, 107–11; and *Army Posture Statement*, 1995, 62.

9. RAND, *Training Readiness*, 107–11.

10. HQDA, DAMO-TRR, "Active Component-Reserve Component Senior Leaders Offsite, Title XI Update Briefing," January 3, 1996.

11. NGB, *Annual Review*, 992, 30–32, 38.

12. Ibid.

13. NGB, *Annual Review*, 1993, 37–40.

14. *National Guard*, July 1989, 4; and *National Guard*, August 1989, 22.

15. Ibid.; and Nickey W. Philpot, "National Guard Involvement in Counterdrug Operations and Its Impact on Readiness," U.S. Army War College, Strategy Research Project, September 11, 1998, 1–7.

16. NGB, *Annual Review*, 1990, 17.

17. NGB, *Annual Review*, 1993, 27–30, 60, 116; and Philpot, 11.

18. NGB, *Annual Review*, 1998, 22–24; and ARNG, *Posture Statement*, 2000, 3–4.

19. Duncan, 4.

20. Chairman, JCS, *National Military Strategy of the United States*, January 1992, 19; and *Army Posture Statement*, 1994, 19.

21. NGAUS and AGAUS, *Roles and Missions*, 6.

22. *National Guard*, April 1988, 34–36; Director, ARNG, All-States Memorandum #I90-0385, "FY 91–94 Force Structure Reductions," September 10, 1990; NGB, *Annual Review*, 1992, 36; and NGB, *Annual Review*, 1993, 37.

23. NGB, *Annual Review*, 1993, 37; ARNG Force Management Division, Information Paper, "Army National Guard Force Structure Allowance and End Strength, FY '87–'03," n.d.; and ARNG Force Management Division, Information Paper, "ARNG Combat Brigades Inactivated Since FY 1991," n.d.

24. NGB, *Annual Review*, 1993, 45–46; and NGB, *Annual Review*, 1998, 45–46.

25. John R. D'Araujo, Jr. "Off-Site Agreement," Informal Memorandum, October 25, 1999, 1–4.

26. Ibid.

27. Ibid.

28. NGB, *Annual Review*, 1994, 50.

29. NGB, *Annual Review*, 1995, 39; and *Army Posture Statement*, 1997, 26.

30. William C. Bilo, interview by the author, "Artillery Transfer to the Army National Guard," December 9, 1999, Army National Guard Readiness Center, Arlington, VA.

31. Powell, 550.

32. Department of Defense, *The Bottom-Up Review*, September 1, 1993, 1–2.

33. Ibid, 10–12, 94; and Department of Defense, *The Bottom-Up Review* Press Briefing, September 1, 1993, Charts 14, 18.

34. Author's personal knowledge

35. NGB, *Annual Review*, 1994, 49–50.

36. NGB, *Annual Review*, 1996, 35.

37. Chairman, JCS, *National Military Strategy of the United States of America: a Strategy of Flexible and Selective Engagement*, 1995, i–iii, 8–9.

38. NGB, *Annual Review*, 1996, 3–4; and NGB, *Annual Review*, 1997, 30.

39. NGB, *Annual Review*, 1994, 37.

426 Notes to pages 354–368

40. Ibid.; NGB, Annual Review, 1995, 29; and NGB, Annual Review, 1996, 26.

41. NGB, *Annual Review*, 1995, 1, 29, 36; and *Reserve Component Soldiers as Peacekeepers*, vii–xxii, 1–12.

42. Ibid.

43. *Home Station Mobilization: An Assessment of the Direct Deployment of the 41st Personnel Services Company (Oregon Army National Guard) in the Second Rotation of Operation JOINT ENDEAVOR* (McLean, VA: Science Applications International Corporation, January 6, 1997), 1; and NGB, *Annual Review*, 1996, i and Appendix E, Table 2.

44. NGB, *Annual Review*, 1997, 28 and Appendix E, Table 2; *Home Station Mobilization*, iii–viii and Annex A (Chronology); and *Mobilizing an Infantry Company: The Experience of Calling Up C/3-116th Infantry (Virginia Army National Guard) for Operation JOINT GUARD* (McLean, VA: Science Applications International Corporation, August 25, 1998), v–vi, 1–5 and Annex A (Chronology).

45. NGB, *Annual Review*, 1998, 27–28; and ARNG Mobilization Readiness Division, Information Paper, "The Army National Guard in Stability and Support Contingency Operations," February 17, 2000, 1–9.

46. Conaway, 204–210; NGB, *Annual Review*, 1992, 89; and *National Guard*, January 1993, 128.

47. Conaway, 210–212; and NGB, *Annual Review*, 1992, 29, 89.

48. Conaway, 225–227; NGB, *Annual Review*, 1993, 3, Appendix G; and *ARNG Posture Statement*, 1996, 5–6.

49. *National Guard*, June 1995, 14–20, 23–24.

50. NGB, *Annual Review*, 1996, 36.

51. *ARNG Posture Statement*, 1999, 3–5.

52. Conaway, 201; NGB, *Annual Review*, 1991, 8–9; NGB, *Annual Review*, 1993, 10; and *ARNG Posture Statement*, 2000, 42–43.

53. NGB, *Annual Review*, 1993, 3, 33.

54. *ARNG Posture Statement*, 2000, 46–50.

55. U.S. General Accounting Office, Report to the Secretary of the Army, *Army National Guard: Combat Brigades Ability to Be Ready for War in 90 Days is Uncertain*, June 1995, 1–7; Youngman, 2–4, 16–19; and NGB, *Annual Review*, 1995, 38.

56. Ibid.; and U.S. Congress, "Hearings on National Defense Authorization Act for Fiscal Year 1993 and Oversight of Previously Authorized Programs," Committee on Armed Services, House of Representatives, 22 February 1992, 347.

57. Ibid.

58. Department of Defense, *Report of the Commission on Roles and Missions of the Armed Forces: Directions for Defense*, May 24, 1995, i–viii, 2-23 – 2-25.

59. *ARNG Posture Statement*, 1996, 11; and NGB, *Annual Review*, 1998, 31.

60. NGB, *Annual Review*, 1998, 39.

61. Department of Defense, *Report of the Quadrennial Defense Review*, May 1977, i–x.

62. Ibid., 29, 32–33.

63. William A. Navas, Jr., "Input for the ARNG Official History: 1997 Quadrennial Defense Review (QDR)," Informal Memorandum, January 16, 2000, 1–4; and *National Guard*, December 1996, 8, 30–31.

64. Ibid.

65. Ibid.; and Director, ARNG, All-States Memorandum #I99-0063, "Army National Guard (ARNG) 17K Force Structure Adjustment Impacts," May 3, 1999, 1–2 and Enclosure.

66. *ARNG Posture Statement*, 2001, 17; and *National Guard*, February 2000, 18–19.

67. *ARNG Posture Statement*, 2001, 44; and Department of Defense, Office of the Assistant Secretary of Defense, Press Release, "Cohen Defers Decision to Cut Army Reserve Components," December 20, 1999.

68. *National Guard*, January 2000, 18–19; and ARNG Mobilization Readiness Division, Information Paper, "Stability and Support," n.d., 3–6.

69. *ARNG Posture Statement*, 2001, 2–7.

70. Ibid.

Selected Bibliography

Primary Sources

Legislative Publications

Fifty-Fifth Congress, Session II, 1902, "An Act to Promote the Efficiency of the Militia and for Other Purposes," Public Law No. 33, January 21, 1903.

Goldich, Robert L. Congressional Research Service, *Report for Congress: The Army's Roundout Concept After the Persian Gulf War.* Washington, DC: Library of Congress, 1991.

Medal of Honor Recipients, 1863–1978. Washington, DC: United States Senate, Committee On Veterans Affairs, 1979.

Role of the Reserves in the Total Force Policy, Testimony of Richard A. Davis, Director, Army Issues, National Security and International Affairs Division, before the Subcommittee on Readiness, House Committee on Armed Services, February 23, 1989.

Second Congress, Session I, Chapter 28, 1792.

Seventy-Seventh Congress, Committee on Military Affairs, U.S. Senate. *The National Defense Act, Approved June 3, 1916; as Amended to January 1, 1942, Inclusive.* Washington, DC: Government Printing Office, 1942.

Sixty-Sixth Congress, Session II, Chapter 227, 1920.

The Statutes At Large of the United States of America from December 1901 to March 1903. Published by Authority of Congress, Volume XXXII, Part 1. Washington, DC: Government Printing Office, 1903.

War Department/Department of Defense Publications

Adjutant General of the Army. *Correspondence Relating to the War With Spain, Including the Insurrection in the Philippine Islands and the China Relief Expedition, April 15, 1898 to July 30, 1902.* 2 Volumes (1993 reprint by U.S. Army Center of Military History of Adjutant General's Office 1902 printing). Washington, DC: Government Printing Office, 1993.

Adjutant General of the Army. *Strength Of Volunteer Forces Called Into Service During The War With Spain With Losses From All Causes.* Washington, DC: Government Printing Office, 1899.

Army National Guard After Action Report, OPERATION DESERT SHIELD-OPERATION DESERT STORM. Arlington, VA: National Guard Bureau, 1991.

Army National Guard Vision 2010. Arlington, VA: National Guard Bureau, n.d.

Chief, Militia Bureau, *Annual Reports,* 1911–1931.

Chief, National Guard Bureau, *Annual Reports* and *Annual Reviews,* 1932–2000.

Conduct of the Persian Gulf Conflict: An Interim Report to Congress. Washington, DC: Department of Defense, 1991.

Currie, James T. and Richard B. Crossland. *Twice the Citizen: A History of the United States Army Reserve, 1908–1995.* Washington, DC: U.S. Army, Office of the Chief of Army Reserve, Department of the Army Pamphlet No. 140-14, 1997.

Department of Defense, Commission on Roles and Missions of the Armed Forces. "Directions for Defense," Report of the Commission on Roles and Missions of the Armed Forces, May 24, 1995.

Division of Militia Affairs, *Annual Reports,* 1908–1910.

Kreidberg, Marvin A. and Merton G. Henry. *History of Military Mobilization in the United States Army, 1775–1945.* Washington, DC: U.S. Army, Department of the Army Pamphlet No. 20-212, 1955.

National Military Strategy of the United States. Washington, DC: Joint Chiefs of Staff, 1992.

National Military Strategy of the United States. Washington, DC: Joints Chiefs of Staff, 1995.

The Posture of the Army and Department of the Army Budget Estimates for Fiscal Years 1982–1991. Washington, DC: U.S. Army, Department of the Army, 1982–1991.

Report to Congressional Committees—ARMY NATIONAL GUARD—Combat Brigades' Ability to Be Ready for War in 90 Days Is Uncertain. Washington, DC: General Accounting Office, June 1995.

Report of the Quadrennial Defense Review. Washington, DC: Department of Defense, May 1997.

Report of the Secretary of the Army-National Guard Peacetime Training Did Not Adequately Prepare Combat Brigades for Gulf War. Washington, DC: General Accounting Office, 1991.

Report to the Secretary of the Army—FORCE STRUCTURE—Army National Guard Divisions Could Augment Wartime Support Capability. Washington, DC: General Accounting Office, March 1995.

Report of the Secretary of Defense to the President and the Congress. Washington, DC: Department of Defense, 991.

Secretary of Defense. Memorandum. "Readiness of the Selected Reserve," August 23, 1973.

Secretary of Defense. *The Guard and Reserve in the Total Force,* June 1975.

Secretary of Defense. *The Bottom Up Review: Forces for a New Era,* September 1993.

Statistical Exhibit of the Strength of Volunteer Forces Called Into Service During the War With Spain With Losses From All Causes. Washington, DC: Adjutant General of the Army, 1899.

Vollmer, Arthur. *Military Obligation: The American Tradition—A Compilation of the Enactments of Compulsion From the Earliest Settlements of the Original Thirteen Colonies in 1607 Through the Articles of Confederation 1789.* Special Monograph No.1, Volume II, Part 1, General Information. Washington, DC: U.S. Selective Service System, 1947.

War Department, *Annual Reports,* 1912 and 1915.

State Military Department Documents

Adjutant General of Ohio. "After Action Report, Kent State University, 29 April - 5 May 1970." Submitted to Chief, National Guard Bureau, 12 June 1970.

Oral Interviews and Written Questionnaires

Bilo, Brig. Gen. William C., (Ret.). Interview by the author, "Artillery Transfer to the Army National Guard," Army National Guard Readiness Center, Arlington, VA, December 9, 1999.

D'Araujo, Maj. Gen. John R., (Ret.). Memorandum, "Off-Site Agreement," October 25, 1999.

Desert Shield/Desert Storm Historical Questionnaires, Arlington, VA: National Guard Bureau, Historical Services Division, 1991. (Historical questionnaires were produced and distributed by the NGB Historical Services Division to each ARNG unit mobilized for the Persian Gulf War. Many were returned with attached unit after action reports and other documents dealing with the mobilization. All documents are on file at the NGB Historical Services Division.)

Greenlief, Maj. Gen. Francis S., (Ret.). Interviewed by Lt. Col. Franklin D. Simmons, Jr. Senior Officer Oral History Program, Carlisle Barracks, PA: U.S. Army Military History Institute, 1982.

Hill, Thomas A. Interviewed by John W. Listman, Jr., Historian, Army National Guard Readiness Center, Arlington, VA, March 2000.

Navas, Maj. Gen. William A., Jr. (Ret.). Memorandum, "Input for the ARNG Official History: 1997 Quadrennial Defense Review (QDR)," January 16, 2000.

Temple, Lt. Gen. Herbert R., Jr. (Ret.). Interviewed by Lt. Col. Edward Daily, Senior Officer Oral History Program, Carlisle Barracks, PA: U.S. Army Military History Institute, 1998.

Special Studies

The Abrams Doctrine: Then, Now and in the Future. Washington, DC: National Guard Association of the United States, July 1993.

Deerin, James B. *The Militia in the Revolutionary War.* Washington, DC: The Historical Society of the Militia and National Guard, 1976.

Doubler, Michael D. *Citizen-Soldiers as Peacekeepers: The Army National Guard in the Balkans.* Washington, DC: The Minuteman Institute for National Defense Studies (MINDS), June 2000.

Doughty, Robert A. *The Evolution of U.S. Army Tactical Doctrine, 1946–76.* Fort Leavenworth, KS: Combat Studies Institute, 1979.

Everett, Dianna. *Historic National Guard Armories: A Brief, Illustrated Review of the Past Two Centuries.* Washington, DC: National Guard Bureau, Historical Services Division, n.d.

Going to War: Mobilizing and Deploying the Army National Guard Enhanced Separate Brigades. McLean, VA: Science Applications International Corporation, April 1999.

Hawes–Dawson, Jennifer, Tessa Kaganoff, J. Michael Polich and Ronald E. Sortor. *1992 Bold Shift Program.* Santa Monica, CA: RAND Corporation, Arroyo Center, 1994.

Home Station Mobilization: An Assessment of the Direct Deployment of the 41st Personnel Services Company (Oregon Army National Guard) in the Second Rotation of Operation Joint Endeavor. McLean, VA: Science Applications International Corporation, January 1997.

Hylton, Renee. *When Are We Going?: The Army National Guard and the Korean War, 1950–1953.* Washington, DC: National Guard Bureau, Historical Services Division, 2001.

Hylton, Renee and Robert K. Wright, Jr. *A Brief History of the Militia and National Guard.* Washington, DC: National Guard Bureau, Historical Services Division, 1993.

Jacobs, Bruce. *Tensions Between the National Guard and the Regular Army.* Washington, DC: The Historical Society of the Militia and National Guard, 1990.

Kondratiuk, Leonid E., and Jeffrey L. Pope. *Army National Guard Lineage Series: Armor Battalions and Cavalry Squadrons of the ARNG.* Washington, DC: National Guard Bureau, Historical Services Division, April 1995.

Lee, Gus C. and Geoffrey Y. Parker. *Ending the Draft—The Story of the All Volunteer Force.* Alexandria, VA: Human Resources Research Organization, 1977.

Lest We Forget: New Mexico's National Guard Heroes on Bataan, 1941–1942. Washington, DC: The Historical Society of the Militia and National Guard, 1992.

Melnyk, Les. *Mobilizing for the Storm: The Army National Guard in Operations Desert Shield and Desert Storm.* Washington, DC: National Guard Bureau, Historical Services Division, 2001.

Mobilizing an Infantry Company: The Experience of Calling up C/3-116th Infantry (Virginia Army National Guard) for Operation Joint Guard. McLean, VA: Science Applications International Corporation, August 1998.

National Guard Association. *Proceedings.* 1st Annual Conference, St. Louis, MO, October 1879.

Nike Quick Look III, Fort Worth, TX: AEROMK, June 1990.

Osato, Timothy. *Militia Missilemen: The Army National Guard in Air Defense, 1951–1967.* Ent Air Force Base, CO: U.S. Army Air Defense Command, 1968.

Report of The National Advisory Commission on Civil Disorders. Washington, DC: Government Printing Office, March 1968.

Roles and Missions of the National Guard. Washington, DC: National Guard Association of the United States and the Adjutants General Association of the United States, November 1992.

Rothstein, Julius. *The Chiefs of the National Guard Bureau.* Washington, DC: National Guard Bureau, Historical Services Division, n.d.

——. *The History of the National Guard Bureau.* Washington, DC: National Guard Bureau, Historical Services Division, n.d.

Sabrosky, Alan N. and Robert L. Sloane, ed. *The Recourse to War: An Appraisal of the Weinberger Doctrine.* Carlisle Barracks, PA: U.S. Army War College, Strategic Studies Institute, 1988.

Sennewald, Robert W. and James D. Blundell. *The Active and Reserve Components: Partners in the Total Army,* Arlington, VA: Association of the U.S. Army, 1989.

Shapiro, Stephen M. and Michael K. Kellogg, Counsel of Record. "On Writ of Certiorari To the United States Court of Appeals for the Eighth Circuit" *Rudy Perpich, Governor of Minnesota, Et Al., Petitioners v. Department of Defense, Et Al., Respondents.* Washington, DC: National Guard Association of the United States, March 1990. (Brief submitted as evidence in the Supreme Court of the United States, October Term, 1989, No. 89-542)

Sortor, Ronald E, Thomas F. Lippiatt, J. Michael Polich and James C. Crowley. *Training Readiness in the Army Reserve Components.* Santa Monica, CA: RAND Corporation, Arroyo Center, 1994.

Stuckey, John D. and Joseph H. Pistorius. "Mobilization of the Army National Guard and the Army Reserve: Historical Perspective and the Vietnam War." Carlisle Barracks, PA: U.S. Army War College, Strategic Studies Institute, September 1984.

The U.S. President's Commission on an All-Volunteer Armed Force. Washington, DC: Government Printing Office, February 1970.

Wright, Robert K., Jr. "Massachusetts Militia Roots." Washington, DC: National Guard Bureau, Historical Services Division, 1986.

Youngman, D. Allen. *Citizen-Soldiers, Combat and the Future: America's Army At War With Itself.* Washington, DC: American Defense Coalition, March, 1998.

Secondary Sources

Articles

Chamberlain, Robert S. "The Northern State Militia." *Civil War History*, June 1958.

Fitzpatrick, David J. "Emory Upton and the Citizen Soldier." *Journal of Military History*, April 2001.

Greene, Francis V. "The New National Guard." *Century Magazine*, February 1892.

Hill, Jim Dan. "Those Civil War Regiments." *National Guardsman*, April 1961.

Listman, John R., Jr. "Not To Be Denied..." *National Guard*, February 2001.

London, Lena. "The Militia Fine, 1830–1860." *Military Affairs*, Fall 1951.

Mahon, John K. "A Board of Officers Considers the Condition of the Militia in 1826." *Military Affairs*, Summer 1951.

McGlasson, W. D. "Mobilization, 1940." *National Guard*, September 1980.

Morton, Louis. "The Origins of American Military Policy." *Military Affairs*, Summer 1958.

Shea, William L. "The First American Militia." *Military Affairs*, February 1982.

Smith, Paul Tincher. "Militia of the United States from 1846 to 1860." *Indiana Magazine of History*, 1919.

Todd, Frederick P. "Our National Guard." *Military Affairs*, I: Summer 1941 and II: Fall 1941.

Stang, Alan. "Kent State: Proof To Serve The Guardsmen," *American Opinion*, June 6, 1974.

Weiner, Frederick Bernays. "The Militia Clause of the Constitution." *Harvard Law Review*, December 1940.

Books

Ambrose, Stephen E. *Upton and the Army.* Baton Rouge, LA: Louisiana State University Press, 1964.

Bacevich, A. J. *The Pentomic Era: The U.S. Army Between Korea and Vietnam.* Washington, DC: National Defense University Press, 1986.

Balkoski, Joseph M. *Beyond the Beachhead: The 29th Infantry Division in Normandy.* Harrisburg, PA: Stackpole Books, 1989.

——. *The Maryland National Guard: A History of Maryland's Military Forces, 1634–1991.* Baltimore, MD: Maryland National Guard, 1991.

Bell, William G. *Commanding Generals and Chiefs of Staff, 1775–1995.* Washington, DC: U.S. Army, Center of Military History, 1997.

Berebitsky, William. *A Very Long Weekend: The Army National Guard in Korea, 1950–1953.* Shippensburg, PA: White Mane Publishing, 1996.

Cave, Dorothy. *Beyond Courage: One Regiment Against Japan, 1941–45.* Las Cruces, NM: Yucca Tree Press, 1992.

Chambers, John Whiteclay, II. *To Raise an Army: The Draft Comes To Modern America.* New York: The Free Press, 1987.

Coffman, Edward M. *The War To End All Wars: The American Military Experience in World War I.* Madison, WI: University of Wisconsin Press, 1986.

Collins, John M. *National Military Strategy, The DOD Base Force and U.S. Unified Command Plan.* Washington, DC: Congressional Research Service, Library of Congress, June 1992.

Conaway, Lt. Gen. (Ret.) John B. and Jeff Nelligan. *Call Out the Guard!* Paducah, KY: Turner Publishing, 1997.

Cooke, James J. *The Rainbow Division in the Great War, 1917–1919.* Westport, CT: Praeger Publishers, 1994.

Cooper, Jerry. *The Rise of the National Guard: The Evolution of the American Militia, 1865–1920.* Lincoln, NE: University of Nebraska Press, 1997.

——. *The Militia and the National Guard in America Since Colonial Times: A Research Guide.* Westport, CT: Greenwood Press, 1993.

Cunliffe, Marcus. *Soldiers & Civilians: The Martial Spirit in America, 1775–1865.* New York: The Free Press, 1973.

Derthick, Martha. *The National Guard in Politics.* Cambridge, MA: Harvard University Press, 1965.

Duncan, Stephen M. *Citizen Warriors: America's National Guard and Reserve Forces and the Politics of National Security.* Novato, CA: Presidio Press, 1997.

Elting, John R. *The Battle of Bunker Hill.* Monmouth Beach, NJ: Freneau Press, 1975.

Fischer, David Hackett. *Paul Revere's Ride.* New York: Oxford University Press, 1994.

Flynn, Jean Martin. *The Militia in Antebellum South Carolina Society.* Spartanburg, SC: The Reprint Company, 1991.

Fowles, Brian Dexter. *A Guard in Peace and War: The History of the Kansas National Guard, 1854–1987.* Manhattan, KS: Sunflower University Press, 1989

Franks, Kenny A. *Citizen Soldiers: Oklahoma's National Guard.* Norman, OK: University of Oklahoma Press, 1984.

Freidel, Frank. *The Splendid Little War.* New York: Dell Publishing Co., 1962.

Galvin, John R. *The Minute Men: The First Fight, Myths and Realities of the American Revolution.* Washington, DC: Brassey's, 1996.

Gordon, Martin K. *Imprint on the Nation: Stories Reflecting the National Guard's Impact on a Changing Nation.* Manhattan, KS: Sunflower University Press, 1983.

Gross, Charles J. *Prelude to the Total Force: The Air National Guard 1943–1969.* Washington, DC: Office of Air Force History,1985.

Hagan, Kenneth J., and William R. Roberts, ed. *Against All Enemies: Interpretations of American Military History from Colonial Times to the Present.* New York: Greenwood Press, 1986.

Hart, Gary. *The Minuteman: Restoring An Army of the People.* New York: The Free Press, 1998.

Hartman, Douglas R. *Nebraska's Militia: The History of the Army and Air National Guard, 1854–1991.* Virginia Beach, VA: The Donning Company, 1994.

Hawk, Robert. *Florida's Army.* Englewood, FL: Pineapple Press, 1986.

Higginbotham, Don. *The War of American Independence: Military Attitudes, Policies and Practice, 1763–1789.* Bloomington, IN: Indiana University Press, 1971.

———. ed. *Reconsiderations on the Revolutionary War: Selected Essays.* Westport, CT: Greenwood Press, 1978.

Higham, Robin. *Bayonets in the Streets: The Use of Troops in Civil Disturbances.* Lawrence, KS: University of Kansas Press, 1969.

Hill, Jim Dan. *The Minute Man In Peace and War: A History of the National Guard.* Harrisburg, PA: Stackpole Books, 1964.

Holley, I.B. *General John M. Palmer, Citizen Soldiers, and the Army of a Democracy.* Westport, CT:Greenwood Press, 1982.

Johnson, Charles, Jr. *African American Soldiers in the National Guard: Recruitment and Deployment During Peacetime and War.* Westport, CT: Greenwood Press, 1992.

Johnson, James M. *Militiamen, Rangers and Redcoats: The Military in Georgia, 1754–1776.* Macon, GA: Mercer University Press, 1992.

Joint War History Commissions of Michigan and Wisconsin. *The 32nd Division in the World War, 1917–1919.* Madison, WI: Wisconsin War History Commission, 1920.

Kohn, Richard H. *Eagle and Sword: The Beginnings of the Military Establishment in America.* New York: The Free Press, 1975.

Leach, Douglas E. *Arms for Empire: A Military History of the British Colonies in North America, 1607–1763.* New York: Macmillan, 1973.

Logan, John A. *The Volunteer Soldier of America.* New York: R. S. Peale & Company, 1887.

Mahon, John K. *History of the Militia and National Guard.* New York: Macmillan, 1983.

——. *The American Militia: Decade of Decision, 1789–1800.* Gainesville, FL: University of Florida, 1960.

Matloff, Maurice. *American Military History.* Washington, DC: U.S. Army, Office of the Chief of Military History, 1969.

McCartney, William F. *The Jungleers: A History of the 41st Infantry Division.* Washington, DC: Infantry Journal Press, 1948.

McPherson, James M. *Ordeal By Fire: The Civil War and Reconstruction.* New York: Alfred A. Knopf, 1982

Michener, James A. *Kent State: What Happened and Why.* Greenwich, CT: Fawcett Crest Books, 1971.

Miller, Ernest B. *Bataan Uncensored.* Long Prairie, MN: Hart Publications, 1949.

Millett, Allan R. and Peter Maslowski. *For the Common Defense: A Military History of the United States of America.* New York: The Free Press, 1984.

Morden, Bettie J. *The Women's Army Corps, 1945–1978.* Washington, DC: U.S. Army, Center of Military History,1990.

National Guard Association of the United States. *The Nation's National Guard.* Buffalo, NY: Baker, Jones, Hausauer, Inc., 1954.

Newland, Sam. *The Pennsylvania Militia: The Early Years, 1669–1792.* Annville, PA: Department of Military and Veterans Affairs, 1997.

Palmer, John McAuley. *America at Arms.* New York: Oxford University Press, 1941.

Powell, Colin L. and Joseph E. Persico. *My American Journey.* New York: Random House, 1995.

Prucha, Francis P. *Sword of the Republic: The United States Army on the Frontier, 1783–1846.* Lincoln, NE: University of Nebraska Press, 1969.

Riker, William H. *Soldiers of the States.* New York: Arno Press, 1979.

Scales, Robert H., Jr. *Certain Victory: The U.S. Army in the Gulf War.* Washington, DC: Brassey's, 1997.

Shea, William L. *The Virginia Militia in the Seventeenth Century.* Baton Rouge, LA: Louisiana State University Press, 1983.

Shy, John. *A People Numerous and Armed: Reflections on the Military Struggle for Independence.* New York: Oxford University Press, 1976.

Skeen, C. Edward. *Citizen Soldiers in the War of 1812.* Lexington, KY: University Press of Kentucky, 1999.

Sorley, Lewis. *Thunderbolt: General Creighton Abrams and the Army of His*

Times. New York: Simon and Schuster, 1992.

Stanton, Shelby. *Order of Battle, U.S. Army, World War II.* Novato, CA: Presidio Press, 1984.

Summers, Harry G. *On Strategy, A Critical Analysis of the Vietnam War.* Novato, CA: Presidio Press, 1982.

———. *On Strategy II: A Critical Analysis of the Gulf War.* New York: Dell Publishing, 1992.

Svingen, Orlan J., ed. *The History of the Idaho National Guard.* Boise, ID: State of Idaho Military Department, 1995.

U.S. News and World Report. *Triumph Without Victory: The Unreported History of the Persian Gulf War.* New York: Random House, 1992.

Upton, Emory. *The Military Policy of the United States.* Washington, DC: U.S. War Department, 1907.

Warner, Ezra J. *Generals in Blue: Lives of the Union Commanders.* Baton Rouge, LA: Louisiana State University Press, 1992.

———. *Generals in Gray: Lives of the Confederate Commanders.* Baton Rouge, LA: Louisiana State University Press, 1999.

Weigley, Russell F. *History of the United States Army.* New York: Macmillan,1967.

Wirls, Daniel. *Buildup: The Politics of Defense in the Reagan Era.* Ithaca, NY: Cornell University Press, 1992.

Wright, Robert K., Jr. *The Continental Army.* Washington, DC: U.S. Army, Center of Military History, 1983.

Manuscripts

Andresen, Martin W. "The New England Colonial Militia and Its English Heritage, 1620–1675." Fort Leavenworth, KS: Master of Military Art and Science Thesis, 1979.

Colby, Elbridge. "The National Guard of the United States." Typed, bound copy held in Library of the National Guard, Washington, D.C., n.d.

Gordon, Martin K. "The Militia of the District of Columbia, 1790–1815." Ph.D. diss., George Washington University, 1975.

"May 4th, 1970 Collection," Kent, OH: Kent State University Library, Kent State University.

McCreedy, Kenneth O. "Palladium of Liberty: The American Militia System, 1815–1861." Ph.D. diss., University of California, Berkeley, 1991.

Philpot, Nickey W. "National Guard Involvement in Counterdrug Operations and Its Impact on Readiness." Carlisle Barracks, PA: U.S. Army War College, Strategy Research Project, 1988.

Rutman, Darrett B. "A Militant New World, 1607–1640." Ph.D. diss., University of Virginia, 1959.

Stentiford, Barry M. "The State Militia In The Twentieth Century." Ph.D. diss., University of Alabama, Tuscaloosa, 1998.

Periodicals

Army, Volumes 31 and 32, 1981–82.

National Guardsman (later *National Guard*) Volumes I-LIV, 1947–2001. (*National Guardsman* ran from 1947 through the Sept/Oct 1978 issue, and then the name changed to *National Guard* starting with the November 1978 issue.)

Index